MW01051365

Table of Contents

Getting Started

Congratulations on working with a Cengage Learning book! *iLrn: Heinle Learning Center* gives you access to a wealth of data about your performance, thereby allowing you to learn more effectively. Moreover, you'll enjoy *iLrn: Heinle Learning Center* because it is easy to use and gives you instant feedback when you complete an exercise. *iLrn: Heinle Learning Center* simply requires you to set up your account with your book key and then to log in each time you use it.

Registration

Creating an Account

To set up your account, follow these steps:

Step 1: Go to *http://ilrn.heinle.com*

Step 2: Click the *Login* button.

Step 3: Click *Create account.*

Step 4: Enter your user information and click *Submit.*

Step 5: You will be prompted to enter your book key printed inside the sleeve that came bundled with your book. Click *Go.* (You can also purchase an access code online from cengagebrain.com)

Step 6: Your book also requires an instructor's course code. You must get the course code from your instructor to gain access to your course. If you already have it, enter it when prompted. Otherwise, you can enter it the next time you login.

Figure 1: Student Workstation: Before entering course code

Login Instructions

To access your book after you have added it to your account, follow these steps:

Step 1: Go to *http://ilrn.heinle.com*

Step 2: Click the *Login* button.

Step 3: Enter your username and password. You are taken to the Student Workstation.

Step 4: Click on the book cover to open the *iLrn: Heinle Learning Center*.

If you experience any problems with setting up your account, ask Quia for help. You can submit a request at http://hlc.quia.com/support.html, email Quia at bookhelp@quia.com or call them at 1-877-282-4400.

Updating Your Profile

When you create your *iLrn: Heinle Learning Center* account, the information you enter, such as your name and email address, is saved in your profile.

To update your profile:

1. Login to the *Student Workstation*.

2. Click *Profile* in the upper right corner of your screen.

3. Update the information and press *Save changes*.

Make sure your email address is current in your profile, as Quia uses this email address to respond to technical support questions and provide forgotten username/password information.

Student Workstation

Once you have entered your book and course keys, the Student Workstation will appear like the screen below each time you login.

Figure 2: Student Workstation: After entering course code

In this view, you can choose one of the five options:

1) Click on book cover to access resources

Click on the book title or cover. This brings you to the *Welcome page* for *iLrn: Heinle Learning Center*, where you have access to all the resources available for your course.

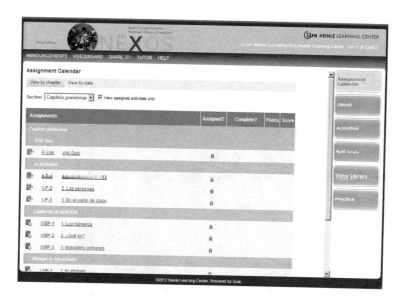

Figure 3: Student Workstation: Assignment Calendar Welcome Screen

From the Welcome page, you have access to these tabs:

▸ *Assignment Calendar*— Provides one place for you to go to access all of your assigments (Text and SAM Activities). Here you can locate all assignments by due date or by chapter.

▸ *eBook*—This page-for-page reproduction of the printed book features embedded audio, video, as well as note-taking and text highlighting capabilities. You can complete textbook activities directly from the ebook interface. You can also see whether it is assigned, completed or graded. Just look for the ⬤ icon to see what is assigned and when it is due. Hover the mouse over the ⬤ icon to see your grade for a completed assignment. The page view can be magnified and the content searched via the index, table of contents, or search functions. Within the ebook, your instructor can also write and post notes and links for the whole class to view. All books published in copyright year 2013 or beyond have an iPad-compatible ebook.

▸ *Activities*— You can locate all assignments (textbook and SAM) here. You can select a chapter and view all of the Textbook and SAM exercises for each chapter. Click on the title to open an activity. Links to the exercises are available here, the Assignment Calendar and directly from the ebook.

▸ *Self-Tests*— You may take an online self-test before or after working through a textbook chapter to get an initial assessment of what you know and what you still need to master. Your results are graded automatically and displayed according to learning outcomes.

A Personalized Study Plan, based on the automatically graded test, directs you to additional study aids that focus your efforts and study time on the areas where you need the most help. Please see the *Self-Tests and Personalized Learning* section for more information.

▸ *Video Library*— For every chapter, you can access accompanying video segments. You can can also turn closed captioning on and off as an aid to understanding. Video segments may be accompanied by pre and post-viewing exercises.

▸ *Practice*—Depending on the title, practice activities might include any or all of the following additional activities: vocabulary flashcards; grammar and pronunciation tutorials; additional auto-graded quizzing; and access to Heinle iRadio's MP3-ready cultural exploration activities.

▸ *Online exams* - Your instructor may choose to make exams available online. If you are in a distance course, this may be the sole method of taking exams in your course. To access your exam, click the book cover from your Student Workstation. On the left-hand navigation bar, click on the ⊞ to expand a chapter. Click on the *Exam* for that chapter. Your instructor can assign times when the exams are available. If the exam is not yet available, you will not be able to access it. If it is available, just click *Start* to begin.

2) Class details

In your Student Workstation you will find the details related to your course including:

▸ Course Information: Name (the title and section), Instructor (with a button to click for easy contact, Code (course number), School, Duration (dates of course)

▸ Book Information: Book title, Publisher, Book duration.

3) Registration options

You can drop a course, transfer to a different class, or transfer to a different course or instructor.

To drop a course:

1. Login to the Student Workstation.

2. Click the *Registration options* button in the course you wish to drop.

3. Click *Drop course* to drop your enrollment in this course. Your instructor will be notified. After dropping this course, you will still be able to view your scores; however, you will no longer be able to access the books in this course.

To transfer to a different course or instructor:

1. Login to the Student Workstation.

2. Click the *Registration options* button in the course you wish to transfer from.

3. Click *Change course/instructor*.

4. Enter the new course code and click *Submit*.

To transfer to a different class:

1. Login to the Student Workstation.

2. Click the *Registration options* button in the course you wish to transfer from.

3. Click *Change class*.

4. Select the class you want to enroll in and click *Submit*.

Assignment Calendar

To access all of your assignments by date:

1. Login to the Student Workstation. Click on the book title or cover.

2. Click on the *Assignment Calendar* tab on the right-hand side. Then click on "View by Date" in the blue toolbar.

Figure 4: Calendar

3. You will see all Textbook and Student Activities Manual assignments that are due. This icon ![icon] indicates a Textbook Activity and this icon ![icon] indicates a SAM Activity.
Click an activity to complete it.

4. You can also check your grades on completed assignments. If you see the ● icon, your assignment needs to be graded by your instructor.

5. To see assignments for previous or future weeks, select a date from the calendar during the week you wish to view.

To access all of your assignments by chapter:

Alternatively, you can view the assignments for each chapter.

1. From the Welcome page, click *Assignment Calendar* tab on the right-hand side. Then click on "View by Chapter" in the blue toolbar.

2. Select a chapter from list to see all assignments for that chapter. A due date will appear under the Due Date column for all assigned activities. If an assignment has been completed, the date will be indicated.

3. Select an activity from the list to open and complete.

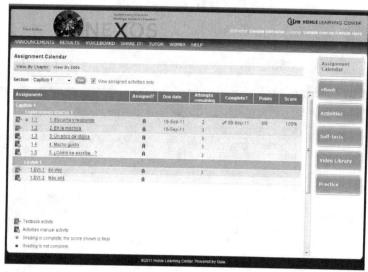

Figure 5: Assignment List

Review & Practice Activities

With enhanced feedback, student are given additional support. At the end of each chapter students will find additional auto-grade grammar activities with specific explanations to their answers. This way students are given direct support and guidance while practicing.

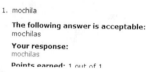

Figure 6: Enhanced Feedback

The **Review It!** button appears with grammar and vocabulary activities and links to relevant resources in the Textbook and Student Activities Manual. Located in the accent toolbar, when a you click the button for an accompanying activity you'll see links to ebook pages covering relevant lessons, flashcards for vocab terms in the activity, podcasts and tutorials that review grammar lessons in the activity, and other resources found in the iLrn for that topic all in one place. This will help you self-correct.

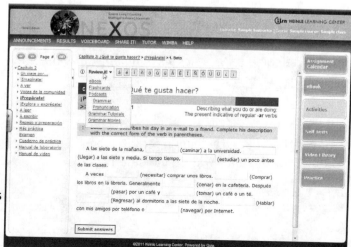

Figure 7: Review it! Button links

Voice-enabled Activities

Voice-enabled activities can be completed alone, with a partner, or with a group. You can talk to your partner or team and write instant messages to work together on the activity, then record a conversation that your instructor will grade. Please note that voice-enabled activities do not work on mobile devices at this time due to technical limitations.

Tips for setting up your computer

It is important that your computer is configured correctly to capture the voice-enabled activities. Here are some tips for ensuring you have the proper setup:

▸ *Microphone* — The latest browser versions and Adobe Flash works best with USB (Universal Serial Bus) connected microphones. Internal microphones, WebCam microphones and the older stereo-jack (male connection) microphones can be problematic.

▸ **Adobe Flash** — You should have the latest version of Adobe Flash installed. Also make sure your Flash settings are configured on your web browser for the program to recognize the microphone being used for Voiceboard. To this follow this steps:

1. Open a voiceboard exercise and right-click on the **Record** button. Select **Settings**.

2. At the bottom of the menu, click the second tab from the left (it looks like a monitor with an eye on it). Make sure the **Allow** option and the **Remember** check box are selected.

3. Click the fourth tab (the one with a microphone on it). Make sure the record volume is up all the way and the correct microphone is selected from the drop-down list.

▸ *"Lab" environment*— In a "Lab" environment, your IT department needs to make sure that the network port "1935" is enabled for voice. If this port is disabled from the school's network voice will not transmit.

Find a partner/team

1. Click on *Voiceboard* at the top of your student Welcome page screen.

2. From the *Voice activities*, select the activity you want to complete.

3. If you need a partner, click the *Find a partner* link at the top of the *Partner Record and Chat box*. This will take you to the partner switchboard where you can invite someone online to partner with you.

Figure 8: Partner Switchboard

4. If you are working with one partner, his or her name will appear at the top of the ***Partner Record and Chat box***.

5. If the assignment requires you to work in teams, you will either need to join an existing team, or invite others to join you. To join an existing team, check the Partnership/Team column and find the name of a person whose team you would like to join. Click his/her name and send him/her a private chat to request an invitation.

6. To form your own team, find an available partner from the Partnership/Team column, click his/her name and the ***Invite to partner*** link. To add more team members, click their names and the ***Invite to team*** link. Note that if you have four teammates, you cannot invite more – teams are restricted to five members.

Complete a voice-enabled activity

1. To send text messages to your partner or team, type in the text box and press Send or press the ***Enter*** key.

2. To talk to your partner or team before recording, press the ***Talk to your partner*** button. Make sure that you and your partner have microphones and a headset or speakers, and that the volume is turned on. Note: Your partner cannot speak to you or hear what you say until he or she presses ***Talk to your partner*** as well. Your conversation will not be recorded unless you click the ***Record*** button.

3. Coordinate with your partner or team on what you'd like to say. When you're ready to record the conversation, press the ***Record*** your conversation button. The computer will start to record your conversation ONLY after all partners or teammates have clicked the ***Record*** button. You will know it is recording because a message in red appears saying "recording..." until either one of the partners presses ***Stop recording***.

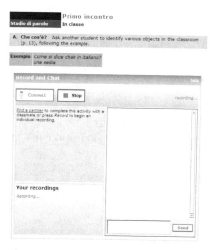

Figure 9: Activity in recording mode

4. Press ***Stop*** when you want to stop recording. You can still talk with your partner or team when the recording stops.

5. To listen to your recording, press ***Play***. You can pause the recording at any time by pressing ***Pause***. If you are not satisfied with your recording, you may record again.

Each recording is saved and you can choose which recording (from a drop-down list) you want to submit.

6. When you are satisfied with your recording, press **Submit answers** to send your recording to your instructor. Note: All partners and teammates must press **Submit** in order for the recording to be counted in all of your grades.

7. If you can't find a partner or team, you can record answers on your own; just press **Record** to record your voice, then stop the recording and submit it when you're done. Check with your instructor to see if an individual recording is acceptable, since these activities are designed to be done with a partner.

Share It!

The new Share It! feature allows you to upload a file, image or video to the Share It! tab where your classmates can comment and rate your file. You can make comments on your classmates files as well, including audio comments.

Your instructor may assign Share It! activities. These will be prompts asking you to upload a file to complete the assignment. When you submit the activity, it will go to the gradebook for your instructor to assign a grade. It will also publish directly the the Share It! tab.

Figure 10: Share It! comment

Self-Tests and Personalized Learning

You may take an online self-test before or after working through a text chapter to get an initial assessment of what you know and what you still need to master. Your results are graded automatically and displayed according to learning outcomes. A Personalized Study Plan, based on the automatically graded test, directs you to additional study aids available in *iLrn: Heinle Learning Center*, including Student Activities Manual activities and pages in the ebook, that focus your efforts and study time on the areas where you need the most help.

> ▸ Step 1 ...Pre-Test (or What Do I Know?) provides an evaluation of what you already know.

> ▸ Step 2 ... Personalized Study Plan (or What Do I Need to Learn?) provides a focus for your work. Chapter sections and additional study materials are chosen to cover concepts that you had problems with in the pre-test.

> ▸ Step 3 ... Post-Test (or What Have I Learned?) provides an evaluation of what you have learned after working through the personalized study plan.

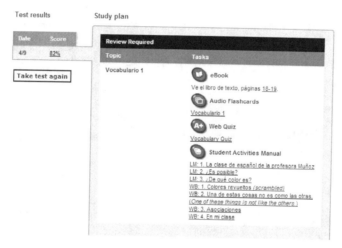

Figure 11: Personalized Study Plan

Using Personal Tutor

What is Personal Tutor?

▸ Personal Tutor provides tutors exclusively from among experienced and qualified instructors. Tutors have achieved high grades in their degrees (many have a Master's degree and higher) and have real classroom teaching experience. All of Personal Tutor's tutors are located in Tampa, FL, and are monitored on-site by a director, who also holds a Ph.D.

How does Personal Tutor work?

▸ Personal Tutor provides whiteboard technology for synchronous tutoring (Q&A sessions) that also includes video and audio capabilities (for those students who want these extra features).

How many hours of tutoring do students get on Personal Tutor?

▸ Personal Tutor provides students with 5 hours of tutoring time.

▸ Students have 3-semesters to use the 5 hours of tutoring

▸ Students have the option of purchasing additional tutoring directly from Personal Tutor if their hours/paper submissions are used up before the end of a semester. The cost is significantly less at $29.99 for an entire month of tutoring versus paying $35 per hour from other services.

When will tutoring be available?

▸ Tutors are available for online tutoring seven days a week, and offline questions and papers can be submitted at any time, 24 hours a day. Online tutoring is available for languages at the times below. Responses to offline questions can take 24 to 48 hours to be returned, however, they are usually returned within one day.

	Spanish	French	Italian	German
MONDAY	9AM-1PM 9PM-12AM			
TUESDAY	9AM-1PM	4-8PM		8PM-Midnight
WEDNESDAY	9AM-1PM 9PM-12AM		6PM-10PM	
THURSDAY	9AM-1PM	4-8PM	8PM-12PM	
FRIDAY	9AM-1PM 5PM-9PM	4-8PM		
SATURDAY	12PM-4PM	4-8PM		
SUNDAY			3PM-7PM	7PM-11PM

Technical Support

▸ Visit *http://hlc.quia.com/support.html*

▸ View FAQs at *http://hlc.quia.com/help/books/faq.html* for immediate answers to common problems.

▸ Send an e-mail to *bookhelp@quia.com*

▸ Call Toll-free 1-877-282-4400

System Requirements

Microsoft® Windows 98, NT, 2000, ME, XP, VISTA, 7
Browsers: Internet Explorer 7.x or higher, or Firefox version 3.x or higher

Macintosh OS X
Browsers: Firefox version 3.x or higher, or Safari 3.x or higher.

Additional Requirements
▸ A high-speed connection with throughput of 256 Kbps or more is recommended to use audio and video components.

▸ Screen resolution: 1024 x 768 or higher

▸ CPU: 233MHz

▸ RAM: 128MB

▸ Flash Player 10 or higher

▸ You will need speakers or a headset to listen to audio and video components, and a microphone is necessary for recording activities.

Exploraciones

Custom Edition for Johnson and Wales University

2nd Edition

Mary Ann Blitt | Margarita Casas

CENGAGE
Learning·

Australia • Brazil • Japan • Korea • Mexico • Singapore • Spain • United Kingdom • United States

Exploraciones: Custom Edition for Johnson and Wales University , 2nd Edition

Exploraciones, 2nd Edition
Mary Ann Blitt | Margarita Casas

© 2016, 2012 Cengage Learning. All rights reserved.

For product information and technology assistance, contact us at
Cengage Learning Customer & Sales Support, 1-800-354-9706
For permission to use material from this text or product,
submit all requests online at **cengage.com/permissions**
Further permissions questions can be emailed to
permissionrequest@cengage.com

This book contains select works from existing Cengage Learning resources and was produced by Cengage Learning Custom Solutions for collegiate use. As such, those adopting and/or contributing to this work are responsible for editorial content accuracy, continuity and completeness.

Compilation © 2015 Cengage Learning

ISBN: 978-1-337-04406-6

WCN: 01-100-101

Cengage Learning
20 Channel Center Street
Boston, MA 02210
USA

Cengage Learning is a leading provider of customized learning solutions with office locations around the globe, including Singapore, the United Kingdom, Australia, Mexico, Brazil, and Japan. Locate your local office at: **www.international.cengage.com/region.**

Cengage Learning products are represented in Canada by Nelson Education, Ltd.

For your lifelong learning solutions, visit **www.cengage.com/custom.**

Visit our corporate website at **www.cengage.com.**

DEDICATORIA

To my parents and closest friends, I am forever grateful for your unconditional love and support

To the Spanish faculty at MCC, thank you for all of your encouragement

Para los estudiantes de español, que aprendan a apreciar el idioma y sus culturas
(Mary Ann)

A mi queridísima familia: A Gordon, a mis padres, a mis hermanos Luis, Alfonso y Fer, a Paty y a mis sobrinos. Gracias por su apoyo y cariño incondicional.

To all my professors and friends at the Foreign Language Department of Colorado State University.

To all our Spanish students!
(Margarita)

Scope and Sequence

Chapter	Objectives	Vocabulary
CAPÍTULO 1 Hola ¿qué tal? 	At the end of the chapter, you will be able to: ■ Greet and say goodbye to people in formal and informal situations ■ Describe your classroom, your friends, and other people ■ Use numbers up to 101, exchange telephone numbers ■ Spell names	**Exploraciones léxicas 1** Greetings, introductions, and goodbyes 4 Classroom 4 Alphabet 5 Numbers 0–101 9, 12 **Exploraciones léxicas 2** Descriptive adjectives 18
CAPÍTULO 2 ¿Cómo es tu vida? 	At the end of the chapter, you will be able to: ■ Describe your family and tell their age ■ Talk about your classes ■ Discuss your routine ■ Express ownership	**Exploraciones léxicas 1** Family members and pets 40 **Exploraciones léxicas 2** Academic subjects 54
CAPÍTULO 3 ¿Qué tiempo hace hoy? 	At the end of the chapter, you will be able to: ■ Talk about the weather and seasons ■ Discuss clothing ■ Express likes and dislikes ■ Communicate dates and time ■ Tell what you and others are going to do in the near future	**Exploraciones léxicas 1** Seasons 78 Weather 78 Clothing 78 Colors 78 **Exploraciones léxicas 2** Days of the week 92 Months 92 Time 92

Scope and Sequence

Chapter	Objectives	Vocabulary
CAPÍTULO 4 ¿Dónde vives? 	At the end of the chapter, you will be able to: ▪ Describe your town or city ▪ Describe your home ▪ Tell where things are located ▪ Request information about the cost of things ▪ Use question words to ask for specific information	**Exploraciones léxicas 1** Places in a city 114 **Exploraciones léxicas 2** Rooms of a house 128 **Exploraciones léxicas 3** Furniture and appliances 128
CAPÍTULO 5 ¿Estás feliz en el trabajo? 	At the end of the chapter, you will be able to: ▪ Describe your feelings, emotions, and physical states ▪ Talk about ongoing actions ▪ Discuss abilities needed for certain jobs and professions	**Exploraciones léxicas 1** Adjectives of emotion and physical states 152 **Exploraciones léxicas 2** Professions 166
CAPÍTULO 6 ¿Cómo pasas el día? 	At the end of the chapter, you will be able to: ▪ Talk about your daily routine ▪ Discuss your hobbies and pastimes ▪ Tell when and how often you do things ▪ Talk about sports ▪ Discuss events that occurred in the past	**Exploraciones léxicas 1** Parts of the body 188 **Exploraciones léxicas 2** Sports 202 Sporting equipment 202

Scope and Sequence

Chapter	Objectives	Vocabulary

Scope and Sequence

Chapter	Objectives	Vocabulary

CAPÍTULO 13

¿Es tu vida una telenovela?

At the end of the chapter, you will be able to:

- Talk about relationships
- Express desires and give recommendations
- Talk about popular culture
- Discuss emotional reactions to events

Exploraciones léxicas 1
Personal relations 448

Exploraciones léxicas 1
Popular culture 462

CAPÍTULO 14

¿Qué haces en una emergencia?

At the end of the chapter, you will be able to:

- Discuss health issues with a doctor
- Discuss hypothetical situations
- Express opinions regarding world issues
- Tell what happened prior to other events in the past

Exploraciones léxicas 1
Health and medical emergencies 484

Exploraciones léxicas 2
Nationalities 498

Political concepts 498

To the student

Most people who study another language would like to be able to speak it. **Exploraciones** will help you do just that. You'll learn to talk about yourself, your community, and the world around you. You'll start out asking and answering questions, then you'll narrate events and make comparisons, and eventually you'll be able to express your opinions. At the same time, you'll read and listen to real-world samples of the language such as radio announcements, interviews, flyers, and magazine articles, and you'll write emails and blog entries in Spanish.

To become a successful language learner, it's important to learn to analyze the language and figure out the rules for yourself. In the grammar sections of **Exploraciones,** you'll be guided through a process of observing the language in use and recognizing the patterns. Eventually, you'll sharpen this skill and be able to use it beyond this textbook.

You can't learn a language without studying the cultures of the people who speak it. In every chapter, you'll learn about the practices of Spanish speakers from around the world and the countries they live in. This will enable you to make cultural comparisons: finding both similarities and differences between these cultures and your own. We hope that you'll find the study of the Spanish language exciting and fun, and that it opens many doors in your future explorations.

Organization of Exploraciones

Exploraciones has fourteen chapters, each consisting of two independent parts that are identical in organization. Each chapter starts with the chapter outline and provides a learning strategy. The remainder of each of the chapters is set up in the following manner:

Exploraciones léxicas

You will be introduced to vocabulary through illustrations and lists. Then, in the **A practicar** section, you will work through a series of activities that will require you to speak minimally at first and then progress to more open-ended communicative activities.

Conexiones culturales

This section has short cultural information pieces and tasks that encourage you to go beyond the reading and research various aspects of the Spanish-speaking world. You will have the opportunity to share some of your findings online with your classmates in Share it!

Exploraciones gramaticales

Through a series of video vignettes, you will meet eight characters from different parts of the Spanish-speaking world. After watching the video you will be asked to analyze a segment of the video transcript to discover the patterns and rules of Spanish grammar in the **A analizar** section. This section is followed by **A comprobar,** in which you can compare your conclusions with the explanation of the rules. Then in the **A practicar** section, you will practice the grammar concept in a variety of activities.

Lectura

This section allows you to learn more about the culture of Spanish-speaking countries while improving your reading skills. Each section starts with a strategy to help you improve your reading in Spanish.

Redacción

At the end of each chapter, you will develop your writing skills through a process-writing exercise in which you are guided to brainstorm, write a draft, and revise it.

En vivo

In the first half of the chapter, you will improve your listening skills as you listen to audio segments that you are likely to hear in a Spanish-speaking country, such as commercials and public service announcements. In the second half of the chapter, you will enhance your reading skills through readings from a variety of sources such as magazines and websites.

Exploraciones profesionales

These short career-focused video vignettes allow you to observe the Spanish language within a professional context. The **Vocabulario** section provides useful Spanish vocabulary and expressions that you are likely to use in a field in which you currently work or in which you may intend to work, while the **Datos importantes** feature gives important information about the career such as education, salary and work environment.

Exploraciones de repaso

At the end of each chapter, there are two pages of review activities. The **Exploraciones de repaso: estructuras** provides a structured review of the grammar concepts from the chapter while the **Exploraciones de repaso: comunicación** lets you practice the vocabulary and grammar through communicative partner activities.

Exploraciones literarias

After every second chapter, there is a literary selection that will introduce you to different writers from throughout the Spanish-speaking world and a sample of their work. You will also learn the basics of literary analysis through the **Investiguemos la literatura** box accompanying each selection.

Study Suggestions

1. Study every day. For most students, it is more effective to study for 15–20 minutes 3 times a day, than to spend one full hour on the subject.

2. Listen to the audio recordings. When studying the vocabulary, take time to listen to the pronunciation of the words. It will help your pronunciation, as well as help you learn to spell them properly.

3. Get help when you need it. Learning a foreign language is like learning math; you will continue to use what you have already learned and to build upon that knowledge. So, if you find you don't understand something, be sure to see your instructor or a tutor right away.

4. Participate actively in class. In order to learn the language, you have to speak it and to learn from your mistakes.

5. Make intelligent guesses. When you are reading, listening to your instructor, or watching a video make intelligent guesses as to the meaning of words you do not know. Use the context, cognates (words that look or sound like English words), intonation, and if possible visual clues such as body language, gestures, facial expressions and images, to help you figure out the meaning of the word.

6. Study with a friend or form a study group. Not only might you benefit when your friend understands a concept that you have difficulty with, but you will have more opportunities to practice speaking as well as listening.

7. Find what works for you. Use a variety of techniques to memorize vocabulary and verbs until you find the ones that are best for you. Try writing the words, listening to recordings of the words, and using flash cards.

8. Review material from previous lessons. Because learning a language is cumulative, it is important to refresh your knowledge of vocabulary, verbs, and structures learned in earlier lessons.

9. Avoid making grammar comparisons. While it is helpful to understand some basic grammar concepts of the English language, such as pronouns and direct objects, it is important not to constantly make comparisons, but rather to learn the new structures.

10. Speak Spanish. Try to use Spanish for all your classroom interactions, not just when called on by the instructor or answering a classmate's question in a group activity. Don't worry that your sentence may not be structurally correct; the important thing is to begin to feel comfortable expressing yourself in the language.

Acknowledgments

We would like to express our most sincere gratitude and appreciation to everybody who has played a role in the making of **Exploraciones,** and to those who have supported us on this edition. In particular, we are grateful to the instructors and students who used **Exploraciones** in its previous edition, and helped us to improve it.

We wish to thank everybody who has worked so hard at Cengage to make this project a success. In particular we would like to give thanks Kim Beuttler, our content developer, Heather Bradley Cole, our product manager, and Beth Kramer, our product director. A huge thank you goes to Esther Marshall—we do not know how the project would have been completed without her. Our thanks also go to Michelle Williams, Linda Jurras, and Julie Allen; Hermann Mejia for his superb illustrations, Katy Gabel from Lumina Datamatics for her dedicated work and professional contribution; Lupe Ortiz, the copyeditor; Margaret Hines, the proofreader; and the skilled freelance professionals who worked on this project: Photo researcher Poyee Oster, and text permissions researcher Melissa Flamson.

Reviewers and Contributors

Special thanks go to the following instructors who have written the outstanding supplements to accompany the text:

Clara Burgo, *Loyola University Chicago* – Composition activities
Clara Vega, *Alamance Community College* – PowerPoint presentations, games, worksheet activities
Christina García – Testing Program

We are thankful to the following members of the **Exploraciones** Advisory Board who provided thoughtful commentary on the manuscript through detailed reviews during its development.

Frances Alpren, *Vanderbilt University*
Shannon Hahn, *Durham Technical Community College*
Martine Howard, *Camden County College*
Yolanda González, *Valencia College*
Todd Hernández, *Marquette University*
Joshua Hoekstra, *Bluegrass Community College*
Mercedes Meier, *Miami Dade College*
José Morillo, *Marshall University*
Dolores Pons, *University of Michigan – Flint*
Laura Ruiz-Scott, *Scottsdale Community College*
José Sandoval, *Coastal Carolina Community College*
Bethany Sanio, *University of Nebraska – Lincoln*
Roger Simpson, *Clemson University*

We are also grateful for the valuable feedback and suggestions offered by the following professors through their participation in live and virtual focus groups, one-on-one interviews, and chapter reviews.

Claudia Acosta, *College of the Canyons*
Maria Luisa Akrabova, *Metropolitan State University of Denver*
Susana Alaiz Losada, *Queensborough Community College*
Alma Alfaro, *Walla Walla University*
Frances Alpren, *Vanderbilt University*
Tim Altanero, *Austin Community College*
Elizabeth Amaya, *Millikin University*
Sandra Anderson, *College of DuPage*
Gunnar Anderson, *SUNY Potsdam*
Lisette Balabarca, *Siena College*
Susan Bangs, *Harrisburg Area Community College*
Vania Barraza, *University of Memphis*
Philip Benfield, *Horry Georgetown Technical College*

Patricia Betancourt, *Palm Beach State College*
Georgia Betcher, *Fayetteville Technical Community College*
Rosa Bilbao, *Alamance Community College*
Marie Blair, *University of Nebraska*
Silvia Bliss, *Morrisville State College*
Graciela Boruszko, *Pepperdine University*
Ana J. Caldero Figueroa, *Valencia College*
Wendy Caldwell, *Francis Marion University*
Aurelie Capron, *McKendree University*
Lindsey Carpenter, *Durham Technical Community College*
F. Eduardo Castilla Ortiz, *Missouri Western State University*
Esther Castro, *San Diego State University*
Thomas Claerr, *Henry Ford Community College*
Sheri Cochran-Alejo, *Utah State University / Cottonwood HS*
Judy Cortes, *California State University Monterey Bay*
David Counselman, *Ohio Wesleyan University*
Angela Cresswell, *Holy Family University*
Daniel D'Arpa, *Mercer County College*
Luis Delgado, *Olive-Harvey College*
Lisa DeWaard, *Clemson University*
Oscar Díaz, *Middle Tennessee State University*
Conxita Domenech, *University of Wyoming*
Indira Dortolina, *Lone Star College - Cy Fair*
Jabier Elorrieta, *New York University*
Luz Marina Escobar, *Tarrant County College – Southeast*
Erin Farb, *Community College of Denver*
Ronna Feit, *Nassau Community College*
Arlene Fuentes, *Southern Virginia University*
Elena Gandía García, *University of Nevada, Las Vegas*
Gerardo García-Muñoz, *Prairie View A&M University*
Margarita Garcia-Notario, *SUNY Plattsburgh*
Christina Garitselov, *State University of New York College at Brockport*
Deborah Gill, *Penn State DuBois*
Sara Goke, *Massasoit Community College*
Inmaculada Gómez Soler, *University of Memphis*
Arcides Gonzalez, *California University of Pennsylvania*
Marvin Gordon, *University of Illinois at Chicago*
Manuel Guzman, *Imperial Valley College*
Sergio Guzmán, *College of Southern Nevada*
Shannon Hahn, *Durham Technical Community College*
Patricia Harrigan, *Community College of Baltimore County*
Ruth Heath, *MCC Penn Valley*
Florencia Henshaw, *University of Illinois at Urbana-Champaign*
Todd Hernández, *Marquette University*
Suzanna Hernandez, *Wilson Community College*
Joshua Hoekstra, *Bluegrass Community and Technical College*
Esther Holtermann, *American Univesity*
Walter Hopkins, *Michigan State University*
Martine Howard, *Camden County College*
Casilde Isabelli, *University of Nevada, Reno*
Becky Jaimes, *Austin Community College*
Roberto Jiménez-Arroyo, *University of South Florida Sarasota-Manatee*
Hilda M. Kachmar, *St. Catherine University*
Esther Kahn, *North Virginia Community College*
Laura Kahn, *Suffolk Community College*
Brian Keady, *Linn-Benton Community College*

Kristin Kiely, *Francis Marion University*
Kelly Kingsbury Brunetto, *University of Nebraska-Lincoln*
Julie Kleinhans-Urrutia, *Austin Community College*
Melissa Knosp, *Johnson C. Smith University*
Kevin Krogh, *Utah State University*
Barbara Kruger, *Finger Lakes Community College*
Carol Kuznacic, *Metropolitan Community College - Longview*
Luis Latoja, *Columbus State Community College*
Alejandro Lee, *Central Washington University*
Jessica Lee, *Utah State University*
Lucy Lee, *Truman State University*
Roxana Levin, *St. Petersburg College*
Clara Lipszyc-Arroyo, *Case Western Reserve University*
Regina Lira, *Imperial Valley College*
Domenico Maceri, *Allan Hancock College*
Jorge Majfud, *Jacksonville University*
Debora Maldonado-DeOliveira, *Meredith College*
Marilyn Manley, *Rowan University – Glassboro*
Donna Marques, *Cuyamaca College*
Carol Marshall, *Truman State University*
Karen Martin, *Texas Christian University*
Francisco Martinez, *Northwestern Oklahoma State University*
Carlos Martinez, *New York University*
Mercedes Meier, *Miami Dade College*
Marco Mena, *MassBay Community College*
Ana Menendez-Collera, *Suffolk County Community College Ammerman Campus*
Joseph Menig, *Valencia College*
Jerome Miner, *Knox College*
Nancy Minguez, *Old Dominion University*
Geoff Mitchell, *Maryville College*
José Morillo, *Marshall University*
Melissa Murphy, *University of Texas*
Jerome Mwinyelle, *East Tennessee State University*
Rosalinda Nericcio, *San Diego State University*
Christine Núñez, *Kutztown University*
Jeffrey Oxford, *Midwestern State University*
Yelgy Parada, *Los Angeles City College*
Anne Pasero, *Marquette University*
Teresa Perez-Gamboa, *University of Georgia*
Inma Pertusa, *Western Kentucky University*
Ana Piffardi, *Eastfield College*
Dolóres Pons, *University of Michigan-Flint*
Sofia Ramirez Gelpi, *Allan Hancock College*
Alma Ramirez-Trujillo, *Emory & Henry College*
Gladys Robalino, *Messiah College*
Jennifer Rogers, *Metropolitan Community College - Blue River*
Marta Rosso-O'Laughlin, *Marta Rosso-O'Laughlin*
David Rubi, *Paradise Valley Community College*
Laura Ruiz-Scott, *Scottsdale Community College*
Josue Sanchez, *Paine College*
Jaime Sanchez, *Volunteer State Community College*
Alex Sandoval, *Coastal Carolina Community College*
Lester Sandres Rapalo, *Valencia College*
Bethany Sanio, *University of Nebraska-Lincoln*
Roman Santos, *Mohawk Valley Community College*
Sarah Schaaf, *College of Saint Benedict & Saint John's University*

Nina Shecktor, *Kutztown University*
Roger Simpson, *Clemson University*
Andrea M Smith, *Shenandoah University*
Michael Smith, *Norfolk State University*
Stuart Smith, *Austin Community College*
Alfredo Sosa-Velasco, *Southern Connecticut State University*
Stacy Southerland, *University of Central Oklahoma*
Maria Luisa Spicer-Escalante, *Utah State University*
Kathleen Sullivan, *Marquette University*
March Sustarsic Harvey, *Pikes Peak Community College*
Joe Terantino, *Kennesaw State University*
Silvina Trica-Flores, *Nassau Community College*
Luziris Turi, *Rice University*
Felix Versaguis, *North Hennepin Community College*
Bernardo Viano, *CUNY-Lehman College*
Oswaldo Voysest, *Beloit College*
Sandra Watts, *University of North Carolina at Charlotte*
Valerie Watts, *AB Technical Community College*
Carolyn Woolard, *Milligan College*
Renee Wooten, *Vernon College*
Mary Yetta McKelva, *Grayson County College*
Itzá Zavala-Garrett, *Morehead State University*

In addition to the instructors listed above, hundreds of additional instructors took the time to respond to surveys gathering information about preferred supplementary items, product packaging formats, and other critical issues. We appreciate their time and advice.

We are especially grateful for the feedback and suggestions we have received from thousands of students who used the book in the classroom. Their comments and suggestions have informed every aspect of this program. In addition to students who learned from the first edition, students from the following schools offered extremely useful suggestions about preferences on content, design and the use of technology during focus groups and surveys:

Austin Community College, Bradley University, Butler University, Central Michigan University, Central Piedmont Community College, Cincinnati State and Technical College, Clemson University, College of Charleston, DePaul University, George Washington University, Kansas State University, Minnesota State University, North Lake College, Oklahoma University, Rock Valley College, Saint Louis University, Temple University, Trinity College, University of Maryland—College Park, University of Wisconsin—Milwaukee, University of Dallas, University of Texas—Arlington, Washington State University

Learning Strategy

Study frequently

When learning a foreign language it is important to study every day. Aside from any written homework you may have, plan to spend some time each day learning the current vocabulary and verbs. For most students, it is more effective to study for 15–20 minutes three times a day than to spend a full hour on the subject. It might also be a lot easier for you to find time to study if you break it into smaller periods of time.

In this chapter you will learn how to:

- Greet and say goodbye to people in formal and informal situations
- Describe your classroom, your friends, and other people
- Use numbers up to 100 and exchange telephone numbers
- Spell names

Hola, ¿qué tal?

© Image Source Plus/Alamy

Exploraciones léxicas

Este es el salón de clases de Mariana. ¿Qué hay en la clase?

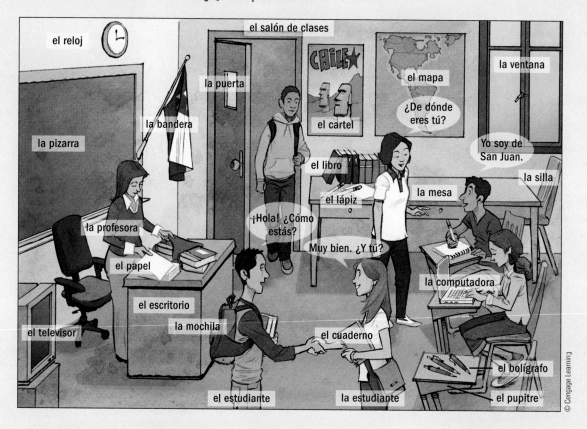

Saludos formales

Buenos días.
Buenas tardes.
Buenas noches.
¿Cómo está (usted)?

Respuestas

Buenos días.
Buenas tardes.
Buenas noches.
Bien, gracias. / Mal. / Regular, gracias.
¿Y usted?

Saludos informales

¡Hola!
¿Cómo estás (tú)?
¿Qué tal?
¿Qué hay de nuevo?
¿Qué pasa?

Respuestas

¡Hola!
Bien, gracias. / Mal. / Regular, gracias. ¿Y tú?
Nada.

Nada.

Despedidas

Adiós.	Goodbye.
Chao.	Goodbye. (informal)
Hasta luego.	See you later.
Hasta pronto.	See you soon.
Hasta mañana.	See you tomorrow.
¡Nos vemos!	See you later!
¡Que tengas un buen día!	Have a nice day! (informal)

Presentaciones

¿Cómo te llamas?	What is your name? (informal)
Me llamo...	My name is . . .
Le presento a...	I'd like to introduce you to . . . (formal)
Te presento a...	I'd like to introduce you to . . . (informal)

Encantado(a).	Nice to meet you.
Mucho gusto.	Nice to meet you.
¿Cómo se escribe...?	How do you spell . . . ?

Palabras interrogativas

¿Dónde?	Where?
¿Cuándo?	When?
¿Cuántos(as)?	How many?
¿Qué?	What?
¿Quién?	Who?
¿Por qué?	Why?

INVESTIGUEMOS EL VOCABULARIO

Vocabulary often varies from one Spanish-speaking country to another. For example, here are three different terms for the word for *pen*:

el bolígrafo (Spain)   **la pluma** (Mexico)   **el lapicero** (Peru)

Another word that has variations is *computer*:

la computadora (Latin America)   **el ordenador** (Spain)

A practicar

1.1 **Escucha y responde** Listen to the following list of common classroom items. If the item is in your classroom, give a thumbs-up; if it is not, give a thumbs-down.

🔊 1-2

1.2 **En la mochila** Indicate which of these items could go into a student's backpack: **la pizarra, el cuaderno, el papel, la silla, el bolígrafo, el escritorio, la puerta, los lápices**

1.3 **Un poco de lógica** Match each question or statement with a logical response.

1. ¿Cómo te llamas?
2. ¿De dónde eres?
3. ¿Cómo estás?
4. ¿Qué hay de nuevo?
5. Te presento a Jairo.

a. Soy de California.
b. Me llamo Marcos.
c. Nada.
d. Mucho gusto.
e. Bien, gracias. ¿Y tú?

> **INVESTIGUEMOS EL VOCABULARIO**
> When making introductions, male speakers use the form **encantado**. Female speakers use the form **encantada**.

1.4 **Mucho gusto** Read the dialogue aloud with a partner. Then, read it again, substituting all the parts in italics with your own information or greetings/farewells.

Estudiante 1: *¡Hola!*
Estudiante 2: *¡Hola!*
Estudiante 1: Me llamo *Rafael*. ¿Y tú? ¿Cómo te llamas?
Estudiante 2: Me llamo *Carlos*.

Estudiante 1: Mucho gusto, *Carlos*. ¿De dónde eres?
Estudiante 2: Soy de *México*. ¿Y tú?
Estudiante 1: Yo soy de *Argentina*.
Estudiante 2: ¡Qué bien!
Estudiante 1: Bueno... *¡adiós!*
Estudiante 2: *¡Chao!*

> **INVESTIGUEMOS EL VOCABULARIO**
> According to the Real Academia, **ch, ll,** and **rr** are not independent letters, so they are not listed as part of the Spanish alphabet. Additional changes made to the alphabet are the names of the letters **v, w,** and **y.** However, it is likely to hear the former letter names used as well.

🔊 El alfabeto
1-3

Letra	Nombre de la letra	Letra	Nombre de la letra	Letra	Nombre de la letra	Letra	Nombre de la letra
A	a	H	hache	Ñ	eñe	U	u
B	be	I	i	O	o	V	uve
C	ce	J	jota	P	pe	W	doble uve
D	de	K	ka	Q	cu	X	equis
E	e	L	ele	R	ere	Y	ye
F	efe	M	eme	S	ese	Z	zeta
G	ge	N	ene	T	te		

1.5 **Correo electrónico** You and your partner are in charge of your school's Club Internacional. You have information for half of the new members on this page and your partner has the other half in Appendix B. Ask each other questions to complete the tables. You will need the following words: **arroba** (@) and **punto** (*dot*).

Modelo Estudiante 1: *¿Cuál es el correo electrónico de Pilar?*
Estudiante 2: *pilybonita@uden.es → p-i-l-y-b-o-n-i-t-a, arroba, u-d-e-n, punto, e-s*

Nombre	Correo electrónico
1. Marina	
2. Gabriel	gabmuñoz@inter.cl
3. Alejandro	
4. Valeria	valelapeña@clarotodo.pr

Conexiones culturales

Latinos e hispanos en el mundo

Conexiones... a la geografía

Look at the map and write the names of all Spanish-speaking countries that you can locate. Then indicate in what region each country is located: North America (**América del Norte**), Central America (**América Central**), South America (**América del Sur**), the Caribbean (**el Caribe**), Europe (**Europa**), or Africa (**África**). When you finish your list, match each of the countries with its capital city from the box below. **¡OJO!** One of the countries has two capital cities.

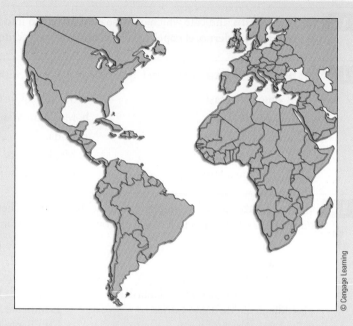

Asunción	La Paz	San Juan
Bogotá	Lima	San Salvador
Buenos Aires	Madrid	Santiago
Caracas	Malabo	Santo Domingo
Ciudad de Guatemala	Managua	Sucre
Ciudad de México	Montevideo	Tegucigalpa
Ciudad de Panamá	Quito	
La Habana	San José	

You can learn more about these countries in **Appendix A: Exploraciones del mundo hispano.**

Comparaciones

How different is the Spanish used in Spain from the Spanish spoken in Latin American countries? It is important to understand that it is the same language and both will be understood in every country where Spanish is spoken. However, there are regional differences in vocabulary as well as accents, just as there are between the English spoken in England and the English used in the United States. Come up with a list of five or six regional vocabulary variations in English and compare your list with a partner's. Do your words fit into specific categories (food, clothing, etc.)? What factors do you think influence differences in vocabulary within the same language? Write five words that you would expect to vary in Spanish-speaking countries. For some variations, check **Investiguemos el vocabulario** on page 4.

Cultura

Cultural practices and products of Spanish-speaking countries vary from country to country. Putting aside preconceived ideas will help you gain a better understanding of these cultures. Work in groups of three or four to determine if the statements below are true or false. Then, search the Internet to correct the false statements.

1. All Latin Americans speak Spanish.
2. Flamenco is a popular dance throughout South America.
3. The majority of the population in Spanish-speaking countries is Catholic.
4. **Tortillas** are a typical dish in Spain.
5. Some indigenous people in Mexico and Guatemala still wear traditional clothing.
6. Chiles are a cooking staple in Paraguay, Uruguay, and Argentina.
7. Soccer is the most popular sport in South America.
8. In many Spanish-speaking countries, children can attend school in the morning or the afternoon.
9. Bullfighting is a popular sport in Cuba.
10. In most Spanish-speaking countries, the main meal is between 5:00 and 7:00 P.M.

© sportgraphic/Shutterstock

Many people assume that the same foods are eaten in all of Latin America and Spain. Choose a country from the **Exploraciones del mundo hispano** section in **Appendix A** and research some of the typical dishes from that country. Share an image and the name of a dish you'd like to try and list the ingredients needed.

Comunidad

If there are any international students or ESL students in your school that are native Spanish speakers, introduce yourself to one of them and find out where he or she is from. You may want to become conversation partners.

INVESTIGUEMOS LA MÚSICA

Find the song "Latino" by Adolescent's Orquesta on the Internet and listen to it. What Latin American countries are named?

© Kolett/Shutterstock

Exploraciones gramaticales

Throughout the program, you will be given examples of grammatical structures in Spanish and asked to discover the patterns of use based on those examples. This process not only helps you to remember how to use particular structures but will also help you to develop important skills such as inference and pattern recognition, which will make you a better language learner.

A analizar

Professor Tobar is in his classroom making sure he has everything ready for the first day of classes. Watch the video and note whether there is one or more than one of everything you see. Read the passage and underline the vocabulary words. Then answer the questions.

> Este es el salón de clases. Hay muchos estudiantes en la clase. Hay una pizarra. No hay carteles, pero hay un mapa. Hay muchas sillas. También hay un escritorio, hay lápices y bolígrafos en el escritorio... ¡no hay una computadora!

© Cengage Learning

1. Which words that you underlined refer to more than one item (are plural)? How do you know?
2. Find the word above that is similar to **lápiz**. What differences do you notice?

A comprobar
Gender and number of nouns

1. A noun (**sustantivo**) is a person, place, or thing. In order to make a noun plural:

   - add an -**s** to words ending in a vowel   libro → libros   silla → sillas
   - add an -**es** to words ending in a consonant   profesor → profesores   papel → papeles
   - change a final -**z** to -**c** and add an -**es**   lápiz → lápices

2. You will notice that some nouns lose an accent mark or gain an accent mark when they become plural. You will learn more about accent marks in **Capítulo 2**.

   televisión → televisiones
   salón → salones
   examen → exámenes

3. In Spanish, nouns have a gender. In other words, they are either masculine or feminine.

   The endings of nouns not referring to people often indicate a word's gender.

   > Masculine nouns:
   > - often end in -**o**, such as **el libro** and **el cuaderno**
   > - can refer to a man, such as **el profesor** and **el estudiante**
   >
   > Feminine nouns:
   > - often end in -**a**, such as **la silla** and **la pizarra**
   > - can refer to a woman, such as **la profesora** and **la estudiante**

   There are some exceptions such as:

Masculine	Feminine
el día	la mano
el mapa	la foto
el problema	la moto

4. Here are the numbers from 0 to 20.

Los números					
0	cero	7	siete	14	catorce
1	uno	8	ocho	15	quince
2	dos	9	nueve	16	dieciséis
3	tres	10	diez	17	diecisiete
4	cuatro	11	once	18	dieciocho
5	cinco	12	doce	19	diecinueve
6	seis	13	trece	20	veinte

A practicar

1.6 **De singular a plural** Change the following vocabulary words from singular to plural.

Modelo cuaderno → *cuadernos*

1. mochila
2. lápiz
3. papel
4. pupitre
5. reloj
6. bandera
7. libro
8. cartel
9. televisor
10. examen

© MARCELODLT/Shutterstock

1.7 **Género** Using the rules that you have learned, decide whether the following words are masculine (**M**) or feminine (**F**).

	M	F
1. saludo	_____	_____
2. actriz	_____	_____
3. cafetería	_____	_____
4. rosa	_____	_____
5. doctor	_____	_____
6. teatro	_____	_____
7. día	_____	_____
8. supervisora	_____	_____
9. mapa	_____	_____
10. autor	_____	_____

1.8 **En la clase** Listen to Carolina describe how many of the following items are in her classroom. As you listen, write the number next to each item. Then tell how many of each of the items there are in your classroom.

1-4

Modelo   You will hear: *Hay once escritorios.*
You will write: _____11_____ escritorios

1. _____ estudiantes
2. _____ pizarras
3. _____ sillas
4. _____ ventanas
5. _____ mapas
6. _____ computadoras

1.9 **Los útiles** Look at the pictures below and identify the plural classroom items you have learned, telling how many there are. Then work with a partner and take turns identifying the school supplies you each have. **¡OJO!** Pay attention to singular and plural forms of the vocabulary words.

1.10 **La clase de matemáticas** Work with a partner and take turns saying the following mathematical equations in Spanish and giving their solutions. You will need the following words: **más (+)**, **menos (–)**, and **son (=)**.

Modelo $6 + 10 =$
Seis más diez son dieciséis.

1. $4 + 5 =$
2. $16 - 6 =$
3. $20 - 2 =$
4. $7 + 9 =$
5. $3 + 12 =$
6. $11 - 4 =$
7. $13 + 1 =$
8. $14 + 5 =$

A analizar

Profesor Tobar is in his classroom. Watch the video again. Then read the paragraph below and answer the questions that follow.

Este es el salón de clases. Hay muchos estudiantes en la clase. Hay una pizarra. No hay carteles, pero hay un mapa. Hay muchas sillas. También hay un escritorio, hay lápices y bolígrafos en el escritorio... ¡no hay una computadora! ¡¿Donde está la computadora?! Necesito hablar con el director.

© Cengage Learning

1. Write the word that comes before each of the following nouns. Do these words change according to the nouns that follow? Explain.

_____ salón de clase   _____ escritorio

_____ pizarra   _____ computadora

_____ mapa   _____ director

2. What do you think **hay** means?

A comprobar

Definite and indefinite articles and **hay**

1. The definite article *the* is used with a specific noun or a noun that has previously been mentioned. In Spanish, the definite article indicates whether a noun is masculine or feminine as well as whether it is singular or plural. It can be expressed in four different ways.

Artículos definidos

	masculino	femenino
singular	el	la
plural	los	las

¿De dónde es **el** profesor?
*Where is **the** professor from?*

2. The indefinite articles *a/an* or *some* are used when referring to a noun that is not specific or that has not previously been mentioned. They also indicate gender (masculine/feminine) and number (singular/plural), and can be expressed in four different ways in Spanish.

Artículos indefinidos

	masculino	femenino
singular	un	una
plural	unos	unas

¿Hay **una** ventana en el salón de clases?
*Is there **a** window in the classroom?*

3. **Hay** means *there is* or *there are*. It is used with the indefinite article to talk about singular nouns and to indicate *some* with plural nouns. The indefinite article is often omitted after **hay** in plural expressions.

Hay un escritorio.   No hay lápices.
There is a desk.   *There are no pencils.*

Hay (unas) ventanas.   No hay una pizarra.
There are (some) windows. *There isn't a board.*

4. When using **hay** with numbers, do not use an article. You already know numbers 0–20; numbers 21 through 101 are below.

No hay tres libros.
There aren't three books.

Hay cinco libros.
There are five books.

21	veintiuno	28	veintiocho	60	sesenta
22	veintidós	29	veintinueve	70	setenta
23	veintitrés	30	treinta	80	ochenta
24	veinticuatro	31	treinta y uno	90	noventa
25	veinticinco	40	cuarenta	100	cien
26	veintiséis	50	cincuenta	101	ciento uno
27	veintisiete				

Numbers below 30 are only one word, whereas numbers above 30 take the word **y** *(and),* for example, **treinta y uno.** With the numbers 21, 31, etc., **uno** changes to **un** when followed by a masculine noun: **Hay treinta y un libros** and **una** when followed by a feminine noun: **Hay treinta y una sillas.** Note that **veintiún** has an accent over the letter **u.**

A practicar

1.11 **¿Lógico o no?** Read the statements and decide if they are logical or not.

1. Hay un cuaderno en la mochila.
2. No hay una puerta en la clase.
3. Hay una estudiante en la clase.
4. Hay cinco libros en el escritorio.
5. Hay unos papeles en la mesa.
6. Hay una pizarra en la silla.

1.12 **Los artículos** Read the paragraph and decide if you need the definite article or the indefinite article. Circle the correct answer.

David es estudiante en (**1.** una / la) universidad de los Estados Unidos. En su salón de clases hay (**2.** unos / los) carteles y (**3.** una / la) ventana. (**4.** Una / La) ventana es muy grande. En (**5.** una / la) mochila de David hay (**6.** unos / los) libros. También hay (**7.** un / el) cuaderno para (**8.** una / la) clase de español de David.

David es estudiante.

1.13 **¿Cuántos hay?** Look at the picture below and take turns answering the following questions.

© Cengage Learning

1. ¿Cuántos mapas hay?
2. ¿Cuántas sillas hay?
3. ¿Cuántos libros hay?

4. ¿Cuántos lápices hay?
5. ¿Cuántas banderas hay?
6. ¿Qué más hay? (*What else is there?*)

1.14 **¿Qué hay?** With a partner, take turns asking and answering the questions about the items in your classroom. If you have them in your classroom, tell how many there are. Remember, if there is only one item, you must use **un** or **una.**

Modelo ¿Hay mesas?
    Estudiante 1: *¿Hay mesas?*
    Estudiante 2: *Sí, hay una mesa. / Sí, hay dos mesas. / No, no hay mesas.*

1. ¿Hay relojes?
2. ¿Hay pizarras?
3. ¿Hay banderas?
4. ¿Hay mapas?

5. ¿Hay ventanas?
6. ¿Hay carteles?
7. ¿Hay computadoras?
8. ¿Hay sillas?

© Christopher Futcher/Shutterstock

1.15 **El número, por favor** Look at the directory for a university in Nicaragua. Tell what numbers you would need to call to reach the following areas.

1. la oficina de admisión
2. las diferentes facultades *(departments)*
3. para participar en actividades

Contáctenos

Oficina de admisión 2214 7300

Facultades
Ciencia y Tecnología 2297 7210
Psicología 2249 3765
Sociología 2278 4403
Humanidades y Filosofía 2251 2030
Arquitectura 2259 8215

Deportes y cultura
Fútbol 2264 3911
Karate 2255 1290
Volibol 2213 8616
Ballet folclórico 2233 0961
Grupo de teatro 2292 4718

© Cengage Learning

1.16 **En la librería** It is the end of the year, and employees are taking inventory at the bookstore. Tell how many items they have using the verb **hay**.

1. 50 cuadernos
2. 85 diccionarios
3. 100 bolígrafos
4. 78 lápices
5. 21 computadoras
6. 94 paquetes de papel
7. 31 libros de español
0. 62 mapas
9. 49 calculadoras
10. 51 mochilas

© Monkey Business Images/Shutterstock

Entrando en materia

Where do you buy your school supplies?

Comprando artículos escolares

🔊 Maricarmen will start school next week, and she is looking for supplies at good
1-5 prices. Listen to two commercials where she can buy what she needs: the first one for Papelería El Gigante and the second one for La Bodega.

Vocabulario útil

los artículos escolares	*school supplies*	**gratis**	*for free*
la copiadora	*copier*	**la impresora**	*printer*
el descuento	*discount*		

Comprensión

Listen to the commercials again and indicate where Maricarmen would get a better price for the following articles.

Maricarmen needs . . .   She should buy at . . .

1. cuadernos   Papelería El Gigante   La Bodega
2. lápices   Papelería El Gigante   La Bodega
3. papel   Papelería El Gigante   La Bodega
4. una computadora   Papelería El Gigante   La Bodega
5. bolígrafos   Papelería El Gigante   La Bodega
6. una mochila   Papelería El Gigante   La Bodega

Más allá

What supplies do you use for your classes? Using the vocabulary in this chapter, make a list in Spanish and use Share It! to post a written or recorded list to share with the class.

© Nattika/Shutterstock

Lectura

Reading Strategy: Cognates

Look at the following list of words: **elefante, fotografía, oficina, bicicleta.** Chances are you have never seen them before but that you can figure out what they mean because they look similar to English words. Words that are similar in two languages are called cognates (**cognados**). While there are some false cognates (words that look like English words but have different meanings), most of the time, the meaning will be the same. When you are reading, you will not understand every word, but use cognates to help you understand the general idea.

Antes de leer

Look at the advertisement for a school. Using the cognates to help you, answer the questions.

LINGUAMAX

Establecido en 1980, **Linguamax** ofrece clases de inglés y francés para adolescentes y adultos.

- Profesores nativos con mucha experiencia
- Clases con un máximo de 5 estudiantes
- Precios razonables

Los cursos comienzan el 1° de junio

Para más información llame al 951-23-45-67 o visite **Linguamax** en la Avenida Bolívar, 203

¡Cursos de lenguas con garantía de calidad!

Obtenga un descuento del 10% al mencionar este anuncio.

---

1. When was the school established?
2. What classes are offered at the school?
3. Who can take classes?
4. What are three benefits of taking classes at this school?
5. When do classes begin?
6. How can you get more information?
7. How can you receive a discount?

Now look at the reading on the next page. The red, bold words are cognates. What do they mean?

© Keith Dannemiller / Alamy

A leer

La escuela es para todos

En los **países** latinoamericanos y en España, **la educación** es un **derecho** de los niños. En unos países la escuela **primaria** y la **secundaria** son **obligatorias.** En otros países la **preparatoria** es obligatoria. Para satisfacer la **demanda,** muchas escuelas tienen dos **turnos:** unos niños **asisten** a la escuela por la mañana, y otros por la tarde.

countries/right

3 year pre-university course
shifts/attend

> [la educación es un
> derecho de los niños]

Por lo **general**, los libros de texto son **gratuitos**, pero las familias **deben comprar** otros **útiles** escolares. También en muchos **casos** las **familias** necesitan comprar **uniformes** para los niños porque es **común** usarlos.

free
must buy
supplies

Una escuela en Cuba

© AFP/Getty Images

Comprensión

Decide whether the following statements are true (**cierto**) or false (**falso**).

1. En Latinoamérica la escuela primaria es obligatoria.
2. Todos *(All)* los niños están en la escuela por la mañana.
3. Es necesario comprar *(to buy)* los libros para la escuela.
4. Muchos niños usan uniformes.

Después de leer

Even though school is free, there are many expenses associated with it, such as purchasing uniforms, lab coats, fees for special equipment, etc. What expenses are associated with K–12 in the United States? Can you think of other hidden expenses?

el hombre | la mujer

calvo(a)

alto(a)

rubio(a)

bajo(a)

viejo(a)

pelirrojo(a)

moreno(a)

feo(a)

grande

delgado(a)

la niña

el niño

bonito(a)

pequeño(a)

joven

© Cengage Learning

Las descripciones de la personalidad

bueno(a) / malo(a)
cruel / cariñoso(a)
generoso(a) / egoísta
idealista / realista
inteligente / tonto(a)
interesante / aburrido(a)
optimista / pesimista
liberal / conservador(a)
paciente / impaciente
serio(a) / cómico(a)
tímido(a) / sociable

Más adjetivos

agresivo(a)	aggressive
atlético(a)	athletic
antipático(a)	unfriendly
amable	kind
corto(a)	short (length)
difícil	difficult
divertido	funny; fun
fácil	easy
famoso(a)	famous
gordo(a)	fat

guapo(a)	good-looking
honesto(a)	honest
largo(a)	long
nuevo(a)	new
perezoso(a)	lazy
pobre	poor
rico(a)	rich
simpático(a)	nice
trabajador(a)	hardworking

Palabras adicionales

muy	very
pero	but
un poco	a little
también	also
y	and

INVESTIGUEMOS EL VOCABULARIO

The word **gordo** is often used in Spanish endearingly, such as between spouses, and parents often call their children **gordito** or **gordita**. People often describe themselves using the diminutive as well: **Soy (un poco) gordito.** Another word commonly used instead of **delgado** is **flaco.**

A practicar

1.17 **Escucha y responde** Look at the picture and listen to the different adjectives. Write the letter **D** on one piece of paper and the letter **S** on another. If the adjective you hear describes Don Quijote, hold up the **D**. If it describes Sancho Panza, hold up the **S**.

🔊 1-6

© Cengage Learning

1.18 **Identificaciones** Look around the classroom and identify someone that fits the following descriptions.

1. pelirrojo
2. alto
3. joven
4. guapo
5. moreno
6. rubio
7. bajo
8. delgado

1.19 **Sinónimos** Identify a word from the vocabulary list that has a similar meaning.

1. afectuoso
2. introvertido
3. sincero
4. tolerante
5. complicado
6. atractivo
7. simple
8. positivo

1.20 **La personalidad y las profesiones** Make a list of the ideal personality traits for the following jobs.

Modelo profesor
paciente, interesante, inteligente

1. policía
2. estudiante
3. actor
4. espía (*spy*)
5. político
6. doctor

1.21 **Veinte preguntas** Follow the steps below to play "twenty questions."

Paso 1 In groups of three, write a list of names of famous men who are familiar to everybody in the group.

Paso 2 One person in the group chooses a name from the list but doesn't say which name it is. The other two members of the group guess the name by asking yes/no questions.

Modelo *¿Es (Is he) joven?* *¿Es rubio?* *¿Es alto?*

1.22 **La fila** Work with a partner to figure out the names of the people in the stands. One of you will look at this page, and the other will look at the picture in Appendix B. Take turns giving the name of a person and a description, so your partner will know who it is.

Cultura

Francisco de Goya was a Spanish painter who made a living for many years painting portraits of the Spanish royal family. Goya painted *La familia de Carlos IV,* shown below, in 1800.

Pick three different people in the painting and describe them in Spanish using vocabulary from the chapter. You might speculate what their personalities are like.

La familia de Carlos IV, por Francisco de Goya

Research a different portrait painter from a Spanish-speaking country. Find a painting you like and upload the image to Share It! along with a description in Spanish of one of the people in the painting.

Comparaciones

There is great cultural diversity among Spanish-speaking countries. One thing all Hispanic countries have in common is that Spanish is spoken by the majority of the population, although it is not always an official language, and in most cases, it is not the only language. Why do you think there are "official" languages, and what impact do they have on communities? Look at the information below. How can you explain the variety of languages in these countries? What do you think is the difference between a "national" language and an "official" language?

SPAIN

Official language:	Spanish
Official regional languages:	Galician, Basque (Euskara), Catalan, Valenciano
Other languages spoken:	14

MEXICO

National language:	Spanish
Other languages spoken:	298 (nahuatl is the only one spoken by over one million speakers)

GUATEMALA

Official language:	Spanish
Other languages spoken:	55

BOLIVIA

Official languages:	Spanish, Quechua, Aymara
Other languages spoken:	45

UNITED STATES

National languages:	English (official in some states)
Regional languages:	Hawaiian, Spanish (in New Mexico)
Other languages spoken:	178

Sources: The Ethnologue Report, Almanaque Mundial 2010

INVESTIGUEMOS EL MUNDO HISPANO

You can learn more about these countries and their Spanish-speaking populations in Appendix A: **Exploraciones del mundo hispano**.

Conexiones... a la geografía

The people in the photos are all from Latin America. In Spanish, tell what country each person is from and describe him or her. If possible, locate the countries using Google Earth. Why do you think there is such great ethnic diversity in Latin America?

Rigoberta Menchú, Guatemala, activista política

Paulina Rubio, México, cantante

Evo Morales, Bolivia, presidente

David Ortiz, República Dominicana, beisbolista

Keiko Fujimori, Perú, política

Lionel "Leo" Messi, Argentina, futbolista

Comunidad

Interview a Spanish speaker from your school or community. Introduce yourself and ask him/her to describe the diversity in his/her home country: You may want to start by asking: **¿Cómo es la gente** *(people)* **en tu país?**

A analizar

Rosa is going to introduce herself and her friend Santiago.
After watching the video, read the following paragraph,
paying attention to the words in bold.

Yo **soy** Rosa y **soy** de El Salvador. Mi mejor amigo
es de España y se llama Santiago. Yo **soy** muy
sociable, pero Santiago no; él **es** un poco tímido,
pero nosotros **somos** muy buenos amigos… ¿Y tú?
¿Cómo **eres** tú?

© Cengage Learning

1. In the paragraph, who does **yo** refer to? Who does **él** refer to? Does **nosotros** refer
   to one person or more than one person?

2. The verb **ser** *(to be)* is used throughout the paragraph. Its forms are in bold.
   Write the appropriate form that is used with each of the following pronouns.

   yo _____   él _____

   tú _____   nosotros _____

3. Look at the following conversations, paying attention to the use of **tú** and **usted.**
   Both mean *you* in English. What do you think the difference is?

© Cengage Learning

A comprobar

Subject pronouns and the verb ser

singular		plural	
yo	*I*	**nosotros/nosotras**	*we*
tú	*you (familiar)*	**vosotros/vosotras**	*you (familiar in Spain)*
usted	*you (formal)*	**ustedes**	*you*
él	*he*	**ellos**	*they (group of males or a mixed group)*
ella	*she*	**ellas**	*they (group of females)*

1. When addressing one person, Spanish speakers use either **tú** or **usted** (sometimes abbreviated **Ud.**). **Tú** is informal. It is used with family, friends, classmates, and children. It denotes familiarity. **Usted** is formal. It is used with people in a position of authority, older people, strangers, and people in a professional setting. It denotes respect and more distance.

2. When referring to groups of females, use **nosotras** and **ellas,** and when referring to groups of males, use **nosotros** and **ellos.** When the groups are mixed, use the masculine forms **nosotros** and **ellos,** as they have a generic meaning that implies the presence of both genders.

3. In Spain, **vosotros** and **vosotras** are used to address a group of people and denote familiarity, and follow the same rules as **nosotros** and **nosotras** with regard to gender; **ustedes** is used to address a group of people and denotes respect. In Latin America, **ustedes** (sometimes abbreviated **Uds.**) is used to address any group of people, regardless of the relationship.

4. The verb **ser** means *to be.* Just as there are different forms of the verb *to be* in English (*I am, you are,* etc.), there are also different forms of the verb **ser** in Spanish. Changing a verb into its different forms to indicate who is doing the activity is called *conjugating.*

INVESTIGUEMOS LA GRAMÁTICA

In Spanish **ser** and **estar** both mean *to be.* You will learn more about **estar** in **Capítulo 4.**

ser					
yo	**soy**	*I am*	**nosotros/nosotras**	**somos**	*we are*
tú	**eres**	*you are*	**vosotros/vosotras**	**sois**	*you (all) are*
usted	**es**	*you are*	**ustedes**	**son**	*you all are*
él/ella	**es**	*he/she is*	**ellos/ellas**	**son**	*they are*

5. Use **ser**
   - to describe what someone is like.
     Él **es** alto, pero ellos **son** bajos.
     *He **is** tall, but they **are** short.*
   - to identify someone or something
     Yo **soy** Manolo.   *I **am** Manolo.*
   - to ask or say where someone is from.
     ¿De dónde **eres** tú?   Yo **soy** de Lima, Perú.
     Where are you from?   *I **am** from Lima, Peru.*

A practicar

1.23 **¿Tú o usted?** Which pronoun would you use **to address** each of the following people?

Modelo un niño → *tú*

1. un policía
2. un profesor
3. mamá
4. un amigo
5. el presidente
6. un estudiante en la clase de español

1.24 Sustituciones Which pronoun would you use **to talk about** the following people?

Modelo Rebeca → *ella*

1. Felipe
2. Silvia y Alicia
3. tu amigo y Ricardo
4. Regina

5. la señora Marcos
6. Javier y yo
7. Lola, Ana, Sara y Luis
8. Miguelito

1.25 Parejas Match the subject with the remainder of the sentence.

1. Yo
2. Rafael y Carlos
3. La profesora
4. Tú
5. Maite y yo

a. es joven.
b. somos trabajadores.
c. soy optimista.
d. eres inteligente.
e. son guapos.

1.26 El verbo *ser* Complete the paragraph with the necessary form of the verb **ser**.

¡Hola! Yo (1) _____ Antonio y (2) _____ de Santiago, Chile. Mis amigos (3) _____ Laura y Víctor. Nosotros (4) _____ estudiantes en la Universidad de Santiago. Laura (5) _____ estudiante de biología y Víctor y yo (6) _____ estudiantes de ciencias políticas. Y tú, ¿también (7) _____ estudiante?

1.27 ¿De dónde son? In groups of three, look at the map and complete the following sentences telling where the different people are from. Then, find out from the other members of your group where they are from. Be sure to use the correct forms of the verb **ser**.

Modelo Carolina...
Carolina es de Chile.

1. Margarita...
2. Arturo...
3. Cecilia...
4. Carolina y Pilar...

5. Antonio y yo...
6. Tú...
7. Ustedes...
8. Ricardo y Anita...
9. El profesor Gómez...

América Latina
Golfo de México
Océano Atlántico
Mar Caribe
Océano Pacífico
Océano Atlántico

© Cengage Learning

A analizar ▶

Rosa is going to introduce herself and her friend Santiago. Watch the video. Then read the paragraph that follows and underline the adjectives.

Yo soy Rosa y soy de El Salvador. Mi mejor amigo es de España y se llama Santiago. Yo soy muy sociable, pero Santiago no; él es un poco tímido, pero nosotros somos muy buenos amigos. Santiago es inteligente, muy simpático e idealista. Yo también soy inteligente y simpática pero no soy idealista. Soy realista, muy trabajadora y también soy liberal. Además, Santiago es alto, rubio y atlético, y yo soy baja y morena. Santiago y yo somos muy diferentes, pero lo importante es que somos buenos amigos.

© Cengage Learning

Note the forms already filled in the chart and use the adjectives you underlined as well as what you learned about **encantado** and **encantada** in the box on page 5, to complete the chart.

masculine singular	masculine plural	feminine singular	feminine plural
bajo	_____	_____	_____
_____	inteligentes	_____	_____
_____	_____	idealista	_____
liberal	_____	_____	_____
_____	_____	_____	trabajadoras

A comprobar

Adjective agreement

Adjectives describe a person, place, or thing. In Spanish, adjectives must agree with the person or the object they describe both in gender (masculine/feminine) and in number (singular/plural).

Singular masculine adjectives		singular	plural
ending in **-o**	masculine	simpático	simpáticos
	feminine	simpática	simpáticas
ending in **-a**	masculine	idealista	idealistas
	feminine	idealista	idealistas
ending in **-e**	masculine	sociable	sociables
	feminine	sociable	sociables
ending in a consonant*	masculine	ideal	ideales
	feminine	ideal	ideales
*exception: ending in **-or**	masculine	trabajador	trabajadores
	feminine	trabajadora	trabajadoras

Mi amigo es simpático, sociable e idealista.

Mi amiga también es simpática, sociable e idealista.

Mis amigos son simpáticos, sociables e idealistas.

INVESTIGUEMOS LA PRONUNCIACIÓN

For pronunciation purposes, **y** *(and)* becomes **e** when followed by a word beginning with the letter(s) **i** or **hi.**

A practicar

1.28 **¿Quién es?** Listen to the six descriptive statements and decide which person is being described. In some cases, the description may apply to both. Place a check mark in the appropriate blanks. **¡OJO!** Pay attention to the adjective endings!

1-7

1. _____ Jennifer López   _____ Pitbull
2. _____ Lorena Ochoa   _____ Rafael Nadal
3. _____ Sofía Vergara   _____ George López
4. _____ Isabel Allende   _____ Gabriel García Márquez
5. _____ Christina Aguilera   _____ Gael García Bernal
6. _____ Penélope Cruz   _____ Mario López

1.29 **La atracción de los opuestos** Complete each sentence with an adjective that has the opposite meaning of the underlined word. **¡OJO!** Be sure the adjectives agree with the subject they are describing.

1. Susana es <u>generosa</u> y su esposo *(spouse)* es _____.
2. Fernando es <u>tímido</u> y su esposa es _____.
3. Mis amigas son <u>delgadas</u> y sus esposos son _____.
4. Marcos es <u>trabajador</u> y su esposa es _____.
5. Mis amigos son <u>cómicos</u> y sus esposas son _____.
6. Mi amigo es _____ y su esposa es _____.
   (Choose adjectives not used in the sentences above.)

1.30 **En el café** Work with a partner and take turns giving true/false statements about the people in the drawing. You should correct any false statements. **¡OJO!** Be sure the adjectives agree with the subject they are describing.

Modelo Estudiante 1: *Vicente es calvo.*
         Estudiante 2: *Falso, él es rubio.*

© Cengage Learning

1.31 **Los ideales** Complete the following statements expressing your own opinion regarding the ideal characteristics of each subject. Then compare your list with a partner's and come to an agreement on two characteristics for each.

1. La profesora ideal es… No es…
2. El estudiante ideal es… No es…
3. Los amigos ideales son… No son…
4. La madre (mother) ideal es… No es…
5. Los políticos ideales son… No son…
6. Las mascotas (pet) ideales son… No son…

1.32 **El horóscopo** Find your astrological sign below and read the descriptions. Choose two characteristics that describe you. You may use those listed for your sign or choose others that are more accurate. Then, talk to three classmates and find out their signs and the characteristics that describe them.

Modelo Estudiante 1: *¿Cuál es tu signo?*
Estudiante 2: *Yo soy Aries.*
Estudiante 1: *¿Cómo eres tú?*
Estudiante 2: *Yo soy extrovertido y muy emocional.*

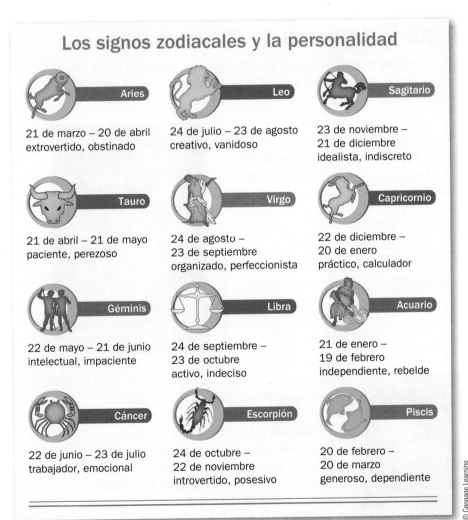

Los signos zodiacales y la personalidad

Aries
21 de marzo – 20 de abril
extrovertido, obstinado

Leo
24 de julio – 23 de agosto
creativo, vanidoso

Sagitario
23 de noviembre –
21 de diciembre
idealista, indiscreto

Tauro
21 de abril – 21 de mayo
paciente, perezoso

Virgo
24 de agosto –
23 de septiembre
organizado, perfeccionista

Capricornio
22 de diciembre –
20 de enero
práctico, calculador

Géminis
22 de mayo – 21 de junio
intelectual, impaciente

Libra
24 de septiembre –
23 de octubre
activo, indeciso

Acuario
21 de enero –
19 de febrero
independiente, rebelde

Cáncer
22 de junio – 23 de julio
trabajador, emocional

Escorpión
24 de octubre –
22 de noviembre
introvertido, posesivo

Piscis
20 de febrero –
20 de marzo
generoso, dependiente

© Cengage Learning

Lectura

Antes de leer

Write a list of names of famous contemporary U.S. citizens in the fields of pop culture, politics, movies, and sports. Why are they famous? Compare lists with a classmate. Together, try to come up with names of famous contemporary citizens of Spanish-speaking countries. What are their professions?

A leer

Algunos famosos de Latinoamérica

Muchas personas de países hispanos se distinguen en todas las áreas y es difícil escribir una lista corta. A continuación hay descripciones de algunas personas muy populares en el mundo contemporáneo.

Deportes
Manu Ginóbili (julio 1977), deportista argentino, es un excelente jugador de básquetbol de la NBA de los Estados Unidos. Habla fluidamente español, inglés e italiano y tiene su propia página en el Internet.

© Bob Pearson/epa/Corbis

> Muchas personas de países hispanos se distinguen en todas las áreas y es difícil escribir una lista corta.

© Alastair Grant/AP Images

teach reading

Cine
Gael García Bernal (noviembre 1978) es actualmente uno de los actores latinoamericanos más famosos, gracias a su participación en filmes como *Los diarios de motocicleta* (2004), *El crimen del Padre Amaro* (2002) y *Babel* (2006). Un dato interesante es que Gael participó en campañas para **enseñar a leer** a los indígenas huicholes en el norte de México.

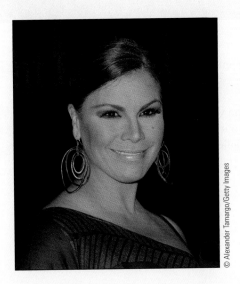

© Alexander Tamargo/Getty Images

Música

Olga Tañón (abril 1967) es una cantante y actriz de Puerto Rico. Es famosa en Latinoamérica por su música rítmica, y ahora planea **grabar** música en inglés. Tañón participó en la controversial versión en español del himno estadounidense en 2006.

to record

© AFP/Getty Images

Política

Michelle Bachelet (septiembre 1951) es presidente de Chile, doctora pediatra y también la primera mujer presidente de este país (2006–2010; 2014–2018). Es muy popular entre los chilenos y es la **segunda vez** que es elegida presidente. *Forbes* la considera una de las mujeres más influyentes del mundo. Bachelet se distingue por su trabajo para conseguir la **igualdad** entre hombres y mujeres.

second time

equality

Comprensión

To which of the people mentioned in the reading does the statement refer?

1. Es famosa por su música.
2. Estudió medicina.
3. Es un actor popular.
4. Es atlético.
5. Es puertorriqueña.
6. Juega al básquetbol.

Después de leer

What other famous people do you know from Spanish-speaking countries? Work with a partner to come up with a list of names, then choose one of the people on your list and write a short description of him/her. Read your description to the class and have them guess whom you are describing.

INVESTIGUEMOS LA MÚSICA

Find the Mocedades song "Eres tú" on the Internet and listen to it. Write down as many cognates as you can as well as words you recognize. What do you think the theme of the song is?

Redacción

Write a paragraph in which you describe yourself and your best friend.

Paso 1 Create a Venn diagram such as the one below. In the middle section where the circles overlap, write any adjectives that are common to both yourself and your best friend. Write any adjectives that are unique to yourself in the circle on the left and adjectives that are unique to your best friend in the circle on the right.

yo   mi mejor amigo

liberal   simpático   conservador

Paso 2 Write a sentence in which you introduce your reader to yourself and to your best friend.

Paso 3 Using the information you generated in **Paso 1,** continue your paragraph with two or three sentences in which you describe the qualities that you and your friend have in common and another two or three sentences where you describe the qualities that are unique to you and unique to your best friend.

© Francesco Ridolfi/Shutterstock

Paso 4 Write a conclusion sentence that wraps up the paragraph.

Paso 5 Edit your paragraph:

1. Do the adjectives agree with the person they describe?
2. Check your spelling, including accent marks.
3. Are there any sentences that could be joined with either **y** or **pero**?
4. Can you vary some of the sentences by using expressions like **también** and **los/las dos** *(both of us)*?

Entrando en materia

Look at the following sketches of people. Write down two or three adjectives that describe each person.

A   B   C   D   E   F

© Cengage Learning

En busca de talento

A television network is looking for talent to participate in a new sitcom. The show requires several Hispanic characters, and they have a very specific idea of what they should look like. The descriptions that follow have been distributed to agents in the hopes of finding an exact match. Match the headshots to the descriptions.

NUEVO PROGRAMA BUSCA TALENTOS

Buscamos nuevos talentos para actuar en una comedia original. Es indispensable hablar español e inglés.

Leyre Morales Blanco

Edad: 5 años
Estatura: 1.10 **mts.**
Descripción: Delgada, morena, **pelo** largo. Leyre es
               tímida y seria, pero aventurera.

Rocío Leyva Zamora

Edad: 30 años
Estatura: 1.55 mts.
Descripción: Delgada, con pelo corto. Rocío es
               bonita, extrovertida y amable.

meters
hair

Aymar Ibañez Sodi

Edad: 12 años
Estatura: 1.50 mts.
Descripción: Alto para su edad, pelo negro y corto.
               Aymar es atlético, independiente y muy
               sociable. Es alérgico a los animales.

Florián González Calva

Edad: 75 años
Estatura: 1.60 mts.
Descripción: Bajo, calvo y un poco gordito. Carácter
               tímido y serio.

Comprensión

Which headshot corresponds to which description?

Más allá

 Think of a person you know well and describe that person to your partner, who will draw a portrait according to your description. Be sure to include the person's name and key identifiers such as height, hair color, etc. Switch roles so that you each have a turn to describe and draw.

> Now use the drawing you have just created to post a brief corresponding description to Share It! Don't forget to use correct adjective forms!

Narración de voz en off

Vocabulario

Sustantivos

el acento	*accent*
la grabación	*recording*
el guión	*script*
el/la hablante nativo(a)	*native speaker*
la lengua meta	*target language*

Adjetivos

bilingüe	*bilingual*
neutro(a)	*neutral*

Verbos

ensayar	*to practice*
grabar	*to record*
hablar	*to speak*

Frases útiles

¡Grabando!	*Recording!*
¡Probando!	*Testing!*
Más despacio, por favor.	*Slowly, please.*
Repite la última oración.	*Repeat the last sentence.*

Más despacio, por favor.

© Cengage Learning

DATOS IMPORTANTES

Educación: Título universitario en comunicación; Los hablantes nativos de la lengua meta tienen preferencia; Es necesario producir un acento neutro en inglés y español

Salario: Promedio: $45.000/año – $33–50/hora

Dónde se trabaja: Empresas de publicidad, canales de televisión, editoriales, estudios de grabación

Vocabulario nuevo Choose the most logical answer.

1. Yo hablo (*I speak*) español pero mi _____ es muy fuerte.
   a. grabación
   b. acento
   c. lengua
2. Cuando hablo otro idioma, no hablo (*I don't speak*) rápido, hablo _____.
   a. bilingüe
   b. neutro
   c. despacio
3. Jorge habla italiano y español. Él es _____.
   a. acento
   b. meta
   c. bilingüe

Elisa Solís, voz en off

Elisa Solís, a voiceover professional, is going to work at a recording studio. Felipe Hernández is the studio technician. In the video, you will watch a segment of Elisa's recording session and observe Felipe's instructions.

© Cengage Learning

Antes de ver

Bilingual voiceover professionals deliver messages and announcements and narrate videos, documentaries, and commercials. Voiceover narrators are heard but never seen. They must be professionally trained and speak the target language, such as Spanish, perfectly. What type of instruction do you think a voiceover professional receives at the recording studio? How long do you think it takes to record a one-minute commercial? Do you believe that voiceover professionals should be native speakers of English or of the target language? Why?

Comprensión

Decide whether the following statements are true (**cierto**) or false (**falso**).

1. El técnico se llama José.

2. Elisa no habla inglés.

3. Elisa es de Cuba.

4. El video es sobre *(about)* un festival.

5. Elisa quiere *(wants)* ensayar.

Después de ver

With a partner, play the roles of a voiceover professional and a recording studio technician. Write a short recording script using the vocabulary and expressions on page 32. The technician should give instructions and correct the voiceover professional when needed. Include both English and Spanish in the script. Determine who is the target audience and what is the message. Be creative!

1.33 **¿Qué hay?** A student is in her room studying. Mention five items that are in the room, and then mention one thing that is not.

Modelo *Hay unos libros.*

© Sofos Design/Shutterstock

1.34 **Los famosos** Tell where the following famous people are from. Search online for information on anyone you don't know.

1. Enrique y Julio Iglesias
2. Ricky Martin
3. Salma Hayek
4. Daisy Fuentes y Gloria Estefan
5. Carlos Mencia
6. Shakira y Juanes

1.35 **Mi amiga Mónica** Complete the paragraph with the appropriate forms of the verb **ser** and the adjectives, as indicated by the words in parentheses.

¡Buenos días! Yo (**1.** ser) _____ Jacobo y ella (**2.** ser) _____ Mónica. Nosotros (**3.** ser) _____ estudiantes en la Universidad Central de Venezuela. Mónica (**4.** ser) _____ estudiante de literatura, y es muy (**5.** inteligente) _____ y (**6.** trabajador) _____. Las clases (**7.** ser) _____ muy (**8.** difícil) _____, pero los profesores son (**9.** bueno) _____ y (**10.** simpático) _____.

1.36 **Entrevista** Talk to three different classmates to gather the following information about them.

1. What are their first and last names and how are they spelled?

2. Where they are from?

3. What they are like? (two descriptions each)

1.37 **Diferencias** Working with a partner, one of you will look at the picture on this page, and the other will look at the picture in Appendix B. Take turns describing the pictures using the expression **hay,** numbers, and the classroom vocabulary. Find the eight differences.

Modelo Estudiante 1: *En A hay una computadora.*
Estudiante 2: *Sí. En B, hay una silla.*
Estudiante 1: *No, en A no hay una silla.*

© Cengage Learning

1.38 **Somos similares** Work with a partner to identify the personality traits that you have in common.

Paso 1 Make a list of 7–8 adjectives that describe your personality. **¡OJO!** Pay attention to the adjective endings.

Paso 2 Take turns describing your personalities using the adjectives on your lists. Be sure to use complete sentences. When you determine a trait that you both have in common, circle it on your lists.

Paso 3 Report to the class on how you are similar by sharing the characteristics that you have in common.

CAPÍTULO 1

Vocabulario 1

1-8

Saludos

bien	*fine*
Buenas noches.	*Good night.*
Buenas tardes.	*Good afternoon.*
Buenos días.	*Good morning.*
¿Cómo estás (tú)?	*How are you?* (informal)
¿Cómo está (usted)?	*How are you?* (formal)
gracias	*thank you*
hola	*hello*
mal	*bad*
nada	*nothing*
¿Qué hay de nuevo?	*What's new?*
¿Qué pasa?	*What's going on?*
¿Qué tal?	*How's it going?*
regular	*so-so*
¿Y tú?	*And you?* (informal)
¿Y usted?	*And you?* (formal)

Presentaciones

Encantado(a).	*Nice to meet you.*
Me llamo...	*My name is . . .*
Mucho gusto.	*Nice to meet you.*
Le presento a...	*I'd like to introduce you to . . .* (formal)
Te presento a...	*I'd like to introduce you to . . .* (informal)

Despedidas

Adiós.	*Goodbye.*
Chao.	*Bye.*
Hasta luego.	*See you later.*
Hasta mañana.	*See you tomorrow.*
Hasta pronto.	*See you soon.*
Nos vemos.	*See you later.*
¡Que tengas un buen día!	*Have a nice day!*

El salón de clases

la bandera	*flag*
el bolígrafo	*pen*
el cartel	*poster*
la computadora	*computer*
el cuaderno	*notebook*
el diccionario	*dictionary*
el escritorio	*teacher's desk*
el (la) estudiante	*student*
el lápiz	*pencil*
el libro	*book*
el mapa	*map*
la mesa	*table*
la mochila	*backpack*
el papel	*paper*
la pizarra	*chalkboard*
el (la) profesor(a)	*professor*
la puerta	*door*
el pupitre	*student desk*
el reloj	*clock*
el salón de clases	*classroom*
la silla	*chair*
el televisor	*television set*
la ventana	*window*

Palabras interrogativas

¿Dónde?	*Where?*
¿Cuándo?	*When?*
¿Cuántos(as)?	*How many?*
¿Qué?	*What?*
¿Quién?	*Who?*
¿Por qué?	*Why?*

Los números *See pages 9, 12*

Palabras adicionales

¿De dónde eres tú?	*Where are you from?*
hay	*there is/there are*
Yo soy de...	*I am from . . .*

◀)) Vocabulario 2

Adjetivos para describir la personalidad

aburrido(a)	*boring*		interesante	*interesting*
agresivo(a)	*aggressive*		liberal	*liberal*
amable	*kind*		malo(a)	*bad*
antipático(a)	*unfriendly*		optimista	*optimist*
atlético(a)	*athletic*		paciente	*patient*
bueno(a)	*good*		perezoso(a)	*lazy*
cariñoso(a)	*loving*		pesimista	*pessimist*
cómico(a)	*funny*		pobre	*poor*
conservador(a)	*conservative*		realista	*realist*
cruel	*cruel*		rico(a)	*rich*
egoísta	*selfish*		serio(a)	*serious*
famoso(a)	*famous*		simpático(a)	*nice*
generoso(a)	*generous*		sociable	*sociable*
honesto(a)	*honest*		tímido(a)	*timid, shy*
idealista	*idealist*		tonto(a)	*dumb*
impaciente	*impatient*		trabajador(a)	*hardworking*
inteligente	*intelligent*			

Adjetivos para describir el aspecto físico

alto(a)	*tall*		guapo(a)	*good-looking*
bajo(a)	*short*		joven	*young*
bonito(a)	*pretty*		moreno(a)	*dark-skinned/ dark-haired*
calvo(a)	*bald*			
delgado(a)	*thin*		pelirrojo(a)	*red-haired*
feo(a)	*ugly*		pequeño(a)	*small*
gordo(a)	*fat*		rubio(a)	*blond(e)*
grande	*big*		viejo(a)	*old*

Otros adjetivos

corto(a)	*short (length)*		fácil	*easy*
difícil	*difficult*		largo(a)	*long*

Verbos

ser	*to be*

Palabras adicionales

el hombre	*man*		pero	*but*
la mujer	*woman*		un poco	*a little*
muy	*very*		también	*also*
el (la) niño(a)	*child*		y	*and*

Diccionario personal

_____

_____

Learning Strategy

Listen to and repeat vocabulary

When studying vocabulary, take time to listen to and repeat the pronunciation of the words. It will help your pronunciation, which in turn will help you learn to spell the words properly. You may click on the vocabulary in the eBook to hear it pronounced or you may want to download the audio files onto your MP3 player or cell phone, so they will be more accessible.

In this chapter you will learn how to:

- Describe your family and talk about ages
- Discuss your classes
- Discuss your routine
- Express ownership

¿Cómo es tu vida?

© Ariel Skelley/Corbis

Esta es la familia de Hernán. ¿Cuántas personas hay en la familia?

Burbuja
el pez

la abuela — el abuelo

la abuela — el abuelo

Silvestre
el gato

ALBERTO

Fabiola — Alberto   Clara — Leonardo

la madre   el padre   el tío   la tía

Nacho
el pájaro   Suyapa — Orlando   Jacobo — Lucero   Oso
el perro

el hermano   yo   la hermana   el primo   la prima

Juan Pablo   Hernán   Belén   Lorenzo   Ana

Pinto
el caballo

Timoteo
el ratón

© Cengage Learning

La familia

los parientes	*relatives*
esposo(a)	*spouse*
hijo(a)	*son / daughter*
nieto(a)	*grandson / granddaughter*
sobrino(a)	*nephew / niece*
hermanastro(a)	*stepbrother / stepsister*
madrastra	*stepmother*
padrastro	*stepfather*
medio(a) hermano(a)	*half brother / half sister*
suegro(a)	*father-in-law / mother-in-law*

Palabras adicionales

(mejor) amigo(a)	*(best) friend*
¿Cómo se llama...?	*What is the name of . . . ?*
la mascota	*pet*
novio(a)	*boyfriend / girlfriend*

INVESTIGUEMOS EL VOCABULARIO

Remember that most of the words in the vocabulary can be used to refer to a female by changing the final **o** to an **a**. When talking about a mixed group, the masculine plural form is used:

hijos   *sons and daughters*

hermanos   *brothers and sisters*

padres   *parents*

La mascota is used for both male and female pets.

A practicar

2.1 **Escucha y responde** Listen to the following statements about Hernán's family. Based on the drawing, give a thumbs up if the statement is true or a thumbs down if it is false.

1-10

2.2 **¿Cómo se llama...?** Give the names of the following people using the information provided in the drawing on p. 40.

1. la madre de Suyapa
2. el padre de Lorenzo
3. los padres de Orlando y Jacobo
4. la hermana de Juan Pablo
5. los tíos de Lorenzo
6. la mascota de Hernán

2.3 **¿Quién es?** Complete the following sentences about Hernán's family with the appropriate vocabulary word.

1. Suyapa es la _____ de Lorenzo.
2. Fabiola es la _____ de Suyapa.
3. Hernán es el _____ de Orlando.
4. Belén es la _____ de Lorenzo.
5. Jacobo y Orlando son _____.
6. Hernán es el _____ de Jacobo.
7. Clara es la _____ de Leonardo.
8. Fabiola es la _____ de Juan Pablo.

2.4 **En busca de...** Circulate throughout the classroom and find students to whom the following statements apply. Find a different student for each statement. **¡OJO!** Remember that the masculine word is used in a generic sense. For example **¿Tienes hermanos?** is asking if you have any siblings, which could include sisters as well as brothers.

Modelo Tiene gatos. *(Has cats.)*
Estudiante 1: *¿Tienes gatos?* (Do you have cats?)
Estudiante 2: *No, no tengo gatos. / Sí, tengo un gato.*
(No, I don't have cats. / Yes, I have a cat.)

1. Tiene hijos.
2. Tiene hermanos.
3. Tiene primos.
4. Tiene caballos.
5. Tiene abuelos.
6. Tiene mascotas.
7. Tiene tíos.
8. Tiene sobrinos.

INVESTIGUEMOS LA CULTURA

In most countries where Spanish is spoken, families use two last names. Typically the first last name comes from the father's side, and the second last name comes from the mother's side. These are not middle names.

INVESTIGUEMOS LA MÚSICA

Pimpinela is an Argentine brother-sister duo whose songs are often conversations between a man and a woman. Find their song "Señorita" online and write down any family vocabulary words you hear in the song. Then, look up the words of the song online and check your understanding. To find lyrics, just type the word **letra** after the title of the song.

2.5 **Una familia** You and your partner each have half of the information about the Sofía Navarro family. One of you will look at the drawing on this page, the other one will look at the drawing in Appendix B. Take turns asking the names of the different people.

Modelo
Estudiante 1: *¿Cómo se llama la madre de Sofía?*
Estudiante 2: *Se llama Gloria.*

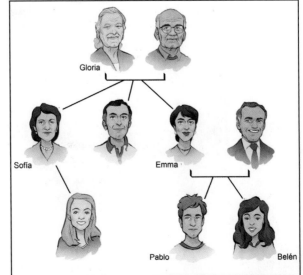

Gloria

Sofía Emma

Pablo Belén

© Cengage Learning

Conexiones culturales

El papel de la familia y su valor

Cultura

What determines whether a group is considered a family? The painting entitled *La familia presidencial* (1965) was created by Colombian artist Fernando Botero. With this painting, the artist consolidated his now famous signature style of inflated, round figures. Look at the painting. Do you think that they are blood relatives, or are they related in a different way? Can you think of any other groups of people who are considered to be like families?

 Discover some other famous Colombians and identify their professions in **Exploraciones del mundo hispano.**

 Carmen Lomas Garza has painted numerous works depicting Hispanic families in the U.S. Find a painting you like. Why do you like it? Post the painting and your opinion on Share It!

familia presidencial, Fernando Botero

Comunidad

Find a native speaker of Spanish in your university or community who is willing to be interviewed and ask the following questions: **¿Tu familia es grande o pequeña? ¿Cuántas personas hay en tu familia? ¿Quiénes son? ¿Cuántos primos hay en tu familia extendida?**

 Post your findings to Share It! and read the information posted by your classmates.

Comparaciones

What are some of the important events that bring families together in the United States? In Spain and Latin America, numerous events allow families to get together. Some are religious celebrations such as Christmas (**Navidad**) and Holy Week (**Semana Santa**); others are non-religious occasions such as Mother's Day, Father's Day, Children's Day, and any family birthday or anniversary. The **quinceañera** celebration or **los quince años,** which marks a girl's 15th birthday, is a particularly important celebration.

Fiesta de quince años

While many of these days are also observed in the U.S., there are some important differences. For example, in Mexico, El Salvador, and Guatemala, Mother's Day is always on May 10, so it could fall on any day of the week. Paraguay and Nicaragua also have set dates in May, and Costa Rica in August. Many companies organize activities to honor mothers, and often allow employees to leave early so they can take their mothers out to eat. If the date falls on a weekend, many people will have a larger celebration with food and music.

The date to mark Children's Day also varies. For example, it is celebrated on June 1 in Ecuador and Nicaragua, April 12 in Bolivia, August 16 in Paraguay, and December 25 in Guinea Ecuatorial. It is usually celebrated with big parties at schools, city parades for children, and other types of entertainment. Many organizations will give away toys or other items for children on this day. This photo and the one on the previous page are of family events in Latin America. How are these photos similar to ones you might take during your own family events? How are they different?

Conexiones... a la sociología

In Spanish-speaking countries the family is very important and people tend to dedicate a lot of time to their family members. It is not uncommon for children to live with their parents until they marry. How can this impact other areas of society (for example, housing, jobs, eating habits, etc.)? Does it have any impact on the life of college students? What do you think are some advantages and disadvantages of living with your family until getting married?

Es común vivir con la familia hasta casarse.

A analizar ▶

Rosa talks to Paula about her family. After watching the video, read part of their conversation, and note the words in bold. Then answer the questions below.

Paula:	¿Es esta una foto de **tu** familia, Rosa?
Rosa:	Sí. Esa foto es del Día de la Madre. Aquí está **mi** hermano Miguel y aquí está **mi** hermana Susana con **su** esposo Jaime. Este es **su** hijo Tomás. Y ellos son **mis** padres...
Paula:	¡¿Y este gato en la mesa?!
Rosa:	Es Bibi, **nuestra** gata. Es cómica y muy cariñosa... ¡pero muy mala con **nuestro** pobre perro!

© Cengage Learning

The words in bold are used to show possession.

1. What are the two ways of expressing *my* in Spanish in the conversation above? What is the difference between the two forms? Why do you think they are different?

2. What are the two forms of **nuestro** in the conversation? What is the difference between the two forms? Why do you think they are different?

3. In the conversation the word **su** has two different meanings. Find the two uses of **su** above. How are they different?

A comprobar

Possessive adjectives

mi(s)	*my*	**mi** hermano, **mis** hermanos
tu(s)	*your*	**tu** primo, **tus** primos
su(s)	*his, her, its, your*	**su** mascota, **sus** mascotas
nuestro(s), nuestra(s)	*our*	**nuestro** primo, **nuestros** primos, **nuestra** prima, **nuestras** primas
vuestro(s), vuestra(s)	*your*	**vuestro** tío, **vuestros** tíos, **vuestra** tía, **vuestras** tías
su(s)	*their, your*	**su** abuelo, **sus** abuelos

> **INVESTIGUEMOS LA GRAMÁTICA**
>
> When using possessive adjectives in Spanish, keep in mind that the subject pronouns **tú, usted, vosotros,** and **ustedes** all mean *you*. Each of the possessive adjectives that indicate *your* corresponds to a different subject pronoun.
>
> tú → tu(s)
> usted → su(s)
> vosotros/vosotras → vuestro(s)/vuestra(s)
> ustedes → su(s)

1. Similar to other adjectives, possessive adjectives agree in number (singular / plural) with the noun they modify (that is, the object that is owned or possessed).

   Mi familia es muy grande.
   My family is very large.

   Sus padres hablan italiano.
   His parents speak italian.

2. **Nuestro** and **vuestro** agree in gender (masculine / feminine) as well as in number.

   Nuestra gata se llama Lili.
   ***Our cat** is named Lili.*

   ¿Cómo se llaman **vuestras hijas**?
   *What are **your daughters'** names?*

3. In Spanish, the 's does not exist. Instead, if you want to be more specific about who possesses or owns something, it is necessary to use **de** *(of)*. Notice that in this structure the item owned comes before the person who owns it.

Es la casa **de mi hermano.**	Es **su** casa.
*It is **my brother's** house.*	*It is **his** house.*
Ellas son las hijas **de Patricia.**	Ellas son **sus** hijas.
*They are **Patricia's** daughters.*	*They are **her** daughters.*

4. Just as there are contractions in English (can't, don't), there are also contractions in Spanish. However, these contractions are not optional. When using **de** in front of the masculine article **el,** it forms the contraction **del** (**de + el = del**).

Macarena es la esposa **del** profesor.
Macarena is the professor's wife.

De does not contract with the other articles.

Max es el perro **de la** familia Pérez.
Max is the Pérez family's dog.

A practicar

2.6 **Mi familia** Indicate whether each of the sentences requires **mi** or **mis**.

1. (Mi/Mis) madre es bonita.
2. (Mi/Mis) padre es alto.
3. (Mi/Mis) hermanas son cómicas.
4. (Mi/Mis) perro es pequeño.
5. (Mi/Mis) abuelos son simpáticos.
6. (Mi/Mis) amigos son inteligentes.

2.7 **Su familia** Complete the following paragraph with the correct form of **su** or **sus**.

Alberto, David y Óscar son hermanos y tienen un apartamento en Lima. **(1.)** _____ apartamento es pequeño, pero confortable. Alberto y David comparten *(share)* un cuarto *(bedroom)* y hay muchos carteles en **(2.)** _____ cuarto. **(3.)** _____ hermano, Óscar, tiene un cuarto pequeño. Él tiene dos gatos y un perro. **(4.)** _____ mascotas molestan *(bother)* mucho a **(5.)** _____ hermanos porque **(6.)** _____ perro siempre está en el sofá y **(7.)** _____ gatos siempre están en la mesa.

El perro siempre está en el sofá.

© Bryan Firestone/Shutterstock

2.8 **¿Qué tienen?** With a partner, take turns completing the sentences to tell what your friends and family have. You may complete the sentences with a person (**un hermano, un novio,** etc.), a pet (**un perro, un gato,** etc.), or an object (**una casa, un auto, una clase,** etc.). Then describe the person, pet, or object using a possessive pronoun and an adjective, as in the model.

Modelo La profesora tiene...
    La profesora tiene un gato. Su gato es bonito.

1. Yo tengo...
2. Mi amigo tiene...
3. Mi familia tiene...
4. Mis amigos tienen..

2.9 **Andrés y Ana** Andrés and Ana are siblings, and they have left their things in the living room. Tell whether the items belong to Andrés or Ana.

Modelo los CDs   *Los CDs son de Andrés.*

1. la pizza	**4.** la mochila	**7.** los papeles
2. los bolígrafos	**5.** el cuaderno	**8.** el cartel
3. el diccionario	**6.** los libros	**9.** la soda

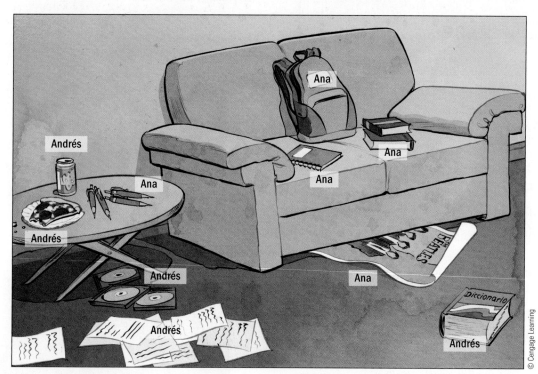

© Cengage Learning

2.10 **¿De quién es?** Andrés' mother is cleaning the living room where her children have left their things. She is unsure about what belongs to him and what belongs to his sister, Ana. With a partner, take turns playing Andrés and his mother. Look at the picture in Activity 2.9 to decide how Andrés answers her questions. Be sure to use the correct possessive adjective in the proper form.

Modelo Estudiante 1 (madre): *¿De quién (Whose) es el cuaderno?*
Estudiante 2 (Andrés): *Es su cuaderno.*
Estudiante 2 (madre): *¿De quién son los papeles?*
Estudiante 1 (Andrés): *Son mis papeles.*

1. ¿De quién es la mochila?	**5.** ¿De quién son los bolígrafos?
2. ¿De quién son los libros?	**6.** ¿De quién es la soda?
3. ¿De quién es el diccionario?	**7.** ¿De quién es la pizza?
4. ¿De quién es el cartel?	**8.** ¿De quién son los CDs?

2.11 **¿Cómo son?** Describe the following items that your family owns and ask your partner about the items his/her family owns.

Modelo el televisor
Estudiante 1: *Nuestro televisor es nuevo. ¿Cómo es su televisor?*
Estudiante 2: *Nuestro televisor es pequeño.*

1. la casa/el apartamento	**3.** la mascota	**5.** los primos
2. el auto/los autos	**4.** la computadora	**6.** la familia

A analizar

Rosa talks about her family with Paula. After watching the video, read part of their conversation, paying attention to the endings of the words in bold. Then answer the questions.

Paula:	¿Dónde **trabajan** ellos?
Rosa:	Mi madre **trabaja** en la universidad. Ella es profesora de historia. Y mi padre **trabaja** en una compañía internacional y viaja a los Estados Unidos con frecuencia.
Paula:	¡Qué interesante! ¿Tú **trabajas** también?
Rosa:	No, yo no **trabajo**.

1. What does the word **trabajar** mean?
2. You have learned that the verb **ser** has different forms depending upon the subject. The verb **trabajar** also has different forms. Looking at the forms of the verb **trabajar** in the conversation, complete the following chart.

yo _____   nosotros(as) trabajamos

tú _____   vosotros(as) trabajáis

él, ella, usted _____   ellos, ellas, ustedes _____

A comprobar

Regular -ar verbs

1. An infinitive is a verb in its simplest form. It conveys the idea of an action, but does not indicate who is doing the action. The following are verbs in their infinitive form. You will notice that their English translations are all to _____.

ayudar	to help	**estudiar**	to study	**necesitar**	to need
bailar	to dance	**hablar (por**	to talk (on	**practicar**	to practice; to
buscar	to look for	**teléfono)**	the phone)	**(deportes)**	play (sports)
caminar	to walk	**limpiar**	to clean	**preguntar**	to ask
cantar	to sing	**llamar**	to call	**regresar**	to return
cocinar	to cook	**llegar (a)**	to arrive (at)	**(a casa)**	(home)
comprar	to buy	**mandar (un**	to send (a	**tomar**	to take; to drink
desear	to want,	**mensaje)**	message)	**(café)**	(coffee)
	to desire	**manejar**	to drive	**trabajar**	to work
enseñar	to teach	**mirar (la tele)**	to look, to	**usar**	to use
escuchar	to listen		watch (TV)	**viajar (a)**	to travel (to)
esquiar	to ski	**nadar**	to swim		

2. Although it also means *to drink*, the verb **tomar** is used in many of the same ways that the verb *to take* is used in English.

tomar un examen *to take a test*	**tomar una siesta** *to take a nap*
tomar fotos *to take photos*	**tomar un taxi** *to take a taxi*
tomar notas *to take notes*	**tomar vacaciones** *to take a vacation*

3. You learned that the verb **ser** must be conjugated in agreement with the subject. In other words, different forms of the verb indicate who the subject is. The verbs in the list on page 47 all end in **-ar** and are all conjugated in the same way. To form a present tense verb, the **-ar** is dropped from the infinitive and an ending is added that reflects the subject (the person doing the action).

llegar

yo	-o	llego	nosotros(as)	-amos	llegamos
tú	-as	llegas	vosotros(as)	-áis	llegáis
él, ella, usted	-a	llega	ellos, ellas, ustedes	-an	llegan

4. When using two verbs together that are dependent upon each other, the second verb remains in the infinitive.

> Él **necesita viajar** mucho.
> He **needs to travel** a lot.

> Ellas **desean estudiar** inglés.
> They **want to study** English.

However, notice that both verbs are conjugated in the following sentences because they are not dependent on each other.

> Yo **estudio** en la universidad y **trabajo** en un restaurante.
> I **study** in the university and **work** in a restaurant.

> Édgar **nada, esquía** y **practica** el tenis.
> Édgar **swims, skis,** and **plays** tennis.

5. When creating a negative statement, place the word **no** in front of the verb.

> Ella **no** baila bien.
> She **doesn't** dance well.
> No, yo **no** trabajo.
> No, I **don't** work.

6. In order to create a simple yes/no question, it is not necessary to use helping words. Simply place the subject after the verb and change the intonation, raising your voice at the end.

> ¿Estudias tú mucho?
> *Do you study a lot?*

> ¿Habla usted español?
> *Do you speak Spanish?*

> **INVESTIGUEMOS LA GRAMÁTICA**
>
> When the recipient of the action (direct object) is a person or a pet, an **a** is used in front of the object. This is known as the **a personal.** It is not translated into English. You will learn more about this concept in **Capítulo 5.**
>
> Los estudiantes buscan **a** la profesora.
> Los niños llaman **a** los perros.

A practicar

2.12 **Mi familia y yo** Decide which of the two phrases best completes the sentences. ¡OJO! You must decide which verb ending agrees with the subject.

1. Mi padre...
   a. mira la tele mucho   **b.** miran la tele mucho

2. Mis padres...
   a. manejamos un auto viejo   **b.** manejan un auto viejo

3. Mi esposo...
   a. baila bien   **b.** bailo bien

4. Mi hermana y yo...
   a. tomamos mucho café   **b.** toman mucho café

5. ¿Tú...?
   a. estudia mucho   **b.** estudias mucho

2.13 La familia de Gabriela Complete the paragraph with the appropriate form of the verb in parentheses.

Yo (**1.**) _____ (ser) Gabriela. Mi esposo se llama Nicolás y él (**2.**) _____ (trabajar) en un hospital. Él (**3.**) _____ (pasar – *to spend*) mucho tiempo en el trabajo. Nuestros dos hijos Dora y Ernesto (**4.**) _____ (estudiar) en la universidad. Mi esposo necesita (**5.**) _____ (trabajar) mucho, pero nosotros siempre (*always*) (**6.**) _____ (tomar) vacaciones en julio. La familia (**7.**) _____ (viajar) a Bariloche, Argentina, y nosotros (**8.**) _____ (esquiar). Yo no (**9.**) _____ (esquiar) muy bien, pero es muy divertido.

2.14 El fin de semana Working in pairs, find out if your partner does the following activities on the weekend.

Modelo hablar por teléfono
Estudiante 1: *¿Hablas por teléfono?*
Estudiante 2: *Sí, hablo por teléfono. / No, no hablo por teléfono.*

1. trabajar
2. estudiar español
3. limpiar la casa
4. tomar una siesta
5. practicar deportes

6. bailar en un club
7. mirar la tele
8. cantar en un coro (*choir*)
9. cocinar para (*for*) amigos
10. caminar con (*with*) el perro

2.15 En los Estados Unidos The following statements describe what some Spanish speakers in different countries often do. Using the **nosotros** form, state what we generally do in the United States.

Modelo Los colombianos practican fútbol.
   Nosotros practicamos fútbol americano.

1. Los argentinos hablan español.
2. Los chilenos estudian inglés.
3. Los españoles viajan a Francia de vacaciones.
4. Los mexicanos escuchan música en inglés y español.
5. Los cubanos bailan salsa.
6. Los paraguayos esquían en Argentina.

Los cubanos bailan salsa.

Aleksandar Todorovic/Shutterstock

2.16 **Un día ocupado** Fedra and Bruno are very busy. Look at the drawings and describe what they do on a typical day.

Modelo *Fedra y Bruno toman un café.*

1.

2.

3.

4.

5.

6.

© Cengage Learning

2.17 **¡Yo también!** Place a check mark next to four of the following activities that you do. Then, find four different classmates, each of whom also does one of those activities. When you are finished, report to the class something that you and another classmate both do using the **nosotros** form.

_____ buscar un trabajo

_____ viajar con frecuencia (*frequently*)

_____ mirar la tele mucho

_____ trabajar en un restaurante

_____ cantar bien

_____ cocinar

_____ mandar muchos mensajes

_____ llamar a un amigo con frecuencia

_____ escuchar la radio

_____ usar la computadora

_____ nadar

_____ comprar muchos regalos (*gifts*)

_____ esquiar

_____ ¿?

2.18 **¿Quién?** Interview your partner to find out if he/she or someone he/she knows does the following activities. **¡OJO!** When asking the question you will need to use the **él/ ella** form of the verb. When answering, be sure that the verb agrees with the subject.

Modelo viajar mucho

        Estudiante 1: *¿Quién viaja mucho?*

        Estudiante 2: *Mis padres viajan mucho. / Mi mejor amigo y yo viajamos mucho.*

1. manejar un auto nuevo

2. trabajar en un restaurante

3. practicar tenis

4. enseñar

5. estudiar biología

6. escuchar música clásica

7. cocinar bien

8. mandar muchos textos

En vivo ◀)))

Entrando en materia

¿Celebras tú el Día de la Madre ¿y el Día del Niño?

Celebrando a la familia

◀))) You are going to hear a fragment of a radio show. Listen carefully, then answer the
1-11 questions below.

Vocabulario útil

fecha fija	*fixed date*	**razón**	*reason*
mayo	*May*	**tercer domingo**	*third Sunday*
junio	*June*		

Comprensión

After listening to the radio announcers, read the statements below and decide if each one is
true (**cierto**) or false (**falso**).

1. Hoy es 30 de mayo.
2. El 30 de mayo es el Día del Padre en Nicaragua.
3. En Nicaragua no celebran el Día de la Suegra.
4. En Argentina el Día de la Suegra es el 17 de octubre.
5. En Perú, Colombia y Ecuador no celebran el Día del Padre.

Más allá

Look for another date that is celebrated in a Spanish-speaking country. What is the
celebration? Where does it take place? When? Here are a few keywords to help with your
search: **Independencia, Acción de Gracias, Día Nacional.**

Record your findings and post a brief summary to Share It!

El día de la Madre es importante en muchos países.

© mnoa357/Shutterstock

Lectura

Antes de leer

What does the modern American family look like? What do you think the modern Latin American family looks like?

A leer

La familia típica latinoamericana

Es difícil hablar de una familia típica latinoamericana, especialmente porque Latinoamérica es una región muy grande que comprende muchos países diferentes. Sin embargo, en todas las sociedades las familias **cambian** para adaptarse a los tiempos modernos. La familia típica latinoamericana urbana tiene pocos hijos, y el hombre y la mujer trabajan. Las familias extendidas son muy importantes, pero en la mayoría de las casas no **viven** muchos familiares. Por ejemplo, en Chile viven un **promedio** de 3.5 personas por casa; en México, viven 3.9 y en Colombia viven 4.2. En Colombia y en México en el 74% de las casas viven solamente los padres y los hijos o una pareja sin hijos. Solo en el 24% de las casas viven otros miembros de la familia **como** abuelos, nietos u otros familiares. **Es decir**, para muchos latinoamericanos es muy importante ayudar a los miembros de la familia, solo en una de cuatro casas vive un miembro de la familia extendida. Ahora también hay muchas familias donde los hijos viven con solo uno de sus padres, o **ninguno**. También hay muchas casas donde dos adultos cohabitan (viven **juntos** pero no están **casados**). En Colombia el 39% cohabitan, en México el 21% y en Chile el 12%.

change

live
average

such as
In other words

neither

together
married

> [las familias extendidas son muy importantes]

© Andy Dean Photography/Shutterstock

Otro cambio importante en toda la región es el del **papel** de la mujer. La mayoría de las familias **está encabezada por** hombres, pero el número de familias encabezadas por mujeres **está aumentando** rápidamente.

role

is headed by

is increasing

En varios países latinoamericanos el divorcio es **cada vez más frecuente**. En Chile el divorcio es legal desde 2004 y ahora hay más divorcios que **casamientos**. En 2013 Chile fue el 3er país con más divorcios en el mundo con una tasa de 170% de divorcios. En México la tasa de divorcios es 16%, y en Colombia 24%.

increasingly more frequent

marriages

© Monkey Business Images/Shutterstock

Otra estadística interesante que habla de la importancia de la familia es la frecuencia con que las familias comen juntas. En toda Latinoamérica comer juntos es importante. En Argentina el 86% de las familias come junta, en contraste con Perú, donde solo el 69% come junta. En Estados Unidos el número es aproximadamente el 65%.

Sources: Sistema Nacional para el Desarrollo Integral de la Familia; Instituto Nacional de Estadística y Geografía; Instituto Nacional de Estadísticas; RevistaCredencial.com

Comprensión

Decide whether the following statements are true (**cierto**) or false (**falso**). Correct any false statements.

1. Las mujeres latinoamericanas no trabajan.
2. La familia extendida es muy importante en Latinoamérica.
3. Ahora hay más (*more*) familias encabezadas por mujeres.
4. En la mayoría de las casas viven tres generaciones (los abuelos, los padres y los hijos).
5. En Chile pocos matrimonios terminan (*end*) en divorcio.
6. En Colombia muchos adultos prefieren vivir juntos sin (*without*) estar casados.

Después de leer

1. In groups of three or four, discuss the following questions in English.
   - Did any information surprise you? Why?
   - How does this information about Latin American families compare with U.S. families in general?

2. In the same groups, discuss the following questions in Spanish.
   - ¿Es importante la familia para ti?
   - ¿Qué personas consideras tú como parte de tu familia?
   - ¿Qué actividades haces (*do you do*) con tu familia?

¿Cómo es tu universidad?

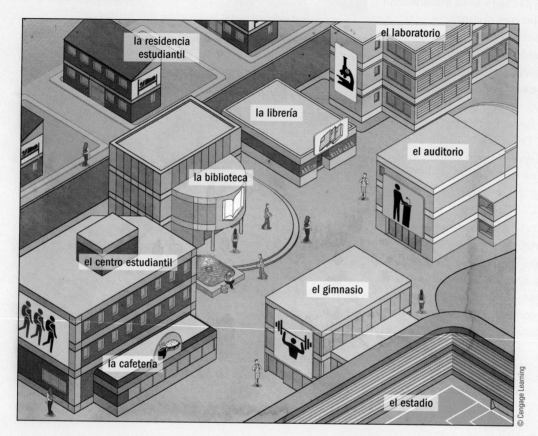

Las materias académicas	Academic subjects	las ciencias sociales	social studies
el álgebra	algebra	la física	physics
el arte	art	la economía	economics
el cálculo	calculus	la geografía	geography
la criminología	criminology	la historia	history
la educación física	physical education	la psicología	psychology
la expresión oral	speech	la química	chemistry
la filosofía	philosophy		
la geografía	geography	**Las lenguas**	**Languages**
la informática	computer science	el alemán	German
la ingeniería	engineering	el español	Spanish
la literatura	literature	el francés	French
las matemáticas	mathematics	el inglés	English
la música	music	el italiano	Italian
los negocios	business		
el periodismo	journalism	**Palabras adicionales**	
la redacción	writing, composition	el/la compañero(a)	classmate
el teatro	theater	de clase	
		la nota	grade
Las ciencias naturales	**Natural science**	el semestre	semester
la biología	biology	la tarea	homework
las ciencias políticas	political science	el trimestre	quarter

Estrategia

Listen to and repeat vocabulary

When studying vocabulary, take time to listen to and repeat the pronunciation of the words included on the audio recordings. It will help your pronunciation, which in turn will help you learn to spell the words properly. You may want to download the audio files onto your MP3 player or cell phone so they will be more accessible.

A practicar

2.19 **Escucha y responde** Listen to the statements about activities that can be done at the university. Raise your right hand if the activity typically occurs in the classroom; raise your left hand if it typically occurs in another part of the campus, such as the cafeteria, gym, or stadium.

🔊 1-12

2.20 **Relaciones** Match each course from the first column with a related topic from the second column.

1. _____ periodismo
2. _____ ciencias políticas
3. _____ química
4. _____ alemán
5. _____ veterinaria
6. _____ informática

a. los animales
b. la computadora
c. los eventos internacionales
d. los elementos
e. los verbos
f. los presidentes

2.21 **En la universidad** Look at the list and determine where on campus students would do each activity.

1. tomar una siesta
2. escuchar un concierto
3. comprar libros
4. mirar un partido *(match)* de fútbol

5. tomar café con unos amigos
6. estudiar en silencio
7. usar un microscopio
8. practicar deportes

2.22 **Opiniones** With a classmate, take turns completing the sentences with a word from the vocabulary list and finishing the sentences logically.

1. Me gusta *(I like)* la clase de _____ porque *(because)* es...
2. No me gusta mucho la clase de _____ porque es...
3. El profesor/La profesora de la clase de _____ es...
4. Los exámenes en la clase de _____ son...
5. El libro para la clase de _____ es...
6. La tarea de la clase de _____ es...

> **INVESTIGUEMOS LA GRAMÁTICA**
>
> In order to talk about a specific class or a specific instructor, you can use the expressions **La clase de...** or **El profesor de...**
>
> **El profesor de historia es inteligente.**
> *The history instructor is intelligent.*

2.23 **La graduación** In order to graduate, each student must take one class in each of the following categories: natural science, social science, math, humanities (**las humanidades**), and language. You and your partner must check the transcripts of four students to determine which courses they have taken, and which ones they need. One of you will look at the information on this page and the other will look at Appendix B.

> **Modelo** Estudiante 1: ¿*Tiene* (has) *Raúl Ruiz Costa una clase de ciencias naturales?*
> Estudiante 2: *Sí, Raúl tiene una clase de biología.*

Ramón Ayala Pérez	Andrea Gómez Ramos	Diana Salazar Casas	Hugo Vargas Díaz
	ingeniería		biología
	física		geometría
	alemán		economía
	cálculo		negocios

Cultura

One of the largest universities in the world is the **Universidad Nacional Autónoma de México (UNAM).** The university is so large that the applicants have to take their admission exam in a sports stadium. UNAM is considered one of the best universities in the world and is free for Mexican citizens.

The Central University City Campus of UNAM is one of three universities in the world that was designated as a World Heritage site by UNESCO in 2007. It was designed by over 60 architects, engineers, and artists, and is an exceptional display of twentieth-century modernism. The campus has numerous impressive works of art, and is known especially for its murals and mosaics.

Is there art at your school or university? Where? What do you think of it? How many students attend your university?

Do an online search to explore a historic university in Spain or Latin America. Find out when it was built and what makes it special. Post an image of it on Share It! and share what you learned. Here are some keywords to help with your search: **universidad, histórica, primera, fundada, establecida.**

Sources: Times Higher Education; UNESCO; www.topuniversities.com

Comunidad

Find an international student from a Spanish-speaking country and ask him or her for additional information about their school system. Ask which subjects they study, the price of textbooks, and the number of hours they spend at school every day. The following are some possible questions for your interview:

¿De dónde eres?
¿Qué clases tienes?
¿Es similar la universidad en ____*(country)*____?
¿Cuántas horas están en la escuela los estudiantes de primaria/secundaria/preparatoria?

¿Qué clases tienes?

Comparaciones

While in the United States students are required by law to attend school until they are 16, in Chile students are legally required to attend school only until they complete **nivel básico** at age 14. After that, students can choose the type of **liceo** they want to attend. Those who continue to **educación superior** can attend an **instituto profesional** and learn a trade, or attend university. Recently, however, several reforms have been introduced and are being implemented. These reforms call for a redistribution of the number of years spent in **nivel básico** and **enseñanza media**, and seek to update the system, improve the quality of education, and provide better access to education for everyone. How does the education system of the United States compare to the Chilean system? Complete the table with the U.S. equivalents.

Edad	Chile	Estados Unidos
2–6 años	preescolar (kinder)*	_____
6–14 años	nivel básico (8 años)*	_____
14–18 años	enseñanza media (liceo) (4 años)**	_____
18+	educación superior (instituto profesional/universidad) (2–4 años)	_____
	diplomados	_____
	maestría	_____
	doctorado	_____

* Compulsory
** Education can become specialized at this point. Students can choose between Humanities and Sciences, technical programs, or the Arts.

For more information on Chile, refer to Appendix A: **Exploraciones del mundo hispano.**

Conexiones... a la educación

In Spanish-speaking countries, elementary and secondary students commonly wear uniforms to school. What are the advantages and disadvantages of using them? Did you ever wear a uniform to school? Are uniforms popular in the United States? Why?

Niñas cubanas en sus uniformes

A analizar ▶

Paula and Santiago are talking about their classes. After watching the video, read Paula's comments, paying particular attention to the forms of the verb **tener** in bold. Then answer the questions below.

> **Tengo** dos clases de psicología este semestre y son muy difíciles. **Tengo** que estudiar mucho. Nosotros **tenemos** mucha tarea y hay varios estudiantes que **tienen** miedo de recibir una mala nota. ¿**Tienes** tú una clase difícil este semestre?

1. What does the verb **tener** mean?
2. Using the examples in the paragraph, complete the chart with the forms of the verb **tener**.

   yo _____   nosotros, nosotras _____

   tú _____   vosotros, vosotras **tenéis**

   él, ella, usted _____   ellos, ellas, ustedes _____

3. Using context clues to help you, what does the expression **tener miedo** mean?

   a. to have to   **b.** to need   **c.** to be afraid

A comprobar

The verb **tener**

tener (to have)

yo	**tengo**	nosotros(as)	**tenemos**
tú	**tienes**	vosotros(as)	**tenéis**
él, ella, usted	**tiene**	ellos, ellas, ustedes	**tienen**

*Notice that the original vowel **e** changes to **ie** in some of the forms. This is what is known as a stem-changing verb. You will learn more about stem-changing verbs in **Capítulo 3**.

1. There are a number of expressions in which the verb **tener** is used where *to be* would be used in English. The following are noun expressions with the verb **tener**:

tener... años	*to be . . . years old*
tener (mucho) calor	*to be (very) hot*
tener (mucho) cuidado	*to be (very) careful*
tener (mucho) éxito	*to be (very) successful*

tener (mucho) frío	*to be (very) cold*
tener ganas de + infinitive	*to feel like doing something*
tener (mucha) hambre	*to be (very) hungry*
tener (mucho) miedo	*to be (very) afraid*
tener (mucha) prisa	*to be in a (big) hurry*
tener que + infinitive	*to have to do something*
tener (mucha) razón	*to be right*
tener (mucha) sed	*to be (very) thirsty*
tener (mucho) sueño	*to be (very) sleepy*
tener (mucha) suerte	*to be (very) lucky*

2. Unlike adjectives, noun expressions do not change in gender and number.

   Mis hermanos tienen frío.
   My brothers are cold.

   Mi hermana tiene sueño.
   My sister is sleepy.

A practicar

2.24 **¿Qué tienen?** Match the sentences to the appropriate picture.

a.

b.

c.

d.

e.

f.

1. _____ Tenemos hambre.
2. _____ Tienen miedo.
3. _____ Tengo 5 años.

4. _____ Tiene sed.
5. _____ ¿Tienes sueño?
6. _____ Tiene prisa.

2.25 **¿Tienes ganas?** Read the the list of activities that Carla will do this week and decide whether each one is something she feels like doing (**tiene ganas de**) or has to do (**tiene que**).

1. estudiar para el examen de español hasta *(until)* las tres de la mañana
2. hablar con unos amigos en el centro estudiantil
3. trabajar por 18 horas
4. comprar los libros para sus clases en la librería
5. viajar a España
6. limpiar la casa
7. bailar en el club
8. mirar la tele con un amigo

2.26 **¿Cuántos años tienes?** Complete the paragraph with the correct forms of the verb **tener**.

Yo soy estudiante en la Universidad de Salamanca y (**1.**) _____ 20 años. Mis amigos Sara y Fernando (**2.**) _____ 19 años. Sara y yo (**3.**) _____ nuestros cumpleaños *(birthday)* en noviembre. Fernando (**4.**) _____ su cumpleaños en diciembre. ¿Y tú? ¿Cuántos años (**5.**) _____?

INVESTIGUEMOS LA MÚSICA

Find the song "Tengo tu love" by Puerto Rican singer and songwriter El Sie7e online and listen to it. What does he say that he has? What are some of the things he mentions that others have?

2.27 ¿Cuántos años tiene? Ask your partner how old the following people are. If you are not sure, guess and use the expression **probablemente.**

Modelo tu profesor de inglés

      Estudiante 1: *¿Cuántos años tiene tu profesor de inglés?*
      Estudiante 2: *Mi profesor (probablemente) tiene 35 años.*

1. tú
2. tu mejor amigo
3. tu profesor de la clase de español
4. el presidente de los Estados Unidos
5. tu actor favorito (¿Cómo se llama?)
6. tu actriz favorita (¿Cómo se llama?)

2.28 ¿Qué tienen? Describe the scenes using expressions with **tener.**

Modelo Ronaldo
      Ronaldo tiene razón.

1. Lola y yo

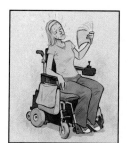

2. Marcia

3. yo

4. Isabel y Mar

5. tú

6. Rosario

© Cengage Learning

2.29 Entrevista Interview a classmate using the questions below.

En la casa

1. ¿Tienes mucho sueño en la noche?
2. ¿Tienes ganas de invitar a amigos a tu casa?
3. ¿Quién (*Who*) tiene que cocinar?

En la universidad

4. ¿En qué clase tienes éxito en los exámenes?
5. ¿Tienes miedo de un profesor? ¿Cómo se llama?
6. ¿Para qué clases tienes que estudiar mucho?

A analizar ▶

Paula and Santiago are talking about their classes. Watch the video again. Then read part of the conversation between Paula and Santiago and identify the adjectives. Then, answer the questions below.

Paula: Tengo dos clases de psicología este semestre y son muy difíciles. Tengo que estudiar mucho. Nosotros tenemos mucha tarea y hay varios estudiantes que tienen miedo de recibir una mala nota. ¿Tienes tú una clase difícil este semestre?

Santiago: Para mí, historia es una clase interesante pero muy difícil. ¡Tenemos exámenes muy largos! Afortunadamente tengo un buen profesor con mucha experiencia. Además es un hombre simpático e inteligente.

1. List all the adjectives you identified.

_____   _____   _____   _____

_____   _____   _____   _____

2. Where are the adjectives placed in relation to the noun they describe? What are the exceptions?

A comprobar

Adjective placement

1. In Spanish, adjectives are generally placed *after* the nouns they describe.

> El cálculo es una clase **difícil**.
> *Calculus is a **difficult** class.*

> La señora Muñoz es una profesora **interesante**.
> *Mrs. Muñoz is an **interesting** professor.*

2. However, adjectives such as **mucho** (*a lot*), **poco** (*few*), and **varios** (*several*) that indicate quantity or amount are placed in front of the object.

> **Muchos** estudiantes estudian francés.
> ***Many** students study French.*

> Tengo **varios** libros para esta clase.
> *I have **several** books for this class.*

> Hay **pocos** estudiantes en clase hoy.
> *There are **few** students in class today.*

3. **Bueno** and **malo** are likewise generally placed in front of the noun they describe. They drop the **o** when used in front of a masculine singular noun.

> Él es un **buen** estudiante.   Ellos son **buenos** estudiantes.
> *He is a **good** student.*   *They are **good** students.*

> Es una **mala** clase.   Son **malas** clases.
> *It's a **bad** class.*   *They are **bad** classes.*

4. When using more than one adjective to describe an object, use commas between adjectives and **y** (*and*) before the last adjective.

> Tengo un cuaderno pequeño **y** rojo.
> *I have a small, red notebook.*

> El profesor es un hombre honesto, serio **e** inteligente.
> *The professor is an honest, serious, **and** intelligent man.*

A practicar

2.30 **Mi clase de español** Listen to the statements about your Spanish class and decide whether they are true (**cierto**) or false (**falso**).

1-13   **Modelo** *(you hear)* La clase de español tiene estudiantes simpáticos.
Cierto

2.31 **¿Cómo son?** Complete the sentences with a logical adjective from the list on the right.

Modelo Eva Longoria es una actriz... talentosa.
Eva Longoria es una actriz talentosa.

1. Victor Cruz es un hombre...   **a.** largo.
2. Santana es un grupo...   **b.** atlético.
3. Sofía Vergara es una mujer...   **c.** guapa.
4. "Bésame mucho" es una canción *(song)*...   **d.** musical.
5. *Don Quijote de la Mancha* es un libro...   **e.** argentina.
6. Buenos Aires es una ciudad...   **f.** mexicana.
7. Puerto Rico es una isla...   **g.** altos.
8. Manu Ginobili y Rudy Fernández son basquetbolistas...   **h.** pequeña.

2.32 **Mis clases** With a classmate, complete each of the following sentences with the name of a class and an appropriate adjective.

Modelo En la clase de _____ hay un profesor _____.
En la clase de historia hay un profesor inteligente.

1. El profesor de _____ es un hombre _____.
2. La profesora de _____ es una mujer _____.
3. En la clase de _____ tenemos un libro _____.
4. En la clase de _____ hay unos estudiantes _____.
5. En la clase de _____ tenemos exámenes _____.
6. _____ es una clase _____.
7. En la clase de _____ tenemos tarea _____.
8. En la clase de _____ hay un estudiante _____.

> **¿TE ACUERDAS?**
>
> Remember that adjectives must agree in both number (singular and plural) and gender (masculine and feminine) with the object they describe.

2.33 **En busca de...** Circulate throughout the classroom and find eight different students to whom one of the following statements applies. Be ready to report to the class; so remember to ask for the names of your classmates if you don't know them.

Modelo Tiene un lápiz nuevo
Estudiante 1: *¿Tienes un lápiz nuevo?*
Estudiante 2: *Sí tengo un lápiz nuevo.*

1. Tiene una clase difícil.
2. Tiene mucha tarea este semestre.
3. Tiene un profesor rubio.
4. Tiene una computadora nueva.
5. Tiene pocos libros en la mochila hoy *(today)*.
6. Siempre *(Always)* tiene notas excelentes.
7. Tiene un muy buen profesor este semestre.
8. Tiene un compañero de clase muy inteligente.

© wavebreakmedia/Shutterstock

2.34 **¿Cierto o falso?** Complete the statement below to form four true / false statements that describe the people and objects in the classroom. Then read your statements to your partner, who will tell you whether they are true (**cierto**) or false (**falso**). **¡OJO!** Pay attention to the position of the adjective.

En la clase hay...

Modelo Estudiante 1: *En la clase hay un estudiante calvo.*
Estudiante 2: *Falso.*

© Cengage Learning

2.35 **Hablemos de las clases** Interview a classmate with the following questions.

1. ¿Tienes muchas clases hoy? ¿Qué clases tienes?
2. ¿Tienes un profesor muy simpático este semestre? ¿Cómo se llama?
3. ¿Tienes una clase con pocos estudiantes? ¿Cuántos estudiantes hay?
4. ¿Tienes una clase favorita? ¿Qué clase es?
5. ¿En qué clase tienes exámenes muy largos?
6. ¿En qué clase tienes tarea difícil?

2.36 **¿Tienes...?** Use different adjectives to talk about the following items with a partner. Possible adjectives: **inteligente, simpático, viejo, nuevo, grande, pequeño, difícil, fácil, interesante, aburrido, largo, corto.**

Modelo una computadora
Estudiante 1: *¿Tienes una computadora?*
Estudiante 2: *Sí, tengo una computadora nueva.*
Estudiante 1: *Yo tengo una computadora vieja. / Yo también
tengo una computadora nueva.*

1. una casa / un apartamento
2. un auto
3. clases

4. profesores
5. una familia
6. un amigo

Reading Strategy: Predicting
Before you read a text, pay attention to the title and any visual clues there might be. You might want to write three possible topics based on the title or list adjectives in Spanish to describe photos. This will help you anticipate the kind of ideas that might be mentioned.

Antes de leer 👥

1. The title of this article is **"Otros sistemas universitarios."** Use your knowledge of cognates to deduce what it means, and then mention three ideas that you would expect to find in a text with this title.

2. Work with a partner to ask and answer the following questions.
   a. ¿Cuántas clases tienes este semestre?
   b. ¿Qué clases tomas?

A leer

Otros sistemas universitarios

world Las universidades en diferentes partes del **mundo** usan diversos sistemas de educación. En muchas universidades de España y Latinoamérica los estudiantes no necesitan obtener un cierto número de créditos para graduarse.

Instead of **En vez de** usar créditos tienen un "plan de estudios", que es una lista de las clases que los estudiantes

each tienen que tomar **cada** semestre. A veces las universidades combinan el plan de estudios con el sistema de créditos, especialmente para ayudar a los estudiantes internacionales.

La Universidad de la Habana en Cuba

© Liset Alvaez/Shutterstock

[en muchas universidades no hay clases de educación general]

En muchas universidades no hay clases de educación general. Un estudiante de literatura tiene diferentes clases de literatura y otras materias relacionadas, pero no necesita estudiar matemáticas ni ciencias si no son parte de su plan de estudios. En consecuencia, cuando un estudiante inicia **la licenciatura,**

bachelor's degree

tiene que especializarse inmediatamente en su área y toma casi todas sus clases en una sola **facultad.** Cuando un estudiante **termina** la licenciatura, puede usar el título de licenciado. En muchas partes del mundo, la educación universitaria es un **derecho** y es prácticamente **gratuita.** Sin embargo, un estudiante **puede** asistir a una universidad privada si lo prefiere y si tiene suficiente dinero.

department / finishes

right / free
can

Comprensión

Decide whether the statements are true (**cierto**) or false (**falso**). Correct the false statements.

1. En muchas universidades hispanas no existen los créditos.
2. La lista de clases que los estudiantes necesitan tomar se llama "el plan de estudios".
3. Los estudiantes en Latinoamérica y España necesitan tomar clases de educación general.
4. Normalmente los estudiantes tienen clases en diferentes facultades.
5. Las universidades privadas son gratuitas.

Después de leer

Look for a university in a Spanish-speaking country. Then find your major in the index and answer the following questions.

1. ¿Cuántos años de estudios son necesarios para completar la carrera?
2. ¿Qué cursos necesitan tomar?

La Universidad de Guanajuato en México

Redacción

Write an email to a new friend and tell him or her about your family and your classes.

Paso 1 Jot down a list of the members of your family.

Paso 2 Choose two family members and beside each one, write down his or her age and two adjectives that describe the person. Be sure to use different adjectives for each person so your paragraph will not be repetitive.

Paso 3 Jot down a list of the classes you are taking.

Paso 4 Choose one of the classes in the list and write an adjective to describe it (**fácil, difícil, aburrido, interesante,** etc). Then jot down a series of phrases about it including the following: how many students are in the class and what they are like, and who the teacher is and what he or she is like.

Paso 5 Start your email with **Hola** or **¿Qué tal?** *(How's it going?)* and introduce yourself. Tell him/her something about yourself, such as where you are from, your age, or what you are like.

Paso 6 Tell him/her whether you have a large or small family. Then tell who each of the members of your family are and give details about two of them using the ideas you generated in **Paso 2.**

Paso 7 Begin a second paragraph telling your friend that you are a student and where you are studying.

Paso 8 Tell your friend what classes you have this semester. Then introduce the class you brainstormed ideas for in **Paso 4,** giving your opinion of the class.

Paso 9 Using the information you generated in **Paso 4,** describe the class.

Paso 10 Finish the letter with **Hasta pronto** or **Tu amigo(a).**

Paso 11 Edit your letter:

1. Are there any sentences that are irrelevant to the topic? If so, get rid of them.
2. Are there any spelling errors?
3. Do adjectives agree with the person or object they describe?
4. Do verbs agree with the person doing the action?
5. Are there any sentences you can join using **y** or **pero**?

En vivo

Entrando en materia

How many classes does a full-time student in the United States usually take?

Un plan de estudios

Look at the plan of study for a technical program from a school in Colombia.

Programas técnicos: Auxiliar de oficina

Plan de estudios

Semestre 1: Recepción de Información (336 horas, 7 créditos)
1. Desarrollo de habilidades comunicativas.
2. Utilización de los equipos de oficina.
3. Digitación de textos.
4. Manipulación y aplicación de herramientas informáticas I.
5. Formación Humana: Conciencia e identidad del ser integral.

Semestre 2: Procesamiento y disposición de la información (336 horas, 7 créditos)
1. Aplicación de técnicas de archivo.
2. Aplicación de las técnicas de correspondencia comercial.
3. Manipulación y aplicación de herramientas informáticas II.
4. Manejo de bases de datos en Access.
5. Construcción de valores para la vida, el liderazgo y la autonomía.

Semestre 3: Manejo de la información (288 horas, 6 créditos)
1. Aplicación de técnicas comerciales de oficina.
2. Servicio al cliente.
3. Etiqueta y protocolo empresarial.
4. El emprendedor y la empresa.

Semestre 4: Formación y práctica laboral (672 horas, 14 créditos)
1. Proyecto empresarial.
2. Práctica laboral.

Intensidad horaria semanal:
Estudia entre 14 y 16 horas semanales de **clase presencial.**

contact hours

Comprensión

1. ¿Qué programa es?
2. ¿Cuántas clases hay en el primer *(first)* semestre? ¿y en el tercer *(third)* semestre?
3. ¿Cuántas horas de clases hay por semana?

 Más allá

Choose another major or technical program and list classes you think would be appropriate for the first two semesters of study. Post your major and list of classes to Share It! and find out what your classmates have chosen.

© Chris Fredriksson / Alamy

Asistente de oficina ▶

© Yuri Arcurs/Shutterstock

Vocabulario

Sustantivos

buena presencia	*good appearance*
la cita	*appointment*
el formulario	*form*
la oficina	*office*
la reunión	*meeting*

Verbos

contestar el teléfono	*to answer the phone*
inscribir	*to register*
interpretar	*to interpret*
preparar informes	*to prepare reports*

Frases útiles

¿En qué puedo servirle?
How can I help you?

Un momento, por favor.
One moment, please.

Está ocupado. ¿Desea hacer una cita?
He is busy right now. Would you like to make an appointment?

¿Cuál es su número de teléfono?
What is your phone number?

Más despacio, por favor.
Slower, please.

Disculpe
Excuse me. / I'm sorry.

Necesita hablar con...
You need to speak to . . .

¿Con quién quiere hablar?
Whom do you want to speak to?

Tiene que ver a...
You have to see . . .

DATOS IMPORTANTES

Educación: Escuela secundaria con entrenamiento especial en tecnología o *community college;* algunos puestos *(some positions)* requieren una licenciatura *(bachelor's degree)*

Salario: Entre $23 000 y $36 000

Dónde se trabaja: Variedad de organizaciones; aproximadamente 90% de los asistentes trabajan en la industria de servicio, como *(like)* la educación, el gobierno *(government),* la salud *(health)* y ventas *(retail)*

Vocabulario nuevo Match the comments or questions from the first column with a logical response from the second column.

1. ¿En qué puedo servirle?
2. ¿Con quién quiere hablar?
3. ¿Cuál es su número de teléfono?
4. Tengo que ver al señor Gómez.
5. Disculpe...

a. Está ocupado.
b. Tengo una cita con el señor Pérez.
c. Necesito hablar con la Sra. Ávila.
d. Un momento, por favor.
e. Es el 555-333-2222.

▶ María Bravo, secretaria ejecutiva

María Bravo es secretaria ejecutiva y trabaja en una escuela privada. Allí hay muchos estudiantes de otros países *(countries)*. Ella necesita comunicarse en inglés y en español continuamente. María se encarga de *(is in charge of)* los trabajos administrativos de la escuela y ayuda a los padres y estudiantes que necesitan información. En el video, María habla con el padre de un estudiante que no habla inglés.

© Cengage Learning

Antes de ver

Administrative assistants and executive secretaries are the connections between a company and their clients. What questions do you think a parent would ask a secretary at a private school? How important do you think it is to have bilingual administrative personnel in a school? Why?

Comprensión

Answer the following questions according to the video.

1. ¿Qué tiene que hacer *(to do)* el Sr. Molina?
2. ¿De dónde son el Sr. Molina y su familia?
3. ¿Cuántos años tiene el hijo del Sr. Molina?
4. Según la Sra. Bravo, ¿a qué grado entra el hijo del Sr. Molina?
5. ¿Cuántos maestros *(teachers)* bilingües hay?

Después de ver

With a partner, play the roles of the parent of a Latin American student who has just arrived in the United States and the secretary of a school. Greet and introduce yourself to the secretary. The secretary should ask how he/she can help you. Explain what you need.

Begin your answer with this phrase.

Quiero inscribir a...   *I want to register . . .*

2.37 **La Universidad de Puerto Rico** Complete the paragraph with the appropriate form of the verb or the possessive in parentheses.

(**1.**) _____ (mi) hermana Victoria y yo (**2.**) _____ (estudiar) en la Universidad de Puerto Rico. (**3.**) _____ (nuestro) clases son difíciles y nosotras (**4.**) _____ (tener) mucha tarea. Los profesores son muy amables y (**5.**) _____ (ayudar) mucho. Yo (**6.**) _____ (tener) tres clases: cálculo, biología e inglés. La clase de inglés es muy interesante, y yo (**7.**) _____ (hablar) bien. Victoria (**8.**) _____ (tener) cuatro clases. Ella (**9.**) _____ (tomar) historia, filosofía, literatura y francés. (**10.**) _____ (su) clases favoritas son las de historia y de literatura.

2.38 **Así es mi familia** Add the adjectives in parentheses to the sentences. Be sure to put them in the proper place and in the proper form (masculine, feminine, singular, plural).

1. Tengo una familia. (interesante)
2. Tengo dos hermanas. (pequeño)
3. No tenemos mascotas. (mucho)
4. Tenemos un perro. (cariñoso)
5. Tenemos una gata. (perezoso)
6. Tengo parientes en la ciudad (*city*) donde vivo. (varios)

2.39 **¿Cómo son?** Using the descriptive adjectives in parentheses and the possessive adjectives (**mi, tu, su,** etc.), tell what the family members and pets of the people below are like. ¡OJO! Be sure to use the correct form of the possessive and descriptive adjectives.

Modelo Natalia tiene perros. (agresivo)   *Sus perros son agresivos.*
Mi hermano tiene una esposa. (rubio)   *Su esposa es rubia.*

1. Geraldo tiene una hermana. (simpático)
2. Mis abuelos tienen gatos. (cariñoso)
3. Nosotros tenemos un caballo. (viejo)
4. Tú tienes primos. (cómico)
5. Yo tengo una sobrina. (bonito)
6. Rufina tiene hijos. (grande)

Mi caballo es bonito.

2.40 **En familia** In groups of three, each student chooses a different photo to describe to the rest of the group. Imagine the following about the people in the photo: their names, what their relationship is, how old they are, what they are like, and what they are doing.

2.41 **Datos personales** Working with a partner, look at the chart below while your partner looks at the chart in Appendix B. Take turns asking questions to fill in the missing information.

Modelo ¿Cuántos años tiene Diego?   Diego tiene veinte años.
           ¿Qué parientes hay en la familia de Diego?   Diego tiene dos hermanos.
           ¿Qué clase tiene Diego?   Diego tiene informática.

Nombre	Edad	Familia	Clase
Diego	20	dos	informática
Alonso	18		química
Magdalena	22	padrastro	
Cristina			historia
Pablo		dos hijos	arte
Gabriel		una hermana	
Rufina	41		

2.42 **Buscando un amigo** You are looking to find some new friends to do things with.

Paso 1 Circle 5 or 6 activities below that you like to do.

bailar en un club   escuchar un concierto   nadar
caminar en el parque   esquiar   practicar deportes
cantar karaoke   hablar por teléfono   tomar café
cocinar   manejar una motocicleta   tomar fotos
comprar ropa *(clothing)* mirar la tele   viajar

Paso 2 Interview your partner to find out whether he/she does the activities that you have circled.

Paso 3 Decide whether you and your partner are compatible and would be good friends. Share your decision with the class.

◄)) Vocabulario 1

1–14

La familia

el (la) abuelo(a)	*grandfather / grandmother*
el (la) amigo(a)	*friend*
el (la) esposo(a)	*spouse*
el (la) hermanastro(a)	*stepbrother / stepsister*
el (la) hermano(a)	*brother / sister*
el (la) hijo(a)	*son / daughter*
la madrastra	*stepmother*
la madre (mamá)	*mother*
el (la) medio(a) hermano(a)	*half brother / half sister*

el (la) nieto(a)	*grandson / granddaughter*
el (la) novio(a)	*boyfriend / girlfriend*
el padrastro	*stepfather*
el padre (papá)	*father*
la pareja	*couple; partner*
el pariente	*relative*
el (la) primo(a)	*cousin*
el (la) sobrino(a)	*nephew / niece*
el (la) suegro(a)	*father-in-law / mother-in-law*
el (la) tío(a)	*uncle / aunt*

Las mascotas

el caballo	*horse*
el (la) gato(a)	*cat*
el pájaro	*bird*

el (la) perro(a)	*dog*
el pez	*fish*
el ratón	*mouse*

Los verbos

ayudar	*to help*
bailar	*to dance*
buscar	*to look for*
caminar	*to walk*
cantar	*to sing*
cocinar	*to cook*
comprar	*to buy*
desear	*to wish*
enseñar	*to teach*
escuchar	*to listen*
esquiar	*to ski*
estudiar	*to study*
hablar (por teléfono)	*to talk (on the phone)*
limpiar	*to clean*
llamar	*to call*
llegar	*to arrive*

mandar (un mensaje)	*to send (a message)*
manejar	*to drive*
mirar (la tele)	*to look, to watch (TV)*
nadar	*to swim*
necesitar	*to need*
practicar (deportes)	*to practice; to play (sports)*
preguntar	*to ask*
regresar (a casa)	*to return (home)*
tomar (café)	*to take; to drink (coffee)*
trabajar	*to work*
usar	*to use*
viajar	*to travel*

Diccionario personal

_____

_____

_____

_____

Vocabulario 2

Las materias académicas

el alemán	*German*
el álgebra	*algebra*
el arte	*art*
la biología	*biology*
el cálculo	*calculus*
las ciencias naturales	*natural science*
las ciencias políticas	*political science*
las ciencias sociales	*social science*
la criminología	*criminology*
la economía	*economics*
la educación física	*physical education*
la expresión oral	*speech*
la filosofía	*philosophy*
la física	*physics*
el francés	*French*
la geografía	*geography*
la geometría	*geometry*

la historia	*history*
la informática	*computer science*
la ingeniería	*engineering*
el inglés	*English*
el italiano	*Italian*
las lenguas	*languages*
la literatura	*literature*
las matemáticas	*mathematics*
la música	*music*
los negocios	*business*
el periodismo	*journalism*
la psicología	*psychology*
la química	*chemistry*
la redacción	*writing, composition*
el teatro	*theater*
la veterinaria	*veterinary medicine*

Los lugares en la universidad

el auditorio	*auditorium*
la biblioteca	*library*
la cafetería	*cafeteria*
el centro estudiantil	*student center*
el estadio	*stadium*

el gimnasio	*gymnasium*
el laboratorio	*laboratory*
la librería	*bookstore*
la residencia estudiantil	*residence hall*

Expresiones con *tener*

tener… años	*to be . . . years old*
tener (mucho) calor	*to be (very) hot*
tener (mucho) cuidado	*to be (very) careful*
tener (mucho) éxito	*to be (very) successful*
tener (mucho) frío	*to be (very) cold*
tener ganas de + infinitive	*to feel like doing something*
tener (mucha) hambre	*to be (very) hungry*

tener (mucho) miedo	*to be (very) afraid*
tener (mucha) prisa	*to be in a (big) hurry*
tener que + infinitive	*to have to do something*
tener (mucha) razón	*to be right*
tener (mucha) sed	*to be (very) thirsty*
tener (mucho) sueño	*to be (very) sleepy*
tener (mucha) suerte	*to be (very) lucky*

Palabras adicionales

el (la) compañero(a) de clase	*classmate*
el examen	*exam*
mucho	*a lot*
la nota	*grade*

poco	*few*
el semestre	*semester*
la tarea	*homework*
el trimestre	*quarter*
varios	*several*

© Felipe Rodríguez/age fotostock

Gustavo Adolfo Bécquer

Biografía

Gustavo Adolfo Bécquer (1836–1870) was a Spanish writer associated with the post-romanticism movement. Some of his recurrent topics are the night, love, human fragility, and death. His best known book, *Rimas y leyendas*, is a collection of poems and tales that has become essential reading for anyone studying Spanish literature.

Antes de leer

1. In your opinion, what is poetry?

2. Have you ever written a poem?

3. Based on the title, what do you think this poem is going to be about?

¿Qué es poesía?

you say while you pierce

¿Qué es poesía?, **dices mientras clavas**
En mi pupila tu pupila azul.
¡Qué es poesía! ¿Y tú me lo preguntas?
Poesía eres tú.

Source: Gustavo Adolfo Bécquer, "Rima XXI," *Rimas*.

Después de leer

A. Comprensión

1. To whom is the poetic voice talking?

2. In your opinion, what is meant by the last line, "Poesía eres tú"?

B. Conversemos

Why do people write poetry?

Investiguemos la literatura: La voz poética

The poetic voice is the person that speaks in the poem. It would be incorrect to say that the poet is actually speaking. He or she usually takes on the persona of someone in a particular situation. As you read through a poem, it is important to ask yourself who is speaking.

© OlgaLis/Shutterstock

Gloria Fuertes
Biografía
Gloria Fuertes (1917–1998) was a Spanish writer born in Madrid. She wrote her first poem at the age of 14 and published her first poems in 1935. She continued writing during the Spanish Civil War (1936–1939) while working as an accountant and a secretary. The civil war had a profound effect on her as she struggled to understand how modern civilizations could go to war over things of little importance and with no concern for the children destroyed by it. As a result, a large percentage of her works were written for children.

Antes de leer

1. What do you know about Somalia?
2. What would you expect a poet to write about children in Somalia?

Niños de Somalia

eat

Yo **como**
Tú comes
Él come
Nosotros comemos
Vosotros coméis
¡Ellos no!

Source: Authorized by Luz María Jimenez, heiress of Gloria Fuertes.

Después de leer

A. Comprensión

1. According to the poem, who eats? Who does not?
2. What do you think is the message of the poem?

B. Conversemos

1. Both Becquer's and Fuertes' poems are simple, but they are very different in style. Which poem do you prefer? Why?
2. Do you enjoy reading poetry? Why?

Investiguemos la literatura: Interpretación

It is important to realize that there are often multiple interpretations of a literary piece. Each reader brings his or her own experiences to the reading, and these experiences influence his or her interpretation. So don't be afraid to express your ideas. Look for ways to support them with a part or parts of the text.

Learning Strategy

Understand before moving on

Learning a foreign language is like learning math: you will continue to use what you have already learned and will build upon that knowledge. Therefore, if you find you don't understand something, make an appointment to see your instructor or a tutor right away in order to get some extra help. For help with grammar topics, you can also watch the tutorials in iLrn.

In this chapter you will learn how to:

- Talk about the weather and seasons
- Discuss clothing
- Express likes and dislikes
- Communicate dates and times
- Tell what you and others are going to do in the near future

¿Qué tiempo hace hoy?

Christopher Pillitz/Getty Images

¿Qué estación es? ¿Qué ropa llevas?

el invierno — el gorro — el abrigo — los guantes — la bufanda — las botas

la primavera — el paraguas — la blusa — el suéter — la falda — los zapatos

el verano — el sombrero — la camiseta — los pantalones cortos — las sandalias — el traje de baño

el otoño — la chaqueta — la camisa — los bluyines — los tenis

© Cengage Learning

El tiempo

Hace (muy) buen tiempo.	The weather is (very) nice.
Hace (muy) mal tiempo.	The weather is (very) bad.
Hace (mucho) calor.	It's (very) hot.
Hace fresco.	It is cool.
Hace (mucho) frío.	It's (very) cold.
Hace sol.	It's sunny.
Hace (mucho) viento.	It's (very) windy.
Está nublado.	It is cloudy.
Está despejado.	It is clear.
Llueve.	It's raining. / It rains.
Nieva.	It's snowing. / It snows.

La ropa

la bolsa	handbag
los calcetines	socks

el cinturón	belt
la corbata	tie
el impermeable	raincoat
los lentes	glasses
los pantalones	pants
la pijama	pajamas
el traje	suit
el vestido	dress

Verbos

llevar	to wear; to carry; to take
llevar puesto(a)	to be wearing
tomar el sol	to sunbathe

Palabras adicionales

cómodo(a)	comfortable

Los colores

amarillo(a)	yellow
anaranjado(a)	orange
azul	blue
blanco(a)	white
café	brown
gris	gray
morado(a)	purple
negro(a)	black
rojo(a)	red
rosado(a)	pink
verde	green

INVESTIGUEMOS EL VOCABULARIO

Many Latin Americans use the word **el clima** to refer to the weather. Additionally, it is possible to say either **llevar** or **llevar puesto(a)** to say what you wear.

The following are lexical variations for clothing items:

handbag	**el bolso** (Spain), **la cartera**	tennis shoes	**las zapatillas de deportes** (Spain), **los campeones** (Paraguay)
jacket	**la chamarra** (Mexico)		
glasses	**las gafas** (Spain), **los anteojos**	jeans	**los pantalones de mezclilla** (Mexico), **los mahones** (Puerto Rico), **los vaqueros** (Spain)
socks	**las medias** (Central and South America)		
skirt	**la pollera** (Panama and South America)		

A practicar

3.1 **Escucha y responde** You are going to hear a list of different articles of clothing. If you wear the clothing when it is hot, give a thumbs up. If not, give a thumbs down.

1-16

3.2 **¿Qué tiempo hace?** Which season do you associate with each of the weather conditions?

1. Hace viento.
2. Nieva.
3. Hace mucho calor.
4. Está despejado.
5. Hace fresco.
6. Llueve.
7. Hace mucho sol.
8. Hace mucho frío.

3.3 **Identificaciones** Find a classmate who is wearing one of the articles of clothing in the list. For number 10, choose another item of clothing. Then, report to the class who is wearing what.

1. unos calcetines blancos
2. una chaqueta
3. un suéter
4. unas botas
5. una camiseta
6. una falda
7. unos pantalones negros
8. un vestido
9. unos tenis
10. ¿?

> **INVESTIGUEMOS LA GRAMÁTICA**
>
> Notice that the indefinite article is used when talking about what you are wearing, not the definite article. Articles can be omitted altogether if the clothing item is plural.
> **Llevo pantalones y una camisa.**

> **INVESTIGUEMOS LA MÚSICA**
>
> El Grupo Niche is a Colombian salsa band. Listen to their song "Gotas de lluvia" and write down any vocabulary words you hear.

3.4 **De vacaciones** With a partner, take turns asking about the weather in the following destinations, and the clothing that you need.

Modelo Cancún / julio
> Estudiante 1: *¿Qué tiempo hace en Cancún en julio?*
> Estudiante 2: *Hace mucho calor y está despejado.*
> Estudiante 1: *¿Qué ropa necesitas?*
> Estudiante 2: *Necesito pantalones cortos, sandalias y un traje de baño.*

1. Buenos Aires / diciembre
2. Anchorage / abril
3. Miami / agosto
4. Londres / junio
5. La Habana / septiembre
6. Chicago / marzo

3.5 **Los regalos** A friend sent a care package for the rest of your friends but forgot to label who everything was for, so you and a classmate need to clarify. One of you will look at the drawing on this page, and the other at the drawing in Appendix B.

Modelo Estudiante 1: *¿Para quién (For whom) son los calcetines rojos?*
> Estudiante 2: *Los calcetines rojos son para Emilia.*

Irma José Lola
Ricardo
Sara

Conexiones culturales

El clima y la ropa

Cultura

Write a list in Spanish of colors and other things you associate with spring. Then read aloud the first verse of "De colores," a popular song in many Spanish-speaking countries. Afterward, answer the questions that follow.

De colores, de colores se visten los **campos**[1] en la primavera

De colores, de colores son los pajaritos que vienen de afuera

De colores, de colores es el **arco iris**[2] que vemos **lucir.**[3]

Y por eso los grandes amores de muchos colores me gustan a mí.[4]

Y por eso los grandes amores de muchos colores me gustan a mí.

Write your own one-stanza poem about colors and post to Share It!

[1]*fields*   [2]*rainbow*   [3]*to shine*   [4]*I like*

1. In your opinion, which of the following words best describe the song? Why?

   triste *(sad)*   alegre *(happy)*   nostálgica   rítmica   rápida   lenta *(slow)*

2. Go back to your list of associations for spring. Did any of the words appear in the song? If so, what words?

Comunidad

Find a native Spanish speaker in your community who is open to answering a few questions. Remember to use **usted** forms if you don't know the person. Ask the person where he/she is from, and what words from the lexical variations shown in **Investiguemos el vocabulario** on page 78 are most used in that country. Ask questions such as these:

¿De dónde eres? / ¿De dónde es usted?

En Puerto Rico, ¿cómo se dice...?

En Granada, España

Comparaciones

Clothing in different regions of the Spanish-speaking world varies widely depending on a number of factors such as age, socioeconomic status, community size, and rural versus urban locations. The photographs below show two groups of college students. Read the information, study the photos, and answer the questions that follow.

1. ¿Qué ropa llevan los estudiantes en las fotos? ¿Es similar a la ropa que llevan los estudiantes en tu universidad? ¿Piensas que *(Do you think that)* los españoles y los latinoamericanos usan ropa similar a la tuya *(yours)*? Describe las similitudes *(similarities)* y diferencias.

2. La segunda foto es de una celebración. ¿Hay diferencias entre *(between)* la ropa que llevan a la universidad y la ropa que llevan a la fiesta? ¿Tu ropa es diferente cuando *(when)* estás en una fiesta? ¿Cuáles son las diferencias?

Courtesy of Fernando Casas, ITESO

Dmitriy Shironosov/Shutterstock

Conexiones...
a la redacción

With a partner, choose a season and write a list of adjectives, activities, and expressions that you associate with it. Then, write a stanza of four lines dedicated to that season. Remember that poems normally don't have complete sentences and that it isn't necessary to have a rhyme.

LianeM/iStockphoto

A analizar ▶

Nicolás is going to introduce himself and talk about his likes and dislikes. Watch the video, then read his introduction, paying particular attention to the verb **gustar,** and answer the questions that follow.

> **Me gusta** la universidad y también **me gustan** las clases... son muy interesantes y mis profesores son buenos. ¡Pero no **me gusta** el frío en el invierno! ¡Tampoco **me gusta** caminar en la nieve ni llevar abrigo, gorro, guantes, bufanda, botas... ¡uy! **Me gustan** más el sol y el calor de Puerto Rico.

1. The verb **gustar** is used to express likes and dislikes. What do you think **me gusta** means?
2. Notice that **gusta** and **gustan** are both used. Now find the words that follow **gustan** each time it is used. How are these words different from the ones that follow **gusta**?

A comprobar

The verb **gustar**

1. The Spanish equivalent of *I like* is **me gusta,** which literally means *it pleases me.* The expression **me gusta** is followed by singular nouns.

> **Me gusta** *tu vestido.*
> *I like your dress. (Your dress **pleases me.**)*
> **Me gusta** *el verano.*
> *I like summer. (Summer **pleases me.**)*

2. When followed by a plural noun or multiple nouns, it is necessary to use **gustan.**

> **Me gustan** *los zapatos negros.*
> *I like black shoes. (Black shoes **please me**.)*
> **Me gustan** *el otoño y la primavera.*
> *I like spring and fall. (Spring and fall **please me**).*

3. When followed by a verb or a series of verbs, the singular form **gusta** is always used.

> Me **gusta** nadar y esquiar. *I like to swim and ski.*
> No me **gusta** llevar lentes. *I don't **like** wearing glasses.*

4. **Gustar** can also be used to ask about or indicate what other people like.

me gusta(n)	*I like*	nos gusta(n)	*we like*
te gusta(n)	*you like*	os gusta(n)	*you like (plural, Spain)*
le gusta(n)	*he/she likes*	les gusta(n)	*they, you (plural) like*

> **¿Te gustan** mis botas?
> *Do you like my boots?*
> **Nos gusta** el otoño.
> *We like fall.*

5. Contrary to English, when using **gustar** with a noun, you must use the definite article as well.

> Le gustan **los bluyines.**
> *He likes **blue jeans.***
> ¿Les gusta **el invierno?**
> *Do you (all) like **winter?***

6. When clarifying who *he, she* or *they* are, it is necessary to use **a** in front of the name.

> **A Mario** le gustan los pantalones cómodos.
> *Mario likes comfortable pants.*

7. To express different degrees, use the terms **mucho** *(a lot),* **un poco** *(a little),* and **para nada** *(not at all).*

> Me gusta **mucho** el color rojo.
> *I like the color red **a lot.***
> A Alba le gustan **un poco** las sandalias.
> *Alba likes the sandals **a little bit**.*
> ¡No nos gusta el frío **para nada!**
> *We don't like the cold **at all!***

INVESTIGUEMOS EL VOCABULARIO

When using **gusta** with people, it has a romantic implication. In **Capítulo 8** you will learn the expression **caer bien,** which is used to say that you like a person.

> **Me gusta Juan.**
> *I like Juan (as a romantic interest).*

A practicar

3.6 **Me gusta el verano** Renata loves everything about summer in her home country, Argentina, but doesn't like anything about winter. Listen to her statements and decide if they are logical or not by replying **lógico** or **ilógico**.

🔊
1-17

3.7 **Combinaciones lógicas** Decide which phrases in the second column best complete those in the first column.

1. En el restaurante me gustan...   **a.** la clase de inglés.
2. En el restaurante no me gusta...   **b.** los menús variados.
3. En la universidad me gusta...   **c.** ayudar a mis hijos con su tarea.
4. En la universidad no me gustan...   **d.** el servicio malo.
5. En casa me gusta...   **e.** los exámenes difíciles.
6. En casa no me gustan...   **f.** las tareas domésticas (chores).

3.8 **¿Qué te gusta?** Complete the following mini-dialogues with **me** or **te** and **gusta** or **gustan**.

1. Elena: Sonia, ¿ _____ _____ comprar zapatos?

   Sonia: Sí, _____ _____ mucho comprar zapatos.

   Elena: ¿ _____ _____ los tenis?

   Sonia: No, _____ _____ más las sandalias.

2. Hugo: ¿ _____ _____ esquiar, Raúl?

   Raúl: No, para nada. No _____ _____ el frío.

   Hugo: ¿ _____ _____ practicar deportes en verano?

   Raúl: Sí, _____ _____ el golf y el tenis.

3.9 **¿Te gusta... ?** Circulate throughout the classroom and talk with 10 different students about their likes and dislikes. Be sure to use some of the following expressions: **mucho, un poco,** and **para nada.**

Modelo bailar

> Estudiante 1: ¿Te gusta bailar?
> Estudiante 2: Sí, me gusta (mucho) bailar. No, no me gusta bailar (para nada).

1. el color azul
2. las clases de ciencias
3. llevar tenis
4. la música rock
5. los caballos
6. hablar por teléfono y mandar mensajes
7. los chocolates
8. las novelas románticas
9. el invierno
10. ¿?

¿Te gusta el invierno?

© Alvaro Pantoja/Shutterstock

3.10 Nuestros gustos Look at the pictures below and, using the expression **le(s) gusta(n),** tell what Octavio and Olivia like and don't like.

Modelo *A Octavio no le gusta estudiar.*

1.

2.

3.

4.

5.

6.

© Cengage Learning

3.11 En común Choose four of the following items that you like. Then circulate throughout the classroom and interview your classmates to find out if they like the same things. For each of the items you chose, find at least one other classmate who shares your opinion.

Modelo Estudiante 1: *¿Te gusta cantar?*
        Estudiante 2: *Sí, me gusta (mucho) cantar. / No, no me gusta cantar.*

____ los colores pastel   ____ la primavera

____ esquiar   ____ los deportes de invierno

____ la ropa de verano   ____ el fútbol y el béisbol

____ los bluyines de marca *(name brand)*   ____ nadar y tomar el sol

____ llevar pantalones cortos   ____ ¿?

3.12 La universidad You are going to find out what both you and your partner like about your school.

Paso 1 Write a list of 6 items or activities that you like at your school.

Paso 2 With a partner, take turns asking if the other likes the items or activities on the list and check the items that you both like.

Paso 3 Using **Nos gusta(n)...** report to the class the items you have in common.

Modelo *Nos gustan la historia, la geografía y el español.*

A analizar

Now watch again as Nicolás introduces himself and talks about his likes and dislikes. Then read his introduction and this time pay attention to the forms of the verb **vivir** that he uses.

> Me llamo Nicolás y soy de Puerto Rico. Mi familia **vive** en San Juan, bueno, mis padres **viven** en San Juan con mi hermana, pero yo **vivo** en Nueva York con mis tíos porque estudio en la Universidad de Nueva York. Nosotros **vivimos** en un apartamento en el Bronx.

© Cengage Learning

Vivir is an **-ir** verb. Use what you have learned about **-ar** verbs on page 48 and the examples in the paragraph above to complete the chart.

yo _____   nosotros(as) _____

tú _____   vosotros(as) vivís

él, ella, usted _____   ellos, ellas, ustedes _____

A comprobar

Regular -er and -ir verbs

1. In **Capítulo 2** we learned the forms of verbs whose infinitives end in **-ar.** The following are regular **-er** and **-ir** verbs:

Los verbos -er

aprender (a + *infinitive*)	*to learn (to do something)*	creer	*to believe*
		deber (+ *infinitive*)	*should (do something)*
beber	*to drink*		
comer	*to eat*	leer	*to read*
comprender	*to understand*	vender	*to sell*
correr	*to run*		

Los verbos -ir

abrir	*to open*	escribir	*to write*
asistir (a)	*to attend*	recibir	*to receive*
decidir	*to decide*	vivir	*to live*

2. Regular **-er** and **-ir** verbs follow a pattern very similar to regular **-ar** verbs.

beber					
yo	**-o**	beb**o**	nosotros(as)	**-emos**	beb**emos**
tú	**-es**	beb**es**	vosotros(as)	**-éis**	beb**éis**
él, ella, usted	**-e**	beb**e**	ellos, ellas, ustedes	**-en**	beb**en**

escribir					
yo	**-o**	escrib**o**	nosotros(as)	**-imos**	escrib**imos**
tú	**-es**	escrib**es**	vosotros(as)	**-ís**	escrib**ís**
él, ella, usted	**-e**	escrib**e**	ellos, ellas, ustedes	**-en**	escrib**en**

Remember the following rules:

a. To form negative sentences, the word **no** is placed in front of the conjugated verb.

Los niños **no comprenden** inglés. *The children **don't understand** English.*

b. When using two verbs together, the second verb stays in the infinitive.

Debemos **estudiar** en la biblioteca. *We should **study** in the library.*

Los estudiantes aprenden a **hablar** español. *The students are learning **to speak** Spanish.*

c. To form simple questions, place the subject after the conjugated verb and add the question marks at the beginning and end of the question.

¿Vive Alfredo en Bogotá? *Does Alfredo live in Bogota?*

A practicar

3.13 **¿Qué tienen?** Choose the most logical verb to complete the sentence.

1. Cuando tengo hambre, yo _____ un sándwich.
   a. como   **b.** creo   **c.** corro

2. Vanesa y Nelson tienen prisa y _____ a clase.
   a. comprenden   **b.** escriben   **c.** corren

3. Cuando tienen calor, mis padres _____ las ventanas.
   a. deciden   **b.** asisten a   **c.** abren

4. Belinda y yo tenemos éxito en la clase de cálculo y _____ buenas notas.
   a. vendemos   **b.** recibimos   **c.** aprendemos

5. Cuando Leopoldo tiene sed, _____ agua.
   a. debe   **b.** come   **c.** bebe

3.14 **Mis amigos y yo** Complete the sentences with the forms of the verbs indicated.

1. **(leer)** Mi amigo Gustavo y yo **(a.)** _____ muchos libros. Yo **(b.)** _____ novelas de ciencia ficción y él **(c.)** _____ novelas de suspenso.

2. **(vender)** Mi amiga Patricia y yo trabajamos en una tienda *(store)* y nosotros **(a.)** _____ ropa para mujeres. Yo **(b.)** _____ vestidos y Patricia **(c.)** _____ zapatos.

3. **(abrir)** En clase, la profesora **(a.)** _____ su libro. Los estudiantes **(b.)** _____ sus libros también. A Elena no le gusta estudiar y no desea **(c.)** _____ su libro.

3.15 **Un día en la vida de Antonio** With a partner, take turns describing Antonio's activities. Use the **-er** and **-ir** verbs from this lesson as well as other verbs you have learned.

3.16 **En busca de...** Find classmates who do the following activities. Be sure to find a different person for each activity.

1. leer novelas románticas
2. recibir buenas notas
3. correr en la mañana
4. beber mucho café

5. vivir en un apartamento
6. escribir muchos mensajes de texto
7. asistir a conciertos
8. comer en la cafetería

3.17 **¿Qué hacen?** Tell your partner about the things you and others do. Choose a subject from the first column and combine it with a verb from the second column. Be sure to add a phrase from the parentheses to complete your sentence. **¡OJO!** Pay attention to the form of the verb.

yo
mis compañeros de clase
mis amigos y yo
mi mejor amigo
mi profesor de español
mi familia

deber (estudiar, escribir la tarea, leer el libro)
recibir (buenas notas, muchos mensajes, cartas)
asistir a (clase de español, muchos conciertos, muchas fiestas)
vivir en (una casa, un apartamento, el campus)
comprender (el español, las matemáticas, el inglés)
comer (en restaurantes, en la cafetería, mucha pizza)

3.18 **Entrevista** Take turns asking and answering the following questions.

1. Normalmente ¿asistes a clases en el verano?
2. ¿Comprendes al profesor de español?
3. ¿Lees mucho? ¿Lees novelas o revistas *(magazines)*?
4. ¿Dónde vives? ¿Vives con otra persona?
5. ¿Bebes mucho café?
6. ¿Recibes muchos mensajes? ¿De quién? *(From whom?)*
7. ¿Debes escribir muchas composiciones para *(for)* tus clases? ¿Para qué clases?
8. ¿Crees que *(that)* aprender español es fácil o difícil? ¿Por qué?

3.19 **¿Qué debe hacer?** With a partner, come up with recommendations for what the following people should do. Use the verb **deber** and one of the following verbs.

aprender	asistir	buscar	comer	correr	decidir
estudiar	hablar	practicar	ser	trabajar	viajar

Modelo Carla tiene problemas con su novio.
Ella debe hablar con su novio.

1. Julio y Claudia tienen malas notas en sus clases.
2. A Mónica no le gusta su ropa pero no tiene dinero para comprar ropa nueva.
3. Me gusta el frío pero vivo en Puerto Rico.
4. El señor Ortíz desea estar más sano *(healthy)*.
5. Pablo y yo no tenemos muchos amigos.
6. La señorita García desea ser doctora.

3.20 **Yo también** Using some of the verbs below, tell your partner what you do. Your partner will tell you if he or she does the same activities or not. Then report to the class the activities that you and your partner both do.

abrir	aprender	asistir	beber	comer	comprender
correr	deber	decidir	leer	recibir	vender

Modelo correr
Estudiante 1: *Yo corro en el gimnasio.*
Estudiante 2: *¡Yo también! / Yo no corro. No me gusta correr.*

Estrategia

Understand before moving on

Do you feel comfortable using **gustar** as well as **-er** and **-ir** verbs? If there is anything you're still not sure about, now is a good time to check in with your instructor for help. For more support, you can also view the tutorials for **gustar**, **-er** verbs and **-ir** verbs in iLrn.

© ArtmannWitte/Shutterstock

Entrando en tema

¿Te gusta ir de compras *(to go shopping)*? ¿Dónde prefieres comprar ropa? ¿Por qué?

De compras

◀)) You are going to hear a commercial. Listen carefully and then answer the comprehension
1-18 questions.

Vocabulario útil

ahora mismo	*right now*	**el precio**	*price*
barato(a)	*cheap*	**¿Vienes conmigo?**	*Would you come with me?*
de moda	*fashionable*		

Comprensión

1. ¿De qué es el comercial?
2. ¿Qué ropa lleva puesta la chica? ¿Le gusta esa *(that)* ropa a su amigo?
3. ¿Qué otros artículos de ropa compró *(bought)* la chica?
4. ¿Cuánto cuesta *(costs)* la blusa?

⊞ Más allá

Write your own commercial for a store. Keep it simple! Just give the name of the store, a couple of reasons to buy there, and three or four examples of items they sell. Once you are satisfied with your commercial, record it and post to Share It! and find out what your classmates are advertising.

© Dmitry Kalinovsky/Shutterstock

Lectura

Antes de leer

The people in the photos below are wearing traditional clothing. With a classmate match the photos with the country where you think they are from (**Argentina, Perú,** or **Cuba**). Then answer the questions below based on your own experience.

© Don Tremain/JupiterImages

© Kobby Dagan/Shutterstock

© Joel Shawn/Shutterstock

1. ¿Qué factores consideran para relacionar las fotografías con los países?

2. ¿Hay ropa tradicional en el estado / la región donde vives? ¿Cómo es?

A leer

La ropa tradicional

show

Muchas regiones del mundo hispano tienen una gran variedad de trajes tradicionales que **muestran** su cultura y sus tradiciones, y también reflejan su historia y su clima. En muchas culturas es posible determinar de qué región o comunidad es una persona solamente por el traje y los colores que lleva, como es el caso de Guatemala.

> En muchas culturas es posible determinar de dónde es una persona solamente por el traje

Nevertheless
cities

Sin embargo, no todas las personas llevan sus trajes tradicionales todo el tiempo. En las **ciudades** las personas prefieren usar ropa moderna como camisas, faldas, vestidos y bluyines. Muchos indígenas que van a vivir a las ciudades prefieren no usar su ropa tradicional para **evitar** la discriminación.

avoid

Sin embargo, es posible ver la **belleza** de la ropa tradicional en muchas partes. Por ejemplo, a muchas mujeres en la región andina de Bolivia y Ecuador les gusta llevar puesta su ropa tradicional: una pollera (falda) larga, una blusa en color **llamativo** y un **sombrero de bombín**. Este **conjunto** es un signo

beauty

flashy
bowler hat
outfit

© vlad0209/Shutterstock

de distinción y elegancia. Gracias a esta ropa, estas mujeres, **conocidas como** Cholitas, se identifican como un grupo, **fomentando** la solidaridad y su identidad cultural.

known as
promoting

Otro ejemplo de ropa tradicional es el de las blusas de las mujeres Kuna Yala, en la costa de Panamá. Sus blusas se llaman molas y están decoradas con **motivos** geométricos del océano y de animales, pero las molas **están cambiando** y ahora muchos **diseños** reflejan la interacción con el mundo moderno.

motifs
are changing
designs

La ropa indígena refleja las **creencias** y los valores de una comunidad, y muchas veces el estado civil o social de una persona. Para muchos indígenas, la ropa tradicional es una parte vital de su identidad, y una conexión a sus **antepasados**. ¿Qué valores refleja tu ropa?

beliefs

ancestors

© rj lerich/Shutterstock

Comprensión

1. ¿Qué reflejan los trajes tradicionales?
2. ¿Qué ropa prefieren llevar las personas en las ciudades?
3. ¿Qué ropa llevan las Cholitas de Bolivia?
4. ¿Qué son las molas? ¿Quiénes usan las molas?

Después de leer

With a partner, describe a traditional outfit that reflects the climate, culture, and history of a region of your country. What would the men wear? And the women? What colors are the outfits? What do the colors represent?

¿Cuál es la fecha? ¿Qué día es hoy?

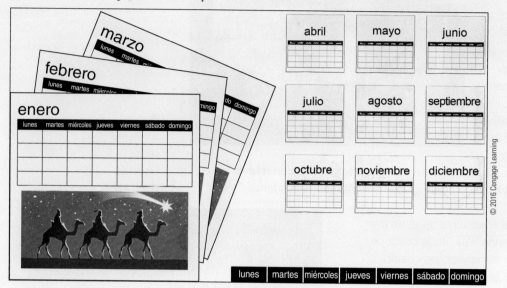

calendars: marzo, febrero, enero; abril, mayo, junio; julio, agosto, septiembre; octubre, noviembre, diciembre; lunes martes miércoles jueves viernes sábado domingo

© 2016 Cengage Learning

Estrategia

Understand before moving on Be sure to make an appointment to see your instructor or a tutor right away in order to get some extra help if you don't understand something.

Palabras adicionales

ahora	now	**la fecha**	date	**por la tarde**	in the afternoon	**terminar**	to end
el Año Nuevo	New Year	**hoy**	today	**por la noche**	in the evening	**todos los días**	every day
el día feriado	holiday	**mañana**	tomorrow	**Navidad**	Christmas		
el cumpleaños	birthday	**por la mañana**	in the morning				

1. To tell time, the verb **ser** is used. Use **es la** with **una** and **son las** with all other hours.

   ¿Qué hora es?   *What time is it?*

   Son las tres.   *It's three o'clock.*   **Es** la una.   *It's one.*

2. To tell time from the hour to the half hour (1–30 minutes), use **y** between the hour and the minutes. To tell time after the half hour (31–59 minutes), use **menos** and the minutes until the next hour.

   Son las siete **y** cinco.   Son las tres **menos** veinte.

   It's 7:05.   *It's 2:40.*

3. Use **cuarto** to express a quarter before or after the hour, and use **media** to express half past the hour.

   Son las diez y **cuarto.**   Son las once menos **cuarto.**   Son las ocho y **media.**

   It's 10:15   *It's 10:45.*   *It's 8:30.*

4. It is also common to express time as read on a digital clock.

   Es la una y cincuenta.   *It's 1:50.*   **Son las seis y quince.**   *It's 6:15.*

5. To ask or tell at what time something is done, use the preposition **a.**

   ¿A qué hora trabajas?   *At what time do you work?*

   Trabajo **a** las cuatro de la tarde.   *I work at 4:00 in the afternoon.*

6. To express that an event goes from a certain time to another specific time, use **de las… a las…**

   Trabajo **de las** 2:00 **a las** 5:00 de la tarde.   *I work from 2:00 to 5:00 in the afternoon.*

7. To express A.M. or P.M., use the following expressions: **de la mañana** *(in the morning)*, **de la tarde** *(in the afternoon)*, and **de la noche** *(in the evening)*. To express *noon* use **mediodía** and to express *midnight* use **medianoche.**

8. When talking about dates, use the phrase:

   Es *(number)* **de** *(month)*.

   Hoy **es** once **de** julio.   *Today is the eleventh of July.*

9. To talk about the first of the month use **primero.**

   Es **primero** de julio.   *It is the first of July.*

Notice that the names of the months and days of the week are not capitalized in Spanish.

INVESTIGUEMOS EL VOCABULARIO

When talking about days and dates:

- use the definite article (**el** or **los**) to talk about something that happens on a particular day or days.

  El examen es **el** miércoles.
  The test is on Wednesday.

  Trabajo **los** viernes y sábados.
  I work on Fridays and Saturdays.

- other than **sábado** and **domingo,** the plural form for other days of the week is the same as the singular form.

  el sábado   los sábados
  el lunes   los lunes

In some Spanish-speaking countries, calendars show the first day of the week as Monday (**lunes**).

A practicar

3.21 **Escucha y responde** Escribe la palabra **mes** en un papel y **día** en otro. Escucha la lista de meses y días. Si escuchas un mes, levanta el papel que dice **mes**. Si escuchas un día, levanta el papel que dice **día**. *(Write the word **mes** on one piece of paper and **día** on another. Listen to a list of months and days. If you hear a month hold up **mes**; if you hear a day of the week, hold up **día**.)*

🔊 1-19

3.22 **En orden** Completa las secuencias con la palabra que falta. *(Complete the following sequences with the missing word.)*

1. enero, febrero, marzo, _____

2. viernes, sábado, _____

3. lunes, miércoles, _____

4. septiembre, octubre, _____

5. lunes, martes, _____

6. junio, julio, _____

7. jueves, sábado, _____

8. mayo, agosto, noviembre, _____

3.23 **¿Qué hora es?** Mira los celulares y di qué hora es. *(Look at the cell phones and tell what time it is.)*

1. **2.** **3.** **4.** **5.** **6.**

3.24 **Entrevista** En parejas túrnense para preguntar y responder las siguientes preguntas. *(Working with a partner, take turns asking and answering the following questions.)*

1. ¿Cuándo es tu cumpleaños? Y el cumpleaños de tu mejor *(best)* amigo?

2. ¿Cuál es tu día feriado *(holiday)* favorito? ¿En qué mes es?

3. ¿Cuál es tu mes favorito? ¿Por qué?

4. ¿Qué días tienes clases? ¿A qué hora es tu primera clase de la semana?

5. ¿Trabajas? ¿Qué días trabajas? ¿A qué hora trabajas normalmente?

3.25 **La tele** En parejas túrnense para preguntar a qué hora son los programas y en qué canal son. Uno mira la programación y las preguntas aquí y el otro mira el **Apéndice B**. *(With a partner, take turns asking what times the shows are on and on what channel. One will look at the guide and questions here, and the other will look at Appendix B.)*

Modelo Estudiante 1: ¿A qué hora es Veredicto final?
Estudiante 2: Veredicto final *es a las dos de la tarde.*
Estudiante 1: ¿En qué canal es?
Estudiante 2: *Es en Canal 5.*

INVESTIGUEMOS LA CULTURA

Here are some holidays that are commonly celebrated in most Spanish-speaking countries: **el Día de los Muertos** *(Day of the Dead)*, **el Día de los Reyes Magos** *(Three Kings Day)*, **la Pascua** *(Easter, Passover)*, **la Navidad** *(Christmas)*, **la Nochebuena** *(Christmas Eve)*, **la Semana Santa** *(Holy Week)*.

INVESTIGUEMOS EL VOCABULARIO

In Spain and in many parts of Latin America, the 24-hour clock is used when posting hours for businesses and for schedules, such as school schedules, flight schedules, and movie and television schedules. To convert the 24-hour clock, subtract 12:00 from 13:00 and later, so that 14:30 would be 2:30 in the afternoon.

PROGRAMACIÓN ● Películas ● Especiales ● Deportes ● Nuevos

Jueves 10 de agosto			14:00	14:30	15:00	15:30	16:00	16:30	17:00	17:30	18:00	18:30	19:00
	Galavisión	Cable 10	Héroe		El Amor no	El Chapulín Colorado	Laura en América				La Oreja		
	Canal 22	Cable 22	TV UNAM	De Cine	Película se Anunciará			México	La Magia de la Naturaleza		Ciencia Cierta		
	Movie City	Digital 480	(1:40) ★★"Dos Ilusiones" (2004)			(:35) "A los 30 Años" (Francia, 2004)			(:20) ★ "Gritos del Más Allá (2005)				
	Canal 5		Veredicto final		Será anunciada				Difícil de creer		Quiero amarte		

© Cengage Learning

¿A qué hora es... ?

1. *Los Archivos del FBI*

2. *Adictos*

3. *Aprendiendo a vivir*

4. *Durmiendo con el enemigo*

Conexiones culturales
Las celebraciones

Cultura

José Guadalupe Posada was a Mexican artist who produced numerous engravings depicting skeletons in everyday scenes, usually having fun. Although Posada's intention originally was satirical, as his work dealt with political and social issues, his art has been consistently used by Mexicans to decorate and celebrate **el Día de los Muertos.**

 Find out when *El Día de los Muertos* is celebrated and learn more about Mexico in **Exploraciones del Mundo Hispano** in Appendix A.

INVESTIGUEMOS LA MÚSICA

"La Llorona" is a well-known Mexican legend associated with the Day of the Dead. Listen to the song "La Llorona" sung by Lila Downs, a Mexican-American artist whose music is influenced by the music of Mixtec, Zapotec, Maya, and Nahuatl cultures. What is the tone of the song? What words can you understand?

© Giraudon/Art Resource, NY

Explore other works by José Guadalupe Posada. Choose a favorite, then post to Share It! with a caption. Tell the class what you like about it in Spanish. Here are some keywords to help with your search: **grabado** *(engraving)*, **ilustración, caricatura.**

Comparaciones

The following are celebrations in Spain or Latin American countries. Are there similar celebrations in the United States? If so, when are they celebrated? Can you think of holidays that are unique to the United States?

San Fermín	el 7 de julio	Los españoles corren con los toros.
El Día de los Muertos	el 1 y 2 de noviembre	Los mexicanos honran *(honor)* a sus antepasados.
El Día de los Inocentes	el 28 de diciembre	Los hispanos hacen bromas *(jokes)*.
El Carnaval	la semana antes *(before)* del Miércoles de Cenizas *(Ash Wednesday)*	Los hispanos cantan y bailan en las calles.
San Juan	el 24 de junio	Los paraguayos juegan *(play)* con fuego *(fire)*.
El Año Nuevo	el 1° de enero	Los latinos celebran la llegada del nuevo año.
La Tomatina	el último *(last)* miércoles de agosto	Los españoles pelean *(fight)* con tomates.
El Día del Estudiante	el 21 de septiembre	Los estudiantes argentinos tienen fiestas en el parque y juegan al fútbol.

Conexiones... a la religión

Another Catholic tradition widely observed throughout the Spanish-speaking world is the celebration of **el santo.** Each day of the year is attributed to a particular saint, and it is common practice to give a baby the name of the saint of the day when he or she was born. For babies who do not share the name of the patron saint of their birthday, their **santo** is celebrated like a second birthday. For example, suppose a child born on October 31 is named Fernando. Fernando will always celebrate his birthday on October 31 as well as his **santo** on May 30, **día de San Fernando.**

Look at the calendar and determine when these people would celebrate their **santo.**

Óscar de la Renta (diseñador *[designer]*, República Dominicana, 1932)
Rómulo Gallegos (autor, Venezuela, 1884–1969)
Gilberto Santa Rosa (cantante, Puerto Rico, 1962)
Marta Sánchez (cantante, España, 1966)
Rufino Tamayo (pintor, México, 1899–1991)

If someone in your family has a Christian name, find out when you would celebrate his/her **santo.**

Óscar de la Renta

Febrero

1. San Cecilio	11. Nuestra Sra. de Lourdes	20. San Eugenio
2. San Cornelio	12. San Damián	21. San Pedro Damián
3. San Óscar	13. Santa Maura	22. Santa Leonor
4. San Gilberto	14. San Valentín	23. Santa Marta de Astorga
5. Santa Felicia	15. San Faustino	24. San Sergio
6. Santa Dorotea	16. San Elías	25. San Valerio
7. Santa Juliana	17. San Rómulo	26. San Alejandro
8. San Lucio	18. San Eladio	27. San Basilio
9. San Abelardo	19. San Gabino	28. San Rufino
10. San Jacinto		29. Santa Emma

Comunidad

 Find a native Spanish speaker in your community who is willing to answer your questions. Ask him/her what holidays are celebrated in his/her country of origin and which are his/her favorites. Post your findings on Share It!

Ask questions such as these:

¿Qué días festivos celebran en su país?
¿Cuál es su favorito? / ¿Cuáles son sus favoritos?

A analizar ▶

Rosa y Paula hablan de su día. Después de ver el video, lee su conversación y observa las formas del verbo **ir**. Luego contesta las preguntas que siguen. *(Rosa and Paula talk about their day. After watching the video, read their conversation and observe the forms of the verb **ir**. Then answer the questions that follow.)*

Rosa: ¡Hola Paula! ¿Cómo estás?

Paula: Bien, ¿y tú Rosa?

Rosa: Bien. ¿Adónde **vas**?

Paula: **Voy** a clase ahora. Después **voy** a la biblioteca porque tengo que estudiar para un examen de historia...

Rosa: ¿Y si tú y yo **vamos a comer** al Café Rústico? Tienen muy buenas pizzas.

Paula: ¡Qué buena idea... **vamos**!

Rosa: ¡Excelente! ¡Hasta luego!

1. The forms **voy, vas,** and **vamos** in the conversation are forms of the verb **ir.** Is the verb regular like **vivir** or irregular like **ser**? Explain why.

2. Using the forms presented in the conversation and what you already know about verbs, complete the chart.

   ir

yo _____	nosotros _____
tú _____	vosotros vais
él, ella, usted _____	ellos, ellas, ustedes _____

3. Why do you think the verb **ir** is not conjugated in the phrase **necesito ir?**

A comprobar
The verb ir

ir *(to go)*			
yo	**voy**	nosotros(as)	**vamos**
tú	**vas**	vosotros(as)	**vais**
él, ella, usted	**va**	ellos, ellas, ustedes	**van**

1. The verb **ir** is used to tell where someone goes and often requires the preposition **a** *(to)*. When asking where someone goes, the preposition **a** is added to the word **dónde** *(adónde)*.

   ¿Adónde van ustedes después de la clase?
   ***Where do you go** after class?*
   Vamos a la biblioteca. ***We go** to the library.*

2. Just as there are contractions in English *(can't, don't)*, there are also contractions in Spanish. In Spanish, however, these contractions are not optional. Similar to the contraction **del,** when using the preposition **a** in front of a masculine definite article, it combines with **el** to form the contraction **al (a + el = al).** The **a** does not contract with the other articles.

   Los sábados yo voy **al** estadio con mis amigos.
   *Saturdays I go **to the** stadium with my friends.*

   Al mediodía mis amigos van **a la** cafetería.
   *At noon my friends go **to the** cafeteria.*

3. It is common to use the verb **ir** in the present tense to tell where someone is going at that moment.

> Mi amiga **va** a la universidad ahora.
> My friend **is going** to the university now.
>
> Nosotros **vamos** al gimnasio.
> We **are going** to the gym.

4. The verb **ir** is used in a variety of expressions.

ir de compras	*to go shopping*
ir de excursión	*to go hiking*
ir de paseo	*to go for a walk*
ir de viaje	*to take a trip*

A practicar

INVESTIGUEMOS LA MÚSICA

Julieta Venegas is a popular Mexican singer, songwriter, and musician. Listen to her song "Me voy." Why do you think she is leaving?

3.26 **Las vacaciones de verano** Todos viajan este verano. Lee las siguientes oraciones y di qué países van a visitar. Sigue el modelo. *(Everyone is traveling this summer. Read the following sentences and tell which countries they will visit. Follow the model.)*

> **Modelo** Adriana va a Santiago.
> *Adriana va a Chile.*

Argentina	**Costa Rica**	**España**
Perú	**Puerto Rico**	**la República Dominicana**

1. Yo voy a San Juan.
2. Manuela va a Buenos Aires.
3. Jorge y Horacio van a San José.
4. Marina y yo vamos a Santo Domingo.
5. La familia Montalvo va a Lima.
6. Los hermanos Castro van a Madrid.

3.27 **Después de las clases** Completa el párrafo con la forma apropiada del verbo **ir**. *(Complete the paragraph with the appropriate form of the verb **ir**.)*

Después de *(After)* las clases, mis compañeros (1) _____ a casa,

y yo (2) _____ a la biblioteca con mi amigo Fernando. Nosotros

(3) _____ al café después para tomar algo. Luego, él (4) _____

a su casa, y yo (5) _____ al centro estudiantil para trabajar. ¿Adónde

(6) _____ tú después de las clases?

3.28 **A clase** Usando el vocabulario de las clases del **Capítulo 2** y el verbo **ir**, explica adónde van las siguientes personas para hacer las actividades indicadas. *(Using class subject vocabulary from **Capítulo 2** and the verb **ir**, explain where the following people go to do the indicated activities.)*

> **Modelo** Tú aprendes a escribir bien.
> *Vas a la clase de redacción.*

1. Yo estudio los mapas y aprendo las capitales.
2. Elisa tiene que hablar enfrente de sus compañeros de clase hoy.
3. Gael y Damián leen una novela de Mario Vargas Llosa.
4. Tú estudias los elementos y haces experimentos.
5. Valentín y yo aprendemos de las plantas y los animales.
6. La profesora Arango enseña las teorías de Freud.
7. Paolo es actor en el nuevo drama de la universidad.
8. Tú estudias los eventos importantes del pasado *(past)*.
9. Yo tengo que analizar figuras como el triángulo.
10. Germán y tú aprenden de Sócrates y Platón.

3.29 **¿Adónde van?** Usando la forma apropiada del verbo **ir,** di adónde van las siguientes personas. **¡OJO!** Usa la contracción **al** cuando sea necesario. *(Using the appropriate form of the verb **ir**, tell where the following people are going. **¡OJO!** Remember to use the contraction **al** when necessary.)*

1. yo

2. el profesor Rosales

3. Ricardo y yo

4. tu amigo y tú

5. mis amigos

6. tú

© Cengage Learning

3.30 **¿Adónde vas?** Escribe adónde vas para hacer las siguientes actividades. Usa palabras del vocabulario o el nombre del lugar. Luego busca compañeros que vayan a los mismos lugares. *(Write down where you go to do the following activities. Use vocabulary words or the name of the place. Then find classmates who go to the same places.)*

Modelo para *(in order to)* nadar
　　　　Estudiante 1: *¿Adónde vas para nadar?*
　　　　Estudiante 2: *Yo voy a City Fitness. / Yo voy al gimnasio. / Yo no nado.*

1. para comer

2. para estudiar

3. para tomar un café

4. para leer

5. para mirar la tele

6. para escuchar música

7. para caminar o correr

8. para bailar

A analizar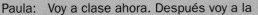

Rosa y Paula hablan de sus actividades. Después de ver el video, lee su conversación y observa las expresiones en negritas. Luego contesta las preguntas que siguen. *(Rosa and Paula are talking about their activities. Watch the video again. Then read their conversation and look at the boldface expressions. Then answer the questions that follow.)*

Paula:	Voy a clase ahora. Después voy a la biblioteca porque tengo que estudiar para un examen de historia.
Rosa:	Yo también tengo que ir a la bibioteca hoy. **Voy a buscar** unos libros para una investigación. ¿Qué **vas a hacer** después?
Paula:	Nada. **Voy a comer** en la cafetería.
Rosa:	¿Y si tú y yo **vamos a comer** al Café Rústico? Tienen muy buenas pizzas.
Paula:	¡Qué buena idea... vamos!

1. Do the phrases in bold express past, present, or future?
2. What patterns do you notice?

A comprobar

Ir + a + *infinitive*

1. Similar to the English verb *to go,* the verb **ir** can be used to talk about the future. To tell what someone is *going to do,* use the following structure:

ir	+	**a**	+	*infinitive*
Voy		a		viajar.
Van		a		trabajar.

   Vamos a estudiar esta noche.
   We are going to study tonight.

   Juan **va a ir** al café con Elena.
   Juan is going to go to the café with Elena.

2. To ask what someone is going to do, use the verb **hacer** in the question. When responding, the verb **hacer** is not necessary.

   ¿Qué vas a hacer (tú)?
   What are you going to do?

   (Yo) Voy a estudiar (trabajar, comer, etcétera).
   I am going to study (work, eat, etc.).

   > **Note:** You will learn the forms of the verb **hacer** in **Capítulo 5.**

© Cengage Learning

A practicar

3.31 **Un poco de lógica** Varias personas van a diferentes lugares en el campus. Selecciona la respuesta apropiada de la segunda columna para indicar lo que van a hacer cuando llegan. *(Various people are going to different places on campus. Select the appropriate answer from the second column to tell what they are going to do when they get there.)*

1. Yo voy a la librería.
2. Raquel va al gimnasio.
3. Mis amigos van a la cafetería.
4. Sergio va a clase.
5. Paloma y yo vamos al estadio.
6. Agustina y Octavio van a la biblioteca.

   a. Van a comer.
   b. Vamos a mirar fútbol
   c. Voy a comprar un libro.
   d. Va a tomar un examen.
   e. Van a estudiar.
   f. Va a correr.

3.32 **El cumpleaños de Merche** Hoy es el cumpleaños de Merche y tiene un día muy ocupado. Usando **ir** + **a** + infinitivo, explica lo que va a hacer hoy y a qué hora. *(Today is Merche's birthday, and she has a busy day. Using **ir** + **a** + infinitive, tell what she is going to do today and what time she is going to do it.)*

© Cengage Learning

3.33 **¿Qué vas a hacer mañana?** Pregúntale a tu compañero qué va a hacer mañana a las siguientes horas. *(Ask your partner what he/she is going to do tomorrow at the following times.)*

Modelo 2:00 P.M.
    Estudiante A: *¿Qué vas a hacer mañana a las dos de la tarde?*
    Estudiante B: *(Yo) Voy a correr en el parque.*

1. 8:00 A.M.
2. 10:30 A.M.
3. 12:00 P.M.
4. 1:15 P.M.
5. 3:30 P.M.
6. 6:45 P.M.
7. 8:15 P.M.
8. 10:00 P.M.

3.34 **¿Qué vas a hacer?** Trabaja con un compañero para preguntarse sobre sus planes. *(Work with a partner asking about each others' plans.)*

Modelo ahora
> Estudiante 1: *¿Qué vas a hacer ahora?*
> Estudiante 2: *Voy a comer en la cafetería, ¿y tú?*
> Estudiante 1: *Voy a estudiar.*

1. esta *(this)* noche
2. mañana por la mañana
3. mañana por la noche
4. el sábado
5. el domingo
6. la próxima *(next)* semana
7. este verano
8. el próximo semestre

3.35 **De vacaciones** El curso de primavera terminó y vas a ir de vacaciones con un amigo. Mira el anuncio y con un compañero decidan cómo van a contestar las siguientes preguntas. *(The spring semester is ending and you are going to go on vacation with a friend. With a classmate, look at the advertisement and decide how you will answer the following questions.)*

Modelo Estudiante 1: *¿Adónde vamos a ir?*
> Estudiante 2: *Vamos a Puerto Rico.*
> Estudiante 1: *No me gusta el calor. Vamos a...*

1. ¿Adónde van a ir?
2. ¿Cuándo van a viajar?
3. ¿Qué ropa van a necesitar?
4. ¿Qué van a hacer?
5. ¿Cuándo van a regresar?

Agencia de Viajes Vagabundo

San Juan, Puerto Rico (5 días) $650
Hotel Miramar ★ ★ ★ ★
Playa *(beach)* privada

Bariloche, Argentina (7 días) $1850
Hotel Nevada ★ ★ ★
Estación de esquí a 5 kilómetros

Cuzco, Perú (8 días) $1475
Hotel Tierra Andina ★ ★ ★ ★
En el centro, cerca del *(near)* mercado y tiendas *(stores)*

Madrid, España (9 días) $1995
Hotel Príncipe ★ ★ ★
Cerca de museos y teatros

3.36 **Tiempo libre** En parejas túrnense para preguntar lo que van a hacer en las siguientes situaciones. *(In pairs take turns asking what you are going to do in the following situations.)*

Modelo Es domingo y no tienes mucha tarea.
> Estudiante 1: *¿Qué vas a hacer?*
> Estudiante 2: *Voy a tomar un café con mi amiga.*

1. Mañana no hay clases y no necesitas trabajar.
2. La clase de español termina a las diez y tu siguiente *(next)* clase es a las doce.
3. Son las vacaciones de primavera y vas a recibir un cheque de $800 de los impuestos *(taxes)*.
4. Es sábado y hace buen tiempo.
5. Recibes un cheque de 50 dólares por tu cumpleaños.
6. Es viernes por la noche.

Lectura

Antes de leer

In many countries there are important celebrations and holidays that are unique to the country. Make a list of the holidays that are important in the United States. Which ones do you celebrate and why? Look back at the celebrations mentioned in **Conexiones culturales.** Do you know other celebrations from a Spanish-speaking country? The following reading is about Christmas, a particularly important celebration because the majority of the population in Spain and Latin America is Catholic.

A leer

La Navidad en algunos países hispanos

Muchas de las tradiciones en Latinoamérica son religiosas y tienen sus orígenes en tradiciones españolas. Una de estas tradiciones es la de la Navidad. Para muchos, la celebración de la Navidad se inicia **antes** del 25 de diciembre. Desde noviembre es posible escuchar **villancicos** en los

before

Christmas carols

© Fer Gregory/Shutterstock

> [...les gusta cantar villancicos, comer comida tradicional y romper piñatas.]

comerciales de televisión y de la radio. En varios países las fiestas inician el 16 de diciembre y continúan todas las noches hasta el 24 de diciembre. Estas fiestas se llaman *posadas*. En las posadas muchas personas visitan otras casas en la comunidad.

Durante estas fiestas, a las personas les gusta cantar villancicos y comer **comida** tradicional. A los niños les gusta mucho romper piñatas. A veces también hay *pastorelas*, que son similares a pequeñas **obras de teatro** con lecciones religiosas o morales.

food

plays

En muchos países las personas van a la **iglesia** el 24 de diciembre (Nochebuena), comen con su familia y, a la medianoche, abren los regalos de Navidad. Las celebraciones de Navidad terminan el 6 de enero, el Día de los Reyes Magos. En algunos países los niños reciben regalos de los **Tres Reyes Magos,** y todos comen la famosa **rosca** de reyes.

Rosca de reyes

church

the Three Kings
ring-shaped bread

Comprensión

Decide si las siguientes afirmaciones son ciertas o falsas. Corrige las oraciones falsas. *(Decide whether the following statements are true or false. Correct any false statements.)*

1. En toda Latinoamérica las celebraciones de Navidad inician el 25 de diciembre.
2. Las pastorelas son fiestas en las que las personas cantan villancicos.
3. Es tradicional ir a la iglesia en Nochebuena.
4. En algunos países, los niños reciben regalos el Día de los Reyes Magos.
5. La rosca de reyes es una comida tradicional.

> **INVESTIGUEMOS LA MÚSICA**
>
> "Los peces en el río" is a simple Christmas carol. Find the version by the Gipsy Kings on the Internet and listen to it.

Después de leer

En el Diccionario personal al final del capítulo escribe una lista de 5 palabras en inglés que asocias con Navidad, Jánuca, Kuanza, otra celebración del solsticio invernal o el Año Nuevo. Después, usa un diccionario para saber cómo se dice en español y comparte tu vocabulario nuevo en Share It! y lee las palabras de tus compañeros. *(In the personal dictionary at the end of the chapter, write 5 words in English that you associate with Christmas, Hanukkah, Kwanzaa, another winter solstice celebration or the New Year. After, use a dictionary to look up how to say the words in Spanish and share your new vocabulary words on Share It! and read your classmates' words.)*

En Jánuca, celebramos con la familia.

Redacción

An international student from a Spanish-speaking country is going to attend your university. Write an e-mail to the student explaining what the climate in your area is like, what people often do, and advise him/her as to what clothing he or she will need.

Paso 1 Write down the current season. Then write a list of the types of weather you experience in your area during that time.

© Chris Schmidt/iStockphoto

Paso 2 Jot down things people do in your area during that time.

Paso 3 Decide whether you are writing to a male or a female student. Then write down a list of clothing items that people wear in your area. Think about what they would wear to school, to go out, and to do any of the activities you wrote down in **Paso 2.**

Paso 4 Start your e-mail by writing the date in Spanish and greeting the student using the expression **Querido(a)** *(Dear)*. Remember to use **Querido** if it is a male student and **Querida** if it is a female student.

Paso 5 Begin your first paragraph by introducing yourself to the international student and telling him or her where you study. Then, using the information you generated in **Pasos 1** and **3,** tell him or her what season it is, what the weather is like in your area, and what particular clothing items he/she needs for that climate.

Paso 6 Using the information you generated in **Pasos 2** and **3,** begin a second paragraph and tell him or her what students usually wear to class. Then explain what kinds of activities people do in their free time and any particular clothing items he or she would need.

Paso 7 Conclude your letter with **Hasta pronto** or **Tu nuevo(a) amigo(a).**

Paso 8 Edit your e-mail:

1. Do your sentences use a friendly, inviting, and conversational tone?
2. Are your paragraphs logically organized or do you skip from one idea to the next?
3. Are there any short sentences you can combine by using **y** or **pero**?
4. Are there any spelling errors?
5. Do adjectives agree with the objects they describe?
6. Does each verb agree with its subject?

En vivo

Entrando en materia

¿En qué meses hay muchos anuncios de agencias de viajes?

Un anuncio de una agencia de viajes

Lee el anuncio y contesta las preguntas que siguen.

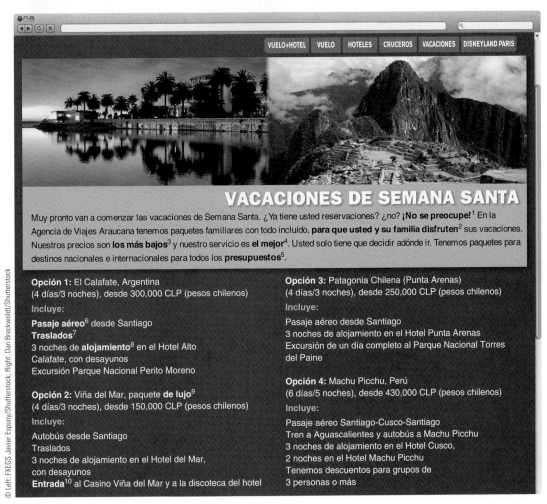

VUELO+HOTEL   VUELO   HOTELES   CRUCEROS   VACACIONES   DISNEYLAND PARIS

VACACIONES DE SEMANA SANTA

Muy pronto van a comenzar las vacaciones de Semana Santa. ¿Ya tiene usted reservaciones? ¿no? **¡No se preocupe!**[1] En la Agencia de Viajes Araucana tenemos paquetes familiares con todo incluído, **para que usted y su familia disfruten**[2] sus vacaciones. Nuestros precios son **los más bajos**[3] y nuestro servicio es **el mejor**[4]. Usted solo tiene que decidir adónde ir. Tenemos paquetes para destinos nacionales e internacionales para todos los **presupuestos**[5].

Opción 1: El Calafate, Argentina
(4 días/3 noches), desde 300,000 CLP (pesos chilenos)

Incluye:

Pasaje aéreo[6] desde Santiago
Traslados[7]
3 noches de **alojamiento**[8] en el Hotel Alto
Calafate, con desayunos
Excursión Parque Nacional Perito Moreno

Opción 2: Viña del Mar, paquete **de lujo**[9]
(4 días/3 noches), desde 150,000 CLP (pesos chilenos)

Incluye:

Autobús desde Santiago
Traslados
3 noches de alojamiento en el Hotel del Mar,
con desayunos
Entrada[10] al Casino Viña del Mar y a la discoteca del hotel

Opción 3: Patagonia Chilena (Punta Arenas)
(4 días/3 noches), desde 250,000 CLP (pesos chilenos)

Incluye:

Pasaje aéreo desde Santiago
3 noches de alojamiento en el Hotel Punta Arenas
Excursión de un día completo al Parque Nacional Torres
del Paine

Opción 4: Machu Picchu, Perú
(6 días/5 noches), desde 430,000 CLP (pesos chilenos)

Incluye:

Pasaje aéreo Santiago-Cusco-Santiago
Tren a Aguascalientes y autobús a Machu Picchu
3 noches de alojamiento en el Hotel Cusco,
2 noches en el Hotel Machu Picchu
Tenemos descuentos para grupos de
3 personas o más

[1]Don't worry!   [2]so that you and your family enjoy   [3]the lowest   [4]the best   [5]budgets
[6]airfare   [7]transfers   [8]lodging   [9]luxury   [10]admittance

Comprensión

1. ¿Cómo se llama la Agencia de Viajes?
2. ¿A qué lugares *(places)* sugiere viajar la agencia?
3. ¿Cuál es el viaje más barato *(least expensive)*?
4. De los cuatro destinos ¿cuál te gusta más y por qué?

Más allá

Investiga otro destino turístico interesante en Sudamérica. ¿En qué país está? ¿Qué atracciones turísticas hay? ¿Cuántos días recomiendas para visitarlo? ¿En qué mes o estación es mejor ir? Comparte tus recomendaciones en Share It! *(Explore another interesting tourist destination in South America. What country is it in? What attractions are there? How many days do you you recommend visiting? What month or season is best to go? Share your recommendations on Share It!)*

Vocabulario

Sustantivos

el clima	*climate*
el descuento	*discount*
la devolución	*return*
el ecosistema	*ecosystem*
el ecoturismo	*ecotourism*
el medio ambiente	*environment*
la naturaleza	*nature*
el pago	*payment*
la reserva	*reservation*
el seguro	*insurance*
la temporada	*season*

Adjetivos

caluroso(a)	*hot*
diligente	*diligent*
educado(a)	*polite*
húmedo(a)	*humid*
lluvioso(a)	*rainy*
responsable	*responsible*
seco(a)	*dry*

Verbos

averiguar	*to find out*
cobrar	*to charge*
confirmar	*to confirm*
devolver	*to return*
pagar	*to pay*
recorrer	*to go through*

Frases útiles

Tenemos descuento para grupos familiares.
We have family discount plans.

Es temporada alta/baja.
This is high/low season.

¿Me da su número de tarjeta de crédito?
May I have your credit card number?

Este es su número de confirmación.
This is your confirmation number.

© Andresr/Shutterstock

DATOS IMPORTANTES

Educación: Estudios secundarios. Certificación de agente de turismo por escuelas privadas o universidades. Algunas universidades ofrecen licenciatura en viajes y turismo. Se requieren conocimientos *(knowledge)* de computación y se prefieren estudios complementarios en negocios.

Salario: Promedio *(Average)* de $50 000, comisiones de hasta 25% y bonos

Dónde se trabaja: Agencias de viaje, corporaciones, hoteles y oficinas nacionales de turismo

Vocabulario nuevo Completa las oraciones con la palabra apropiada de la lista de vocabulario. *(Complete the sentences with the appropriate vocabulary word from the list.)*

1. Muchos turistas visitan España en el verano porque es _____ alta.

2. Debes tener un paraguas porque España tiene un clima _____.

3. No llueve mucho en esa parte de México porque tiene un clima _____.

4. Costa Rica tiene una gran diversidad de plantas y animales y por eso _____ es muy popular.

5. Si pagas antes de ir, recibes _____ del 10%.

Marcela Díaz, agente de turismo

Marcela Díaz trabaja en una importante agencia de turismo. Vende paquetes de ecoturismo a distintos lugares de Latinoamérica. En el video vas a ver a Marcela preparando un viaje por teléfono para un nuevo cliente. *(Marcela works at an important travel agency. She sells ecotourism packages to different places in Latin America. In the video you are going to see Marcela on the phone planning a trip with a new client.)*

© Cengage Learning

Antes de ver

Muchos vendedores trabajan por comisión y reciben dinero extra por cada venta que hacen. Para ellos, los clientes son muy importantes. Necesitan ser educados y diligentes con ellos. Según tu experiencia si una persona habla con una agente de viajes, ¿qué tipo de preguntas específicas hace? *(Many salespeople work on commission and receive extra money for each sale they make. For them, clients are very important and salespeople must be polite and diligent with them. Based on your experience, what specific questions does the agent ask?)*

Comprensión

1. ¿Qué mira Carlos en la televisión normalmente?
2. ¿Qué país le recomienda Marcela?
3. ¿Qué animal especial vive en El Yunque?
4. ¿Cómo es el clima en Puerto Rico en esa temporada?
5. ¿Qué hacen en Luquillo?
6. ¿Adónde van el último *(last)* día?

Después de ver

En parejas, representen a un agente de viajes y a un cliente que quiere hacer ecoturismo por un país de Latinoamérica. El agente recomienda un lugar de acuerdo con los gustos del cliente. Consideren el clima y hagan recomendaciones de ropa para llevar. *(In pairs, role-play a travel agent and a client that wants to do ecotourism in a Latin American country. The agent should recommend a place according to the client's tastes. Think about the climate and make recommendations of what clothing to wear.)*

3.37 Un día en el centro Escoge el verbo apropiado y completa los párrafos con la forma necesaria. *(Choose the appropriate verb and complete the paragraphs with the necessary form.)*

A Teresa le (**1.**) _____ (gusta/gustan) mucho comprar ropa y
(**2.**) _____ (tener/ser) que buscar un vestido porque ella
(**3.**) _____ (abrir/deber) asistir a un evento importante el viernes. Ella
(**4.**) _____(ir/vivir) a una tienda *(store)* con ropa bonita. A Teresa le
(**5.**) _____ (gusta/gustan) los zapatos y al final compra unos zapatos y
un vestido elegante.

Después de sus compras, Teresa (**6.**) _____ (tener/ser) hambre. Ella y
su amiga van a (**7.**) _____ (comer/beber) en el restaurante Río Grande.
Ellas (**8.**) _____ (correr/creer) que el restaurante (**9.**) _____
(vende/leer) los mejores *(best)* tacos. Las dos chicas (**10.**) _____ (decidir/
recibir) comer tacos y (**11.**) _____ (deber/beber) agua.

3.38 ¿Qué van a hacer? Di lo que van a hacer estas personas según el tiempo que hace donde viven. Debes usar el futuro (**ir** + **a** + infinitivo). *(Indicate what the following people are going to do according to the weather where they live. You should use the future [**ir** + **a** + infinitive].)*

1. Yo vivo en Antigua y hoy llueve.
2. Carla vive en Santo Domingo y hoy hace buen tiempo.
3. Yago y Matilde viven en Granada y hoy nieva.
4. Zoila y yo vivimos en Tegucigalpa y hoy hace calor.
5. Hugo y Marisabel viven en Caracas y hoy hace mal tiempo.
6. Cándido vive en Asunción y hoy hace mucho frío.
7. Yo vivo en Bogotá y hoy hace fresco.
8. Ulises vive en La Paz y hoy hace viento.
9. Renata y yo vivimos en San Juan y hoy hace sol.
10. ¿Dónde vives tú? ¿Qué tiempo hace? ¿Qué vas a hacer hoy?

3.39 Explicaciones Lee las oraciones y usa **gustar** para explicar por qué estas personas no hacen ciertas actividades. *(Read the sentences and then, using the verb **gustar**, explain why these people don't do certain activities.)*

Modelo Frank no estudia. → *No le gustan sus clases.*
Miguel y Ofelia no miran la tele. → *Les gusta leer en la noche.*

1. Yo no como chocolates.
2. Tú no comes en restaurantes.
3. Laura y Ángel no limpian su casa.
4. Tomasa no lleva pantalones cortos.
5. Felipe no recibe muchos mensajes electrónicos.
6. Nuria y yo no estudiamos en la biblioteca.

3.40 **Descripción de fotos** Escoge una de las fotos y contesta las siguientes
preguntas. (*Choose one of the photos and answer the following questions.*)

1. ¿Qué estación es?
2. ¿Qué tiempo hace?
3. ¿Cuál es la relación entre las personas?
4. ¿Qué ropa llevan?
5. ¿Qué hacen? (*What are they doing?*)

3.41 **Ocho diferencias** Trabaja con un compañero. Uno mira la ilustración aquí y
el otro mira la ilustración en el Apéndice B. Túrnense para describir su ilustración
y buscar las ocho diferencias. (*Work with a partner. One of you will look at the
illustration on this page and the other will look at the illustration in Appendix B. Take
turns describing the illustrations to find the eight differences.*)

3.42 **Mi agenda** Tu compañero y tú tienen que encontrar una hora para estudiar español.
(*You and your partner have to find a time to study Spanish.*)

Paso 1 On a piece of paper write down your schedule for the week (Monday through
Friday). You should include your classes, work, and other activities.

Paso 2 Work with a partner to find a time to study Spanish together. Using the expression
¿Qué tal. . . ? (*How about . . . ?*), take turns asking if a free time will work for the
other. Continue until you find a time.

Paso 3 Share with the class the day and time you will study together.

🔊 Vocabulario 1

1-20

La ropa y los accesorios

el abrigo	*coat*
la blusa	*blouse*
los bluyines	*blue jeans*
la bolsa	*purse*
las botas	*boots*
la bufanda	*scarf*
los calcetines	*socks*
la camisa	*shirt*
la camiseta	*T-shirt*
la chaqueta	*jacket*
el cinturón	*belt*
la corbata	*tie*
la falda	*skirt*
el gorro	*cap*
los guantes	*gloves*
el impermeable	*raincoat*
los lentes	*glasses*
los pantalones	*pants*
los pantalones cortos	*shorts*
el paraguas	*umbrella*
la pijama	*pajamas*
las sandalias	*sandals*
el sombrero	*hat*
el suéter	*sweater*
los tenis	*tennis shoes*
el traje	*suit*
el traje de baño	*swimming suit*
el vestido	*dress*
los zapatos	*shoes*

El tiempo

Está despejado.	*It is clear.*
Está nublado.	*It is cloudy.*
Hace buen tiempo.	*The weather is nice.*
Hace calor.	*It's hot.*
Hace fresco.	*It is cool.*
Hace frío.	*It's cold.*
Hace mal tiempo.	*The weather is bad.*
Hace sol.	*It's sunny.*
Hace viento.	*It is windy.*
Llueve.	*It rains. / It is raining.*
Nieva.	*It snows. / It is snowing.*

Las estaciones

el invierno	*winter*
el otoño	*fall*
la primavera	*spring*
el verano	*summer*

Los verbos

abrir	*to open*
aprender (a + infinitive)	*to learn (to do something)*
asistir (a)	*to attend*
beber	*to drink*
comer	*to eat*
comprender	*to understand*
correr	*to run*
creer	*to believe*
deber	*should, ought to*
decidir	*to decide*
escribir	*to write*
leer	*to read*
recibir (un regalo)	*to receive (a gift)*
tomar el sol	*to sunbathe*
vender	*to sell*
vivir	*to live*

Los colores see p. 78

Expresiones importantes

me gusta	*I like*
te gusta	*you like*
le gusta	*he/she likes*
nos gusta	*we like*
os gusta	*you (plural) like (Spain)*
les gusta	*they, you (plural) like*

Palabras adicionales

cómodo(a)	*comfortable*
llevar	*to wear, to carry; to take*
llevar puesto(a)	*to be wearing*

🔊 Vocabulario 2

Los días de la semana

el lunes	*Monday*		el viernes	*Friday*
el martes	*Tuesday*		el sábado	*Saturday*
el miércoles	*Wednesday*		el domingo	*Sunday*
el jueves	*Thursday*			

Los meses

enero	*January*		julio	*July*
febrero	*February*		agosto	*August*
marzo	*March*		septiembre	*September*
abril	*April*		octubre	*October*
mayo	*May*		noviembre	*November*
junio	*June*		diciembre	*December*

Los verbos

ir	*to go*		terminar	*to finish*

Palabras adicionales

ahora	*now*		la medianoche	*midnight*
el Año Nuevo	*New Year*		el mediodía	*noon*
el cumpleaños	*birthday*		Navidad	*Christmas*
el día	*day*		la semana	*week*
el día feriado	*holiday*		por la mañana / tarde / noche	*in the morning / afternoon / evening*
la fecha	*date*			
el fin de semana	*weekend*		todos los días	*every day*
hoy	*today*			
mañana	*tomorrow*			

Diccionario personal

_____

_____

_____

_____

_____

_____

Learning Strategy

Participate

Participate in class. You cannot learn another language simply by observing. You must be willing to use the language actively, and to learn from the mistakes you make.

In this chapter you will learn how to:

- Describe your town or city
- Describe your home
- Tell where things are located
- Request information about the cost of things
- Use question words to ask for specific information

¿Dónde vives?

© PhotoLink/JupiterImages

El señor Ramírez tiene media hora para ir al banco y hacer otras diligencias
(*errands*). ¿Qué más puede hacer en el centro de la ciudad?

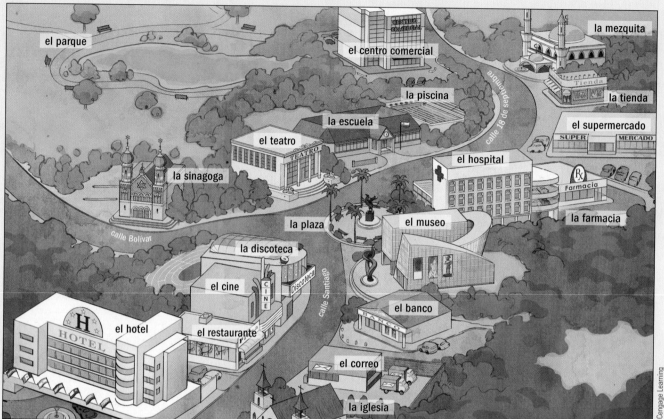

Otros lugares	Other places			Los verbos	
el aeropuerto	airport	el negocio	business	depositar dinero	to deposit money
el bar	bar	la oficina	office	mandar una carta /	to send a letter /
el café	cafe	la playa	beach	un paquete	a package
el club	club	el templo	temple	mirar una película	to watch a movie
el edificio	building	el zoológico	zoo	rezar	to pray
el mercado	market				

INVESTIGUEMOS EL VOCABULARIO

The suffix **-ería** is often used to indicate stores where certain products are sold. What is sold in the following stores?

chocolatería   frutería   papelería   tortillería

INVESTIGUEMOS EL VOCABULARIO

In the Spanish-speaking world, there are variations in the words that describe places to shop. For example, a department store could be referred to as **el almacén** or **la tienda de departamentos**. A supermarket could be **la bodega, el supermercado,** or **la tienda de autoservicio.**

A practicar

4.1 **Escucha y responde** Vas a escuchar una lista de lugares. Indica con el pulgar hacia arriba si es posible comprar un producto en el lugar. Si no es posible, indica con el pulgar hacia abajo.
1-22

4.2 **¿Cierto o falso?** Decide si las oraciones son ciertas o falsas. Corrige las oraciones falsas.

1. En la playa compramos ropa.
2. En la discoteca miramos animales.
3. Nadamos en la piscina.
4. Miramos películas en el cine.
5. En el parque compramos medicinas.
6. Estudiamos y aprendemos en la tienda.
7. En la plaza rezamos.
8. Mandamos cartas en el banco.

4.3 **¿Con qué frecuencia... ?** Para cada actividad, habla con un compañero diferente y pregúntale con qué frecuencia hace la actividad.

Modelo ir a la playa
        Estudiante 1: *¿Con qué frecuencia vas a la playa?*
        Estudiante 2: *Voy a la playa una vez al año.*

1. comprar comida en el mercado
2. rezar en el templo
3. caminar en el parque
4. mirar películas en el cine
5. enviar cartas en el correo
6. depositar cheques en el banco
7. ir al zoológico
8. bailar en una discoteca

<aside>
INVESTIGUEMOS EL VOCABULARIO

When saying how often you do something, use the word **vez.**

una vez a la semana
once a week

dos veces al mes
two times a month

To say you never do something, use the word **nunca** in front of the conjugated verb.

Yo **nunca** voy al museo.
I never go to the museum.
</aside>

4.4 **Conversemos** Entrevista a tu compañero. Túrnense con las siguientes preguntas.

1. ¿Cuál es tu supermercado favorito?
2. ¿Hay un banco cerca de *(nearby)* tu casa? ¿Cómo se llama?
3. ¿Te gusta ir al cine?
4. ¿Cuál es tu restaurante favorito?
5. ¿En qué tienda prefieres comprar tu ropa?
6. ¿Adónde prefieres ir con tus amigos?
7. ¿Te gusta ir a museos? ¿Cómo se llama tu museo favorito?
8. ¿Te gusta ir al parque? ¿Por qué?

<aside>
Estrategia

Participate in class.

The activities on this page offer many opportunities to use Spanish actively in class and to learn from your mistakes instead of worrying about making one.
</aside>

4.5 **Planes para el fin de semana** Trabaja con un compañero. para descubrir cuáles son las actividades de Jazmín, Lila y Arturo durante el fin de semana y dónde las hacen. Uno de ustedes va a ver la información en esta página, y el otro va a ver la información en el **Apéndice B.**

Modelo Estudiante 1: *¿Qué hace Jazmín el sábado por la mañana?*
        Estudiante 2: *Jazmín compra fruta.*
        Estudiante 1: *¿Dónde compra fruta?*
        Estudiante 2: *En el mercado.*

	Jazmín	**Lila**	**Arturo**
sábado por la mañana	comprar fruta (mercado)		rezar (la sinagoga)
sábado por la tarde		comprar ropa (el centro comercial)	
sábado por la noche			mirar una película (el cine)
domingo por la mañana	nadar (la playa)	visitar a un amigo (el hospital)	

Cultura

Las grandes ciudades del mundo generalmente tienen museos muy importantes. Dos museos de fama internacional son El Prado en Madrid, España, y el Museo del Oro *(Gold)* en Bogotá, Colombia. El Museo del Prado tiene una de las colecciones de arte más importantes del mundo, especialmente de pintores europeos de los siglos *(centuries)* XVI al XIX. El Museo del Oro tiene una colección impresionante de artículos prehispánicos hechos de *(made of)* oro y otros metales, con instalaciones modernas y exposiciones con multimedia.

© Pat_Hastings/Shutterstock

Courtesy of Margarita Casas

¿De qué artistas crees que hay cuadros en El Prado?

¿Qué civilizaciones prehispánicas crees que están representadas en el Museo del Oro?

¿Qué otros museos de todo el mundo son muy famosos y por qué?

 Busca los nombres de artistas españoles y colombianos en **Exploraciones del mundo hispano** en el **Apéndice A.**

Investiga en Internet los sitios web oficiales del Museo del Prado y del Museo del Oro. Identifica una obra que te guste de uno de los museos. Sube *(Upload)* a Share It! la obra que te gusta y comparte *(share)* el nombre del artista y de la obra.

Comunidad

Busca a una persona de un país donde se habla español y haz una entrevista con las siguientes preguntas: **¿Dónde compras comida generalmente? ¿Dónde prefieres comprar ropa? ¿Son diferentes las tiendas en tu país?** Repórtale la información a la clase.

© Claudiu Marius Pascalina/Dreamstime.com

Comparaciones

Las ciudades pequeñas son diferentes a las grandes ciudades no solo por su tamaño *(size)*. Observa el mapa de Puno, una pequeña ciudad al lado del lago Titicaca, en Perú. ¿Hay algún edificio que no haya en tu ciudad? ¿Cuál? ¿Cuáles son los lugares turísticos principales?

Si llegas a Puno por tren, ¿debes caminar mucho para ver los lugares de interés?

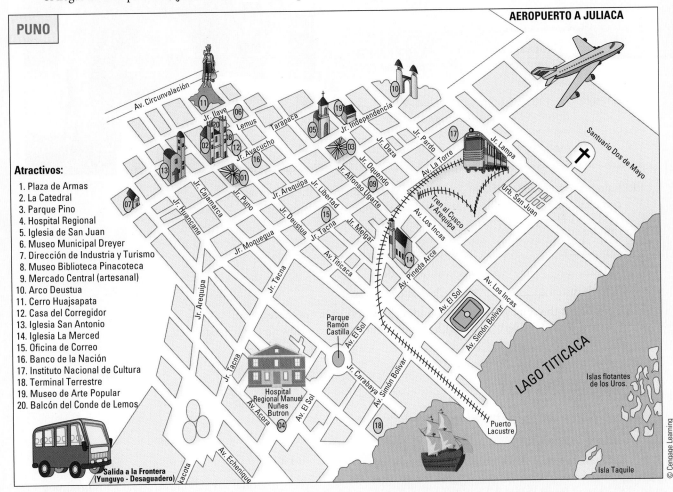

PUNO

AEROPUERTO A JULIACA

Atractivos:
1. Plaza de Armas
2. La Catedral
3. Parque Pino
4. Hospital Regional
5. Iglesia de San Juan
6. Museo Municipal Dreyer
7. Dirección de Industria y Turismo
8. Museo Biblioteca Pinacoteca
9. Mercado Central (artesanal)
10. Arco Deustua
11. Cerro Huajsapata
12. Casa del Corregidor
13. Iglesia San Antonio
14. Iglesia La Merced
15. Oficina de Correo
16. Banco de la Nación
17. Instituto Nacional de Cultura
18. Terminal Terrestre
19. Museo de Arte Popular
20. Balcón del Conde de Lemos

LAGO TITICACA

Islas flotantes de los Uros.

Isla Taquile

Salida a la Frontera (Yunguyo - Desaguadero)

Puerto Lacustre

Hospital Regional Manuel Nuñes Butron

Parque Ramón Castilla

Santuario Dos de Mayo

Tren al Cusco y Arequipa

© Cengage Learning

Conexiones... a las relaciones internacionales

Muchas ciudades del mundo participan en un programa de ciudades hermanas. La Asociación Internacional de Ciudades Hermanas es una organización que promueve el respeto mutuo, la comprensión y la cooperación. Por ejemplo, Miami, Florida, es ciudad hermana de Managua, Nicaragua. El objetivo del programa es conectar a dos ciudades semejantes *(similar)* en superficie que están en diferentes zonas del mundo para fomentar *(to encourage)* el contacto humano. ¿Cuál es la ciudad hermana de la capital de tu estado? ¿Qué actividades y eventos tienen?

Managua, la capital de Nicaragua, es ciudad hermana de Miami.

Image Source/Getty Images

Exploraciones gramaticales

A analizar

Nicolás y Santiago hablan de sus planes. Después de ver el video, lee parte de su conversación y observa las formas del verbo **poder.**

> Nicolás: ¿**Puedes** ir conmigo? Como está cerca del restaurante cubano, **podemos** comer después.
>
> Santiago: Uy, me gustaría, pero no **puedo.** Tengo que ir a la biblioteca ahora. Voy a estudiar con Paula para el examen de ciencias políticas.

© Cengage Learning

1. Using your knowledge of verb conjugation and the forms in the conversation, complete the chart with the correct forms of the verb **poder.**

   poder

yo _____	nosotros(as) _____
tú _____	vosotros (as) podéis
él, ella, usted _____	ellos, ellas, ustedes _____

2. Now look at the conjugated forms of **poder** above. Which forms have a stem (the first part of the verb) that is different from the infinitive? How do they change?

A comprobar

Stem-changing verbs (o → ue)

1. There are a number of verbs that have changes in the root or stem. They are called stem-changing verbs. Notice in the verbs below, that the **o** changes to **ue** in all forms except the **nosotros** and **vosotros** forms. The endings are the same as other **-ar**, **-er**, and **-ir** verbs.

almorzar *(to eat lunch)*

yo	alm**ue**rzo	nosotros(as)	almorzamos
tú	alm**ue**rzas	vosotros(as)	almorzáis
él, ella, usted	alm**ue**rza	ellos, ellas, ustedes	alm**ue**rzan

volver *(to return)*

yo	v**ue**lvo	nosotros(as)	volvemos
tú	v**ue**lves	vosotros(as)	volvéis
él, ella, usted	v**ue**lve	ellos, ellas, ustedes	v**ue**lven

dormir *(to sleep)*

yo	d**ue**rmo	nosotros(as)	dormimos
tú	d**ue**rmes	vosotros(as)	dormís
él, ella, usted	d**ue**rme	ellos, ellas, ustedes	d**ue**rmen

Los niños **duermen** en este dormitorio.
*The children **sleep** in this bedroom.*

Gloria y yo **almorzamos** en la cafetería.
*Gloria and I **eat lunch** in the cafeteria.*

The verbs listed below are also **o → ue** stem-changing verbs.

costar	*to cost*
devolver	*to return (something)*
encontrar	*to find*
llover	*to rain*
morir	*to die*
poder	*to be able to*
recordar	*to remember*
soñar (con)	*to dream (about)*

2. The verb **jugar** is conjugated similarly to the **o → ue** stem-changing verbs, changing the **u** of its stem to **ue**.

jugar *(to play)*

yo	**jue**go	nosotros(as)	jugamos
tú	**jue**gas	vosotros(as)	jugáis
él, ella, usted	**jue**ga	ellos, ellas, ustedes	**jue**gan

A practicar

4.6 **Un poco de lógica** ¿Qué verbo completa mejor la oración?

1. Matilde siempre _____ a la casa después de trabajar.
   a. llueve **b.** vuelve **c.** almuerza

2. Los niños _____ con el perro en el parque.
   a. juegan **b.** sueñan **c.** encuentran

3. Nosotros _____ en el café.
   a. dormimos **b.** volvemos **c.** almorzamos

4. Renata no _____ un vestido bonito en la tienda.
   a. sueña **b.** encuentra **c.** vuelve

5. Mis amigos _____ mirar una película en el cine.
   a. juegan **b.** cuestan **c.** pueden

6. Mi esposo y yo _____ en un hotel en Montevideo.
   a. dormimos **b.** podemos **c.** encontramos

7. Yo _____ el libro a la biblioteca.
   a. encuentro **b.** vuelvo **c.** devuelvo

8. La ciudad es confusa y no _____ dónde está el hotel.
   a. recuerdo **b.** puedo **c.** duermo

La ciudad es confusa.

Peter Bernik/Shutterstock

4.7 **Nuestros sueños** Completa el siguiente párrafo con las formas necesarias del verbo **soñar.**

Todos tienen sueños *(dreams)* para el año nuevo. Yo **(1)** _____ con un trabajo y mi esposo **(2)** _____ con comprar un auto nuevo. Nosotros también **(3)** _____ con comprar una casa nueva. Mis hermanos **(4)** _____ con unas vacaciones en la playa. Y tú ¿con qué **(5)** _____?

¿Sueñas con comprar un auto?

© Monkey Business Images/Shutterstock

4.8 **¿Cuánto cuesta?** Estás en una tienda de ropa en España. Con un compañero, túrnense para preguntar cuánto cuestan los objetos.

35€

Modelo Estudiante 1: *¿Cuánto cuesta el sombrero negro?*
Estudiante 2: *Cuesta treinta y cinco euros.*

32€
70€

1.

28€
19€

2.

47€
15€

3.

52€
61€

4.

© Cengage Learning

4.9 **¿Quién puede?** Usando el verbo **poder**, explícale a tu compañero quién puede o no puede hacer las siguientes actividades.

Modelo viajar este verano
Yo puedo viajar este verano.
Mi esposo no puede viajar este verano.

1. tocar el piano   **4.** hablar francés   **7.** votar *(to vote)*

2. bailar bien   **5.** nadar   **8.** comer mucho

3. jugar al golf   **6.** ir a bares   **9.** cocinar bien

4.10 **En busca de…** Busca a ocho compañeros diferentes que hagan una de las siguientes actividades.

1. Normalmente (dormir) ocho horas.

2. (Volver) a casa después de las clases.

3. (Almorzar) en un restaurante una vez a la semana.

4. (Jugar) al tenis.

5. (Soñar) con un auto nuevo.

6. (Poder) cantar muy bien.

7. (Devolver) ropa a la tienda con frecuencia.

8. (Encontrar) a amigos en el cine.

INVESTIGUEMOS LA MÚSICA

Rakim y Ken-Y es un grupo de reggaetón de Puerto Rico. Escucha su éxito "Un sueño" en Internet. ¿Cuál es el sueño del que hablan?

A analizar

Santiago le explica a Nicolás dónde está el correo. Mira el video otra vez. Después lee parte de su conversación y observa las formas del verbo **estar**.

> Nicolás: ¡Hola Santiago! ¿Cómo **estás**?
>
> Santiago: **Estoy** muy bien, ¿y tú?
>
> Nicolás: Bien, pero no sé dónde **está** el correo y tengo que mandar este paquete a mis padres.
>
> Santiago: No **está** muy lejos. Mira, **estamos** en la calle San Pedro y el correo **está** en la calle Santa Rosa, enfrente del restaurante cubano.

© Cengage Learning

1. You learned some of the forms of the verb **estar** in **Capítulo 1**. The boldfaced verbs are also forms of the verb **estar**. From what you have already learned and by looking at the examples above, fill in the following chart.

   estar

   yo _____   nosotros(as) _____

   tú _____   vosotros(as) _____

   él, ella, usted _____   ellos, ellas, ustedes _____

2. **Estar** is used in the conversation for two different purposes. Can you identify them?

A comprobar

The verb **estar** with prepositions of place

Las preposiciones de posición					
a la derecha de	*to the right of*	**dentro de**	*inside*	**enfrente de**	*in front of, facing*
a la izquierda de	*to the left of*	**detrás de**	*behind*	**entre**	*between*
al lado de	*beside, next to*	**en**	*in, on, at*	**fuera de**	*outside*
cerca de	*near*	**encima de**	*on top of*	**lejos de**	*far from*
debajo de	*below*				

1. Notice that most of the prepositions include the word **de** (*of*).

   You will remember from **Capítulo 2** that the **de** in front of a masculine noun combines with **el** to become **del (de + el = del)**, and that it does not contract with the other articles.

   > Mi casa está al lado **del** café.
   > *My house is next to the café.*

   > El cine está a la derecha **de** la tienda.
   > *The movie theater is to the right of the store.*

2. The verb **estar** is used to express position; therefore, it is used with all prepositions of place.

estar *(to be)*			
yo	**estoy**	nosotros(as)	**estamos**
tú	**estás**	vosotros(as)	**estáis**
él, ella, usted	**está**	ellos, ellas, ustedes	**están**

A practicar

4.11 **Actividades en la ciudad** Lee las oraciones. ¿Qué actividades pueden hacer *(do)* las personas en el lugar donde están?

1. Yo estoy en la plaza.
2. Mis hijos están en la escuela.
3. Tú estás en el aeropuerto.
4. Mi esposa está en la oficina.
5. Mis amigos están en el café.
6. Mi hermano está en el correo.
7. Mi madre y yo estamos en el parque.
8. Tú estás en el banco.

4.12 **En la capital** Completa las oraciones con la forma necesaria del verbo **estar.** Luego identifica los países donde están las ciudades.

Modelo Mario ____*está*____ en Santiago. *Está en Chile.*

1. Yo _____ en Lima.
2. Usted _____ en San José.
3. Gloria y yo _____ en La Habana.
4. Joaquín y Héctor _____ en San Juan.
5. Hugo _____ en Caracas.
6. Tú _____ en Tegucigalpa.
7. Cristina _____ en Quito.
8. Los Gardel _____ en Buenos Aires.

4.13 **¿Dónde están?** Usa la forma apropiada del verbo **estar** y el vocabulario para explicar dónde están las diferentes personas. Luego explica qué hacen *(they do)* allí.

Modelo los niños
Los niños están en el zoológico. Miran los animales.

1. Ricardo

2. mis amigos

3. la señora Montero

4. mis amigos y yo

5. tú

6. tu perro y tú

© Cengage Learning

4.14 **En la ciudad** Mira el plano, escucha la descripción de la ciudad y decide si cada oración es cierta o falsa. Corrige las oraciones falsas.

1-23

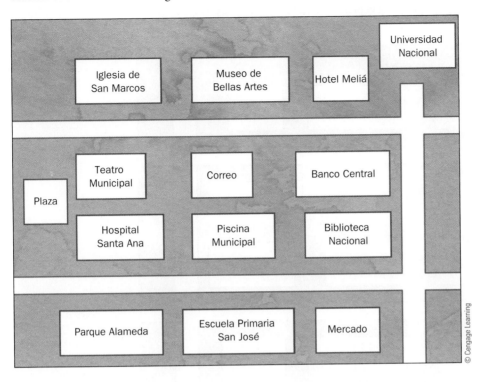

4.15 **El plano** En parejas inventen tres oraciones más sobre el plano. Las oraciones pueden ser ciertas o falsas y deben incluir las preposiciones. Después van a leer las oraciones para la clase y los otros compañeros van a decidir si son ciertas o falsas.

4.16 **¿Dónde está... ?** En parejas túrnense para hacer y contestar preguntas sobre el dibujo. Usen todas las preposiciones posibles para cada pregunta.

Modelo el café

Estudiante 1: *¿Dónde está el café?*
Estudiante 2: *El café está al lado de la librería.*

1. el banco   **3.** el automóvil   **5.** el gimnasio   **7.** el parque
2. la librería   **4.** la bicicleta   **6.** el perro   **8.** la tienda

4.17 Creando una ciudad Con un compañero túrnense para decidir dónde están los edificios en la ciudad en el plano *(city map)* abajo. Después de describir dónde están, escriban los nombres de los edificios en el plano. Al final tu plano y el plano de tu compañero deben ser idénticos.

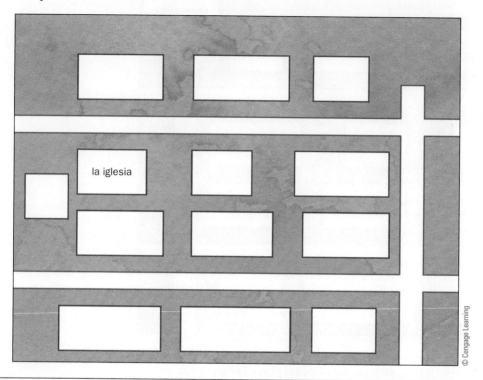

la iglesia

4.18 ¿Es cierto? En parejas túrnense para hacer oraciones ciertas o falsas sobre las posiciones de los edificios, los coches y la piscina en la ilustración. El otro estudiante debe decidir si la afirmación es cierta y corregir las afirmaciones falsas.

Modelo Estudiante 1: *Hay un coche detrás del banco.*
Estudiante 2: *Falso, está enfrente del banco.*

Escuela San José

¡A comer!

CRÉDITO POPULAR

Entrando en materia

¿Adónde te gusta ir en la ciudad o pueblo donde vives?

Turismo local en Ecuador

🔊 Escucha el reportaje *(news report)* sobre los esfuerzos *(efforts)* para promover el turismo
1-24 local en Ecuador.

Vocabulario útil

la comida	food	los eventos	events
compartir	to share	las noticias	news
disfrutar	to enjoy	el portal	web page

Comprensión

Decide si las afirmaciones son ciertas o falsas. Corrige las oraciones falsas.

1. Según las noticias, a muchos habitantes de Quito les gusta pasar tiempo en las calles de la ciudad.
2. La Compañía de Turismo de Ecuador tiene un nuevo portal en Internet.
3. En el portal las personas pueden compartir recomendaciones.
4. El fin de semana hay un concierto en el cine frente a la plaza principal.
5. El locutor *(announcer)* piensa que el portal es una mala idea.

© Noamfein/Dreamstime.com

🏙 Más allá

Escribe una reseña *(review)* de un lugar que te gusta visitar en tu ciudad. ¿Qué tipo de lugar es? ¿Cómo se llama? ¿Dónde está? ¿Por qué es bueno?

Comparte tu reseña en Share It! y, si es posible, incluye fotos. Luego lee las recomendaciones de los otros estudiantes.

Lectura

Antes de leer

¿Qué cosas hay en todas las grandes ciudades? ¿Cómo imaginas que son las capitales de España y los países latinoamericanos?

A leer

Algunas ciudades únicas de Latinoamérica

were / before

La mayoría de las grandes ciudades latinoamericanas combina lo moderno con lo histórico. Algunas de las ciudades **fueron** fundadas mucho **antes** de la llegada de los españoles, como es el caso de Cuzco, la capital del imperio Inca en Perú, y de la Ciudad de México, fundada por los aztecas con el nombre de Tenochtitlán. Hoy día en las dos ciudades se pueden ver ruinas de civilizaciones indígenas al lado de edificios coloniales de hasta 400 años de antigüedad. Por supuesto, en España y Latinoamérica también hay muchas ciudades modernas, con **rascacielos** y otras maravillas de la ingeniería, como **puentes** y avenidas de circulación rápida.

skyscrapers
bridges

[Un elegante ejemplo de modernidad se encuentra en Buenos Aires...]

as

was

subdivisions

Un elegante ejemplo de modernidad se encuentra en Buenos Aires, la capital de Argentina y su ciudad más importante. Con más de doce millones de habitantes. "Baires", **como** la llaman los argentinos, **fue** fundada en 1536 con el nombre original de "Puerto de Nuestra Señora Santa María del Buen Aire". Los **barrios** de la ciudad reflejan su pasado de inmigrantes. Es una ciudad cosmopolita y llena de cultura. Es famosa por sus monumentos, como

Puerto Madero, en Buenos Aires

el Obelisco, y por tener la avenida **más ancha** del mundo: la Avenida 9 de julio.

widest

Otra ciudad moderna y de **hermosa** arquitectura es Bogotá. La ciudad de Bogotá es la capital de Colombia y en 2006 fue declarada "capital del libro del mundo" por la UNESCO, gracias a las increíbles bibliotecas de la ciudad.

beautiful

La ciudad de Bogotá

Cada una de estas ciudades es especial por su arquitectura, sus monumentos, parques, restaurantes, cafés, tiendas y boutiques. Sin duda, como muchas otras ciudades latinoamericanas, son muy atractivas para el turismo.

Comprensión

Contesta las preguntas.

1. ¿Qué combinan muchas de las ciudades de Latinoamérica?
2. ¿Cómo se llamaba la capital del imperio Inca en Perú?
3. ¿Cómo llaman los argentinos a su capital?
4. ¿Por qué es famosa Buenos Aires?
5. ¿Por qué fue declarada "la capital del libro del mundo" Bogotá?

Después de leer

Busca una página en Internet con información para turistas en una ciudad de España o Latinoamérica. Después contesta las preguntas.

1. ¿Qué actividades puedes hacer?
2. ¿Te gustaría visitar la ciudad? ¿Por qué?

La ciudad de Cuenca, en Ecuador, es famosa por sus iglesias.

Esta es la casa de Lola. ¿Qué hay en su casa?

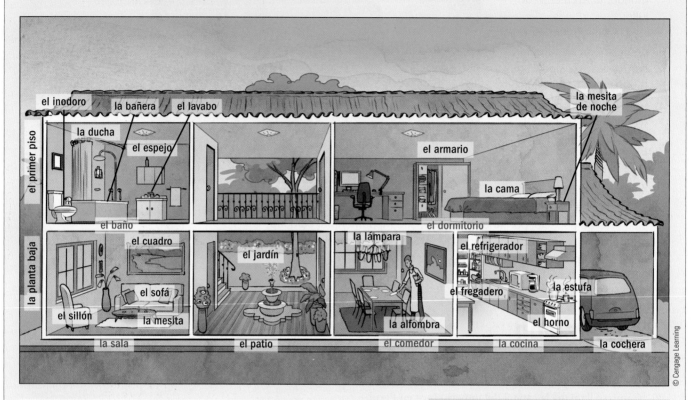

alquilar	*to rent*	el (horno de)	*microwave (oven)*
el apartamento	*apartment*	microondas	
la cafetera	*coffee maker*	la lavadora	*washer*
las cortinas	*curtains*	el lavaplatos	*dishwasher*
la dirección	*address*	los muebles	*furniture*
el electrodoméstico	*appliance*	las plantas	*plants*
la flor	*flower*	la secadora	*dryer*
la habitación	*room*		

INVESTIGUEMOS LA GRAMÁTICA

You learned in **Capítulo 2** that adjectives that express quantity, such as **mucho, poco,** and **varios,** are placed in front of the noun they describe. **Primero** is another adjective that precedes nouns. Notice that in the masculine singular form it becomes **primer** when in front of a noun.

Mi dormitorio está en el **primer** piso.
*My bedroom is on the **first** floor.*

Es la **primera** casa en la calle.
*It is the **first** house on the street.*

INVESTIGUEMOS EL VOCABULARIO

Notice that **el primer piso** refers to what people in the United States would call the second floor. In many Spanish-speaking countries the first floor is referred to as the ground floor, or **la planta baja.**

A practicar

4.19 **Escucha y responde** Vas a escuchar algunas oraciones. Indica con el pulgar hacia arriba si la oración es lógica. Si no es lógica, indica con el pulgar hacia abajo.

CD 1-25

4.20 **¿Dónde están?** ¿En qué habitación de la casa están los siguientes muebles o aparatos?

1. el horno
2. el sillón
3. el lavabo
4. el lavaplatos
5. el armario
6. la cafetera
7. la mesita de noche
8. la cama
9. el inodoro

4.21  **¡Qué desastre!** La casa es un desastre y no puedes encontrar nada. Con un compañero, túrnense para preguntar dónde están los objetos perdidos (lost).

Modelo la corbata

Estudiante 1: *¿Dónde está la corbata?*
Estudiante 2: *Está encima de la cama.*

1. el teléfono
2. el libro
3. la bota
4. el suéter

5. el paraguas
6. el cuaderno
7. los peces
8. el gato

4.22 **Adivinanza** Mira el dibujo al inicio de la lección. Vas a elegir y a describir tres objetos en dos o tres oraciones. No debes mencionar el objeto en tu descripción. Usa **es para** para describir la función del aparato. Con un compañero túrnense para adivinar el objeto que el otro describe.

Modelo Estudiante 1: *Está en la cocina. Está debajo de la estufa. Es para cocinar.*
Estudiante 2: *¡Es el horno!*

4.23 **Comparemos** Trabaja con un compañero. Uno de ustedes mira la casa en esta página mientras el otro mira la casa en el **Apéndice B.** Túrnense para describir las casas y busquen las seis diferencias.

la casa de Alberto

Cultura

Entre las atracciones turísticas de cada ciudad, es común que haya alguna casa en donde vivió *(lived)* una persona destacada para la historia o la cultura de ese país. Muchas de las casas de personas famosas son transformadas en *(are converted into)* museos. Por ejemplo, Pablo Neruda, el famoso poeta de Chile, tuvo casas en Santiago de Chile, en Valparaíso y en Isla Negra. Hoy en día todas sus casas son museos que se pueden visitar. En ellas hay muchas obras de arte y objetos que pertenecieron a *(belonged to)* Neruda.

Otra casa muy visitada es la de Ernesto "Ché" Guevara, famoso revolucionario que participó en la Revolución Cubana. Al igual que Neruda el Che vivió en varias casas que ahora lo homenajean *(pay tribute to him)*. Una de las más populares es el Museo Casa del Ché en Alta Gracia, Argentina donde vivió de niño *(as a child)*.

La siguiente es una lista de otras casas de personas famosas. Busca en Internet para decir quiénes fueron *(were)* estas personas y dónde están sus casas.

La Casa-Museo de Federico García Lorca

El Museo Casa natal de Rubén Darío

La Casa-Museo Quinta de Simón Bolívar

 Busca a un escritor colombiano en **Exploraciones del mundo hispano** en el **Apéndice A** y después investiga si tiene una casa-museo.

Casa de Pablo Neruda en Valparaíso

© Yoann Combronde/Shutterstock

Comunidad

Entrevista a una persona de un país hispanohablante acerca de su casa. ¿Qué habitaciones hay? ¿Qué hay en las habitaciones? Toma notas y luego observa qué variaciones léxicas de la página 129 usa la persona que entrevistas. ¿Notas otras variaciones? Repórtale a la clase la información más relevante.

Casa de Ernesto Guevara

© Juan José Pascual/age fotostock

Comparaciones

Una expresión común en la cultura hispana es una que se usa para dar la bienvenida a un visitante: "Está usted en su casa", o "Mi casa es su casa". Hay muchas expresiones en español que hablan de la casa. Otro ejemplo es "Candil (*lamp*) de la calle, obscuridad de su casa", una expresión que se usa para hablar de una persona que es muy amable con las personas fuera de su casa, pero no con las de su familia. Los siguientes son otros refranes (*proverbs*) que se refieren a la casa. ¿Cuál de las fotos asocias con cada refrán? ¿Por qué? ¿Qué valores reflejan? ¿Estás de acuerdo con ellos? ¿Hay equivalentes en inglés?

Casa sin hijos, higuera (*fig tree*) sin higos (*figs*).

Cuando de casa estamos lejanos, más la recordamos.

En la casa en que hay un viejo, no faltará (*lack*) un buen consejo (*advice*).

La ropa sucia (*dirty*) se lava en casa.

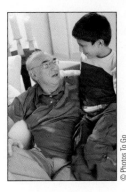   

¿Cuáles son algunos refranes en inglés que hablan de la casa? ¿Qué valores reflejan?
¿Reflejan valores semejantes o diferentes a los refranes en español?

Conexiones... a la arquitectura

Algunos de los arquitectos más famosos del mundo son españoles. Un ejemplo histórico es el de Antonio Gaudí (1852–1926) y un ejemplo moderno es el de Santiago Calatrava (1951– ...). Gaudí era un hombre muy sencillo y religioso. Su obra maestra (*masterpiece*) es la Catedral de la Sagrada Familia, en Barcelona, que todavía está en construcción. Su arquitectura es considerada modernista, pero su estilo es único en el mundo. Por otra parte está Santiago Calatrava. Aunque no es arquitecto sino (*but*) ingeniero, sus edificios se caracterizan por conjuntar (*bring together*) la ingeniería y la arquitectura. Calatrava es particularmente famoso por sus puentes (*bridges*), estaciones de trenes y estadios. ¿Qué estilo prefieres? ¿Tienes un arquitecto o un estilo arquitectónico favorito? ¿Quién o cuál?

Casa Milá en Barcelona, una obra de Gaudí

Museo diseñado por Santiago Calatrava, Valencia, España

A analizar ▶

Santiago habla con una señora sobre un apartamento que ella desea alquilarle. Después de ver el video, lee parte de su conversación y contesta las preguntas que siguen.

Santiago:	¿Cómo es el apartamento?
Señora:	Bueno, la sala es bonita y muy grande. Hay un dormitorio con una cama matrimonial y un escritorio donde puede estudiar. También hay una cocina pequeña y un cuarto de baño con ducha y lavabo.
Santiago:	¿Qué electrodomésticos hay en la cocina?
Señora:	Hay una estufa, un refrigerador y una lavadora.
Santiago:	¿Cuánto cuesta al mes?
Señora:	$750 e incluye el gas pero no el agua.
Santiago:	Y ¿cuál es la dirección?
Señora:	Está en la calle 8, número 53, cerca del hospital.

© Cengage Learning

1. Punctuation for questions is different in Spanish and English. What is the difference?
2. Identify the interrogatives (question words) in the conversation. What do all of the question words have in common?

A comprobar

Interrogatives

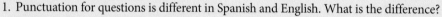

¿cómo?	how?	¿adónde?	to where?	¿quién(es)?	who?	¿cuántos(as)?	how many?
¿cuándo?	when?	¿de dónde?	from where?	¿qué?	what?	¿cuánto(a)?	how much?
¿dónde?	where!	¿por qué?	why?	¿cuál(es)?	which?		

*Notice that all question words have an accent.

1. In most questions:
- the subject is placed after the verb.
- the question word is often the first word of the question.
- it is not necessary to have a helping word such as *do* or *does*.
- it is necessary to have an inverted question mark at the beginning of the question and another question mark at the end.

interrogative + verb + subject		
¿Cuál	es	tu casa?
¿Dónde	vives	tú?

2. Prepositions (**a, con, de, en, por, para,** etc.) cannot be placed at the end of the question as is often done in English. They *must* be in front of the question word.

> **¿Con** quién vives?
> *Who (Whom) do you live with?*

3. Quién and **cuál** must agree in number with the noun that follows, and **cuánto** and **cuántos** must agree in gender.

> **¿Cuántas habitaciones tiene la casa?**
> *How many rooms does the house have?*

> **¿Quiénes son tus compañeros de casa?**
> *Who are your roommates?*

4. There are two ways to express *What?* or *Which?*

When asking *which*, use **qué** in front of a noun and **cuál** in front of a verb or with the preposition **de**.

¿Qué electrodomésticos necesitas?
What (Which) appliances do you need?

¿Cuáles son sus camas?
Which (ones) are their beds?

¿Cuál de estos apartamentos te gusta?
Which of these apartments do you like?

When asking *what*, use **cuál** with the verb **ser** with the exception of the question **¿Qué es?** *(What is it?)*. Use **qué** with all other verbs.

¿Cuál es tu número de teléfono?
What is your phone number?

¿Qué buscas en la sala?
What are you looking for in the living room?

A practicar

4.24 **La respuesta lógica** Lee las preguntas y decide cuál es la respuesta más lógica.

1. _____ ¿Cómo es la casa?
2. _____ ¿Cuántos baños hay?
3. _____ ¿Dónde está la casa?
4. _____ ¿Qué hay en la cocina?
5. _____ ¿Quién vive en la casa ahora?
6. _____ ¿Por qué venden la casa?

a. Uno.
b. Hay una estufa y un refrigerador.
c. Ella tiene un nuevo trabajo en otra ciudad.
d. Es pequeña, pero muy cómoda.
e. Una madre con sus dos hijos.
f. Está en el centro.

4.25 **¿Qué o cuál?** Decide si debes usar **¿Qué?** o **¿Cuál(es)?** para completar las preguntas.

1. ¿_____ dormitorio te gusta más?
2. ¿En _____ calle está el apartamento?
3. ¿_____ es tu casa, la casa blanca o la casa azul?
4. ¿_____ muebles hay en la sala?
5. ¿_____ son los electrodomésticos que necesitas?
6. ¿En _____ piso están los dormitorios?
7. ¿_____ de los apartamentos está más cerca?
8. ¿_____ es la dirección de la casa?

4.26 **Una conversación por teléfono** Escuchas parte de una conversación telefónica entre el señor Ruiz y Magdalena sobre un apartamento que él tiene para alquilar. Completa la conversación telefónica con las preguntas lógicas de ella. Inventa la última pregunta y la respuesta.

Señor Ruiz: ¿Bueno?
Magdalena: Buenos días. 1. ¿ _____?
Señor Ruiz: Estoy bien, gracias.
Magdalena: 2. ¿ _____?
Señor Ruiz: El apartamento está en la calle Montalvo.
Magdalena: 3. ¿ _____?
Señor Ruiz: Hay tres dormitorios.
Magdalena: 4. ¿ _____?
Señor Ruiz: Cuesta 2000 pesos al mes.
Magdalena: 5. ¿ _____?
Señor Ruiz: Usted puede visitar el apartamento hoy mismo.
Magdalena: 6. ¿...?
Señor Ruiz: _____ Bueno, adiós.

¿Bueno?

© toocanimages/Shutterstock

4.27 **Una casa** Trabaja con un compañero. Mira la foto e inventa preguntas sobre la casa y las personas que viven allí. Luego inventa respuestas para las preguntas de tu compañero.

Modelo *¿Cuántas personas viven aquí?*

Las casas en Valaparaíso, Chile, son famosas por sus colores.

4.28 **Información, por favor** Imagínate que trabajas en una oficina dónde alquilan apartamentos y necesitas completar el formulario con la información de un cliente nuevo. Debes hacerle algunas preguntas a tu compañero para completar el formulario. En donde dice preferencias, el cliente debe imaginar dos o tres características que quiere en una casa, por ejemplo **Necesita tener dos baños.** Cuando terminen, cambien de papel *(change roles)*.

Modelo Nombre
　　　　Estudiante A: *¿Cómo se llama Ud.?*
　　　　Estudiante B: *Me llamo…*

FORMULARIO PARA ALQUILAR UN APARTAMENTO	
Nombre	
Edad *(Age)*	
Dirección	
Origen	
Nombre de esposo(a)	
Número de hijos	
Trabajo	
Preferencias	

A analizar

Santiago habla con una señora sobre un apartamento que ella tiene para alquilar. Después de ver el video lee esta parte de su conversación y observa las formas del verbo **preferir**.

Santiago:	Me gustaría ver *(see)* el apartamento.
Señora:	Bueno, mi esposo y yo **preferimos** recibir a las personas interesadas durante el fin de semana. ¿Qué día **prefiere** usted, el sábado o el domingo?
Santiago:	**Prefiero** el sábado por la mañana si es posible.
Señora:	Bueno, ¿qué tal el sábado a las once?
Santiago:	¡Perfecto! Hasta el sábado.

1. Using the examples from the conversation and your knowledge of conjugating stem-changing verbs, complete the table with the verb **preferir**.

   preferir

   yo _____   nosotros(as) _____

   tú _____   vosotros(as) _____

   él, ella, usted _____   ellos, ellas, ustedes _____

2. How do the **nosotros** and **vosotros** forms of the verb differ from the other forms?

A comprobar

Stem-changing verbs e → ie and e → i

1. In **Exploraciones gramaticales 1** you learned that some verbs have changes in the stem. Notice that in the verbs below the **e** changes to **ie** and that the endings are the same as other -**ar, -er,** and -**ir** verbs.

cerrar *(to close)*

yo	cierro	nosotros(as)	cerramos
tú	cierras	vosotros(as)	cerráis
él, ella, usted	cierra	ellos, ellas, ustedes	cierran

querer *(to want)*

yo	quiero	nosotros(as)	queremos
tú	quieres	vosotros(as)	queréis
él, ella, usted	quiere	ellos, ellas, ustedes	quieren

mentir *(to lie)*

yo	miento	nosotros(as)	mentimos
tú	mientes	vosotros(as)	mentís
él, ella, usted	miente	ellos, ellas, ustedes	mienten

The verbs listed below are also **e → ie** stem-changing verbs.

comenzar (a)	*to begin (to do something)*
nevar	*to snow*
empezar (a)	*to begin (to do something)*
pensar	*to think*
encender	*to turn on*
perder	*to lose*
entender	*to understand*
preferir	*to prefer*

2. **Pensar en** means *to think about* and **pensar de** means *to think of* (opinion). **Pensar** + an infinitive means *to plan to do something.*

> Ella **piensa** mucho **en** sus hijos.
> *She thinks about her children a lot.*

> ¿Qué **piensas de** la casa?
> *What do you think of the house?*

> Yo **pienso** buscar un apartamento.
> *I plan to look for an apartment.*

3. There are some **-ir** verbs in which the **e** in the stem changes to **i**. As with the **e → ie** stem-changing verbs, these verbs also change in all forms except **nosotros** and **vosotros,** and the endings are the same as regular **-ir** verbs.

repetir (*to repeat*)

yo	repito	nosotros(as)	repetimos
tú	repites	vosotros(as)	repetís
él, ella, usted	repite	ellos, ellas, ustedes	repiten

The verbs listed below are **e → i** stem-changing verbs like **repetir.**

competir	*to compete*	servir	*to serve*
pedir	*to ask for*	sonreír	*to smile*
reír	*to laugh*		

4. Notice that the verb **reír** requires an accent mark on the **i** when it is conjugated. The same rule applies for **sonreír.**

reír (*to laugh*)

yo	**río**	nosotros(as)	**reímos**
tú	**ríes**	vosotros(as)	**reís**
él, ella, usted	**ríe**	ellos, ellas, ustedes	**ríen**

5. **Pedir** means *to ask for (something)* and **preguntar** means *to ask (a question).* The preposition *for* is part of the verb **pedir,** so you should not use **por** or **para** with it.

> Los niños **piden** permiso de sus padres.
> *Children ask permission from their parents.*

> Él **pregunta** si van a vender su casa.
> *He is asking if they are going to sell their house.*

A practicar

4.29 **En la tienda de muebles** Todos quieren comprar algo nuevo. ¿Para qué habitación son los objetos que quieren comprar?

1. Mi esposo y yo queremos comprar una cama.
2. Raúl quiere comprar un auto.
3. Carlota y Esteban quieren comprar una mesa con cuatro sillas.
4. Jimena quiere comprar un sofá.
5. Yo quiero comprar un horno de microondas.

4.30 **¿Qué piensan hacer más tarde?** Usando el verbo **pensar,** explica qué piensan hacer las personas, cuándo y dónde.

Modelo mi hermana
Mi hermana piensa leer un libro en el patio a las dos y media.

1. yo

2. mi esposa

3. mis hijos

4. mi esposa y yo

5. mi abuelo

6. Y tú ¿qué piensas hacer más tarde?

© Cengage Learning

4.31 **Somos iguales** Marca cuatro de las siguientes oraciones que sean ciertas *(are true)* para ti. Después, busca cuatro diferentes compañeros para quienes una de las oraciones también sea cierta.

__ Sirvo la comida en mi casa.

__ Quiero viajar a otro país.

__ Sonrío en las fotos.

__ No miento.

__ Enciendo la radio cuando estudio.

__ Normalmente empiezo a estudiar después de *(after)* las ocho de la noche.

__ A veces *(Sometimes)* pierdo la tarea.

__ Pienso comer en un restaurante hoy.

__ Entiendo otra lengua.

__ Pido ayuda con la tarea de español.

4.32 **Entrevista** Con un compañero túrnense para entrevistarse con las siguientes preguntas.

Los estudios

1. ¿Dónde prefieres estudiar?

2. Normalmente ¿a qué hora empiezas a estudiar?

3. ¿Entiendes al profesor de español?

4. ¿A veces pides ayuda con la tarea de español? ¿A quién?

El tiempo libre

5. ¿Enciendes la tele en la noche? ¿Qué te gusta mirar?

6. ¿Compites en un deporte? ¿Cuál?

7. ¿Qué piensas hacer este fin de semana?

8. ¿Quieres viajar en el verano? ¿Adónde?

¿Adónde quieres viajar?

herjua/Shutterstock

Lectura

Antes de leer

¿Cómo crees que van a ser las casas en el futuro?

A leer

Soluciones a la vivienda

Debido a las diferencias en el clima y la cultura de los diferentes países, las viviendas pueden ser muy diferentes. A continuación aparecen algunos ejemplos.

Los palafitos

Los palafitos (casas hechas sobre pilares) se pueden ver en países como Argentina, Chile, Colombia, Perú y Venezuela. Son comunes en zonas **fluviales** *of rivers* de corrientes tranquilas, donde el nivel del agua varía notablemente durante el año. En el caso de Venezuela, los palafitos son unas de las viviendas más antiguas del país. De hecho, el nombre de este país viene del

Chile

nombre Venecia, ya que el descubridor Alonso de Ojeda observó este tipo de casa a su llegada a la región, en 1499.

Las columnas sobre las que se construyen las casas generalmente están hechas de **madera,** *wood* aunque en algunos lugares se usan ahora materiales sintéticos prefabricados y **acero,** *steel/life* para alargar la **vida** de las casas. La arquitectura de estas casas permite habitar regiones que de otra forma serían inhabitables. Sin embargo, existen algunas desventajas, como problemas de **salud** *health* a causa de la contaminación del agua o la humedad.

La ruca mapuche

Los mapuches son los habitantes originales del territorio que hoy es Chile. La Ruca es la construcción más importante dentro de la arquitectura mapuche y está fabricada con materiales de la región. Las rucas tradicionales son **redondas** *round* u ovaladas, aunque también pueden ser rectangulares. Son muy grandes, pero tienen solo una habitación. A los

Ruca en Chile

lados están las camas y provisiones y en el centro se pone un fogón para cocinar; algunos utensilios **cuelgan del techo.** En la actualidad se están **desarrollando** programas de etno-turismo que permitirán conocer la cultura mapuche conviviendo y **hospedándose** con ellos.

hang from the ceiling
developing

lodging

Las islas flotantes de los uros
Este tipo de vivienda es única de los uros, un grupo étnico del Perú que vive en el lago Titicaca. Puede decirse que estas casas son una combinación de palafitos y rucas. Desde hace cientos de años los uros viven en islas flotantes construidas a base de una planta de la región (la totora). Encima de las islas están sus casas, una especie de cabañas similares a las rucas mapuches (con una habitación solamente), pero mucho más pequeñas. Estas viviendas también se construyen con la totora. Sin embargo, los uros cocinan fuera de sus casas para **evitar incendios.** Una desventaja de este tipo de casa es la alta humedad, la cual ocasiona problemas de reumas entre la población.

to avoid fires

La casa cueva
Una casa **cueva** es una vivienda que tiene al menos una parte en la **tierra** o en una estructura natural, como una cueva. Su mayor ventaja es su carácter ecológico y su temperatura agradable: fresca en el verano y cálida en el invierno. Gracias a sus características, **ahorra** energía y protege mejor de vientos o lluvias fuertes. Las casas cueva son muy flexibles y pueden adaptarse a las necesidades de familias diferentes. Mucha gente piensa que son viviendas **obscuras,** pero no es verdad: se distinguen por su luminosidad. Las casas cueva nos acercan al **medio ambiente** proporcionando al mismo tiempo todas las comodidades de la vida moderna.

cave
land

saves

dark
environment

En España las casas cueva se utilizan desde hace **miles** de años. Probablemente las más famosas sean las que están cerca de la ciudad de Granada, que **hoy en día** funcionan como hoteles. La mayor **desventaja** de estas viviendas es que requieren de más espacio para **albergar** a una familia, a diferencia de otras soluciones como los edificios de apartamentos.

thousands

nowadays/disadvantage
to house

Comprensión

Decide si las oraciones son ciertas o falsas. Corrige las oraciones falsas.

1. Gracias a los palafitos, algunas personas pueden vivir en zonas fluviales.
2. Las rucas son un tipo de vivienda que se usa en el lago Titicaca.
3. En las rucas hay múltiples habitaciones.
4. La totora es la casa de los uros.
5. Las casas cueva son viviendas obscuras.
6. Las casas cueva ahorran energía.

Después de leer

¿Te gustaría *(Would you like)* vivir en una de las casas en el artículo? ¿Cuál? ¿Por qué?

Redacción

You are going to write an email to a new friend in which you tell him or her about where you live. One approach to descriptive writing is to begin with a general idea and to then become more specific. That is what you will do in this email. In the first paragraph, you will discuss the town or city where you live; in the second paragraph you will describe your home in general, and in the last paragraph you will discuss your favorite room.

Paso 1 Jot down as many adjectives as you can think of that you would use to describe the town or city where you live. Write a list of the things your town or city has to offer: businesses, museums, etc.

Paso 2 Jot down as many phrases as you can about your home in general. Think about the following questions: Do you live in an apartment or a house? Whom do you live with? How would you describe your home (color, big, old, comfortable, etc.)? What rooms does it have?

Paso 3 Decide which room you like best. Jot down as many phrases as you can about that room. Think about the following questions: Why is it your favorite room? What items do you like in that room? How much time do you spend there? What do you do there?

Paso 4 After your greeting, begin your first paragraph by telling where you live. Then develop the paragraph in which you describe your city or town using the ideas you generated in **Paso 1.**

Paso 5 Write a transition sentence in which you tell where your home is located, such as the street you live on or what you live near. Then, develop the rest of the paragraph in which you describe your home using the information you generated in **Paso 2.**

Paso 6 Begin your third paragraph with a transition sentence that connects the second paragraph with the new idea to be discussed (your favorite room).

> **Modelo** *Hay muchas habitaciones en mi casa, pero mi habitación favorita es la sala.*

Paso 7 Develop the rest of the paragraph using the ideas you generated in **Paso 3.** Be sure to have a concluding statement at the end of the third paragraph. At the end of your email, ask your new friend two or three questions about where he/she lives.

Paso 8 Edit your essay:

1. In each paragraph, do all of your sentences support the topic sentence?
2. Are your paragraphs logically organized or do you skip from one idea to the next?
3. Are there any short sentences you can combine by using **y** or **pero**?
4. Are there any spelling errors?
5. Do adjectives agree with the objects they describe?
6. Do verbs agree with their subjects?

En vivo

Entrando en materia

¿Qué información hay en la sección de anuncios para apartamentos y casas en el periódico (*newspaper*)?

Casas en venta

Estos son anuncios para unas casas en venta en Ponce, Puerto Rico.

URBANIZACIÓN COLINAS DEL VALLE

CASAS EN VENTA
En una de las mejores zonas de Ponce, cerca de parques y un centro comercial

Modelo Bugambilia
- 3 habitaciones
- 2 baños y medio
- cocina integral
- sala-comedor amplia
- acabados de lujo
- estacionamiento cubierto para un auto

Modelo Rosal
- 4 habitaciones
- 2 baños
- cocina con desayunador
- sala
- comedor
- acabados de lujo
- terraza
- estacionamiento para un auto

Todo lo que necesita para vivir cómodamente.

Visite nuestras casas modelos todos los días de 9:00 A.M. a 9:00 P.M.

© Cengage Learning

Comprensión

1. ¿Qué crees que es un "medio baño"?
2. ¿Qué piensas que significa "estacionamiento cubierto"?
3. ¿Cuál de las dos casas prefieres? ¿Por qué?

Más allá

Imagina que encuentras el anuncio de tu casa ideal en el periódico. Escribe el anuncio incluyendo dónde está y la lista de todo lo que tiene la casa. Comparte tu anuncio en Share It! y lee los anuncios de tus compañeros. ¿Irías a ver *(Would you go to see)* una de las casas de los anuncios?

La arquitectura ▶

¡Manos a la obra!

Vocabulario

Sustantivos

la calefacción central	*central heat*
los cimientos	*foundation*
el (la) dueño(a)	*owner*
la entrada	*entrance*
la fecha de inicio	*starting date*
la finalización	*completion*
el frente	*façade*
la grúa	*crane*
el ladrillo	*brick*
la maqueta	*scale model*
el plano	*blueprint*

Adjetivos

apurado(a)	*in a hurry*
construido(a)	*built*
creativo(a)	*creative*
preparado(a)	*ready, prepared*
retrasado(a)	*late*

Verbos

cavar	*to dig*
conectar	*to connect*
demoler	*to demolish*
diseñar	*to design*
instalar	*to install*
construir	*to built*

Frases útiles

Con vista a...
With a view to . . .

Les presento el nuevo proyecto.
I'm pleased to introduce the new project.

¿Cuántos pisos tiene el edificio?
How many stories are in the building?

El edificio tiene cien unidades.
The building has one hundred units.

Estas son las dimensiones.
These are the dimensions.

Usamos materiales de primera calidad.
We use top-quality materials.

¡Manos a la obra!
Let's get to work!

DATOS IMPORTANTES

Educación: Estudios universitarios completos en arquitectura; Experiencia en compañías constructoras; Capacidad de trabajo en equipo

Salario: Entre $100 000 y $200 000, dependiendo de la responsabilidad del proyecto de construcción

Dónde se trabaja: Compañías constructoras, Departamento de Obras Públicas del gobierno, contratistas, consultorías

---

Vocabulario nuevo Completa las oraciones con la palabra apropiada de vocabulario.

1. Si vives en un clima frío es necesario tener _____.

2. _____ es donde está la puerta de la casa.

3. _____ es un modelo en tres dimensiones.

4. Es necesario ser _____ para diseñar una casa.

5. Estamos _____ y no vamos a completar la construcción a tiempo *(on time)*.

Briana Vásquez, Arquitecta

Briana Vásquez es arquitecta y trabaja para una importante compañía constructora. Ella es responsable de la obra de construcción de edificios de apartamentos. También debe comunicarse con los dueños del edificio. En el video vas a ver a la arquitecta Vásquez mientras habla con uno de los dueños.

Antes de ver

Los arquitectos desarrollan *(develop)* los proyectos de construcción. Luego supervisan a los trabajadores de la construcción para realizar los planos a la perfección.

1. ¿En qué tipo de proyectos trabaja un arquitecto?
2. Imagínate que quieres construir un edificio. ¿Qué preguntas le haces al arquitecto?

Comprensión

1. ¿Qué tipo de apartamentos quiere ofrecer el Sr. Sierra?

2. ¿Qué vista tienen los apartamentos de tres habitaciones?

3. ¿Cómo son los apartamentos de dos habitaciones?

4. ¿Cuántos pisos va a tener el edificio?

5. ¿Qué va a estar al lado de la entrada principal del edificio?

6. ¿Cuándo es la fecha de finalización de la construcción?

Después de ver

En grupos pequeños, representen una reunión entre un arquitecto asociado, un trabajador que es el jefe de construcción y un dueño. El dueño piensa construir un edificio de apartamentos. Hagan un diálogo entre las tres personas. Deben explicarle al arquitecto lo que quieren tener en su apartamento. El arquitecto puede hacer preguntas específicas.

4.33 **En casa** Completa el párrafo con la forma apropiada del verbo entre paréntesis.

Toda la familia (**1.**) _____ (estar) en casa hoy. Mi esposa y yo (**2.**) _____
(estar) en la cocina. Nosotros siempre (**3.**) _____ (almorzar) a esta hora, y hoy
yo (**4.**) _____ (pensar) preparar unos sándwiches. Los niños (**5.**) _____
(estar) en casa también. Ellos no (**6.**) _____ (poder) jugar en el jardín porque
(**7.**) _____ (llover) hoy. Vicente (**8.**) _____ (dormir) en su habitación,
y Marisa (**9.**) _____ (jugar) unos videojuegos en la sala. Después de *(After)*
comer, mis hijos (**10.**) _____ (querer) ir al cine con sus amigos. Mi esposa y yo
(**11.**) _____ (preferir) mirar una película aquí en casa.

4.34 **En tu salón de clase** Usando las preposiciones, identifica donde están las
personas y objetos en tu salón de clase.

Modelo al lado de
    La pizarra está al lado de la ventana.

1. enfrente de
2. cerca de
3. encima de
4. a la derecha de
5. dentro de
6. debajo de
7. entre
8. detrás de

La pizarra está cerca de la ventana.

4.35 **Comprensión de lectura** Imagínate que eres profesor y tienes que escribir
cinco preguntas de comprensión para los estudiantes sobre este párrafo. ¡**OJO**! Las
respuestas a las preguntas deben estar en el párrafo.

Soy Rómulo y vivo en Montevideo, Uruguay.
Vivo en un apartamento en el centro de
la ciudad con mi amigo Pablo. Nuestro
apartamento no es muy grande pero es
cómodo. Tiene dos dormitorios y un baño.
También tiene una sala pequeña donde Pablo
y yo miramos la tele. Mi habitación favorita es
mi dormitorio. Allí *(there)* me gusta escuchar
música y leer.

Me gusta leer en mi dormitorio.

4.36 **¡Adivina dónde estoy!** Vas a trabajar con un compañero. Uno de ustedes debe imaginar que está en un lugar en la casa o en la ciudad. El otro debe hacer hasta *(up to)* diez preguntas para adivinar *(to guess)* dónde está, pero la respuesta debe ser solo **sí** o **no.** Túrnense para contestar.

Modelo | Estudiante 1: *¡Adivina dónde estoy!* | Estudiante 2: *¿Hay libros y mesas?*
| Estudiante 2: *¿Comes en este lugar?* | Estudiante 1: *Sí.*
| Estudiante 1: *No.* | Estudiante 1: *¿Estás en la biblioteca?*
| | Estudiante 2: *Sí.*

4.37 **Seis diferencias** Trabaja con un compañero. Uno mira el dibujo aquí y el otro mira el dibujo en el **Apéndice B.** Túrnense para describirlos y buscar seis diferencias.

© Cengage Learning

4.38 **Buscando un apartamento** Con un compañero van a decidir dónde quieren vivir.

Paso 1 Escribe una lista de lo que es importante para ti a la hora de decidir dónde quieres vivir. Luego mira los anuncios y decide cuál de los apartamentos prefieres.

Paso 2 Tu compañero y tú necesitan escoger *(choose)* uno de los apartamentos. Convence a tu compañero de que tu selección es donde deben vivir.

Paso 3 Tomen una decisión y compártenla *(share it)* con la clase. Deben explicar por qué seleccionaron el apartamento.

Apartamento amueblado, un dormitorio grande con dos camas, baño con bañera y ducha, sala-comedor, cocina con lavadora, en la línea del autobús, $750 al mes	Cerca de la universidad, apartamento con dos dormitorios, baño con ducha, medio baño, sala amplia, cocina con espacio para comer, $950 al mes	Apartamento en tercer piso con balcón, dos dormitorios, baño con ducha, sala, comedor, cocina con lavaplatos, aire acondicionado, $875 al mes	Apartamento en planta baja, tres dormitorios, dos baños con ducha, sala-comedor, acceso a piscina y gimnasio, $1050 al mes	Apartamento muy céntrico con acceso a restaurantes y tiendas, dos dormitorios, un baño con bañera, sala, cocina grande, espacio reservado para un coche, $900 al mes

🔊 Vocabulario 1
1-26

Los lugares	**Places**
el aeropuerto	*airport*
el banco	*bank*
el bar	*bar*
el café	*cafe*
la calle	*street*
el centro comercial	*mall, shopping center*
el cine	*movie theater*
el club	*club*
el correo	*post office*
la discoteca	*nightclub*
el edificio	*building*
la escuela	*school*
la farmacia	*pharmacy*
el hospital	*hospital*
el hotel	*hotel*
la iglesia	*church*

el mercado	*market*
la mezquita	*mosque*
el museo	*museum*
el negocio	*business*
la oficina	*office*
el parque	*park*
la piscina	*swimming pool*
la playa	*beach*
la plaza	*city square*
el restaurante	*restaurant*
la sinagoga	*synagogue*
el supermercado	*supermarket*
el teatro	*theater*
el templo	*temple*
la tienda	*store*
el zoológico	*zoo*

Los verbos

almorzar (ue)	*to have lunch*
costar (ue)	*to cost*
depositar	*to deposit*
devolver (ue)	*to return (something)*
dormir (ue)	*to sleep*
encontrar (ue)	*to find*
estar	*to be*

jugar (ue)	*to play*
llover (ue)	*to rain*
morir (ue)	*to die*
poder (ue)	*to be able to*
recordar (ue)	*to remember*
rezar	*to pray*
soñar (ue) (con)	*to dream (about)*
volver (ue)	*to come back*

Palabras adicionales

la carta	*letter*
el dinero	*money*

el paquete	*package*
la película	*movie*

Las preposiciones

a la derecha de	*to the right of*
al lado de	*beside, next to*
a la izquierda de	*to the left of*
cerca de	*near*
debajo de	*under*
dentro de	*inside*
detrás de	*behind*

en	*in, on, at*
encima de	*on top of*
enfrente de	*in front of*
entre	*between*
fuera de	*outside*
lejos de	*far from*

Diccionario personal

_____

_____

◀))) Vocabulario 2
1-27

Habitaciones de la casa

el baño	bathroom		el dormitorio	bedroom
la cochera	garage		el jardín	garden
la cocina	kitchen		el patio	patio
el comedor	dining room		la sala	living room

Muebles, utensilios y aparatos electrodomésticos

la alfombra	carpet		el (horno de) microondas	microwave (oven)
el armario	closet, armoire		el inodoro	toilet
la bañera	bathtub		la lámpara	lamp
la cafetera	coffee maker		el lavabo	bathroom sink
la cama	bed		la lavadora	washer
las cortinas	curtains		el lavaplatos	dishwasher
el cuadro	painting, picture		la mesita	coffee table
la ducha	shower		las plantas	plants
el espejo	mirror		el refrigerador	refrigerator
la estufa	stove		la secadora	dryer
la flor	flower		el sillón	armchair
el fregadero	kitchen sink		el sofá	couch
el horno	oven			

Los verbos

alquilar	to rent		nevar (ie)	to snow
cerrar (ie)	to close		pedir (i)	to ask for
comenzar (ie) (a)	to begin (to do something)		pensar (ie)	to think
			perder (ie)	to lose
competir (i)	to compete		preferir (ie)	to prefer
empezar (ie) (a)	to begin (to do something)		reír (i)	to laugh
			repetir (i)	to repeat
encender (ie)	to turn on		querer (ie)	to want
entender (ie)	to understand		servir (i)	to serve
mentir (ie)	to lie		sonreír (i)	to smile

Palabras adicionales

el apartamento	apartment		el mueble	furniture
la dirección	address		la planta baja	ground floor
la habitación	room		el (primer) piso	(first) floor

Palabras interrogativas

¿adónde?	to where?		¿de dónde?	from where?
¿cómo?	how?		¿dónde?	where?
¿cuál(es)?	which?		¿por qué?	why?
¿cuándo?	when?		¿qué?	what?
¿cuánto(a)?	how much?		¿quién(es)?	who?
¿cuántos(as)?	how many?			

Juan Ramón Jiménez:

Biografía

Juan Ramón Jiménez (1881–1958) nace (*born*) en Moguer, España. Estudia derecho (*law*) en la Universidad de Sevilla, pero decide no practicar. Con la ayuda del poeta modernista Rubén Darío, Jiménez publica su primer libro en 1900, a la edad (*age*) de 10 años. Durante su carrera trabaja como crítico literario y editor de varias revistas (*magazines*) literarias y pasa (*spends*) tiempo en diferentes países como Francia, Portugal y Estados Unidos. Cuando empieza la Guerra (*War*) Civil, viaja a las Américas. Vive en Cuba, los Estados Unidos y más tarde en Puerto Rico donde muere en 1958. Su poesía es muy visual, y el verde y el amarillo son los colores dominantes.

Antes de leer

1. ¿Qué colores asocias con el otoño?
2. Examina el poema. ¿Qué palabras (*words*) se refieren a elementos de la naturaleza?

Departure

path/gold/blackbirds

Ida* de otoño

Por un **camino** de **oro** van los **mirlos**... ¿Adónde?
Por un camino de oro van las rosas... ¿Adónde?
Por un camino de oro voy...
¿Adónde, otoño? ¿Adónde, pájaros y flores?

Después de leer

A. Comprensión

1. ¿Qué color es dominante en el poema?
2. ¿Qué acción hay en el poema?
3. ¿Qué quiere saber (*to know*) la voz poética?
4. Si las estaciones del año son símbolos para las fases de la vida ¿qué representan las cuatro estaciones?

B. Conversemos

 Habla con un compañero para compartir (*share*) sus respuestas a las preguntas.

1. ¿Qué colores asocian con el verano? ¿y con la primavera y el invierno?
2. ¿Cuál es su estación favorita? ¿Por qué?

Antes de leer

1. ¿Con qué estación se asocian las canciones *(songs)* de los pájaros?

2. ¿Adónde van los pájaros en el invierno?

Canción de invierno

Cantan. Cantan.
¿Dónde cantan los pájaros que cantan?

It has rained/branches **Ha llovido**. Aún las **ramas**
without/leaves están **sin hojas** nuevas. Cantan. Cantan
los pájaros. ¿En dónde cantan
los pájaros que cantan?

cages No tengo pájaros en **jaulas**.
No hay niños que los vendan. Cantan.
valley/Nothing El **valle** está muy lejos. **Nada**...

know Yo no **sé** dónde cantan
los pájaros-cantan, cantan-
los pájaros que cantan.

© Aleksey Stemmer/Shutterstock

Juan Ramón Jiménez, "Canción de Invierno," *Juan Ramón Jiménez para niños y niñas—y otros seres curiosos*. Ediciones de la Torre, 2010.
By permission of the Herederos de Juan Ramón Jiménez.

Después de leer

A. Comprensión

1. ¿Piensas qué la voz poética escucha las canciones de los pájaros? ¿Por qué?

2. ¿Qué piensas que representan los pájaros?

3. La voz poética pregunta dónde cantan los pájaros que cantan. ¿Dónde están los pájaros que cantan?

4. El poema es repetitivo. ¿Qué efecto creen que el autor quiere transmitir con la repetición?

5. ¿Cuál es el tono del poema?

B. Conversemos

 Habla con un compañero para compartir sus respuestas a las siguientes preguntas.

1. ¿Te gusta el poema? ¿Por qué?

2. ¿Qué estación crees que inspira más a los poetas? ¿Por qué?

3. ¿Conoces *(Do you know)* un poema en inglés o en español sobre una estación? ¿Cuál?

Investiguemos la literatura: El tono

The tone of a work refers to the attitude that a writer communicates toward a particular subject through the work. It can be playful, formal, angry, loving, etc. You can often identify the tone of a work by paying attention to the author's word choice. Does the author use words or expressions that are positive, negative, or neutral?

Learning Strategy

Guess intelligently

When you are listening to audio recordings or your instructor, or when watching a video, make intelligent guesses as to the meaning of words you do not know. Use context, intonation, and if possible, visual clues such as gestures, facial expressions and images to help you figure out the meaning of words.

In this chapter you will learn how to:

- Describe your feelings, emotions, and physical states
- Talk about ongoing actions
- Discuss abilities needed for certain jobs and professions

¿Estás feliz en el trabajo?

© Aaron Mccoy/Getty Images

Laura trabaja en el Café Simón. Es un lugar muy popular en el centro histórico de la ciudad. ¿Cómo están las personas en el café?

Los estados de ánimo

estar alegre	to be happy	**estar divertido(a)**	to be entertained, to be in a good mood	**estar frustrado(a)**	to be frustrated
estar celoso(a)	to be jealous			**estar interesado(a)**	to be interested
estar contento(a)	to be happy, to be content			**estar ocupado(a)**	to be busy
		estar enfermo(a)	to be sick	**estar sano(a)**	to be healthy
estar deprimido(a)	to be depressed	**estar equivocado(a)**	to be wrong	**estar seguro(a)**	to be sure
		estar feliz	to be happy		

A practicar

5.1 **Escucha y responde** Escucha los adjetivos de emoción. Indica con el pulgar hacia arriba *(thumbs up)* si es una emoción positiva o con el pulgar hacia abajo *(thumbs down)* si es una emoción negativa.

1-28

5.2 **¿Lógica o ilógica?** Indica si las siguientes oraciones son lógicas o ilógicas.

1. Vamos a tener un examen difícil y estamos felices.
2. Tus amigos te preparan una fiesta sorpresa y estás celoso.
3. Nuestro hijo está muy enfermo. Estamos preocupados.
4. Después de correr 15 kilómetros estás cansado.
5. Estás sano porque tienes una F en matemáticas.

5.3 **¿Cómo estás?** Con un compañero, túrnense para expresar sus reacciones ante estas situaciones.

Modelo Tienes tres exámenes y recibes una A en todos.
Estudiante 1: *¡Estoy contento! ¿Y tú?*
Estudiante 2: *¡Yo estoy sorprendido!*

1. Vas de vacaciones a las islas Canarias y pierdes tu pasaporte.
2. Tú y tu novio se casan (*get married*) hoy.
3. Recibes un kilo de chocolates y los comes todos en un día.
4. Necesitas trabajar pero no puedes encontrar un trabajo.
5. Llegas tarde al aeropuerto y pierdes tu vuelo (*flight*).
6. Hay una persona que no conoces (*that you don't know*) en la sala de tu casa.

Estamos enamorados.

5.4 **Asociaciones** Habla con un compañero para explicar la emoción que asocian con las situaciones de la lista. Explica por qué.

Modelo Estoy en la clase de matemáticas.
Estoy frustrado porque no comprendo los problemas de matemáticas. / Estoy feliz porque me gustan las matemáticas.

1. Es lunes.
2. Es verano.
3. Estoy en la clase de historia.
4. Tengo un examen final.
5. Es el Día de San Valentín.
6. Llueve.
7. Estoy en el templo.
8. Estoy en la universidad.

5.5 **¿Y tú?** Con un compañero, túrnense para completar las oraciones con mucha información. En la última (*last*) oración, ustedes deciden el estado de ánimo.

Modelo Cuando estoy cansado yo... ¿y tú?
Estudiante 1: *Cuando estoy cansada, yo duermo en mi sofá con mi gato ¿y tú?*
Estudiante 2: *Yo también duermo, pero prefiero tomar una siesta en mi cama.*

1. Cuando estoy enamorado, yo... ¿y tú?
2. Cuando estoy triste, yo... ¿y tú?
3. Cuando estoy aburrido, yo... ¿y tú?
4. Cuando estoy enojado, yo... ¿y tú?
5. Cuando estoy enfermo, yo... ¿y tú?
6. Cuando estoy _____ ¿? _____ , yo... ¿y tú?

5.6 **Los chismes (gossip)** Imagina que tu compañero y tú están intercambiando información sobre cómo están todos sus amigos. Pregúntense para completar la información. Uno de ustedes va a ver la información en esta página, y el otro en el **Apéndice B**. **¡OJO!** ¡Presta atención a la concordancia (*agreement*)!

Modelo Estudiante 1: *¿Cómo está Ramira?*
Estudiante 2: *Está contenta.*
Estudiante 1: *¿Por qué?*
Estudiante 2: *Porque va a ir de vacaciones a Venezuela.*

Nombre	¿Cómo está(n)?	¿Por qué?
Ramira	contento	Va a ir de vacaciones a Venezuela.
Emanuel y Arturo	ocupado	
Gisela	enojado	Sus amigas no hablan con ella.
Alex		Su hijo es agresivo con otros niños de su escuela.
Karina e Iliana		
Gerardo	preocupado	
Javier y Manuel		No tienen actividades para el fin de semana.

Cultura

Emociones fuertes como la tristeza, la depresión o la alegría pueden resultar en obras *(works)* de arte en las manos *(in the hands)* de una artista talentosa como la pintora mexicana Frida Kahlo (1907–1954). Kahlo es famosa por sus autorretratos *(self-portraits),* los que muestran su sufrimiento. Cuando tenía 17 años, sufrió un accidente en un tranvía *(streetcar)* y se fracturó la espina dorsal *(spinal cord)* y varios huesos *(bones).* Como resultado, pasó mucho tiempo en el hospital, nunca pudo tener hijos y sufrió de dolor *(pain)* por el resto de su vida *(life).*

Observa el cuadro de Frida Kahlo. ¿Qué emociones produce? ¿Por qué? ¿Qué colores usa?

Pensando en la muerte, de Frida Kahlo

Muchas de las obras del pintor ecuatoriano Osvaldo Guayasamín también muestran sufrimiento. Investiga en Internet obras de Osvaldo Guayasamín. Sube a Share It! una pintura que te gusta y explica: ¿Cómo se llama la pintura? ¿Qué emociones produce?

Comunidad

Entrevista a una persona de un país hispanohablante. Pregúntale quién es su artista favorito, de dónde es y cómo son sus pinturas. Después repórtale la información a la clase.

¿Quién es tu artista favorito?

Busca una pintura del artista favorito de la persona que entrevistaste. Sube la pintura a Share it! y explica: **¿Quién es el artista? ¿Qué hay en la pintura? ¿Qué emociones produce? ¿Cuál es el mensaje de la pintura? ¿Te gusta?**

Comparaciones

Con un compañero, hagan *(make)* una lista de cinco supersticiones populares en la cultura de ustedes. Después lean la lista de supersticiones del mundo hispano. ¿Hay supersticiones similares a las que mencionaron?

1. Pasar por debajo de una escalera *(ladder)* trae mala suerte.
2. Abrir un paraguas dentro de una casa trae mala suerte.
3. Romper un espejo trae siete años de mala suerte.
4. Cruzarse con un gato negro trae mala suerte.
5. Sentir comezón *(itch)* en la mano es señal de que se va a recibir dinero.
6. Para tener un buen año con el dinero, uno debe usar calzoncillos *(underwear)* amarillos para recibir el año nuevo.

Si encontraste *(If you found)* supersticiones parecidas *(similar)*, ¿cómo puedes explicar la similitud?

Conexiones... a la literatura

Generalmente, ¿qué emociones puede provocar la poesía? Piensa en un poema que conoces. ¿Qué emociones te provoca?

Alfonsina Storni (1892–1938), poeta argentina, fue *(was)* la primera mujer reconocida entre los grandes escritores de su época. Uno de los temas más frecuentes en sus poemas es el feminismo.

El siguiente es un poema en el cual una mujer habla con el hombre con quien tiene una relación.

Hombre pequeñito

Hombre pequeñito, hombre pequeñito,
Suelta a tu canario que quiere **volar**...   *release / to fly*
Yo soy el canario, hombre pequeñito,
Déjame saltar.   *Let me jump*

Estuve en tu **jaula**, hombre pequeñito,   *cage*
Hombre pequeñito que jaula me das.
Digo pequeñito porque no me entiendes,   *I say*
Ni me entenderás.

Tampoco te entiendo, pero mientras tanto
Ábreme la jaula que quiero escapar;
Hombre pequeñito, **te amé** media hora,   *I loved you*
No me pidas más.

INVESTIGUEMOS LA MÚSICA

Listen to the song "La Negra Tomasa" by Los Caifanes. What emotions are mentioned in the song?

¿Qué emoción te produce este poema? Da ejemplos concretos de las palabras o frases que producen la emoción.

Busca el nombre de otro poeta argentino y aprende más sobre Argentina en **Exploraciones del mundo hispano** en el **Apéndice A.**

A analizar ▶

Mira el video. Después lee parte de la conversación entre Camila y Vanesa y observa los verbos en negritas. Luego contesta las preguntas que siguen.

> Vanesa: ¡Hola Camila! ¿Cómo estás?
>
> Camila: Bien, pero estoy muy ocupada hoy.
>
> Vanesa: ¿Por qué? ¿Qué **estás haciendo**?
>
> Camila: Mis suegros van a llegar de Colombia esta noche y **estoy preparando** comida. Afortunadamente no tengo que limpiar la casa. Rodrigo está en casa hoy y **está limpiando** la sala y los baños.
>
> Vanesa: ¿Y los niños?
>
> Camila: **Están escribiendo** su tarea... Bueno, ¿y cómo estás tú, Vanesa?
>
> Vanesa: ¡Estoy muy feliz!

© Cengage Learning

1. How are the verbs in bold formed?

2. In **Capítulo 4,** you learned to use the verb **estar** to indicate location. Look at the conversation again. In what other two ways is the verb **estar** used here?

A comprobar

Estar with adjectives and the present progressive

1. Remember that **estar** is an irregular verb:

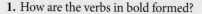

estar *(to be)*			
yo	**estoy**	nosotros	**estamos**
tú	**estas**	vosotros	**estáis**
él, ella, usted	**está**	ellos, ellas, ustedes	**están**

2. In addition to indicating location as you learned in **Capítulo 4,** the verb **estar** is also used to express an emotional, mental, or physical condition.

   Mis padres están felices.
   *My parents **are** happy.*

   Yo estoy cansado hoy.
   *I **am** tired today.*

   Nosotros estamos muy ocupados.
   *We **are** very busy.*

3. The verb **estar** is also used with present participles to form the present progressive. The present progressive is used to describe actions in progress at the moment.

To form the present participle, add **-ando** (**-ar** verbs) or **-iendo** (**-er** and **-ir** verbs) to the stem of the verb.

> hablar → habl**ando**
> comer → com**iendo**
> vivir → viv**iendo**

El profesor **está hablando** con Tito ahora.
*The professor **is talking** to Tito now.*

4. The present participle of the verb **ir** is **yendo.** However, it is much more common to use the present tense of the verb when the action is in progress.

   Voy a la iglesia. / **Estoy yendo** a la iglesia.
   I'm going to church.

You will recall from **Capítulo 4** that to say where someone is going in the future, it is necessary to use the verb **ir** in the present tense or to use the structure **ir + a + infinitive.**

   Vamos (a ir) a una fiesta mañana.
   *We **are going (to go)** to a party tomorrow.*

5. When the stem of an **-er** or an **-ir** verb ends in a vowel, **-yendo** is used instead of **-iendo**.

> leer – le**yendo**   oír *(to hear)* – o**yendo**
> traer *(to bring)* – tra**yendo**

6. Stem changing **-ir** verbs have an irregular present participle. An **e** in the stem becomes an **i**, and an **o** in the stem becomes a **u**.

> mentir – m**i**ntiendo   pedir – p**i**diendo
> repetir – rep**i**tiendo   servir – s**i**rviendo
> dormir – d**u**rmiendo   morir – m**u**riendo

7. In the present progressive, the verb **estar** must agree with the subject; however, you will notice that there is only one form for each present participle. It does NOT agree in gender (masculine/feminine) or number (singular/plural) with the subject.

> Mis hijos están estudiando inglés.
> *My children are studying English.*
>
> Sandra está leyendo su libro de química.
> *Sandra is reading her chemistry book.*

A practicar

5.7 **¿Cierto o falso?** Escucha las oraciones sobre el dibujo y decide si cada oración es cierta o falsa.

1-29

© Cengage Learning

5.8 **La fiesta** Estás en una fiesta en la casa de Dalia. Un amigo llama por teléfono y tú describes lo que está pasando en la fiesta. Usa los verbos entre paréntesis en la forma del presente progresivo para explicar lo que están haciendo todos.

Modelo   yo (hablar por teléfono)
         Estoy hablando por teléfono.

1. Dalia (servir la comida)
2. Luis y Alfonso (comer pizza)
3. María Esther (beber una soda)
4. Felicia, Marciano y Mateo (jugar a las cartas)
5. Fernando (bailar con su novia)
6. los padres de Dalia (dormir)
7. la hermana de Dalia (leer una novela)
8. el hermano de Dalia (¿?)

5.9 **¿Qué están haciendo?** Con un compañero de clase, decidan dos actividades que las personas de la lista están haciendo.

Modelo Los estudiantes están en la biblioteca.
            Están estudiando.
            Están buscando libros.

1. El chef Pepín está en la cocina.
2. El presidente está en Camp David.
3. Juanes y Shakira están en el estudio.
4. El profesor de español está en la oficina.
5. Miguel Cabrera está en el parque.
6. Tú estás en la clase de biología.
7. Isabel Allende está en su oficina.
8. Sonia Sotomayor está en Washington, D.C.

Miguel Cabrera, jugador de béisbol

© Aspen Photo/Shutterstock

5.10 **En la oficina** Usando el presente progresivo, describe lo que están haciendo en la oficina.

© Cengage Learning

5.11 **Un amigo curioso** Trabaja con un compañero. Imaginen que uno de ustedes llama por teléfono a las siguientes horas y pregunta **¿Qué estás haciendo?** Túrnense para ser el amigo curioso y para responder

Modelo 8:00 de la mañana
            Estudiante 1: *¿Qué estás haciendo?*
            Estudiante 2: *Estoy tomando café.*

1. 9:00 de la mañana
2. mediodía
3. 2:00 de la tarde
4. 5:00 de la tarde
5. 8:00 de la noche
6. medianoche

¿Qué estás haciendo?

© Jason Stitt/Shutterstock

A analizar ▶

Mira el video otra vez. Después lee parte de la conversación entre Camila y Vanesa y observa los usos de los verbos **ser** y **estar**.

© Cengage Learning

Camila:	Mis suegros van a llegar de Colombia esta noche y **estoy** preparando comida. Afortunadamente no tengo que limpiar la casa. Rodrigo **está** en casa hoy y **está** limpiando la sala y los baños…
Vanesa:	¿Y cómo **son** tus suegros? ¿Tienes una buena relación con ellos?
Camila:	Pues, sí, nos llevamos bien. **Son** simpáticos, en particular mi suegra. Ella también **es** maestra. Mi suegro **es** un poco difícil con la comida. Él **es** de Uruguay y no le gusta mucho la comida colombiana. Bueno, ¿y cómo **estás** tú, Vanesa?
Vanesa:	¡**Estoy** muy feliz! ¡Carlos Vives viene a dar un concierto!
Camila:	¿De veras? ¿Cuándo?
Vanesa:	Va a **estar** en el auditorio municipal el once de mayo. ¿Quieres ir?
Camila:	¡Por supuesto! **Es** mi artista favorito. Oye, ¿qué hora **es**?
Vanesa:	**Son** las tres y media.

1. What are the uses of **estar** you have learned so far? Find examples in the paragraph.
2. Look at the verb **ser** in the paragraph. What are the different ways in which it is used?

A comprobar

Ser and estar

1. The verb **ser** is used in the following ways:

   a. to describe characteristics of people, places, or things

   La profesora **es** inteligente.
   The professor is intelligent.

   Mi coche **es** muy viejo.
   My car is very old.

   b. to identify a relationship, occupation, or nationality

   Esta **es** mi novia; **es** peruana.
   This is my girlfriend; she is Peruvian.

   Ellos **son** mecánicos.
   They are mechanics.

   c. to express origin

   Yo **soy** de Cuba.
   I am from Cuba.

   d. to express possession

   Este libro **es** de Álvaro.
   This book belongs to Álvaro.

   e. to tell time and give dates

   Es tres de marzo y **son** las dos.
   It is the third of March, and it is two o'clock.

2. The verb **estar** is used in the following ways:

   a. to indicate location

   El perro **está** enfrente de la casa.
   The dog is in front of the house.

   b. to express an emotional, mental, or physical condition

   Estoy muy feliz.
   I am very happy.

   Mi madre **está** enferma hoy.
   My mother is sick today.

   Las secretarias **están** ocupadas.
   The secretaries are busy.

   c. in the present progressive

   Estoy estudiando.
   I am studying.

3. It is important to realize that the use of **ser** and **estar** with some adjectives can change the meaning of those adjectives. The use of **ser** indicates a characteristic or a trait, while the use of **estar** indicates a condition. Here are some common adjectives that change meaning:

estar aburrido(a) *to be bored*

ser aburrido(a) *to be boring*

estar alegre (feliz) *to be happy (emotion)*

ser alegre (feliz) *to be a happy person*

estar bueno(a)/ malo(a) *to be (taste) good/bad (condition)*

ser bueno(a)/malo(a) *to be good/bad (general quality)*

estar guapo(a) *to look handsome/pretty (condition)*

ser guapo(a) *to be handsome/pretty (characteristic)*

estar listo(a) *to be ready*

ser listo(a) *to be clever*

estar rico(a) *to be delicious*

ser rico(a) *to be rich*

> **INVESTIGUEMOS LA GRAMÁTICA**
>
> While **estar** is generally used to indicate location, if you want to say where an event takes place, use **ser**.
> La fiesta **es** en la casa de Alejandro.
> *The party **is** at Alejandro's house.*

Carlos **es** alegre.

Carlos is happy. (a happy person) (personality)

Graciela **está** alegre.

Graciela is happy. (emotion)

La fruta **es** buena.

Fruit is good. (general quality)

Los tomates **están** buenos.

The tomatoes are (taste) good. (present condition)

A practicar

5.12 **¿Es posible?** Mira la foto y lee las oraciones. Decide si son posibles o no.

1. Son amigos.
2. Están enojados.
3. Están en la universidad.
4. Son muy viejos.
5. Están hablando.
6. Son de Puerto Rico.

© Alberto L. Pomares G./iStockphoto

5.13 **¿Cómo son o cómo están?** Decide qué expresiones pueden completar las oraciones correctamente. Hay más de una posibilidad para cada oración.

1. Yo estoy…
   - **a.** cansada
   - **b.** en clase ahora
   - **c.** estudiante
   - **d.** enamorado

2. Javier y Marta son…
   - **a.** mis amigos
   - **b.** enfermos
   - **c.** colombianos
   - **d.** enfrente de la clase

3. Madrid es…
   - **a.** en Europa
   - **b.** cosmopolita
   - **c.** muy bonita
   - **d.** la capital de España

4. El profesor de español está…
   - **a.** en la oficina
   - **b.** interesante
   - **c.** rubio
   - **d.** ocupado

5. Nosotros somos…
   - **a.** inteligentes
   - **b.** de Chile
   - **c.** hermanos
   - **d.** preocupados

6. Mis primos son…
   - **a.** profesores
   - **b.** cerca de la casa
   - **c.** guapos
   - **d.** estudiando

7. Tú estás…
   - **a.** mi amigo
   - **b.** contenta
   - **c.** inteligente
   - **d.** detrás del hotel

8. Mi hermano está…
   - **a.** hablando
   - **b.** listo
   - **c.** peruano
   - **d.** simpático

5.14 **Una foto** En parejas, contesten las preguntas sobre la foto. Inventen la información que no es evidente. **¡OJO!** Atención al uso de los verbos **ser** y **estar**.

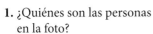

1. ¿Quiénes son las personas en la foto?
2. ¿Cómo están hoy?
3. ¿Cómo son?
4. ¿De dónde son?
5. ¿Dónde están?
6. ¿Qué están haciendo?

© StockLite/Shutterstock

5.15 ¿Ser o estar? Completa el párrafo con la forma apropiada del presente del indicativo de **ser** o **estar.**

Hoy (1) _____ primero de septiembre, el primer día de clases. (2) _____ las once y media y yo (3) _____ en la clase de inglés. Yo (4) _____ un poco nervioso porque es mi primera clase de inglés. Laura (5) _____ mi amiga y ella (6) _____ en la clase también. Nosotros (7) _____ muy interesados en aprender inglés. El profesor de la clase (8) _____ el señor Berg. Él (9) _____ alto, delgado y moreno. Es evidente que él (10) _____ simpático. Creo que va a (11) _____ un buen semestre.

5.16 ¿Cómo eres y cómo estás? Decide cuáles de los siguientes adjetivos te describen a ti. Después pregúntale a tu compañero si esos adjetivos también lo describen a él. Atención al uso de **ser** y **estar,** y a las formas de los adjetivos.

© schwarzhana/Shutterstock

Modelo	contento	Estudiante 1: *¿Estás contento?*
		Estudiante 2: *Sí, estoy contento. /*
		No, no estoy contento.
	rico	Estudiante 1: *¿Eres rica?*
		Estudiante 2: *Sí, soy rica. / No, no soy rica.*

1. enamorado   6. romántico
2. triste   7. enfermo
3. inteligente   8. atlético
4. tímido   9. preocupado
5. cansado   10. optimista

5.17 Una historia interesante Con un compañero de clase, escojan uno de los dibujos y describan la escena. Contesten las siguientes preguntas usando los verbos **ser** y **estar.** ¿Quiénes son las personas? ¿Cuál es su relación? ¿Dónde están? ¿Cómo están? ¿Qué está pasando? ¡Sean creativos!

Modelo *El hombre es Tomás y la mujer es Graciela. Son buenos amigos.*
Están en la sala de espera (waiting room) *del hospital porque la madre de Graciela está enferma.*
Ellos están muy preocupados...

© Cengage Learning

Entrando en materia

¿Quién es tu actor favorito y cómo es su personalidad? ¿Qué le preguntarías *(would you ask)* si pudieras *(if you could)* hablar con él o ella?

Entrevista de un actor

◄)) Vas a escuchar un fragmento de una entrevista *(interview)* con el actor Francisco Méndez.
1-30 Escucha con atención y después responde las preguntas.

Vocabulario útil

las admiradoras	*fans*
conociéndonos	*getting to know each other*
el maquillaje	*makeup*
los milagros	*miracles*
parecer	*to seem*

Estrategia

Guess intelligently

Make intelligent guesses as to the meaning of words you do not know, and use context and intonation to help you figure out the meanings of words.

Comprensión

1. ¿En qué evento están? ¿dónde?
2. ¿Cómo es la personalidad de Francisco, según él *(according to him)*?
3. ¿Cómo está Francisco cuando debe hablar frente a muchas personas?
4. ¿Cómo es la novia de Francisco?
5. ¿Francisco está enamorado de su novia?

Más allá

Imagina que puedes entrevistar a un actor, a una actriz o a un artista que te gusta mucho. Piensa en cinco preguntas que harías *(that you would ask)* en tu entrevista. Comparte el nombre del actor o del artista y tus preguntas en Share it! Lee las preguntas de tus compañeros. ¿Conoces a todos los actores y artistas?

Tengo muchos admiradores.

© wassiliy-architect/Shutterstock

Lectura

Reading Strategy: Guessing verb tenses

A useful strategy for understanding a text is to not worry about the exact meaning of a word and to make an educated guess instead. In the case of verbs, if you know the meaning of the verb, you will be able to guess from the context if it refers to the past or to the future. Look at the second-to-last paragraph. The verb **concluir** is translated for you. From the context of the paragraph, is the verb used to refer to the past or the future?

Antes de leer

Contesta las preguntas.

1. En general ¿qué necesitas para ser feliz?
2. ¿En qué países piensas que las personas son más felices? ¿Por qué?

A leer

¿Quiénes son más felices?

Gracias a muchas **investigaciones** *(research)* **se sabe** *(it is known)* que la felicidad no depende del dinero, **sino** *(but rather)* de la calidad de las relaciones entre las personas. Aunque hay muchos estudios sobre la felicidad con resultados diferentes, en la mayoría de estos estudios los latinos **aparecen** *(appear)* entre las personas más felices del planeta. En estas páginas hablaremos sobre los resultados de tres estudios sobre la felicidad.

© Monkey Business Images/Shutterstock

El primero fue publicado por la revista *Forbes*. En este estudio no hay ningún país latinoamericano y los Estados Unidos aparecen en el 10º lugar. Los primeros puestos son todos para países europeos y para Canadá, Australia y Nueva Zelandia. Sin embargo, este estudio se basa solamente en estadísticas económicas como **sueldos** *(salaries)* altos y oportunidades de empleo, y no en la opinión de las personas entrevistadas. Un problema con este criterio es que **se ha comprobado** *(it has been proven)* experimentalmente que la economía no tiene relación con el nivel de la felicidad **una vez que** *(once)* se pueden satisfacer las necesidades básicas.

[los latinos aparecen entre las personas más felices del planeta]

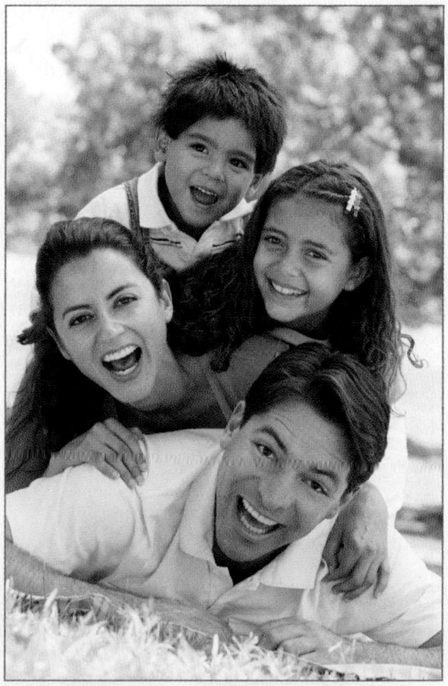

El segundo estudio lo publica el índice del Planeta Felíz *(Happy Planet Index),* que da periódicamente sus resultados según criterios de **sustentabilidad** y de la percepción (subjetiva) de felicidad de los encuestados. En sus resultados del 2012, Costa Rica está en el primer lugar y 17 de los 25 países más felices del mundo están en Latinoamérica. Otros países en la lista son Colombia, todos los países centroamericanos, Venezuela, Cuba, Argentina, Chile y México. Los Estados Unidos están en el puesto 114, cerca del final de la lista.

sustainability

© Jacob Wackerhausen/iStockphoto

El tercer estudio, **hecho** por Global Research en 2012, está basado completamente en preguntarles a las personas si son muy felices, felices, poco felices o infelices. De acuerdo

done

a las respuestas obtenidas, entre los primeros 25 países hubo 3 países latinoamericanos (Venezuela, Argentina y Uruguay). España está también entre esos países. Chile y México siguen de cerca. Esta investigación **concluyó** que Latinoamérica es la región más felíz del mundo, mientras que Europa está en el **último** lugar (solo el 15% dijo ser muy felíz). Los Estados Unidos están en el lugar 13° en la lista, a pesar de que otro estudio *(Harris Poll,* 2013) encontró que en los Estados Unidos solo el 33% de las personas piensa que es feliz.

concluir to conclude

last

Curiosamente, de entre todas las estadísticas demográficas, el único factor que parece afectar la felicidad es estar casado: las personas que están casadas **dicen** ser más felices.

claim

Sources: http://www.nationmaster.com/graph/lif_hap_net-lifestyle-happiness-net
Nationmaster.com; Ipsos-na.com; *El Ciervo*

Comprensión

1. ¿Cuál es el tema del artículo?
2. Según el artículo ¿de qué depende la felicidad?
3. Según *Forbes* ¿qué condiciones son necesarios para ser felíz?
4. Según el índice del Planeta Felíz, ¿cuál es el país más felíz? ¿Qué países latinoamericanos están en la lista de los más felices según el índice del Planeta Felíz?
5. ¿Hay similitudes en los tres estudios?

Después de leer

Con un compañero, escriban una lista de cuatro o cinco cosas que pueden hacer para ser más felices.

2
Exploraciones léxicas

Luisa es fotógrafa y asiste a una reunión de aniversario de su graduación para ver a sus compañeros. ¿Qué profesiones tienen ellos?

REUNIÓN DE LA GENERACIÓN DEL 98

la enfermera · el músico · el médico · la mesera · el mecánico · la fotógrafa · la cocinera · el pintor · el actor · el asistente de vuelo · el piloto · el policía · el científico · el deportista

© Cengage Learning

Las profesiones

el (la) abogado(a)	lawyer	el (la) periodista	reporter
la actriz	actress	el (la) político(a)	politician
el (la) agente de viajes	travel agent	el (la) psicólogo(a)	psychologist
el amo(a) de casa	homemaker	el (la) secretario(a)	secretary
el (la) arquitecto(a)	architect	el (la) trabajador(a) social	social worker
el bailarín/la bailarina	dancer	el (la) vendedor(a)	salesperson
el (la) cantante	singer	el (la) veterinario(a)	veterinarian
el (la) contador(a)	accountant		
el (la) consejero(a)	counselor	**Palabras adicionales**	
el (la) dependiente	store clerk	el (la) cliente	client
el (la) diseñador(a)	designer	la entrevista	interview
el (la) escritor(a)	writer	ganar	to earn; to win
el (la) ingeniero(a)	engineer	la solicitud	application; want ad
el jefe/la jefa	boss		
el (la) maestro(a)	teacher	el sueldo	salary
el (la) modelo	model	el trabajo	job

INVESTIGUEMOS EL VOCABULARIO

In Latin America, **el (la) asistente de vuelo** refers to a flight attendant regardless of gender; however, in Spain **la azafata** is used for a female flight attendant and **el auxiliar de vuelo** is used for male flight attendants.

El (La) mesero(a) is used in Latin America to refer to a waiter/waitress; another word used in some South American countries is **el (la) mozo(a).** In Spain **el (la) camarero(a)** is used.

INVESTIGUEMOS LA GRAMÁTICA

(a) While most nouns ending in **-o** change to **-a** when referring to females, the following do not: **el (la) piloto** and **el (la) modelo.**

(b) Professions ending in **-or** add an **a** to make them feminine: **contadora, diseñadora, escritora,** and **vendedora.**

(c) Professions ending in **-a** maintain the same spelling regardless of the gender of the person, such as **el (la) periodista** and **el (la) deportista.** However, **la mujer policía** is used for female police officers as **la policía** refers to the police in general.

(d) Regardless of gender, **el ama de casa** requires the masculine article for pronunciation purposes. However, any adjectives would agree with the gender of the person: **Sara es el ama de casa perfecta.**

(e) When identifying a person's profession, the indefinite article is not used unless an adjective is added: **Eva es modelo. Adán es un buen actor.**

A practicar

5.18 **Escucha y responde** Vas a escuchar una lista de profesiones. Levanta la mano si una persona que tiene la profesión mencionada lleva uniforme.

🔊 1-31

5.19 **¿Dónde trabajan?** Relaciona a la persona con su lugar de trabajo.

1. _____ un dependiente   **a.** un hospital
2. _____ un cocinero   **b.** un teatro
3. _____ un pintor   **c.** un restaurante
4. _____ un actor   **d.** una tienda
5. _____ un médico   **e.** un estudio

5.20 **¿Qué hacen?** Con un compañero escriban una actividad que hacen las siguientes

personas en su trabajo.

Modelo mesero
    Un mesero sirve café.

1. maestro   **4.** policía
2. secretario   **5.** ama de casa
3. enfermero   **6.** deportista

5.21 **¿Cuál es su profesión?** ¿Puedes identificar las profesiones de las siguientes

personas? Identifica las que sabes *(the ones you know)* y después pregunta a tus compañeros para completar la información. Incluye toda la información adicional posible.

Modelo Jennifer López
    Estudiante 1: *¿Cuál es la profesión de Jennifer López?*
    Estudiante 2: *Es cantante. También es actriz en las películas* Selena, Gigli *y* El cantante.
        Ella es de Puerto Rico.

1. Albert Pujols   **5.** Esmeralda Santiago
2. Carolina Herrera   **6.** Fernando Botero
3. Isabel Allende   **7.** Carlos Santana
4. Antonio Banderas   **8.** Michelle Bachelet

5.22 **Consejero** Imagina que eres consejero y debes recomendarles una profesión a algunos

estudiantes, según sus clases favoritas y sus intereses. Túrnense con un compañero.

Modelo las matemáticas y la química
    Estudiante 1: *Me gustan las matemáticas y la química. ¿Qué profesión debo estudiar?*
    Estudiante 2: *Debes ser científico o ingeniero.*

1. los deportes y la clase de español   **4.** la biología y los animales
2. las clases de historia y de arte   **5.** las fiestas y cocinar
3. la música y bailar   **6.** las leyes *(law)* y la política

> **INVESTIGUEMOS LA MÚSICA**
>
> Listen to the Spanish classic "Cuando seas grande" by Argentinian rocker Miguel Mateos. What does the teenager in the song want to be when he grows up?

5.23 **Personas famosas** Trabaja con un compañero para completar la información. Uno de ustedes debe ver la tabla en esta página, y el otro debe ver la tabla en el **Apéndice B.** Túrnense para preguntar y responder.

Nombre	Profesión	País de origen
Alicia Alonso	bailarina	
Óscar de la Renta		República Dominicana
Andrea Serna	periodista, modelo	Colombia
Baruj Benacerraf		
Gabriela Mistral	escritora, maestra	
Luis Federico Leloir		Argentina

Conexiones culturales
Las profesiones y la economía

Cultura

Las profesiones relacionadas con el arte deben enfrentar un reto *(challenge)* adicional: además de crear su arte, deben también crear un mercado para su arte, es decir, deben encontrar compradores, o empleadores que necesiten bailarines, actores, escritores, etcétera.

Según un estudio publicado en los Estados Unidos, casi la mitad *(almost half)* de los artistas pasan la mayor parte de su tiempo en el sector comercial, buscando oportunidades de darse a conocer *(to make themselves known)* en su comunidad. Uno de los mejores ejemplos de un genio artístico que aprendió a promover *(to promote)* su arte con éxito fue Salvador Dalí, el pintor surrealista, quien usaba su excentricidad para vender su arte. Además, Dalí supo rodearse *(knew how to surround himself)* de personas influyentes. Sin embargo, se debe mencionar que Dalí contó con un mecenas *(sponsor)* muy rico, Edward James. Dalí terminó por romper con *(break away from)* el grupo de artistas surrealistas. Lo acusaron de amar demasiado el dinero y también lo condenaron por no proclamarse contra el fascismo porque Dalí pensaba que el arte puede ser apolítico. Cuando lo expulsaron del grupo surrealista, Dalí respondió simplemente: "El surrealismo soy yo". El tiempo le dio la razón: Salvador Dalí se conoce como el padre del surrealismo.

Observa la obra de Dalí de la fotografía. ¿Te gusta? ¿Por qué?

Persistencia de la memoria, de Salvador Dalí

> Busca en Internet más pinturas de Salvador Dalí. Sube a Share It! una pintura que te gusta. Luego mira las pinturas de tus compañeros. ¿Cuál te gusta más? ¿Por qué?

Comunidad

Entrevista a una persona de un país hispanohablante acerca de su ocupación. Puedes preguntarle en qué y dónde trabaja, si le gusta su trabajo y si quiere tener una ocupación diferente en el futuro. Repórtale a la clase la información.

Comparaciones

¿Piensas que en los Estados Unidos la gente trabaja mucho? ¿Crees que trabajan más en otros países? Mira la información en el cuadro y contesta las preguntas.

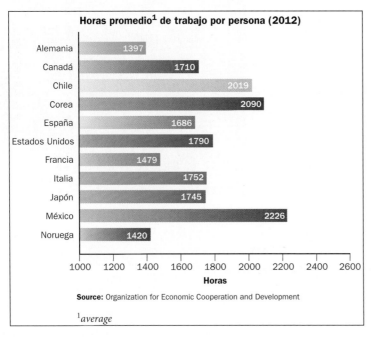

Horas promedio[1] de trabajo por persona (2012)

País	Horas
Alemania	1397
Canadá	1710
Chile	2019
Corea	2090
España	1686
Estados Unidos	1790
Francia	1479
Italia	1752
Japón	1745
México	2226
Noruega	1420

Source: Organization for Economic Cooperation and Development

[1]*average*

En promedio *(On average)*, ¿cuántas horas trabajan al año en Chile y en México? ¿Quiénes trabajan más: los españoles o los estadounidenses? ¿Cómo puedes explicar las diferencias?

Conexiones... a la economía y al comercio

 Hay muchas compañías de los Estados Unidos que tienen fábricas *(factories)* en países en vías de desarrollo *(developing)*. Estas industrias se llaman **maquiladoras,** y hacen todo tipo de productos, como ropa, zapatos, muebles, productos químicos y electrónicos.

Habla con un compañero sobre las siguientes preguntas. Luego investiga qué compañías de los Estados Unidos tienen maquiladoras en otros países y repórtaselo a la clase.

1. ¿Cuáles son las ventajas *(advantages)* y las desventajas para la compañía? ¿y para los empleados?
2. ¿Qué efectos tienen las maquiladoras en la economía de los Estados Unidos? ¿y en la economía de los países donde se establecen?

Investiga en Internet y aprende más sobre los países latinoamericanos donde los Estados Unidos tienen maquiladoras en el **Apéndice A: Exploraciones del mundo hispano.**

Exploraciones **gramaticales**

A analizar ▶

Vanesa habla de su profesión. Mira el video. Después lee el
párrafo y observa las formas de los verbos.

Yo soy fotógrafa y trabajo para esta revista. ¡Me
gusta mucho mi trabajo! Siempre llego a la oficina
a las ocho y **pongo** todo en orden. Durante el día
conduzco a diferentes lugares y **veo** a personas
interesantes. Además tengo suerte porque **salgo**
de viaje con frecuencia. **Traigo** la cámara si la
quieren ver.

1. Look at the paragraph again and find the first person
   (yo) form of the following verbs.

   conducir   poner   salir   traer   ver

2. Do you notice a pattern in any of the **yo** forms of the verbs? What is it?

A comprobar

Verbs with changes in the first person

1. Some verbs in the present tense are irregular only in the first person **(yo)** form. You have
   already seen the verb **hacer.**

   hacer *(to do; to make)*

hago	hacemos
haces	hacéis
hace	hacen

2. The following verbs also have irregular first person forms:

poner *(to put; to set)*	**pongo,** pones, pone, ponemos, ponéis, ponen
salir *(to go out, to leave)*	**salgo,** sales, sale, salimos, salís, salen
traer *(to bring)*	**traigo,** traes, trae, traemos, traéis, traen
conducir *(to drive)*	**conduzco,** conduces, conduce, conducimos, conducís, conducen
dar *(to give)*	**doy,** das, da, damos, dais, dan
ver *(to see)*	**veo,** ves, ve, vemos, veis, ven

   INVESTIGUEMOS A LA GRAMÁTICA

   When telling where someone is
   leaving from, it is necessary to use
   the preposition **de.**

   Salgo **de** la casa a las 7:00.
   I leave the house at 7:00.

3. The following verbs are not only irregular in the first person form, but also have other changes:

decir (to say, to tell)	
digo	decimos
dices	decís
dice	dicen

venir (to come)	
vengo	venimos
vienes	venís
viene	vienen

seguir (to follow; to continue)	
sigo	seguimos
sigues	seguís
sigue	siguen

oír (to hear)	
oigo	oímos
oyes	oís
oye	oyen

A practicar

5.24 **¿Quién soy?** Decide quién hace las siguientes actividades.

> **Modelo** Les doy inyecciones a las mascotas.
> *el veterinario*

1. Hago las reservaciones para personas que quieren viajar.
2. Conduzco un coche con luces *(lights)* rojas y azules. No quieres conducir muy rápido cuando yo estoy cerca.
3. Les traigo la comida a los clientes en el restaurante.
4. Veo a muchas personas enfermas.
5. Escribo artículos, entrevisto a personas famosas y digo la verdad *(truth)*.
6. Oigo los problemas de muchas personas.
7. Muchas personas vienen a mi estudio y yo tomo fotos de ellas.
8. Pongo todo en orden en casa y salgo para comprar comida.

5.25 **Un día ocupado** Completa el párrafo usando los verbos de la lista en la primera persona singular (**yo**).

conducir	hacer	poner	salir	tener	venir

Soy ama de casa y (**1**) _____ que hacer mucho trabajo todos los días.

Primero (**2**) _____ el almuerzo para mis hijos. A las 7:45 ellos suben al

(get into) auto y (**3**) _____ a la escuela. Después, voy al supermercado,

(**4**) _____ a casa y (**5**) _____ la comida en el refrigerador. Más tarde

(**6**) _____ otra vez a la escuela para recoger a mis hijos.

Soy ama de casa.

5.26 **¿Qué hace Rocío?** Rocío es agente de viajes. Con un compañero, describan lo que hace Rocío. Incluyan todos los detalles posibles y usen verbos que conocen (know) y los siguientes verbos : **poner, oír, hacer, decir, salir, conducir.**

© Cengage Learning

5.27 **¿Con qué frecuencia...?** Habla con seis compañeros de clase y pregúntale a cada uno con qué frecuencia hace una de las siguientes actividades. Después, comparte la informacíon con la clase.

siempre (always)   **a veces** (sometimes)   **casi nunca** (almost never)
nunca (never)

Modelo hacer la cama
   Estudiante 1: ¿Con qué frecuencia haces la cama?
   Estudiante 2: Siempre (A veces/Casi nunca/Nunca) hago la cama.

1. seguir las recomendaciones de tus amigos
2. salir los fines de semana
3. ver la televisión por la noche
4. venir tarde a la clase
5. dar respuestas correctas en clase
6. hacer la tarea para la clase de español

5.28 **Los estudios** Entrevista a un compañero de clase para saber (to know) más sobre sus hábitos.

1. ¿Qué coche conduces? ¿Tienes que conducir a la universidad?
2. ¿A qué hora vienes a la universidad? ¿A qué hora regresas a casa?
3. ¿Cuántos libros tienes en tu mochila? ¿Siempre (Always) traes el libro de español a clase?
4. ¿Cuándo haces la tarea? ¿Dónde prefieres hacer la tarea?
5. ¿Pones música cuando estudias? ¿Qué tipo de música escuchas cuando estudias?
6. ¿Sales con compañeros de clase? ¿Con quiénes?

¿Dónde prefieres hacer la tarea?

© wavebreakmedia/Shutterstock

A analizar

Óscar habla de su profesión. Mira el video. Después lee la información y observa el uso de los verbos **saber** y **conocer**.

> Camila: Ahora, vamos a **conocer** al señor Fuentes.
>
> Óscar: Muchas gracias. ¿**Saben** cuál es mi profesión?
>
> Niños: ¡Policía!
>
> Óscar: ¡Exacto! Probablemente ustedes **saben** que mi trabajo es muy importante. **Conozco** a muchas personas que viven aquí y trabajo para protegerlos. Yo **conozco** muy bien la ciudad y las calles. Tengo un coche blanco y azul, y **sé** conducir muy bien. Puedo correr muy rápido si es necesario, y también **sé** hacer karate. ¡Es un trabajo muy interesante!

1. What is the first person form of the verb **saber**? And the verb **conocer**?
2. The verbs **saber** and **conocer** both mean *to know*. Explain the difference in their uses above.

A comprobar

Saber and conocer

1. As with the other verbs in this chapter, **saber** and **conocer** are irregular in the first person form.

saber	**sé**, sabes, sabe, sabemos, sabéis, saben
conocer	**conozco**, conoces, conoce, conocemos, conocéis, conocen

2. While the verbs **saber** and **conocer** both mean *to know*, they are used in different contexts.

   - **Saber** is used to express knowledge of facts or information as well as skills.
   - **Conocer** is used to express acquaintance or familiarity with a person, place, or thing.

   Notice the difference in meaning in the following sentences:

   Ana **conoce** Chile. *(familiarity)*
   Ana **sabe** dónde está Chile. *(fact)*

   Paco **conoce** a Diego. *(acquainted with)*
   Paco **sabe** dónde vive Diego. *(information)*

   Conozco la poesía de Neruda. *(familiarity)*
   Sé que Neruda es un poeta famoso. *(fact)*

3. When using **saber** to mean *to know how to do something,* it is followed by the infinitive.

   El ingeniero **sabe diseñar** edificios.
   *The engineer **knows how to design** buildings.*

   El cantante **sabe cantar.**
   *The singer **knows how to sing.***

4. When expressing some knowledge or familiarity with general concepts or subjects, the verb **conocer** is used.

   El artista **conoce** el arte prehispánico.
   *The artist **knows** (is familiar with) pre-Hispanic art.*

   La enfermera **conoce** la medicina.
   *The nurse **knows** (is familiar with) medicine.*

5. When the recipient of the action (direct object) is a person or a pet, an **a** is used in front of the object. This is known as the **a personal** and is not translated into English. It is not necessary to use it with the verb **tener;** however when using the verb **conocer** to tell that someone knows a person, it is necessary to use the **a personal.**

   La profesora **conoce a** los estudiantes.
   *The professor **knows** her students.*

   El jefe **conoce a** sus empleados.
   *The boss **knows** his employees.*

A practicar

5.29 **¿Lógica o ilógica?** Decide si las siguientes descripciones de profesiones son lógicas. Corrige las oraciones ilógicas.

1. La bailarina sabe jugar al fútbol.
2. El periodista conoce a muchas personas famosas.
3. El médico sabe dónde está la farmacia.
4. El contador sabe cantar bien.
5. El veterinario conoce a unos criminales.
6. La secretaria sabe usar la computadora.
7. El psicólogo conoce bien la cocina del restaurante.
8. El escritor conoce las obras *(works)* más importantes de la literatura.

5.30 **Oraciones incompletas** Decide qué opciones pueden completar las siguientes oraciones. Hay más de una posibilidad para cada oración.

1. El médico conoce...
   a. a sus pacientes.
   b. la medicina.
   c. dar inyecciones.
   d. el hospital.

2. El arquitecto sabe...
   a. al ingeniero.
   b. diseñar casas.
   c. dónde está la casa.
   d. la ciudad.

3. El científico conoce...
   a. las ciencias.
   b. cómo hacer el experimento.
   c. el laboratorio.
   d. que su trabajo es importante.

4. El consejero sabe...
   a. los problemas de sus clientes.
   b. escuchar bien.
   c. a sus clientes.
   d. a qué hora vienen los clientes.

5.31 **¿Saber o conocer?** Primero completen individualmente las siguientes oraciones con las formas necesarias de los verbos **saber** y **conocer.** Después, túrnense para leer las definiciones y decir cuál es una profesión lógica.

Modelo Estudiante 1: *Yo _____sé_____ tocar el piano.*
Estudiante 2: *Un músico.*

1. Yo _____ bien la ley *(law)*.
2. Julio _____ pintar bien.
3. Matilde y Simón _____ a muchos médicos.
4. Fabio _____ al presidente.
5. Daniela y yo _____ tomar buenas fotos.
6. Yo _____ dónde están los buenos hoteles.
7. Mario y Luisa _____ bien a los animales en el zoológico donde trabajan.
8. Tú _____ cocinar muy bien.
9. Yo _____ bailar tango.
10. El señor Montero _____ a sus estudiantes.

5.32 **Puerto Rico** Con un compañero, túrnense para preguntar si saben o conocen las siguientes cosas.

Modelo   Puerto Rico
        Estudiante 1: *¿Conoces Puerto Rico?*
        Estudiante 2: *Sí, conozco Puerto Rico. / No, no conozco*
           Puerto Rico.

        hablar español bien
        Estudiante 1: *¿Sabes hablar español bien?*
        Estudiante 2: *Sí, sé hablar español bien. / No, no sé hablar*
           español bien.

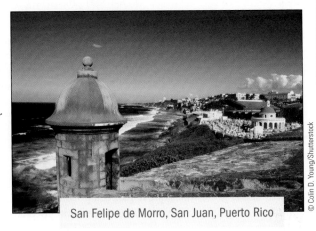

San Felipe de Morro, San Juan, Puerto Rico

1. dónde está Puerto Rico
2. un puertorriqueño
3. la comida puertorriqueña
4. quién es el gobernador de Puerto Rico
5. San Juan
6. la historia de Puerto Rico
7. cuándo es el día de la independencia de Puerto Rico
8. bailar salsa

5.33 **¿Qué saben? ¿Qué conocen?** En parejas, túrnense para completar las siguientes oraciones.

1. **a.** Nosotros conocemos…
   b. Nosotros sabemos…
2. **a.** Los periodistas conocen…
   b. Los periodistas saben…
3. **a.** Un jefe conoce…
   b. Un jefe sabe…
4. **a.** El presidente conoce…
   b. El presidente sabe…

5.34 **En busca de…** Decide qué verbo necesitas usar en cada oración y después busca a ocho compañeros diferentes que respondan positivamente a una de las siguientes preguntas. Después de responder, deben contestar la pregunta adicional. Luego, comparte las respuestas con la clase.

1. ¿(sabes/conoces) a una persona famosa? (¿Quién?)
2. ¿(sabes/conoces) un buen restaurante? (¿Cuál?)
3. ¿(sabes/conoces) hablar otra lengua (¿Cuál?)
4. ¿(sabes/conoces) a una persona de otro país *(country)*? (¿Qué país?)
5. ¿(sabes/conoces) el nombre del presidente de Argentina? (¿Cómo se llama?)
6. ¿(sabes/conoces) cocinar? (¿Cuál es tu especialidad?)
7. ¿(sabes/conoces) muy bien la ciudad donde vives? (¿Cuál es tu lugar favorito?)
8. ¿(sabes/conoces) cuál es la capital de Venezuela? (¿Cuál es?)

Lectura

Reading Strategy: Paying attention to parts of speech

You've learned some concrete strategies to make educated guesses about verbs. To guess the meaning of other words, pay attention to the context and the part of speech of the unknown word (verb, noun, etc.). For example, in the sentence *He walked bumptiously,* we might not know the meaning of *bumptiously,* but we know it is an adverb and it refers to the way in which the person walked. Look at the second-to-last paragraph on page 177. What part of speech do you think the word **potable** is? What do you think it means?

Antes de leer

Menciona dos profesiones que te parecen poco comunes. ¿Por qué piensas que son poco comunes? ¿Conoces a alguien con una profesión poco común?

A leer

Profesiones poco comunes

cambiar: *to change*

En un mundo que está **cambiando** muy rápidamente, los trabajos de la gente también cambian a gran velocidad y muchos trabajos ya casi no existen, pero también aparecen nuevos empleos. Aquí te presentamos algunos trabajos poco comunes y muy modestos. Algunos están desapareciendo, y otros son relativamente nuevos.

thief
law

Ladrón profesional: Este novedoso trabajo es para ladrones que no roban más y están del lado de la **ley**. Muchas tiendas de departamentos contratan a estas personas para descubrir vulnerabilidades con la seguridad y corregirlas para **evitar** robos.

to avoid

> [los trabajos de la gente también cambian a gran velocidad]

La lavandera: Para las personas que no están contentas con su lavadora de ropa, o no tienen una, la lavandera es una gran ayuda. Va a la casa de una persona para lavar **a mano** toda la ropa **sucia**.

by hand / dirty

El organillero: En raras ocasiones, puedes encontrar al organillero en un parque de la ciudad, tocando música con su organillo. No es muy común pero a veces es posible ver a un chimpancé bailando a la música del organillero, y pidiéndole dinero a la gente en la calle. Esta profesión originada en Europa ya es casi algo del pasado.

dice

Inspector de dados: Es muy importante para los casinos no tener dados defectuosos, pues pueden ocasionar muchas **pérdidas.** Por eso los fabricantes de dados y los casinos necesitan personas para probar los dados antes de usarlos en el casino.

losses

© John Mitchell / Alamy

El adivinador: Va por el parque con un pajarito en una **jaula.** Cuando el cliente le paga al adivinador, el pájaro selecciona un papel que dice su suerte, igual que un horóscopo.

cage

Repartidores: Van por toda la ciudad y llevan artículos de gran importancia a las casas de la gente. Hay muchos tipos de repartidores, pero los más importantes son los repartidores de agua potable y los que reparten el gas para cocinar. Otros repartidores llevan **refrescos** o periódicos a las casas.

soft drinks

Limpiador de chicles: Un trabajo relativamente moderno es el de limpiar los chicles de las calles. Aunque, en el caso de Chile **intentaron** limpiar con agua a presión, y productos químicos, nada funciona tan bien como una vieja espátula. En otros países no existe este trabajo tan expecializado, sino que emplean un vehículo especial para limpiar las calles. Esta labor de limpieza es importante porque el chicle (o goma de mascar) es un foco de bacterias y enfermedades: una sola goma puede tener hasta 70 mil bacterias y hongos. Otra consecuencia es que los pájaros mueren después de comer un chicle. Además **afean** la ciudad ¿y a quién le gusta **pisar** uno?

gum

tried

makes it ugly / step on

Sources: Trabajo.about.com; Diario.latercera.com; Eluniversal.com.mx; 3djuegos.com

Comprensión

1. ¿Cuáles de estos trabajos están desapareciendo? ¿Cuáles son relativamente modernos?
2. ¿Quiénes usan los servicios de los ladrones profesionales?
3. ¿Qué hace la lavandera?
4. ¿Dónde trabaja el adivinador y por qué necesita un pájaro?
5. ¿Qué artículos llevan a las casas los repartidores?
6. ¿Por qué es importante limpiar los chicles de las calles?

Después de leer

En grupos de tres, hablen sobre los trabajos que tienen o los trabajos que consideren interesantes. Incluyan lo siguiente: las habilidades (*skills*) necesarias, la preparación necesaria, el sueldo, lo que les gusta del trabajo y lo que no les gusta del trabajo.

Write an email to a friend telling him/her about a new job.

Paso 1 Brainstorm a list of jobs that you think are fun or exciting.

Paso 2 Pick one of the jobs from your list of interesting jobs. Jot down as many things as you can about that job: Why do you find it interesting? Where do professionals in that field work? What do they do? What do they have to know? Who do they work with? How much do they work?

Paso 3 Write a list of emotions that you might feel if you were to have a job like the one you described in **Paso 2**.

Paso 4 Imagine that you have the job you described in **Paso 2**. Begin the email to your friend and ask how he/she is doing. Then say how you are feeling.

Paso 5 Continue your email telling your friend that you have a new job. Then write a paragraph in which you discuss various aspects of the job using the information you generated in **Paso 2**. Also describe how you are feeling about the job using the list you created in **Paso 3**.

Paso 6 Conclude your email.

Paso 7 Edit your email:

1. Is your email logically organized with smooth sentence transitions?
2. Are there any short sentences you can combine by using **y** or **pero**?
3. Do verbs agree with the subjects?
4. Do adjectives agree with the nouns they describe?
5. Did you use **ser** and **estar** properly?
6. Are there any spelling errors?

Entrando en materia

Cuando buscas un trabajo y lees solicitudes de trabajo, ¿qué tipo de requisitos *(requirements)* es común encontrar?

Solicitudes de trabajo

Aquí hay algunas solicitudes de empleo de un periódico de Colombia.

EMPLEO

ARQUITECTO. Empresa solicita Arquitecto o Diseñador. Hombres o mujeres, 25 a 35 años, experiencia programas 3d autocad, etc. Excelente presentación, disponibilidad de horario y para viajar. Interesados comunicarse al 3636-1111 (de 10:00 a 18:00 hrs).

DEPENDIENTE. Mujer honesta y responsable para trabajar en una óptica en Plaza Fancy, turno completo, sin experiencia y preparatoria terminada. Interesadas enviar curriculum vitae a: plazafancy@empleos.com. Sueldo base $4,000 + Comisión.

CAJERO. Administrador de pizzería, hombre, edad máxima 30 años, zona Ciudad Bugambilias. Contratación Inmediata. Comunicarse al: 3693-9393.

SUPERVISOR. Empresa en expansión ofrece oportunidad de trabajo de medio tiempo, de lunes a viernes. Buscamos personas mayores de 17 años para supervisar personal y atender líneas telefónicas. Para mayor información comunicarse al número 467676767 o enviar hoja de vida al correo electrónico empleo@gmail.com preguntar por la señorita Marciano.

SE Solicita Ama de Casa. Para atender señor solo. Tardes libres. Informes al 345-0900- 2636.

CHOFER. Hotel solicita chofer de camioneta. Requisitos: Inglés indispensable, disponibilidad de horario para rotar turnos, actitud de servicio. Interesados presentar solicitud en Avenida Bolívar 7002, en horario de oficina.

ABOGADA. Bufete de abogados e inversionistas requiere abogada titulada. Responsabilidades: Examinar procesos civiles. Informes al 900 800-7000.

DENTISTA o pasante para trabajo en clínica dental de Ortodoncia. Turno completo, sexo femenino. Informes al 987- 5567-8133 a mandar curriculum o: ortodoncia@ortomax.com.

EJECUTIVO(A) de ventas con experiencia, auto compacto y disponibilidad para viajar, 25–35 años. Ofrecemos producto de primera necesidad para la industria hotelera, sueldo base más comisión, y prestaciones de ley. Interesados enviar c.v con foto a: gerencia@ hotelería.com.

ENFERMERA(O). General/técnica, indispensable cédula profesional. Edad: 25–45 años, estado civil indistinto, experiencia comprobable de tres años. Sueldo según aptitudes. Enviar curriculum a: recursoshumanos@ hospitalSanJose.com.

MESEROS y cantineros. Ambos sexos. Requisitos: experiencia mínima de 3 años, excelente presentación, disponibilidad de horario. Presentarse con curriculum o solicitud elaborada en Restaurante Bar Arcoiris, centro histórico, teléfono 987-6543- 4571.

RECEPCIONISTA. Empresa nacional solicita personal mixto para trabajar medio tiempo. Requisitos: responsable y con iniciativa, disponibilidad de horario. Buena presentación, edad 23 a 35 años, manejo de PC, paquete Office. Citas al Tel: 541-5959-6283, extensión 345.

SE solicita Instructor de Yoga. Experiencia mínima de un año, de 20 a 35 años, interesados llamar al cel: 044-33 3403-3466.

Comprensión

1. ¿Qué tipo de trabajos ofrecen las solicitudes de empleo?
2. ¿Qué tipo de requisitos tienen?
3. ¿Qué diferencias hay entre estos anuncios y los de los Estados Unidos?

🔳 Más allá

Escribe un anuncio de empleo para una profesión no representada en estos anuncios. Compártela en Share It! y lee los anuncios de tus compañeros. ¿Te interesa alguno de los anuncios?

El trabajo social

Vocabulario

Sustantivos

el abuso	*abuse*
el alcohol	*alcohol*
la autoestima	*self-esteem*
la custodia	*custody*
la droga	*drug*
la rehabilitación	*rehabilitation*
la violencia	*violence*

Adjetivos

agresivo(a)	*aggressive*
obsesionado(a)	*obsessed*
violento(a)	*violent*

Verbos

dejar de + *infinitive*	*to stop doing something*

Frases útiles

¿En qué puedo ayudarle?
How can I help you?

¿Tiene problemas de salud?
Do you have any health problems?

¿Cuál es su número de seguridad social?
What is your Social Security number?

¿Cómo se llama la persona encargada de su caso?
What is the name of your case worker?

Voy a referirlo a...
I am going to refer you to . . .

Necesitamos hacer una cita con...
We need to make an appointment with . . .

Estrategia

Guess intelligently.

Use context, intonation as well as visual clues such as body language, gestures, facial expressions, and images to help you figure out the meaning of words.

DATOS IMPORTANTES

Educación: Licenciatura en trabajo social o carrera relacionada, aunque muchos puestos requieren una maestría

Salario: Entre $38 000 y $60 000

Dónde se trabaja: Escuelas primarias y secundarias, hospitales, asilos para ancianos, centros para el tratamiento de abuso, agencias para individuos y familias, el gobierno local o estatal

Vocabulario nuevo Completa las oraciones con la palabra apropiada de la lista de vocabulario.

1. Para un alcohólico es difícil _____ beber.
2. La cocaína y la heroína son _____ ilegales.
3. Una persona que no tiene un buen concepto de sí mismo (*himself*) tiene _____ baja.
4. Si los padres son violentos, no pueden tener _____ de sus hijos.
5. Muchas veces es necesario ir a un centro de _____ para poder controlar una adicción.

● Ana Correa, trabajadora social

Ana Correa es trabajadora social y ayuda a personas con diferentes problemas, como la falta de *(lack of)* trabajo, las drogas y la violencia doméstica. En el video vas a ver una entrevista entre Ana y una persona que necesita ayuda.

© Cengage Learning

Antes de ver

1. ¿Cuáles son los problemas sociales más comunes en los Estados Unidos? Existen esos problemas en tu comunidad?
2. ¿Qué tipo de ayuda crees que puede ofrecer un trabajador social para los problemas mencionados en la pregunta número 1?
3. ¿Hay lugares en tu comunidad donde puedes hablar con un trabajador social?

Comprensión

1. ¿Cómo se llama el hombre que habla con Ana Correa y qué problema tiene?

2. ¿Cómo está el hombre en el momento de la entrevista?

3. ¿Qué datos le pide la trabajadora social?

4. ¿Con quién vive el Sr. Gómez?

5. ¿Qué dice la Sra. Correa sobre el alcohol?

6. ¿Es el Sr. Gómez agresivo?

7. ¿Qué debe hacer el Sr. Gómez?

Después de ver

En grupos de tres, representen a una pareja o dos amigos que van a ver a un trabajador social por primera vez. Uno perdió *(lost)* su trabajo y no puede encontrar un nuevo trabajo. El trabajador social debe hacer preguntas y dar consejos.

El consejero debe preguntar sobre:

Nombre de la persona

Dirección y teléfono

Educación

Habilidades y talentos

Preferencias

Preguntas posibles para el consejero:

¿En qué les puedo ayudar?

¿Cómo están ahora?

5.35 **Un día en la vida** Completa el siguiente párrafo con la forma necesaria de la palabra entre paréntesis. A veces debes escoger entre dos palabras. ¡**OJO!** Algunos de los verbos requieren el uso del presente progresivo.

Me llamo Romina. **(1)** _____ (Ser/Estar) de Cuzco, Perú, pero

(2) _____ (ser/estar) en Nueva York. **(3)** _____ (Ser/Estar) cocinera ¡y

me encanta mi trabajo! Ahora estoy **(4)** _____ (trabajar) en un restaurante

con un cocinero francés. Estoy **(5)** _____ (aprender) mucho con él.

Yo **(6)** _____ (saber/conocer) a mis clientes muy bien. Ellos **(7)** _____

(venir) al restaurante con frecuencia y **(8)** _____ (decir) que mi comida es la

mejor en Nueva York. Algún día quiero **(9)** _____ (ser/estar) dueña *(owner)*

de un restaurante andino. Yo **(10)** _____ (saber/conocer) cocinar muy bien...

¡yo **(11)** _____ (hacer) unos platos deliciosos! **(12)** _____ (Ser/Estar)

segura de que puedo tener éxito.

5.36 **Descripción personal** Conjuga el verbo en la primera persona **(yo)**, y completa la oración de una forma original para escribir una descripción personal.

1. (Ser)... **5.** Yo no (saber)...

2. Hoy (estar)... **6.** (Conocer) a...

3. (Venir) a la clase de... **7.** No (hacer)...

4. Los fines de semana (salir)... **8.** (Conducir)...

5.37 **Mensajes de texto** Estás visitando la ciudad de Barcelona, en España, y escribes varios mensajes en tu teléfono celular para decirles a tus amigos lo que estás haciendo en ese momento. Usa el presente progresivo para hablar de tus actividades.

1. 10:30 A.M. – caminar por el parque Güell

2. 1:00 P.M. – comprar recuerdos en las Ramblas

3. 2:00 P.M. – almorzar en el Café 4Gats

4. 4:00 P.M. – visitar el mercado

5. 6:00 P.M. – ver cuadros en el Museo de Picasso

6. 8:00 P.M. – beber y comer en un restaurante de tapas

5.38 **En el trabajo** Explica lo que las siguientes personas saben o conocen según *(according to)* la profesión que tienen.

Modelo Isabel es veterinaria.
　　　　Ella conoce a las mascotas de sus clientes. Sabe cómo ayudar a los animales.

1. Leticia es mesera. **4.** Mario es deportista.

2. Ernesto es secretario. **5.** Alicia es ama de casa.

3. Esmeralda es mujer policía. **6.** Marcelo es maestro.

5.39 **Descripción de fotos** Con un compañero describan las siguientes fotos. Deben determinar quiénes son las personas en las fotos, qué relación tienen, cuáles son sus profesiones, qué están haciendo y qué emociones se muestran en las fotos. **¡OJO** con los verbos **ser** y **estar**!

Modelo *Marta no está contenta. Es escritora y está hablando por teléfono con el editor.*
Él necesita el libro en dos semanas.

5.40 **Información, por favor** Trabaja con un compañero. Uno debe mirar el gráfico en esta página y el otro debe mirar el gráfico en el **Apéndice B.** Túrnense para preguntarse y completar el gráfico con la información necesaria. Necesitan identificar sus profesiones, sus orígenes, dónde están ahora y cómo están. Atención al uso de **ser** y **estar.**

Nombre	Profesión	Origen	Localización	Emoción
Carlota		Madrid	la casa	
Éric			el banco	frustrado
César	periodista	San Juan		cansado
Paloma	abogada		el correo	
Samuel		Managua	la oficina	
Camila	diseñadora			divertida

5.41 **¿Estás feliz?** Tú y tu compañero trabajan para una revista y deben escribir un test de felicidad para los lectores *(readers)*.

Paso 1 Escribe una lista de 5–7 actividades que hace una persona feliz.

Paso 2 Comparte *(Share)* tu lista con tu compañero y decidan 6 actividades que deben incluir en el test.

Paso 3 Tomen el test y descubran si son felices. Después compartan los resultados con el resto de la clase.

🔊 Vocabulario 1

1-32

Los estados de ánimo y otras expresiones con el verbo *estar*

aburrido(a)	*bored*	enojado(a)	*angry*
alegre	*happy*	equivocado(a)	*wrong*
asustado(a)	*scared*	feliz	*happy*
avergonzado(a)	*embarrassed*	frustrado(a)	*frustrated*
borracho(a)	*drunk*	interesado(a)	*interested*
cansado(a)	*tired*	loco(a)	*crazy*
celoso(a)	*jealous*	nervioso(a)	*nervous*
confundido(a)	*confused*	ocupado(a)	*busy*
contento(a)	*happy*	preocupado(a)	*worried*
deprimido(a)	*depressed*	sano(a)	*healthy*
divertido(a)	*entertained; in a good mood*	seguro(a)	*sure*
		sorprendido(a)	*surprised*
enamorado(a) (de)	*in love (with)*	triste	*sad*
enfermo(a)	*sick*		

Palabras adicionales

la salud   *health*

Diccionario personal

_____

_____

_____

_____

_____

_____

_____

_____

_____

🔊 Vocabulario 2

1-33

Las profesiones

el (la) abogado(a)	lawyer
el actor	actor
la actriz	actress
el (la) agente de viajes	travel agent
el amo(a) de casa	homemaker
el (la) arquitecto(a)	architect
el (la) asistente de vuelo	flight attendant
el bailarín/la bailarina	dancer
el (la) cantante	singer
el (la) científico(a)	scientist
el (la) cocinero(a)	cook
el (la) consejero(a)	adviser
el (la) contador(a)	accountant
el (la) dependiente	clerk
el (la) deportista	athlete
el (la) diseñador(a)	designer
el (la) enfermero(a)	nurse
el (la) escritor(a)	writer
el (la) fotógrafo(a)	photographer

el (la) ingeniero(a)	engineer
el jefe/la jefa	boss
el (la) maestro(a)	elementary/ high school teacher
el (la) mecánico(a)	mechanic
el (la) médico(a)	doctor
el (la) mesero(a)	waiter
el (la) modelo	model
el (la) músico(a)	musician
el (la) periodista	journalist
el (la) piloto	pilot
el (la) pintor(a)	painter
el policía/la mujer policía	police officer
el (la) político(a)	politician
el (la) psicólogo(a)	psychologist
el (la) secretario(a)	secretary
el (la) trabajador(a) social	social worker
el (la) vendedor(a)	salesperson
el (la) veterinario(a)	veterinarian

Palabras adicionales

el (la) cliente	client
la entrevista	interview
la solicitud	application; want ad

el sueldo	salary
el trabajo	job

Los verbos

conducir	to drive
conocer	to know, to be acquainted with
dar	to give
decir (i)	to say, to tell
ganar	to earn
hacer	to do, to make
oír	to hear
poner	to put; to set

saber	to know (facts; how to do something)
salir	to go out, to leave
seguir (i)	to follow
traer	to bring
venir (ie)	to come
ver	to see

Learning Strategy

Study with a partner

Study with a friend or form a study group. Not only will you benefit when someone in your group understands a concept that you may have difficulty with, but you can also increase your own understanding by teaching others who need extra help. Group study will provide you with more opportunities to speak and listen to Spanish as well.

In this chapter you will learn how to:

- Talk about your daily routine
- Discuss your hobbies and pastimes
- Talk about when and how often you do things
- Talk about sports
- Discuss events that occurred in the past

¿Cómo pasas el día?

© Caroline Webber/age fotostock

Es temprano por la mañana y la familia Cervantes comienza su día.

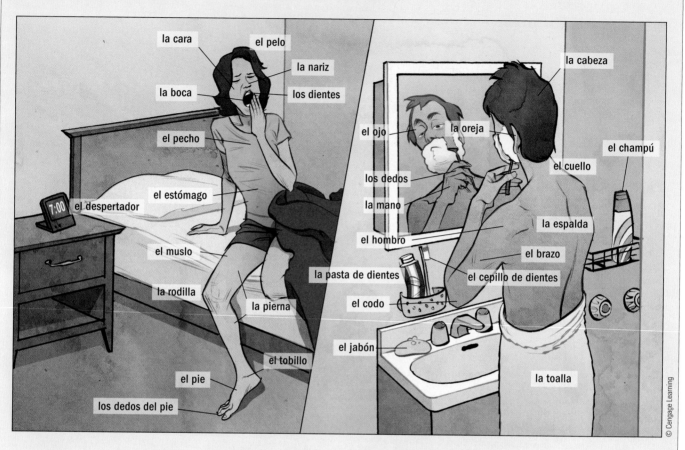

la cara · el pelo · la nariz · la boca · los dientes · el pecho · el estómago · el despertador · el muslo · la rodilla · la pierna · el tobillo · el pie · los dedos del pie · la cabeza · el ojo · la oreja · el champú · el cuello · los dedos · la mano · la espalda · el hombro · la pasta de dientes · el cepillo de dientes · el brazo · el codo · el jabón · la toalla

© Cengage Learning

Verbos

acostarse (ue)	to go to bed, to lie down	**ducharse**	to shower	**verse**	to look at oneself
afeitarse	to shave	**estirarse**	to stretch	**vestirse (i)**	to get dressed
arreglarse	to fix oneself up; to get ready	**lavarse**	to wash		
		levantarse	to get up		
bañarse	to bathe, to take a bath	**maquillarse**	to put on make-up		
cepillarse	to brush	**peinarse**	to comb or style one's hair		
cortarse	to cut				
despertarse (ie)	to wake up	**ponerse (la ropa)**	to put on (clothing)		
divertirse (ie)	to have fun	**quitarse (la ropa)**	to take off (clothing)		
dormirse (ue)	to fall asleep	**secarse**	to dry oneself		
		sentarse (ie)	to sit down		

Palabras adicionales

tarde	late
temprano	early

> **INVESTIGUEMOS EL VOCABULARIO**
>
> In addition to **el pelo**, **el cabello** can also be used to refer to hair.

A practicar

6.1 **Escucha y responde** Vas a escuchar varias partes del cuerpo. Señala la parte del cuerpo que escuches.

 1-34

6.2 **Asociaciones** ¿Qué ropa asocias con las siguientes partes del cuerpo?

1. los pies   3. la cabeza   5. el cuello
2. las piernas   4. las manos   6. la espalda y el pecho

6.3 **¿Qué parte del cuerpo es?** Completa las descripciones.

1. _____ está entre la cabeza y los hombros y sirve para mover la cabeza.

2. Tenemos dos _____, y cada uno tiene cinco dedos. Sirven para caminar y bailar.

3. Usamos _____ para hablar y para comer.

4. Tenemos dos _____ en la cara para ver.

5. _____ está en el brazo, entre la mano y el hombro.

6. Tenemos dos _____. Una está en el lado izquierdo de la cabeza, y la otra en el lado derecho.

7. Yo tengo _____ largo, rubio y rizado *(curly).*

8. _____ es una parte que conecta la pierna con el pie.

6.4 **No corresponde** Trabaja con un compañero. Observen los grupos de palabras y túrnense para decidir cuál es diferente. Expliquen por qué.

Modelo la pierna   la toalla   el pie
la toalla porque no sirve para caminar

1. los pies	las manos	el cuello
2. los dedos	la boca	la nariz
3. el pelo	el codo	la rodilla
4. el estómago	el diente	la espalda
5. el muslo	la oreja	el tobillo
6. el despertador	la pasta de dientes	el jabón

6.5 **¿Cuándo?** Con un compañero, túrnense para explicar en qué situaciones una persona tiene que hacer las siguientes actividades.

Modelo ducharse con agua fría
Estudiante 1: *¿Por qué una persona tiene que ducharse con agua fría?*
Estudiante 2: *La persona tiene mucho calor.*

1. sentarse al frente de la clase

2. acostarse muy tarde

3. vestirse con ropa muy vieja

4. estirarse

5. levantarse muy temprano

6. afeitarse las piernas

7. cortarse el pelo

8. cepillarse los dientes

> **INVESTIGUEMOS EL VOCABULARIO**
>
> In some Latin American countries, **el dentífrico** is used rather than **la pasta de dientes** to say *toothpaste.*
> In Mexico **rasurarse** is used to say *to shave* rather than **afeitarse,** and **bañarse** refers to both showering and bathing.

6.6 **Unos monstruos** Trabaja con un compañero. Uno debe mirar el dibujo en esta página, y el otro va a mirar el dibujo en el **Apéndice B.** Túrnense para describir los monstruos y encontrar las cinco diferencias.

© Cengage Learning

Conexiones culturales

La vida diaria

Cultura

Antonio López García (1936–) es un famoso artista español. Comenzó a pintar influenciado por su tío, quien era pintor. López García escribió: "Una obra nunca se acaba *(is finished)*, sino que se llega al límite de las propias *(own)* posibilidades". Con esta idea describe su propio proceso como pintor, ya que *(since)* a veces toma muchos años para terminar un cuadro. Varias de sus obras reflejan momentos de la vida diaria. Algunos críticos definen su estilo como hiperrealista porque sus cuadros parecen casi fotografías.

Observa su cuadro *Lavabo y espejo*. ¿Qué objetos reconoces? ¿Te gusta? ¿Por qué? ¿Qué sentimientos *(feelings)* te inspira?

Investiga en Internet otras obras de Antonio López García. Sube una que te guste en Share It! con el título de la pintura. Identifica qué hay en la pintura y explica por qué te gusta.

Antonio López García, *Lavabo y espejo*

Comparaciones

Cada país tiene frases y refranes que reflejan la cultura popular. Las siguientes frases populares se relacionan con las partes del cuerpo. Por ejemplo, la frase "cuesta un ojo de la cara" significa que algo cuesta mucho dinero. Si una persona dice "¡Hoy en día *(Nowadays)* la gasolina cuesta un ojo de la cara!" significa que la gasolina es muy costosa. ¿Puedes adivinar el significado de los refranes después de leer los ejemplos? ¿Conoces alguna frase que signifique lo mismo en inglés?

1. **ser codo**
   ¡Mi novio es muy codo! Nunca me invita a cenar.

2. **hacérsele (a uno) agua la boca**
   Mi mamá hace un flan delicioso. ¡Se me hace agua la boca!

3. **tomar el pelo**
   ¿No hay exámenes en la clase de matemáticas? ¿Me estás tomando el pelo?

4. **no tener pies ni cabeza**
   No entiendo la explicación. No tiene ni pies ni cabeza.

5. **no tener pelos en la lengua**
   Mi hermana no tiene pelos en la lengua y siempre dice lo que piensa.

> **INVESTIGUEMOS LA MÚSICA**
>
> Listen to "Mis Ojos" by the Mexican rock group Maná. Write all the parts of the body mentioned in the song. Listen a second time. What is the tone of the song? Why?

Conexiones... a la música

Pin Pon fue originalmente un programa de televisión de Chile en el que un personaje *(character)* llamado Pin Pon le enseña a los niños buenos hábitos y valores *(values)*. La siguiente es una canción infantil de este programa. Pin Pon se conoce en todos los países latinoamericanos.

© Carlos Restrepo/Shutterstock

Pin Pon es un **muñeco**   *doll*
con cara de cartón
se lava la carita
con agua y con jabón.

Se peina los cabellos
con peines de **marfil**   *ivory*
y aunque le den **tirones**   *tugs*
no **llora** ni hace así.   *cry*

Como siempre **obedece**   *obeys*
lo que manda mamá
estudia las lecciones
antes de irse a acostar.

Y cuando las **estrellas**   *stars*
empiezan a **brillar**   *to shine*
Pin Pon se va a la cama
reza y se echa a soñar.

¿Conoces alguna canción en inglés con el mismo propósito *(goal)*? ¿Qué dice la canción?

Busca el nombre de una película chilena y aprende más sobre Chile en **Exploraciones del mundo hispano** en el **Apéndice A.**

Comunidad

Como la canción de Pin Pon, existen muchos libros para niños que enseñan a tener buenos hábitos de higiene. Pregunta en la biblioteca de tu comunidad si tienen un programa para leerles en español a los niños. Si tu biblioteca no tiene un programa, puedes ser voluntario en un programa bilingüe en un jardín de niños o en una escuela primaria. ¡Leer es una magnífica manera de practicar español!

© Rob Marmion/Shutterstock

A analizar

Camila habla con su consejera sobre su rutina. Después de ver el video, lee lo que Camila dice y observa las estructuras de los verbos.

© Cengage Learning

> Todos los días **me despierto** a las seis, **me peino** rápidamente y **me visto**. Después de **arreglarme**, despierto a mi hijo y preparo su cereal… Acuesto al niño y después mi esposo y yo vemos la tele un poco. Antes **de acostarme**, me baño. Prefiero **bañarme** en la noche porque no tengo mucho tiempo en la mañana. **Me acuesto**, leo y **me duermo**.

1. What is the subject of the verbs in bold in the examples above?
2. What do you notice about the verbs in bold in the paragraph above?
3. Notice the different structures of the verbs **acostar** and **despertar** in the examples below. How are they different? Why do you think the structures are different?

   > Todos los días **me despierto** a las seis… / **despierto** a mi hijo y preparo su cereal…

   > **Acuesto** al niño… / **Me acuesto,** leo y me duermo.

A comprobar

Reflexive verbs

1. Many verbs used to discuss daily routines (**bañarse, despertarse, vestirse**, etc.) are known as reflexive verbs. Reflexive verbs are used to indicate that the subject performing the action also receives the action of the verb. In other words, these verbs are used to describe actions we do to ourselves.

   > Ella **se pone** un vestido azul.
   > *She puts on (herself) a blue dress.*

   > Yo **me levanto** temprano.
   > *I get (myself) up early.*

2. Reflexive verbs are conjugated in the same manner as other verbs; however, they must have a reflexive pronoun. The reflexive pronoun agrees with the subject of the verb.

   lavarse *(to wash oneself)*

yo	**me** lavo	nosotros	**nos** lavamos
tú	**te** lavas	vosotros	**os** laváis
él, ella, usted	**se** lava	ellos, ellas, ustedes	**se** lavan

The following verbs from the **Vocabulario** section are verbs with reflexive pronouns:

acostarse* (ue)	divertirse* (ie)	ponerse
afeitarse	dormirse* (ue)	quitarse
arreglarse	ducharse	secarse
bañarse	estirarse	sentarse* (ie)
cepillarse	lavarse	verse
despertarse* (ie)	levantarse	vestirse* (i)

*stem-changing verbs

3. The reflexive pronoun is placed in front of a conjugated verb.

   > Nosotros **nos** acostamos tarde.
   > *We go to bed late.*

   > Yo **me** estoy durmiendo.
   > *I am falling asleep.*

INVESTIGUEMOS LA GRAMÁTICA

Dormirse has a reflexive pronoun, but it is slightly different from the other reflexive verbs. The pronoun indicates a change of state rather than a subject doing something to himself/herself.

4. When using an infinitive, attach the reflexive pronoun to the end. Note that even in the infinitive form, the pronoun agrees with the subject. The pronoun can also be attached to the present participle, but you must add an accent to maintain the original stress.

> ¿Vas a bañar**te** ahora?
> *Are you going to bathe now?*

> Estoy lavándo**me** la cara.
> *I am washing my face.*

5. Many verbs can be used reflexively or nonreflexively, depending on who (or what) receives the action.

> Gerardo **se lava** las manos.
> *Gerardo **washes** his (own) hands.*

> Felipe **lava** el coche.
> *Felipe **washes** the car.*

> (Felipe does not receive the action; the car does.)

> Rebeca **se mira** en el espejo.
> *Rebeca **looks at herself** in the mirror.*

> Los niños miran a la maestra.
> *The children **look at** the teacher.*

> (The children do not receive the action; the teacher does.)

6. When using reflexive verbs, do not use possessive adjectives.

> Silvia se lava **el** pelo.
> *Silvia washes **her** hair.*

7. Some verbs have a slightly different meaning when used with a reflexive pronoun, such as **irse** *(to go away, to leave)* and **dormirse** *(to fall asleep).*

> Liz **se duerme** a las diez todas las noches.
> *Liz falls asleep at ten o'clock every night.*

> Liz **duerme** ocho horas cada noche.
> *Liz sleeps eight hours each night.*

A practicar

6.7 **Conclusiones lógicas** Empareja las columnas para hacer oraciones lógicas.

1. El despertador suena a las ocho y tú...
2. No hay agua caliente y por eso yo...
3. Empieza la clase de aeróbic y la profesora...
4. Son las once de la noche y nosotros...
5. Tengo que ir a una fiesta formal y yo...
6. Después de comer ellos...

a. me pongo un vestido elegante.
b. se estira.
c. se cepillan los dientes.
d. te levantas y te vistes.
e. nos acostamos.
f. prefiero no ducharme.

Estrategia

Form a study group

Reflexive verbs do not exist in English. Study with classmates to be sure that you all understand the concept in Spanish.

6.8 **Mis hábitos** Habla con un compañero sobre tus hábitos. Conjuga el verbo en la forma apropiada y completa las oraciones.

Modelo Yo (lavarse) el pelo...
> Estudiante 1: *Yo me lavo el pelo con Champú Reina, ¿y tú?*
> Estudiante 2: *Yo me lavo el pelo con Champú Brillo.*

1. Los fines de semana yo (acostarse)...
2. Yo (estirarse) cuando...
3. A veces yo (dormirse) cuando...
4. Yo nunca (ponerse)...
5. En clase de español prefiero (sentarse)...
6. Yo (divertirse) cuando...

NotarYES/Shutterstock

6.9 **Entrevista** Entrevista a un compañero con estas preguntas.

1. ¿A qué hora te despiertas de lunes a viernes? ¿y los sábados o domingos?
2. Generalmente, ¿cuánto tiempo necesitas para arreglarte?
3. ¿En qué ocasiones te pones ropa elegante?
4. ¿A veces te duermes en clase? ¿En qué clase?
5. ¿Qué haces para divertirte?
6. ¿Prefieres bañarte o ducharte?

6.10 Una mañana muy apurada Completa el siguiente párrafo con la forma necesaria del verbo apropiado. Después, compara tus respuestas con las de un compañero. **¡OJO!** Unos verbos son reflexivos y otros no.

Carmen (**1.**) _____ (despertar/despertarse) y (**2.**) _____ (mirar/mirarse) el reloj. ¡Las siete de la mañana! Los niños deben estar en la escuela a las ocho. Rápidamente va al cuarto de sus hijos y (**3.**) _____ (despertar/despertarse) a Carlos y Víctor. Ellos (**4.**) _____ (levantar/levantarse) y van al baño. Mientras los niños (**5.**) _____ (bañar/bañarse), Carmen (**6.**) _____ (preparar/prepararse) el desayuno *(breakfast)* para ellos. Cuando Carlos y Víctor entran en la cocina para desayunar, Carmen corre al baño y empieza a (**7.**) _____ (arreglar/arreglarse). Ella (**8.**) _____ (maquillar/maquillarse) y (**9.**) _____ (vestir/vestirse). Después Carmen (**10.**) _____ (llamar/llamarse) a sus hijos. Carlos y Víctor van al baño y (**11.**) _____ (cepillar/cepillarse) los dientes. Carmen (**12.**) _____ (peinar/peinarse) a los chicos y todos salen de la casa a las ocho menos diez.

6.11 Las rutinas ¿Qué están haciendo estas personas?

 **1.**  **2.** **3.**

 **4.**  **5.**  **6.**

6.12 En busca de... Busca a compañeros que hagan las siguientes actividades. Habla con una persona diferente para cada actividad de la lista. **¡OJO!** Tienes que decidir si debes usar la forma reflexiva del verbo o no y conjugarlo para preguntarles a tus compañeros. Luego comparte *(share)* la información con la clase.

Modelo (duchar/ducharse) en la noche
 Estudiante 1: *¿Te duchas en la noche?*
 Estudiante 2: *Sí, me ducho en la noche.*

 1. (levantar/levantarse) temprano los fines de semana
 2. preferir (vestir/vestirse) con ropa cómoda
 3. (lavar/lavarse) la ropa una vez a la semana
 4. normalmente (dormir/dormirse) siete horas
 5. preferir (sentar/sentarse) al frente de la clase
 6. (poner/ponerse) la mesa antes de comer
 7. (afeitar/afeitarse) todos los días
 8. (cepillar/cepillarse) a una mascota

A analizar ▶

Camila habla con su consejera. Mira el video otra vez. Después lee lo que dice Camila y observa las expresiones de tiempo en negritas.

Todos los días me despierto a las seis, me peino rápidamente y me visto. **Después de** arreglarme, despierto a mi hijo y preparo su cereal. Mi mamá **siempre** llega a las siete y media y yo salgo para la escuela. Paso el día en la escuela enseñando y **a veces** tengo reuniones con los otros maestros o con los padres de los niños en la tarde. Normalmente llego a casa **a las cinco** y empiezo a preparar la comida. **Después** mi esposo limpia la cocina mientras yo juego con mi hijo. Acuesto al niño y **después** mi esposo y yo vemos la tele un poco. **Antes de** acostarme, me baño.

1. What form of the verb is used after the expressions **antes de** and **después de**?
2. What form of the verb is used with the other expressions of time?

A comprobar

Adverbs of time and frequency

1. One of the functions of an adverb is to tell when an action occurs. The following are common adverbs of time, some of which you have already learned:

a menudo	*often*
ahora	*now*
hoy	*today*
luego	*later*
mañana	*tomorrow*
más tarde	*later*
pronto	*soon*
todos los días	*every day*

> **Más tarde** ellos van a arreglarse para salir.
> *Later they are going to get ready to go out.*
>
> Carmina está duchándose **ahora**.
> *Carmina is showering now.*

Notice that it is possible to use the adverb either before or after the action.

2. The following adverbs of time usually come before the verb:

a veces*	*sometimes*
mientras*	*while*
normalmente	*normally, usually*
(casi) nunca	*(almost) never*
(casi) siempre	*(almost) always*
todavía	*still*
ya	*already*
ya no	*no longer*

*If using a subject in the sentence, these adverbs are placed in front of the subject.

> **A veces** mi hermana se acuesta después de la medianoche.
> *Sometimes my sister goes to bed after midnight.*
>
> Mi padre **nunca** se afeita los fines de semana.
> *My father **never** shaves on the weekend.*

3. To say what someone does before or after another activity, use the expressions **antes de** + *infinitive* and **después de** + *infinitive*.

> **Antes de acostarse, mi hijo lee un libro.**
> *Before going to bed, my son reads a book.*

> **Los niños necesitan cepillarse los dientes después de comer.**
> *The children need to brush their teeth after eating.*

When using a verb after a preposition (**a, con, de, para,** etc.), it is necessary to use the infinitive. **Antes** and **después** can also be used without the preposition **de;** however, the meaning changes slightly and they are translated as *beforehand* and

afterwards, respectively. They are followed by the conjugated verb.

> **Normalmente tomo un café y después voy a la universidad.**
> *Normally I have coffee and afterwards I go to the university.*

4. When saying how often you do something, use the word **vez** *(time)*.

> Él se corta las uñas **una vez a la semana.**
> *He cuts his nails **once a week.***

> Me cepillo los dientes **tres veces al día.**
> *I brush my teeth **three times a day.***

Notice that this adverbial expression comes after the activity.

A practicar

6.12 **¿Cierto o falso?** Habla con un compañero y dile *(tell him/her)* si las oraciones son ciertas o falsas para ti. Corrige las oraciones falsas para que sean *(so that they are)* ciertas.

1. Normalmente me seco el pelo con una secadora.
2. Me cepillo los dientes diez veces al día.
3. Me afeito todos los días.
4. Me ducho y luego me acuesto.
5. Escucho música mientras me arreglo.
6. Me visto después de cepillarme los dientes.
7. A menudo me despierto antes de escuchar el despertador.
8. Nunca me maquillo.

6.13 **¿Qué haces?** Completa las oraciones con las actividades que haces con la frecuencia indicada.

Modelo Siempre... *tomo café antes de la clase de español.*

1. Todos los días...
2. Una vez al día...
3. A veces...
4. Una vez al mes...
5. Una vez al año...
6. Ya no...
7. Casi nunca...
8. Nunca...

Siempre tomo café antes de la clase de español.

© beginwithaspin/Shutterstock

6.14 **¿Cuándo?** Mira las ilustraciones y explica cuándo las personas hacen una de las actividades en relación a la otra.

Modelo *Antes de ponerse un sombrero, se peina. /*
Después de peinarse, se pone un sombrero.

1.

2.

3.

4.

5.

6.

6.15 **¿Con qué frecuencia?** Con un compañero, pregúntense con qué frecuencia hacen las actividades de la lista.

Modelo cepillarse los dientes
Estudiante 1: *¿Con qué frecuencia te cepillas los dientes?*
Estudiante 2: *Me cepillo los dientes tres veces al día.*

1. levantarse antes de las ocho
2. bañarse (en la bañera)
3. ponerse ropa elegante
4. cortarse el pelo
5. lavarse la cara
6. dormirse con la tele encendida *(turned on)*
7. afeitarse
8. acostarse tarde

6.16 **¿Qué haces antes?** Con un compañero, túrnense para contestar las preguntas sobre sus actividades anteriores.

Modelo antes de levantarse
Estudiante 1: *¿Qué haces antes de levantarte?*
Estudiante 2: *Antes de levantarme apago* (turn off) *el despertador y escucho un poco de música.*

1. antes de salir para la universidad
2. antes de tomar un examen
3. antes de hacer ejercicio
4. antes de comer
5. antes de salir con amigos
6. antes de acostarse
7. antes de hacer un viaje
8. antes de comprar un coche

6.17 **Opuestas** Elisa y Florencia son muy diferentes y comparten *(share)* un apartamento. Con un compañero, túrnense para comparar sus hábitos. Usen algunos de los adverbios de tiempo.

Modelo Elisa lava la ropa todas las semanas pero Florencia casi nunca lava la ropa.

Elisa

Florencia

© Cengage Learning

6.18 **Entrevista** Con un compañero, túrnense para responder las preguntas y describir sus rutinas. Usen los adverbios de tiempo para explicar la secuencia de actividades.

1. ¿Cómo es tu rutina por la mañana?
2. ¿Cómo es tu rutina por la noche?
3. ¿Cómo es un día típico en la universidad?
4. ¿Cómo es un día típico en el trabajo?
5. ¿Cómo es un sábado típico?
6. ¿Cómo es un domingo típico?
7. ¿Cómo es una cita romántica típica?
8. ¿Cómo es una típica celebración de Año Nuevo?

6.19 **Una vida sana** En un grupo de 3–4 estudiantes van a decidir quién tiene la vida más sana.

Paso 1 Escribe una lista de 7–8 hábitos y actividades que consideras sanas.

Paso 2 Comparte tu lista con los otros de tu grupo. Luego decidan 6 o 7 hábitos y actividades que piensan que son las más importantes para mantener una vida sana.

Paso 3 Pregúntense *(Ask each other)* con qué frecuencia hacen las actividades de la lista. Luego repórtenle a la clase quién tiene la vida más sana y por qué.

Entrando en materia

¿Qué le puedes decir a un niño que te pregunta por qué debemos lavarnos las manos?

Cómo mantenernos sanos

🔊 Vas a escuchar un fragmento de un programa para niños en donde hablan sobre buenos
1-35 hábitos de higiene personal. Escucha con atención y responde las preguntas que siguen.

Vocabulario útil

contagiarse	*to become infected*	**frotar**	*to rub*
enfermarse	*to become sick*	**los gérmenes**	*germs*
la enfermedad	*illness*	**la higiene**	*hygiene*
estornudar	*to sneeze*	**los resfriados**	*colds*
la época	*era, time*	**toser**	*to cough*

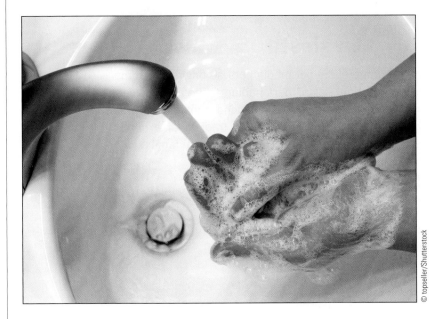

© topseller/Shutterstock

Comprensión

1. ¿Quién es el invitado *(guest)* al programa de hoy?
2. ¿Cuál es el tema del programa?
3. ¿Cómo llegan al cuerpo los gérmenes y bacterias?
4. ¿Qué significa "lavarse bien las manos"?
5. ¿Qué debe (o no) hacer una persona enferma para no contagiar a otros?

🖧 Más allá

Escoge una de las siguientes opciones, escribe una explicación para niños y compártela en
Share It!

1. por qué deben lavarse los dientes
2. por qué deben lavarse el pelo y peinarse

Lectura

Take notes while you read to improve your focus and comprehension of the material. Use the margins to write down phrases or key words that summarize the main idea of each paragraph in Spanish. The more you use the language actively without translating, such as by taking notes in Spanish, the closer you will be to feeling comfortable with Spanish and becoming more fluent.

Antes de leer

1. ¿Qué personas crees que toman siestas más frecuentemente y por qué?
2. ¿En qué países piensas que se toman siestas y por qué?

A leer

La siesta

La costumbre de dormir durante el día por media hora se originó en Roma, donde se usaba la expresión "hora sexta" para hablar del tiempo dedicado a dormir y descansar después de cinco horas de mucho trabajo. En España *became* "la hora sexta" **se convirtió** en *la siesta.* En el horario tradicional, exportado después a los países latinoamericanos, la gente come con su familia al mediodía y después descansa un poco antes de volver a trabajar.

Este tiempo es importante porque la comida al mediodía es la comida principal en muchos de

[recomiendan la siesta como algo positivo]

estos países, y es saludable tomar tiempo para digerir. Además, en los meses cuando hace mucho calor, nadie quiere salir a la calle durante *the warmest* estas horas, **las más calurosas** del día. Muchos estudios científicos recomiendan la siesta como algo positivo para la salud *as* **ya que** previene problemas cardiacos, ayuda a la digestión y

Casi nadie sale durante la hora de la siesta.

disminuye el estrés. Aún más, aunque las personas no siempre usan la siesta para dormir, la interrupción de las labores permite a las familias reunirse y pasar más tiempo juntas.

En algunos países hay empresas que entienden el valor de la siesta, y dan a sus trabajadores un espacio donde pueden descansar por algunos minutos para incrementar su productividad. Desafortunadamente, la hora dedicada a la siesta es una costumbre que está desapareciendo en muchos países. La gente ya casi nunca tiene tiempo para descansar debido principalmente a la presión de la vida en las ciudades, en donde el tiempo es poco, el tráfico y las distancias son grandes, y los negocios prefieren no cerrar, para tener algunos clientes más.

La siesta coincide con las horas de más calor.

Comprensión

1. ¿Cuál es el origen de la palabra *siesta*?
2. ¿Qué hacen las personas durante la hora de la siesta?
3. ¿Cuáles son los beneficios de tomar una siesta?
4. ¿Por qué está desapareciendo esta costumbre?
5. En tu opinión ¿crees que la costumbre de la siesta va a desaparecer por completo? ¿Por qué?

Después de leer

Habla con un compañero para responder las preguntas.

1. ¿Duermes una siesta a veces? ¿Por qué?
2. ¿Piensas que es una buena idea dormir siestas?
3. ¿Cuáles son las ventajas y las desventajas de dormir la siesta?

¡Es verano! Hace buen tiempo y algunas personas de la ciudad salen a disfrutar del buen tiempo.

esquiar en agua

la tienda de campaña

jugar al fútbol

el fútbol americano

la pelota

pescar

bucear

la raqueta

la red

el bádminton

patinar

los patines

andar en bicicleta

jugar al golf

montar a caballo

© Cengage Learning

Los deportes

el atletismo	track and field
el básquetbol	basketball
el béisbol	baseball
la natación	swimming
el tenis	tennis
el voleibol	volleyball

Los pasatiempos

acampar	to camp
esquiar en tabla	to snowboard
hacer alpinismo	to go mountain climbing
ir de excursión	to go hiking
jugar al ping-pong	to play ping-pong

levantar pesas	to lift weights
patinar en hielo	to ice skate

Palabras adicionales

el (la) aficionado(a)	fan (of a sport)
el campo	field
la cancha	court
el equipo	team; equipment
la entrada	ticket
el lago	lake
el partido	game (sport), match
el saco de dormir	sleeping bag

A practicar

6.20 **Escucha y responde** Vas a escuchar una lista de actividades. En un papel escribe **deporte** y en otro **equipo**. Si escuchas el nombre de un deporte, levanta el papel que dice **deporte**, y si es equipo para jugar, levanta el papel que dice **equipo**.

1-36

6.21 **¿Qué actividad es?** Identifica el nombre del deporte que se necesita para completar las oraciones.

INVESTIGUEMOS LA GRAMÁTICA

In Spanish it is possible to say both **juego fútbol** and **juego al fútbol**. Also, volleyball can be spelled as **volibol** or **voleibol**.

1. Es necesario tener dos equipos de seis personas, una pelota y una red para jugar al _____.
2. Jugamos _____ con raquetas, una mesa, una red y pelotas pequeñas.
3. Cuando vamos a acampar dormimos en_____.
4. Para jugar al fútbol necesitamos dos _____ de once personas.
5. Es necesario tener una _____ para jugar tenis.
6. El deporte más popular en Europa y Latinoamérica es _____.

6.22 **Relaciones** Con un compañero, túrnense para relacionar las palabras de las dos columnas y explicar la relación.

1. la raqueta	a. el básquetbol
2. esquiar	b. la entrada
3. el partido	c. patinar en el hielo
4. el voleibol	d. el equipo
5. la cancha	e. la red
6. el aficionado	f. el campo

6.23 **¿Qué palabra no corresponde al grupo?** Encuentra la palabra que no corresponda (belong), y después compara tus respuestas con las de un compañero. Expliquen por qué no corresponde.

1. pescar	nadar	acampar	bucear
2. la raqueta	la tienda de campaña	la pelota	la red
3. patinar en hielo	jugar al golf	esquiar	esquiar en tabla
4. el fútbol	ir de excursión	el béisbol	el básquetbol
5. el aficionado	el saco de dormir	el partido	la cancha

6.24 **En busca de...** Busca a compañeros en tu clase que hacen las siguientes actividades en su tiempo libre. Deben dar información adicional al responder. Después repórtenle la información a la clase.

Modelo jugar al ping-pong
    Estudiante 1: *¿Juegas al ping-pong?*
    Estudiante 2: *Sí, juego al ping-pong en casa de mis amigos.*

1. jugar al fútbol	5. jugar bien al básquetbol
2. levantar pesas	6. estar en un equipo deportivo
3. acampar en el verano	7. patinar en hielo
4. ver golf en televisión	8. gustar ver fútbol americano

6.25 **Actividades de verano** Los organizadores de los eventos de verano para una pequeña ciudad están intercambiando información sobre el equipo que necesitan y las actividades que tienen planeadas. Trabaja con un compañero para completar la información. Uno de ustedes debe ver la información en esta página, y el otro debe ver la información en el **Apéndice B**.

Evento	Lugar del evento	Equipo que tienen	Equipo/recursos que necesitan
1.		cancha	pelotas
2. Excursión a la playa	Playa Bonita		
3.	la piscina del parque		instructores
4. Torneo de ping-pong		seis mesas	
5.	el estadio universitario	red	

Cultura

El béisbol es muy popular en todos los países de la región del Caribe. Cuba, la República Dominicana y Venezuela son famosos por aportar excelentes jugadores de béisbol a las grandes ligas de los Estados Unidos, como el dominicano David Ortíz. San Pedro de Macorís, en la República Dominicana, es un pequeño pueblo que tiene una gran importancia para el béisbol, pues un gran número de jugadores de la MLB provienen de aquí. Uno de los jugadores más conocidos de este pueblo es Sammy Sosa.

Descubre el nombre de la isla que la República Dominicana comparte con Haití y aprende más sobre el país en **Exploraciones del mundo hispano** en el **Apéndice A.**

> **INVESTIGUEMOS LA MÚSICA**
>
> Similar to the Olympic Games, the FIFA World Cup soccer matches are played every four years. "We Are One" (Ola Ola) was selected as the official song of the 2014 World Cup and was performed by Jennifer López at the opening ceremony. The official anthem "Dar um Jeito" (We Will Find a Way) was performed at the closing ceremony by Carlos Santana, Wyclef Jean, Avicii and Alexandre Pires. Listen to both songs. Which do you like better? Why?

> Busca en Internet quiénes son otros beisbolistas famosos de San Pedro de Macorís y para quién juegan. ¿Cómo crees que afecta a un pueblo pequeño tener tantos deportistas famosos? ¡Comparte tu respuesta y los nombres de los beisbolistas en Share It!

Comunidad

Muchos deportistas en los Estados Unidos vienen de países hispanohablantes. Investiga si hay jugadores de países hispanohablantes en tu universidad y escribe una entrevista para ese deportista. Las siguientes son algunas ideas para la entrevista:

¿Por qué le gusta jugar?

¿Con qué frecuencia practica?

¿Quiere ser profesional? ¿Por qué?

¿Cuándo empezó a jugar?

¿Jugó en un equipo de la escuela secundaria?

¿El deporte le ayudó a llegar a la universidad? ¿Cómo?

Comparaciones

En muchos países de habla hispana se practican deportes en las universidades, pero juegan un papel diferente de los deportes en los Estados Unidos, donde los estudiantes obtienen créditos por practicar deportes. En Latinoamérica los deportes son considerados un entretenimiento y generalmente las personas no mencionan sus actividades deportivas en su curriculum vitae (résumé), excepto los deportistas. Sin embargo, la mayoría de las universidades tienen equipos deportivos que representan a su alma mater con orgullo.

¿Son importantes las actividades deportivas en tu universidad?

¿Hay becas (scholarships) para deportistas en tu universidad?

¿Son importantes las actividades deportivas en tu vida en general?

¿Cuántas horas a la semana practicas deportes?

> Busca una universidad en España o en Latinoamérica en Internet y compara las actividades deportivas que se ofrecen con las actividades de una universidad en los Estados Unidos. Después, comparte los resultados de tu comparación en Share It!

Conexiones... a la antropología

Muchas civilizaciones antiguas practicaban deportes como juegos de pelota, pero el objetivo no era solamente el entretenimiento ya que el juego tenía significados religiosos. Entre las culturas anteriores a los incas, en los Andes, se usaban pelotas de goma (rubber) para jugar juegos parecidos al hockey y al tenis de hoy en día. También llenaban un pequeño saco con arena (sand) y lo decoraban con plumas (feathers) para practicar un juego similar al bádminton de hoy.

En el juego de pelota azteca (Tlachtli) la cancha representaba el mundo, y la pelota el sol o la luna. En este juego, la pelota debía atravesar el aro hecho de piedra (stone). El juego de pelota azteca tenía una gran semejanza (similarity) con el juego Pok-a-tok de los mayas, juego en el que los jugadores debían tocar la pelota solamente con los codos, las rodillas o las caderas (hips).

¿Conoces el origen de otros deportes o juegos?

Juego de pelota de los mayas, en Tikal

Source: http://www.efdeportes.com/efd90/juego.htm

A analizar

Rodrigo habla con Óscar sobre el fin de semana. Mira el video. Después lee lo que dice Rodrigo y observa las formas de los verbos en negritas.

> Óscar: (Yo) Te **llamé** el sábado para invitarte al partido de fútbol, pero no **contestaste**.
>
> Rodrigo: Camila y yo **pasamos** el fin de semana en la casa de sus padres. Viven cerca de un lago, entonces mi suegro y yo salimos en el bote y **pescamos.** A mi suegra no le gusta pescar, así que Camila y ella **nadaron** y **tomaron** el sol. ¡Pero lo mejor del fin de semana fue la comida! ¡Mi suegra es muy buena cocinera y **preparó** unas comidas muy ricas!

© Cengage Learning

1. The boldfaced verbs are in the preterite tense. Do they refer to events that have already happened or that are going to happen in the future?

2. All the boldfaced words are **-ar** verbs. Using the verbs in the paragraph as a model, fill in the blanks with the appropriate verb endings .

-ar

yo	_____	nosotros(as)	_____
tú	-aste	vosotros(as)	-asteis
él, ella, usted	_____	ellos, ellas, ustedes	_____

A comprobar

The preterite

INVESTIGUEMOS LA GRAMÁTICA

Notice that the endings for regular **-er** and **-ir** verbs are identical in the preterite.

1. The preterite is used to discuss actions completed in the past.

> **¿Jugaste** al tenis ayer?
> *Did you **play** tennis yesterday?*
>
> No, **nadé** en la piscina.
> *No, I **swam** in the pool.*

2. To form the preterite of regular **-ar, -er,** and **-ir** verbs, add these endings to the stem of the verb.

comer *(to eat)*

yo	com**í**	nosotros(as)	com**imos**
tú	com**iste**	vosotros(as)	com**isteis**
él, ella, usted	com**ió**	ellos, ellas, ustedes	com**ieron**

hablar *(to speak, to talk)*

yo	habl**é**	nosotros(as)	habl**amos**
tú	habl**aste**	vosotros(as)	habl**asteis**
él, ella, usted	habl**ó**	ellos, ellas, ustedes	habl**aron**

escribir *(to write)*

yo	escrib**í**	nosotros(as)	escrib**imos**
tú	escrib**iste**	vosotros(as)	escrib**isteis**
él, ella, usted	escrib**ió**	ellos, ellas, ustedes	escrib**ieron**

3. -ar and -er verbs that have stem changes in the present tense do not have a stem change in the preterite. You will learn about -ir stem-changing verbs later in this chapter.

cerrar (*to close*)

yo	cerr**é**	nosotros(as)	cerr**amos**
tú	cerr**aste**	vosotros(as)	cerr**asteis**
él, ella, usted	cerr**ó**	ellos, ellas, ustedes	cerr**aron**

volver (*to return*)

yo	volv**í**	nosotros(as)	volv**imos**
tú	volv**iste**	vosotros(as)	volv**isteis**
él, ella, usted	volv**ió**	ellos, ellas, ustedes	volv**ieron**

4. Verbs ending in -**car**, -**gar**, and -**zar** have spelling changes in the first person singular (**yo**) in the preterite. Notice that the spelling changes preserve the original sound of the infinitive for -**car** and -**gar** verbs.

-car	c → qué
tocar	yo **toqué,** tú tocaste, él tocó,...
-gar	g → gué
jugar	yo **jugué,** tú jugaste, él jugó,...
-zar	z → cé
empezar	yo **empecé,** tú empezaste, él empezó,...

5. The third person singular and plural of **leer** and **oír** also have spelling changes. An unaccented **i** always changes to **y** when it appears between two vowels. Notice the use of accent marks on all forms except the third person plural.

leer (*to read*)

yo	leí	nosotros(as)	leímos
tú	leíste	vosotros(as)	leísteis
él, ella, usted	**leyó**	ellos, ellas, ustedes	**leyeron**

oír (*to hear*)

yo	oí	nosotros(as)	oímos
tú	oíste	vosotros(as)	oísteis
él, ella, usted	**oyó**	ellos, ellas, ustedes	**oyeron**

6. The following expressions are helpful when talking about the past:

anoche	last night
ayer	yesterday
la semana pasada	last week

A practicar

6.26 **El orden lógico** Héctor y Gustavo pasaron un muy buen fin de semana. Lee las oraciones sobre sus actividades y ponlas en un orden lógico.

_____ Héctor invitó a Gustavo a ir a la playa por el fin de semana.

_____ Los dos salieron para la playa.

_____ Héctor llamó a su mejor amigo, Gustavo.

_____ Gustavo llegó a la casa de Héctor a las siete.

_____ El viernes Héctor volvió a casa después de trabajar.

_____ Gustavo aceptó la invitación con mucho entusiasmo.

_____ Cuando llegaron a la playa, buscaron un hotel.

6.27 El sábado pasado Usa la información de los dibujos para describir lo que Beatriz hizo *(did)* el sábado pasado con su novio Arturo. Pueden usar los siguientes verbos u otros:

aceptar	beber	comer	comprar	ducharse	encontrarse *(to meet)*	ganar
hablar	invitar	lavarse	llamar	llegar	mirar	perder

INVESTIGUEMOS LOS VERBOS

You will learn irregular preterite verbs in **Capítulo 7**; however you may want to use the verb **ir** in this lesson. It is conjugated in the following manner:

yo	**fui**	nosotros(as)	**fuimos**
tú	**fuiste**	vosotros(as)	**fuisteis**
él, ella	**fue**	ellos, ellas	**fueron**
usted		ustedes	

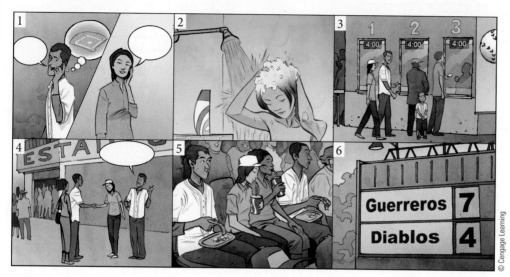

© Cengage Learning

6.28 ¿Qué hiciste? Con un compañero, completen las siguientes oraciones para hablar de su fin de semana. Usen el pretérito. Pueden usar los siguientes verbos u otros verbos.

Modelo Estudiante 1: *Anoche yo comí en un restaurante, ¿y tú?*
Estudiante 2: *Anoche yo cociné para mi familia.*

levantarse	trabajar	salir	estudiar	pasar bien/mal
limpiar	jugar	mirar	escribir	hablar por teléfono

1. El fin de semana pasado yo...
2. El viernes por la noche yo...
3. El sábado yo...
4. El sábado por la noche yo...
5. El domingo yo...
6. El domingo por la noche yo...

6.29 El verano pasado Con un compañero, túrnense para preguntar y contestar las preguntas sobre lo que hicieron *(you did)* el verano pasado.

1. ¿Trabajaste? ¿Dónde? ¿Cuántas horas a la semana?
2. ¿Viajaste? ¿Adónde? ¿Con quién?
3. ¿Tomaste clases? ¿Cuáles?
4. ¿Asististe a un evento (concierto, deporte, etc.)? ¿De qué? ¿Te gustó?
5. ¿Conociste a una persona? ¿A quién?
6. ¿Jugaste un deporte? ¿Cuál?

6.30 La semana pasada Escribe tres actividades que hiciste *(you did)* la semana pasada. Luego busca a tres compañeros diferentes que hicieron una de esas tres actividades también. **¡OJO!** Usa el pretérito.

A analizar

Rodrigo habla con Óscar sobre su fin de semana. Mira el video otra vez. Después lee lo que Rodrigo dice y observa las formas de los verbos.

Fernando **consiguió** unas entradas para el partido de los Toros el sábado pasado. Nos invitó a Vicente y a mí. Fernando y Vicente son grandes aficionados de los Toros y **se vistieron** de rojo, pero yo **me vestí** de los colores de las Chivas, ya sabes, soy gran aficionado de ellos. Después de llegar al estadio y sentarnos, **pedimos** algo de comer. Ellos **pidieron** perros calientes, pero yo pedí nachos. Cuando empezó el partido nos levantamos y gritamos por nuestros equipos. Todos **nos divertimos,** pero creo que ellos **se divirtieron** más porque al final ganaron los Toros.

© Cengage Learning

1. Write out the verb forms you see in bold in the paragraph above and identify how their stems are different from the present tense forms.

2. **Conseguir, vestirse, pedir,** and **divertirse** all have stem changes in the present as well as in the preterite. How are the stem changes different in the preterite?

A comprobar

Stem-changing verbs in the preterite

-ir verbs that have stem changes in the present tense also have stem changes in the preterite. The third person singular and plural (**él, ella, usted, ellos, ellas,** and **ustedes**) change e → i and o → u.

pedir *(to ask for, to request)*

yo	pedí	nosotros(as)	pedimos
tú	pediste	vosotros(as)	pedisteis
él, ella, usted	p**i**dió	ellos, ellas, ustedes	p**i**dieron

Yo **pedí** una quesadilla durante el partido.
Mis amigos **pidieron** tacos.

dormir *(to sleep)*

yo	dormí	nosotros(as)	dormimos
tú	dormiste	vosotros(as)	dormisteis
él, ella, usted	d**u**rmió	ellos, ellas, ustedes	d**u**rmieron

Other common stem-changing verbs:

conseguir (i)	repetir (i)
divertirse (i)	seguir (i)
morir (u)	servir (i)
preferir (i)	vestirse (i)

¿Se **divirtieron** ustedes?
Sí, nos **divertimos** mucho.

Todos **dormimos** en la tienda de campaña.
Mi hermano **durmió** en una hamaca.

A practicar

6.31 Un poco de lógica Decide si las siguientes oraciones son lógicas o no. Si no son lógicas, explica por qué.

1. Alfonso es aficionado al béisbol y consiguió entradas para un partido de su equipo favorito.
2. La mañana del partido se levantó, se vistió y después se bañó.
3. Como prefirió llegar antes de la primera entrada *(inning)*, salió de la casa muy tarde.
4. Sirvieron comida en el estadio y él pidió un taco y una soda.
5. Su equipo ganó y no se divirtió.
6. Cuando volvió a casa estaba cansado y se durmió inmediatamente.

6.32 En los Juegos Panamericanos Tomás, un entrenador, viajó con su equipo de voleibol a Guadalajara, México, para competir en los Juegos Panamericanos. Completa el siguiente párrafo con la forma apropiada del pretérito del verbo indicado. ¡OJO! No todos los verbos tienen cambio en el radical.

El equipo de Tomás Guitiérrez (**1.**) _____ (competir) en los Juegos

Panamericanos de verano. Antes de salir, Tomás llamó al Hotel Bahía y (**2.**) _____

(pedir) habitaciones para todos los jugadores. (**3.**) Las _____ (conseguir) a un

buen precio. Cuando llegaron, estaban muy cansados. (**4.**) _____ (pedir) servicio

a la habitación y (**5.**) _____ (acostarse). Todos (**6.**) _____ (dormir) bien

y (**7.**) _____ (despertarse) temprano para ir al estadio. (**8.**) Ellos _____

(jugar) bien y al final ganaron. Después del partido (**9.**) _____ (volver) al hotel.

Tomás decidió quedarse en la habitación leyendo, pero los jugadores (**10.**) _____

(preferir) relajarse en el sauna. Luego se bañaron y (**11.**) _____ (vestirse) para salir

a celebrar. Salieron a comer y después a bailar; (**12.**) _____ (divertirse) mucho.

6.33 Un día de fútbol Isabel y Mónica son aficionadas al fútbol. En parejas describan el día que fueron a un partido. Incluyan los siguientes verbos: **acostarse, conseguir, divertirse, dormirse, preferir, sentarse, vestirse** y **volver.**

6.34 **En el pasado** Con un compañero, túrnense para conjugar el verbo en el pretérito y completar las oraciones de una forma original. Reporten la información a la clase.

Modelo Ayer yo (jugar)…
Estudiante 1: *Ayer jugué al voleibol con mis amigas, ¿y tú?*
Estudiante 2: *Yo no jugué nada, pero mi hermano jugó al básquetbol.*

1. Anoche yo (dormir)…
2. La última vez *(last time)* que fui a mi restaurante favorito, yo (pedir)…
3. El fin de semana pasado yo (almorzar)…
4. Una vez que cociné, yo (servir)…
5. Esta mañana yo (preferir)…
6. El semestre pasado, yo (conseguir)…
7. Este semestre yo (comenzar)…
8. Una vez yo (perder)…

6.35 **Un evento** Entrevista a un compañero sobre la última vez que asistió a un evento (un partido, una obra de teatro, etcétera).

1. ¿A qué evento asististe?
2. ¿Con quién asististe al evento?
3. ¿Quién consiguió las entradas?
4. ¿Cómo se vistieron para el evento?
5. ¿Sirvieron comida? ¿Qué comida?
6. ¿Se divirtieron en el evento?
7. ¿A qué hora te acostaste?

6.36 **En busca de…** Pregúntales a ocho compañeros si hicieron las siguientes actividades. Habla con un compañero diferente para cada actividad. Tu compañero debe dar información adicional. Después reporten la información a la clase.

Modelo reír mucho el fin de semana (¿Por qué?)
Estudiante 1: *¿Reíste mucho el fin de semana?*
Estudiante 2: *Sí, reí mucho el fin de semana.*
Estudiante 1: *¿Por qué?*
Estudiante 2: *Porque miré una película cómica.*

1. almorzar en un restaurante la semana pasada (¿Cuál?)
2. divertirse durante el fin de semana (¿Dónde?)
3. vestirse elegante recientemente (¿Por qué?)
4. dormir bien anoche (¿Cuántas horas?)
5. pedir ayuda en una clase este semestre (¿Qué clase?)
6. conseguir un trabajo nuevo durante el año pasado (¿Dónde?)
7. servir la cena esta semana (¿Cuándo?)
8. perder algo recientemente (¿Qué?)

Lectura

Reading Strategy: Taking notes

In the first **Lectura** of this chapter you practiced taking notes as you read. Continue practicing this strategy by writing a brief note next to each paragraph of the following reading. Remember to use Spanish for your notes.

Antes de leer

¿Qué deportes piensas que son muy populares en España y Latinoamérica? ¿Sabes el nombre de un deportista famoso de estos lugares?

A leer

Deportistas famosos

pride

A veces un deportista es más que un deportista; a veces los atletas son símbolos de **orgullo** nacional y le dan a la juventud un ejemplo positivo. Tal es el caso de uno de los jugadores más famosos de fútbol, Lionel Messi.

Lionel Messi (1987–) es probablemente el jugador de fútbol argentino más conocido en el mundo desde la época de Diego Maradona. Messi juega para el Club FC Barcelona y el equipo nacional de Argentina. Tiene también la nacionalidad española desde el año 2005. La FIFA nombró a Messi como el mejor jugador del mundo en 2009 y en 2013.

© Maxisport/Shutterstock

> a veces los atletas son símbolos de orgullo nacional

growth

Leo, como se le conoce, nació en Rosario, Argentina. Su carrera como futbolista comenzó a los cinco años, cuando empezó a jugar en un club local. A los once años le diagnosticaron una deficiencia en la hormona del **crecimiento.** Aunque el River Plate —uno de los equipos más populares de la Argentina— estaba interesado en Messi, no quisieron pagar su tratamiento médico. En cambio, FC Barcelona se interesó en él de inmediato. Pagaron el tratamiento médico y Lionel y su familia **se mudaron** a Barcelona, donde Messi empezó a jugar para las categorías inferiores a los 13 años, jugando su primer partido con el equipo oficial a los 16 años.

moved

Además de ganar el título del mayor número de goles en numerosas ocasiones, la revista *Time* lo nombró una de las 32 personas más influyentes en el año 2011 (fue el único deportista de la lista). Messi también es embajador oficial de la UNICEF y tiene una fundación (Fundación Leo Messi) cuyo objetivo es ayudar a los niños y adolescentes en situación de **riesgo** a realizar sus sueños.

risk

Mariana Pajón (1991–) es una deportista colombiana que practica el ciclismo. Aunque su **hazaña** más conocida es haber ganado una medalla en los Juegos Olímpicos de Londres 2012, la trayectoria de Pajón inició cuando ganó una **carrera** a los cuatro años, compitiendo contra niños de cinco y seis años. Mariana viene de una familia de deportistas, ya que su padre practicaba el automovilismo y su madre la **equitación**.

feat

race

horseback riding

Además de la medalla de **oro** en Londres, entre sus **logros,** Mariana ganó medallas de oro en los Juegos Olímpicos Panamericanos (2011), los Juegos Centroamericanos y del Caribe (2010) y los Juegos Sudamericanos (2010). Fue nombrada la atleta del año en Colombia en 2011. En el año 2010, tan solo en los Estados Unidos, Pajón ganó el primer lugar en el *North American Continental Championship* y en la competencia de *Gator Nationals.* Con estos trios Mariana ascendió al segundo **puesto** en la clasificación mundial.

gold
successes

place

Aunque Mariana todavía no tiene una fundación, es conocida en Colombia por dedicar tiempo a labores sociales, especialmente con fundaciones que trabajan para los niños.

Finalmente hay que mencionar a Jefferson Pérez (1974–), un deportista que hizo historia en Ecuador cuando ganó la primera medalla de oro olímpica para este país en el año 1996, en la caminata de 20 kms. Después de ganarla, Jefferson completó un **peregrinaje** de casi 500 kms., desde Quito hasta Cuenca, su ciudad natal. Jefferson volvió a ganar una medalla olímpica de **plata** en 2008, para la misma carrera de 20 kms. Además ganó medallas en los Campeonatos Mundiales de Atletismo de 1999, 2003, 2005 y 2007. Jefferson fue reconocido como el mejor deportista de Ecuador en 2008. Aunque en la actualidad Pérez ya está retirado de las competencias, **dirige** una compañía que se dedica a promover y **apoyar** el talento deportivo en Ecuador y en toda Latinoamérica.

pilgrimage
silver

directs
to support

Comprensión

1. ¿Quiénes son los tres deportistas de los que habla la lectura? ¿De dónde son?
2. ¿Por qué Messi se fue a vivir a Barcelona? ¿Cuál es uno de sus logros?
3. ¿Qué causas promueve *(promotes)* Messi con la UNICEF y con su fundación?
4. ¿Qué deporte practica Mariana Pajón? ¿Qué labor social promueve?
5. ¿Cuál es uno de los logros de Jefferson Pérez?
6. ¿A qué se dedica Pérez ahora?

Después de leer

Con un compañero de clase, escriban una lista de atletas hispanos que conocen y los deportes que juegan. Escojan uno de la lista y busquen detalles interesantes sobre esa persona para compartirlos con la clase.

Write an email to a friend telling him or her about a sporting event.

Paso 1 Think of a sporting event you participated in, attended, or watched on TV. Then jot down a list of things you did. Think about the following questions: What was the event? When was it? Did you have to get tickets or make arrangements? Did you have to get up early or stay up late? What did you do before the event? What happened during the event? Did your team win or lose? What did you do after the event?

© Andresr/Shutterstock

Paso 2 Begin your email with a greeting and ask how your friend is. Then, write a topic sentence using an expression of time to tell your friend when you participated in, attended, or watched the sporting event.

> *El 30 de julio yo...*
> *La semana pasada yo...*

Paso 3 Using the information you generated in **Paso 1,** recount the events of the day. In order to connect your ideas, use some of the expressions you learned in **Exploraciones gramaticales 2** in this chapter.

Paso 4 Write a concluding statement in which you tell how you felt at the end of the day. Then close your email.

Paso 5 Edit your email:

1. Do all of the sentences in each paragraph support the topic sentence?
2. Is the paragraph logically organized with smooth transitions between sentences?
3. Are there any short sentences you can combine with **y** or **pero**?
4. Do verbs agree with the subject? Are they conjugated properly?
5. Are there any spelling errors? Do the preterite verbs that need accents have them?

Entrando en materia

¿Por qué es importante el deporte? ¿Cuáles son algunas cualidades que la gente (en general) admira de los deportistas?

Un reportaje biográfico

Vas a leer un segmento de un reportaje autobiográfico del deportista Javier Gadano. Lee con atención y después responde las preguntas.

Nací en el seno de una familia modesta. Mi papá y mi mamá trabajaron muy duro para **sacarnos adelante** a mis hermanos y a mí. Nunca nos **faltó** comida sobre la mesa, pero no teníamos mucho más de lo necesario. Mis tres hermanos y yo, todos **varones,** dormíamos en una habitación. Desde chico me gustaron mucho los deportes, pero la escuela no me atraía y tuve que repetir el **quinto** año. Debo de confesar que me **saltaba** la escuela cuando tenía la oportunidad.

provide for / lacked
boys

fifth / skipped

Así pasó el tiempo hasta que un día, cuando tenía unos doce años, un entrenador de educación física de nuestro colegio me vio jugar en un partido con mis amigos, después de las clases ese día. Recuerdo que **anoté** dos goles en ese partido, y estaba listo para volver a casa cuando don Genaro —así se llamaba el entrenador—, me alcanzó y me preguntó cómo me llamaba y qué año cursaba. Primero no lo tomé en serio, pero don Genaro comenzó a venir a nuestros juegos regularmente.

scored

Al final de cada partido me buscaba y me preguntaba sobre mi familia, sobre la escuela, sobre mi **vida.** Un día me puse a estudiar matemáticas para salir bien en una **prueba** solo para reportárselo a don Genaro. Fue la primera vez que sentí ganas de triunfar porque alguien más estaba interesado en mí. Me fue muy bien en esa prueba, mis notas empezaron a mejorar.

life
quiz

Un día don Genaro llegó a ver el juego con otro **caballero,** y después hablaron conmigo para invitarme a jugar en una de las ligas de su club deportivo. Me fue bien, y con el **apoyo** de don Genaro seguí estudiando y practicando el fútbol todos los días. Con esta disciplina estaba ocupado todos los días. Nunca me metí en problemas con **la ley** y, como todos saben, llegué a jugar en la primera división muy, muy joven. ¡Todo iba fabuloso! ...Hasta que la fama se me subió a la cabeza. En esos días yo perdí contacto con don Genaro. Con el dinero y la fama empecé a cometer errores graves, como asistir a demasiadas fiestas, emborracharme y... en fin. Empecé a faltar a los entrenamientos. Al final de la temporada el club no extendió mi contrato. Perdí mi casa, mi coche y hasta a mis amigos. Y bueno, pasó un año entero antes de entender la causa de mis problemas. Regresé a entrenar. La disciplina del deporte es algo que me salvó de la ruina y le da dirección a mi vida, además de la oportunidad de ayudar a otros.

gentleman

support

law

© arek_malang/Shutterstock

Comprensión

Decide si las ideas son ciertas o falsas. Corrige las falsas.

1. Javier Gadano creció en una familia con mucho dinero.
2. A Javier siempre le gustó mucho la escuela.
3. Don Genaro motivó a Javier a pasar sus exámenes de matemáticas.
4. Javier perdió su contrato con un equipo de fútbol porque se fracturó una pierna.
5. Javier tiene la oportunidad de ayudar a otros gracias al deporte.

Más allá

¿Admiras a algún deportista? Sube información del deportista a Share It! y explica por qué lo admiras.

La educación física ▶

© iofoto/Shutterstock

Vocabulario

Sustantivos

el (la) adolescente	*teenager*
los aparatos	*exercise machines*
la autoestima	*self-esteem*
el calambre	*cramp*
el calentamiento	*warm-up*
la dieta	*diet*
los ejercicios aeróbicos	*aerobics*
el (la) entrenador(a)	*trainer*
el masaje	*massage*
el músculo	*muscle*
la serie	*series/set*
el sobrepeso	*overweight*

Adjetivos

agotado(a)	*exhausted*
disciplinado(a)	*disciplined*
extenuante	*exhausting*

Verbos

entrenar(se)	*to train oneself*
respirar	*to breathe*
sudar	*to sweat*

Expresiones útiles

estar en buena forma
to be in good shape

Descanse.
Take a break.

Haga abdominales.
Do sit-ups.

Haga flexiones.
Do push-ups.

Haga tres series de...
Do three series of . . .

Tome agua.
Drink some water.

DATOS IMPORTANTES

Educación: Certificación de entrenador personal. Se prefieren profesores de educación física. Otros requisitos adicionales importantes: estudios terciarios y universitarios relacionados con medicina; por ejemplo, asistencia médica, técnica en primeros auxilios, enfermería, etcétera.

Salario: Entre $20 000 y $100 000

Dónde se trabaja: Gimnasios, clubes privados, clubes comunitarios, clubes deportivos profesionales (fútbol, béisbol, boxeo, etcétera)

Vocabulario nuevo ¿Qué palabra o expresión mejor completa cada oración?

1. Para tener brazos fuertes (haga flexiones / tome agua).

2. Para estar en buena forma es importante (respirar / entrenarse).

3. Si usted está agotado, (haga ejercicios aeróbicos / descanse).

4. Es necesario hacer (calentamientos / calambres) antes de hacer ejercicios aeróbicos.

5. Después de hacer mucho ejercicio, estoy muy (agotado/extenuante).

▶ Ricardo Melo, entrenador personal

Ricardo Melo es entrenador personal. Trabaja en un club privado y entrena a personas que quieren bajar de peso o estar en buena forma. En el video vas a ver una entrevista entre Ricardo y la madre de una joven que necesita ir al gimnasio.

Antes de ver

Los entrenadores personales ayudan a personas con diferentes necesidades. ¿Qué tipo de necesidades crees que puede tener una persona que va a un gimnasio? ¿Qué preguntas iniciales le hacen al entrenador? ¿Consideras que el entrenamiento individual es mejor que el entrenamiento en grupo? Explica.

Comprensión

1. ¿Por qué la hija de la Sra. Matos necesita ir al gimnasio?
2. ¿Cuántos años tiene la hija?
3. ¿Dónde hace gimnasia la hija de la Sra. Matos?
4. ¿Qué tipo de ejercicios recomienda el entrenador para empezar a trabajar las piernas?
5. ¿Qué otros ejercicios recomienda el entrenador?
6. Según el entrenador ¿con qué debe combinar el programa de ejercicio?

Después de ver

En parejas, representen a un entrenador personal y a una persona que necesita su ayuda. Expliquen por qué la persona busca al entrenador. ¿Quiere estar en buena forma? ¿Desea fortalecer una parte del cuerpo? ¿Tiene algún problema físico? ¿El médico le recomendó hacer ejercicio? ¿Hay algo que no puede hacer? El entrenador le explica un plan para esa situación.

6.37 **¿Quién lo hace?** Explica quién hace las actividades de la lista.

Modelo cepillarse los dientes tres veces al día
Mi abuela se cepilla los dientes tres veces al día.

1. siempre levantarse temprano
2. vestirse a la moda *(in style)*
3. cortarse el pelo una vez al mes
4. sentarse al frente de la clase
5. a veces dormirse en clase
6. maquillarse en el coche
7. afeitarse la cabeza
8. normalmente acostarse tarde

Las personas famosas se visten a la moda.

6.38 **El órden lógico** Explica el orden lógico de las dos actividades.

Modelo ponerse el pantalón / ponerse los zapatos
Debes ponerte el pantalón antes de ponerte los zapatos. / Debes ponerte los zapatos después de ponerte el pantalón.

1. hacer ejercio / bañarse
2. maquillarse / lavarse la cara
3. comer / cepillarse los dientes
4. acostarse / ponerse la pijama
5. despertarse / levantarse
6. vestirse / ducharse
7. lavarse el pelo / secarse el pelo
8. arreglarse / salir

6.39 **De pesca** Completa la historia con la forma apropiada del pretérito del verbo entre paréntesis.

Esta mañana yo **(1.)** _____ (despertarse) temprano para ir de pesca con mis amigos Alfredo y César. (Yo) **(2.)** _____ (vestirse), **(3.)** _____ (comer) un poco de fruta, **(4.)** _____ (tomar) un café y **(5.)** _____ (salir) de casa. En media hora **(6.)** _____ (llegar) al lago y mis amigos **(7.)** _____ (llegar) un poco después.

　　Nosotros **(8.)** _____ (pasar) toda la mañana en el agua. Alfredo y yo **(9.)** _____ (pescar) unos peces bonitos. ¡Pobre César! Él no **(10.)** _____ (conseguir) pescar nada, pero **(11.)** _____ (divertirse) mucho. A las dos nosotros **(12.)** _____ (decidir) ir a comer. **(13.)** _____ (comer) en un restaurante cerca del lago; luego mis amigos **(14.)** _____ (volver) a sus casas y yo a la mía *(mine)*.

6.40 **Un pasado interesante** Trabaja con un compañero. Túrnense para hacer y contestar las preguntas sobre las fotos. Deben usar el pretérito en todas las respuestas.

1.

2.

3.

a. ¿Qué hizo (*What did he do*) anoche?
b. ¿Por qué durmió en el coche?
c. ¿Qué pasó cuando se despertó?

a. ¿Quién llamó?
b. ¿Qué pasó?
c. ¿Qué hizo la mujer después?

a. ¿Adónde viajaron?
b. ¿Qué hicieron allí (*What did they do there*)?
c. ¿Qué pasó cuando regresaron?

6.41 **¿Qué hizo?** Dante es estudiante de secundaria pero no es muy aplicado. Con un compañero, túrnense para completar la información sobre lo que hizo (*what he did*) esta mañana. Uno de ustedes va a mirar la información en esta página y el otro va a mirar en el **Apéndice B.**

Modelo Estudiante 1: *¿Qué hizo a medianoche?*
Estudiante 2: *Se acostó.*

12:00	acostarse
7:00	
7:30	terminar de escribir la tarea
7:40	afeitarse en la ducha
8:00	
8:55	sentarse en la clase de geografía
9:35	
9:58	
10:10	pedir ir al baño
10:30	
11:00	levantar pesas en el gimnasio

6.42 **La semana pasada** Con un compañero, van a ver si le dedicaron más tiempo a la diversión o a las obligaciones.

Paso 1 Decidan si las siguientes actividades son divertidas u obligatorias. Añadan (*Add*) 4 o 5 otras actividades que hacen en una semana típica y decidan si son divertidas u obligatorias.

asistir a clases	estudiar	practicar un deporte
cocinar	leer	salir con amigos
escribir un ensayo	mirar la tele	trabajar

Paso 2 Averigüen (*Find out*) cuánto tiempo pasaron la semana pasada haciendo las actividades de su lista. ¿Dedicaron más tiempo a la diversión o a las obligaciones?

Paso 3 Repórtenle a la clase sus resultados dando algunos ejemplos.

🔊 Vocabulario 1
1-37

Los verbos reflexivos

acostarse (ue)	*to lie down; to go to bed*
afeitarse	*to shave*
arreglarse	*to fix oneself up; to get ready*
bañarse	*to bathe; to shower (Mex.)*
cepillarse	*to brush*
cortarse	*to cut*
despertarse (ie)	*to wake up*
divertirse (ie)	*to have fun*
dormirse (ue)	*to fall asleep*
ducharse	*to shower*

estirarse	*to stretch*
irse	*to leave, to go away*
lavarse	*to wash*
levantarse	*to get up*
maquillarse	*to put on make-up*
peinarse	*to comb or style one's hair*
ponerse (la ropa)	*to put on (clothing)*
quitarse (la ropa)	*to take off (clothing)*
secarse	*to dry oneself*
sentarse (ie)	*to sit down*
verse	*to look at oneself*
vestirse (i)	*to get dressed*

Las partes del cuerpo

la boca	*mouth*
el brazo	*arm*
la cabeza	*head*
la cara	*face*
el codo	*elbow*
el cuello	*neck*
el dedo	*finger*
el dedo (del pie)	*toe*
el diente	*tooth*
la espalda	*back*
el estómago	*stomach*
el hombro	*shoulder*

la mano	*hand*
el muslo	*thigh*
la nariz	*nose*
el ojo	*eye*
la oreja	*ear*
el pecho	*chest*
el pelo	*hair*
el pie	*foot*
la pierna	*leg*
la rodilla	*knee*
el tobillo	*ankle*

Adverbios

a menudo	*often*
a veces	*sometimes*
ahora	*now*
antes de + infinitive	*before (doing something)*
después de + infinitive	*after (doing something)*
hoy	*today*
luego	*later*
mañana	*tomorrow*

más tarde	*later*
mientras	*while*
normalmente	*normally, usually*
(casi) nunca	*(almost) never*
pronto	*soon*
(casi) siempre	*(almost) always*
todavía	*still*
todos los días	*every day*
ya	*already*
ya no	*no longer*

Palabras adicionales

el cepillo de dientes	*toothbrush*
el champú	*shampoo*
la pasta de dientes	*toothpaste*
el despertador	*alarm clock*

el jabón	*soap*
tarde	*late*
temprano	*early*
la toalla	*towel*

Vocabulario 2

Los deportes

el alpinismo	*mountain climbing*	el fútbol americano	*American football*
el atletismo	*track and field*		
el bádminton	*badminton*	el golf	*golf*
el básquetbol	*basketball*	la natación	*swimming*
el béisbol	*baseball*	el tenis	*tennis*
el fútbol	*soccer*	el voleibol	*volleyball*

El equipo

el equipo	*equipment; team*	la red	*net*
el patín	*skate*	el saco de dormir	*sleeping bag*
la pelota	*ball*	la tienda de campaña	*camping tent*
la raqueta	*racquet*		

Verbos

acampar	*to go camping*	ir de excursión	*to go hiking*
andar en bicicleta	*to ride a bicycle*	jugar al ping-pong	*to play ping-pong*
bucear	*to scuba dive*	levantar pesas	*to lift weights*
esquiar en el agua	*to water-ski*	montar a	*to ride (an animal)*
esquiar en tabla	*to snowboard*	patinar	*to skate*
hacer alpinismo	*to climb mountains*	patinar en hielo	*to ice skate*
		pescar	*to fish*

Palabras adicionales

el (la) aficionado(a)	*fan (of a sport)*	la entrada	*ticket*
anoche	*last night*	el lago	*lake*
ayer	*yesterday*	el partido	*game*
el campo	*field*	la semana pasada	*last week*
la cancha	*court*		

Diccionario personal

_____

_____

_____

_____

_____

_____

_____

© Used by permission of Donato Ndongo

Donato Ndongo

Biografía

Donato Ndongo-Bidyogo (1950–) es un escritor, político y periodista de Guinea Ecuatorial. Su trabajo profesional ha incluido varios puestos en universidades españolas, y más de diez años trabajando para la agencia de noticias (news) EFE en África central. También trabajó como director adjunto del Centro Cultural Hispano-Guineano en Malabo. Dentro de su labor política, destaca como fundador del Partido del Progreso de Guinea Ecuatorial en 1984.

Como escritor, Ndongo es autor de libros de ficción, ensayos y poesía. Algunas de sus obras más destacadas incluyen *Historia y Tragedia de Guinea Ecuatorial* (1977), y la antología de literatura ecuatoguineana titulada *Las tinieblas de tu memoria negra*.

Ndongo ha vivido en el exilio desde 1994, cuando se marchó a España debido a su oposición al gobierno de Teodoro Obiang. Entre 2005 y 2009, Ndongo trabajó como profesor visitante de la Universidad de Missouri en Columbia. Después de su estancia en los Estados Unidos, regresó a España.

Antes de leer

1. El título del poema que vas a leer es "Cántico". ¿Qué piensas que significa esta palabra?
2. El poema habla de lo que un poeta debe hacer. En tu opinión ¿cuáles son los deberes u objetivos de un poeta?

Cántico

© Borderlan s/Alamy

Yo no quiero ser poeta
para cantar a África.
Yo no quiero ser poeta
para glosar lo negro.
5   Yo no quiero ser poeta así.

El poeta no es cantor de
beauties   **bellezas.**
flaunts   El poeta no **luce** la
brillante piel negra.
10   El poeta, este poeta no tiene
voz
undulating gait   para **andares ondulantes** de
hermosas damas
curly / hips   de pelos **rizados** y **caderas**
15   redondas.
land   El poeta llora su **tierra**
inmensa y pequeña
dura y frágil

luminosa y oscura
20   rica y pobre.
Este poeta tiene su mano
atada   *tied*
a las **cadenas** que atan a   *chains*
su gente.
25   Este poeta no siente
nostalgia
de glorias pasadas.
Yo no canto al sexo
exultante

que huele a jardín de rosas.
Yo no adoro **labios gruesos** *thick lips*
que saben a mango fresco.
Yo no pienso en la mujer
encorvada *stooped*
bajo su **cesto** cargado de *basket*
leña *wood*
con un niño chupando la
teta vacía. *empty breast*
Yo describo la triste historia
de un mundo poblado de
blancos
negros
rojos y
amarillos
que saltan de **charca** en *pool*
charca
sin hablarse ni mirarse.
El poeta llora a los muertos
que **matan** manos negras *kill*
en nombre de la Negritud.
Yo canto con mi pueblo
una vida pasada bajo
el cacaotero *cacao tree*
para que ellos
merienden *have a snack*
cho-co-la-te.
Si su pueblo está triste,
el poeta está triste.
Yo no soy poeta por
voluntad divina. *will*
El poeta es poeta por
voluntad humana.
Yo no quiero la poesía
que solo deleita los
oídos de los poetas.
Yo no quiero la poesía
que se lee en noches de
vino tinto
y mujeres **embelesadas.** *spellbound*
Poesía, sí.
Poetas, sí.
Pero que sepan lo que
es el hombre
y por qué sufre el
hombre
y por qué **gime** el *groans*
hombre.

Courtesy of the author, Donato Ndongo.

Después de leer

A. Comprensión

1. Según la voz narrativa, ¿qué es importante decir en las poesías?
2. ¿Cuál es el mensaje del poema?
3. ¿Cuál es el tono? ¿Por qué?
4. ¿Cuál es el tema?
5. Encuentra dos descripciones que hablan de la vida en Guinea Ecuatorial. ¿Qué emoción te producen?

B. Conversemos

1. En tu opinión ¿se debe mezclar *(to mix)* la poesía con la política y los problemas sociales? ¿Por qué?
2. ¿Conoces otros autores que piensan que la poesía debe tener un elemento social? ¿Quiénes?
3. Escribe una lista de temas políticos o sociales que piensas que son buen tema para una poesía.

Investiguemos la literatura: El tema

The theme of a literary text refers to the underlying ideas, what the piece is really about. To find it, look for patterns and ideas that are restated in different parts of the work. It is not the subject of the work, but more of a view of the human experience and attitude. Some common themes include growing up, love, death, and nature.

Learning Strategy

Try a variety of memorization techniques

Use a variety of techniques to memorize vocabulary and verbs until you find the ones that work best for you. Some students learn better when they write the words, others learn better if they listen to recordings of the words while looking over the list, and still others prefer to rely on flashcards.

In this chapter you will learn how to:
- Talk about food
- Order meals at a restaurant
- Use numbers above 100

¿Qué te gusta comer?

© Stuart Pearce/age fotostock

La señora Montero escoge frutas y verduras frescas y baratas en el mercado.

los pepinos · las piñas · los plátanos · el cereal · la mermelada · la mayonesa · la catsup · el brócoli · la mostaza · la sandía · las zanahorias · la leche · los huevos · el melón · los champiñones · las naranjas · la lechuga · las papas · el queso · el pan · las cebollas · los duraznos · el jamón · las manzanas · la mantequilla · las uvas · la crema · las fresas · los pepinillos

© Cengage Learning

En la cocina

el aceite	oil
la fruta	fruit
el maíz	corn
el tomate	tomato
la verdura	vegetable
el yogur	yogurt

Verbos

hornear	to bake

Los números mayores de cien

cien	100
ciento uno	101
doscientos	200
trescientos	300
cuatrocientos	400
quinientos	500
seiscientos	600
setecientos	700
ochocientos	800
novecientos	900
mil	1000
dos mil	2000
un millón	1 000 000

Palabras adicionales

la rebanada	slice

INVESTIGUEMOS EL VOCABULARIO

The names of foods often vary throughout the Spanish-speaking world. Here are some of the variations:

el maíz (Spain; general term) = **el elote** (Mexico), **el choclo** (Argentina, Chile, Paraguay, Peru, and most South American countries)

la fresa (Spain, Mexico) = **la frutilla** (Argentina, Bolivia, Chile, Paraguay, Uruguay)

el plátano (Spain, Mexico) = **la banana** (el Caribe); **el banano** (Central America, Colombia)

la piña (Spain, Mexico) = **el ananá(s)** (Argentina, Paraguay, Uruguay)

la papa (Latin America) = **la patata** (Spain)

el durazno (Latin America) = **el melocotón** (Spain)

la mantequilla (most Spanish-speaking countries) = **la manteca** (Argentina, Paraguay, Uruguay)

A practicar

7.1 **Escucha y responde** Vas a escuchar algunas afirmaciones sobre diferentes frutas, verduras y otras palabras del vocabulario. Indica con el pulgar hacia arriba si la afirmación es cierta, y con el pulgar hacia abajo si es falsa.

🔊 2-2

7.2 **Relaciona las columnas** ¿Qué fruta o verdura corresponde a la descripción?

1. _____ Es una fruta roja, verde o amarilla.
   Es un regalo típico para los profesores.
2. _____ Es verde y la comemos en ensaladas.
3. _____ Es anaranjada y larga. Tiene vitamina A.
4. _____ Es una fruta tropical que se produce mucho en Hawaii.
5. _____ Es una fruta amarilla que crece en un árbol.
6. _____ Las usamos para hacer vino.
7. _____ Es un condimento que ponemos en los sándwiches.
8. _____ Es una fruta pequeña y roja.

a. la zanahoria
b. el plátano
c. la fresa
d. las uvas
e. la mostaza
f. la lechuga
g. la manzana
h. la piña

7.3 **Los ingredientes** Trabaja con un compañero para decidir los ingredientes que se
 necesitan para preparar estas comidas.

Modelo un sándwich
   Para preparar un sándwich necesitamos pan, mayonesa, mostaza, queso y jamón.

1. una ensalada verde
2. una sopa de verduras
3. una quesadilla

4. un omelet
5. unos nachos
6. una ensalada de frutas

7.4 **Descripciones** Trabaja con un compañero. Túrnense para escoger una fruta, un
 vegetal o un ingrediente de la ilustración en la página 226 y describirlo. No deben
decir el nombre de la comida.

Modelo Estudiante 1: *No es una fruta. Es para hacer sándwiches.*
   Estudiante 2: *El pan.*

7.5 **¿Con qué frecuencia?** Trabaja en un grupo de 3 o 4 compañeros y pregúntense
con qué frecuencia hacen las actividades. Después deben reportar a la clase.

1. comer huevos
2. almorzar en la cafetería de la escuela
3. poner catsup en su comida
4. comer cereal

5. pedir papas fritas en un restaurante
6. comer un sándwich con queso
7. beber leche
8. comer verduras

7.6 **¿Cuánto cuesta?** Trabaja con un compañero. Uno de ustedes va a
ver la información en esta página, y el otro debe ver el **Apéndice B**.
Imagínense que están en dos supermercados diferentes en Chile.
Llámense por teléfono para preguntar cuánto cuestan los productos de
cada ilustración. Los precios que tu compañero necesita están abajo, en
el papel. Tomen notas y sumen *(add)* los precios. ¿Quién va a pagar más?

Tu compañero quiere comprar...

un melón, un kilo $620   jamón, 250 gramos $1,743
una lechuga $155   pepinos, 500 gramos $476
huevos, una docena $899   naranjas, 3 kilos $1,634
queso, 500 gramos $867   zanahorias, un kilo $469

Tú quieres comprar...

un kilo

MANTEQUILLA

un kilo

un kilo

un litro   YOGUR

© Cengage Learning

La comida como cultura

Algo muy particular de cada cultura es su comida. Hoy en día, gracias a los eficientes medios de transporte y a tecnologías para preservar los alimentos, podemos comer productos que se producen o cultivan en cualquier parte del mundo. Sin embargo, a pesar de esta globalización de la comida, existen hábitos muy diferentes en las diversas regiones. Hay diferencias en cómo se prepara la comida, en los productos que se usan, dónde se compran y hasta dónde se come, con quién y a qué hora. Identifica las costumbres de la lista con el país o la región donde se hace. Puedes repetir respuestas.

El ceviche es popular en muchos países. Esta foto muestra un plato de ceviche como se prepara en Perú.

Argentina	Chile	Perú
Bolivia	España	Uruguay
Centroamérica	México	toda Latinoamérica

1. Se come más carne que en cualquier otro país.
2. Producen vinos excelentes.
3. Consumen muchos más refrescos (*sodas*) que leche.
4. Son famosos por sus jamones.
5. La comida más importante es por la tarde, entre la 1:00 y las 3:00 PM.
6. Su cocina está muy influenciada por la cocina italiana.
7. Tienen una gran variedad de papas y son muy importantes en su dieta.
8. Prefieren comer con la familia y generalmente encuentran tiempo para hacerlo.
9. Producen y comen una gran variedad de frutas tropicales. El maíz es también importante en su dieta.

Observa la lista nuevamente. ¿Son algunas de estas afirmaciones verdaderas para los Estados Unidos? ¿Cuáles?

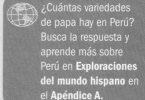

¿Cuántas variedades de papa hay en Perú? Busca la respuesta y aprende más sobre Perú en **Exploraciones del mundo hispano** en el **Apéndice A.**

Comparaciones

En la mayoría de los países donde se habla español la dieta varía por región. Por ejemplo:

- En Sudamérica no se comen chile ni tortillas.
- Los frijoles negros son un alimento básico en Cuba, la República Dominicana, partes de México y Centroamérica.
- En Bolivia se come un cereal muy nutritivo llamado quinoa.
- En Chile y en Argentina frecuentemente se bebe vino con la comida.
- En España, en promedio se comen 7 kilos de queso por persona al año. En Argentina se consumen unos 12 kilos por persona, y en México 3 kilos.
  [Source: CDIC cheese consumption data, 2013]

¿Cómo se comparan tus hábitos alimenticios con los de las personas de los países que se mencionan arriba?

La carne es muy popular en países como Argentina, Paraguay y Uruguay.

Conexiones... a la gastronomía

La comida es una parte muy importante de las tradiciones y cultura de cada país. Los siguientes son algunos ejemplos.

En Argentina, Paraguay y Uruguay se bebe un té que se hace con una yerba llamada mate. Hay varias formas de prepararlo y beberlo, pero en la más tradicional se hace con hojas secas de mate y agua caliente. Se prepara y se bebe en un recipiente hecho con el fruto de la calabaza *(gourd)*, y se bebe con una bombilla *(straw)*. El té se pasa de persona a persona, así que beber mate es una actividad social.

La paella

Gallo Pinto

Un platillo tradicional de Costa Rica es el Gallo Pinto. Este plato se prepara con arroz, pollo, frijoles y otros ingredientes que le dan un sabor *(flavor)* especial, como cebolla y cilantro. Hay muchas variaciones de este platillo. De hecho, el arroz y los frijoles son la base para platillos importantes de otros países, como el platillo Moros y Cristianos, típico de Cuba.

Abajo hay una lista de otros platillos. Escoge cuatro de ellos e investiga qué son y qué ingredientes se necesitan para prepararlos.

Bolivia: chicha
Chile: empanadas
Colombia: buñuelos
Ecuador: ceviche
España: paella

Honduras: baleada
Panamá: chocao panameño
Paraguay: sopa paraguaya
República Dominicana: tostones
Venezuela: hallacas

 En **Exploraciones del mundo hispano** del **Apéndice A** puedes encontrar más platillos tradicionales de cada uno de los países donde se habla español.

Comunidad

Entrevista a una persona de un país donde se habla español. Pregúntale acerca de las comidas típicas de su país, su comida favorita y los ingredientes necesarios. Pregúntale también a qué hora son las comidas en su país y si es común comprar comida rápida.

Un plato típico del Perú es el lomo saltado.

A analizar

Camila y Vanesa van a un café para hablar. Mira el video. Después lee parte de su conversación y observa las formas de los verbos en negritas.

Camila:	(Yo) **Fui** al supermercado para comprar la comida para la fiesta de mi hija. Por ser sábado, había mucha gente y **fue** imposible entrar y salir muy rápido. Y los precios... ¡todo **fue** muy caro, en particular la carne! Un kilo de jamón por veinte dólares...
Vanesa:	¡Guau! ¡Qué caro!... mi día **fue** tranquilo. Por la mañana **fui** de compras y por la tarde un amigo y yo **fuimos** al nuevo restaurante para comer. La comida **fue** excelente y los precios **fueron** muy razonables.

1. The verbs **ser** and **ir** are irregular in the preterite and they have the same conjugated forms. Look at the paragraph above and decide which of the verbs is a form of **ser** and which is a form of **ir.**

2. Using the forms in the paragraph above and what you learned about the preterite in **Capítulo 6,** complete the chart below with the appropriate forms of **ser / ir** in the preterite.

yo _____   nosotros _____

tú _____   vosotros _____

él, ella, usted _____   ellos, ellas, ustedes _____

A comprobar

Irregular verbs in the preterite

1. There are a number of verbs that are irregular in the preterite. The verbs **ser** and **ir** are identical in this tense.

ir *(to go)* / **ser** *(to be)*

yo	**fui**	nosotros(as)	**fuimos**
tú	**fuiste**	vosotros(as)	**fuisteis**
él, ella, usted	**fue**	ellos, ellas, ustedes	**fueron**

Estrategia

Try different memorization techniques

Try some of these techniques to help memorize the verbs and see what works best for you: write out the conjugations, say the conjugations out loud while looking over the list, or make flashcards.

2. The verbs **dar** and **ver** are conjugated similarly.

dar *(to give)*

yo	**di**	nosotros(as)	**dimos**
tú	**diste**	vosotros(as)	**disteis**
él, ella, usted	**dio**	ellos, ellas, ustedes	**dieron**

ver *(to see)*

yo	**vi**	nosotros(as)	**vimos**
tú	**viste**	vosotros(as)	**visteis**
él, ella, usted	**vio**	ellos, ellas, ustedes	**vieron**

3. Other irregular verbs can be divided into three groups. Notice that there are no accents on these verbs and that they all take the same endings (with the exception of the 3rd person plural of the verbs with **j** in the stem).

Verbs with *u* in the stem: poner			
yo	pus**e**	nosotros(as)	pus**imos**
tú	pus**iste**	vosotros(as)	pus**isteis**
él, ella, usted	pus**o**	ellos, ellas, ustedes	pus**ieron**

Other verbs with the same pattern			
andar	**anduv-**	saber	**sup-**
estar	**estuv-**	tener	**tuv-**
poder	**pud-**		

Verbs with *i* in the stem: hacer			
yo	hic**e**	nosotros(as)	hic**imos**
tú	hic**iste**	vosotros(as)	hic**isteis**
él, ella, usted	hiz**o**	ellos, ellas, ustedes	hic**ieron**

Other verbs with the same pattern	
querer	**quis-**
venir	**vin-**

Verbs with *j* in the stem: decir			
yo	dij**e**	nosotros(as)	dij**imos**
tú	dij**iste**	vosotros(as)	dij**isteis**
él, ella, usted	dij**o**	ellos, ellas, ustedes	dij**eron**

Other verbs with the same pattern			
conducir	**conduj-**	traducir	**traduj-**
producir	**produj-**	traer	**traj-**

4. The preterite of **hay** is **hubo** (*there was, there were*).

Hubo un accidente en la cocina.   ***There was** an accident in the kitchen.*

Hubo problemas en el restaurante.   ***There were** problems in the restaurant.*

> **INVESTIGUEMOS LA GRAMÁTICA**
>
> As with the present tense of **haber (hay)**, there is only one form in the preterite **(hubo)** regardless of whether it is used with a plural or singular noun.

A practicar

7.7 **En el restaurante** Lee las oraciones y observa los verbos subrayados (*underlined*) que están en el pretérito. Decide cuál es el infinitivo del verbo.

1. La familia Martínez <u>fue</u> al restaurante Buen Gusto para comer.
2. El mesero <u>vino</u> a la mesa para darnos los menús.
3. El mesero <u>puso</u> el pan en la mesa.
4. Poco después el mesero <u>trajo</u> la comida.
5. El mesero le <u>dio</u> la cuenta (*bill*) al señor Martínez.

7.8 **Fechas importantes** Con un compañero, decidan en qué año ocurrieron los siguientes acontecimientos históricos y después túrnense para hacer oraciones completas con la información.

Modelo Manuel de Falla (componer *to compose*) *El amor brujo.*   1915
Manuel de Falla compuso *El amor brujo en 1915.*

1. Hernán Cortés (estar) en México.   **a.** 1492
2. (Haber) una revolución en Cuba.   **b.** 1808
3. Napoleón (querer) conquistar España.   **c.** 1959
4. Cristóbal Colón (hacer) su primer viaje a las Américas.   **d.** 1519
5. Miguel Hidalgo (dar) el grito (*shout*) de independencia en México.   **e.** 1810

7.9 **La semana pasada** Primero, conjuga el verbo en el pretérito y luego completa la oración de una manera lógica. Después compara tu semana con la de un compañero de clase.

Modelo yo (hacer)…
> Estudiante 1: *La semana pasada hice una fiesta. ¿Qué hiciste tú?*
> Estudiante 2: *La semana pasada yo hice la cena para mi familia.*

La semana pasada…

1. yo (conducir)…
2. mi amigo (estar)…
3. mis amigos y yo (ir)…
4. yo (tener) que…
5. uno de mis profesores (decir) que *(that)*…
6. mis compañeros y yo (poder)…
7. yo (ver)…
8. mis compañeros de clase (traer)…

7.10 **¿Qué pasó?** Con un compañero, túrnense para describir lo que pasó en las escenas. Deben usar los siguientes verbos en el pretérito.

conducir   decir   hacer   ir   poner   querer   traer

1.

2.

3.

4.

7.11 **En busca de…** Pregúntales a ocho compañeros diferentes si hicieron una de las actividades de la lista. Si responden afirmativamente debes perdirles más información.

1. conducir a la universidad hoy (¿A qué hora?)
2. estar en una fiesta durante el fin de semana (¿Dónde?)
3. ir de compras recientemente (¿Qué compró?)
4. traer su almuerzo de la casa hoy (¿Qué comida preparó?)
5. tener un examen la semana pasada (¿En qué clase?)
6. poder hacer la tarea anoche (¿Para qué clase?)
7. ver una buena película recientemente (¿Cuál?)
8. hacer un viaje el año pasado (¿Adónde?)

A analizar ▶

Camila y Vanesa van a un café para hablar. Mira el video otra vez. Después lee parte de su conversación y observa los usos de **por** y **para**.

Camila:	Fui al supermercado **para** comprar la comida **para** la fiesta de mi hija. **Por** ser sábado, había mucha gente y fue imposible entrar y salir muy rápido. Y los precios... ¡todo fue muy caro, en particular la carne! Un kilo de jamón **por** veinte dólares...
Vanesa:	¡Guau! ¡Qué caro!... mi día fue tranquilo. **Por** la mañana fui de compras y **por** la tarde un amigo y yo fuimos al nuevo restaurante **para** comer. La comida fue excelente y los precios fueron muy razonables.
Camila:	¡Qué bueno! A ver si Rodrigo y yo vamos a ese restaurante **para** celebrar su cumpleaños.
Mesera:	Aquí tengo sus cafés. ¿**Para** quién es el capuchino?
Camila:	Es **para** mí. Gracias.
Mesera:	Y el moca **para** usted.

© Cengage Learning

1. Find all of the uses of **por** above and write the words that follow them. What different meanings does **por** express?
2. Now find all of the uses of **para** and write the words that follow them. What different meanings does **para** express?

A comprobar

Por and para and prepositional pronouns

1. **Por** is used to indicate:

a. cause, reason, or motive *(because of, on behalf of)*

   Por la lluvia, no vamos a la piscina hoy.
   Because of the rain, we are not going to the pool today.

   Hicieron sacrificios **por** sus hijos.
   They made sacrifices on behalf of their children.

b. duration, period of time *(during, for)*

   Van a estar en el restaurante **por** dos horas.
   They will be in the restaurant for two hours.

c. exchange *(for)*

   Él compró las piñas **por** 15 pesos.
   He bought the pineapples for 15 pesos.

   Gracias **por** el regalo de cumpleaños.
   Thank you for the birthday gift.

d. general movement through space *(through, around, along, by)*

   Pedro caminó **por** el mercado.
   Pedro walked through (by) the market.

   Para llegar a la piscina, tienes que pasar **por** el gimnasio.
   To get to the pool, you have to pass by the gym.

e. expressions

por ejemplo	*for example*	**por** fin	*finally*
por eso	*that's why*	**por** supuesto	*of course*
por favor	*please*		

2. Para is used to indicate:

a. goal, purpose *(in order to, used for)*

Vamos al mercado **para** comprar fruta.
*We are going to the market (**in order**) **to** buy fruit.*

El pan es **para** hacer sándwiches.
*The bread is **for** making sandwiches.*

b. recipient *(for)*

Ella compró un regalo **para** su amiga.
*She bought a gift **for** her friend.*

c. destination *(to)*

Salen **para** las montañas el sábado.
*They are going **to** the mountains Saturday.*

d. deadline *(for, due)*

La tarea es **para** mañana.
*The homework is **for (due)** tomorrow.*

e. contrast to what is expected *(for)*

Para estar a dieta, él come mucho.
***For** being on a diet, he eats a lot.*

f. expressions

para colmo	*to top it all off*	**para** siempre	*forever*
para nada	*not at all*	**para** variar	*for a change*

3. In **Capítulo 1**, you learned to use subject pronouns (**yo, tú, él,** etc.). Except for **yo** and **tú**, these same pronouns are used after prepositions.

mí	nosotros(as)
ti	vosotros(as)
él	ellos
ella	ellas
usted	ustedes

El regalo es para **ti.**
A **mí** me gustan las fresas. (emphasis)

4. Instead of using **mí** and **ti** with **con, conmigo** and **contigo** are used.

Vamos a comer **contigo.**
*We'll go to eat **with you.***

> **INVESTIGUEMOS LA GRAMÁTICA**
> The negative of **con** is **sin** *(without),* and it takes the same personal pronouns as the other prepositions.
> No quiero comer sin **ti.**

A practicar

7.12 **Una fiesta de cumpleaños** Jacinto llama a un proveedor de comida *(caterer).* Lee las preguntas del proveedor y decide cuál es la respuesta más lógica.

1. ¿Por qué organiza la fiesta?
2. ¿Para cuándo necesita la comida?
3. ¿Para cuántas personas necesita comida?
4. ¿Cuándo van a llegar los invitados?
5. ¿Cuánto tiempo va a durar *(to last)* la fiesta?
6. ¿Cómo prefiere pagar por la comida?

a. El 15 de abril.
b. Con tarjeta de crédito.
c. Por la tarde.
d. Veinticinco.
e. Es el cumpleaños de mi esposa.
f. Por cuatro horas.

¿Para cuándo necesita la comida?

© Ciampiofoto/Shutterstock

7.13 **En el supermercado** Completa el siguiente párrafo con **por** y **para**.

Ayer fui al supermercado **(1.)** _____ comprar la comida de la semana.
Siempre me gusta ir **(2.)** _____ la mañana porque hay menos personas, pero
ayer hubo mucha gente en el supermercado **(3.)** _____ un evento especial
(4.) _____ celebrar los 20 años del negocio. Tenían grandes especiales,
(5.) _____ ejemplo, queso manchego a 100 pesos **(6.)** _____ kilo.
Decidí comprar 2 kilos **(7.)** _____ hacer sándwiches durante la semana. A mi
esposo no le gusta el queso, **(8.)** _____ eso compré jamón **(9.)** _____
él. Al final compré toda la comida **(10.)** _____ la semana y ahorré *(saved)*
mucho dinero.

7.14 **Planes para el día** Fernando llama a su amiga Verónica. Completa la conversación con **por** o **para** o el pronombre preposicional apropiado. **¡OJO!** También es posible usar **conmigo** o **contigo**.

Vamos a tener un picnic.

Fernando: Hola, Verónica. Voy a ir a la playa mañana. ¿Quieres ir **(1.)** _____?

Verónica: ¡A **(2.)** _____ me gusta mucho la playa! ¡**(3.)** _____ (Por/Para) supuesto que voy **(4.)** _____!

Fernando: Vamos a salir temprano **(5.)** _____ (por/para) la mañana **(6.)** _____ (por/para) pasar *(to spend)* todo el día en la playa. También van a ir José, Pablo y Catarina con **(7.)** _____.

Verónica: ¡Qué bueno! ¿Qué quieres que lleve *(take)*?

Fernando: Vamos a tener un picnic, entonces puedes llevar algo **(8.)** _____ (por/para) comer.

Verónica: ¿A **(9.)** _____ te gusta el jamón?

Fernando: Sí, me gusta mucho, pero Catarina es vegetariana.

Verónica: Bueno, voy a llevar jamón y también puedo llevar queso **(10.)** _____ (por/para) **(11.)** _____. No tengo coche hoy. ¿Puedes venir **(12.)** _____ (por/para) **(13.)** _____?

Fernando: No hay problema. Paso **(14.)** _____ (por/para) **(15.)** _____ a las ocho.

Verónica: Bueno, voy a estar lista. ¡Hasta entonces!

7.15 **En la caja** Imagínense que están en la caja *(cash register)* para pagar sus compras en el supermercado. Uno de ustedes es el cliente y el otro es el dependiente que quiere vender una tarjeta con minutos para el celular. Respóndanse las preguntas que aparecen a continuación.

Estudiante 1 (el cliente):

1. ¿Puedo conseguir descuentos por ser mayor de 55 años?
2. ¿Por cuánto tiempo es la oferta del jamón?
3. ¿Puedo usar la tarjeta de crédito para pagar?

Estudiante 2 (el dependiente):

4. ¿Necesita minutos para su teléfono?
5. ¿Para qué compañía telefónica quiere la tarjeta?
6. ¿Por cuántos minutos quiere la tarjeta?

¿Puedo usar la tarjeta de crédito para pagar?

7.16 **Oraciones incompletas** Con un compañero, completen las oraciones. Deben pensar en los usos diferentes de **por** y **para.**

1. **a.** Voy al supermercado por…

   b. Voy al supermercado para…

2. **a.** El chef prepara la comida por…

   b. El chef prepara la comida para…

3. **a.** Por ser un buen chef,…

   b. Para ser un buen chef,…

4. **a.** Quiero los huevos por…

   b. Quiero los huevos para…

5. **a.** El mesero fue a la cocina por…

   b. El mesero fue a la cocina para…

6. **a.** Tenemos una reservación por…

   b. Tenemos una reservación para…

INVESTIGUEMOS LA MÚSICA

Carlos Ponce is a Puerto Rican singer and actor. One of his hit songs is called "Rezo." What do you think the song will be about? Search online, listen to the song and compare your answers. What phrases do you hear with **por**? And with **para**?

7.17 **En la recepción** Con un compañero, túrnense para explicar lo que hicieron Manuel y las otras personas según *(according to)* los dibujos. **¡OJO!** Deben usar el pretérito y **por** o **para.**

© Cengage Learning

7.18 **Una foto** Con un compañero, escojan una de las fotos e inventen una historia basada en la foto. Deben incluir varios usos de **por** y **para** en su historia.

© Monkey Business Images/Shutterstock

© Lewis Tse Pui Lung/Shutterstock

Entrando en materia

¿Qué comidas compras con frecuencia en el supermercado? Si alguien quiere ahorrar dinero en el supermercado ¿qué debe hacer?

Las compras en el supermercado

🔊 Vas a escuchar un programa de radio producido por una organización de protección al
2-3 consumidor. Después de escuchar, responde las preguntas que siguen.

Vocabulario útil

ahorrar	*to save*	los derechos	*rights*
el azúcar	*sugar*	la envoltura	*wrappers, packaging*
caducar	*to expire*	la lata	*can (of food)*
congelado(a)	*frozen*	el sodio	*sodium*
congelar	*to freeze*	la temporada	*season*
dejarse llevar	*to impulse buy*		
por impulsos			

Es importante comprar frutas y verduras de la temporada.

Comprensión

1. En general ¿de qué hablan en este programa de radio?
2. ¿Cuál es la segunda estrategia?
3. ¿Por qué es buena idea hacer un menú para la semana?
4. ¿Por qué recomiendan comprar productos congelados y no en lata?

🖧 Más allá

Escribe una estrategia que usas para ahorrar en el supermercado. Comparte tu estrategia en Share It! y lee las recomendaciones de otros estudiantes.

Lectura

Reading Strategy: Reading out loud

Although you should read silently the first time you read a text for comprehension, try reading it out loud once you have used all the strategies described in previous lessons. Reading out loud will help you to remember new words and build pronunciation skills as well.

Antes de leer

Escribe una lista de comidas que se consumen durante el Día de Acción de Gracias. ¿Qué ingredientes se necesitan para prepararlas? ¿Conoces una comida típica de algún país latinoamericano? ¿Qué comida? ¿Qué ingredientes se necesitan para prepararla?

A leer

Los alimentos del Nuevo Mundo

people
where they used to live

Es obvio que en épocas anteriores **la gente** comía los alimentos que estaban disponibles en la zona **donde habitaban.** Debido a las diferencias climáticas y geográficas, los animales y plantas del Nuevo Mundo (el continente americano) eran muy diferentes a los que existían en Europa.

[¿puedes imaginar el resto del mundo sin chocolate...?]

Hoy en día, gracias al avance en las comunicaciones del mundo y a las nuevas técnicas de transporte y preservación de los alimentos,

were harvested

es posible comer productos que se **cosecharon** o produjeron a miles de kilómetros de distancia. Nuestro

used to be

mundo **era** muy diferente antes de la llegada de los europeos al Nuevo Mundo.

¿Puedes imaginar tu dieta sin leche, sin queso, sin carne de res o sin naranjas ni plátanos? Estos son solo algunos de los productos

were not available

que **no había** en el Nuevo Mundo. Por otra parte, ¿puedes imaginar el resto del mundo sin chocolate, vainilla, tomates, maíz, papas, chiles o **pavos**? La lista de productos americanos es

turkeys

larga y su importancia **va mucho

goes well beyond

más allá** del gusto por estos productos. Un buen ejemplo es el

Las papas son originarias de Sudamérica.

de las papas, las cuales les salvaron la vida a millones de europeos durante el período de escasez que siguió a la Segunda Guerra Mundial en Europa.

Si se piensa en la identidad cultural de algunos países ¿puedes imaginar a Suiza o a Bélgica sin chocolates? ¿Puedes imaginar las típicas pizzas

El cacao y la vainilla son originarios de Mesoamérica.

italianas sin tomate? ¿o la **picante** comida de la India sin chile?

spicy

Tanto el tomate como el maíz, la vainilla y el cacao se originaron en Mesoamérica, el territorio que hoy es parte de México y de Centroamérica. De hecho, las palabras *tomate* y *chocolate* vienen de las palabras del náhuatl *tomatl* y *xocolatl*. *Ahuacatl* y *chilli* son palabras náhuatl para **aguacate** y chile, otras plantas nativas de las Américas.

avocado

Un poco más al sur se originan la papa y la quinoa, un cereal que aunque no es muy conocido en los Estados Unidos, se considera que puede ser la solución al problema del hambre en el mundo, debido a su gran valor nutritivo.

Dos ingredientes centrales en muchos países en Asia son los chiles y los **cacahuates.** Los helados europeos son populares gracias al chocolate y la vainilla, y las papas a la francesa no pueden existir sin papas. Estos productos son solo una pequeña parte de las aportaciones del Nuevo Mundo para el resto del planeta.

peanuts

Comprensión

1. ¿Cuáles son cuatro productos originarios de las Américas que son importantes en las celebraciones culturales de los Estados Unidos?

2. ¿Qué frutos tomaron su nombre del idioma náhuatl, el idioma de los aztecas?

3. ¿Qué es la quinoa y por qué es importante?

4. En tu opinión ¿cuáles son tres productos de América que tienen mucha importancia en la economía mundial? ¿Por qué?

5. ¿Qué productos muy importantes en tu dieta personal no había en América antes de la llegada de los europeos?

Después de leer

Cada región o país tiene su comida típica. Piensa en los factores externos que ayudan a determinar la comida típica de una región. Después considera la comida típica donde vives. Con un compañero, explíquenle al resto de la clase cómo preparar una comida típica de su estado o su región.

Exploraciones léxicas

El señor Buenrostro y su familia salen a comer en un restaurante para celebrar su cumpleaños.

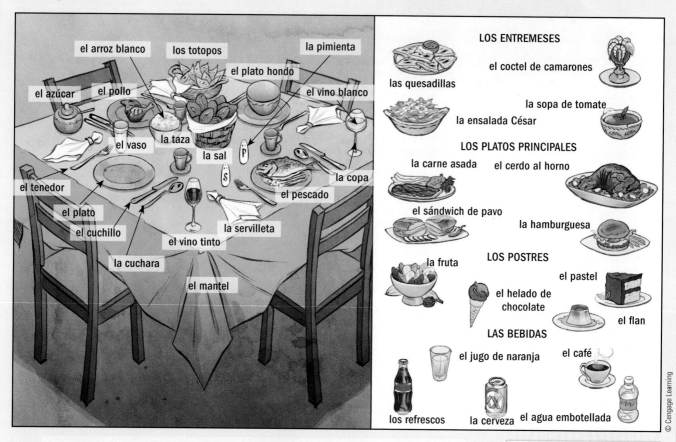

LOS ENTREMESES
el coctel de camarones
las quesadillas
la sopa de tomate
la ensalada César

LOS PLATOS PRINCIPALES
la carne asada   el cerdo al horno
el sándwich de pavo
la hamburguesa

LOS POSTRES
la fruta
el pastel
el helado de chocolate
el flan

LAS BEBIDAS
el jugo de naranja   el café
los refrescos   la cerveza   el agua embotellada

© Cengage Learning

el almuerzo	lunch
la cena	dinner
la cuenta	bill
el desayuno	breakfast
la orden	order
el tazón	serving bowl

Verbos

cenar	to eat dinner
dejar (una propina)	to leave (a tip)
desayunar	to eat breakfast

INVESTIGUEMOS LA GRAMÁTICA

The word **agua** is feminine, and therefore any adjectives need to be in the feminine form; however, it takes the masculine article for pronunciation purposes.

A practicar

7.19 **Escucha y responde** Vas a escuchar los nombres de varias comidas y bebidas. En un papel dibuja un vaso y en otro un tenedor. Si escuchas una bebida, levanta el vaso y si escuchas una comida levanta el tenedor.

🔊 2-4

7.20 **¿Cuál es?** Contesta con la opción más lógica.

1. ¡Tengo mucha sed! Quiero _____.
   a. arroz   b. un pastel   c. un refresco   d. un pollo
2. Mi entremés favorito es _____.
   a. fruta   b. pimienta   c. un café   d. una quesadilla
3. Mi café necesita más _____.
   a. taza   b. azúcar   c. cucharita   d. sal
4. Mi postre favorito es _____.
   a. la cerveza   b. la leche con chocolate   c. el helado   d. el azúcar
5. Para cortar la carne necesito _____.
   a. un cuchillo   b. una cuchara   c. una servilleta   d. la sal

INVESTIGUEMOS EL VOCABULARIO

In Spain, a cake is called **una torta**; however, in Mexico **una torta** is a type of sandwich.

Sándwich, borrowed from English, is commonly used throughout the Spanish-speaking world. The less commonly used Spanish equivalent is **el emparedado**.

7.21 **Relaciones** Relaciona las siguientes palabras con una palabra de la lista. Después, trabaja con un compañero para decir qué relación hay entre las palabras.

la carne   la copa   la cuchara   el plato principal   el postre   la sal   la taza   el vaso

Modelo el café... la bebida → *El café es una bebida.*

1. el cerdo
2. el pastel
3. el vino
4. la sopa
5. el jugo
6. la pimienta
7. las enchiladas
8. el té

7.22 **Encuesta** Encuentra a seis personas que hacen las siguientes actividades. Contesta con oraciones completas y después reporta a la clase.

Modelo desayunar cereal todos los días
    Estudiante 1: *¿Desayunas cereal todos los días?*
    Estudiante 2: *Sí, siempre desayuno cereal todos los días.*

1. pedir postre siempre cuando come en un restaurante
2. su comida favorita es el desayuno
3. saber hacer flan
4. comer carne más de tres veces a la semana
5. no tomar cerveza nunca
6. cenar frente al televisor

> **INVESTIGUEMOS EL VOCABULARIO**
> In some countries, **la comida** is used to refer to the noon meal, which is the main meal of the day.

7.23 **En un restaurante** En parejas, túrnense para hacer el papel *(play the role)* de mesero y de cliente.

Mesero: Buenas tardes, (señor/señorita/señora). ¿Prefiere la sección de fumar o de no fumar?

Cliente: _____

Mesero: ¿Desea una bebida?

Cliente: _____

Mesero: ¿Qué prefiere como plato principal?

Cliente: _____

Mesero: ¿Le gustaría *(Would you like)* un postre?

Cliente: _____

Mesero: ¿Necesita algo más *(something else)*?

Cliente: _____

Mesero: ¡Buen provecho! *(Enjoy!)*

¿Desean una bebida?

7.24 **Comparemos** Trabaja con un compañero. Uno va a mirar el dibujo en esta página y el otro va a mirar el dibujo en el **Apéndice B**. Túrnense para describir los dibujos y encontrar cinco diferencias.

Cultura

A veces un lugar para comer se vuelve casi tan importante como un monumento para una ciudad debido a su comida y a la historia del lugar. Por ejemplo, 4Gats en Barcelona fue un lugar de reunión para muchos artistas famosos, como Pablo Picasso.

Otro ejemplo famoso es La Cabaña, en Buenos Aires. La Cabaña es el restaurante especializado en carnes más viejo de la capital argentina. Su libro de visitas tiene la firma de visitantes muy famosos, entre ellos Charles de Gaulle, Henry Kissinger, Richard Nixon, el Rey Juan Carlos, Joan Crawford y Walt Disney, para mencionar solo a algunos.

En La Habana, Cuba, se distingue un restaurante llamado La Bodeguita del Medio. En parte es famosa por las personas importantes que la han visitado, como Pablo Neruda, Salvador Allende, Marlene Dietrich y Ernest Hemingway. El poeta nacional de Cuba, Nicolás Guillén, le dedicó un verso. Más allá de su fama, la Bodeguita se distingue por ser una especie de museo, ya que de sus paredes cuelgan *(hang)* fotos y artefactos que cuentan la historia de Cuba. Este restaurante también parece ser el lugar donde se inventó el mojito. Aún quienes no se interesan por la historia se sentirán atraídos a un menú con algunas de las mejores especialidades criollas cubanas, como frijoles negros, pierna de puerco asada, yuca con mojo y plátanos fritos.

Piensa en una ciudad de un país hispano que te interesa conocer y busca información sobre algún restaurante o café famoso de esa ciudad.

La Bodeguita del Medio es uno de los restaurantes más conocidos de La Habana.

Busca en Internet otros restaurantes importantes en el mundo hispanohablante. Para buscar, usa palabras como **restaurante, café, pub, taberna, famoso, histórico** y el nombre de un país o una ciudad hispanohablante. Escoge uno y sube la información o el menú a Share It! Explica por qué te gustaría comer en ese restaurante.

Comunidad

Visita un supermercado de tu comunidad y busca la sección de comida de otras partes del mundo. Luego prepara un reporte y usa las siguientes preguntas para guiarte.

¿Hay comida latinoamericana o española?

¿Qué productos encuentras?

Mira las etiquetas *(labels)*. ¿Dónde están hechos *(made)*?

¿Te sorprende la cantidad de productos de otros países? ¿Por qué?

¿Hay otras tiendas con comida de otros países? ¿De qué países?

¿Hay comida latinoamericana o española en tu supermercado?

Conexiones... a la salud

Muchas personas piensan que somos lo que comemos *(we are what we eat)*. En estos tiempos modernos mucha gente no tiene tiempo para preparar comida y esto puede afectar negativamente los hábitos alimenticios. Además, muchas personas compran comidas procesadas que son muy económicas, pero también tienen un alto contenido de calorías, azúcares y sodio. Una consecuencia de estos cambios es la gran cantidad de personas obesas que hay en muchos países. Entre los países industrializados con un mayor porcentaje de obesidad aparecen los Estados Unidos, México, Chile y Australia. El caso de México puede explicarse, en parte, por el dramático consumo de refrescos. Los mexicanos consumen en promedio 149 litros de refrescos por año.

Escribe una lista de productos que piensas que tienen un impacto negativo en la salud *(health)* de las personas. Después entrevista a tres compañeros de la clase para saber si también piensan que estos productos son malos para la salud. Reporta la información a la clase.

La comida rápida no siempre es la más saludable.

Comparaciones

¿Dónde compras la comida? ¿Vas a tiendas especializadas? En España y Latinoamérica siempre ha sido *(it has been)* muy común comprar la comida en diferentes tiendas pequeñas en vez del supermercado. La siguiente es una lista de diferentes tipos de tiendas. ¿Qué productos crees que venden en los siguientes lugares?

1. una tortillería
2. una heladería
3. una panadería
4. una frutería
5. una lechería
6. una carnicería
7. una chocolatería

En una alfajorería se venden alfajores, un postre típico de Argentina.

¿Cuáles son las ventajas *(advantages)* de ir a las tiendas especializadas? ¿y las desventajas? ¿Dónde compras tú esos *(those)* productos? ¿Puedes encontrar estas tiendas especializadas donde vives?

Exploraciones **gramaticales**

A analizar

Rosa y Santiago salen a comer en un restaurante. Mira el video. Después lee parte de su conversación y observa los pronombres de objeto directo en negritas. Después contesta las preguntas que siguen.

Mesero:	Buenas tardes. ¿Están listos?
Rosa:	Sí. Me gustarían los tacos de pescado, por favor.
Mesero:	Lo siento, no **los** tenemos ahora. Ya no hay más pescado.
Rosa:	¡Ay, qué lástima! Bueno, en ese caso quiero las enchiladas suizas. ¿Vienen con salsa verde o salsa roja?
Mesero:	Con salsa verde.
Rosa:	Perfecto, **las** voy a pedir.
Mesero:	¿Y para usted, caballero?
Santiago:	Tengo una pregunta, ¿la sopa de pollo tiene chile?
Mesero:	No, no **lo** tiene.
Santiago:	Bien, **la** voy a pedir entonces.

1. Pronouns take the place of a noun. In the above dialogue, the words in bold are direct object pronouns. Identify what each of the pronouns in the dialogue replaces.

2. What do **lo** and **la** mean in the dialogue above? And **los** and **las**?

3. Where are the pronouns in bold placed?

4. What pronoun would you use to replace **el arroz**? And **las cervezas**?

A comprobar

Direct object pronouns 1

1. A direct object is a person or a thing that receives the action of the verb. It tells to whom or to what something is being done.

   Juan pide **pollo.**
   Juan is ordering chicken. (The chicken is what is being ordered.)

   Elena invita a **Natalia** a comer.
   Elena is inviting Natalia to eat. (Natalia is who is being invited.)

2. In order to avoid repetition, the direct object can be replaced with a pronoun. In Spanish, the pronoun must agree in gender and number with the direct object it replaces.

¿Tienes **las tazas?**	*Do you have **the cups?***
Sí, **las** tengo.	*Yes, I have **them.***

In answering the question, it is not necessary to repeat the direct object, **las tazas;** instead it is replaced with the pronoun **las.**

3. The following are the third person direct object pronouns:

	singular		plural	
masculino	**lo**	*it, him, you (formal)*	**los**	*them, you*
femenino	**la**	*it, her, you (formal)*	**las**	*them, you*

4. The direct object pronoun is placed in front of the conjugated verb.

> ¿Comes carne?
> *Do you eat meat?*
>
> No, no **la** como.
> *No, I don't eat it.*

5. When using a verb phrase that has an infinitive or a present participle **(-ando, -iendo)**, the pronoun can be placed in front of the conjugated verb, or it can be attached to the infinitive or the present

participle. Notice that an accent is necessary when adding the pronoun to the end of the present participle.

> **La** voy a invitar. / Voy a invitar**la.**
> *I am going to invite **her.***
>
> ¿**Lo** quieres comer? / ¿Quieres comer**lo**?
> *Do you want to eat **it**?*
>
> Él **lo** está sirviendo. / Él está sirviéndo**lo.**
> *He is serving **it.***

A practicar

7.25 **En el restaurante** Lee la siguiente conversación e identifica el objeto o la persona que el pronombre reemplaza *(replaces)*.

Sr. Ortega: ¿Quieres el menú?

Sra. Ortega: No, no <u>lo</u> (**1.**) necesito. Ya sé qué quiero.

Sr. Ortega: ¿Sí? ¿Vas a pedir el pollo como siempre?

Sra. Ortega: No, no <u>lo</u> (**2.**) quiero comer hoy. Voy a pedir la carne asada.

Sr. Ortega: Yo voy a pedir<u>la</u> (**3.**) también. ¿Pedimos una botella de vino?

Sra. Ortega: Sí, <u>la</u> (**4.**) podemos pedir.

Sr. Ortega: Bueno, estamos listos. ¿Dónde está el mesero? No <u>lo</u> (**5.**) veo.

Sra. Ortega: Allí está. ¿Por qué no <u>lo</u> (**6.**) llamas?

Sr. Ortega: ¡Señor!

7.26 **La semana pasada** Habla con un compañero sobre quién hizo las siguientes actividades en sus casas la semana pasada. Deben usar los pronombres de objeto directo y el pretérito cuando contesten las preguntas. Es posible responder con **nadie** *(no one)*.

> **Modelo** ¿Quién tomó leche?
> Estudiante 1: *¿Quién tomó leche?*
> Estudiante 2: *Yo la tomé. ¿Y en tu casa?*
> Estudiante 1: *Nadie la tomó.*

1. ¿Quién compró la comida?

2. ¿Quién preparó el desayuno?

3. ¿Quién puso la mesa?

4. ¿Quién cocinó la cena?

5. ¿Quién sirvió la comida?

6. ¿Quién comió postre?

7. ¿Quién lavó los platos?

8. ¿Quién limpió la cocina?

¿Quién comió postre?

© luxmilita/Shutterstock

7.27 **¿Quién lo hace?** Mira los dibujos. Con un compañero, túrnense para hacer y responder preguntas con las palabras. Usen pronombres de objeto directo para responder.

> **Modelo** *(Look at drawing #1)* comer/ensalada
> Estudiante 1: *¿Quién come la ensalada?*
> Estudiante 2: *Eva **la** come.*

1.

a. tomar/sopa **b.** comer/pan

2.

a. servir/tacos **b.** servir/hamburguesas

3.

a. necesitar/tenedor **b.** necesitar/cuchara

4.

a. tomar/cerveza **b.** tomar/refresco

7.28 **Entrevista** Túrnense para hacer y contestar las siguientes preguntas. **¡OJO!** Deben usar pronombres de objeto directo para reemplazar *(replace)* las palabras subrayadas *(underlined)* cuando contesten para evitar la repetición.

1. ¿Desayunaste esta mañana? ¿Tomaste <u>café</u>?

2. ¿Trajiste <u>el almuerzo</u> a la universidad? ¿Qué trajiste?

3. ¿A qué hora cenaste anoche? ¿Quién preparó <u>la cena</u>?

4. ¿Cocinaste esta semana? ¿Preparaste <u>verduras</u>?

5. ¿Comiste <u>postre</u> después de la cena anoche? ¿Qué comiste?

6. ¿Tomaste <u>refrescos</u> con el almuerzo? ¿Qué tomaste?

7. ¿Quién limpió <u>la cocina</u> en tu casa después de la cena anoche? ¿Lavó <u>los platos</u> a mano?

8. ¿Compraste <u>comida</u> en el supermercado esta semana? ¿Qué compraste?

7.29 **¿Para qué es?** Con un compañero, túrnense para explicar lo que hacemos con las siguientes cosas. Deben usar los pronombres de objeto directo y verbos diferentes en las respuestas y dar explicaciones completas.

> **Modelo** el arroz
> Estudiante 1: *¿Qué hacemos con el arroz?*
> Estudiante 2: *Lo servimos con frijoles. / Lo ponemos en la paella. / Lo cocinamos en agua.*

1. el refresco	**3.** la ensalada	**5.** el cuchillo	**7.** la sopa
2. el helado	**4.** las enchiladas	**6.** los totopos	**8.** los tomates

A analizar ▶

Rosa y Santiago salen a comer en un restaurante. Después de ver el video otra vez, lee parte de su conversación y observa los pronombres de objeto directo en negritas.

> Rosa: Gracias por invitar**me** a cenar aquí. **Me** conoces y sabes que este es mi restaurante favorito.
>
> Santiago: Sí, **te** conozco muy bien, Rosa.

1. To whom do the pronouns **me** and **te** refer?
2. How would you translate the sentences above?

A comprobar

Direct object pronouns 2

In the last **Exploraciones gramaticales** section, you learned about third person direct object pronouns. The following are all of the direct object pronouns.

	singular		plural	
first person	**me**	*me*	**nos**	*us*
second person	**te**	*you*	**os**	*you (plural)*
third person	**lo, la**	*it, him, her, you (formal)*	**los, las**	*they, you (plural)*

1. As with the third person direct object pronouns, these pronouns are placed in front of the conjugated verb. They can also be attached to an infinitive or a present participle. Remember that an accent is necessary when adding the pronoun to the present participle.

El mesero **nos** ve.
The waiter sees us.

Te quiero invitar a cenar. / Quiero invitar**te** a cenar.
I want to invite you to dinner.

Ana **me** está llamando. / Ana está llamándo**me**.
Ana is calling me.

2. The following are some of the verbs that are frequently used with these direct object pronouns:

ayudar	felicitar *(to*	querer *(to love)*
buscar	*congratulate)*	saludar
conocer	invitar	*(to greet)*
creer	llamar	ver
encontrar	llevar *(to*	visitar
escuchar	*take along)*	

A practicar

7.30 **¿Qué significa?** Decide cuál es la traducción correcta.

1. No te entiendo.
   a. I don't understand you.   b. You don't understand me.
2. Mi madre me llama todos los días.
   a. My mother calls me every day.   b. I call my mother every day.
3. ¿Te esperan tus amigos?
   a. Are you waiting for your friends?   b. Are your friends waiting for you?
4. No nos ven.
   a. They don't see us.   b. We don't see them.

7.31 **Algunas preguntas** Decide cuál es la respuesta correcta.

1. ¿Quién me llama?
   a. Héctor te llama.   **b.** Héctor me llama.

2. ¿Te comprenden tus padres?
   a. Sí, te comprenden.   **b.** Sí, me comprenden.

3. ¿Me ayudas con la tarea?
   a. Sí, te ayudo.   **b.** Sí, me ayudas.

4. ¿Cuándo te invitan a comer?
   a. Te invitan a comer hoy.   **b.** Me invitan a comer hoy.

5. ¿Vas a visitarnos mañana?
   a. Sí, voy a visitarnos.   **b.** Sí, voy a visitarlos.

6. ¿El profesor los vio a ustedes?
   a. Sí, nos vio.   **b.** Sí, los vio.

7.32 **En clase** Contesta las preguntas referentes a los hábitos del profesor de español. Debes usar el pronombre **nos** en las respuestas.

Modelo ¿El profesor de español los invita a ustedes a fiestas?
   Sí, nos invita a fiestas. / No, no nos invita a fiestas.

¿El profesor de español…

1. los comprende a ustedes?
2. los conoce bien?
3. los ayuda a ustedes con la tarea?
4. los escucha cuando ustedes tienen problemas?
5. los llama a casa?
6. los lleva a comer en un restaurante?
7. los saluda en los pasillos *(hallways)*?
8. los ve fuera de la clase?
9. los invita a ser sus amigos en su página de Facebook?
10. los felicita cuando hacen un buen trabajo?

La profesora siempre nos ayuda.

© Tyler Olson/Shutterstock

7.33 **¡Ayuda!** Completa la siguiente conversación con el pronombre **me, te** o **nos**.

Susana: Simón, ¡yo (**1.**) _____ necesito! ¡No entiendo francés!

Simón: ¿El profesor siempre habla con ustedes en francés?

Susana: Sí, solo nos habla en francés, pero no lo comprendemos a él, ni él (**2.**) _____ comprende a nosotros. ¿(**3.**) _____ ayudas con mi tarea?

Simón: Por supuesto. Yo (**4.**) _____ puedo ayudar esta tarde si quieres.

Susana: ¡Sí! Entonces ¿(**5.**) _____ vas a llamar luego?

Simón: Sí, yo (**6.**) _____ llamo después de trabajar.

Susana: ¡Qué bueno! ¡(**7.**) _____ quiero, Simón!

¿Necesitas ayuda con la tarea?

© Andresr/Shutterstock

7.34 **Una noche en el restaurante** Con un compañero, túrnense para describir lo que pasó anoche en el restaurante. Deben completar lo que dijeron las diferentes personas en cada escena, usando los pronombres de objeto directo **me, te** y **nos.**

7.35 **La telenovela** Imagínate que eres un actor de telenovelas *(soap operas)*. Con un compañero, túrnense para leer las preguntas y las exclamaciones, y para responder de una manera original y dramática. Usen pronombres de objeto directo en las respuestas. ¡Sean creativos!

Modelo ¿Quieres a tu esposa?
Estudiante 1: *¿Quieres a tu esposa?*
Estudiante 2: *No, no la quiero, pero ella es muy rica.*

1. ¿Me quieres?
2. ¿Me vas a querer siempre?
3. ¿Quién te besa *(kiss)* cada noche?
4. ¡¿No nos vas a llevar contigo?!
5. ¡No me comprendes!
6. ¿Me estás engañando *(cheating on)?*
7. ¿Nos vas a abandonar?
8. ¡Nunca me escuchas!

¿Me quieres?

7.36 **Preguntas personales** Entrevista a un compañero de clase con las siguientes preguntas.

Modelo Estudiante 1: *¿Quién te cree siempre?*
Estudiante 2: *Mi esposo (mi madre, mi mejor amigo, etc.) me cree siempre.*

1. ¿Quién te comprende?
2. ¿Quién te quiere mucho?
3. ¿Quién te invita a comer con frecuencia?
4. ¿Quién te llama por teléfono y habla y habla y habla… ?
5. ¿Quién te ayuda con la tarea de español?
6. ¿Quién te visita con frecuencia?
7. ¿Quién te escucha cuando tienes problemas?
8. ¿Quién te busca cuando necesita dinero?
9. ¿Quién los visita a ti y a tu familia con frecuencia?
10. ¿Quién los saluda a ti y a tus compañeros de clase todos los días?

Antes de leer

¿Qué comidas se consideran "comida rápida" en los Estados Unidos? ¿Existe una diferencia entre comida rápida y comida chatarra *(junk food)*? ¿Cuál?

A leer

La comida rápida en Latinoamérica

has changed / century — Todos sabemos que la vida **ha cambiado** mucho en el último **siglo,** especialmente en las grandes ciudades, donde hoy en día hay poco tiempo para hacer todo lo que debemos hacer. ¿Cómo

lack of time — afecta esta **falta de tiempo** nuestros hábitos alimenticios?

Preparar comida consume mucho tiempo, así que mucha

save — gente busca soluciones para **ahorrar** ese tiempo. Las soluciones para este problema son diferentes según el país. Por ejemplo, en muchos países latinos donde pasar tiempo con la familia es muy importante, no

make sense — **tiene sentido** que una persona coma mientras maneja su automóvil. A la hora de la comida muchas amas de casa ocupadísimas se detienen en locales de comida rápida (o "comida corrida") para

homemade — comprar platillos **caseros** para su familia. De esta manera, no tienen que llegar a casa a preparar comida, solamente deben servirla. Los platillos que se compran en estos locales tienen la ventaja de ser variados y de cambiar todos los días. ¿Qué

stews — venden? ¡De todo! Diferentes variedades de sopa, carnes **guisadas**, verduras y hasta postres. Como el negocio no necesita mucho espacio y hay pocos empleados, pueden proveer comida

similar — muy **semejante** a la que se elabora en casa a un precio razonable.

Otra comida rápida popular es el pollo asado.

chains — Hay **cadenas** que lo venden
like — muy barato, **a semejanza** de las grandes compañías en los Estados Unidos que venden hamburguesas.

However — **Sin embargo,** el negocio de la comida rápida no se

> [no tiene sentido que una persona coma mientras maneja]

Las pupusas son un ejemplo de comida típica salvadoreña.

limita a la comida para toda la familia. ¿Quién no tiene hambre a mediodía o a media tarde? Para satisfacer esos **antojos,** en cualquier pueblo o ciudad de Latinoamérica se encuentran puestos en la calle o pequeños locales donde se puede comprar comida barata de acuerdo al gusto local. Por ejemplo, en los países andinos (Perú, Ecuador y Bolivia especialmente) se compran papas en la calle, preparadas de mil maneras diferentes. En El Salvador se venden pupusas, en Puerto Rico

cravings

El chipá paraguayo

los pinchos y en el Paraguay el chipá. Aunque los ingredientes de la comida rápida no son necesariamente los mismos que los de la comida que se compra en los Estados Unidos, los resultados son igual de **apetecibles.**

appetizing

Comprensión

Decide si las siguientes afirmaciones son ciertas o falsas, según la lectura. Corrige las ideas falsas.

1. En Latinoamérica la gente tiene mucho tiempo para cocinar.
2. La gente generalmente no come mientras conduce su automóvil en los países latinos.
3. Los locales de comida rápida venden comida como hamburguesas, pizza y pollo asado.
4. El pollo asado es una comida popular.
5. Las papas pueden ser un tipo de comida rápida en algunos países como Perú y Bolivia.

Después de leer

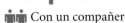 Con un compañero, túrnense para hacer y contestar las preguntas.

1. ¿Comes comida rápida/chatarra con frecuencia? ¿Por qué?
2. ¿Qué comidas rápidas prefieres?
3. ¿Qué más haces para ahorrar tiempo con la comida?

Redacción

Write a blog entry in which you discuss a favorite restaurant.

Paso 1 Think of a restaurant that you like. Jot down some basic information about the restaurant. Where is it located? What are its hours? What is the ambience of the restaurant like? What are the prices like? What kind of food do they serve? What do you recommend?

Paso 2 Think about a time that you visited the restaurant. When did you go and with whom? What did you and the others with you eat? How was the service? How was the food?

Paso 3 Using the information you generated in **Paso 1,** write a paragraph (in the present tense) in which you tell your readers about your favorite restaurant. Be sure to begin your paragraph with a sentence that will catch your readers' attention; a sentence such as *El Café Cielo es mi restaurante favorito.* is not going to encourage someone to continue reading.

Paso 4 Using the information you generated in **Paso 2,** write a second paragraph in which you discuss a time you visited the restaurant. You will need to use the preterite.

Paso 5 Write a brief concluding paragraph in which you sum up your thoughts about the restaurant.

Paso 6 Edit your blog entry:

1. Do all of the sentences in each paragraph support the topic sentence?
2. Are there any short sentences you can combine with **y** or **pero**?
3. Do adjectives agree with the nouns they describe?
4. Do verbs agree with the subject? Did you use the correct forms of the preterite?
5. Are there any spelling errors? Do the preterite verbs that need accents have them?

INVESTIGUEMOS EL VOCABULARIO

Here are some terms for ethnic foods commonly served in restaurants:

comida china	*Chinese food*
comida griega	*Greek food*
comida italiana	*Italian food*
comida japonesa	*Japanese food*
comida mexicana	*Mexican food*

Entrando en materia

¿Lees los comentarios sobre los restaurantes antes de elegir un nuevo lugar para comer? ¿Por qué?

Una reseña de un restaurante

Vas a leer una bitácora que cada semana habla sobre un restaurante de la ciudad. Después de leer decide si la reseña es positiva o negativa.

GUÍA GASTRONÓMICA: COMIDA CRIOLLA

Cuando Cristóbal Colón llegó a América, la historia del mundo cambió… y las opciones para comer se multiplicaron. Aquí en la ciudad gozamos de muchas opciones de cocina internacional, pero la comida tradicional y la cocina criolla siguen siendo las favoritas. El Criollo es un nuevo restaurante que abrió el mes pasado. Antes de hablar sobre los platillos que ofrecen, **valdría la pena** recordar la diferencia entre la comida tradicional y la criolla, para que ustedes sepan qué esperar de este restaurante.

Si pensamos en la historia de Latinoamérica, recordaremos que los criollos eran hijos de europeos, pero **nacieron** en el nuevo mundo y se criaron en él. Generaciones más tarde, los hijos de los criollos siguieron llamándose criollos, hasta que la palabra llegó a significar algo **autóctono** o nacional (justamente en la época que los países latinoamericanos empezaron a independizarse de España). Algo similar ocurrió con la comida: con el intercambio de alimentos, nacieron nuevas cocinas locales que combinaban los nuevos alimentos con las prácticas culinarias locales.

Hoy en día se habla de comida tradicional y comida criolla como sinónimos, pero en realidad hay diferencias importantes. La comida tradicional es la que tradicionalmente consume un grupo cultural o etnográfico. Por ejemplo, se puede hablar de cocina tradicional **judía.** La cocina criolla se basa en una mezcla tanto de ingredientes como de

técnicas para cocinar. En Latinoamérica, la cocina criolla fusiona dos (o más) gastronomías con sus técnicas, tradiciones e ingredientes. En el caso de Latinoamérica, se mezclan tradiciones culinarias prehispánicas con las europeas, las que a su vez estaban mezcladas con las de la cultura árabe y judía, entre otras.

Ahora que está aclarada la diferencia, vale la pena mencionar que en El Criollo no van a encontrar las recetas típicas peruanas, sino platillos **hechos** con ingredientes locales con un toque moderno. Las porciones son pequeñas, pero están elegantemente presentadas. El ambiente del local también es moderno, aunque un poco **ruidoso.** El servicio, para ser honesto, es un poco **lento,** pero los precios son moderados en comparación con otros restaurantes de cocina criolla. Además, El Criollo tiene un estacionamiento muy amplio, así que es un buen lugar para citarse a comer con los amigos.

¿El veredicto? Pienso regresar a El Criollo para comer con mis amigos a un buen precio.

Papas a la huancaina; papas con una salsa picante de queso

it would be worth it

were born

made
indigenous

noisy
slow

Jewish

Comprensión

Decide si las afirmaciones son ciertas o falsas, y corrige las falsas.

1. Después de que Cristóbal Colón encontró el Nuevo Mundo, la comida se homogeneizó en todo el mundo y hubo menos variedad de platillos.
2. Los criollos eran los hijos de europeos que nacieron en América.
3. "Comida criolla" es sinónimo de "comida tradicional".
4. La cocina árabe influye en la gastronomía que trajeron los españoles a Latinoamérica.
5. El autor del blog piensa que los precios de la comida en El Criollo son buenos.
6. Al autor del blog no le gustó el restaurante.

Más allá

Escribe una breve reseña de un restaurante en tu ciudad. ¿Lo recomiendas? ¿Por qué? Sube tu reseña y tu recomendación a Share It!

Exploraciones profesionales
La cocina ▷

Vocabulario

Sustantivos

el berro	*watercress*
el bife de lomo	*sirloin*
la caloría	*calorie*
el (la) camarero(a)	*waiter (waitress)*
el carbón	*charcoal*
la carne (de res)	*beef*
el chimichurri	*Argentine steak sauce*
el choclo	*corn*
el chorizo	*spicy sausage*
el condimento	*spice*
la empanada	*turnover, pasty*
la especialidad	*specialty*
el matambre	*flank steak*

Adjetivos

arrollado(a)	*rolled*
hervido(a)	*boiled*
relleno(a)	*stuffed*
tierno(a)	*tender*
vegetariano(a)	*vegetarian*

Verbos

descubrir	*to discover*

Frases útiles

a fuego lento
low heat

a la parrilla
on the grill

Se corta finito.
Cut in small slices.

Se sirve caliente/frío.
Serve hot/cold.

vuelta y vuelta
cooked on both sides

© Photos To Go

DATOS IMPORTANTES

Educación: Título de chef otorgado por escuelas de cocina internacional o título universitario de licenciatura en artes culinarias y hospedaje. Para trabajar en restaurantes finos se requieren años de experiencia.

Salario: Entre $35 000 y $85 000, dependiendo de la experiencia y la categoría del restaurante

Dónde se trabaja: Restaurantes, hoteles, clubes privados, compañías de servicios para fiestas y eventos, cruceros

Vocabulario nuevo Completa con una palabra lógica.

1. No como carne porque soy _____.

2. Ponemos el chimichurri sobre _____.

3. La _____ del restaurante son las empanadas.

4. El chef va a preparar una papas _____ de carne.

5. La ensalada tiene choclo y _____.

Miguel Casas, chef

Miguel Casas es el chef de un restaurante de especialidades argentinas. Trabaja en ese lugar desde hace diez años y los clientes del restaurante están muy satisfechos con la comida. En el video vas a ver al chef Casas hablar con un cliente.

Antes de ver

Un chef es el supervisor de una cocina. Debe estar al tanto de todos los platos que se preparan para que los clientes queden contentos. ¿Qué instrucciones crees que les da un chef a sus cocineros? ¿Qué tipo de conversación puede tener un chef con un cliente? ¿Qué piensas de la costumbre de algunos chefs de salir al comedor para hablar con los clientes? Explica.

Comprensión

1. ¿En qué tipo de restaurante trabaja el chef Casas?

2. ¿Quién llamó al chef Casas?

3. ¿Cómo cocinan la carne en ese restaurante?

4. ¿Qué tipo de carne comió la señorita?

5. ¿Qué ensalada comió?

6. ¿Qué tipo de vino tomó?

7. ¿Con qué rellenan las empanadas en ese restaurante?

Después de ver

En parejas, representen a un chef que sale a hablar con un cocinero muy joven y sin experiencia que hace muchas preguntas. Otra opción es representar a un chef que sale a hablar con un cliente del restaurante. ¿El cliente se queja *(complains)* o lo felicita? ¿Cómo responde el chef?

7.37 **El cumpleaños de mi esposa** Completa las siguientes oraciones con el pretérito del verbo entre paréntesis. ¡OJO! No todos los verbos son irregulares.

Ayer (**1.**) _____ (ser) el cumpleaños de mi esposa. Para celebrar yo (**2.**) _____ (hacer) una reservación en un restaurante elegante en el centro de la ciudad. Nosotros (**3.**) _____ (tener) que conducir media hora, pero valió la pena *(it was worth it)*. Cuando llegamos, (**4.**) _____ (ir) directamente a la mesa. Nosotros (**5.**) _____ (ver) el menú y luego (**6.**) _____ (pedir) nuestra comida. Cuando el mesero (**7.**) _____ (traer) la comida, yo (**8.**) _____ (estar) muy satisfecho con mi selección. Al terminar de comer, mi esposa (**9.**) _____ (querer) un postre y decidimos pedir un pastel. ¡El pastel (**10.**) _____ (estar) delicioso! Después de comer (**11.**) yo _____ (pagar) la cuenta, (**12.**) _____ (dejar) una buena propina y mi esposa y yo (**13.**) _____ (volver) a casa.

7.38 **Una cena en restaurante** Lee el párrafo sobre una noche que Tomás y Jimena cenaron en un restaurante. Cambia las oraciones y usa los pronombres de objeto directo para evitar *(to avoid)* las repeticiones.

Modelo Ayer fue el cumpleaños de Jimena y Tomás decidió invitar a Jimena a cenar en un restaurante.
Ayer fue el cumpleaños de Jimena y Tomás decidió invitarla a cenar en un restaurante.

(**1.**) El mesero llegó con los menús y Tomás y Jimena miraron los menús.
(**2.**) A Jimena le gusta el pollo asado y decidió pedir pollo asado. (**3.**) Tomás prefirió el pescado y pidió pescado. (**4.**) Las ensaladas parecían *(seemed)* deliciosas y los dos quisieron ensaladas. (**5.**) Tomás vio al mesero y llamó al mesero.
(**6.**) El mesero recomendó el vino blanco, pero ellos no quisieron vino blanco; prefirieron pedir vino tinto. (**7.**) En poco tiempo la comida llegó y ellos disfrutaron *(enjoyed)* la comida. (**8.**) Al final el mesero trajo la cuenta y Tomás pagó la cuenta con su tarjeta de crédito.

7.39 **¿Por o para?** Lee las siguientes oraciones y substituye las palabras en cursiva con **por** o **para.**

1. Ayer Renato decidió ir a un restaurante *a* cenar.
2. A las ocho salió de su casa *al* restaurante.
3. *A causa de* no tener una reservación, no pudo sentarse inmediatamente.
4. Esperó *durante* media hora.
5. *Al* fin, un señor lo llevó a una mesa.
6. Tenían un especial: una pizza de queso *a* 50 pesos y decidió pedirla.
7. Luego pidió un helado *de* postre.

7.40 **Sondeo** En grupos de tres o cuatro contesten las siguientes preguntas. Luego compartan las respuestas con la clase.

1. ¿Prefieres comer en un restaurante o en casa? ¿Por qué?
2. ¿Cuántas veces a la semana almuerzas en un restaurante?
3. ¿Cuántas veces al mes cenas en un restaurante?
4. ¿Cuál es tu restaurante favorito? ¿Qué pides allí?
5. ¿Cuándo fue la última vez *(last time)* que fuiste a un restaurante? ¿Cuál fue?

7.41 **La fiesta** Tu compañero y tú están planeando una cena para unos amigos, pero los invitados tienen algunas restricciones en su dieta. Uno de ustedes mira la información en esta página y el otro mira la información en el **Apéndice B.** Compartan la información sobre sus dietas y luego decidan qué van a servir del menú abajo.

> **aperitivo:** queso, totopos con salsa
>
> **primer plato:** ensalada con vinagreta, sopa de fideos *(noodles)*
>
> **segundo plato:** carne asada con papas fritas, fajitas con tortillas de maíz y verduras asadas
>
> **postre:** ensalada de frutas, pastel de chocolate
>
> **bebida:** té helado, limonada

Invitado	Restricción
Angélica	
Lucas	Es alérgico al chocolate.
Mateo	
Regina	Está a dieta.
Javier	
Gisa	No puede consumir gluten.

7.42 **La lista del supermercado** Con un compañero, van a crear una lista de supermercado. Tienen un presupuesto *(budget)* limitado y solo pueden comprar diez productos.

Paso 1 Escribe una lista de diez productos que quieres comprar. Debes incluir tres verduras, tres frutas y otros cuatro productos.

Paso 2 Compara tu lista con la de tu compañero y explica por qué quieres comprar ciertos productos. Luego pónganse de acuerdo *(agree)* en los diez productos que van a comprar.

Paso 3 Compartan *(Share)* la lista con la clase y expliquen algunas de sus decisiones.

Vocabulario 1

2-5

Frutas

el durazno	*peach*		la piña	*pineapple*
la fresa	*strawberry*		el plátano	*banana*
la manzana	*apple*		la sandía	*watermelon*
el melón	*melon*		las uvas	*grapes*
la naranja	*orange*			

Verduras

el brócoli	*broccoli*		la papa	*potato*
la cebolla	*onion*		el pepino	*cucumber*
la lechuga	*lettuce*		el tomate	*tomato*
el maíz	*corn*		la zanahoria	*carrot*

Lácteos y otros alimentos

la catsup	*ketchup*		la mayonesa	*mayonnaise*
el cereal	*cereal*		la mermelada	*jam*
la crema	*cream*		la mostaza	*mustard*
el huevo	*egg*		el pan	*bread*
el jamón	*ham*		el pepinillo	*pickle*
la leche	*milk*		el queso	*cheese*
la mantequilla	*butter*		el yogur	*yogurt*

Verbos

hornear	*to bake*

Palabras adicionales

la rebanada	*slice*

Los números

cien	*100*		setecientos	*700*
ciento uno	*101*		ochocientos	*800*
doscientos	*200*		novecientos	*900*
trescientos	*300*		mil	*1000*
cuatrocientos	*400*		dos mil	*2000*
quinientos	*500*		un millón	*1 000 000*
seiscientos	*600*			

Diccionario personal

_____

_____

_____

_____

🔊 Vocabulario 2

Los utensilios

la copa	*wine glass*	la servilleta	*napkin*
la cuchara	*spoon*	la taza	*cup*
el cuchillo	*knife*	el tazón	*serving bowl*
el mantel	*tablecloth*	el tenedor	*fork*
el plato	*plate*	el vaso	*glass*
el plato hondo	*bowl*		

La comida

el arroz	*rice*	el jugo	*juice*
el azúcar	*sugar*	el pastel	*cake*
la bebida	*drink*	el pavo	*turkey*
el café	*coffee*	el pescado	*fish*
el camarón	*shrimp*	la pimienta	*pepper*
la carne	*meat*	el pollo	*chicken*
el cerdo	*pork*	el postre	*dessert*
la cerveza	*beer*	el refresco	*soda*
el coctel	*cocktail*	la sal	*salt*
la ensalada	*salad*	el sándwich	*sandwich*
el entremés	*appetizer*	la sopa	*soup*
el flan	*flan*	los totopos	*tortilla chips*
la fruta	*fruit*	el vino blanco	*white wine*
la hamburguesa	*hamburger*	el vino tinto	*red wine*
el helado	*ice cream*		

Verbos

cenar	*to eat dinner*	querer	*to love*
dejar (una propina)	*to leave (a tip)*	llevar	*to take along*
desayunar	*to eat breakfast*	saludar	*to greet*
felicitar	*to congratulate*		

Palabras adicionales

al horno	*baked*	la cuenta	*bill*
el almuerzo	*lunch*	el desayuno	*breakfast*
asado(a)	*grilled*	frito(a)	*fried*
la cena	*dinner*	la orden	*order*
la comida	*food; lunch*	el plato principal	*main dish*

Diccionario personal

_____

_____

Learning Strategy

Review material from previous chapters

Because you continue to use vocabulary, verbs, and grammar that you learned in past chapters, it is important to review this material. Make flashcards for each chapter and review them often, go back to the **Exploraciones de repaso** section in earlier chapters to be sure you can still do the activities, and complete the **Hora de reciclar** activities in your *Student Activities Manual* or iLrn.

In this chapter you will learn how to:

- Talk about household chores
- Talk about your hobbies and pastimes
- Describe what you used to do in the past

¿Qué haces dentro y fuera de la casa?

© Simon Winnall/Getty Images

Exploraciones **léxicas**

Es sábado y la familia Carrillo está limpiando la casa. ¿Qué están haciendo?

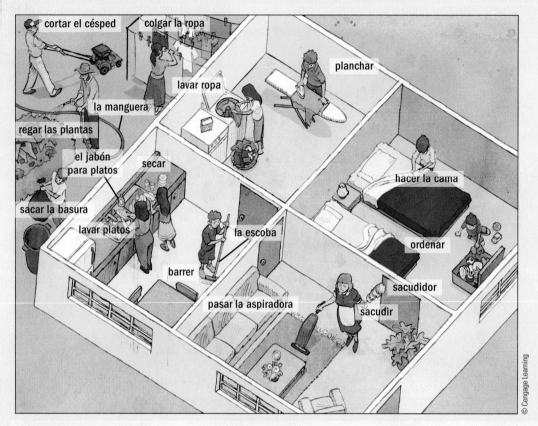

cortar el césped
colgar la ropa
planchar
lavar ropa
la manguera
regar las plantas
el jabón para platos
secar
hacer la cama
sacar la basura
lavar platos
la escoba
ordenar
barrer
sacudidor
pasar la aspiradora
sacudir

© Cengage Learning

La limpieza					Verbos	
el bote de basura	trash can	**el trapeador**	mop		**guardar**	to put away
el cortacésped	lawnmower	**el trapo**	cleaning cloth, rag		**poner la mesa**	to set the table
la plancha	iron				**recoger**	to pick up
los quehaceres	chores	**Adjetivos**			**recoger la mesa**	to clear the table
la tabla de planchar	ironing board	**limpio(a)**	clean		**trapear**	to mop
		sucio(a)	dirty			

A practicar

8.1 **Escucha y responde** Vas a escuchar una serie de quehaceres y de artículos de limpieza. Levanta la mano derecha si el quehacer o producto se relaciona con la cocina, y levanta la mano izquierda si se relaciona con el jardín.

2-7

8.2 **¿Con qué frecuencia?** En parejas túrnense para preguntar con qué frecuencia hacen ustedes los quehaceres de la lista.

Modelo sacudir

Estudiante 1: *¿Con qué frecuencia sacudes en tu casa?*
Estudiante 2: *Sacudo una vez a la semana. / Yo no sacudo, pero mi esposo sacude una vez a la semana.*

1. lavar la ropa
2. planchar
3. barrer el piso de la cocina
4. pasar la aspiradora

5. cortar el césped
6. hacer las camas
7. limpiar los baños
8. sacar la basura

8.3 **Una fiesta** Imagina que vives en la casa de los siguientes dibujos. Tus amigos y tú van a dar una gran fiesta para toda la clase. Con un compañero, decidan lo que deben hacer antes de la fiesta y lo que van a tener que hacer después de la fiesta. Sean creativos.

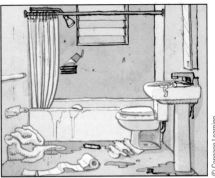

8.4 **Busca a alguien** Busca a compañeros que hacen/hicieron las siguientes actividades. Después repórtale la información a la clase.

1. Lavó la ropa ayer.
2. Nunca riega las plantas.
3. Hizo su cama esta mañana.
4. Detesta lavar los platos.
5. Cuelga la ropa para secarla.
6. Nunca corta el césped.
7. Vive con alguien que limpia el baño.
8. Planchó algo la semana pasada.

8.5 **Una entrevista** Trabaja con un compañero para contestar las preguntas y luego repórtale la información a la clase.

1. ¿Qué quehacer te gusta menos? ¿Cuál te gusta más?
2. En tu opinión ¿qué quehacer es el más importante? ¿Cuál es el menos importante?
3. ¿Tienes quehaceres en el jardín? ¿Cuáles?
4. ¿Crees que los niños deben ayudar en casa? ¿Qué quehaceres deben hacer?
5. ¿Usas productos de limpieza que son buenos para el medio ambiente *(environment)*? ¿Por qué?

8.6 **Compañeros de casa** Javier, Marcos y Emanuel decidieron vivir juntos y quieren organizarse para hacer los quehaceres que les gustan. Trabaja con un compañero para completar la tabla. Uno de ustedes va a ver la información en esta página, y el otro debe ver la información en el **Apéndice B**. Primero completen el gráfico y después decidan quién va a hacer cada quehacer. Cada persona debe tener dos obligaciones.

Quehacer	Javier	Marcos	Emanuel	¿Quién va a hacerlo?
lavar los platos		No le gusta.		
limpiar los baños	No le gusta.		No le gusta.	
trapear la cocina	No le gusta.	Le gusta.		
pasar la aspiradora				
cortar el césped		No le gusta.	No le gusta.	
regar las plantas	No le gusta.		No le gusta.	

Conexiones culturales

Los deberes de la casa

Cultura

Este cuadro del pintor boliviano Melchor Pérez Holguín (1660–1732) muestra a la Virgen María y a José, su esposo, en una pausa durante su viaje a Egipto. La producción de Pérez Holguín se basó en cuadros encargados *(commissioned)* por órdenes religiosas. En sus obras *(works)*, el artista mezcla elementos de la pintura europea de la época con elementos populares y de su país, Bolivia. Por ejemplo, la ropa de la Virgen y la manta *(blanket)* en el suelo son tradicionales de la región de La Paz, Oruro y Cochabamba. Por otra parte, los querubines son tradicionales en el arte europeo.

Observa el cuadro. ¿Qué están haciendo la Virgen y los ángeles en el cuadro? ¿Qué otros quehaceres piensas que tenían que hacer?

 Identifica otra pintora famosa y aprende más sobre Bolivia en **Exploraciones del mundo hispano** en el **Apéndice A.**

 Investiga en Internet otras obras de Melchor Pérez Holguín. Elige una que te guste, súbela a Share It! y explica por qué te gusta. Después lee lo que escribieron tus compañeros.

© Virgen lavandera by Melchor Pérez Holguin. National Art Museum Collection–La Paz, Bolivia. Photo: © National Art Museum Archives.

Comparaciones

De acuerdo a un estudio de una universidad inglesa, las mujeres tendrán que esperar hasta el año 2050 para que los hombres pasen el mismo número de horas haciendo labores de la casa.

¿Cuánto tiempo pasas haciendo quehaceres? ¿Crees que las mujeres pasan más tiempo limpiando que los hombres? El siguiente es un resumen de las horas que los argentinos, los españoles, los mexicanos y los estadounidenses dedican al trabajo doméstico cada semana. Observa la información. ¿Te sorprende? ¿Por qué?

Horas totales de trabajo doméstico semanal para familias con hijos

mujeres argentinas	37,8 horas
hombres argentinos	15,4 horas
mujeres españolas	29,7 horas
hombres españoles	15,9 horas
mujeres mexicanas	32,2 horas
hombres mexicanos	15,3 horas
mujeres estadounidenses	32 horas
hombres estadounidenses	17 horas

Sources: Pew Research Center; Instituto Nacional de Estadística; Instituto Nacional de Estadística y Geografía; ElObservatodo.cl

¿Cómo se pueden explicar las diferencias entre los hombres y las mujeres de todos estos países?

© Andersen Ross/JupiterImages

Comunidad

Entrevista a una persona de un país hispanohablante y averigua (*find out*) quién hace los quehaceres en su casa, qué quehaceres hace y cuánto tiempo dedica a la semana a hacer estos quehaceres. Si la familia tiene niños, incluye el tiempo que se necesita para ellos.

© MJTH/Shutterstock

Conexiones... a la biología

Un nuevo tipo de productos se hace cada vez más popular en los mercados: los productos de limpieza biológicos. En particular, el jabón para lavar ropa hecho con enzimas naturales puede limpiar sin dañar la ropa, el medio ambiente (*environment*) o la salud (*health*).

Las enzimas para quitar manchas se obtienen con bacterias modificadas genéticamente. Su uso comenzó en 1913, cuando el químico alemán Otto Rhöm usó una enzima digestiva del páncreas de animales para mejorar el proceso de limpieza. Así se empezó a fabricar y comercializar el primer jabón enzimático. La producción masiva de enzimas provenientes de bacterias y hongos comenzó a mediados del siglo XX.

Más recientemente, un grupo de investigadores de la Universidad de Chile, descubrió que el krill, un minúsculo habitante del mar antártico, produce enzimas capaces de actuar a solo 20° C. Juan Asenjo, el líder de este grupo de científicos, le explicó al periódico *El Mercurio* el significado de este descubrimiento para la industria de la limpieza:

© Monkey Business Images/Shutterstock

"*Si en nuestro país se lava ropa un millón de veces al día y, en promedio, cada lavado requiere 20 litros de agua a 50ºC, este hallazgo podría reducir a la mitad la energía que se gasta para calentar toda esa agua*".

Según el libro *Biotecnología* (2007) escrito por la doctora en genética María Antonia Muñoz de Malajovich, de nacionalidad argentina, "en la actualidad más del 60% de la producción industrial de enzimas se basa en técnicas de biotecnología moderna". Tan solo en 2009 se calcula que el mercado mundial de enzimas fue de alrededor de 2,4 millones de dólares, y seguirá aumentando, según el pronóstico de Malajovich.

Sources: TecnoCienciaYSalud.com; Biotecnologia.suite101.net

Lee las etiquetas de los productos que tienes en casa para la limpieza de ropa. ¿Cuántos usan enzimas?

A analizar ▶

Camila habla con Vanesa sobre los quehaceres. Después de ver el video, lee parte de lo que dice Camila y presta atención a los verbos en negritas.

> Ahora que Rodrigo tiene un nuevo puesto *(position)* y yo también trabajo, estamos muy ocupados. Antes los dos **limpiábamos** la casa juntos los domingos. Él **barría** la cocina y **sacaba** la basura mientras yo **pasaba** la aspiradora y **sacudía.** Luego en la tarde yo **lavaba** y **secaba** la ropa, y él **limpiaba** el baño.

Using the examples above and your knowledge of verb conjugations, answer the questions.

1. What are the endings of the **-ar** verbs in bold? And the **-er/-ir** verbs?

2. The verbs in bold are in the imperfect tense. Does the imperfect describe actions in the past, present, or future?

A comprobar

The imperfect

1. To form the imperfect of regular verbs, add the following endings to the stem:

-ar verbs	**lavar** *(to wash)*
lav**aba**	lav**ábamos**
lav**abas**	lav**abais**
lav**aba**	lav**aban**

-er/-ir verbs	**barrer** *(to sweep)*
barr**ía**	barr**íamos**
barr**ías**	barr**íais**
barr**ía**	barr**ían**

2. The verbs **ser, ir,** and **ver** are the only irregular verbs in the imperfect.

ser *(to be)*			
yo	**era**	nosotros(as)	**éramos**
tú	**eras**	vosotros(as)	**erais**
él, ella, usted	**era**	ellos, ellas, ustedes	**eran**

ir *(to go)*			
yo	**iba**	nosotros(as)	**íbamos**
tú	**ibas**	vosotros(as)	**ibais**
él, ella, usted	**iba**	ellos, ellas, ustedes	**iban**

ver *(to see)*			
yo	**veía**	nosotros(as)	**veíamos**
tú	**veías**	vosotros(as)	**veíais**
él, ella, usted	**veía**	ellos, ellas, ustedes	**veían**

3. There are no stem-changing verbs in the imperfect. All verbs that have changes in the stem in the present or the preterite are regular.

> Mi madre **cuelga** la ropa afuera.
> Mi abuela también **colgaba** la ropa afuera.

> Mi madre **prefirió** lavar los platos a mano ayer.
> Mi abuela siempre **prefería** lavar los platos a mano.

4. The imperfect of the verb **haber (hay)** is **había.**

> Siempre **había** platos en el fregadero.
> *There were* always plates in the sink.

5. One of the uses of the imperfect is to describe past habits or routines. In English, we frequently use the expression *used to*. It is often used with expressions such as **siempre, todos los días, todos los años, con frecuencia, a menudo, normalmente, generalmente, a veces,** etc.

> De niño, **era** mi responsabilidad sacar la basura.
> *As a child, it **used to be** my responsibility to take out the trash.*

> Todos los sábados **limpiábamos** la casa.
> *Every Saturday we **used to clean** the house.*

6. Another use of the imperfect is to describe an action in progress at a particular moment in the past where there is no emphasis on when the action began or ended.

> ¿Qué **hacías** a las tres?
> *What **were you doing** at three o'clock?*

> Yo **cortaba** el césped.
> *I **was cutting** the grass.*

INVESTIGUEMOS LA GRAMÁTICA

You will recall that the present progressive describes actions in progress in the present. It is also possible to use the imperfect of **estar** with the present participle.

Mi hermano **estaba planchando** su ropa.
*My brother **was ironing** his clothes.*

A practicar

8.7 **En tu adolescencia** Lee las siguientes oraciones e indica si son ciertas o falsas según tu experiencia.

1. No tenía que hacer quehaceres.
2. Sacaba la basura.
3. No me gustaba ordenar mi habitación.
4. Cortaba el césped.
5. Hacía la cama todos los días.
6. Ponía la mesa antes de comer.
7. Lavaba mi ropa.
8. No colgaba mi ropa.

Cuando era niña ayudaba a mis padres con los quehaceres.

© Lane V. Erickson/Shutterstock

8.8 **Mi niñez (childhood)** Cambia el verbo a la forma necesaria del imperfecto y completa las siguientes ideas.

Modelo mi padre me (contar)…
> *Cuando era niña, mi padre me contaba cuentos.*

Cuando era niño(a),…

1. yo (vivir)…
2. mis amigos y yo (comer) mucho…
3. mi familia (ir) con frecuencia a…
4. mis amigos (jugar)…
5. no me (gustar)…
6. mi mejor amigo(a) (ser)…
7. yo (tener) que…

8.9 **¿Qué hacían?** Cristina llamó a la casa de su amiga pero nadie contestó. Con un compañero, túrnense para identificar las actividades que hacían las personas en ese momento.

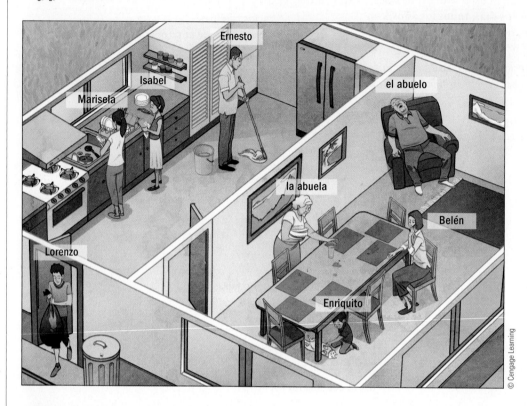

8.10 **Entrevista** Túrnense para entrevistar a un compañero sobre sus actividades mientras estaban en la escuela secundaria. Den mucha información al contestar las preguntas.

1. ¿Qué te gustaba hacer en las vacaciones cuando estabas en la escuela secundaria?
2. ¿Practicabas algún deporte? ¿Cuál?
3. ¿Quién cocinaba? ¿Qué comida preferías?
4. ¿Trabajaban tus padres? ¿Dónde?
5. ¿Salías con amigos los fines de semana? ¿Adónde iban?
6. ¿Cómo se llamaba tu mejor amigo? ¿Qué hacías con él?
7. ¿Qué quehaceres tenías que hacer?
8. ¿Qué hacías después de regresar de la escuela?

8.11 **Una encuesta** En grupos de tres o cuatro van a descubrir quién tenía que trabajar más en su casa cuando era niño.

Paso 1 Con los compañeros del grupo decidan tres quehaceres más para añadir *(to add)* a la lista. Luego usen el imperfecto para preguntar quién hacía las actividades en la lista cuando era niño.

cortar el césped   sacar la basura

limpiar el baño   _____

lavar los platos   _____

poner la mesa   _____

Paso 2 ¿Quién tenía más quehaceres cuando era niño? Repórtenle la información a la clase.

A analizar

Camila habla con Vanesa sobre los quehaceres. Mira el video otra vez. Después lee parte de su conversación y observa las expresiones negativas en negritas.

> ¡Ay, Vanesa! Parece que **nunca** tengo el tiempo que necesito para limpiar la casa. Mis padres van a llegar el sábado para visitarnos ¡y la casa es un desastre! Sé que **no** voy a tener tiempo para limpiar **ni** mañana **ni** el viernes porque tengo mucho trabajo para la escuela. ¿Conoces a alguien que me pueda ayudar a limpiar?
>
> Vanesa: **No** conozco a **nadie**, pero puedo preguntarle a mi hermana.
>
> Camila: Sí, por favor. ¡Ya **no** tengo tiempo de hacer **nada**!

1. How many negative words are there in each sentence?
2. Where is the word **no** placed in relation to the verb it refers to in the sentences?

A comprobar

Indefinite and negative words

1. The following are the most commonly used negative and indefinite words.

Palabras negativas

nadie	*no one, nobody*
nada	*nothing*
nunca	*never*
jamás	*never*
tampoco	*neither, either*
ningún (ninguno), ninguna	*none, any*
ni… ni	*neither . . . nor*

Palabras indefinidas

alguien	*someone, somebody*
algo	*something*
siempre	*always*
también	*also*
algún (alguno), alguna	*some*
o… o	*either . . . or*

2. In Spanish, it is possible to use multiple negative words in one sentence. When a negative word follows the verb, it is necessary to place **no** or another negative word in front of the verb, making it a double negative.

> **No** plancho **nunca.**
> I **never** iron.
>
> **No** hay **ni** escoba **ni** aspiradora aquí.
> There is **neither** a broom **nor** a vacuum here.
>
> **Nunca** le das **nada** a **nadie.**
> You **never** give **anything** to **anyone.**

3. The negative words **nadie, jamás, nunca,** and **tampoco** can be placed directly before the verb. **Nada** can only be placed before the verb if it is used as the subject.

> **Nadie** está lavando ropa ahora.
> *No one is washing clothes now.*
>
> **Tampoco** hago la cama.
> *I don't make my bed **either**.*
>
> **Nada** es imposible.
> *Nothing **is impossible**.*

4. The indefinite words **algún, alguno(s), alguna(s),** and the negative words **ningún, ninguno(s), ninguna(s)** are often used to add emphasis but are not essential. Notice that they must agree in number and gender with the noun they are describing. When using the negative, the singular form is generally used.

> ¿Tienes **algunas** camisas para planchar?
> No, no tengo **ninguna** camisa. (No, no tengo **ninguna**.)

> ¿Tienes trapos?
> No, no tengo **ningún** trapo.
> (No, no tengo **ninguno.**)

*While it is correct to use **algunos(as)** in front of a noun, it is much more common to use **unos(as)** or to omit the article. **Algunos(as)** tends to be used more frequently as a pronoun: **Necesito plantas para el jardín. ¿Tiene algunas?**

A practicar

8.12 **¿Cierto o falso?** Mira el dibujo y decide si estas oraciones son ciertas o falsas.

1. No hay nadie en el comedor.

2. No hay ni platos ni vasos en la mesa.

3. Tampoco hay flores en la mesa.

4. Ninguna mascota está en el comedor.

5. No hay nada debajo de la mesa.

6. Nadie limpia el comedor.

7. El perro no come nada.

8. Hay algo al lado de la mesa.

© Cengage Learning

8.13 **A contratar ayuda** Vas a entrevistar a una persona para limpiar la oficina donde trabajas, pero no es una buena candidata. Para saber qué respuestas dio durante la entrevista, contesta las siguientes preguntas de forma negativa.

1. ¿Siempre llega usted a tiempo *(on time)*?

2. ¿Alguien va a ayudarla a limpiar la oficina?

3. ¿Limpia ventanas y espejos?

4. No tenemos aspiradora. ¿Tiene usted una aspiradora?

5. ¿Tiene algunas cartas de recomendación?

6. ¿Necesita saber algo más sobre nuestra oficina?

No me gusta limpiar ni cocinas ni baños.

© age fotostock / SuperStock

8.14 **Ayuda por favor** La madre de Jorge está limpiando la casa y necesita ayuda, pero él es muy perezoso. Completa la conversación con algunas de estas palabras negativas e indefinidas. **¡OJO! Algún** y **ningún** tienen varias formas.

algo	alguien	algún	siempre	o
nada	nadie	ningún	nunca	ni

Madre: Jorge, ¿puedes guardar **(1.)** _____ de estos libros?

Jorge: No, no quiero guardar **(2.)** _____ libro. Los voy a leer más tarde.

Madre: ¿Puedes ir a la cocina y traerme **(3.)** _____ para limpiar las ventanas?

Jorge: No, no puedo traerte **(4.)** _____ porque estoy ocupado.

Madre: ¿Puedes ayudarme a lavar los platos **(5.)** _____ a secarlos después?

Jorge: No quiero lavar los platos **(6.)** _____ secarlos, tengo que hacer la tarea.

Madre: ¿Vas a hacer la tarea con **(7.)** _____ de tu clase?

Jorge: No, no la voy a hacer con **(8.)** _____ . Voy a hacerla solo.

Madre: Entonces sí puedes hacer **(9.)** _____ quehaceres antes de hacerla.

Jorge: No puedo hacer **(10.)** _____ porque necesito tomar una siesta primero.

Madre: ¡Jorge! ¡**(11.)** _____ tienes una excusa y **(12.)** _____ ayudas en la casa!

8.15 **Un sondeo** En grupos de cuatro o cinco, túrnense haciendo las preguntas para averiguar *(find out)* quién hace las siguientes actividades. Luego reporten a la clase.

Modelo no tiene ninguna clase de matemáticas
Estudiante 1: *¿Quién no tiene ninguna clase de matemáticas?*
Estudiante 2: *Yo no tengo ninguna clase de matemáticas.*

1. no tiene ninguna otra clase
2. no estudia con nadie
3. nunca olvida *(forgets)* su tarea
4. siempre hace la tarea para la clase de español
5. no entiende nada en alguna clase
6. jamás se sienta al frente de la clase

8.16 **Preguntas personales** Entrevista a un compañero con las siguientes preguntas. Si es posible, continúa la conversación con la pregunta entre paréntesis.

1. ¿Vives con alguien? (¿Con quién?)
2. ¿Tienes un perro o un gato? (¿Cómo se llama?)
3. ¿Con qué frecuencia limpias la casa? (¿Alguien te ayuda?)
4. ¿Hay algún quehacer que no te gusta para nada? (¿Cuál?)
5. ¿Tienes que hacer algo hoy que no quieres hacer? (¿Qué es?)
6. ¿Siempre haces tu cama? (¿Por qué?)

¿Siempre haces tu cama?

8.17 **En casa** Mira los dibujos. Después escucha las oraciones y decide si son ciertas
o falsas. Si son falsas, corrígelas. Después, usando las expresiones negativas e
indefinidas, inventa tres oraciones y compártelas con un compañero, quien va a
decidir si son ciertas o falsas.

🔊 2-8

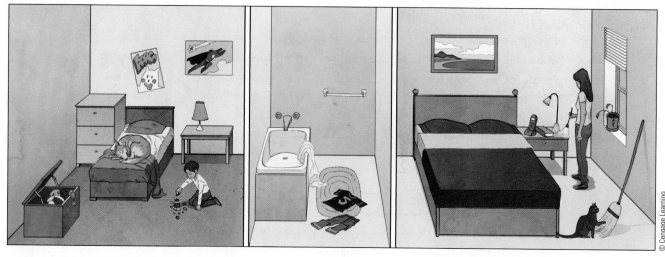

8.18 **¿Qué debo hacer?** Con un compañero, túrnense para pedir consejos para
conseguir los objetivos de la lista. Cuando das los consejos, menciona lo que debe o
no debe hacer tu compañero usando una palabra afirmativa o negativa.

Modelo ayudar a otros

Estudiante 1: *¿Qué debo hacer para ayudar a otros?*

Estudiante 2: *Debes buscar algunas oportunidades para trabajar como voluntario.*

1. ahorrar *(save)* dinero
2. conocer a más personas
3. tener buenas notas
4. conseguir un nuevo trabajo
5. estar más sano
6. divertirme más

8.19 **De mal humor** Trabaja con un compañero y túrnense para proponerle *(to propose)*
unas ideas. Cuando el primer estudiante propone algo, el segundo estudiante que está
de mal humor *(bad mood)* debe responder con expresiones negativas.

Modelo Estudiante 1: *Siempre estudio en la biblioteca. ¿Quieres ir conmigo?*

Estudiante 2: *Nunca estudio en la biblioteca.*

Estudiante 2: *Leo algunos libros antes de dormirme. ¿Quieres un libro?*

Estudiante 1: *No leo ningún libro antes de dormirme.*

Leemos algunos libros antes de acostarnos.

En vivo ◀))

Entrando en tema

En tu opinión ¿cuáles son las labores domésticas más fastidiosas (*bothersome*)?

Un programa de televisión sobre la limpieza

◀))
2-9

Vas a escuchar un segmento de un programa de televisión donde se dan recomendaciones para ayudar con la limpieza de la casa. Escucha con atención y después responde las preguntas.

Vocabulario útil

el bicarbonato	*bicarbonate (baking soda)*	**el polvo**	*dust*
		profundo(a)	*deep*
la cáscara	*skin of a fruit*	**quemado(a)**	*burnt*
las hojas	*leaves*	**reluciente**	*shining, sparkling*
la limpieza	*cleaning*	**el vinagre**	*vinegar*
el medio ambiente	*environment*		

Detesto planchar.

© Chamille White/Shutterstock

Comprensión

Decide si las oraciones son ciertas o falsas según lo que escuchaste. Corrige las falsas.

1. En este programa dan consejos para ahorrar (*to save*) dinero comprando productos de limpieza más baratos.
2. Para ahorrar tiempo limpiando el horno se pueden usar productos químicos más fuertes (*strong*).
3. Para planchar más fácilmente se debe colgar la ropa inmediatamente después de plancharla.
4. Las cáscaras de plátano sirven para limpiar las ventanas.
5. Con bicarbonato, vinagre y limón se pueden hacer muchas tareas de limpieza.

Más allá

Escribe tu propia lista de cinco consejos para hacer más fáciles algunas labores de la casa y súbela a Share It! Lee los consejos de otros compañeros. ¿Encontraste información útil?

Lectura

Antes de leer

¿Cómo se promueve *(promote)* la limpieza en tu ciudad? ¿y en tu universidad?

A leer

La ciudad es nuestra casa

"Tan limpio es quien limpia como quien no ensucia"
"Jugá limpio"
"Te quiero limpia"
"Cuento contigo"
"Ensuciar cuesta dinero"

> [Ensuciar cuesta dinero]

Todos estos son eslogans usados en diversas ciudades de países hispanos en sus campañas para mantener limpias las calles de sus ciudades, pero muchas de estas campañas van **más allá** *[beyond]* de limpiar. Uno de sus objetivos principales es educar a sus comunidades para mantener su ciudad limpia y **acogedora** *[welcoming]* para todos. No se trata simplemente de no tirar basura a la calle, aunque esto es importante. Entre las diversas campañas hay objetivos tan variados como pintar muros en barrios que lo necesitan, organizar asociaciones de **vecinos,** *[neighbors]* poner contenedores para reciclar y educar a las personas sobre cómo reciclar correctamente, separando **desechos** *[waste]* orgánicos de los materiales reciclables. Algunas ciudades también organizan campañas de voluntarios para recoger excrementos de perros, y promueven educar a los dueños para recoger los excrementos de sus mascotas usando bolsas de plástico.

Un caso en el que el trabajo de los ciudadanos va más allá de mantener la ciudad en orden es el de la Fundación Ciudad Limpia, en Chaco, Argentina. Entre sus muchos éxitos se cuentan los siguientes: recuperaron miles de libros y los donaron a bibliotecas; hicieron una campaña para **evitar** *[to avoid]* la contaminación de la ciudad con propaganda política ("Si ensucia... no lo voto"); dieron **charlas** *[talks]* en sus escuelas; recolectaron más de una **tonelada** de **pilas** *[ton / batteries]* para neutralizarlas; participaron en el cuidado de espacios públicos, como

Contenedores para reciclar

© Mikhail Zahranichny/Shutterstock

parques y plazas; limpiaron grafiti y hasta ayudaron a un grupo de niños de las calles a encontrar oportunidades de educación para aprender un **oficio,** y les ofrecieron oportunidades de recreación deportiva. Todos estos objetivos fueron logrados con la participación de voluntarios de la región y con sus donaciones. Para los habitantes de esta ciudad mantener limpia su ciudad significa mantener una comunidad que ofrece oportunidades para todos sus habitantes.

trade

Comprensión

Decide si las afirmaciones son ciertas o falsas y corrige las falsas.

1. El objetivo principal de las campañas de limpieza que se describen es no tirar basura.
2. Algunas campañas enseñan a las personas a reciclar.
3. La Fundación Ciudad Limpia tiene campañas de propaganda política.
4. La Fundación Ciudad Limpia ofrece oportunidades de recreación y educativas a los jóvenes.

Después de leer

1. ¿Hay campañas de limpieza en tu comunidad? ¿Qué actividades proponen estas campañas? ¿Participaste alguna vez?
2. Busca tres o cuatro anuncios en español de una campaña de limpieza en YouTube. ¿Cuál es tu favorito y por qué?

¿Participaste alguna vez en una campaña de limpieza?

Los tiempos cambian, así como también cambian las actividades favoritas de los niños y de los adultos.

Estrategia

Review material from previous chapters

The theme for this section of the chapter is pastimes. It might be helpful to review the sports and hobbies vocabulary from **Capítulo 6** to discuss favorite activities.

Juegos y juguetes	Games and toys
el ajedrez	chess
el carrito	toy car
las cartas	cards
las damas	checkers
el dominó	dominos
el rompecabezas	puzzle

Verbos	
andar en patineta/ motocicleta	to ride a skateboard/ motorcycle
chatear	to chat on the Internet
contar (ue) (cuentos, historias, chistes)	to tell (short stories, stories, jokes)
cuidar a (niños)	to care for (children)
dar la vuelta	to take a walk or a ride

dibujar	to draw
hacer jardinería	to garden
ir de paseo	to go for a walk/ride
navegar en Internet	to surf the Internet
pasar tiempo	to spend time
pelear	to fight, to argue
portarse (bien / mal)	to behave (well / badly)
salir (a + *infinitive*)	to go out (to do something)
volar una cometa	to fly a kite

Palabras adicionales	
la niñera	babysitter
el permiso	permission
el piano	piano
el (teléfono) celular	cell phone

INVESTIGUEMOS EL VOCABULARIO:

Spanish terms for illustrated stories vary depending on how or where they are published and who their audience is. For example, the Sunday comics are known as **tiras cómicas.** Weekly or monthly publications purchased independently are known as **historietas** or **tebeos** (Spain). In some places they are just called **cómics.** For adult readers, the term **novela gráfica** is used. If the cartoons are animated for television they are called **dibujos animados** or **caricaturas.** A movie for children is **película de animación,** but if the intended audience is older it might be **animé.**

A practicar

8.20 **Escucha y responde** Vas a escuchar una serie de actividades. Si es una actividad que hacemos generalmente dentro de una casa o edificio, indica con tu pulgar hacia arriba. Si es una actividad al aire libre *(outdoors),* indica con el pulgar hacia abajo.

2-10

8.21 **¿Cierto o falso?** Mira el dibujo de **Exploraciones léxicas** y decide si las siguientes oraciones son ciertas o falsas. Corrige las oraciones falsas.

1. La abuela está jugando a los bolos.
2. Tres niños tocan la guitarra.
3. Una niña salta la cuerda en el jardín.
4. El padre juega videojuegos.
5. Un niño trepa un árbol.
6. Los gatos tejen.

8.22 **¿Qué dicen estos niños del tercer año?** Completa las ideas con una palabra de la lista de vocabulario (no las necesitas todas). Si es un verbo, debes conjugarlo.

andar	cometa	contar	cuento	dominó
juguete	pelear	permiso	saltar	videojuegos

Juanito: Mi mamá dice que soy malo cuando _____ con mis hermanas.

Anita: Los fines de semana me gusta _____ la cuerda con mis amigas.

Luisito: Mis hermanos y yo _____ chistes.

Mónica: Yo _____ en patineta en el parque cerca de mi casa.

Roberto: Cuando hace viento, me gusta ir al parque y volar una _____.

Sarita: Si quiero salir con mis amigas, tengo que pedirle _____ a mi mamá o a mi papá.

Emilia: Yo prefiero jugar _____ con mis amigos en la computadora.

8.23 **Asociaciones** Con un compañero, decidan qué palabra no pertenece al grupo y expliquen por qué.

1. el dominó — el ajedrez — el permiso — las damas
2. jugar — dibujar — las damas — volar
3. el rompecabezas — el carrito — el cuento — la muñeca
4. la niñera — las cartas — los bolos — las escondidas
5. andar en patineta — tocar el piano — volar una cometa — trepar árboles

8.24 **Explicaciones** En parejas, túrnense para elegir una palabra del vocabulario en la página anterior. Deben explicar la palabra sin decir cuál es y adivinar qué palabra es.

8.25 **Las actividades favoritas** Irma y Mario tienen que cuidar a varios niños todo el sábado. Irma quiere ir de excursión con la mitad de los niños, pero Mario quiere cuidarlos desde su casa porque tiene que trabajar. Habla con un compañero para saber qué actividades les gustan a los niños y después decidir cuáles son los 3 niños que van a ir con Irma y quiénes se van a quedar con Mario. Un compañero debe mirar la tabla en el **Apéndice B**.

Modelo *¿Cuál es la actividad favorita de Manuela?*
¿A quién le gusta volar cometas?

Niño	Actividad favorita	¿Con quién debe pasar el sábado?
Manuela	volar cometas	
Jimena	ir de paseo	
	nadar	
Alejandro		
Juan Carlos	dibujar	
Edmundo	trepar árboles	
	jugar juegos de mesa	

Cultura

¿A quién no le gusta la música? La música es un elemento cultural de todas las sociedades. Algunos géneros musicales se originaron en otros lugares del mundo, y luego se popularizaron por todo el planeta. Lo que conocemos como música latina es, en realidad, una mezcla de géneros y culturas. Por ejemplo, el danzón es un género de música bailable que se originó en Cuba a finales del siglo XIX. Otro ejemplo es el tango, que también es un baile. El tango se originó en Argentina y Uruguay, y se caracteriza por el uso del bandoneón (*a type of accordion*). Uno de los más importantes artistas del tango, Enrique Santos Discépolo, lo definió como "un pensamiento triste que se baila".

A continuación aparece una lista de otros géneros musicales que se escuchan en España y Latinoamérica. ¿Cuáles conoces? ¿Conoces grupos o cantantes de los Estados Unidos que incorporen estos ritmos en su música?

la salsa (popular en los países del Caribe, especialmente Cuba)
el bolero (especialmente popular en España y México)
el vallenato (originario de Colombia)
los corridos (originarios de México)
la samba (música brasileña)
los sones (hay tipos diferentes de sones, en particular los cubanos y los mexicanos)
el mambo (baile cubano)
el merengue (popular en países del Caribe, Centroamérica, Colombia y Venezuela)
la cumbia (muy popular en Panamá, Venezuela, Perú y sobre todo en Colombia)

Mira la sección **Exploraciones del mundo hispano** en el **Apéndice A** y busca un cantante o un músico de un país hispanohablante. Investiga en Internet qué tipo de música toca o canta.

> Sube un video del artista del **Exploraciones del mundo hispano** que investigaste y comparte la información del artista. Luego escucha la música de las selecciones de tus compañeros. ¿Cuál te gusta más?

Comunidad

Entrevista a una persona de tu comunidad que sea originaria de un país donde se habla español. Pregúntale acerca de las actividades favoritas de niños y adultos en su país. Pregúntale también acerca de los tipos de música más populares en su país de origen. Después repórtale la información a la clase.

Músicos cubanos

Comparaciones

La industria de las historietas se mantiene viva en muchos países gracias a la tradición, pero también gracias a la creatividad de nuevos talentos que publican tiras *(strips)* con nuevos personajes *(characters)*. Condorito está entre las historietas clásicas que todavía se pueden adquirir en muchos países latinoamericanos. Condorito es una creación del artista chileno René Ríos Boettiger, más conocido como Pepo. Esta historieta fue publicada por primera vez en 1949.

Otra historieta que sigue siendo popular a pesar de que ya no se publica es Mafalda, creada por el caricaturista argentino Joaquín Salvador Lavado, mejor conocido como Quino. Mafalda es una tira sobre una niña y su grupo de amigos, pero también es una radiografía *(x-ray)* de los temas políticos y sociales que sobresalían *(stood out)* en los años setentas. Hoy en día Mafalda se consigue fácilmente en todos los países hispanos, publicada en diversas colecciones que se venden en cualquier librería.

Mafalda, de Quino

En la actualidad existe una gran variedad de historietas modernas. La mayoría de ellas se pueden conseguir en tiendas especializadas.

Argentina: Boogie el aceitoso; Gaturro; Catalina
Bolivia: Cascabel; El duende y su camarilla
Chile: Barrabases
Colombia: Copetín; Dina Salomón; Pionero
Cuba: El curioso cubano; Supertiñosa

España: Florita; Mortadelo y Filemón; El Coyote
México: Memín Pinguín; La Familia Burrón; Rolando el rabioso
Perú: Supercholo, El Cuy
Uruguay: Pelopincho y Cachirula; El viejo

Investiga en Internet de qué trata y de qué época es una de las historietas de la lista, o investiga otras historietas o novelas gráficas (¡hay cientos!). Después, sube la información a Share It!

Busca un ejemplo de Condorito o Mafalda en Internet. ¿Es similar a alguna historieta en inglés?

Conexiones... a la comunicación

En el mundo hispano las telenovelas no son siempre sinónimo de programas cursis *(corny)* de entretenimiento para amas de casa. De hecho, muchas telenovelas se presentan en los mejores horarios de televisión, y algunas de ellas incluso han ayudado a cambiar una sociedad. Las telenovelas latinoamericanas se caracterizan por ser adictivas, y muchas de ellas han tenido un gran éxito en todo el mundo. De lo que pocos hablan es de cómo algunas de ellas han contribuído al cambio social. Por ejemplo, *Enseñando a coser (Teaching how to sew)*, una telenovela peruana de 1969, contó la historia de una empleada doméstica que se superó *(bettered herself)* gracias a su trabajo con una máquina de coser. En México, *Ven conmigo* le dio un gran impulso a un programa que el gobierno tenía para alfabetizar *(to teach to read and write)* adultos, esto debido a una escena emotiva en la que un hombre mayor consigue leer una carta de su hija por primera vez.

En 1977 la cadena Televisa comenzó a tratar temas ecológicos. En ese año se habló de reciclar la basura en la telenovela *Pacto de amor*. En el año 2001, esta importante productora de televisión lanzó una iniciativa para que todas sus producciones informaran y educaran al público sobre temas de salud *(health)*, educación y otros temas de interés social.

¿Conoces algún programa que además de entretener educa al público?

Algunos actores de la telenovela "Cielo Rojo"

Sources: BBC Mundo; Univisión

A analizar

Santiago habla con Rosa sobre lo que debe comprar para su sobrina. Después de ver el video, lee parte de su conversación y presta atención al objeto indirecto en negritas.

Rosa:	¿**Le** gustan los juegos de mesa?
Santiago:	Yo creo que sí, y sé que a sus padres **les** gusta jugarlos con ella.
Rosa:	Entonces **le** puedes comprar un juego de mesa a tu sobrina.
Santiago:	Sí, se lo voy a comprar. Gracias por tu ayuda.
Rosa:	¿**Te** molesta si voy a la tienda contigo?
Santiago:	¡Para nada! ¡Vamos!

1. You've learned that a direct object is a thing or person acted upon directly, for example, **Compré <u>una cometa</u>** or **Busco <u>una niñera</u>.** What do you think an indirect object is?

2. Why is the verb **gustar** conjugated in the third person plural form in the first sentence? Why is it singular in the second sentence?

A comprobar

Indirect object pronouns

1. An indirect object is not affected directly by the action of the verb. It is usually a person and tells **to whom** or **for whom** something is done.

   > Él siempre le dice la verdad **a su novia.**
   > *He always tells the truth **to his girlfriend.***
   > (**to whom** the truth is told)

   > Le compro un regalo **a mi amigo.**
   > *I am buying a gift **for my friend.***
   > (**for whom** the gift is bought)

2. When using the indirect object pronoun, it is possible to add **a** + *prepositional pronoun* or **a** + *noun* to either clarify or emphasize. Although it may seem repetitive, it is necessary to include the indirect object pronoun, even if the indirect object is clearly identified.

   > Alberto **le** dio una cometa **a su sobrino.**
   > *Alberto gave a kite **to his nephew.***

   > Jorge **me** escribió **a mí.**
   > *Jorge wrote **to me.** (not to someone else)*

3. Indirect object pronouns

yo	me	nosotros(as)	nos
tú	te	vosotros(as)	os
él, ella, usted	le	ellos, ellas, ustedes	les

4. As with the direct object pronoun, the indirect object pronoun is placed in front of a conjugated verb or can be attached to an infinitive or a present participle.

   > **Le** pregunté cuánto cuesta.
   > *I asked **him/her** how much it costs.*

   > Voy a contar**te** un chiste.
   > *I'm going to tell **you** a joke.*

   > Mi hijo está mostrándo**le** su nueva patineta a su amigo.
   > *My son is showing his new skateboard to his friend.*

5. The following are some of the verbs that are frequently used with indirect object pronouns:

contar (ue)	pedir
dar	preguntar
decir	prestar
devolver (ue)	servir
mostrar (ue) *to show*	

6. In **Capítulo 3** you learned the verb **gustar. Gustar** always takes the indirect object pronoun and is conjugated according to the subject that follows it.

A él **le gustan** los carritos.
He **likes** the cars. (The cars are **pleasing to him.**)

A los niños no **les gusta** esta historia.
The children don't like this story.

The following are verbs similar to **gustar.** They also take an indirect object pronoun and are conjugated according to the subject.

aburrir	*to bore*
caer bien / caer mal	*to like / dislike a person*
encantar	*to really like, to enjoy immensely*
fascinar	*to fascinate*
importar	*to be important*
interesar	*to interest*
molestar	*to bother*

Me encanta su nueva muñeca.
*I **love** her new doll. (Her new doll **delights me**.)*

¿**Te interesa** aprender a tejer?
*Does it **interest you** to learn to knit?*

A practicar

8.26 **¿Es lógico?** Lee las oraciones y decide si son lógicas o no.

1. A la niñera le caen bien los niños simpáticos.
2. A los abuelos les gusta comprar juguetes ruidosos *(noisy)* para sus nietos.
3. A los padres les importa contratar a una niñera irresponsable.
4. A la maestra le caen mal los niños perezosos.
5. Al pediatra le importa la salud *(health)* de los adultos.

8.27 **Sondeo** En grupos de cuatro o cinco, hablen sobre sus pasatiempos usando los verbos y las expresiones indicados. Cada estudiante debe escribir el número de estudiantes que contestan **sí** y el número que contestan **no.** Después, repórtenle la información a la clase.

Modelo gustarle los juegos de mesa
Estudiante 1: *¿A quién le gustan los juegos de mesa?*
Estudiante 2: *Me gustan mucho.*
Estudiante 3: *No me gustan (para nada).*

	sí	no
molestarle los chistes de mal gusto	_____	_____
fascinarle leer las historietas	_____	_____
encantarle los rompecabezas	_____	_____
interesarle aprender tocar un instrumento	_____	_____
importarle ser activo	_____	_____
aburrirle los videojuegos	_____	_____
gustarle el ajedrez	_____	_____

8.28 **Oraciones incompletas** Selecciona la conclusión más lógica para las siguientes oraciones. Luego explica a quién se refiere el pronombre indicado.

1. A Rosa le gusta jugar a la mamá por eso…
2. Jorge fue a la tienda con su abuela y…
3. A Tomás le gusta jugar en el jardín por eso…
4. Como llueve los niños no pueden jugar afuera y…
5. Cecilia y Eva van a acostarse y…
6. A Rebeca le encanta la música por eso…

a. ella **le** compró un carrito.
b. su tía **le** enseña a tocar el piano.
c. su papá **les** va a leer un cuento.
d. sus abuelos **le** van a regalar una muñeca.
e. su papá **le** dio una cometa.
f. su madre **les** trae unos juegos de mesa.

8.29 **Tu mejor amigo** Entrevista a un compañero sobre su mejor amigo.

Modelo ¿Le sirves una bebida a tu mejor amigo cuando te visita? *Sí, le sirvo una bebida.*

1. ¿Le cuentas tus secretos a tu mejor amigo?
2. ¿Le prestas dinero a tu mejor amigo?
3. ¿Siempre le dices la verdad a tu mejor amigo?
4. ¿Le das regalos a tu mejor amigo?
5. ¿Le pides consejos *(advice)* a tu mejor amigo?
6. ¿Le escribes mensajes de texto a tu mejor amigo?

8.30 **La cena** Completa la conversación entre una mujer y su nieto con los pronombres de objeto indirecto. Luego explica qué pasó usando el pretérito de los verbos indicados.

1.

desear, pedir

2.

dar, gustar, decir

3.

mostrar

8.31 **Entrevista** Entrevista a un compañero con las siguientes preguntas.

1. ¿Quién te importa mucho? ¿A quién le importas mucho?
2. ¿A quién siempre le dices la verdad? ¿Quién siempre te dice la verdad a ti?
3. ¿A quién le pides ayuda con la tarea de español? ¿Quién te pide ayuda a ti?
4. ¿A quién le escribes cartas o mensajes electrónicos? ¿Quién te escribe a ti? ¿Alguien te escribe cartas de amor?
5. ¿A quién le pides consejos *(advice)*? Normalmente ¿te dan buenos consejos? ¿Alguien te pide consejos a ti?
6. ¿Quién te da regalos para tu cumpleaños? ¿A quién le das regalos de cumpleaños?
7. ¿Qué les prestas a tus amigos? ¿Siempre te devuelven tus cosas? ¿Qué te prestan tus amigos a ti?
8. ¿Quién te cae bien a ti? ¿A quién le caes muy bien?

A analizar

Santiago habla con Rosa sobre lo que debe comprar para su sobrina. Mira el video otra vez. Después lee las siguientes oraciones de su conversación y presta atención a los pronombres en negritas.

> **Rosa:** Entonces le puedes comprar un juego de mesa a tu sobrina.
>
> **Santiago:** Sí, **se lo** voy a comprar. Gracias por tu ayuda.

1. What do each of the pronouns in bold refer to?
2. Which pronoun is the direct object in the second sentence? Which one is the indirect object?

A comprobar

Double object pronouns

Remember the direct and indirect object pronouns.

Direct object pronouns	
me	nos
te	os
lo, la	los, las

Indirect object pronouns	
me	nos
te	os
le	les

1. When using both object pronouns with the same verb, the indirect object comes before the direct object.

    ¿Quién **te lo** dio? *Who gave **it to you**?*
    Paulina **me lo** dio. *Paulina gave **it to me**.*

2. When using both the direct and the indirect object pronouns, the same rules for placement of single object pronouns apply. They are both placed before a conjugated verb or can be attached to the end of an infinitive or a present participle. The two pronouns cannot be separated. You will notice that an accent is added when two pronouns are attached to an infinitive or a present participle.

    La profesora **nos lo** va a explicar.
    La profesora va a explicár**noslo.**
    *The professor is going to explain **it to us**.*

    Gerardo **me las** está mostrando.
    Gerardo está mostrándo**melas.**
    *Gerardo is showing **them to me**.*

3. When using the third person indirect object pronoun together with the direct object pronoun, change the pronoun from **le** or **les** to **se**.

le se		lo
	+	la
les se		los

—¿**Le** prestas tu ropa a tu amiga?
—*Do you lend your clothing to your friend?*
—Sí, **se la** presto.
—*Yes, I lend **it to her**.*

—¿Su niñera **les** dio un videojuego?
—*Their babysitter gave them a video game?*
—Sí, **se lo** dio para la Navidad.
—*Yes, she gave **it to them** for Christmas.*

> **Estrategia**
>
> **Review material from previous chapters**
>
> You will be combining indirect and direct object pronouns in this section. It will be helpful to review the direct object pronouns from **Capítulo 7**.

A practicar

8.32 Identificaciones Lee las conversaciones e indica a qué o a quién se refieren los pronombres subrayados *(underlined)*.

Modelo Arsenio: ¿Me muestras tu historieta?
Emilio: Sí, <u>te la</u> muestro.
te* es tú *(Arsenio); **la** es la **historieta

1. Isaura: ¿Me prestas tus muñecas?
Aimée: Sí, <u>te las</u> presto.

2. Eduardo: ¿Les pediste permiso a tus padres?
Enrique: No, no <u>se lo</u> pedí.

3. Gonzalo: ¿Tus padres te dieron los videojuegos?
Javier: Sí, <u>me los</u> dieron.

4. Luz: Maestra, ¿nos vas a contar la historia de Pinocho?
Maestra: Sí, <u>se la</u> voy a contar.

8.33 Respuestas lógicas Decide qué respuesta corresponde a la pregunta.

1. ¿Les prestas tu teléfono celular a tus amigos?
2. ¿Tus padres te dan regalos para tu cumpleaños?
3. ¿Me muestras tu colección de muñecas?
4. ¿Tu profesor te da ayuda?
5. ¿Me prestas tu patineta?
6. ¿Le muestras la tarea a la profesora?

a. Sí, me los dan.
b. No, no te la presto.
c. Sí, me la da.
d. Sí, se la muestro.
e. No, no se lo presto.
f. Sí, te la muestro.

8.34 Buenos amigos Trabaja con un compañero y túrnense para preguntar y responder. **¡OJO!** Deben usar pronombres de objeto directo e indirecto al responder.

Modelo prestarme tu lápiz
Estudiante 1: *¿Me prestas tu lápiz?*
Estudiante 2: *Sí, te lo presto. / No, no te lo presto.*

1. prestarme tu coche
2. darme cinco dólares
3. explicarme la gramática
4. contarme tus secretos

5. decirme la verdad
6. mostrarme tu tarea
7. darme tu libro de español
8. prestarme tu tarjeta de crédito

¿Me prestas tu bolígrafo?

© Jamie Duplass/Shutterstock

8.35 **Prestado** Cuando era niño, Elián siempre les prestaba sus cosas *(things)* a todos. Con un compañero, túrnense para preguntarse a quiénes se las prestaba. Responde las preguntas usando los pronombres de objeto directo e indirecto.

Modelo ¿A quién le prestaba la pelota?
   Estudiante 1: *¿A quién le prestaba la pelota?*
   Estudiante 2: *Se la prestaba a Ariel.*

1. ¿A quién le prestaba la patineta?
2. ¿A quién le prestaba los videojuegos?
3. ¿A quién le prestaba el teléfono celular?
4. ¿A quién le prestaba las cartas?
5. ¿A quién le prestaba los libros?
6. ¿A quién le prestaba la cometa?
7. ¿A quién le prestaba la guitarra?
8. ¿A quién le prestaba el carrito?

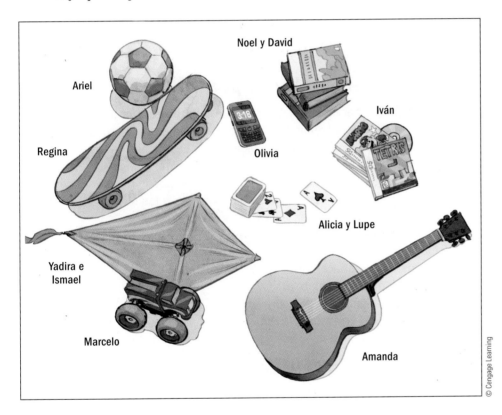

8.36 **En la escuela secundaria** Entrevista a un compañero sobre su experiencia en la escuela secundaria con las siguientes preguntas. Tu compañero debe contestar usando los pronombres de objeto directo e indirecto.

1. ¿Quién te escribía poemas románticos?
2. ¿A quién le escribías correos electrónicos con frecuencia?
3. ¿A quién le prestabas dinero?
4. ¿Quién te pedía consejos?
5. ¿A quién le contabas tus secretos?
6. ¿Quién te daba regalos para tu cumpleaños?
7. ¿Quién te pedía ayuda con la tarea?
8. ¿A quién le decías mentiras?

Lectura

Antes de leer

¿Cuáles son tus pasatiempos favoritos? ¿Cuáles eran tus pasatiempos favoritos cuando eras niño?

A leer

Todos necesitamos un pasatiempo

Hay muchas razones para tener un pasatiempo. Para empezar, es divertido tenerlo, pero según muchos estudios un pasatiempo también ayuda a reducir el estrés y nos **distrae** de los problemas de la vida diaria. En muchos casos, un pasatiempo ayuda a reducir síntomas de depresión y eliminar energía negativa. Si el pasatiempo **involucra** actividad física también puede mejorar **la salud.** Un pasatiempo ofrece la oportunidad de enseñarles a los niños lecciones importantes, entre ellas tener disciplina y mejorar sus habilidades para resolver problemas y para enfocarse. Algunos pasatiempos también hacen que una persona conozca nuevas personas con intereses similares, quienes pueden convertirse en buenos amigos. Otros pasatiempos ayudan a unir más a la familia.

> [Un pasatiempo ayuda a reducir el estrés.]

distracts
involves
health

Por todas estas razones los pasatiempos son comunes en todos los grupos sociales y entre las personas de todas las edades. ¿Cuáles son los más populares? Esto depende más de la **edad** de las personas que de su nacionalidad. **Sin embargo,** algunos estudios indican que en algunos países se tiene preferencia por ciertos deportes o pasatiempos. Aquí se presentan algunos de los favoritos:

age
Nevertheless

El dominó
Este juego es popular en muchas partes del mundo, pero en la República Dominicana, Venezuela, Cuba y otros países del Caribe existe una gran **afición** a este juego. En la República Dominicana el dominó es considerado un juego nacional. Aunque es más popular entre hombres que entre mujeres, este juego atrae a personas de

passion

Un grupo de amigos cubanos se divierte jugando dominó.

todos los sectores de la sociedad. Entre sus ventajas está que promueve la socialización, la **agudeza** mental (al contar puntos mentalmente), y hasta se sabe que retarda la aparición del Alzheimer.

sharpness

Juegos de mesa

Se juegan en España y por toda Latinoamérica. Son una forma divertida de pasar el tiempo en familia y con amigos. Algunos requieren **destrezas,** otros son simplemente divertidos. ¿Los más populares? Además del ajedrez y el dominó, figuran las cartas (entre ellas la **baraja** española), el juego de la **oca,** las damas y, en los últimos años, el sodoku. A muchos adultos les encantan los **rompecabezas.** También destacan por su popularidad los juegos de palabras, como la sopa de letras, los **crucigramas** y el Scrabble.

skills

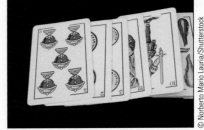

La baraja española

deck of cards / snakes and ladders

crosswords

Coleccionistas

Coleccionar objetos es naturaleza humana. Por muchos años la filatelia —coleccionar sellos postales— fue un pasatiempo obligado de muchas generaciones. Hoy en día, sin embargo, la industria del correo está en decadencia. Si bien la filatelia sigue siendo un pasatiempo favorito de las generaciones anteriores, los jóvenes de hoy tienen muchas más opciones gracias a los intereses comerciales. Se pueden coleccionar tarjetas de jugadores de todos los deportes, **fósforos, corcholatas, conchas,** monedas… ¡las posibilidades son infinitas!

matches / bottle caps / shells

El fútbol

Una sola estadística sobre el fútbol puede ser elocuente: 2 billones 400 mil millones (2.000.400.000) de personas vieron la última Copa del Mundo. Según la FIFA, 270 millones de personas en el mundo juegan el fútbol de forma regulada. Por cada persona que lo practica, hay muchas más que lo siguen. En la lista de los diez países que venden más entradas para ver fútbol en los estadios aparecen México, España y Brasil. Quizás se trate de la industria del entretenimiento más grande del mundo… si el fútbol fuera un país, sería la 17 economía más grande del planeta.

Comprensión

1. ¿Cuáles son dos razones por las que los pasatiempos son buenos para la salud?
2. ¿Cuáles son dos habilidades que los niños pueden aprender mediante pasatiempos?
3. ¿En qué países es muy popular el dominó?
4. ¿Cuál es un ejemplo de un juego de palabras?
5. ¿Qué es la filatelia y de quién era un pasatiempo favorito?
6. Según el artículo ¿cuál es el pasatiempo más popular de los que se listan?

Después de leer

1. ¿Sabes jugar dominó? ¿Te gustan los rompecabezas y los crucigramas? ¿Juegas con ellos?
2. El dominó es el deporte nacional de la República Dominicana. En tu opinión ¿cuál es el deporte nacional de los Estados Unidos y por qué?

Redacción

Write a blog entry about your childhood memories.

Paso 1 Decide whether you would like to write about your childhood or adolescence. Then write a list of some of the activities you used to enjoy doing during that time of your life. Do not write down specific things you only did once, such as a trip to the beach one summer. Rather, write down things that you used to do often, such as playing on a basketball team.

Paso 2 Look over your list and pick one item that you feel you can expand upon. Create a simple mind map and write down ideas related to the activities.

ser muy bueno

siempre ganar

jugar al básquetbol

jugar con mi hermanito

mi hermanito llorar

© Cengage Learning

Paso 3 Write a list of the things you used to have to do (around the house, for school, etc.). Did you particularly dislike any of the chores?

Paso 4 Look at the idea you selected in **Paso 2** and write a topic sentence that would tell your readers something about what you were like when you were younger.

> **Modelo** *Yo era un adolescente muy activo.*

Paso 5 Tell your reader some of the things you used to do when you were younger. Then develop the remainder of the paragraph giving some of the details of one of your activities using the information you developed in **Paso 2.**

Paso 6 Write a transition statement that connects the first paragraph to the second, in which you are going to tell your reader about some of the things you used to have to do when you were younger. Then, using the information you generated in **Paso 3** develop that paragraph.

© GWImages/Shutterstock

Paso 7 Conclude your entry with a few questions encouraging your readers to add their own comments about their childhood.

Paso 8 Edit your entry:

1. Do all of your sentences in each paragraph support the topic sentence?
2. Do you have smooth transitions between sentences? Between paragraphs?
3. Do verbs agree with the subjects? Are they conjugated properly?
4. Are there any spelling errors? Do you have accents on the **-er** and **-ir** imperfect forms?

En vivo

Entrando en materia

1. ¿Qué tipo de negocios hay en los centros comerciales?
2. ¿Quiénes los frecuentan más? ¿Vas tú con frecuencia? ¿Por qué?

El nuevo centro comercial Siglo 22

El siguiente es un anuncio que busca inversionistas para poner sus negocios en un nuevo centro comercial. ¿Qué ideas piensas que se van a presentar para atraer nuevos negocios?

Siglo^{22}

¿Sabía usted que el pasatiempo favorito de muchas personas es comprar y salir con los amigos y la familia? ... y hay un lugar que puede atraer a todo tipo de clientela:

¡El Centro Comercial Siglo 22 abre sus puertas!

Excelente oportunidad de inversión

- Si usted es inversionista[1] y está buscando oportunidades para abrir un nuevo negocio, no busque más. Apresúrese[2] a llamarnos antes de que se agoten[3] los nuevos locales[4] comerciales del Centro Comercial Siglo 22.

- El nuevo centro comercial es el más grande de la ciudad y se convertirá en el más visitado. Está localizado en una zona de fácil acceso, rodeada de hoteles de categoría y otros comercios bien establecidos. El centro cuenta con una serie de servicios que atraerán[5] a un gran número de personas, aumentando sus posibilidades de obtener clientela.

- Para asegurar la afluencia de clientes, la Plaza cuenta con seis salas cinematográficas de lujo[6], dos tiendas departamentales de gran prestigio y dos centros de videojuegos con las máquinas más modernas del mercado. Además hay un boliche[7], numerosas boutiques, restaurantes y tiendas especializadas... ¡Solamente hace falta su negocio!

• locales de 80 m^2 hasta 2000 m^2	• diseño vanguardista
• todos los servicios[8]	• asesoría de mercadotecnia[10]
• amplio estacionamiento[9]	• financiamiento flexible

Lo invitamos a una sesión informativa el próximo 24 de abril, en donde se hablará de los negocios que más demanda tienen. Hablarán también representantes de algunas de las franquicias[11] más exitosas del país.

Para mayores informes, envíenos un mensaje a Siglo22@localesenventa.com.

[1]investor [2]Hurry [3]are taken [4]establishments [5]will attract [6]luxury [7]bowling alley
[8]utilities [9]parking [10]marketing [11]franchises

Comprensión

1. ¿Qué quieren vender con este anuncio?
2. ¿Cómo se llama el nuevo centro comercial?
3. ¿Qué tipo de entretenimiento hay en este centro comercial?
4. ¿De qué van a hablar en la sesión informativa de abril?

Más allá

Imagina que vas a abrir un nuevo negocio en el centro comercial. Escribe una descripción del tipo de negocio, piensa en un nombre y explica por qué crees que va a tener éxito. Comparte tu descripción en Share It! y después decide cuál de los negocios de tus compañeros es el más original.

Exploraciones profesionales

La mercadotecnia

Vocabulario

Sustantivos

la campaña	*campaign*
la encuesta	*survey*
la firma	*firm*
la lata	*can*
el presupuesto	*budget*
el puesto	*stand / booth*

Adjetivos

atractivo(a)	*attractive*

Verbos

anunciar	*to advertise*
convencer	*to convince*
invertir	*to invest*
probar	*to try*
superar	*to overcome, to beat*

Frases útiles

estrategia de mercadotecnia	*marketing strategy*

Necesitamos mucha publicidad.

© Andresr/Shutterstock

DATOS IMPORTANTES

Educación: Título universitario en mercadotecnia o administración de empresas; Bilingüe en español e inglés

Salario: Promedio: $ 40.000–120.000/año

Dónde se trabaja: Restaurantes, supermercados, empresas de publicidad, compañías de servicios (transporte, educación, medicina, etcétera)

Vocabulario nuevo Completa las oraciones con la palabra más apropiada de la lista de vocabulario.

1. No sé cómo es la bebida. ¿La puedo _____ ?

2. Necesitamos un plan económico porque tenemos un _____ muy limitado.

3. Vamos a hacer una _____ para saber cuántas personas prefieren productos naturales.

4. Es necesario _____ varios obstáculos para establecer un nuevo producto en el mercado.

5. La meta *(goal)* de una _____ de mercadotecnia es convencer a la gente de comprar un producto.

Julia García, licenciada en mercadotecnia

Julia García es licenciada en mercadotecnia. Está en su oficina hablando con la señora Campos, una ejecutiva que quiere vender su producto en el mercado hispano en los Estados Unidos. En el video, vas a ver las ideas que la Sra. García tiene para promover el producto de la compañía de la Sra. Campos.

Antes de ver

Los profesionales en mercadotecnia ayudan a los empresarios *(entrepreneurs)* a vender sus productos. Ellos conocen las necesidades de los clientes y las estrategias de venta. Generalmente hablan dos idiomas para trabajar con compañías internacionales.

¿Qué tipo de productos compra más la gente? ¿Cuál crees que es una buena estrategia de venta? ¿Prefieres comprar un producto caro o un producto económico? Explica.

Comprensión

1. ¿En dónde están hablando la Sra. García y la Sra. Campos?

2. ¿Para qué firma trabaja la Sra. Campos?

3. ¿Qué tipo de producto quiere vender la Sra. Campos?

4. ¿Dónde quiere hacer la encuesta la Sra. García?

5. ¿Qué información quiere conseguir de la encuesta?

6. ¿Dónde debe regalar el producto la Sra. Campos?

7. ¿Por qué la Sra. García va a contactar a la Sra. Campos la siguiente semana?

Después de ver

Con un compañero, representen a un licenciado en mercadotecnia y a una persona que quiere vender un producto. La persona explica qué tipo de producto es. El licenciado le hace preguntas y le da consejos. ¿Para qué sirve el producto? ¿Es económico? ¿A quién se lo quieren vender? ¿Qué estrategia de venta va a usar? ¿Esperan un alto porcentaje de ganancia?

8.37 **Repetitivo** Primero indica si las palabras subrayadas son objetos directos o indirectos. Luego reemplaza los objetos directos con pronombres para evitar la repetición, haciendo los cambios necesarios a los objetos indirectos.

Modelo El 2 de mayo es el cumpleaños de Pablito y va a celebrar <u>su cumpleaños</u> en casa.
el cumpleaños *es objeto directo* → *El 2 de mayo es el cumpleaños de Pablito y lo va a celebrar en casa.*

1. Tiene muchos amigos y quiere invitar a <u>sus amigos</u> a su fiesta.

2. Su mamá escribe las invitaciones para sus amigos y <u>les</u> manda <u>las invitaciones</u> a <u>sus amigos.</u>

3. Los amigos de Pablito quieren comprar regalos y llevar<u>le</u> <u>los regalos</u> a <u>Pablito</u> el día de la fiesta.

4. Los padres de Pablito compran una patineta y <u>le</u> dan <u>la patineta</u> la mañana de su cumpleaños.

5. El día de la fiesta los amigos de Pablito llegan con regalos y <u>le</u> dan <u>los regalos</u> a <u>él</u>.

6. Pablito recibe muchos juguetes de sus amigos y <u>les</u> muestra <u>los juguetes</u> a <u>sus padres.</u>

8.38 **¿A quién...?** Combina los elementos para hacer oraciones completas indicando a quién le gustan (molestan / interesan / etc.) los siguientes temas o personas.

Modelo gustar / las películas de terror
A Stephen King le gustan las películas de terror.

1. interesar / la política
2. encantar / el invierno
3. molestar / los cigarros
4. fascinar / las ciencias
5. importar / mucho el dinero
6. aburrir / las personas que hablan mucho
7. caer bien / los niños
8. importar / tener buenas notas

8.39 **La juventud de los famosos** Decide cuáles eran las actividades de estas personas famosas cuando eran más jóvenes. Si no las reconoces a todas, usa la lógica para adivinar *(guess)*. Luego forma oraciones completas usando el imperfecto de los verbos.

1. Jorge Luis Borges
2. Selena
3. Rafael Nadal
4. Pablo Picasso
5. Ellen Ochoa
6. Miguel Cabrera
7. Sofía Vergara
8. Carolina Herrera

a. encantarle jugar al béisbol con su padre y su tío
b. gustarle dibujar y pintar
c. vivir en Baranquilla, Colombia
d. jugar al tenis y al fútbol
e. ir a muchas fiestas elegantes
f. cantar en un grupo con sus hermanos
g. leer mucho
h. ser excelente en la clase de matemáticas

8.40 **Hace 50 años** Mucho ha cambiado *(has changed)* en los últimos 50 años. Con un compañero, expliquen las diferencias entre hoy y el pasado. Deben usar el presente y el imperfecto.

> **Modelo** el transporte
>> Estudiante 1: *Hoy muchas familias tienen dos o más coches, pero en el pasado muchas familias solo tenían un coche.*
>> Estudiante 2: *Es cierto, y hoy la gasolina cuesta mucho, pero en el pasado no costaba mucho.*

1. la familia
2. el trabajo
3. la comunicación
4. la comida
5. los pasatiempos
6. los restaurantes

8.41 **Regalos** Necesitas comprar regalos para el cumpleaños de los hijos gemelos *(twins)* de un amigo (un niño y una niña). Encontraste buenos regalos en un sitio web, pero no dan los precios. Llamas y preguntas cuánto cuestan los juguetes para decidir qué les vas a comprar. Tu compañero deber mirar el **Apéndice B** para dar los precios. No puedes gastar más de $50.

> **Modelo** *¿Cúanto cuesta el muñeco azul?*
> *Cuesta $32.*

© Cengage Learning

8.42 **¿Cómo eran?** Con un compañero, van a hablar de las actividades de su niñez.

> **Paso 1** Decidan si las siguientes actividades son activas o sedentarias. Luego añadan *(add)* 4 actividades más que hacen los niños y también clasifíquenlas.
>
> | | | |
> |---|---|---|
> | andar en patineta | leer historietas | trepar árboles |
> | dibujar | saltar la cuerda | volar cometas |
> | jugar videojuegos | tocar el piano | |
>
> **Paso 2** Con tu compañero, pregúntense si hacían las actividades en su lista para determinar si eran niños activos o tranquilos.
>
> **Paso 3** Repórtenle sus resultados a la clase.

🔊 Vocabulario 1

2-11

La limpieza

la basura	*trash, garbage, litter*
el bote de basura	*trash can*
el cortacésped	*lawnmower*
la escoba	*broom*
el jabón para platos	*dish soap*
la manguera	*hose*

la plancha	*iron*
el quehacer	*chore*
el sacudidor	*duster*
la tabla de planchar	*ironing board*
el trapeador	*mop*
el trapo	*cloth, rag*

Verbos

barrer	*to sweep*
colgar (ue)	*to hang*
cortar (el césped)	*to cut; to mow (the lawn)*
guardar	*to put away*
hacer la cama	*to make the bed*
lavar platos	*to wash the dishes*
lavar ropa	*to do laundry*
ordenar	*to tidy up, to straighten up*

pasar la aspiradora	*to vacuum*
planchar	*to iron*
poner la mesa	*to set the table*
recoger (la mesa)	*to pick up (to clear the table)*
regar (ie)	*to water*
sacar la basura	*to take the trash out*
sacudir	*to dust*
secar	*to dry*
trapear	*to mop*

Adjetivos

limpio(a)	*clean*
sucio(a)	*dirty*

Palabras negativas e indefinidas see p. 269

Diccionario personal

_____

_____

_____

_____

_____

_____

_____

_____

_____

_____

_____

_____

◀)) Vocabulario 2

Juegos y juguetes   *Games and toys*

el ajedrez	*chess*
el carrito	*toy car*
las cartas	*playing cards*
el chiste	*joke*
la cometa	*kite*
el cuento	*story*
la cuerda	*(jumping) rope*
las damas	*checkers*
el dominó	*dominos*

las escondidas	*hide and seek*
la historieta	*comic book*
el juego de mesa	*board game*
la motocicleta	*motorcycle*
la (el) muñeca(o)	*doll*
el osito	*teddy bear*
la patineta	*skateboard*
el videojuego	*video game*

Verbos

aburrir	*to bore*
andar en	*to ride*
caer (bien / mal)	*to like / dislike a person*
chatear	*to chat (online)*
contar (ue)	*to tell (a story); to count*
dar la vuelta	*to take a walk or a ride*
dibujar	*to draw*
encantar	*to really like, to enjoy immensely*
fascinar	*to fascinate*
hacer jardinería	*to garden*
importar	*to be important*
interesar	*to interest*
ir de paseo	*to go for a walk*
jugar a los bolos	*to go bowling*
molestar	*to bother*
mostrar (ue)	*to show*

navegar el Internet	*to surf the web*
pasar tiempo	*to spend time*
pelear	*to fight; to argue*
portarse (bien / mal)	*to behave (well / badly)*
prestar	*to lend*
salir (a + infinitive)	*to go out (to do something)*
saltar	*to jump*
tejer	*to knit*
tocar (el piano / la guitarra)	*to play (the piano / the guitar)*
trepar (un árbol)	*to climb (a tree)*
volar	*to fly*

Palabras adicionales

el juguete	*toy*
la niñera	*babysitter*

el permiso	*permission*
el teléfono celular	*cell phone*

Diccionario personal

_____

_____

_____

_____

_____

_____

© Photos 12 /Alamy

José Martí

Biografía

José Martí (1853–1895) fue un poeta, ensayista y periodista cubano. Publicó sus primeros poemas en el periódico de su escuela. Martí empezó a resentir a los españoles cuando el gobierno de España, que en ese tiempo controlaba Cuba, cerró las escuelas. Poco después el gobierno español lo envió *(sent)* a prisión por seis años acusado de subversión *(treason)*. Después de estar exiliado en España, Martí fue a los Estados Unidos, en donde formó el Partido Revolucionario Cubano y promovió la independencia de España. En 1895 regresó a Cuba y murió unos meses después en la Batalla de Dos Ríos, antes de que Cuba consiguiera su independencia. Hoy es conocido como el poeta nacional de Cuba y el Padre de la Independencia.

Antes de leer

1. Probablemente, la obra más conocida de José Martí es "Versos sencillos" *(Simple verses)*. Estos versos se hicieron muy famosos cuando fueron convertidos en una canción popular llamada "Guantanamera". ¿Sabes dónde está Guantánamo? ¿Qué crees que significa "Guantanamera"?

2. ¿De qué piensas que puede hablar un poema titulado "Versos sencillos"?

Investiguemos la literatura: El verso

Verse refers to a written work with rhyme and sometimes with meter (the basic rhythmic structure of a line). It can refer to one line or to a complete poem. A verse or a stanza is generally called **una estrofa.**

Versos sencillos

                Yo soy un hombre sincero

grows   De donde **crece** la palma,

                Y antes de morirme quiero

to cast / soul   **Echar** mis versos del **alma.**

     5   Con los pobres de la tierra

                Quiero yo mi suerte echar:

creek / mountain range El **arroyo** de la **sierra**

gives pleasure / sea Me **complace** más que el **mar.**

© Vojko Kavcic/Shutterstock

Mi verso es de un verde claro

bright red 10 Y de un **carmín encendido:**

injured deer Mi verso es un **ciervo herido**

mountain / ayuda Que busca en el **monte amparo.**

Yo quiero salir del mundo

Por la puerta natural:

leaves 15 En un carro de **hojas** verdes

They should take me when I die **A morir me han** de **llevar.**

Darkness No me pongan en lo **oscuro**

A morir como un traidor:

¡Yo soy bueno, y como bueno

20 Moriré de cara al sol!

Yo pienso, cuando me alegro

Como un escolar sencillo,

En el canario amarillo,—

¡Que tiene el ojo tan negro!

25 Yo quiero, cuando me muera,

Sin **patria,** pero sin **amo,** *country / master*

Tener en mi **losa** un ramo *grave*

De flores,— ¡y una bandera!

Cultivo una rosa blanca,

30 En julio como en enero,

Para el amigo sincero

Que me da su mano franca.

Y para el cruel que **me arranca** *tears out*

El corazón con que vivo,

35 **Cardo** ni **ortiga** cultivo: *thistle / nettle*

Cultivo la rosa blanca.

Tiene el leopardo un abrigo

En su monte seco y **pardo:** *dark*

Yo tengo más que el leopardo,

40 Porque tengo un buen amigo.

Estatua de José Martí en la Habana, Cuba

Versos sencillos, José Martí

Después de leer

A. Comprensión

1. Basándote en el texto ¿qué es muy importante para la voz poética?

2. ¿Qué palabras usa el poeta para describir a Cuba?

B. Conversemos

1. Martí menciona ideas importantes para él en este poema. ¿De qué hablarías *(would speak)* tú en un poema?

2. En estos versos, Martí describe a su país. ¿Cuáles son algunos adjetivos que puedes usar en un poema para describir a tu país?

CAPÍTULO 9

Learning Strategy

Remember that Spanish and English have different structures

Grammar is an essential part of any language. While it is helpful to understand and compare basic concepts of the English language, such as pronouns and direct objects, it is important to learn the new structures and avoid translating directly from English to Spanish.

In this chapter you will learn how to:

- Describe past events in detail
- Talk about holidays and celebrations
- Give the details of an accident

¿Qué pasó?

© Henrik Sorensen/Getty Images

1

Exploraciones léxicas

En todas las épocas del año hay celebraciones para divertirse y pasar tiempo con la familia y los amigos.

Celebraciones

el bautizo	baptism
la boda	wedding
el brindis	toast
los desfiles	parades
el festejo	party, celebration
los fuegos artificiales	fireworks
los novios	bride and groom
las posadas	a nine-day celebration before Christmas
los quince años	a girl's fifteenth birthday celebration
la quinceañera	a girl celebrating her 15th birthday

el santo	saint's day (similar to a second birthday, based on the saint's name)
la serenata	serenade

Verbos

casarse (con)	to get married (to)
celebrar	to celebrate
cumplir años	to turn (x) years old
decorar	to decorate
disfrutar	to enjoy
romper	to break
terminar	to finish

A practicar

9.1 **Escucha y responde** En un papel dibuja un pastel y en otro una bandera. Si escuchas una palabra relacionada con un cumpleaños, levanta el pastel. Si es una palabra relacionada con la celebración del Día de la Independencia, levanta la bandera. Levanta los dos si la palabra está relacionada con las dos celebraciones.

2-13

> **INVESTIGUEMOS EL VOCABULARIO**
> While in most of Latin America **bocadillos** means *appetizers*, in Spain a **bocadillo** is a sandwich on a baguette.

9.2 **¿Qué es?** Relaciona las palabras en la segunda columna con las oraciones en la primera columna.

1. _____ Los usamos para decorar.
2. _____ Lo comemos después de apagar las velas.
3. _____ La rompemos para obtener muchos dulces.
4. _____ Las mandamos a los amigos cuando vamos a dar una fiesta.
5. _____ Son las dos personas que se van a casar.
6. _____ Los comemos durante las fiestas y las celebraciones.
7. _____ Lo servimos para el brindis del Año Nuevo.
8. _____ Muchas personas caminan por la calle y hay música.

a. la piñata
b. el champán
c. los globos
d. el pastel
e. el desfile
f. los bocadillos
g. las invitaciones
h. los novios

9.3 **¿Qué celebraron las siguientes personas?** Completa las oraciones con una palabra apropiada del vocabulario.

1. Mi hermana se casó con su novio y tuvieron _____ muy grande.

2. Mi mejor amiga cumple quince años hoy y va a tener una fiesta de _____.

3. En una ceremonia en la iglesia le dimos un nombre a nuestro hijo. Fue su _____.

4. En muchos países predominantemente católicos las nueve fiestas antes de la Navidad se llaman _____.

5. ¡Terminé mis estudios en la universidad! Celebro mi _____ hoy.

6. Mis padres se casaron hace treinta años. Mañana es su _____.

7. Hoy es el cumpleaños de mi novia y quiero darle _____ con un grupo de mariachis.

8. Para celebrar el Año Nuevo y la Independencia, muchas veces hay _____ por la noche. ¡Son espectaculares!

INVESTIGUEMOS LA MÚSICA

Listen to the song "Abriendo Puertas" by Cuban singer Gloria Estefan. The song talks about the New Year. What is the tone of the song? What are some of the things the New Year will bring?

9.4 **En busca de...** Busca a ocho compañeros que hicieron las siguientes actividades. Pide información adicional para reportársela a la clase. Usa el pretérito.

Modelo   una serenata alguna vez (¿cuándo?)
　　　　Estudiante A: *¿Participaste en una serenata alguna vez?*
　　　　Estudiante B: *Sí, participé una vez.*
　　　　Estudiante A: *¿Cuándo?*
　　　　Estudiante B: *El 15 de abril, porque fue el cumpleaños de mi novia.*

1. tener una fiesta en su último *(last)* cumpleaños (¿cuándo?)

2. darle un regalo a alguien recientemente (¿a quién?)

3. preparar una fiesta para niños recientemente (¿por qué?)

4. cenar en un restaurante para celebrar su cumpleaños (¿cuál?)

5. asistir a una boda recientemente (¿de quiénes?)

6. preparar un pastel de cumpleaños para un amigo (¿qué tipo?)

7. romper una piñata en una fiesta (¿qué fiesta?)

8. tener más de quince invitados en una celebración (¿qué celebración?)

9.5 **Las tradiciones** Hay muchas tradiciones interesantes con las que las personas reciben el año nuevo. Trabaja con un compañero. Uno de ustedes va a ver la ilustración en esta página, y el otro va a describir la ilustración en el **Apéndice B**. Describan sus ilustraciones (sin ver la otra) para encontrar las seis diferencias.

© Cengage Learning

Cultura

Las corridas de toros *(bullfights)* son una tradición milenaria. En España, durante la Edad Media, la aristocracia se divertía toreando *(bullfighting)* a caballo. En el siglo XVIII se abandonó esta tradición y se empezó a torear a pie.

La corrida de toros todavía es parte de la cultura de España, México, Colombia, Ecuador y Perú, aunque se prohíbe en algunas regiones de estos países. Por ejemplo en Cataluña, España, no se permiten las corridas desde el año 2012. El toreo en su forma tradicional es controversial y es probable que en el futuro más países la prohíban.

Para algunos, torear es un arte.

Hay gente contra el toreo.

Hoy en día existen diversos eventos con toros como exhibiciones acrobáticas que no involucran matar al animal o hacerle daño *(harm)* en modo alguno.

> Investiga en Internet el movimiento contra las corridas de toros. Decide si estás de acuerdo y sube tus comentarios a Share It!

Conexiones... a la literatura

Octavio Paz (1914–1998) fue un notable poeta y ensayista mexicano, ganador del Premio Nobel de Literatura (1990). Entre las muchas obras de importancia que escribió se encuentra el libro de ensayos *El laberinto de la soledad*. El libro se compone de nueve ensayos y habla de lo que Octavio Paz consideraba la psicología del mexicano. Aunque fue escrito en 1950 y las condiciones en el país han cambiado significativamente, esta obra continúa siendo lectura obligada para muchos porque analiza el efecto psicológico que tuvo la conquista en el pueblo mexicano. El siguiente es un extracto de ese libro:

> El solitario mexicano ama las fiestas y las reuniones públicas. Todo es ocasión para reunirse. Cualquier pretexto es bueno para interrumpir la marcha del tiempo y celebrar con festejos y ceremonias hombres y acontecimientos... Los países ricos tienen pocas [fiestas populares]: no hay tiempo, ni humor.

Octavio Paz

De acuerdo con tus conocimientos ¿qué opinas sobre lo que expresa Paz en la cita mencionada arriba? ¿Es cierto también para tu cultura?

Comunidad

Entrevista a una persona de un país hispano. Pregúntale sobre los festejos que son importantes en su país. ¿Cuándo se celebran? ¿Qué hace la gente? ¿Cuál es su celebración favorita? Repórtale a la clase la información.

La celebración de San Bartolomeo, en Bolivia

Comparaciones

¿Sabes qué es un carnaval? ¿Alguna vez fuiste a uno? ¿Qué hacía la gente? En Latinoamérica hay algunos carnavales que tienen fama internacional. Por ejemplo, el Carnaval de Panamá es un evento muy esperado *(anticipated)* en ese país. El carnaval dura cuatro días y cinco noches y en algunas ciudades de Panamá, como en Las Tablas, hay desfiles con carros alegóricos *(floats)*. Además, miles de personas se reúnen al aire libre para celebrar los culecos, bailes populares en los que se arroja agua sobre los participantes, quienes terminan empapados *(drenched)*. Otro gran ejemplo es el Carnaval de Montevideo en Uruguay. Es el carnaval más largo del mundo y tiene un sabor original, gracias a la influencia africana.

Investiga un poco más sobre los carnavales en Latinoamérica y explora cómo se comparan con el Mardi Gras de Nueva Orleans. ¿En qué aspectos son semejantes? ¿Cómo son diferentes? ¿Cuándo se celebran y por cuánto tiempo?

Carnaval en Montevideo, Uruguay

Una murga del Carnaval de Montevideo

 Para saber más sobre otras celebraciones en España y Latinoamérica consulta la lista de fiestas en la sección **Exploraciones del mundo hispano** en el **Apéndice A**. Elige una y busca información adicional en Internet. Después escribe una síntesis de la celebración y compártela en Share It! Lee las selecciones de tus compañeros. ¿A cuáles de estas celebraciones te gustaría asistir?

A analizar

Santiago habla de algunos recuerdos del Año Nuevo. Mira el video. Después lee los siguientes párrafos y observa los diferentes usos del pretérito y el imperfecto.

> Ella **se llamaba** Fátima y **era** muy guapa, con el pelo largo y negro. **Llevaba** un vestido rojo y **estaba** sentada en el sofá, hablando con una amiga.
>
> **Me acerqué** a ella. Le **pedí** bailar conmigo y aceptó. **Pasamos** el resto de la noche hablando. Al final de la noche, le **pedí** su número de teléfono y me lo **dio.**

1. Which of the paragraphs provides background information? Is the preterite or the imperfect tense used?

2. Which paragraph has actions that tell what happened? Is the preterite or the imperfect tense used?

A comprobar

A comparison of the preterite and imperfect

Imperfect

1. As you learned in **Capítulo 8** the imperfect is used to express past actions in progress or habitual actions in the past.

   > Todos **bailaban** en la fiesta.
   > *Everyone **was dancing** at the party.*

   > Siempre **tenía** una piñata en mis fiestas.
   > *I always **used to have** a piñata at my parties.*

2. The imperfect is also used to describe conditions, people, and places in the past. When telling a story, it communicates background information or details. The order in which these sentences occur is often unimportant.

   > **Era** medianoche y **llovía.**
   > *It **was** midnight, and it **was raining.***

   > Ella **tenía** quince años y **era** alta.
   > *She **was** fifteen and **was** tall.*

   > **Se llamaba** Lourdes.
   > ***Her name was** Lourdes.*

   > La sala **estaba** decorada con globos.
   > *The living room **was** decorated with balloons.*

Preterite

The preterite is used to narrate the main events of a story that have already happened. In other words, they are the past actions that advance the story. Unlike the imperfect, the order of events is important.

> Él **entró** en el café, **pidió** un café con leche, lo **tomó** y le **pagó** al mesero.
> *He **entered** the café, **ordered** a coffee with milk, **drank** it, and **paid** the waiter.*

> Sandra **cortó** el pastel y se lo **sirvió** a los invitados.
> *Sandra **cut** the cake and **served** it to the guests.*

A practicar

9.6 **Los cumpleaños** Sandra celebra su cumpleaños todos los años, pero el año pasado fue una ocasión especial porque celebró sus quince años. Lee las oraciones y decide cuáles se refieren a las celebraciones cuando era niña y cuáles se refieren a su fiesta de quince años. ¡OJO! Presta atención a los verbos.

1. Bailó el vals con su novio.
2. Rompía una piñata.
3. Sus padres la despertaban con "Las mañanitas".
4. Su madre le compró un vestido elegante.
5. Había un payaso *(clown)* con globos.
6. Su padre hizo un brindis durante la fiesta.

9.7 **La fiesta sorpresa** Completa las siguientes oraciones con la forma necesaria del pretérito o imperfecto del verbo indicado, según el caso.

Descripciones:

1. _____ (ser) el ocho de agosto.
2. _____ (ser) mi cumpleaños.
3. Ya _____ (tener) treinta años.
4. _____ (ser) las siete de la tarde.
5. Yo _____ (llevar) ropa de trabajo.
6. Yo _____ (estar) un poco triste.
7. No _____ (haber) luces en la casa.

Acciones principales:

1. Yo _____ (abrir) la puerta.
2. Yo _____ (encender) la luz.
3. Mis amigos _____ (gritar): "¡Sorpresa!"
4. Mi novio me _____ (besar, to kiss).
5. Nosotros _____ (comer) pastel.
6. Todos me _____ (dar) regalos.

9.8 **¡Qué sorpresa!** Mira el dibujo. En parejas, túrnense para describir lo que pasaba cuando los padres de Claudia llegaron a casa.

9.9 **¿Qué pasó?** Este es el comienzo de una historia. Son las descripciones de la escena. Con un compañero, completen el párrafo con cuatro o cinco oraciones que cuenten lo que pasó. **¡OJO!** Deben usar el pretérito porque van a narrar la historia.

Era el 10 de junio, el día de la boda de Alejandra y Rafael. Rafael llevaba un traje negro y estaba frente a la iglesia. Todos los invitados esperaban la llegada de la novia. A las 10:00...

9.10 **Una entrevista** Piensa en la última fiesta en que estuviste. Luego, hazle las siguientes preguntas a un compañero y contesta sus preguntas. Deben usar pretérito e imperfecto.

Descripciones:

1. ¿Qué ropa (llevar) tú?

2. ¿Cuántas personas (haber) en la fiesta?

3. ¿Cómo (ser) el lugar de la fiesta?

4. ¿Cómo (estar) tú ese día?

Acciones principales:

1. ¿A qué hora (llegar) tú a la fiesta?

2. ¿Qué (hacer) después de llegar?

3. ¿(Pasar) algo interesante en la fiesta?

4. ¿A qué hora (volver) a tu casa?

9.11 **La fiesta** Este grupo de jóvenes estaba en una fiesta cuando sacaron la foto que aparece a continuación. Con un compañero inventen los detalles de la fiesta. Primero describan la fiesta usando el imperfecto (¿Qué tiempo hacía? ¿Cuántas personas había? ¿Qué ropa llevaban?). Luego, cuenten qué pasó en la fiesta usando el pretérito y las expresiones **primero, después, luego** y **entonces.**

© Photos To Go

Exploraciones gramaticales

A analizar

Santiago habla de algunos recuerdos del Año Nuevo. Mira el video otra vez. Después lee las oraciones de Santiago y observa los verbos.

> Invitamos a muchos amigos, decoramos la sala con globos y preparamos unos bocadillos. Los primeros invitados llegaron mientras yo ponía la mesa... Unos (invitados) comían mientras otros hablaban.

1. Identify the verb tense in each of the sentences above.
2. Explain why that particular tense was used.

A comprobar

Uses of the preterite and the imperfect

When telling a story or relating a past event, the action usually can be expressed in one of three ways:

1. Two simultaneous actions:

    When there are two actions going on at the same time in the past, they are both in progress, and therefore both verbs will be conjugated in the imperfect. The conjunctions **mientras** and **y** are often used in these sentences. This can be visually represented in the following manner:

    ≈

    Él **escuchaba** mientras ella **hablaba.**
    *He **listened** while she **spoke.***

    Todos **bailaban** y **cantaban.**
    *Everyone **was dancing** and **singing.***

2. A series of completed actions:

    When there is a series of separate and complete actions in the past, the verbs will all be conjugated in the preterite. This series of completed actions can be visually represented in the following manner with each arrow corresponding to a different verb (action):

    ↓   ↓   ↓   ↓   ↓

    La señora Cisneros **llevó** el pastel a la mesa. Los niños **cantaron** "Las mañanitas" y después Rosita **apagó** las velas. La señora **cortó** el pastel y se lo **sirvió** a los niños.
    *Mrs. Cisneros **took** the cake to the table. The children **sang** "Las mañanitas," and then Rosita **blew out***

the candles. Mrs. Cisneros **cut** the cake and **served** the children.

3. One action in progress when another begins:

    In the past, when an action is in progress and a second action begins or is completed, both the preterite and the imperfect are used. The imperfect is used for the action in progress and the preterite is used for the new action that began or interrupted the first action. This can be visually represented in the following manner:

    ↯

    Mientras **terminábamos** las preparaciones, los invitados **empezaron** a llegar.
    *While we **were finishing** the preparations, the guests **began** to arrive.*

    Todos **se divertían** en la fiesta cuando **llegó** la policía.
    *Everyone **was having fun** at the party when the police **arrived.***

Estrategia

Remember that Spanish and English have different structures

You will see that there are differences in how past actions are communicated in English and in Spanish. Remember to learn the new structures and to avoid translating directly from English to Spanish.

A practicar

9.12 **Fotos y descripciones** Empareja las oraciones con las fotos.

    1. En 1980 tuve un hijo.

    2. En 1980 tenía dos hijos.

   a.    **b.**

    3. Mientras Sara hablaba por teléfono tomaba café.

    4. Mientras Susana hablaba por teléfono le sirvieron un café.

   a.    **b.**

    5. Gema leía cuando Rocío le hizo una pregunta.

    6. Rosendo leía mientras Gilda hacía una llamada.

   a.    **b.**

9.13 **La fiesta de cumpleaños** El sábado pasado Felipe celebró su cumpleaños. Para saber lo que pasó, completa las oraciones con la forma apropiada del verbo entre paréntesis. **¡OJO!** Presta atención al uso del pretérito y el imperfecto.

Dos acciones simultáneas

    1. Alicia y Ernesto bailaban mientras el grupo musical (tocar) un vals.

    2. Mientras sus padres hablaban, Carlitos (dormir).

Dos acciones consecutivas

    3. Jimena se rió cuando Rudy le (contar) un chiste.

    4. Hugo se levantó e (hacer) un brindis por el cumpleaños de Felipe.

Una acción en progreso cuando comienza una nueva acción

    5. El mesero le sirvió pastel a Jimena mientras ella (hablar) con Rudy.

    6. Mientras los invitados disfrutaban de la fiesta, Delia le (dar) un regalo a Felipe.

9.14 **¡Acción!** Túrnense para escoger y actuar una de las oraciones de cada par *(pair)* sin decirle a su compañero cuál se está actuando. El otro estudiante debe decidir cuál de las dos oraciones está presentando su compañero. Después decidan cómo actuar las otras oraciones.

1. **a.** Se estiró y se levantó.

   b. Se estiraba mientras se levantaba.

2. **a.** Escribía su tarea cuando sonó el teléfono y lo contestó.

   b. Escribía su tarea mientras hablaba por teléfono.

3. **a.** Se sentó y leyó un libro.

   b. Estaba sentado y leía un libro.

4. **a.** Mientras dibujaba una flor dijo: "Me gusta".

   b. Dibujó una flor y dijo: "Me gusta".

5. **a.** Tomó una copa de champán y se durmió.

   b. Se dormía mientras tomaba una copa de champán.

6. **a.** Bailaba mientras comía su pastel de cumpleaños.

   b. Comió su pastel de cumpleaños y bailó.

9.15 **Cuéntame** Con un compañero miren las siguientes fotos. Túrnense para describir lo que pasó usando los verbs indicados. **¡OJO!** Presten atención al uso del pretérito y el imperfecto.

1.

© AVAVA/Shutterstock

   a. llevar el pastel, cantar

   b. apagar *(to blow out)* las velas, cortar

2.

© Karin Hildebrand Lau/Shutterstock

   a. pegarle a *(to hit),* mirar

   b. romper, correr

3.

© Image Source/Getty Images

   a. tocar un vals, bailar

   b. terminar, aplaudir

4.

© angelo gilardelli/Shutterstock

   a. casarse, salir

   b. salir, tirar arroz

9.16 Los quince años Mayra celebró sus quince años ayer. Completa las oraciones para explicar lo que pasó ese día. ¡OJO! Presta atención al uso del pretérito y del imperfecto.

> Modelo Por la mañana Mayra se cortó el pelo mientras su familia...
> *organizaba los últimos detalles de la fiesta.*

1. Eran las tres de la tarde cuando Mayra...
2. Mientras ella se arreglaba, sus padres...
3. Cuando Mayra llegó a la iglesia, sus amigos...
4. Cuando la misa *(mass)* terminó, todos...
5. Los invitados empezaron a llegar a la fiesta mientras...
6. Mientras el grupo musical tocaba el vals, Mayra...
7. Después de que cortaron el pastel,...
8. Cuando la fiesta terminó...

9.17 Unas fiestas Con un compañero, escojan una de las secuencias y den muchos detalles para relatar lo que pasó. Usen el pretérito y el imperfecto e inventen un final. Para elegir entre el pretérito y el imperfecto, piensen en lo siguiente: ¿es una serie de acciones consecutivas, una acción en progreso cuando comienza una nueva acción o dos acciones simultáneas?

1.

2.

3.

Entrando en materia

¿De qué hablan generalmente los programas sobre personalidades famosas?

La farándula (Show business)

🔊 Vas a escuchar un segmento de un programa sobre personalidades famosas. Los locutores
2-14 hablan sobre un gran evento. Escucha con atención y después responde las preguntas.

Vocabulario útil

los aretes	*earrings*	**las perlas**	*pearls*
el collar	*necklace*	**recién casados**	*just married*
lujoso(a)	*luxurious*	**la reseña**	*report*

Comprensión

1. ¿Cómo se llama el programa de radio?
2. ¿Cuál es el evento del que hablan?
3. ¿Cuántos invitados asistieron? ¿Quién es una persona famosa que fue a la recepción?
4. ¿Qué ropa vistió la novia?
5. ¿Qué pasó durante el brindis?
6. ¿Invitaron los novios a los locutores (announcers) a su boda?

Más allá

Imagina que eres un reportero para la sección de sociedad de un periódico local. Debes escribir la reseña de una gran fiesta de aniversario o de una boda. Después compártela en Share It! y lee las reseñas de tus compañeros. ¿Cuál te gusta más y por qué?

Fue una boda muy elegante.

© infinity21/Shutterstock

Lectura

Antes de leer

¿Conoces alguna celebración de un país hispano? ¿Qué celebración? ¿Qué se hace?

A leer

El Día de los Muertos

Latinoamérica tiene una gran reputación por sus numerosas y variadas celebraciones. Muchas de ellas son de origen religioso, y otras son el resultado de la historia y de la mezcla de tradiciones particulares de cada nación. Entre las celebraciones más conocidas está el Día de los Muertos, festividad que celebraban los mayas, los aztecas y otras culturas mesoamericanas antes de la llegada de los españoles al Nuevo Mundo. Estas culturas precolombinas creían que existía la vida después de la muerte, así que enterraban a sus seres

El Día de los Muertos se celebra en México y Centroamérica.

offerings / jewelry

queridos con **ofrendas** como cerámica y **joyas.** También pensaban que los muertos podían regresar a este mundo un día al año. La celebración ocurría aproximadamente a la mitad del año, se piensa que en julio o agosto. Sin embargo, cuando los europeos llegaron e impusieron su religión, insistieron en cambiar la fecha para noviembre, el Día de Todos los Santos en la religión católica. Los españoles esperaban que, con los años, los indígenas comenzaran a observar la celebración católica y dejaran sus creencias atrás. Esto nunca ocurrió: las creencias europeas se mezclaron con las de los indígenas. Hoy en día el Día de los Muertos se celebra en todo México y los países de Centroamérica.

> [Creían que los muertos podían regresar un día al año.]

Según la tradición, se piensa que el Día de los Muertos es cuando los muertos regresan a este mundo. Ellos son bienvenidos y esperados por todos. Sus familias limpian sus tumbas, llevan flores y preparan comidas especiales para este día.

La parte más típica de la celebración es la creación de ofrendas con todo lo que le gustaba a la persona cuando vivía: música, comida, flores y otros elementos tradicionales, como velas y **cempasúchitl.** Un elemento que no puede faltar en ninguna celebración es el pan de muertos, un pan que se prepara solamente para esta ocasión y se come en todas partes. El Día de los Muertos no es un día triste, sino un día para celebrar a los **seres queridos** que han muerto, en compañía de aquellos que todavía están con nosotros.

marigolds

loved ones

Comprensión

Decide si las afirmaciones son ciertas o falsas, y corrige las falsas.

1. Todas las celebraciones de Latinoamérica se originan en la religión.
2. Los aztecas creían que después de esta vida no había nada.
3. Los españoles crearon la celebración del Día de los Muertos para ayudar a convertir a los aztecas al catolicismo.
4. El Día de los Muertos combina creencias mesoamericanas y europeas.
5. Muchas familias limpian las tumbas de sus familiares en este día.
6. El pan de muertos se come durante todo el año en honor a los muertos.

Después de leer

En México durante la celebración del Día de los Muertos se escriben *calaveras,* poemas cómicos que se burlan de *(make fun of)* figuras famosas. Lee la calavera dedicada a Salma Hayek. ¿Cómo se describe a Salma Hayek? Con un compañero escriban una calavera original.

SALMA HAYEK

This mexican señorita
que es tan *pretty* y tan bonita
a todo el *world* presumía
los *gifts* de la cirugía

When la Muerte *came for* ella
que se monta *on her* burro:
-*Don't* me lleves -dijo ella.
But la Muerte, en un susurro:
-*So you think you're great* estrella,
but you filmas puro churro...

© Calavera: Salma Hayek, authorized by José Hernández.

En la ciudad hay que tener mucho cuidado y prestar atención al tráfico.

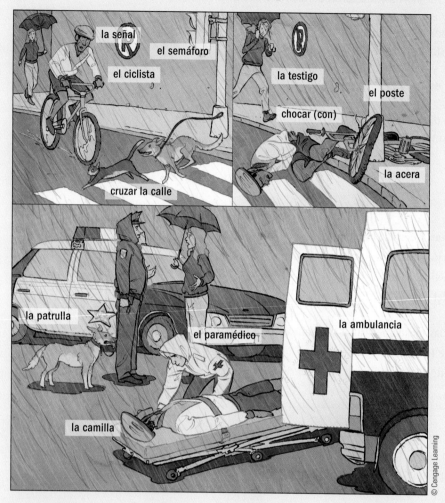

la señal · el semáforo · el ciclista · la testigo · el poste · chocar (con) · la acera · cruzar la calle · la patrulla · el paramédico · la ambulancia · la camilla

© Cengage Learning

INVESTIGUEMOS EL VOCABULARIO

Some countries refer to parking meters as **estacionómetros.** Other common terms for *driver* are **el automovilista** and **el chofer.** Likewise, the verb **aparcar** is used in some countries rather than **estacionarse.**

la carretera	highway	**Los verbos**	
el (la) conductor(a)	driver	atravesar (ie)	to cross
el cruce	crosswalk	atropellar	to run over
la esquina	corner	bajar de	to get out of (a vehicle)
el límite de velocidad	speed limit	caer(se)	to fall
la multa	fine, ticket	dañar	to damage
el parquímetro	parking meter	distraerse	to get distracted
el peatón (la peatona)	pedestrian	esperar	to wait
el puente	bridge	estacionarse	to park
el servicio de emergencias	emergency service	parar	to stop
		pasarse un semáforo en rojo	to run a red light

pasarse una señal de PARE	to run a stop sign
subir a	to get into (a vehicle)
tropezar (ie)	to trip

Expresiones adicionales

de repente	suddenly
estar dañado(a)	to be damaged
estar herido(a)	to be injured

A practicar

9.18 Escucha y responde Vas a escuchar algunas ideas sobre el tráfico en la ciudad y los accidentes. Si la idea es lógica, indícalo con el pulgar hacia arriba. Si la idea no es lógica, señala con el pulgar hacia abajo.

2-15

9.19 **¿Qué palabra es más lógica?** Escoge la palabra que completa la oración lógicamente.

1. El policía me dio una (patrulla/multa) por conducir a exceso de velocidad.
2. Cuando el semáforo está en rojo, es necesario (parar/pasarse).
3. El ciclista (atravesó/atropelló) la calle con cuidado.
4. Los peatones deben caminar por la (señal/acera).
5. El automovilista (se cayó/se distrajo) y no vio a los peatones en (el cruce/el semáforo).
6. Hay mucho tráfico en la (carretera/esquina) hoy.

9.20 **El testigo** Mira el dibujo del accidente en la página 314. Lombardo se pegó en la cabeza y no está seguro de lo que le pasó. Lee las declaraciones que Lombardo le dio al paramédico y decide si son ciertas o falsas. Después corrige las oraciones falsas.

1. Cuando iba en mi bicicleta, un perro se atravesó enfrente de mí.
2. Para no atropellar al perro, di vuelta a la izquierda y choqué con una señal.
3. Por suerte, había una ambulancia estacionada en la calle.
4. Un testigo llamó por teléfono para informarle a la policía de mi accidente.
5. En la calle no había señales de tráfico.
6. Afortunadamente mi bicicleta no se dañó.

9.21 **Una conversación** Habla con un compañero sobre las preguntas. Después repórtenle su conversación a la clase.

1. ¿Cuándo conseguiste tu licencia de conducir? ¿Chocaste el coche de tus padres cuando estabas aprendiendo a conducir?
2. Cuando conduces un auto ¿respetas a los peatones? Cuando caminas por la calle ¿te respetan los automovilistas?
3. ¿Respetas siempre todas las señales de tráfico? ¿el límite de velocidad?
4. ¿Es difícil estacionarse donde vives? ¿Es caro?
5. ¿Siempre atraviesas la calle en los cruces o en las esquinas?
6. ¿Prefieres conducir, andar en bicicleta o usar el transporte público? ¿Por qué?

9.22 **Contradicciones** Tu compañero y tú son testigos de un accidente, pero hay diferencias entre sus dos versiones. Uno de ustedes va a observar la ilustración en esta página y el otro va a observar la ilustración en el **Apéndice B.** Encuentren las cinco diferencias.

© Cengage Learning

El tráfico y los accidentes

Cultura

"Yo sufrí dos accidentes graves en mi vida, uno en el que un autobús me tumbó al suelo *(knocked me down)*… el otro accidente es Diego".

Aunque parezca increíble, fue gracias a un accidente automovilístico que surgió una de las grandes figuras del arte en México: Frida Kahlo. Frida tenía apenas unos dieciocho años cuando, un día, mientras regresaba de la escuela, el tranvía *(streetcar)* en el que viajaba se accidentó. Frida se fracturó la columna vertebral,

El Camión, Frida Kahlo

la clavícula, la pelvis, una pierna y varias costillas *(ribs)*. Pasó mucho tiempo en el hospital, y nunca pudo recuperarse completamente de este accidente. Mientras estaba en reposo *(rest)* absoluto después del accidente, empezó a pintar, actividad que marcó el resto de su vida.

Además de ser una gran pintora, Frida se distinguió como una de las intelectuales más distinguidas de la época y promovió *(promoted)* el amor por su patria *(native homeland)* de muchas maneras, incluyendo la ropa que vestía. Además, tanto Kahlo como Rivera participaron activamente en la política. Por ejemplo, cuando comenzó la Guerra Civil en España, Frida se organizó con otras mujeres para crear un comité de ayuda a los Republicanos españoles. Otro ejemplo conocido es que ambos pintores intercedieron por León Trotsky para que el gobierno mexicano le concediera el exilio político. La vida de esta artista fue polémica e influyente mucho más allá del arte que creó.

Investiga más sobre la vida de Frida Kahlo después del accidente.

> Investiga en Internet sobre el artista Diego Rivera. Elige una obra de Rivera que te guste, súbela a Share It! y escribe por qué te gusta.

Comparaciones

¿Sabías que en los Estados Unidos hay casi 800 vehículos motorizados por cada mil habitantes? Este número incluye automóviles, camiones y autobuses. Observa la información que sigue sobre el número de vehículos por cada mil habitantes en algunos países de habla hispana. ¿Cuál se aproxima más a los Estados Unidos? ¿Cómo se puede explicar? ¿En qué países hay menos vehículos? En tu opinión ¿qué aspectos de la vida diaria pueden ser diferentes en países donde hay muchos menos automóviles?

Argentina 267
Chile 184
Costa Rica 177
Ecuador 71
España 593
Guatemala 68
Guinea Ecuatorial 13

México 275
Nicaragua 57
Panamá 132
Perú 73
Puerto Rico 635
Uruguay 200

Source: The World Bank (2009-2013)

Con un buen sistema de transporte público los automóviles son menos necesarios, como en Santiago de Chile.

Conexiones... a la ingeniería

Uno de los grandes proyectos de la ingeniería es la construcción de una carretera que comunique todos los países de América, desde Alaska hasta Chile. Este proyecto, de hecho, está casi completo. Se llama la carretera Panamericana y es un sistema colectivo de carreteras que recorren más de veinticinco mil kilómetros. Solamente falta un pequeño tramo (*stretch*) para completarla.

La carretera pasa por montañas, selvas (*jungles*) y desiertos, y ofrece vistas increíbles. Como resultado de pasar por diferentes zonas con climas y terrenos variados, la carretera no es uniforme. En algunas épocas (*times*) del año se cierran porciones porque son peligrosas a causa de la lluvia.

Parque Nacional Tierra del Fuego BAHIA LAPATAIA República Argentina Aqui finaliza la Ruta Nac. Nº3 Buenos Aires 3.079 Km. Alaska 17.848 Km.

© meunierd/Shutterstock

La carretera Panamericana termina en la Patagonia argentina. ¿Sabes dónde comienza?

Investiga en Internet qué países atraviesa la carretera Panamericana, dónde está el tramo que falta y por qué algunas personas se oponen a su construcción. ¿Qué efecto tienen en el medio ambiente y en la economía las grandes carreteras?

Comunidad

Entrevista a una persona de un país hispanohablante acerca del sistema de transporte en su país. Pregúntale si muchas personas usan el transporte público, si piensa que es eficiente, qué tipos de transporte público existen, cuánto cuesta usarlo y cómo se compara a la ciudad en la que vive en los Estados Unidos.

© Jane Sweeney/Getty Images

Entre sus medios de transporte público, Medellín cuenta con un metro, tranvía y metrocable.

A analizar

Óscar habla con un señor que fue testigo de un accidente. Mira el video. Después lee las siguientes oraciones de su conversación y observa los diferentes usos de los verbos.

Me **sentía** feliz porque hacía sol.

Me **sentí** muy mal cuando vi que la señora en el coche negro estaba herida.

Había un señor en la otra acera.

Hubo un accidente.

1. Look at the first set of sentences. Which sentence communicates an ongoing emotion? Which sentence communicates a change in emotion? Explain.

2. Based on the second set of sentences, explain how the meaning of **haber** changes with the use of the imperfect or preterite.

A comprobar

Preterite and imperfect with emotions and mental states

You learned in the first part of the chapter that past actions in progress are expressed in the imperfect, and that the preterite is used to relate new or completed actions in the past. The same concept is applied to emotions or mental states.

> Era un día bonito y ella **se sentía** feliz.
> *It was a beautiful day and she **felt** happy.*
> (an ongoing emotion)

> Cuando escuché la noticia **me sentí** mal.
> *When I heard the news, I **felt** bad.*
> (a change in emotion)

1. The following verbs are often used to express a change in emotion or feeling and are usually used with the preterite:

aburrirse	to become bored
alegrarse	to become happy
asustarse	to become frightened
enojarse	to become angry
frustrarse	to become frustrated
sorprenderse	to be surprised

> **Me asusté** cuando vi el accidente.
> *I was (**became**) **frightened** when I saw the accident.*

> Los testigos **se alegraron** cuando descubrieron que nadie estaba herido.
> *The witnesses **were** (**became**) **happy** when they discovered that nobody was hurt.*

2. The verb **sentirse** is a stem-changing verb and is often used to express how one feels

> Hoy **me siento** bien.
> *I **feel** fine today.*

> **Se sintieron** tristes cuando se fue.
> *They **felt** sad when he left.*

3. It is also common to use the verb **ponerse** *(to become)* to express a change of emotion.

> **ponerse** + *adjective* (**triste, feliz, furioso, nervioso,** etc.)

> Cuando se murió mi perro **me puse** triste.
> *When my dog died, I **became** sad.*

4. The verbs **conocer, saber, haber, poder,** and **querer** are not action verbs but rather they refer to mental or physical states. As with action verbs, using them in the imperfect implies an ongoing condition, whereas using them in the preterite indicates the beginning or completion of the condition.

Estrategia

Remember that Spanish and English have different structures.

As you have noticed, there are differences in how past actions are communicated in English and in Spanish. To improve your fluency, avoid translating directly from English to Spanish.

	imperfect	preterite
conocer	to know, to be acquainted with	to meet
saber	to know (about)	to find out
haber	there was/were (descriptive)	there was/there were (occurred)
poder	was able to (circumstances)	succeeded in
no poder	was not able to (circumstances)	failed to
querer	wanted	tried to
no querer	didn't want	refused to

Cuando llegué no **conocía** a nadie, pero más tarde **conocí** a Inma.
*When I arrived, I didn't **know** anyone, but later I **met** Inma.*

A practicar

9.23 Reacciones lógicas Decide qué verbo completa mejor la oración.

1. Cuando vi el coche pasarse el semáforo en rojo, yo...
2. Cuando chocó con mi coche, yo...
3. Cuando vi el daño a mi coche, yo...
4. Cuando la policía le dio una multa, el otro conductor...
5. Cuando recibí el cheque del seguro *(insurance),* yo...

   a. me alegré
   b. me asusté
   c. me sorprendí
   d. me puse triste
   e. se enojó

9.24 ¿Cómo estaba? Usando expresiones con **tener** o **estar,** explica cómo estaba Renato ayer, según sus actividades.

Modelo Desayunó cuatro huevos, cereal, dos plátanos y un vaso de leche.
    Tenía hambre.

1. Se puso un suéter, guantes y un gorro.
2. Mientras conducía, escuchaba música.
3. Tenía un examen de álgebra.
4. Visitó a su abuela en el hospital.
5. Salió con su novia a cenar.
6. Estaba en una fiesta.
7. Se acostó muy tarde.
8. Tuvo una pesadilla *(nightmare).*

9.25 ¿Cuándo fue? Con un compañero túrnense para preguntar sobre la última vez que sintieron las siguientes emociones. Deben explicar las circunstancias de la situación. ¡Atención al uso del pretérito y del imperfecto en las explicaciones!

Modelo asustarse
    Estudiante 1: *¿Cuándo fue la última vez que te asustaste?*
    Estudiante 2: *Me asusté el lunes porque no podía encontrar mi composición.*

¿Cuándo fue la última vez que... ?

1. enojarse
2. aburrirse
3. ponerse triste
4. alegrarse
5. preocuparse
6. frustrarse
7. ponerse nervioso
8. sorprenderse

9.26 **Una entrevista** En parejas, túrnense para responder las preguntas.

1. Tus amigos
   a. ¿Cuándo conociste a tu mejor amigo? ¿Qué hacían?
   b. ¿Supiste algo interesante de tu mejor amigo recientemente? ¿Qué?
2. Tus clases y tu universidad
   a. ¿Conocías a alguien en la clase de español antes de este curso? ¿A quién?
   b. ¿Ya sabías hablar español cuando comenzaste a estudiar en esta universidad? ¿Por qué?
3. Tu vida diaria
   a. ¿Hiciste ayer algo que no querías hacer? ¿Qué?
   b. ¿Hubo un buen concierto en tu comunidad recientemente? ¿De qué?

9.27 **Mini-conversaciones** Completa las conversaciones con la forma del pretérito o del imperfecto del verbo indicado, según el caso.

1. —Cuando salí para la universidad esta mañana, _____ (haber) mucho hielo *(ice)* en las calles.
   —Sí, y escuché en la radio que _____ (haber) muchos accidentes.
2. —¿ _____ (Saber) tú que Manuel tuvo un accidente la semana pasada?
   —Sí, lo _____ (saber) cuando llegué a la oficina.
3. —¿ _____ (Poder) tú conseguir *(get)* el coche de tu hermano?
   —No, él no _____ (querer) prestármelo.
4. —Fui a una fiesta el sábado.
   —¿ _____ (Conocer) a alguien?
   — Yo ya _____ (conocer) a muchas de las personas en la fiesta, pero _____ (conocer) a una chica que se llama Dora.

> **INVESTIGUEMOS EL VOCABULARIO**
>
> In **Capítulo 6** you learned to use the word **ya** to mean *already* and *any more*. When used in a question, it can mean *yet*.
>
> ¿**Ya** llegaron?
> *Have they arrived yet?*
>
> ¿**Ya** terminaste la tarea?
> *Have you finished your homework yet?*

9.28 **Cuéntame** Yadira tuvo un accidente el fin de semana pasado y les cuenta a sus amigos lo que pasó. Cuenta lo que pasó cambiando los verbos en negritas al pretérito o al imperfecto, según sea necesario.

Es[1] sábado por la noche. **Estoy conduciendo**[2] a casa y **estoy**[3] muy nerviosa porque **hay**[4] mucha lluvia y no **puedo**[5] ver bien. De repente un animal **cruza**[6] la calle enfrente de mi coche y yo **me sorprendo**[7]. No **sé**[8] qué tipo de animal **es**[9], pero no **quiero**[10] atropellarlo. **Intento** *(try)*[11] **frenar** *(to brake)*, pero no **puedo**[12] controlar el coche. El coche **empieza**[13] a salirse de la calle y **me asusto**[14]. Afortunadamente solo **termino**[15] en una zanja *(ditch)* y no **choco**[16] con nada.

9.29 **El accidente de Teo** Describe lo que le pasó a Teo. Usa el pretérito y el imperfecto, y los verbos indicados, según el caso.

Vocabulario útil: **el cigarrillo** *cigarette* **la cima** *top (of the mountain)* **la serpiente** *snake*

1. haber, conocer, sentirse
2. ofrecer, querer
3. saber, poder, alegrarse
4. ver, asustarse, caerse
5. estar triste, querer, poder

A analizar ▶

Óscar habla con un señor que fue testigo de un accidente.
Mira el video otra vez. Después lee parte de su conversación y
observa los verbos en el pretérito y el imperfecto.

Óscar:	Buenas tardes, señor. ¿Usted **fue** testigo del accidente?
Señor:	Sí, señor...
Óscar:	¿Qué **hacía** usted cuando **ocurrió** el accidente?
Señor:	Siempre **caminaba** por la calle Sol con mi perrito en las tardes. **Me gustaba** porque **podía** llegar fácilmente al parque, pero la semana pasada **decidí** cambiar mi ruta porque ahora hay mucho tráfico.
Óscar:	Sí, señor, pero ¿qué **hacía** usted en la calle Naranjos hoy?
Señor:	**Caminaba** con mi perrito Negrito. **Me sentía** feliz porque **hacía** sol. Mientras **caminaba**, **miraba** las flores en los jardines. De repente oí un ruido terrible y vi que **hubo** un accidente. **Me sentí** muy mal cuando **vi** que la señora en el coche negro **estaba** herida.
Óscar:	¿Sabe usted qué **pasó**?
Señor:	No **pude** ver mucho porque no **llevaba** mis gafas puestas, pero me parece que el coche negro **se pasó** el semáforo en rojo...
Óscar:	Bueno, gracias por su ayuda, señor.

© Cengage Learning

1. Write a list of the circumstances in which you would use preterite and in which you would use imperfect.

2. Can you find any examples of the uses you listed in the dialogue above?

A comprobar

Preterite and imperfect: A summary

You have already learned that the preterite is the narrative past and is used to express an action that is *beginning* or *ending*, while the imperfect is the descriptive past that is used to express an action *in progress (middle)*. Here is an overview of how the two tenses are used:

Preterite

1. A past action or series of actions that are completed as of the moment of reference

    Vi el accidente y **llamé** a la policía.

2. An action that is beginning or ending

    Empezó a estudiar a las siete.

    Vivimos en Madrid por tres años.

3. A change of condition or emotion

    Tuve miedo cuando escuché el ruido *(noise)*.

Imperfect

1. An action in progress with no emphasis on the beginning or end of the action

    Llovía y hacía viento.

2. A habitual action

    Siempre **leía** antes de acostarme.

3. Description of a physical or mental condition

    Era alto y moreno y **tenía** el pelo largo.

    Estaba muy nervioso.

4. Other descriptions, such as time, date, and age

    Eran las tres de la tarde.

    Era el primero de octubre.

    Tenía sesenta años.

A practicar

9.30 **Esquí en Bariloche** Pon las siguientes oraciones en el orden correcto para contar lo que hizo Rogelio.

1. _____ El invierno pasado cumplió 20 años y fue a Bariloche para esquiar con sus amigos.

2. _____ Cuando Rogelio era niño, iba a esquiar con su familia durante las vacaciones de invierno.

3. _____ Mientras Rogelio bajaba la pista *(slope)* un chico cruzó enfrente de él y se asustó y se cayó.

4. _____ El primer día de esquí, Rogelio y sus amigos se levantaron temprano, se vistieron y fueron a la pista.

5. _____ Hablaban y se reían mientras esperaban su turno para subir *(to go up)* la montaña.

6. _____ Rogelio estaba frustrado y tenía frío, entonces se quitó los esquíes y regresó al hotel para tomar un chocolate caliente.

9.31 **Un accidente en bicicleta** Mayda habla sobre un accidente que tuvo con su bicicleta. Completa las oraciones con la frase apropiada para saber lo que pasó.

1. Tenía una bicicleta roja cuando...
   a. era niña.
   b. fui niña.

2. Cuando salía con mi bicicleta, siempre...
   a. tenía mucho cuidado.
   b. tuve mucho cuidado.

3. Ese día...
   a. hacía mucho sol.
   b. hizo mucho sol.

4. Yo iba por la calle cuando...
   a. un coche se pasaba un alto.
   b. un coche se pasó un alto.

5. Me atropelló porque...
   a. no podía parar.
   b. no pude parar.

6. Cuando el conductor vio que estaba herida...
   a. se preocupaba.
   b. se preocupó.

7. Él me hablaba mientras...
   a. esperábamos la ambulancia.
   b. esperamos la ambulancia.

9.32 **Un accidente** Completa el siguiente párrafo con la forma necesaria del pretérito o del imperfecto del verbo indicado.

Esta mañana (**1.**) _____ (haber) un accidente a las ocho y media. En ese momento yo (**2.**) _____ (caminar) por la calle Montalvo con mi amiga Reina. De repente, nosotros (**3.**) _____ (oír) un ruido *(noise)* y (**4.**) _____ (ver) que un coche acababa de *(just)* chocar contra un árbol. Un hombre mayor (**5.**) _____ (bajar) del coche. Él (**6.**) _____ (estar) muy pálido y (**7.**) _____ (tener) una herida en la cabeza. Nosotros lo (**8.**) _____ (ayudar) a sentarse en la acera. Mientras él (**9.**) _____ (descansar *to rest*), Reina (**10.**) _____ (llamar) a una ambulancia. Nosotros (**11.**) _____ (estar) muy preocupados por él, pero (**12.**) _____ (calmarse) un poco cuando (**13.**) _____ (llegar) la ambulancia. Los paramédicos lo (**14.**) _____ (poner) en la camilla y lo (**15.**) _____ (llevar) al hospital.

9.33 **Experiencias personales** Habla con un compañero sobre tus experiencias y túrnense para completar las oraciones. Atención al uso del pretérito y del imperfecto.

1. Mientras aprendía a conducir...
2. Cuando conseguí la licencia de conducir...
3. La primera vez que conduje...
4. Una vez que conducía...
5. Vi un accidente y...
6. Conozco a alguien que tuvo un accidente porque...

9.34 **El venado** *(The deer)* Con la ayuda de tu compañero describe lo que les pasó a Margarita y a Marián. Usa el pretérito y el imperfecto e incluye muchos detalles. Decidan lo que pasó al final.

© Cengage Learning

Lectura

Antes de leer

¿Cuál es la diferencia entre una leyenda y un cuento? ¿Qué es una leyenda urbana? ¿Conoces alguna leyenda urbana? ¿Cuál?

A leer

Leyendas urbanas

Una leyenda se puede definir como un relato que no se puede comprobar que se basa en personas, hechos o lugares que realmente existen o existieron. Es decir, es un relato fantástico con un fondo histórico que pretende explicar el presente. Un tipo de leyenda muy común es aquella en donde se explica cómo apareció un elemento geográfico importante para una comunidad, como un volcán o una montaña. Un ejemplo es la leyenda paraguaya de origen guaraní de cómo apareció el pájaro ñandú en la Tierra o el Salto del Guairá. Otro tipo de leyenda trata de dar una lección moral, como en el caso de "El padre Almeida" y "Mariangula", ambas leyendas del Ecuador.

En contraste, las leyendas urbanas son historias relativamente modernas que no intentan explicar el presente. Generalmente se trata de historias con elementos increíbles que circulan sin ninguna evidencia de que sean verdaderas. Adquieren relevancia en una comunidad porque **se supone** *supposedly* que son eventos que le ocurrieron a alguien de esa comunidad. Ocasionalmente están basadas en un hecho que realmente llegó a ocurrir, pero se cuenta de forma muy distorsionada.

Un pájaro ñandú

© Worakit Sirijinda/Shutterstock

Son muchas y muy variadas las leyendas urbanas que se escuchan hoy en día. Curiosamente, muchas veces las mismas historias se escuchan en países diferentes. A veces el escenario de la historia es España, a veces Ecuador, Paraguay, Puerto Rico o cualquier otro país. A continuación se cuenta la leyenda de *La muchacha de la curva,* leyenda urbana de la que existen numerosas versiones.

La muchacha de la curva

Era una noche oscura y llovía muy fuerte. Un automovilista conducía solo por la carretera cuando vio a una muchacha haciendo autostop. La chica estaba empapada y tiritaba. Él se detuvo y la dejó subir a su automóvil. Le preguntó adónde iba. La muchacha le dio una

soaked / shivering

> "¡Es ella!", exclamó.

dirección cerca de allí, y el automovilista la llevó hasta su casa. **Se despidió** de ella y la vio caminar hacia la puerta. Después arrancó y continuó su camino.

said goodbye

Al día siguiente el hombre decidió regresar para buscar a la muchacha para saber si estaba bien. Cuando llegó a la casa en donde la había dejado la noche anterior, tocó a la puerta. Una mujer vieja le abrió. El hombre preguntó por la muchacha y la mujer respondió que allí no vivía ninguna joven. Sin embargo, la

... un automovilista vio a una muchacha...

mujer invitó al hombre a entrar. En la sala, el hombre vio una fotografía de la muchacha en la pared. "¡Es ella!", exclamó.

La mujer le dijo al hombre: "Era mi hija. **Hace veinte años** ella iba conduciendo por la carretera. Estaba muy obscuro y llovía. Entonces llegó a la curva donde usted la recogió. Esa noche llovía tanto que ella no vio las señales. Su auto **resbaló** y mi hija perdió el control y chocó. Murió inmediatamente. Ahora, cada año, el mismo día, en el mismo lugar y a la misma hora en que ocurrió el accidente, mi hija aparece y le pide a algún conductor que la **traiga** a casa, que es adonde ella iba esa noche".

Twenty years ago

slid

bring

Comprensión

1. ¿Cuáles son algunas diferencias entre una leyenda y una leyenda urbana?
2. ¿Por qué piensas que las mismas historias se escuchan en diferentes países?
3. En la leyenda de la chica de la curva ¿qué hizo el automovilista cuando vio a una chica haciendo autostop?
4. ¿Qué supo el automovilista al final de la historia?

Después de leer

Investiga una leyenda tradicional o una leyenda urbana. Sube la leyenda a Share It! y lee las leyendas de tus compañeros. ¿Cuál te gusta más? ¿Por qué?

INVESTIGUEMOS LA MÚSICA

Spanish singer Julio Iglesias' song "Pájaro Chogüí" recounts a Paraguayan legend. Listen to the song and tell what the legend is.

Redacción

A magazine has asked readers to write in and tell about a day that was particularly memorable. ¡OJO! You will need to use the preterite and the imperfect.

Paso 1 Think about an event that was particularly memorable. It might be a special day such as a birthday or your wedding, or it might be a day something terrible happened such as an accident.

Paso 2 Jot down a list of phrases that set the scene. Consider how you were feeling as the day began, where and when the event took place, and what the weather was like.

Paso 3 Write a list of chronological events that took place that day.

Paso 4 Begin your story using the information you generated in **Paso 2** to set the scene.

Paso 5 Write a few paragraphs that narrate the story using the information you generated in **Paso 3.** Be sure to elaborate on the chronological development of the event by adding details such as descriptions and emotions.

Paso 6 Conclude your account telling how the event ended and how you felt at the end.

Paso 7 Edit your essay:

1. Is the information clearly organized?
2. Did you include ample details?
3. Is the narration logically organized with smooth transitions between sentences?
4. Are there any short sentences you can combine with **y** or **pero**?
5. Do verbs agree with the subject? Are they conjugated properly?
6. Did you use the preterite and the imperfect accurately?
7. Are there any spelling errors? Do the preterite verbs that need accents have them?

En vivo

Entrando en materia

Cuando eres peatón en las calles de la ciudad ¿qué medidas *(measures)* tomas para caminar seguro *(safely)* por la ciudad? ¿Qué debes hacer para tomar un autobús?

Aviso para peatones

Vas a leer alguna información publicada para enseñar a los peatones a caminar seguros.

Aprenda a caminar seguro por ciudad y por carretera

¡Bienvenido a nuestra ciudad! Estamos orgullosos de ser una de las urbes latinoamericanas con mejores servicios para peatones, ciclistas y automovilistas, pero es importante que todos hagan su parte para evitar accidentes y tener una ciudad segura. Por eso, aclaramos a continuación cuál es la forma indicada de proceder en algunas de las situaciones más frecuentes.

SEGURIDAD PEATONAL Las zonas peatonales están claramente indicadas con líneas blancas, también conocidas como pasos de cebra[1]. Cuando hay zonas peatonales disponibles se debe caminar por ellas y nunca cruzar a la mitad[2] de la calle. Si no hay una zona peatonal nunca se debe bajar de la acera y se debe esperar a cruzar en las esquinas. Es obligación de los automovilistas no invadir las zonas peatonales y prestar atención a los peatones.

ESTACIONAMIENTOS Si un automóvil entra o sale de un estacionamiento, debe cederle[3] el paso a los peatones que circulan por la acera.

PARADAS DE AUTOBUSES El sistema de autobuses ofrece paradas claramente indicadas. Los autobuses no pueden recoger pasajeros en ningún otro lugar. En estas paradas también se indican los números de las rutas que pasan por allí. Usted puede comprar pases mensuales[4] para tomar un número ilimitado de autobuses y en el sistema del metro. Estos pases se pueden adquirir en los quioscos de periódicos o en las tabaquerías. Si usted no necesita pases, es su responsabilidad pagar con el cambio exacto a la hora de abordar el autobús. El conductor no puede darle cambio[5].

© Radu Razvan/Shutterstock

CICLISTAS Aunque hay muchas avenidas con vías para ciclistas, todavía falta mucho por hacer. Los conductores de bicicleta deben circular por la calle, como los otros vehículos, nunca por la acera. Los automovilistas deben tratar a los ciclistas como a otros vehículos motorizados. Es obligación del ciclista llevar un casco[6] como medida de seguridad, así como luces[7] y ropa que lo haga claramente visible, aún en condiciones de lluvia y niebla[8].

[1]*zebra* [2]*middle* [3]*yield* [4]*monthly* [5]*change* [6]*helmet* [7]*lights* [8]*fog*

Comprensión

Lee las siguientes oraciones y decide si son ciertas o falsas, según la lectura.

1. Cuando no hay una zona peatonal, los peatones pueden cruzar a la mitad de la calle.
2. Cuando un automóvil sale de un estacionamiento, los peatones deben cederle el paso.
3. Los autobuses solamente recogen pasajeros en las paradas establecidas.
4. Con los pases para autobuses se puede usar el sistema del metro también.
5. No se le puede pagar al chofer del autobús por el pasaje.
6. Los ciclistas deben conducir por la acera para evitar el peligro de los automóviles.

🖳 Más allá

Ahora escribe una lista de tres consejos para andar en bicicleta por la ciudad. Después comparte tu lista en Share It! y lee los consejos de tus compañeros. ¿Hay algo que aparezca en todas las listas de consejos?

Modelo *Los ciclistas deben llevar ropa clara porque los conductores pueden verlos mejor.*

Exploraciones profesionales

El orden público

Vocabulario

Sustantivos

la audiencia	*hearing*
el cinturón de seguridad	*seat belt*
la corte	*court*
los derechos	*rights*
la infracción de tráfico	*traffic violation*
la licencia de conducir	*driver's license*
la placa	*license plate*
el registro	*registration*
el vehículo	*vehicle*

Adjetivos

imparcial	*impartial*
justo(a)	*fair*

Verbos

apelar	*to appeal*
averiguar	*to find out*
cometer	*to commit*

Frases útiles

licencia de conducir y registro del vehículo
driver's license and registration

dar una advertencia
to give a warning

exceso de velocidad
speeding

prohibido girar en U
no U-turn

Tiene el derecho de apelar.
You have the right to appeal.

DATOS IMPORTANTES

Educación: Estudios secundarios completos. Algunos departamentos requieren uno o dos años de cursos universitarios. En ciertos casos se exige título universitario. Se recomiendan cursos complementarios relacionados con educación física.

Salario: Entre $65 000 y $140 000, dependiendo de la agencia, el estado y la experiencia

Dónde se trabaja: Departamentos de Policía Estatal

Vocabulario nuevo Completa las oraciones con la palabra apropiada de la lista de vocabulario.

1. Debes ponerte el _____ para protegerte si tienes un accidente.

2. El policía quiere ver mi _____ y _____ de mi auto.

3. Tienes el derecho de _____ la decisión de la corte.

4. El policía no le dio una multa, solo le dio una _____.

5. Puedes recibir una multa si cometes una _____.

© Hill Street Studios/Blend Images/Getty Images

Robert Licata, policía estatal

Robert Licata es un policía estatal. Trabaja en las autopistas para que los conductores respeten las reglas de tránsito. En el video vas a ver al Sr. Licata hablando seriamente con una conductora.

Antes de ver

Los policías estatales deben ser imparciales cuando hablan con los conductores que cometen infracciones. Simplemente les dicen qué infracción cometieron, los derechos que tienen y lo que deben hacer. También deben tener cuidado porque no saben si las personas que están en los vehículos pueden atacarlos. ¿Cómo te sientes si un policía detiene tu vehículo? ¿Crees que es conveniente hablar mucho con el policía? ¿Cómo reaccionas si crees que no cometiste ninguna infracción?

Comprensión

1. ¿Qué le pide el policía a la conductora cuando se acerca al auto?
2. ¿En dónde cometió infracciones la conductora?
3. ¿Qué infracciones cometió?
4. ¿Qué excusa da la conductora por las infracciones cometidas?
5. ¿Por qué cantidad es la multa que le da el policía?
6. ¿Por qué el policía no le dio una advertencia?
7. ¿Qué averiguó el policía con la placa del vehículo?
8. ¿Qué solución posible le da el policía a la conductora?

Después de ver

En parejas, representen a un policía y a una persona que hizo algo incorrecto. Demuestren cómo debe actuar el policía, lo que le pide a la persona, qué preguntas le hace y cómo le responde la persona.

9.35 **Una fiesta de quince años** Completa el párrafo con la forma necesaria del pretérito o del imperfecto del verbo entre paréntesis.

El sábado pasado yo (**1.**) _____ (ir) a una fiesta de quince años.

(**2.**) _____ (Haber) muchas personas y yo (**3.**) _____ (conocer) a

Rosaura. Yo (**4.**) _____ (hablar) con la quinceañera Zulema cuando la

(**5.**) _____ (ver) entrar. (**6.**) _____ (Ser) muy guapa y (**7.**) _____

(llevar) un vestido azul. Zulema me (**8.**) _____ (decir) que (**9.**) _____

(ser) su prima. Yo (**10.**) _____ (querer) conocerla y Zulema nos

(**11.**) _____ (presentar). Yo le (**12.**) _____ (pedir) bailar y ella

(**13.**) _____ (aceptar). Nosotros (**14.**) _____ (bailar) toda la noche y

(**15.**) _____ (divertirse) mucho. Ahora Rosaura es mi novia.

9.36 **Un día en el parque** Decide cuál es la relación de las dos acciones. Luego combínalas en una oración usando la forma apropiada del pretérito o del imperfecto.

Modelo Hacer sol / Mateo estar aburrido en casa
   Hacía sol y Mateo estaba aburrido en casa.

1. Mateo querer jugar en el parque / Él invitar a su amigo Ariel a jugar
2. Ariel pedirle permiso a su mamá / Ella decirle que sí
3. Los niños hablar y reír / Ellos caminar al parque
4. Mateo y Ariel llegar al parque / Ellos decidir trepar un árbol
5. Ariel trepar el árbol / Mateo mirarlo
6. Una rama *(branch)* romperse / Ariel caerse
7. Ariel no poder levantarse / Él llorar
8. Mateo asustarse / Él correr a buscar a la mamá de Ariel

9.37 **El Año Nuevo** Ramiro habla de la fiesta del Año Nuevo. Completa sus oraciones para contar lo que pasó. Deben usar el pretérito y el imperfecto.

1. Cuando era niño siempre…
2. El año pasado decidí hacer una fiesta y…
3. Los invitados empezaron a llegar mientras yo…
4. Me alegré mucho cuando…
5. Algunas personas bailaban mientras otras…
6. Cuando el reloj dio la medianoche, todos…

Fuegos artificiales sobre Chichén Itzá

9.38 **Una historia interesante** Con un compañero escojan fotos diferentes y describan lo que pasó usando las preguntas como guía. ¡**OJO!** Presta atención al uso del pretérito y del imperfecto.

1. ¿Dónde estaban? ¿Por qué?
2. ¿Qué hacían?
3. ¿Qué pasó?
4. ¿Cómo se resolvió la situación?

9.39 **El periodista** Un periodista habla con un testigo sobre el accidente que vio. Trabaja con un compañero. Uno de ustedes es el periodista y hace las siguientes preguntas, prestando atención al uso del pretérito o el imperfecto. El otro es el testigo y mira los dibujos en el **Apéndice B** para responder las preguntas.

1. ¿Qué tiempo (hacer)?
2. ¿Quién (conducir) el coche rojo?
3. ¿A qué hora (ocurrir) el accidente?
4. ¿Qué (pasar)?
5. ¿(Haber) testigos?
6. ¿Cuándo (llegar) la ambulancia?

9.40 Con un compañero van a organizar una fiesta.

Paso 1 Decidan qué van a celebrar. Luego necesitan planear todos los detalles:

¿Dónde y cuándo va a ser la celebración?
¿A quiénes van a invitar?
¿Cómo van a decorar?
¿Qué van a ofrecerles a los invitados para beber y comer?
¿Qué actividades va a haber en la fiesta (música viva, baile, juegos, etcétera)?
¿A qué hora va a empezar y a terminar su fiesta?

Paso 2 Repórtenle a la clase los detalles de su fiesta.

Vocabulario 1

En la fiesta

los banderines	*streamers*
los bocadillos	*snacks*
el brindis	*toast*
el champán	*champagne*
el desfile	*parade*
los dulces	*candies*
el festejo	*party, celebration*
los fuegos artificiales	*fireworks*
los globos	*balloons*
el grupo de música	*music group/ band*

la invitación	*invitation*
el invitado	*guest*
los novios	*bride and groom*
el pastel	*cake*
la piñata	*piñata*
la quinceañera	*girl celebrating her fifteenth birthday*
el regalo	*gift*
la serenata	*serenade*
la vela	*candle*

Las celebraciones

el aniversario	*anniversary*
el bautizo	*baptism*
la boda	*wedding*
el cumpleaños	*birthday*
la graduación	*graduation*
las posadas	*nine-day celebration before Christmas*

los quince años	*a girl's fifteenth birthday celebration*
el santo	*saint's day*

Verbos

brindar	*to toast*
casarse (con)	*to get married (to)*
celebrar	*to celebrate*
cumplir años	*to turn (x) years old*

decorar	*to decorate*
disfrutar	*to enjoy*
romper	*to break*
terminar	*to finish*

Diccionario personal

_____
_____
_____
_____
_____
_____
_____
_____
_____

◀)) Vocabulario 2

En la calle

la acera	*sidewalk*
la ambulancia	*ambulance*
la camilla	*stretcher*
la carretera	*highway*
el (la) ciclista	*cyclist*
el (la) conductor(a)	*driver*
el cruce	*crosswalk*
la esquina	*corner*
el límite de velocidad	*speed limit*
la multa	*fine, ticket*
el paramédico	*paramedic*
el parquímetro	*parking meter*
la patrulla	*police car*
el peatón (la peatona)	*pedestrian*
el poste	*post*
el puente	*bridge*
el semáforo	*traffic light*
la señal	*sign*
el servicio de emergencias	*emergency service*
el (la) testigo	*witness*

Los verbos

aburrirse	*to become bored*
alegrarse	*to become happy*
asustarse	*to become frightened*
atravesar (ie)	*to cross*
atropellar	*to run over*
bajar de	*to get out of (a vehicle)*
caer(se)	*to fall*
chocar (con)	*to crash (into)*
cruzar	*to cross*
dañar	*to damage*
distraerse	*to get distracted*
enojarse	*to become angry*
esperar	*to wait*
estacionarse	*to park*
frustrarse	*to become frustrated*
pasarse un semáforo en rojo	*to run a red light*
pasarse una señal de PARE	*to run a stop sign*
sentirse	*to feel*
sorprenderse	*to be surprised*
subir a	*to get into (a vehicle)*
tropezar (ie)	*to trip*

Expresiones adicionales

de repente	*suddenly*
estar dañado(a)	*to be damaged*
estar herido(a)	*to be injured*

Diccionario personal

_____

_____

_____

_____

_____

_____

Learning Strategy

Use Spanish every time you talk in class

Try to use Spanish for all your classroom interactions, not just when called on by the instructor or answering a classmate's question in a group activity. Don't worry that your sentences may not be structurally correct; the important thing is to begin to feel comfortable expressing yourself in the language. You might even initiate a conversation with your instructor or another classmate before or after class.

In this chapter you will learn how to:

- Give and receive directions
- Make travel arrangements
- Book and talk about hotel accommodations
- Suggest activities
- Make informal and formal requests

¿Adónde vas a viajar?

© Digital Vision/JupiterImages

La señora Torres no viaja con frecuencia, pero sabe que es mejor viajar con poco equipaje.

Para viajar en avión o tren

el (la) agente de seguridad	security agent
el cinturón de seguridad	safety (seat) belt
el coche cama	sleeping car
la conexión	connection
la escala	layover
la litera	bunk bed
la parada	stop
el pase de abordar	boarding pass
el reclamo de equipaje	baggage claim
el vuelo	flight

Verbos

abordar	to board
aterrizar	to land
despegar	to take off
doblar	to turn
pasar por seguridad	to pass through security
perder	to miss (a flight, a train)
seguir derecho	to go straight

Palabras adicionales

a tiempo	on time
la aduana	customs

el asiento	seat
la estación de autobuses	bus station
la llegada	arrival
retrasado(a)	delayed
la sala de espera	waiting room
la salida	departure
la visa	visa

INVESTIGUEMOS EL VOCABULARIO

In Latin America, a plane or train ticket is **un pasaje** or **un boleto; un boleto** also refers to a ticket for an event. However, in Spain, a train or a plane ticket is **un billete,** and a ticket for an event is **una entrada.** It is also important to note that while **primera clase** is used for both trains and airplanes, **segunda clase** is used only for trains. For air travel, coach class is known as **clase turista.**

A practicar

10.1 **Escucha y responde** Vas a escuchar una serie de ideas sobre viajar por tren o por avión. Indica con el pulgar hacia arriba si son lógicas, y con el pulgar hacia abajo si son ilógicas.

2-18

10.2 **A viajar** Escribe la palabra lógica del vocabulario que mejor complete la oración.

En el aeropuerto:

1. Debemos obtener un _____ antes de subir a un avión.

2. En el mostrador de la aerolínea, un dependiente nos pregunta si preferimos ventanilla o _____.

3. Antes de _____ y de aterrizar debemos ponernos _____.

En la estación de trenes:

4. Este tren va directamente a su destino, no hace ninguna _____.

5. Compramos un boleto en _____ y después caminamos al _____ para abordar el tren.

6. _____ nos pide nuestros boletos en el tren.

7. Llevamos nuestra ropa en _____ cuando viajamos.

10.3 **Asociaciones** Con un compañero, relacionen las palabras de las dos columnas y expliquen la relación entre ellas.

1. _____ retrasado		**a.** el equipaje
2. _____ la taquilla		**b.** el revisor
3. _____ la ventanilla		**c.** a tiempo
4. _____ aterrizar		**d.** la salida
5. _____ facturar		**e.** el boleto
6. _____ el asistente de vuelo		**f.** la visa
7. _____ la llegada		**g.** el pasillo
8. _____ el pasaporte		**h.** despegar

10.4 **Conversación** Trabaja con un compañero para contestar las preguntas.

1. ¿Alguna vez viajaste por tren? ¿Cuándo? ¿Adónde? ¿Te gustó la experiencia? ¿Por qué?
2. ¿Alguna vez viajaste en autobús? ¿Adónde fuiste? ¿Te dieron un buen servicio?
3. ¿Viajas por avión con frecuencia? ¿Por qué?
4. ¿Qué te gusta y qué no te gusta de viajar por avión?
5. ¿Qué es necesario hacer para tener un buen viaje por avión? ¿Y por tren?
6. ¿Piensas que trabajar en un avión o un tren es un buen trabajo? ¿Por qué?
7. ¿Cuáles son las ventajas de viajar por tren? ¿Por avión? ¿Por autobús?

10.5 **Situaciones** En parejas, túrnense para hablar sobre las fotografías. Usen las preguntas de la lista e inventen todos los detalles.

¿Quiénes son las personas y dónde están?   ¿Adónde van a viajar?

¿Qué están haciendo y por qué?   ¿Cómo crees que va a ser su viaje?

© Losevsky Pavel/Shutterstock

© Patryk Kosmider/Shutterstock

10.6 **¿Vamos por tren o por avión?** Tu compañero y tú están estudiando en Quito, Ecuador, y quieren viajar este fin de semana. Deben decidir si van a viajar por avión a Cuenca, o por tren a Latacunga. Uno de ustedes puede ver la información para viajar por avión en esta página y el otro va a ver la información para viajar por tren en el **Apéndice B.** Intercambien la información y tomen notas. Después van a ponerse de acuerdo *(agree)* en cómo van a viajar y a qué hora. Compartan toda la información antes de decidir.

> **INVESTIGA LA MÚSICA**
>
> Charly García is a famous rock singer from Argentina. Look for his song "No voy en tren, voy en avión" on the Internet. Why do you think he prefers to travel by plane?

AEROPUERTO INTERNACIONAL DE QUITO

Ruta Quito–Cuenca:	Salida	Llegada	Regreso*	Precio por pasajero
	4:35 AM	5:27 AM	6:00 AM	$129,00
	7:50 AM	8:40 AM	1:30 PM	$138,00
	10:00 PM	10:50 PM	11:00 PM	$145,99
*Horario de regreso el día siguiente				

Cultura

Los festivales son una buena oportunidad para ver la cultura de un país y una oportunidad para atraer turistas. Dos ejemplos conocidos de España son el Festival de San Fermín, en Pamplona, y el de la Tomatina, en Buñol. Sin embargo, hay muchos más festivales y carnavales de gran interés en otros países hispanos. Por ejemplo, en Bolivia se celebra el Festival de Oruro, una de las más grandes celebraciones de la cultura andina. El carnaval es un ejemplo de sincretismo (la combinación de diferentes creencias), ya que originalmente celebraba a la Pachamama (una diosa inca que representa a la madre naturaleza), pero se mezcló con tradiciones católicas de los europeos cuando los españoles impusieron su religión. La celebración se centra ahora alrededor de la Virgen del Socavón, virgen que apareció en una importante mina de plata (silver) en 1789.

Investiga y escribe una descripción de uno de estos festivales.

El Carnaval de Barranquilla, Colombia

El Carnaval del País (Carnaval de Gualeguaychú), Argentina

El Festival Casals, Puerto Rico

El Festival del Tango de Buenos Aires, Argentina

El Festival Iberoamericano de Teatro, Colombia

El Festival Internacional Cervantino, Guanajuato, México

Un desfile durante el Festival de Oruro, en Bolivia

 Después de investigar una de estas fiestas o un festival del **Apéndice A**, sube tu descripción del festival y una foto a Share It! Lee las descripciones de tus compañeros. ¿A cuáles de las fiestas te gustaría asistir?

Investiga otros festivales que se celebran en los países hispanohablantes como Cuba, El Salvador o España, en **Exploraciones del mundo hispano** en el **Apéndice A.**

Comparaciones

A veces es necesario obtener una visa para visitar ciertos países. El requisito depende de la nacionalidad del viajero y del tiempo que va a permanecer (to stay) de visita en otro país. Los ciudadanos de los Estados Unidos generalmente no necesitan visa para visitar España ni para viajar a la mayoría de los países hispanoamericanos si su visita va a durar menos de tres meses, pero hay excepciones como Paraguay, país que requiere visa. Para conseguirla se debe completar una solicitud que se puede obtener fácilmente en las páginas web del Consulado de Paraguay. La solicitud debe enviarse al consulado junto con el pasaporte, dos fotografías y la cuota (fee) debida. En realidad, la obtención de la visa es sencilla comparada con los requisitos de otros países.

Paraguay es uno de los países que les pide visa a los ciudadanos de los Estados Unidos que visitan este país.

Si tienes amigos latinoamericanos, pregúntales qué requisitos hay para visitar los Estados Unidos. Si no conoces a ningún latinoamericano, investiga en Internet. Averigua (Find out) si los requisitos son los mismos para los ciudadanos de España. Repórtale a la clase la información sobre los requisitos.

Conexiones... a la economía

De acuerdo con la UNWTO (*United Nations World Tourism Organization*), más de 50 millones de personas visitan España cada año (la cifra fue de casi 60,6 millones en el 2013) y unos 22 millones visitan México anualmente. Estos son los dos países hispanos más visitados en el mundo, pero para muchos otros países hispanos los ingresos económicos que trae el turismo son una parte fundamental de su economía, como es el caso de Costa Rica, Cuba y la República Dominicana. ¿Qué efecto piensas que tiene el turismo en países que reciben a muchos visitantes extranjeros? ¿Cuánto dinero gastas tú cuando vas de vacaciones? ¿Quién crees que trabaja más en carreras relacionadas con el turismo: los hombres o las mujeres? ¿Qué porcentaje de personas en el mundo crees que trabaja en turismo? A continuación puedes leer algunas estadísticas sorprendentes sobre el turismo:

Aeropuerto Internacional Ministro Pistarini, en Buenos Aires, más conocido como Ezeiza

- En 2012 las llegadas de turistas internacionales en todo el mundo fueron más de 1000 millones, lo que significa que la industria del turismo sigue creciendo.
- Se calcula que entre el 6 y el 7% del total de puestos de trabajo en el mundo están relacionados con el turismo. Se calcula que en el año 2013 el turismo representó casi el 3% de la economía mundial.
- También en el año 2013 más de la mitad de los viajeros llegó a sus destinos mediante transporte aéreo (52%), y el 48% viajó por carretera, por ferrocarril (tren) o por barco.

Comunidad

Visita un lugar turístico o un hotel de tu comunidad y entrevista a un turista. Si es posible, elige a alguien que hable español. Averigua de dónde es, por qué está en los Estados Unidos y por cuánto tiempo, qué lugares visitó y qué lugares va a visitar, lo que le gusta de Estados Unidos y lo que no le gusta. Recuerda ser respetuoso con el turista y explicarle que es una tarea para tu clase y que necesitas solamente unos pocos minutos. Después repórtale la información a la clase. Puedes empezar con estas preguntas:

¿De dónde es usted?
¿Por qué está de visita en los Estados Unidos?
¿Por cuánto tiempo va a estar en los Estados Unidos?

¿De dónde son ustedes?

A analizar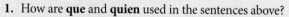

Santiago va a viajar con Nicolás a Puerto Rico. Mira el video. Después lee parte de su conversación y observa el uso de los pronombres **que** y **quien** y contesta las preguntas que siguen.

Nicolás: A mis padres siempre les gusta conocer a las personas con **quienes** estudio en Nueva York. Además, mi hermana quiere conocer al amigo guapo **que** está en las fotos conmigo.

Santiago: ¡Puerto Rico es un país **que** siempre he querido *(have wanted)* conocer!

Nicolás: Estoy seguro que te va a gustar. Tiene playas **que** son muy bonitas y varios lugares turísticos **que** debes conocer.

1. How are **que** and **quien** used in the sentences above?

2. Look at the nouns immediately preceding each use of **que** and **quienes**. How do you determine whether you should use **que** or **quien**?

A comprobar

Relative pronouns and adverbs

1. The relative pronouns **que** and **quien** are used to combine two sentences with a common noun or pronoun into one sentence.

> Rodrigo tiene un coche.
> *Rodrigo has a car.*
>
> El coche no consume mucha gasolina.
> *The car doesn't consume a lot of gas.*
>
> Rodrigo tiene un coche **que** no consume mucha gasolina.
> *Rodrigo has a car **that** doesn't use much gas.*

2. **Que** is the most commonly used relative pronoun. It can be used to refer to people or things.

> Este es el tren **que** va a Córdoba.
> *This is the train **that** goes to Córdoba.*
>
> El hombre **que** tiene la camisa azul es el conductor.
> *The man **that** has the blue shirt is the driver.*

3. In English, the relative pronoun can sometimes be omitted; in Spanish, however, it must be used.

> Los boletos **que** compraste son para primera clase.
> *The tickets **(that)** you bought are for first class.*

4. **Quien(es)** refers only to people and is used after a personal **a** or a preposition (**a, con, de, para, por, en**).

> Esta es la señora **a quien** le debes dar el boleto.
> *This is the lady **to whom** you should give the ticket.*
>
> Las personas **con quienes** viajo están en mi clase.
> *The people **with whom** I am traveling are in my class.*

5. **Quien(es)** may replace **que** when the dependent clause is set off by commas.

> Los pasajeros, **quienes/que** viajan en este vuelo, ya abordaron.
> *The passengers, **who** are traveling on this flight, already boarded.*

6. When referring to places, you will need to use the relative adverb **donde**, without an accent.

> La parada **donde** debes esperar está al otro lado de la calle.
> *The stop **where** you should wait is on the other side of the street.*

*Notice that the pronouns **donde, que,** and **quien(es)** do not have accents.

A practicar

10.7 **¿Es lógico?** Lee las oraciones y decide si son lógicas o no.

1. El pasajero es la persona que viaja.
2. La taquilla es el papel que necesitas para abordar el avión.
3. El andén es el lugar donde debes esperar el autobús.
4. El revisor, quien trabaja en el aeropuerto, necesita ver el pasaporte.
5. El asistente de vuelo es la persona a quien le debes pedir la bebida.
6. Un vuelo que hace escala es directo.

10.8 **Ciudad del Este** Completa el siguiente párrafo con los pronombres relativos **que** y **quien(es).**

Matilde es la amiga con (**1.**) _____ paso mucho tiempo los fines de semana. El fin de semana pasado decidimos visitar a una amiga (**2.**) _____ vive en Ciudad del Este. Nos encontramos en la estación de autobús (**3.**) _____ está en el centro. Allí compramos los boletos y subimos al autobús (**4.**) _____ estaba estacionado. El autobús estaba lleno y tuve que sentarme al lado de una señora (**5.**) _____ viajaba con su hijo (**6.**) _____ lloró todo el viaje.

Matilde es la amiga con quien fui a Ciudad del Este.

Después de unas horas llegamos a Ciudad del Este y vimos a nuestra amiga Pilar, (**7.**) _____ estaba muy contenta de vernos. Cuando llegamos a la casa, Teresa y Daniela, las chicas con (**8.**) _____ vive Pilar, abrieron la puerta. Pasamos horas charlando en la sala; nos contamos historias de nuestras familias, de los chicos con (**9.**) _____ salimos, de las clases (**10.**) _____ tenemos este semestre... de todo. Finalmente, a las dos de la mañana decidimos (**11.**) _____ era hora de acostarnos.

10.9 **Oraciones cortas** Con un compañero, usen los relativos **donde, que** y **quien(es)** para combinar las dos oraciones.

Modelo Tengo una maleta. La maleta es muy grande. *Tengo una maleta que es muy grande.*

1. Tengo el boleto. Compré el boleto en la taquilla.
2. Los pasajeros subieron al autobús. El autobús llegó a la parada.
3. Zacarías es un amigo. Yo voy a viajar con Zacarías.
4. El revisor les pidió los boletos a los pasajeros. Los pasajeros viajaban en tren.
5. El agente miró mi pasaporte. El agente estaba sentado detrás del mostrador.
6. Ella es la agente. Puedes hablar con ella.
7. Aquí está el asiento. El asiento corresponde a tu boleto.
8. Tienes que ir a la aduana. En la aduana van a revisar tu equipaje.

10.10 **Oraciones incompletas** Trabaja con un compañero para completar las siguientes oraciones de una forma original. Usen los pronombres relativos **que** o **quien(es)**.

Modelo Tuve una clase...
    Estudiante 1: *Tuve una clase que fue muy difícil, ¿y tú?*
    Estudiante 2: *Tuve una clase que no me gustó.*

1. Tengo el boleto...

2. Conozco a una persona...

3. Tengo un amigo...

4. Mi mejor amigo es la persona...

5. Hay muchas personas...

6. Vi una película...

7. Tuve un profesor...

8. Tengo unos amigos...

10.11 **Definiciones** Con un compañero, túrnense para dar una definición de una de las siguientes palabras y el otro debe decidir cuál es la palabra que se está definiendo. Deben usar **donde, que** y **quien(es)**.

Modelo el asistente de vuelo → *Es la persona que sirve refrescos en un avión.*
    el asiento → *Es el lugar donde te sientas en el avión o el tren.*

el boleto   el pase de abordar   el pasajero

el revisor   el andén   la taquilla

el piloto   el equipaje   la litera

La asistente de vuelo es la persona que ayuda a los pasajeros en un avión.

10.12 **A conocernos** En parejas, túrnense para preguntar y responder. Comiencen sus respuestas con las palabras entre paréntesis y usen los relativos **donde, que** y **quien(es)** como en el modelo. Deben explicar sus respuestas.

Modelo ¿Qué día de la semana estás más ocupado? (el día de la semana)
    Estudiante 1: *¿Qué día de la semana estás más ocupado?*
    Estudiante 2: *El día de la semana que estoy más ocupado es el lunes porque tengo cuatro clases.*

1. ¿Qué música te gusta? (la música)

2. ¿Con quién hablas cuando tienes problemas? (la persona)

3. ¿Qué materia es muy difícil para ti? (la materia)

4. ¿Qué día feriado te gusta más? (el día feriado)

5. ¿Para quiénes compras muchos regalos? (las personas)

6. ¿Qué tienda prefieres para comprar ropa? (la tienda)

7. ¿Qué profesión te parece *(seems)* interesante? (la profesión)

8. ¿A quién le dices tus secretos? (la persona)

A analizar

Santiago va a viajar con Nicolás a Puerto Rico. Mira el video otra vez. Después lee parte de la bienvenida que el asistente de vuelo les da a los pasajeros y contesta las preguntas que siguen.

> Por favor **pongan** su equipaje de mano debajo de sus asientos, o en los compartimientos en la parte superior de la cabina, y **tengan** cuidado si abren los compartimientos durante el vuelo. **Suban** las bandejas plegables *(tray tables)*, regresen sus asientos a su posición vertical y pónganse el cinturón de seguridad. Por favor, **miren** hacia el frente y **escuchen** con atención las instrucciones sobre lo que deben hacer en caso de emergencia.

1. The verbs in bold are commands. What are the infinitives for those verbs?

2. What do you notice about how the verbs are conjugated?

A comprobar

Formal and **nosotros** commands

1. When we tell someone to do something, we use commands, known as **mandatos** in Spanish. Formal commands are used with people you would address with **usted** and **ustedes**; however, these personal pronouns must be left out when using commands. To form these commands, drop the **-o** from the present tense first person (**yo** form) and add the opposite ending [**-e(n)** for **-ar** verbs, and **-a(n)** for **-er** and **-ir** verbs].

present tense first person		formal command
hablo	→	habl**e(n)**
hago	→	hag**a(n)**
sirvo	→	sirv**a(n)**

Pida más información en el mostrador.
Ask for more information at the counter.

Facturen su equipaje primero.
Check in your bags first.

*Notice that verbs that have a stem change or are irregular in the present tense follow the same pattern in formal commands.

2. Negative formal commands are formed by placing **no** in front of the verb.

> **No** pierdan los pasaportes.
> *Don't lose the passports.*

3. Infinitives that end in **-car** and **-gar** have spelling changes in order to maintain the same sound as the infinitive. Infinitives that end in **-zar** also have a spelling change.

-**car**	buscar → bus**que(n)**
-**gar**	llegar → lle**gue(n)**
-**zar**	empezar → empie**ce(n)**

4. The following verbs have irregular command forms.

dar	**dé (den)**
estar	**esté(n)**
ir	**vaya(n)**
saber	**sepa(n)**
ser	**sea(n)**

5. To make suggestions with *Let's,* use commands in the **nosotros** form. **Nosotros** commands are very similar to formal commands. Add **-emos** for **-ar** verbs, and **-amos** for **-er** and **-ir** verbs.

infinitive	formal command	*nosotros* command
sacar	saque(n)	saqu**emos**
beber	beba(n)	beb**amos**
venir	venga(n)	veng**amos**

Estamos atrasados. **¡Corramos!**
*We are late. **Let's run!***

Salgamos por la mañana.
***Let's leave** in the morning.*

6. The **nosotros** forms of the irregular verbs are also similar to the formal commands.

dar	**demos**
estar	**estemos**
saber	**sepamos**
ser	**seamos**

7. Ir has two different **nosotros** command forms. The present tense **vamos** is commonly used with affirmative commands and **vayamos** is used with negative commands.

¡Vamos a Perú!
***Let's go** to Peru!*

No vayamos en tren.
***Let's not go** by train.*

8. -Ar and **-er** verbs with stem changes do not change in **nosotros** commands. However, **-ir** verbs do have a stem change.

infinitive	present tense	*nosotros* command
cerrar	cerramos	cerremos
volver	volvemos	volvamos
pedir	pedimos	p**i**damos
dormir	dormimos	d**u**rmamos

A practicar

10.13 **¿Qué hago?** Pablo y Verónica van a hacer su primer viaje internacional y un amigo les explicó lo que tienen que hacer. Ordena sus instrucciones lógicamente.

_____ Pasen por la aduana.

_____ Compren el boleto.

_____ Lleguen al aeropuerto dos horas antes del vuelo.

_____ Consigan un pasaporte.

_____ Facturen las maletas.

_____ Confirmen el vuelo el día anterior.

10.14 **¿Qué dicen?** En parejas, túrnense para dar un mandato lógico de lo que las siguientes personas dirían *(would say)*. Usen los verbos entre paréntesis.

Modelo el agente de la aduana a un turista (abrir) *Abra su maleta.*

1. un asistente de vuelo a los pasajeros (poner)

2. un agente de seguridad a un pasajero (venir)

3. un agente de viajes a un cliente (conseguir)

4. un agente en el aeropuerto a un pasajero (ir)

5. un piloto a los asistentes de vuelo (volver)

6. un policía a un automovilista (conducir)

7. un guía a un grupo de turistas (mirar)

8. un revisor en el tren a un pasajero (comprar)

10.15 **Instrucciones** Estás en el hotel y le preguntas al recepcionista cómo llegar a varios destinos. Mira el plano y lee las instrucciones. Debes indicar dónde estás al final.

Vocabulario útil: la cuadra *block*

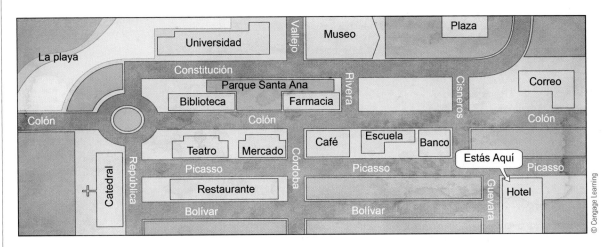

1. Siga derecho por la calle Guevara. Doble a la izquierda en la calle Picasso. Siga derecho hasta la calle República. Está enfrente.

2. Siga derecho en la calle Bolívar hasta la calle República y doble a la derecha. Pase la biblioteca y en la calle Constitución, doble a la derecha otra vez. Está a la izquierda.

3. Siga derecho en la calle Bolívar hasta la calle Córdoba. Doble a la derecha. Cruce la calle Picasso y luego doble a la izquierda en la calle Colón. Pase el parque y está a la derecha.

10.16 **Perdidos** Imagínense que son turistas y no conocen la ciudad. Túrnense para preguntarse y responderse cómo llegar del hotel a los diferentes lugares. Usen el plano de la **Actividad 10.15.**

Modelo   el café
Estudiante 1: *¿Cómo llego al café?*
Estudiante 2: *Atraviese la calle y vaya a la calle Bolívar. Camine hasta la calle Córdoba. Doble a la derecha y siga una cuadra más. El café está en la esquina de la calle Córdoba y la calle Picasso.*

1. el museo   4. el restaurante   7. el correo
2. la playa   5. la catedral   8. el teatro
3. el banco   6. la biblioteca   9. la plaza

10.17 **¿Qué recomiendas?** Trabaja con un compañero para darle recomendaciones a cada una de las siguientes personas. Usen los mandatos formales.

Modelo   El señor Sánchez va a salir de viaje.
Lleve poco equipaje.

1. La señorita Laredo siempre se aburre en los vuelos largos.

2. La señora Ramírez tiene miedo de viajar en avión.

3. Los señores Márquez siempre tienen mucha hambre cuando viajan.

4. El señor Vargas siempre olvida cosas cuando viaja.

5. La señora Castro va a viajar en tren por primera vez.

6. Los señores Gómez van a viajar con sus hijos pequeños en autobús.

7. Está nevando y la aerolínea canceló el vuelo de Miguel.

8. José Ramón está viajando de México a Madrid y el pasajero a su lado ronca *(snores).*

INVESTIGUEMOS LA MÚSICA

Mecano was a Spanish pop group. Listen to their song "No me enseñen la lección." What does the student ask of the teacher? Can you identify with this student's experience?

10.18 **Un viaje** Con un compañero, hagan planes para hacer un viaje. Usen los mandatos en la forma de **nosotros** para expresar sus deseos.

Modelo adónde quieren ir

    Estudiante 1: *Vamos a Cancún.*

    Estudiante 2: *¡Buena idea! / No vayamos a Cancún, vamos a Puerto Rico.*

1. adónde quieren ir
2. cuándo quieren salir
3. cuánto dinero quieren llevar
4. cómo quieren viajar
5. dónde quieren dormir
6. qué quieren hacer
7. qué recuerdos *(souvenirs)* desean comprar

10.19 **Una escena** Con un compañero, escojan una de las fotos e inventen el diálogo. Usen mandatos en la conversación.

En vivo

Entrando en materia

Imagina que un amigo va a viajar por avión por primera vez y no sabe cómo prepararse. ¿Qué le recomiendas?

Un mensaje de la Secretaría de Transporte

2-19 Anticipando un gran número de pasajeros debido al *(due to)* período vacacional, la Secretaría de Transporte preparó el mensaje que vas a escuchar a continuación. Escucha el mensaje y responde las preguntas que siguen.

Vocabulario útil

la cuota	*fee*	las joyas	*jewelry*
el dolor de cabeza	*headache*	el (la) menor de edad	*minor, underage*
la etiqueta	*label*	el tamaño	*size*

© Sveta San/Shutterstock

Comprensión

1. ¿Cuántas maletas puede llevar un pasajero como equipaje de mano si viaja por avión?
2. ¿Qué artículos se recomienda llevar en el equipaje de mano?
3. ¿Por qué recomiendan tomar agua?
4. ¿Cuál es el tamaño máximo de geles o líquidos en el equipaje de mano?
5. ¿Qué necesitan los menores de edad para viajar?
6. ¿Con cuánto tiempo de anticipación recomiendan llegar antes de un vuelo internacional?

Más allá

Decide si prefieres viajar en avión, coche, autobús o por tren y explica por qué. Después escribe una lista de cinco recomendaciones lógicas para viajar (en avión, coche, autobús o por tren) y compártela con tus compañeros en Share It! Lee las recomendaciones de los otros.

Lectura

Antes de leer

¿Qué sitios de Latinoamérica o España piensas que son los más populares entre los turistas? ¿Por qué?

A leer

¿Adónde ir de vacaciones?

Todos los países en donde se habla español ofrecen una cantidad impresionante de atractivos turísticos, ya sea por su geografía o por su interés cultural, e incluso por su interés deportivo. El turismo es importante para la economía de muchos países hispanos. Un ejemplo es España, país que recibe *around* **alrededor** de 60 millones de visitantes al año. Esta cifra es más significativa porque la población total de España es de aproximadamente unos 40 millones de habitantes. En México, tan solo en la ciudad de Cancún hay alrededor de 30 000 habitaciones para turistas. Esta ciudad recibe más de dos millones y medio de visitantes cada año. El turismo es la mayor fuente de ingresos en Costa Rica, donde le da trabajo a más del 13% de la población del país. Sería imposible resumir en un artículo breve la gran diversidad de lugares de interés, así que en este espacio vamos a describir solamente tres destinos turísticos que son poco conocidos entre los turistas estadounidenses.

[El turismo es importante para la economía de muchos países]

© Ramiro Olaciregui/Getty Images

Bariloche, Argentina
Esta ciudad está en la Patagonia argentina, en una zona montañosa. Casi inmediatamente después de su fundación empezaron a llegar los primeros turistas. Sin embargo, fue con la construcción de los medios de transporte que Bariloche se hizo popular. Aunque en 1912 llegó el primer avión a este lugar, cuando se hizo realmente popular fue con la llegada de *railways* los **ferrocarriles** en 1934. En esta época se iniciaron en esta zona los deportes invernales como el esquí y el snowboard.

surrounded by   Hoy en día Bariloche es una hermosa ciudad turística, **rodeada de** paisajes increíbles, ideal para practicar deportes invernales y para hacer innumerables actividades como ir de excursión, visitar museos, montar a caballo y practicar el rafting.

Cartagena, Colombia

Cartagena es una ciudad especial por muchas razones. Su centro histórico fue declarado Patrimonio de la Humanidad por la UNESCO en 1985. Debido a su localización y al hecho de ser puerto y **bahía,** en Cartagena se guardaban **el oro** y otros tesoros antes de embarcarlos a España. En consecuencia, la ciudad prosperó mucho, pero desafortunadamente también atrajo los ataques frecuentes de piratas. Por eso, para finales del siglo XVIII, casi toda la ciudad estaba rodeada por 19 kilómetros de **murallas** que la protegían. Algunos muros llegaron a tener 15 metros de ancho y 12 metros de alto.

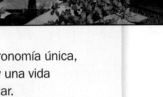

bay
gold

walls

Cartagena fue también el principal puerto al que llegaron los esclavos traídos de África, lo que explica el rico legado cultural de ritmos y arte africanos que se encuentra en la región.

Cartagena es actualmente el puerto de exportación más importante de Colombia, y le ofrece al turista una bellísima ciudad histórica, hoteles de primera clase, una gastronomía única, museos de interés y una vida nocturna espectacular.

El Sunzal, El Salvador

Para los amantes de surfear, El Sunzal es un nombre mundialmente reconocido. La industria del turismo de El Salvador es la que más rápido se está desarrollando en Centroamérica. Además de las bellas playas que este país ofrece, El Salvador también cuenta con volcanes y montañas, parques nacionales y oportunidades para hacer ecoturismo.

Tiene además atracciones históricas, como Joya de Cerén, una comunidad que se conoce como "la Pompeya de Centroamérica" debido a que fue **cubierta** por una erupción volcánica en el año 600 antes de Cristo.

covered

Comprensión

1. ¿Dónde está Bariloche y cuándo se hizo popular?
2. Aparte de los deportes invernales ¿qué otras actividades ofrece Bariloche?
3. ¿Por qué fue importante Cartagena durante la época colonial?
4. ¿Por qué la mayor parte de Cartagena está dentro de murallas?
5. ¿Cuáles son los atractivos de El Salvador para los turistas?

Después de leer

Piensa en una ciudad fascinante que visitaste alguna vez, y escribe una lista de ideas por las que piensas que es una ciudad especial. Primero, comparte tus ideas con un compañero y escucha las suyas. Después suban sus ideas a Share It! y lean las ideas de otros compañeros.

2
Exploraciones léxicas

El señor y la señora Buendía acaban de llegar a su hotel en Bogotá. Se van a quedar cuatro días y esperan tener unas vacaciones fabulosas.

el alojamiento	*lodging*		el (la) turista	*tourist*
la clase turista	*economy class*		de lujo	*luxurious*
disponible	*available*			
el (la) gerente	*manager*		**Verbos**	
la habitación	*single / double /*		alojarse	*to lodge, to stay*
sencilla /	*triple room*			*(in a hotel)*
doble / triple			bajar	*to go down, to take*
el Internet	*wireless Internet*			*(something) down*
inalámbrico			pagar	*to check out*
la sala de	*conference*		(y marcharse)	
conferencias	*center*		quedarse	*to stay*
el servicio a la	*room service*		registrarse	*to check in*
habitación			subir	*to go up, to take (something) up*

INVESTIGUEMOS EL VOCABULARIO

In Latin America, **la camarera** is a maid; in Spain, however, **la camarera** is a waitress.
Another difference in Spain is that **sauna** is feminine but speakers say **el sauna** in most of Latin America. Also, in several South American countries, the verb **cancelar** is used instead of **pagar** to mean *to pay*.

A practicar

10.20 **Escucha y responde** Vas a escuchar cinco comentarios. Decide si los dice el recepcionista o el huésped.

10.21 **En el hotel** Completa las ideas con las palabras del vocabulario que aparecen abajo. No necesitas usarlas todas.

alojamiento	huéspedes	ascensor	sauna	centro de negocios
recepción	recepcionista	botones	habitación	camarera

1. Para entrar en nuestra _____ necesitamos una llave.

2. Cuando llegamos a un hotel, hablamos con el _____.

3. El _____ es la persona que lleva nuestras maletas a la habitación.

4. Los _____ de la habitación 415 desean pedir un taxi.

5. Nuestra habitación está en el décimo piso. ¿Hay _____? Preferimos no usar las escaleras porque tenemos muchas maletas.

6. ¡Qué habitación tan limpia! Debemos recordar darle una buena propina a la _____.

10.22 **Relaciona las palabras** Empareja una palabra de la primera columna con una de la segunda. Después trabaja con un compañero. Túrnense para comparar sus respuestas y explicar la relación entre las dos palabras. Es posible relacionar con más de una palabra.

Modelo la toalla
  la camarera
  La camarera trae las toallas a la habitación.

1. la habitación	**a.** el recepcionista
2. el botones	**b.** la puerta
3. el ascensor	**c.** el sauna
4. la recepción	**d.** las maletas
5. el baño	**e.** las escaleras
6. la llave	**f.** sencilla
7. el huésped	**g.** la camarera

10.23 **Entrevista** Trabaja con un compañero para conversar sobre las siguientes preguntas.

1. ¿Cuándo fue la última vez que te alojaste en un hotel? ¿Por qué te quedaste en el hotel? ¿Recuerdas cuánto pagaste por la habitación?

2. De los hoteles que conoces ¿qué hotel te gusta más y por qué?

3. En tu opinión ¿quién tiene el trabajo más difícil en un hotel (el recepcionista, el botones o el camarero)? ¿Por qué?

4. En tu opinión ¿qué servicios o artículos son muy importantes en una habitación? ¿Y en el hotel?

10.24 **¿Qué hotel elegir?** Tu compañero y tú están planeando unas vacaciones en Costa Rica y hablan por teléfono para decidir qué hotel elegir. Hay solamente dos hoteles que tienen habitaciones disponibles. Uno de ustedes va a mirar la información en esta página y el otro debe mirar el **Apéndice B.** Pregúntense sobre los servicios y decidan al final en qué hotel van a quedarse.

Hotel Monteverde Natural

Descripción: 20 habitaciones disponibles, independientes y rodeadas de jardines

Servicios: baño privado, agua caliente, televisor en todas las habitaciones, vista al Parque Nacional. Desayuno continental incluído en el precio.

Precio: 120.000 colones (habitación doble)

Notas: Para acceder a las habitaciones se debe caminar por senderos y subir escalones. No hay servicio de botones.

Cultura

En España, existen hoteles muy originales que se llaman paradores. Los paradores son hoteles ubicados *(located)* en castillos, monasterios, fortalezas u otros edificios históricos. De esta manera, los españoles conservan sus monumentos nacionales y artísticos y los convierten en un atractivo turístico. Los paradores son económicamente razonables y tienen un estándar de servicio muy alto. Un parador muy famoso es el Parador San Francisco, en Granada. El edificio data del siglo *(century)* XIV, y sirvió como convento en el siglo XV. Este parador es uno de muy pocos en España que recibe la clasificación de Parador Museo.

En Internet o en una guía turística, busca información sobre otro parador en España para saber:
¿Qué tipo de edificio histórico es?
¿Qué servicios ofrece?
¿Cuánto cuesta?

El Parador San Francisco en Granada, España

> Investiga en Internet sobre otros paradores de España y comparte la información y una foto en Share It! Lee la información que subieron dos compañeros sobre otros paradores. ¿Qué parador te gusta más? ¿Por qué?

Comparaciones

Los hoteles no siempre son una opción disponible cuando se quiere visitar lugares remotos o diferentes. Por ejemplo, los visitantes que desean pasar la noche en las islas artificiales de los Uros en el lago Titicaca, en Perú, deben pasar la noche con una familia en una casa hecha en su totalidad de totora, la planta con la que también están hechas las islas.

Para otra visita excepcional, es posible visitar las cuevas *(caves)* Pedro Antonio de Alarcón, en Granada, España, donde los moros se refugiaron durante su expulsión de Granada hace cientos de años. Hoy en día cada cueva es un apartamento con una cocina, un dormitorio y un baño. Algunas cuevas tienen incluso un lujoso jacuzzi o chimenea.

Hotel de Sal en el Salar de Uyuni, Bolivia

Otro hotel poco usual es el Hotel de Sal en el Salar de Uyuni en Bolivia. Este hotel está hecho completamente de sal, incluyendo todos los muebles del hotel.

¿Sabes de hoteles poco convencionales en los Estados Unidos? ¿Por qué son diferentes y dónde están?

Conexiones... a la economía

En muchos países donde se habla español el turismo es un motor importante de la economía. España, por ejemplo, es el tercer país más visitado del mundo, ya que recibe cada año más turistas que su población total. Muchos países latinoamericanos son también importantes destinos turísticos. Entre ellos destaca Costa Rica, país que promueve el ecoturismo. Costa Rica recibe al año más de dos millones de visitantes, lo que significa la mitad de la población de este país. Para Cuba el turismo también es una parte importante de la economía y ha tenido gran influencia en la transformación de la isla. Las playas cubanas son famosas en Europa.

¿Qué impacto crees que el turismo puede tener en la economía de una región y en su cultura?

El turismo es muy importante para la economía de Costa Rica.

 Mira las páginas de **Exploraciones del mundo hispano** en el **Apéndice A.** ¿Cuál es uno de los países qué te gustaría visitar? ¿Por qué?

Comunidad

Visita un hotel en tu comunidad y encuentra un empleado hispano. Hazle preguntas sobre el hotel. Por ejemplo, averigua cuántos empleados hablan español u otros idiomas, en qué áreas trabajan y si reciben muchos huéspedes hispanos. ¿De qué países vienen? Recuerda ser respetuoso y no tomar mucho tiempo. Puedes empezar con estas preguntas.

¿Cuántos empleados en su hotel hablan español?
¿Cuántos empleados en su hotel hablan otros idiomas? ¿Cuáles son?

¿Hay muchos empleados que hablan español?

A analizar

Rosa y Paula se quedaron en un hotel y Rosa está haciendo su maleta. Mira el video. Después lee su conversación, observa las formas de los verbos en negritas y contesta las preguntas.

Rosa:	Necesito mis zapatos rojos. **Mira** debajo de la cama, por favor.
Paula:	No están aquí.
Rosa:	¿Ay, dónde pueden estar?
Paula:	¡Los encontré!
Rosa:	¡Ay, qué bueno!
Paula:	**Toma... Espera,** no la **cierres.** Aquí está tu pañuelo.
Rosa:	¡Ay, gracias Paula! Ya estoy lista. **Llama** al botones, por favor. ¡Mi maleta pesa mucho!
Paula:	Ay, Rosa, tú y tus zapatos. ¡La próxima vez no **traigas** tantos zapatos!

© Cengage Learning

In the conversation above, the informal (**tú**) commands are in bold.

1. How are the affirmative commands formed?
2. How are the negative commands formed?

A comprobar

Informal commands

1. Informal commands are used with people you would address with **tú.** To form the affirmative informal commands, use the third person singular (**él/ella**) of the present tense.

infinitive	affirmative *tú* command
bajar	baja
correr	corre
subir	sube

Llama el hotel para hacer una reservación.
Call the hotel to make a reservation.

Pide* servicio a la habitación.
Ask for room service.

*Notice that stem-changing verbs keep their changes in the informal command forms.

2. The following verbs have irregular forms for the affirmative informal commands.

decir	**di**	salir	**sal**
hacer	**haz**	ser	**sé**
ir	**ve**	tener	**ten**
poner	**pon**	venir	**ven**

Haz la cama, por favor. *Make the bed, please.*

3. When forming negative informal commands use the formal **usted** commands and add an **-s.**

infinitive	usted command	negative *tú* command
ayudar	**ayude**	**no ayudes**
poner	**ponga**	**no pongas**
conducir	**conduzca**	**no conduzcas**
decir	**diga**	**no digas**
ir	**vaya**	**no vayas**

No dejes la llave en la puerta.
Don't leave the key in the door.

No cuelgues las toallas sucias.
Don't hang up the dirty towels.

4. In Spain, **ustedes** commands are formal. To give commands to two or more friends or family members, the Spanish use the informal **vosotros** commands. **Vosotros** affirmative commands are formed by dropping the **-r** from the infinitive and replacing it with a **-d**. Negative commands are formed by using the base of the **usted** commands and adding the **vosotros** ending (**-éis, -áis**).

infinitive	affirmative *vosotros* command	negative *vosotros* command
cerrar	cerr**ad**	**no cerréis**
hacer	hac**ed**	**no hagáis**
ir	**id**	**no vayáis**

A practicar

10.26 **¿Lógico o ilógico?** La familia Domínguez está de viaje y se queda en un hotel. Lee los siguientes mandatos que la señora Domínguez le da a su hijo de 5 años y decide si son lógicos o no. Corrige los mandatos ilógicos.

1. No hagas mucho ruido *(noise).*

2. Salta en la cama.

3. Busca tu traje de baño para ir a la piscina.

4. No corras por el pasillo.

5. Ve a la recepción por toallas.

6. Pierde la llave.

7. No duermas en la cama.

8. No juegues en el ascensor.

10.27 **La nueva empleada** Íngrid tiene un nuevo trabajo como camarera en un hotel y Gabino, otro camarero, le da consejos sobre lo que debe y no debe hacer. Escribe los mandatos informales necesarios para completar las recomendaciones de Gabino.

1. _____ (Llegar) al trabajo a tiempo.

2. _____ (Saludar) a los huéspedes en los pasillos.

3. _____ (Dejar) abierta la puerta mientras limpias la habitación.

4. _____ (Hacer) la cama antes de limpiar el cuarto.

5. _____ (Recoger) las toallas sucias para lavarlas.

6. _____ (Poner) toallas limpias en el baño todos los días.

7. No _____ (abrir) las maletas de los huéspedes.

8. No _____ (fumar) en las habitaciones.

9. No _____ (entrar) a la habitación sin tocar *(to knock).*

10. No _____ (hablar) por celular durante las horas de trabajo.

11. No _____ (traer) comida a las habitaciones.

12. No _____ (salir) del trabajo temprano.

10.28 **Te lo pido** Habla con ocho compañeros diferentes y usa mandatos para pedirles que hagan una de las siguientes actividades.

1. saltar como un conejo *(rabbit)*

2. cerrar los ojos

3. escribir su nombre en la pizarra

4. contar hasta veinte en español

5. bailar

6. dibujar una flor

7. subir un pie

8. apagar y encender la luz

10.29 **Un conflicto moral** Cuando tomamos decisiones, a veces hay un conflicto en la conciencia. Con un compañero, túrnense para hacer los papeles *(play the roles)* de la conciencia.

Modelo Estudiante 1 (el diablo): ¡*Toma la cerveza!*
Estudiante 2 (el ángel): ¡*No tomes la cerveza!*

1.

2.

3.

4.

5.

6.

© Cengage Learning

10.30 **Tengo un problema** Trabaja con un compañero para dar dos mandatos informales lógicos (uno afirmativo y otro negativo) para cada una de las siguientes situaciones.

1. La mascota de tu compañero de casa es un lobo *(wolf)*.
2. Una amiga tiene problemas en su matrimonio.
3. A un amigo no le gusta su trabajo.
4. Tu hermano quiere hacer un viaje, pero no sabe adónde ir.
5. Un compañero de clase recibe malas notas en los exámenes de español.
6. Una amiga quiere perder peso *(weight)*.
7. Un amigo tiene dolor de cabeza *(headache)*.
8. Tu vecino *(neighbor)* siempre tiene fiestas hasta las 3 de la mañana.

A analizar

Rosa y Paula se quedaron en un hotel y Rosa está haciendo su maleta. Mira el video otra vez. Después lee parte de su conversación y observa los mandatos en negrita y la posición de los pronombres.

Rosa: **Ayúdame**, ¿sí?
Paula: Claro. ¿Qué necesitas?
Rosa: Necesito mis zapatos rojos. Mira debajo de la cama, por favor.
Paula: No están aquí.
Rosa: ¿Ay, dónde pueden estar? **Búscalos** en el baño.
Paula: ¡Los encontré!
Rosa: ¡Ay, qué bueno! **Dámelos,** por favor.
Paula: Toma....
Espera, **no la cierres.** Aquí está tu pañuelo.

1. Identify the pronouns in the paragraph above.
2. Where are the pronouns in relation to the verbs?

A comprobar

Commands with pronouns

1. When using affirmative commands, the pronouns are attached to the end of the verb.

   Ponla en el armario.   **Hazlo** ahora mismo.
   ***Put it** in the closet.*   ***Do it** now.*

2. When using negative commands, the pronouns are placed directly before the verb.

   Compra los chocolates, pero **no los comas.**
   *Buy the chocolates, but **don't eat them.***

   Es mi suéter; **no te lo pongas.**
   *It's my sweater; **don't put it on.***

   Cerrad vuestras maletas; **no las dejéis** abiertas.
   *Close your suitcases; **don't leave them** open.*

3. When adding the pronoun(s) creates a word of three or more syllables, an accent is added to the syllable where the stress would normally fall.

lava	lávalos
limpia	límpiala
da	dámelo

   Hagan las maletas y **pónganlas** en el coche.
   *Pack the suitcases and **put them** in the car.*

   Busca la llave y **tráemela.**
   *Look for the key and **bring it to me.***

> **INVESTIGUEMOS LA ORTOGRAFÍA**
>
> When the pronoun **nos** follows a plural command, there is not a double **n.**
> ¿Les ayudamos con las maletas? Sí, **ayúdenos** por favor.

A practicar

10.31 **¿Te ayudo?** Tu amigo y tú están de vacaciones en un hotel. Tu amigo te hace varias preguntas. Mira sus preguntas y escoge la respuesta lógica.

1. ¿Pongo tu maleta allí *(there)*?   **a.** Sí, ciérrala.
2. ¿Pido más toallas?   **b.** No, no las cierres.
3. ¿Cierro la puerta?   **c.** Sí, ponla allí.
4. ¿Pongo las llaves allí?   **d.** No, no las pongas allí.
5. ¿Cierro tus maletas?   **e.** Sí, pídelo.
6. ¿Pido servicio a la habitación?   **f.** No, no las pidas.

10.32 **De salida** Félix y Óscar fueron de vacaciones y se quedaron en un hotel. Ahora tienen que salir del hotel. Félix ya está listo pero Óscar no. Completa las ideas de Félix con el mandato informal y el pronombre.

¡Óscar! ¡**(1.)** _____ (Despertarse)! Tenemos que salir del hotel en 30 minutos.

¡Mira! Toda tu ropa está en el piso. **(2.)** _____ (Recogerla) y **(3.)** _____ (ponerla) en tu maleta. Tu cepillo de dientes y tu desodorante están en el baño; no

(4.) _____ (olvidarlos). Y tus zapatos, ¿dónde están? No **(5.)** _____ (dejarlos); **(6.)** _____ (buscarlos) debajo de la cama. ¡No **(7.)** _____ (mirarme) así! ¡Vamos, **(8.)** _____ (levantarse) tenemos prisa!

10.33 **El gerente** Imagina que trabajas como gerente de un hotel. Contesta las preguntas de tus empleados usando mandatos formales y los pronombres apropiados.

Modelo ¿Tengo que sacar la basura?
  Sí, sáquela ahora. / No, no la saque ahora, puede sacarla más tarde.

La camarera

1. ¿Tengo que hacer las camas?

2. ¿Qué hago con las toallas sucias?

3. ¿Dónde pongo las toallas limpias?

4. ¿Está bien si tomo vacaciones este mes?

El botones

5. ¿Ayudo a estos *(these)* huéspedes?

6. ¿Dónde pongo las maletas de los huéspedes?

7. ¿Les llevo la comida a los huéspedes?

8. ¿Está bien si bebo un café ahora?

10.34 **¿Qué dicen?** Usa los verbos indicados en forma de mandato formal o informal y los pronombres apropiados para decir lo que las personas quieren en cada ilustración.

Modelo hacer → *Hágala.*

1. llevar, subir

2. apagar *(to shut off)*, no mirar

3. limpiar, colgar

4. poner, abrir

5. secarse, vestirse

6. tomar, divertirse

10.35 Consejos Con un compañero, túrnense para pedir y dar consejos *(advice)*. Contesten las preguntas con mandatos informales y los pronombres necesarios.

Modelo Roberto dejó su CD en mi casa. ¿Le devuelvo *(to return)* el CD?
Estudiante 1: *Roberto dejó su CD en mi casa. ¿Le devuelvo el CD?*
Estudiante 2: *Sí, devuélveselo. / No, no se lo devuelvas.*

1. Encontré el diario de mi novia. ¿Lo leo?

2. Puedo obtener las respuestas para el examen de matemáticas. ¿Las obtengo?

3. El jueves es el cumpleaños de Patricia y hay una gran fiesta. Tengo un examen en la clase de biología el viernes. ¿Estudio biología?

4. Tengo un buen amigo que quiere usar mi coche, pero tiene un mal récord de conducir. ¿Le presto mi coche?

5. Vi al novio de María besando a otra chica. ¿Le digo algo a María?

6. Quiero ir a esquiar con mis amigos pero tengo que trabajar. Puedo decirle a mi jefe que estoy enfermo. ¿Le miento?

7. Tengo que comprar un regalo para mi abuela, pero quiero comprar una nueva camisa para mí. No tengo dinero para los dos. ¿Me compro la camisa?

8. Rafael quiere copiar mi tarea para la clase de inglés. ¿Le doy mi tarea?

10.36 Cuida la casa Un amigo se va de vacaciones por dos semanas y tú vas a cuidar su casa. Con un compañero, túrnense para preguntar sobre las responsabilidades en la casa y para responder usando el mandato informal y los pronombres necesarios.

Modelo el gato
Estudiante 1: *¿Le doy de comer al gato?*
Estudiante 2: *Sí, dale de comer.*

1. el césped	**3.** el pájaro	**5.** el correo	**7.** las ventanas
2. las plantas	**4.** los perros	**6.** el periódico	**8.** las luces

---

10.37 Con un compañero, imagínense que están de viaje y llegan a un hotel. Túrnense para hacer el papel *(role)* del esposo y de la esposa. Usen mandatos para decirle al otro lo que debe o no debe hacer.

© Andresr/Shutterstock

Antes de leer

Aparte de los hoteles ¿qué diferentes tipos de alojamiento *(lodging)* conoces? ¿Por qué unos tipos de alojamiento son más caros que otros?

A leer

¿Dónde quedarse: hoteles, moteles, pensiones o albergues?

to choose

Cuando vamos de viaje, a la hora de **elegir** un hotel probablemente lo primero en que pensamos es en el dinero, pero hay otras decisiones importantes como la privacidad y la comodidad. Para seleccionar mejor nuestro alojamiento es importante entender la clasificación internacional.

Hoteles: Un hotel es un edificio entero con habitaciones para los turistas. El precio depende del lujo y de los servicios que se ofrecen. Casi todos los países clasifican los hoteles con un *stars* sistema de cinco **estrellas;** mientras más estrellas tiene un hotel, es mejor. Los hoteles de cuatro y cinco estrellas siempre tienen aire acondicionado y *heat* **calefacción** en las habitaciones, y además tienen tiendas, buenos restaurantes y otras *high quality facilities* **instalaciones de calidad.** Un hotel

Un hotel de lujo en El Salvador

de cinco estrellas tiene habitaciones muy grandes, pero un hotel de una estrella tiene habitaciones muy pequeñas. Aunque la mayoría de los países usan el sistema de

[mientras más estrellas tiene un hotel, es mejor]

estrellas para catalogar los hoteles, hay diferencias en la clasificación de un país a otro. Por ejemplo, un hotel de tres estrellas en España puede ser muy diferente a un hotel de tres estrellas en Costa Rica. Algunos países usan categorías adicionales, como "Gran Turismo", "Diamante" o "Turismo

Mundial" para distinguir los hoteles más lujosos y exclusivos.

Moteles: En general, los moteles están situados fuera de los núcleos urbanos y cada habitación tiene una entrada independiente. Las áreas comunes (salones, comedores, etcétera) son más pequeñas que las de los hoteles.

Hostales y pensiones: Los hostales y pensiones no cumplen con requisitos de los hoteles como tener habitaciones grandes y un restaurante. **Sin embargo,** siempre tienen agua caliente, recepción y un salón social con televisión, y al menos un baño para cada cinco habitaciones.

Albergues juveniles: Uno de los alojamientos más económicos que existe son los albergues juveniles. **Pese a** su nombre, no son solamente para jóvenes; personas de todas las edades pueden hacerse miembros y quedarse allí por la noche. Generalmente ofrecen literas en cuartos para varias personas, y a veces uno debe traer sus propias **sábanas.** Generalmente hay una cocina para el uso de los huéspedes y, sobre todo, hay muchas oportunidades para conocer a personas de otros países. Los albergues casi siempre tienen también un salón de TV, biblioteca, sala de estar y cuarto de lavandería.

Un hostal en España

Nevertheless

© J.D. Dallet/age fotostock

Despite

sheets

Comprensión

Decide si las oraciones son ciertas o falsas. Corrige las afirmaciones falsas.

1. Los hoteles de tres estrellas siempre tienen aire acondicionado.
2. Los mejores hoteles que hay en todo el mundo son los de cinco estrellas.
3. Los hostales y pensiones ofrecen baños privados en cada habitación.
4. Los moteles son iguales a los hoteles, pero más baratos.
5. Los albergues juveniles no tienen baños privados.
6. Los albergues juveniles no son solamente para jóvenes.

Después de leer

Imagina que tú y tu compañero van a viajar a un país hispanohablante. En Internet o en una guía turística, busquen un ejemplo de cada uno de los siguientes alojamientos: un hotel, un motel, un hostal o una pensión y un albergue juvenil. Lean los detalles de cada alojamiento y escriban una lista de los beneficios de cada uno. Decidan en cuál prefieren quedarse y expliquen por qué.

Redacción

Imagine you have just returned from an all-inclusive vacation that you booked with a travel company. Write a review on the travel company's website about your experience.

Paso 1 Decide whether you plan to write a positive or a negative review. Then jot down some ideas to include in your review. Think about the following: How was the trip? Did you have any problems with the airline (lost luggage, delayed flights, etc.)? If you had any problems, how were they taken care of? How was the hotel? Were the installations satisfactory (pool, gym, restaurant, etc.)? Were the hotel employees helpful?

© PlusONE/Shutterstock

Paso 2 Brainstorm some suggestions you would give to people planning to take this trip in the future. Would you recommend they use this company?

Paso 3 Write your initial paragraph in which you tell about your experience on the trip using the information you generated in **Paso 1.**

Paso 4 Write a second paragraph in which you give your recommendations to future clients using the information you generated in **Paso 2.**

Paso 5 Edit your review:

1. Do you have smooth transitions between sentences? Between the two paragraphs?
2. Do verbs agree with the subject?
3. Did you use preterite and imperfect appropriately?
4. Do your adjectives agree with the items they describe?
5. Have you used the proper forms for any commands?
6. Are there any spelling errors? Do you have accents where needed?

En vivo

Entrando en materia

Cuando un estudiante decide estudiar en el extranjero *(abroad)*, una opción muy popular es quedarse con una familia. En tu opinión, ¿cuál es la ventaja *(advantage)* de quedarse con una familia?

Hospedaje para estudiantes de idiomas

El siguiente es un folleto *(brochure)* que explica las opciones que tienen los estudiantes para hospedarse durante sus estudios en el extranjero. Léela y responde las preguntas que siguen.

OPCIONES DE ALOJAMIENTO

Estimado estudiante: Felicitaciones por haber sido aceptado en el programa de español. Para asegurar que todos los estudiantes tengan la mejor experiencia posible, contamos con tres formas de alojamiento, como se explica a continuación.

Residencia universitaria

Les recomendamos las residencias a los estudiantes que quieren mantener una total independencia y vivir en un ambiente estimulante y divertido con otros estudiantes de varias partes del mundo. Las ventajas de vivir en una residencia son que el desayuno y la comida están incluídos de lunes a viernes, para que te concentres en tus estudios. Hay teléfono en cada habitación y acceso gratuito a Internet inalámbrico. Además se ofrece servicio de limpieza por un precio muy económico. Si deseas un baño privado, también están disponibles por solamente 40 euros adicionales por semana.

Con esta opción podrás conocer a muchos estudiantes locales y extranjeros que también se hospedan en nuestras residencias.

Hospedaje con familias

Esta es la mejor forma de alojamiento para conocer la cultura española más de cerca. Todas las familias anfitrionas[1] están seleccionadas cuidadosamente para asegurar una experiencia positiva. Además, todas las casas están localizadas cerca de la universidad. Con esta opción se logra conocer mejor la cultura y la gastronomía del país, ya que muchas familias cocinan platillos tradicionales. Otra ventaja es que no tendrías que preocuparte tampoco por lavar tu ropa. Generalmente este tipo de alojamiento culmina en amistades para toda la vida. Por si

fuera poco, es una opción económica y se puede contratar por el número de semanas que el estudiante prefiera.

Todas las familias ofrecen una habitación con baño privado.

Condominios

Esta es la mejor opción si deseas tener mayor privacidad. Los condominios son pisos[2] económicos con un dormitorio, un baño y una cocineta. Están amueblados y el precio incluye el servicio de limpieza una vez a la semana. Entre las ventajas están que los estudiantes pueden cocinar sus propias comidas y comer cuando lo deseen.

Los condominios están cerca del metro, por lo que el acceso a la universidad es rápido y económico. El alquiler puede contratarse por mes, y si se necesitan más días existe la opción de alargar la estancia[3] a una tarifa especial por cada día extra.

Para más información sobre las tres opciones y el costo de cada una, contacta a la oficina de alojamiento: alojamiento@estudiosdeespanol.es

[1]host [2]apartments [3]stay

Comprensión

1. ¿Qué comidas no están incluídas en el alojamiento en residencias?
2. ¿Qué se debe hacer para tener un baño privado en una residencia?
3. ¿Por cuánto tiempo se puede alquilar una habitación con una familia?
4. ¿Qué tipo de comida ofrecen las familias?
5. ¿Cómo pueden llegar los estudiantes a la universidad si se hospedan en un condominio?

▒ Más allá

Decide cuál de estas opciones prefieres. Publica tu decisión en Share It! y explica por qué.

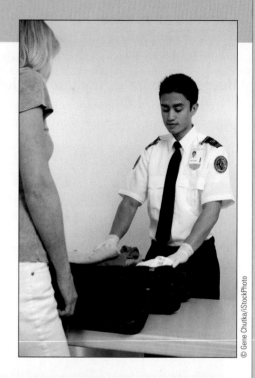

© Gene Chutka/iStockPhoto

Vocabulario

Sustantivos

la Administración de Seguridad en el Transporte	*Transportation Security Administration (TSA)*
la bandeja	*tray*
la cinta transportadora	*conveyor belt*
la computadora portátil	*laptop computer*
el detector de metales	*metal detector*
el envase	*container*
el equipo de rayos X	*X-ray machine*
la requisa	*pat down inspection, body search*
la máquina de Avanzada Tecnología de Imágenes	*Advanced Imaging Technology (AIT) machine*
el proceso de revisión	*screening process*

Verbos

colocar	*to place*
detectar	*to detect*
permanecer inmóvil	*to remain still*

Frases útiles

Coloque su computadora portátil en la bandeja, por favor.
Please place your laptop in the tray.

No se permite llevar envases de líquido o gel en el equipaje de mano.
Carrying containers of liquid or gel in your carry-on luggage is not permitted.

Hay que ponerlos en una bolsa de plástico transparente con capacidad para un cuarto de galón.
You must put them in a quart-sized transparent plastic bag.

Entre a la máquina y permanezca inmóvil.
Enter the machine and remain still.

DATOS IMPORTANTES

Educación: Estudios secundarios completos o el equivalente. Algunos trabajos requieren por lo menos un año de experiencia en seguridad o seguridad de aeropuertos. Se recomiendan cursos complementarios relacionados con la seguridad.

Salario: Entre $17 200 y $157 100

Dónde se trabaja: En aeropuertos

Vocabulario nuevo Completa las oraciones con una palabra del vocabulario.

1. Por favor, ponga su computadora portátil en la _____.
2. Usted no debe moverse mientras está en el detector de rayos X, es decir, permanezca _____.
3. Si no quiere entrar a la máquina, puede solicitar una _____ con un guardia en privado.
4. Este _____ de líquido no se puede poner en el equipaje de mano.
5. Con el equipo de rayos X el agente puede _____ objetos sospechosos *(suspicious)*.

Abdel Meyers, agente de seguridad

© Cengage Learning

Enrique Santiago llega tarde al aeropuerto. Tiene prisa pero antes de abordar el avión, tiene que pasar por seguridad. En el video, Abdel Meyers, el agente que trabaja para la Administración de Seguridad en el Transporte, le explica el proceso de revisión.

Antes de ver

Los consejos que les da la Administración de Seguridad en el Transporte a los pasajeros son ir al aeropuerto temprano y tener paciencia. El proceso de revisión puede ser largo, pero es necesario. ¿Siempre llegas al aeropuerto temprano? ¿Qué consejos puedes darle a una persona que piensa viajar en avión?

Comprensión

1. ¿Con quién habla Enrique por teléfono?
2. ¿Por qué tiene prisa Enrique?
3. ¿Dónde se pone el equipaje de mano?
4. ¿Por qué no puede llevar Enrique la botella de agua a la puerta de salida?
5. ¿Qué tiene que hacer Enrique con los zapatos?
6. ¿Qué le da Enrique al agente en vez del pase de abordar?

Después de ver

En parejas, representen a un agente de la Administración de Seguridad en el Transporte y a un pasajero en el aeropuerto. El agente debe explicarle al pasajero el proceso de revisión. El pasajero debe hacerle preguntas: ¿Puedo llevar este envase? ¿Me quito el cinturón? ¿Dónde pongo mi computadora portátil?

10.38 **¿Qué tiene que hacer?** Trabajas en un hotel y hay un nuevo empleado. Dile lo que tiene que hacer usando mandatos formales.

Modelo subir → *Suba las toallas extras a la habitación.*

1. llegar
2. ser
3. llevar
4. colgar
5. hacer
6. lavar
7. poner
8. ayudar

10.39 **Sugerencias** Un amigo va a viajar en avión por primera vez. Completa las sugerencias para él usando los mandatos informales. **¡OJO!** Hay mandatos afirmativos y negativos.

1. No _____ (tener) miedo.
2. _____ (Sentarse) al lado de la ventanilla.
3. _____ (Poner) los líquidos en el equipaje que vas a facturar.
4. No _____ (llegar) tarde al aeropuerto.
5. _____ (Ir) a la sala de espera después de conseguir el pase de abordar.
6. No _____ (levantarse) durante el despegue.
7. _____ (Beber) mucha agua durante el vuelo.
8. Si es posible, _____ (dormir) durante el vuelo.
9. No _____ (traer) mucho equipaje de mano.
10. _____ (Llevar) comida si vas a tomar un vuelo largo.

10.40 **La recepcionista** Usa los relativos **donde, que** y **quien(es)** para formar una oración, incorporando la segunda oración a la primera.

Modelo Hay muchas personas. Esas personas se quedan en el hotel.
Hay muchas personas que se quedan en el hotel.

1. Hay una nueva recepcionista en el hotel. Yo trabajo en el hotel.
2. La mujer se llama Florinda. El gerente contrató a la mujer.
3. Florinda tiene mucha experiencia. Consiguió la experiencia en un centro turístico.
4. Hay otro recepcionista. Ella va a trabajar con el otro recepcionista.
5. Ella va a ayudar a las personas. Las personas llegan al hotel.
6. A ella le gusta hablar con los huéspedes. Los huéspedes vienen de diferentes partes del mundo *(world)*.

10.41 **Al viajar** Entrevista a un compañero con las siguientes preguntas.

1. ¿Con qué frecuencia viajas?
2. ¿Prefieres viajar en avión o en coche? ¿Por qué?
3. ¿Alguna vez viajaste en tren? ¿Adónde fuiste?
4. ¿Alguna vez viajaste en primera clase? ¿Vale la pena (*Is it worth it*) pagar más para viajar en primera clase?
5. ¿Qué haces para pasar el tiempo durante el viaje?
6. ¿Te sientes nervioso antes de viajar? ¿Por qué?
7. ¿Prefieres visitar lugares turísticos, o lugares poco conocidos? ¿Por qué?

¿Alguna vez viajaste en tren?

10.42 **En la agencia de viajes** Trabaja con un compañero. Uno de ustedes es el agente de viajes y mira la información en esta página. El otro es el cliente y mira la información en el **Apéndice B.** El cliente llama al agente de viajes para comprar un boleto. El agente de viajes debe intentar encontrar el mejor boleto para el cliente y pedirle su información (nombre, teléfono, etcétera) y su tarjeta de crédito.

> **El agente de viaje**
> Los siguientes asientos para Santiago, Chile están disponibles *(available)*:
>
> - Vuelo 514–Sale el jueves a la 1:00 de la tarde con una escala en Caracas, y llega a las 11:15 de la noche. Hay un asiento en el pasillo. ($675)
>
> - Vuelo 386–Sale el jueves a las 8:20 de la mañana directo a Santiago, y llega a las 4:05 de la tarde. Hay un asiento en la ventanilla. ($750)
>
> - Vuelo 624–Sale el miércoles a las 2:45 de la tarde directo a Santiago, y llega a las 10:30 de la noche. Hay un asiento en la ventanilla. ($775)

10.43 **Un compañero de viaje** Tu compañero y tú van a decidir si pueden viajar juntos *(together)*.

Paso 1 Decide qué importancia tiene lo siguiente cuando viajas.

| 1 – no es importante | 2 – es importante | 3 – es muy importante |

una habitación separada en un hotel   el horario del vuelo
acceso a buenos restaurantes   el costo
tener una variedad de actividades planeadas   contar con un guía *(guide)*

Paso 2 Escribe otros tres factores que consideras importante cuando viajas.

Paso 3 Habla con tu compañero para saber qué considera importante. ¿Creen que pueden viajar juntos? Repórtenle a la clase su decisión y expliquen por qué.

◀)) Vocabulario 1
2-21

De viaje

a tiempo	*on time*
la aduana	*customs*
el asiento	*seat*
el boleto	*ticket*
la conexión	*connection*
el equipaje	*luggage*
el equipaje de mano	*hand luggage*
la llegada	*arrival*

el (la) pasajero(a)	*passenger*
el pasaporte	*passport*
el pasillo	*aisle*
la primera clase	*first class*
retrasado(a)	*delayed*
la sala de espera	*waiting room*
la salida	*departure*
la segunda clase	*second class*
la ventanilla	*window*

En el aeropuerto

el aeropuerto internacional	*international airport*
el (la) agente de seguridad	*security agent*
el cinturón de seguridad	*safety (seat) belt*
la escala	*layover*
la maleta	*suitcase*
el mostrador	*counter*

el pase de abordar	*boarding pass*
la puerta (de salida)	*gate*
el reclamo de equipaje	*baggage claim*
la revisión de equipaje	*luggage screening*
la visa	*visa*
el vuelo	*flight*

En la estación de tren

el andén	*platform*
el coche cama	*sleeping car*
la litera	*bunk*
la parada	*stop*

el (la) revisor(a)	*controller*
la taquilla	*ticket window*
el vagón	*car, wagon*

Los verbos

abordar	*to board*
aterrizar	*to land*
despegar	*to take off*
doblar	*to turn*
facturar equipaje	*to check luggage*

pasar por seguridad	*to go through security*
perder	*to miss (a flight, a train)*
seguir derecho	*to go straight*

Diccionario personal

_____

_____

_____

_____

_____

◀)) Vocabulario 2

El hotel

el alojamiento	*lodging*	la llave	*key*
el ascensor	*elevator*	la recepción	*reception (desk)*
el (la) botones	*bellhop*	el (la) recepcionista	*receptionist*
el (la) camarero(a)	*housekeeping*	la sala de conferencias	*conference center*
el centro de negocios	*business center*	el sauna	*sauna*
las escaleras	*stairs*	el servicio a la habitación	*room service*
el (la) gerente	*manager*	el transporte	*transportation*
la habitación	*room*	el (la) turista	*tourist*
el (la) huésped	*guest*		
el Internet inalámbrico	*wireless Internet*		

Verbos

alojarse	*to lodge, to stay (in a hotel)*	quedarse	*to stay*
bajar	*to go down, to take something down*	registrarse	*to register*
		subir	*to go up, to take something up*
pagar (y marcharse)	*to check out*		

Palabras adicionales

la clase turista	*economy class*	de lujo	*luxurious*
disponible	*available*	sencillo(a)	*single*
doble	*double*	triple	*triple*

Diccionario personal

_____

_____

_____

_____

_____

_____

_____

_____

Exploraciones **literarias**

Public Domain

Marco Denevi
Biografía
Marco Denevi (1922–1998) nació en Buenos Aires. Fue un importante novelista, dramaturgo, abogado y periodista que se destacó *(stood out)* por sus cuentos cortos. Recibió el Premio Kraft en 1955 por su primera novela *Rosaura a las diez*. Más tarde ganó el Primer Premio en la revista *Life* en español y el Premio Argentores, los cuales le hicieron ganar prestigio internacional. En 1980 empezó a practicar el periodismo, escribiendo artículos sobre temas políticos y problemas sociales.

Antes de leer

1. ¿Qué efecto pueden tener los celos en una relación?
2. ¿Te consideras una persona celosa?

No hay que complicar la felicidad

Un parque. Sentado bajo los árboles, ella y él se besan.

Él: Te amo.

Ella: Te amo.

Vuelven a besarse.

5   **Él:**   Te amo.

Ella: Te amo.

Vuelven a besarse.

Él: Te amo.

Ella: Te amo.

10   *Él se pone violentamente de pie.*

Él: ¡Basta! ¿Siempre lo mismo? ¿Por qué, cuando te digo que te amo, no contestas que amas a otro?

Ella: ¿A qué otro?

feed   **Él:**   A nadie. Pero lo dices para que yo tenga celos. Los celos **alimentan** al amor.

Deprived / fades   15   **Despojado** de este estímulo, el amor **languidece.** Nuestra felicidad es demasiado simple, demasiado monótona. Hay que complicarla un poco. ¿Comprendes?

guessed   **Ella:**   No quería confesártelo porque pensé que sufrirías. Pero lo has **adivinado.**

Él: ¿Qué es lo que adiviné?

Ella se levanta, se aleja unos pasos.

20   **Ella:**   Que amo a otro.

to please me   **Él:**   Lo dices para **complacerme.** Porque te lo pedí.

Ella: No. Amo a otro.

© Tudor Voinea/Shutterstock

	Él:	¿A qué otro?
	Ella:	No lo conoces.
25	*Un silencio. Él tiene una expresión sombría.*
	Él:	Entonces ¿es verdad?
	Ella:	*(Dulcemente)* Sí. Es verdad.
	Él se pasea haciendo ademanes de furor.
pretend	**Él:**	Siento celos. No **finjo,** créeme. Siento celos. Me gustaría matar a ese otro.
30	**Ella:**	*(Dulcemente)* Está allí.
	Él:	¿Dónde?
	Ella:	Allí, detrás de aquellos árboles.
	Él:	¿Qué hace?
	Ella:	Nos espía. También él es celoso.
35	**Él:**	Iré en su busca.
	Ella:	Cuidado. Quiere matarte.
	Él:	No le tengo miedo.
	Él desaparece entre los árboles. Al quedar sola, ella ríe.
	Ella:	¡Qué niños son los hombres! Para ellos, hasta el amor es un juego.
shot	40	*Se oye **el disparo** de un revolver. Ella deja de reír.*
	Ella:	Juan.
	Silencio.
	Ella:	*(Más alto)* Juan.
	Silencio.
45	**Ella:**	*(Grita)* ¡Juan!
	Silencio. Ella corre y desaparece entre los árboles. Al cabo de unos instantes se oye el grito
bloodcurdling	***desgarrador*** *de ella.*
	Ella:	¡Juan!
curtain	*Silencio. Después desciende **el telón.***

Investiguemos la literatura: Lector activo

Active reading is a literary technique that does not give the reader all of the information, thus forcing him/her to become actively involved in the reading and to come to his/her own conclusions.

Después de leer

A. Comprensión

1. ¿Por qué se queja *(complains)* él de la relación?
2. ¿Qué recomienda él para mejorar la relación?
3. ¿Por qué siente celos él?
4. En tu opinión ¿qué pasa al final?
5. ¿Qué significa el título?

B. Conversemos

1. En el drama "él" dice que "Los celos alimentan el amor". ¿Estás de acuerdo? ¿Por qué?
2. ¿Te identificas con el hombre o con la mujer de la historia? ¿Por qué?

Learning Strategy

Find ways to use your language in real-life settings

Seek out international students from Spanish-speaking countries or, if possible, visit a local restaurant or shop where you may have the opportunity to initiate a conversation with native speakers of Spanish. Explore opportunities to travel or to study abroad. Using the language in different social interactions will help to increase your proficiency as well as your confidence.

In this chapter you will learn how to:

- Express preferences and make comparisons
- Describe the state of objects and people
- Inform and give instructions
- Talk about unplanned occurrences

¿Es la moda arte?

© Marcelo Del Pozo/Reuters/Corbis

Esta semana hay buenas rebajas en los centros comerciales y muchos clientes van de compras.

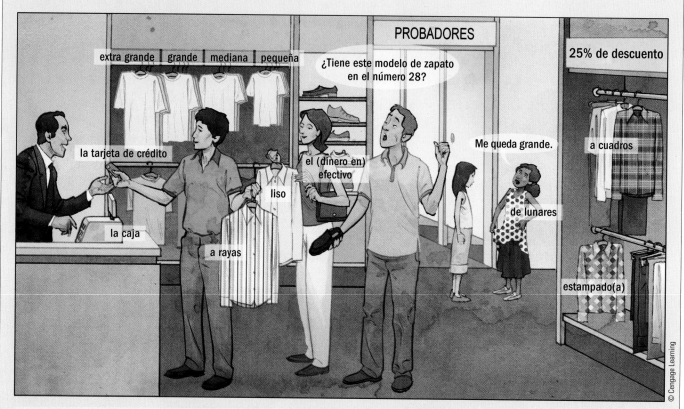

Las telas	Fabrics
el algodón	cotton
la lana	wool
el lino	linen
la mezclilla	denim
la piel	leather
la seda	silk

Adjetivos	
apretado(a)	tight
barato(a)	cheap, inexpensive
caro(a)	expensive
de marca	name brand

(estar) a la moda	(to be) fashionable
(estar) rebajado(a)	(to be) on sale
hecho(a) a mano	handmade

Verbos	
elegir (i)	to choose
hacer juego	to match
probarse (ue)	to try on
quedar	to fit

Expresiones útiles

¡Qué bien te queda esa falda!	That skirt really fits you well!
¡Qué caros!	How expensive!

¡Qué color tan bonito!	What a pretty color!
¡Qué pantalones tan elegantes!	What elegant pants!
¡Qué lindos zapatos!	What pretty shoes!

Palabras adicionales

la oferta	sale (event, reduction of prices)
por ciento	percent
la prenda	garment
la talla	size (clothing)
la venta	sale (transaction)

INVESTIGUEMOS LA GRAMÁTICA

The verb **quedar** can be used with an adjective or an adverb to tell how a piece of clothing fits someone or looks on someone. Like the verb **gustar**, it requires the indirect object pronoun and is conjugated in the third person singular or plural in agreement with the subject.

El vestido **me queda** muy bonito.	The dress **looks** pretty **on me.**
Los pantalones **te quedan** bien.	The pants **fit you** well.

A practicar

11.1 **Escucha y responde** Vas a escuchar seis ideas relacionadas con las compras. Indica con el pulgar hacia arriba si es lógica, y con el pulgar hacia abajo si es ilógica.

2-23

11.2 **La palabra que falta** Lee las siguientes oraciones y completa las ideas con una palabra lógica del vocabulario.

1. ¡Mira! Estas blusas están rebajadas. Tienen un _____ del 20%.

2. ¡Qué cara! Voy a necesitar mi _____ para pagar la blusa.

3. Los bluyíns generalmente están hechos de _____.

4. La falda me _____ muy bien. ¡Voy a comprarla!

5. No me gustan los estampados a rayas ni a cuadros. Prefiero la ropa _____.

6. Mi sobrino es muy alto. Creo que le voy a comprar la talla _____, pero mi sobrina no es muy pequeña ni muy alta; ella necesita una camiseta de talla _____.

11.3 **Una conversación desordenada** Con un compañero, decidan cuál es el orden correcto de la conversación. Después lean el diálogo cambiando las palabras en cursivas para hacer una conversación original.

Dependiente

1. ¿Desea algo más?
2. Puede pagar en la caja, y gracias por su compra.
3. Tenemos *unos zapatos* muy *elegantes* y están rebajados.
4. Buenas tardes. ¿Puedo ayudarlo?
5. ¿Cuál es su *número*?
6. Sí, claro. ¿Cómo le quedan?

Cliente

a. Uso *el número 39 o 39 ½*.
b. No, es todo. ¿Dónde pago?
c. ¿Puedo probármelos?
d. Me quedan *bien*. *¡Me los llevo!*
e. Sí, por favor. Busco *unos zapatos negros, formales*.
f. Muy amable, adiós.

11.4 **Conversemos** Conversa con un compañero y hablen de sus opiniones sobre las compras de ropa. Piensen en lo siguiente: ¿Les gusta vestir a la moda? ¿Dónde prefieren comprar ropa y por qué? ¿Qué estilos y telas prefieren? ¿Cómo prefieren pagar por sus compras? ¿Cuándo fue la última vez que fueron de compras? ¿Adónde fueron y qué compraron?

11.5 **Diferencias** Trabaja con un compañero para encontrar las ocho diferencias. Uno de ustedes va a mirar la ilustración en esta página y el otro va a mirar el dibujo en el **Apéndice B.** Túrnense para describir la escena y encontrar las diferencias.

© Cengage Learning

Conexiones culturales
La moda

Cultura

En todo el mundo existen grupos étnicos y culturales que son fácilmente reconocibles por vestirse de una forma particular. Uno de estos grupos es el de las llamadas cholas, mujeres indígenas bolivianas. Según parece, la historia de las cholitas comienza durante la Colonia, cuando muchas mujeres indígenas inmigraron a las ciudades. Estas campesinas querían adaptarse a la vida de la ciudad y comenzaron a vestirse elegantemente y a usar el típico sombrero de bombín que usaban las europeas en esos tiempos, aunque solo las mujeres casadas tenían derecho a usarlo. Otros elementos indispensables de la vestimenta de las cholas eran, y siguen siendo, la pollera (falda), blusa, manta *(poncho)* y botas negras. Mientras que la moda de las mujeres europeas cambió mucho a través de los años, las cholitas continúan apegadas a su elegante moda, aunque ha habido *(there have been)* algunos pequeños cambios.

¿Puedes pensar en otros grupos de personas que sean fácilmente reconocibles por su ropa? ¿Quiénes son? ¿Qué ropa llevan? ¿Hay algún grupo semejante en tu área geográfica?

Cholitas de Bolivia

 Lee más sobre Bolivia en **Exploraciones del mundo hispano** en el **Apéndice A.** ¿Qué idiomas crees que hablan las cholitas?

 Elige un país hispano e investiga en Internet sobre trajes tradicionales de ese país. Luego comparte la información y una foto en Share It!

Comunidad

No todas las personas tienen la ropa que necesitan para su familia. Considera organizarte con otros estudiantes y donar ropa a alguna institución de caridad que se encargue de distribuirla a personas necesitadas. Pongan etiquetas en español e inglés en las cajas donde pongan la ropa. O si prefieren, pueden buscar una organización que envíe ropa a zonas pobres de países en desarrollo. Estas son algunas palabras que te pueden ayudar en tu búsqueda: **donaciones** + **ropa** + (nombre de país).

Se puede donar ropa a personas que la necesiten.

Comparaciones

Vestirse apropiadamente es un concepto relativo, ya que depende del lugar donde está una persona, de su género, edad e incluso religión. Una persona puede estar vestida apropiadamente con unos pantalones cortos y una camiseta si está en la playa, pero la misma combinación es probablemente poco deseable en una iglesia, o para trabajar en una oficina.

En el contexto de los estudiantes universitarios, aunque se deben evitar las generalizaciones, puede decirse que los estudiantes en países hispanos prefieren llevar ropa cómoda como bluyines, pero los combinan con ropa más formal que una simple camiseta.

En grupos, contesten las siguientes preguntas sobre su universidad.

1. ¿Qué ropa llevan los estudiantes de la fotografía? ¿Es similar o diferente a la ropa que llevan los estudiantes en tu universidad? Explica cualquier diferencia.

2. ¿Creen que es importante la moda en su universidad? ¿Por qué lo creen? Den ejemplos concretos.

3. ¿Les gusta comprar ropa? ¿Compran ropa de moda o de marcas prestigiosas?

4. ¿Qué ropa es apropiada para estudiar en su universidad?

Después de hablar sobre las preguntas, busquen a estudiantes universitarios de algún país hispanohablante (en su universidad o en Internet) y háganles las mismas preguntas. ¿Hay diferencias importantes? ¿Qué diferencias?

Muchos estudiantes de la Universidad Nacional Autónoma de México se visten informalmente.

Conexiones... al diseño

¿Puedes nombrar a cinco diseñadores famosos? Carolina Herrera es una diseñadora venezolana que nació en la alta sociedad de Venezuela, y se distinguió por su apariencia física y su buen gusto para vestir. No fue sino hasta 1980, cuando ya tenía cuarenta años, que Herrera decidió iniciarse como diseñadora.

La siguiente es una lista de otros diseñadores hispanos. Algunos de ellos son muy populares en los Estados Unidos. ¿Los conoces?

Óscar de la Renta
Paloma Picasso
Roberto Giordano
Ángel Sánchez
Ágatha Ruíz de la Prada
Esteban Cortázar
Narciso Rodríguez

Un desfile de moda con los diseños de Carolina Herrera en Nueva York

Mira la sección **Exploraciones del mundo hispano** en el **Apéndice A.** ¿Qué otros diseñadores hay de España y Latinoamérica?

Busca la biografía y algunos de los diseños de uno de estos diseñadores. Después comparte la información en Share It! con algunas fotos de los diseños. ¿Te gustan los diseños? ¿Por qué?

A analizar

Paula acompaña a Rosa a la tienda para buscar un traje.
Mira el video. Despúes lee parte de su conversación y
observa los verbos en negritas.

Paula: En esta tienda **se venden** trajes de buena
calidad a buen precio.

Rosa: Este traje **se ve** muy bonito y está rebajado.

Paula: ¡Qué bien! Debes probarte ese. Busca una
blusa que combine con él. Mira este traje.
Se puede combinar con una blusa azul claro.

Rosa: ¡Me gusta!

Paula: Bueno, ya tienes un traje. Ahora lo que más te gusta... vamos a buscar zapatos.

Rosa: ¡Ay, sí! ¡Ya sé donde **se venden** los mejores zapatos!

1. In what singular and plural forms (person) are the verbs conjugated?

2. What pronoun is used in all of the highlighted verbs? Does the pronoun
have a reflexive meaning like the verbs **sentarse** and **lavarse**?

3. Look again at the verb forms. How do you decide whether to use the singular
or the plural form?

A comprobar

Passive **se** and impersonal **se**

1. The pronoun **se** is used when the person or
thing performing an action is either unknown or
unimportant. The verb is then conjugated in the third
person form. The singular form is used with singular
nouns and the plural form with plural nouns. Notice
that the subject can either precede or follow the verb.

   En esa tienda no **se aceptan** tarjetas de crédito.
   *In that store credit cards **are** not **accepted**.*

   Esta ropa **se hace** en Guatemala.
   *This clothing **is made** in Guatemala.*

2. When the verb is not used with a noun, it is
conjugated in the third person singular. The pronoun
se translates to *one, you,* or *they* in English.

   Se dice que no es necesario pagar mucho para
   tener ropa bonita.
   ***They say** that it is not necessary to pay a lot to have
   nice clothing.*

En la clase **se aprende** sobre los tejidos de la gente
indígena.
*In the class **you learn** about the weavings of the
indigenous people.*

Se ve que ella sabe vestirse bien.
***One can see** that she knows how to dress well.*

3. When using a verb such as **deber** or **poder** that is
followed by an infinitive and a noun, the verb is
conjugated in agreement with the noun because it
is the subject. If there is no noun, then the verb is
conjugated in the singular form.

   Se **pueden** ver los nuevos vestidos en la vitrina.
   ***One can** see the new dresses in the display window.*

   No **se debe** ir de compras ahora.
   ***One should** not go shopping now.*

A practicar

11.6 **Un poco de lógica** Mira los siguientes pasos para ir de compras y decide cuál es un orden lógico.

    a. _____ Se buscan prendas.

    b. _____ Se paga con tarjeta de crédito o con dinero en efectivo.

    c. _____ Se pide la opinión del amigo.

    d. _____ Se espera en la cola *(line)* para pagar.

    e. _____ La ropa se prueba en un probador.

    f. _____ Se va a la tienda con un amigo.

    g. _____ Se llevan las compras a casa.

11.7 **En la tienda** Mira las fotos. ¿Qué ropa se vende en las tiendas?

11.8 **A la moda** Lee el siguiente artículo con algunos consejos para estar a la moda y luego comenta lo que se debe hacer y lo que no se debe hacer. Usa una construcción con **se.**

Consejos para estar a la moda

Para estar a la moda no se tiene que gastar mucho dinero en ropa de marca, pero sí es necesario tener algunas prendas básicas en el armario. ¿Qué se debe hacer para estar segura de tener la ropa esencial?

- Buscar una blusa blanca de estilo clásico, preferiblemente de algodón.
- Usar bluyines de un corte clásico cómo el tipo recto[1].
- Elegir un traje elegante en un color neutro de lino o de algodón.
- Encontrar suéteres de lana para la temporada fría.
- Conseguir un vestido negro del corte que mejor le queda a su figura.
- Comprar un impermeable para lucir a la moda cuando hace fresco o llueve.
- Obtener un blazer; es versátil para situaciones formales o informales.
- Tomar en cuenta[2] la comodidad y el estilo a la hora de comprar calzado[3].

[1]straight leg   [2] Take into account   [3]footwear

11.9 **La boda perfecta** Una tienda de vestidos para novias creó este folleto *(brochure)* para explicar los pasos para tener la boda perfecta. Con un compañero, túrnense para explicar los pasos necesarios usando el **se** pasivo.

11.10 **¿Qué se hace?** Con un compañero, túrnense para escoger una de las siguientes palabras y explicar qué se hace con él. Tu compañero debe adivinar cuál es la palabra que escogiste. Usen una construcción con **se**.

Modelo los zapatos

Se ponen en los pies. Muchas veces se hacen de piel.

la bolsa	la caja	la corbata	la seda
la bufanda	el cinturón	la mezclilla	la tarjeta de crédito

11.11 **¿Cómo se hace?** Con un compañero, escojan una de las siguientes metas *(goals)*, o inventen su propio tema y escriban un mínimo de 5 acciones que se pueden hacer para lograrlo *(achieve it)*. Deben usar una construcción con **se**.

Modelo perder peso

Se va al gimnasio todos los días. Se camina en el parque. Se comen muchas frutas y verduras. Se toman menos refrescos. Se pide comida saludable en los restaurantes.

1. hacerse millonario
2. conquistar a un hombre o a una mujer
3. conseguir una A en la clase de español
4. hacer una cena romántica perfecta
5. conseguir un buen trabajo
6. tener una fiesta sorpresa para alguien
7. terminar los estudios universitarios en tres años
8. comprar un coche nuevo

INVESTIGUEMOS LA MÚSICA

Laura Pausini, an Italian singer, has recorded numerous songs in Spanish. Search online, listen to her song, "Cuando se ama," and write down the **se** constructions that you hear.

A analizar

Paula acompaña a Rosa a la tienda para buscar un traje.
Mira el video otra vez. Después, lee parte de su conversación
y observa las expresiones de comparación.

> **Paula:** Creo que el traje negro es **más bonito que** el traje azul.
>
> **Rosa:** Tienes razón, y el traje negro es **más cómodo que** este. ¡Y [el traje negro] también cuesta **menos que** este traje!
>
> **Paula:** Bueno, ya tienes un traje. Ahora lo que más te gusta... vamos a buscar zapatos.

© Cengage Learning

1. Look at the statements about the black suit. In Spanish, tell how the black suit compares to the blue suit.

2. What words are used to make the comparisons?

A comprobar

Comparisons

1. Comparisons of equality

The following construction is used to compare two people or things that have equal qualities:

> **tan** *(as)* + adjective/adverb + **como** *(as)*
>
> $\left.\begin{matrix} \textbf{tanto(s)} \\ \textbf{tanta(s)} \end{matrix}\right\}$ *(as much, many)* + noun + **como** *(as)*
>
> verb + **tanto como**

Adjective:	La blusa roja es **tan bonita como** la azul. *The red blouse is **as pretty as** the blue one.*
Adverb:	Yo no canto **tan bien como** mi esposo. *I don't sing **as well as** my husband.*
Noun:	Ella tiene **tantos zapatos como** Esmeralda. *She has **as many shoes as** Esmeralda.*
Verb:	Él trabaja **tanto como** ella. *He works **as much as** she does.*

2. Comparisons of inequality

The following constructions are used to compare two people or things that have unequal qualities:

> **más** *(more)*/**menos** *(less)* + adjective + **que** *(than)*
>
>   noun
>
>   adverb
>
> verb + **más/menos** + **que**

Adjective:	La seda es **más cara que** el algodón. Silk is **more expensive than** cotton.
Noun:	Pilar compró **menos ropa que** su hermana. Pilar bought **less clothing than** her sister.
Adverb:	Pancho conduce **más rápido que** Iván. Pancho drives **faster than** Iván.
Verb:	El sombrero **cuesta menos que** los guantes. The hat **costs less than** the gloves.

3. The following adjectives and adverbs do not use **más** or **menos** in their constructions:

bueno/bien	→	**mejor**	*better*
joven	→	**menor**	*younger*
malo/mal	→	**peor**	*worse*
viejo (age of a person)	→	**mayor**	*older*

Aquí tienen **mejores precios que** allí.
*Here they have **better prices than** there.*

Diana es **menor que** Federico.
*Diana is **younger than** Federico.*

4. Superlatives

Superlatives are used when someone or something is referred to as *the most, the least, the best,* etc. This is expressed through the following construction:

el/ la/ los/las + (noun) + **más/menos** + adjective

Este traje es **el traje más caro** de esta tienda.
*This suit is **the most expensive suit** in the store.*

Esta talla es **la más grande**.
*This size is **the biggest**.*

Notice that it is not always necessary to use the noun in these structures.

As with the other comparisons, when using **bueno/ bien, malo/mal, joven,** and **viejo** (age), you must use the irregular constructions **mejor, peor, menor,** and **mayor.**

Esta tienda tiene **las mejores** ofertas.
*This store has **the best** sales.*

5. The preposition **de** is often used with superlatives to express *in* or *of.*

Este vestido es el más bonito **de** todos.
*This dress is the prettiest **of** all.*

Son las mejores ofertas **del** año.
*They are the best sales **of** the year.*

> **INVESTIGUEMOS LA GRAMÁTICA**
>
> When **más** or **menos** is used with numbers or quantities it is followed by **de,** not **que.**
>
> La falda cuesta menos **de** veinte dólares
> *The skirt costs less **than** twenty dollars.*

A practicar

11.12 ¿Qué piensas? Lee las siguientes oraciones y decide si estás de acuerdo o no. Debes explicarle tus razones a la clase.

1. Una camisa a cuadros es más bonita que una camisa a rayas.
2. Pagar en efectivo es mejor que pagar con una tarjeta de crédito.
3. La ropa rebajada no es tan buena como la ropa a precio normal.
4. El precio de la ropa es menos importante que la calidad *(quality)*.
5. Las mujeres gastan *(spend)* tanto dinero en la ropa como los hombres.
6. La ropa hecha *(made)* en El Salvador es más cara que la ropa hecha en los Estados Unidos.
7. Una chaqueta de piel cuesta tanto como una chaqueta de lana.
8. La ropa de marca es mejor que la ropa sin marca.
9. Comprar ropa en Internet es más fácil que comprar en una tienda.
10. La moda es menos importante para los hombres que para las mujeres.

¿Quién gasta más en ropa?

© Deklofenak/Shutterstock

11.13 **A comparar** Mira las vitrinas *(display windows)* de una tienda. Con un compañero, túrnense para comparar dos artículos, usando las expresiones **más… que, menos… que** y **tan… como.** Pueden usar estos adjetivos o seleccionar otros: **bonito, feo, barato, caro, largo, corto, grande, pequeño, elegante.**

Modelo *La blusa rosada es más cara que la camisa a rayas.*

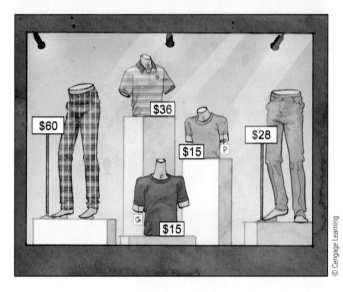

© Cengage Learning

11.14 **Opiniones** Con un compañero, expresen sus opiniones sobre los siguientes temas. Escojan dos ideas dentro de cada categoría y compárenlas.

Modelo la ropa — estilos
    Estudiante 1: *La ropa lisa es más bonita que la ropa estampada.*
    Estudiante 2: *En mi opinión las camisas a rayas son tan bonitas como las camisas lisas.*

1. la ropa
   • telas   • prendas   • tiendas de ropa

2. la educación
   • universidades • clases   • profesores

3. el tiempo libre
   • restaurantes   • grupos de música • deportes

11.15 **Comparaciones de grupo** En grupos de tres o cuatro, contesten las siguientes preguntas sobre los integrantes de su grupo.

© riekephotos/Shutterstock

¿Quién es más alta?

1. ¿Quién es el mayor?
2. ¿Quién es el menor?
3. ¿Quién es el más alto?
4. ¿Quién es el más bajo?
5. ¿Quién es el mejor artista?
6. ¿Quién es el mejor atleta?
7. ¿Quién tiene el pelo más largo?
8. ¿Quién tiene la familia más grande?

11.16 **El mundo hispanohablante** Decide cuál de los tres países, ciudades o conceptos en cada *(each)* lista es el más grande, pequeño, antiguo *(old)*, etcétera. Debes usar los adjetivos enfrente de la línea para crear cada superlativo.

Modelo grande: Santiago / Buenos Aires / Ciudad de México
La Ciudad de México es la más grande.

1. grande: México / Argentina / Chile
2. pequeño: El Salvador / la República Dominicana / Puerto Rico
3. antiguo: la civilización maya / la civilización azteca / la civilización inca
4. nuevo: Perú / Panamá / Cuba
5. poblado *(populated)*: Argentina / Colombia / Venezuela
6. alto: Cuzco / Quito / Santiago

11.17 **El mejor** En parejas, expresen sus opiniones usando las palabras indicadas y los superlativos.

Modelo interesante / libro
Estudiante 1: *El libro más interesante es* Don Quijote.
Estudiante 2: *En mi opinión los libros más interesantes son los libros de Harry Potter.*

1. rápido / coche
2. caro / restaurante
3. bueno / actor o actriz
4. difícil / materia
5. tonta / película
6. malo / programa de televisión
7. talentoso / grupo musical
8. bueno / equipo de fútbol americano

© Jason Stitt/Shutterstock

¿Cuál es el libro más interesante?

Entrando en materia

¿Alguna vez viste a una cadena de radio o de televisión transmitiendo en vivo? ¿Cuál era el evento? ¿Cuál crees que puede ser el objetivo de transmitir en vivo desde un centro comercial?

Control remoto con ofertas

🔊 El Centro Comercial Condesa contrató a una estación de radio para hacer un control
2-24 remoto y atraer clientes nuevos. Vas a escuchar un segmento de este control remoto. ¿Qué tipo de anuncios crees que van a hacer?

Vocabulario útil

el autógrafo	*autograph*	**el (la) radioescucha**	*listener*
la cita	*appointment*	**el reto**	*challenge*
el control remoto	*live radio event*	**transmitir**	*to broadcast*

Comprensión

1. ¿Desde *(From)* dónde está transmitiendo la estación de radio y por cuánto tiempo?
2. ¿Qué cantante va a regalar su último CD?
3. ¿Qué premio van a recibir las personas después de cumplir con el reto?
4. ¿Cuál es uno de los descuentos incluidos en el libro de cupones?
5. ¿Cuál es el reto para poder conseguir el premio?

🔳 Más allá

Imagina que trabajas para una estación de radio y decides hacer un control remoto. Sube tu plan a Share It! ¿Desde dónde van a transmitir? ¿Cómo van a atraer a muchas personas?

© Natursports/Shutterstock

Lectura

Antes de leer

Trabaja con un compañero para responder las siguientes preguntas.

1. ¿Qué significa **escandalosa**?
2. ¿Por qué razones se puede clasificar alguna ropa como escandalosa?
3. Actualmente *(Currently)*, ¿hay ropa que se considera escandalosa? ¿Por qué?
4. Lee el título del artículo. ¿Qué creen que va a decir el artículo?

A leer

Las tapadas: una moda escandalosa

Durante la época de la Colonia en Lima, la capital de Perú, nació una moda que fue producto de la competencia entre las mestizas (de descendencia indígena y europea) y las criollas (descendientes de europeos). Por una parte, las criollas preferían usar vestidos europeos que acentuaban su

waist **cintura.** Por su parte, las mestizas, quienes eran generalmente de talla más grande, comenzaron a usar sayas, que eran faldas muy amplias que solo dejaban ver los pies. Estas faldas eran de seda y normalmente de color azul, café, negro o verde. Las mujeres

belt que seguían esta moda llevaban una **correa** a la cintura y, lo más

cloak importante, usaban un **manto**

covered que les **cubría** parte de la cara, la cabeza y la parte superior del cuerpo, por lo que solamente era posible verles un ojo. Con esta moda, las mestizas

La moda de las tapadas

hid ocultaban sus defectos, y era imposible distinguir a una mujer de otra. En otras palabras, este traje hacía a las mujeres completamente anónimas, ya que no era posible distinguir a la

covered ones persona. Se conocen muchas historias de **tapadas** que "atraparon" a sus

> estos vestidos les dieron a las tapadas de Lima una gran libertad en esta época

propios maridos **coqueteando** con ellas. Hay que recordar que sus caras estaban tapadas, así que los hombres no sabían que estaban hablando con sus esposas. El anonimato de estos vestidos les dio a las tapadas de Lima una gran libertad en esa **época**: podían beber alcohol en público, ir a las corridas de toros y pasear por la ciudad.

flirting

at that time

El **comportamiento** de las tapadas fue considerado obsceno, y desde 1561 tanto los **virreyes** del Perú como la Iglesia Católica quisieron prohibir el uso de su vestimenta, imponiendo multas a las mujeres que usaban el manto. Sin embargo, la prohibición solo aumentó su uso. No fue hasta finales del siglo XIX, con la llegada de la moda francesa, que empezaron a desaparecer tanto la saya como el manto.

behavior
viceroys

Durante la existencia de las tapadas en Lima, estas mujeres fueron el tema de muchas obras de arte y también de varias comedias del dramaturgo Manuel Ascencio Segura. Además, participaron en el inicio de la revolución peruana, ayudando a pasar mensajes a los revolucionarios, usando sus trajes para no ser identificadas. Como se puede ver, la moda de las tapadas tuvo singular importancia en la historia del Perú.

Comprensión

Decide si las siguientes afirmaciones son ciertas o falsas, y corrige las falsas.

1. Las criollas y las mestizas de Lima usaban una moda diferente en la época colonial.
2. Las mestizas, en general, eran mujeres más pequeñas que las criollas.
3. Las criollas usaban un manto para cubrir sus defectos.
4. La moda de las tapadas les permitió tener más libertad.
5. La moda de las tapadas desapareció en el siglo XVI.

Después de leer

Habla con un compañero de clase sobre las siguientes preguntas.

1. ¿Te parece escandalosa la moda de las tapadas? ¿Por qué?
2. ¿Hay alguna moda actual que te parezca *(that seems to you)* escandalosa? ¿Por qué?
3. Piensen en ropa que en otra época o en otra cultura se considera (consideraba) escandalosa. ¿Por qué es (era) escandalosa?

¿Te parecen escandalosas?

Photos © Mihai Blanaru/Shutterstock

A Gabriela le encanta el arte y va a todas las exhibiciones que ofrece el museo de arte de la ciudad donde vive.

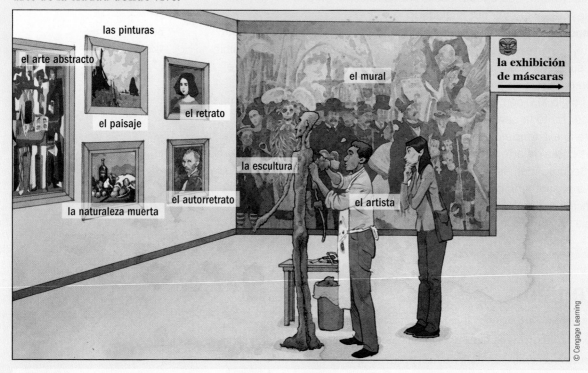

las pinturas

el arte abstracto

el paisaje

el retrato

la naturaleza muerta

el autorretrato

la escultura

el mural

la exhibición de máscaras

el artista

© Cengage Learning

El arte

la galería	gallery
el grabado	engraving; print
la luz	light
el (la) modelo	model
la obra	work (of art, literature, theater, etc.)
el óleo	oil painting
la paleta	palette
el pincel	paintbrush
la tinta	ink

Verbos

apreciar	to appreciate; to enjoy
diseñar	to design
esculpir	to sculpt
exhibir	to exhibit
posar	to pose

Adjetivos

abstracto(a)	abstract
claro(a)	light, pale
complicado(a)	complex

cubista	cubist
extraño(a)	strange, odd
impresionista	impressionist
obscuro(a)	dark
pastel	pastel
sencillo(a)	simple
surrealista	surrealist
tradicional	traditional
vanguardista	revolutionary; avant-garde

A practicar

11.18 **Escucha y responde** Primero, escribe "A" en un pedazo de papel y "B" en otro. Después vas a escuchar una serie de adjetivos para describir el arte que aparece en la **Actividad 11.22** en la siguiente página. Para cada adjetivo, levanta el papel correspondiente si la descripción se refiere a la foto A o a la B.

2-25

11.19 **¿Cuál es la palabra?** Completa con una palabra lógica del vocabulario.

1. En _____ se exhiben muchas obras de arte.

2. No puedo escribir porque no hay _____ en mi bolígrafo.

3. Cuando un artista pinta un cuadro de él mismo, el cuadro se llama _____.

4. Una pintura hecha sobre una pared *(wall)* tiene el nombre de _____.

5. Muchas ciudades tienen en sus calles _____ de personas famosas.

6. Un _____ es una persona que posa para un artista.

11.20 **La lógica** Las siguientes ideas son ilógicas. Corrígelas de manera que sean lógicas.

> Modelo El artista compró muchas de sus obras en la exhibición.
> *El artista <u>vendió</u> muchas de sus obras.*

1. Muchas galerías asisten a exhibiciones de arte.
2. El escultor posa para una escultura.
3. La naturaleza muerta es un cuadro en el que aparecen animales muertos.
4. Un muralista es una obra que el artista pinta en una pared.
5. El pintor usa la paleta para pintar en el pincel.
6. Un cuadro surrealista es un cuadro en el que un pintor se pinta a sí mismo.

11.21 **¡A adivinar!** En parejas, túrnense para elegir una palabra del vocabulario y explicársela a tu compañero sin decirla. El estudiante que está adivinando *(guessing)* puede hacer preguntas.

> Modelo Estudiante 1: *Es la persona que posa para el artista.*
> Estudiante 2: *Es el modelo.*

11.22 **Un análisis de arte** Trabaja con un compañero para hablar sobre dos pinturas muy diferentes. Usen las siguientes preguntas para ayudar con su análisis.

¿En qué estilo se pintó?   ¿Qué emoción evoca?   ¿Qué hay en la pintura?

En tu opinión ¿qué quiere decir el artista?   ¿Qué colores usó el artista?

© Erich Lessing / Art Resource, NY

© Schalkwijk / Art Resource, NY . Art © Tamayo Heirs/Mexico/Licensed by VAGA, New York, NY.

11.23 **Una exhibición de arte** Un museo local quiere montar una exhibición con obras de diferentes artistas hispanos, pero solo tiene el presupuesto *(budget)* para tres artistas diferentes. Tu compañero y tú deben compartir la información sobre los artistas y después decidir qué artistas presentar. Estén preparados para explicar por qué.

INVESTIGUEMOS LA MÚSICA

Listen to the Spanish pop group Mecano's song "'Eungenio' Salvador Dalí." In what ways does the person express admiration for the artist and his work?

Artista	Medio	País	Año	Nombre del cuadro y estilo
1. Oswaldo Guayasamín	pintura		1967	
2. Mario Carreño	pintura	Cuba		
3. Joan Miró		España	1961	*Blue I,* abstracto
4. Marisol Escobar		Venezuela		
5. Diego Rivera	murales			*Baile en Tehuantepec,* cubista
6. Roberto Matta			1941	*Sin título,* abstracto

Cultura

El arte no se limita a la pintura y a las esculturas que se exhiben en los grandes museos. La mayoría de las culturas tiene expresiones artísticas muy particulares. En esta sección vamos a explorar las molas y los alebrijes.

Una mola de Panamá

En las islas de San Blas, Panamá, existe una tribu indígena conocida como los kunas, quienes son famosos por sus molas, una forma de arte textil hecho por las mujeres kunas. Las molas se hacen con fragmentos de tela de colores vivos, y muchas veces tienen diseños abstractos y geométricos. En el pasado las molas se usaban solamente para vestir, pero hoy en día se usan también como artículos decorativos.

Un alebrije de Oaxaca, México

En el estado de Oaxaca, en México, algunos artistas especializados se dedican a crear animales fantásticos, hechos de madera. Los artesanos tallan la madera y la decoran en colores brillantes. Los alebrijes casi siempre son una combinación de diferentes partes de animales. Por ejemplo, un alebrije puede tener el cuerpo de una jirafa, las patas (pies de un animal) de un caballo, la cabeza de un pájaro y la cola de un gato. No hay dos iguales.

Investiga los kunas y aprende más sobre Panamá en **Exploraciones del mundo hispano** en el **Apéndice A.** Busca en Internet otros ejemplos de molas y alebrijes.

> Investiga otra forma de arte típico de un país hispanohablante. Sube una foto a Share It! y escribe una descripción de la obra o forma de arte. Incluye el nombre del artista o grupo, su país de origen, los materiales que se usan y otros detalles.

Comunidad

Entrevista a una persona de España o Latinoamérica sobre sus artistas favoritos de su país. ¿Quiénes son? ¿Qué tipo de arte hacen? Después repórtale a la clase.

Estrategia

The **Comunidad** activities in your text are a great way to initiate a conversation with native speakers in order to build confidence as well as your proficiency.

Fernando Botero posando frente a uno de sus cuadros

Comparaciones

A pesar de que hay innumerables culturas diferentes dentro de los países donde se habla español, el orgullo por sus artistas es muchas veces internacional. Las grandes obras de arte, inclusive las de literatura, unen (*unite*) a la gente de todos estos países.

Sería imposible mencionar a todos los grandes artistas, entre los que hay numerosos escritores. Sin embargo, en ninguna lista se puede dejar de mencionar a Pablo Neruda (1904–1973), ganador del Premio Nobel de Literatura y autor de algunos de los poemas más hermosos que se han escrito en español. Neruda, además, estuvo comprometido con ideales políticos y sociales que lo hicieron muy popular entre los latinoamericanos. Aún a treinta años de su muerte, Pablo Neruda era tan querido que para celebrar los cien años de su nacimiento, algunos de los cantantes más populares de España y Latinoamérica le dedicaron un disco lleno de homenajes a Neruda y a su poesía: "Neruda en el Corazón".

Otra autora importante, muy anterior a Neruda, fue la poetisa mexicana Sor Juana Inés de la Cruz (1648–1695), quien decidió hacerse monja (*nun*) para poder seguir estudiando. Sor Juana escribió poesía, teatro y ensayos. Quizás su poema más conocido es uno en el que les reclama a los hombres su doble estándar para juzgar (*to judge*) a la mujer y al hombre. El gobierno de México ha honrado la memoria de Sor Juana, poniendo su retrato en uno de los billetes del país.

¿Hay autores en la literatura escrita en inglés que sean reconocidos y admirados por todos los países en donde se habla inglés? ¿Quiénes son y por qué se hicieron tan importantes?

Billete chileno que conmemora a la escritora Gabriela Mistral

Conexiones... a la filosofía

La siguiente es una colección de citas sobre el arte que dan varios artistas famosos de países diferentes. Expliquen con sus propias palabras qué quieren decir, y después digan si están de acuerdo con ellas y por qué.

El arte es una mentira que nos acerca a la verdad. **Picasso**

El arte es el mediador de lo inexpresable. **Goethe**

El arte no reproduce lo visible, sino que hace visible lo que no siempre lo es. **Paul Klee**

Canto para no morir, porque el arte es la lucha (*struggle*) contra la muerte. **Carlos Cano**

Los espejos se emplean para verse la cara; el arte para verse el alma (*soul*). **G. B. Shaw**

El arte es inútil, pero el hombre es incapaz de prescindir de (*to do without*) lo inútil. **E. Ionesco**

En Andalucía se vive el arte, en Inglaterra o en los Estados Unidos se cuelga en las paredes. **Lindsay Kemp**

En los mejores días del arte no existían los críticos del arte. **Oscar Wilde**

Estampilla postal que conmemora el arte nicaragüense

Exploraciones gramaticales

A analizar ▶

Vanesa se encuentra con Camila para tomar un café. Mira el video. Después lee parte de su conversación y observa las palabras en negritas.

> **Vanesa:** El museo tiene una nueva exposición. Este mes van a tener una colección de obras de Picasso. ¿Te interesa ir conmigo el sábado?
>
> **Camila:** ¡Por supuesto! Estoy muy **interesada** en las obras de Picasso, especialmente las de su período rosado.
>
> **Vanesa:** Entonces ¿a qué hora vamos?
>
> **Camila:** ¡Ay, se me olvidó que el sábado estoy **ocupada**! ... ¿Sabes si el museo está **abierto** el viernes por la tarde?
>
> **Vanesa:** Sí, solo está **cerrado** los lunes. Podemos ir a las cinco si quieres.

© Cengage Learning

1. The words in bold are adjectives. Identify the verb that each of the adjectives is derived from.
2. Except for **abierto,** the adjectives in bold are derived from **–ar** verbs.
   What is the adjective form of **sorprender**? And **aburrir**?

A comprobar

Estar with the past participle

1. To form the past participle, place **-ado** on the end of the stem of **-ar** verbs and **-ido** on the stem of **-er** and **-ir** verbs.

hablar	habl**ado**
beber	beb**ido**
vivir	viv**ido**

The following verbs have irregular past participles:

abrir	**abierto**	hacer	**hecho**
cubrir	**cubierto**	morir	**muerto**
decir	**dicho**	romper	**roto**
despertar	**despierto**	poner	**puesto**
devolver	**devuelto**	ver	**visto**
escribir	**escrito**	volver	**vuelto**

INVESTIGUEMOS LA GRAMÁTICA

Notice that the common irregular participles end in **-to** or **-cho.** Other irregular past participles end in **-so,** such as **imprimir** → **impreso** (printed).

2. The past participle can be used as an adjective to indicate condition and is often used with the verb **estar.** You have already learned some of them, such as **aburrido, cansado,** and **preocupado.** Like other adjectives, they must agree in gender and number with the nouns they describe.

> Los estudiantes **están interesados** en el arte.
> *The students **are interested** in art.*

> La galería no **está abierta** los lunes.
> *The gallery **is** not **open** on Mondays.*

3. As is common with most adjectives in Spanish, the past participles can also be placed after the noun they describe.

> Me gustan más sus obras **pintadas.**
> *I like his **painted** works better.*

> Salvador Dalí es un pintor **conocido.**
> *Salvador Dalí is a **well-known** painter.*

A practicar

11.24 Mi salón de clases Mira alrededor de tu salón de clases y decide si las oraciones son ciertas o falsas.

1. Hay una ventana rota.
2. Las luces están apagadas.
3. Hay algo escrito en la pizarra.
4. La puerta está abierta.
5. Las sillas están hechas de plástico.
6. Todos los estudiantes están despiertos.

11.25 La casa Entrevista a un compañero con las siguientes preguntas.

Mis plantas no están muertas.

© Monkey Business Images/Shutterstock

1. ¿Está hecha tu cama? ¿Quién la hizo?
2. ¿Está ordenado tu cuarto? ¿Por qué?
3. ¿Están abiertas las ventanas de tu casa? ¿Por qué?
4. ¿Están encendidas las luces de tu casa? ¿Por qué?
5. ¿Está lavada tu ropa? ¿Quién la lava?
6. ¿Están muertas las plantas en tu casa? ¿Por qué?
7. ¿Tienes algo que está roto? ¿Qué es?
8. ¿Tienes algo hecho en otro país? ¿Qué es y de dónde es?

11.26 ¿Qué ves? Túrnense con un compañero para preguntar si ven lo siguiente. **¡OJO!** Recuerden que el participio necesita concordar con el objeto que se describe.

Modelo algo abierto
    Estudiante 1: *¿Ves algo abierto?*
    Estudiante 2: *Sí, la puerta está abierta. / No, no hay nada abierto.*

1. algo escrito en inglés
2. algo hecho de metal
3. alguien casado
4. algo colgado en la pared
5. algo roto
6. alguien cansado
7. algo pintado de rojo
8. algo encendido

11.27 La clase de arte Lee las siguientes oraciones sobre una clase de arte y explica las condiciones de los sujetos, usando el verbo **estar** y el participio pasado del verbo subrayado *(underlined)*.

Modelo La planta del profesor <u>murió</u>.
    La planta del profesor está muerta.

1. Cuando el profesor entró en la clase, <u>encendió</u> las luces y <u>cerró</u> la puerta.
2. Él <u>colgó</u> su suéter.
3. Luisa <u>se sentó</u> al lado de Julián.
4. Ella <u>tiene mucho interés</u> en Julián.
5. Pero Julián <u>se ocupa</u> de su pintura.
6. Inés, la chica al lado de Julián, <u>se aburre</u> en la clase.
7. Ella <u>se durmió</u> en la clase.
8. El profesor <u>escribió</u> la tarea en la pizarra.
9. Al escribir la tarea, <u>rompió</u> la tiza *(chalk)*.
10. El profesor <u>se frustró</u> y terminó la clase temprano.

11.28 **Preocupado** Es medianoche y tu pareja no te deja dormir porque está muy preocupada. Con un compañero, túrnense para preguntar si su pareja hizo lo siguiente. Debe responder con el participio pasado. **¡OJO!** Recuerden que el participio necesita concordar con el objeto que se describe.

Modelo ¿Abriste la ventana?
Estudiante 1: *¿Abriste la ventana?*
Estudiante 2: *Sí, está abierta. / No, no está abierta.*

1. ¿Estás despierto?
2. ¿Apagaste las luces en la sala?
3. ¿Cerraste la puerta?
4. ¿Encendiste la alarma?
5. ¿Colgaste tu ropa?
6. ¿Guardaste los platos limpios?
7. ¿Preparaste el almuerzo para mañana?
8. ¿Escribiste el cheque para el alquiler?

11.29 **El teatro** Con un compañero, túrnense para describir el escenario del teatro usando los participios como adjetivos. Busquen las cinco diferencias.

Vocabulario útil: **el perchero** *coat rack* **vivo** *alive*

© Cengage Learning

A analizar ▶

Vanesa se encuentra con Camila para tomar un café. Mira
el video otra vez. Después lee parte de su conversación y
observa las estructuras de los verbos en negritas.

Vanesa:	Disculpa que haya llegado tarde. **Se me perdieron** las llaves, y no pude salir de casa sin ellas... Este mes van a tener una colección de obras de Picasso. ¿Te interesa ir conmigo el sábado?
Camila:	¡Por supuesto! ...
Vanesa:	Entonces ¿a qué hora vamos?
Camila:	¡Ay, **se me olvidó** que el sábado estoy ocupada! ...
Camila:	Bueno, ¿nos vamos?
Vanesa:	Sí. Señorita, ¿cuánto le debo?
Mesera:	Seis cincuenta, por favor.
Vanesa:	¿Dónde está mi dinero? ¡Ay, **se me quedó** la billetera en casa! ¿Te molesta pagar?

© Cengage Learning

1. Recalling some of the ways that **se** can be used, how do you think it is used here?
2. In which person (1st, 2nd, or 3rd) have the highlighted verbs been conjugated? Why?
3. What pronouns appear before the verbs?

A comprobar

Se to indicate accidental occurrences

1. Earlier in the chapter, you learned to use the pronoun **se** in order to indicate that the subject is either unknown or unimportant. To indicate unintentional or accidental occurrences, you will use a similar construction that also includes the indirect object pronoun.

> **se** + indirect object pronoun + verb

Se me rompió el plato.   *I broke the plate (accidentally).*
A Diego **se le** perdieron las llaves.   *Diego lost his keys (unintentionally).*

Notice that the verb agrees with subject (**el plato** and **las llaves**) and that the person affected by the event becomes the indirect object (**me** and **A Diego... le**).

2. The following are common verbs used with this construction.

acabar	*to finish*	**caer**	*to fall*
Se me acabó la gasolina.	*I ran out of gas.*	**Se les cayeron** los libros.	*They dropped their books.*
apagar	*to turn off*	**descomponer**	*to break down (a machine)*
Se les apagó la computadora.	*Their computer went out.*	**Se me descompuso** el coche.	*My car broke down.*

olvidar	to forget	quedar	to remain (behind)
A ella **se le olvidó** el lápiz.	*She forgot her pencil.*	**Se me quedó** el dinero en casa.	*I left the money at home.*
perder	to lose (an object)	romper	to break
Se nos perdió la tarea.	*We lost our homework.*	**¿Se te rompió** el vaso?	*Did you break the glass?*

A practicar

11.30 **El pintor olvidadizo** El pintor no pudo terminar su obra porque le ocurrieron muchos accidentes. Combina los elementos de las dos columnas para formar oraciones lógicas.

1. Al pintor se le olvidó...   **a.** las luces
2. Al pintor se le apagaron...   **b.** los pinceles
3. Al pintor se le acabaron...   **c.** el número de teléfono del modelo
4. Al pintor se le rompieron... **d.** la paleta
5. Al pintor se le perdió...   **e.** las pinturas
6. Al pintor se le quedó...   **f.** el óleo en casa

11.31 **Un mal día** Completa el párrafo con la forma apropiada del verbo entre paréntesis.

¡Ayer tuve una exposición de mi arte en una galería y todo me salió mal! Primero
(1.) _____ (perder) las obras de cerámica que tenía que llevar a la
galería. **(2.)** _____ (olvidar) que las puse en un lugar seguro. Por fin las
encontré y salí para la galería. A medio camino *(On the way)* **(3.)** _____
(acabar) la gasolina. ¡Tuve que caminar un kilómetro a la gasolinera más cercana!
Al llegar me di cuenta de que la billetera *(wallet)* **(4.)** _____ (quedar)
en casa. Afortunadamente tenía un poco de dinero en mi pantalón y pude pagar la
gasolina. Llegué a la galería tarde. Mientras llevaba las piezas del coche a la sala de
exposición, **(5.)** _____ (caer) una y **(6.)** _____ (romper).
Por fin comenzó la exposición y vendí unas piezas. Por lo menos la noche terminó bien.

11.32 **¿Qué pasó?** Trabaja con un compañero para describir la situación y expliquen lo que les pasó a las personas.

Modelo *El hombre pintaba un mural cuando se le acabó la pintura. No tenía dinero para comprar más.*

11.33 **No se hizo** Estas personas no pudieron hacer su trabajo por diferentes razones. Explica lo que les pasó usando el verbo indicado con el **se** accidental.

Modelo el piloto / descomponer
        Al piloto se le descompuso el avión.

1. la profesora / acabar
2. los estudiantes / olvidar
3. el ama de casa / romper
4. el periodista / descomponer
5. los cocineros / caer
6. el pintor / perder
7. las bailarinas / quedar
8. los actores / apagar

11.34 **En busca de...** Hazles las siguientes preguntas a diferentes compañeros. Busca a alguien que responda afirmativamente a la primera pregunta. Después hazle la pregunta entre paréntesis. Usa la expresión **alguna vez** en la pregunta.

Modelo acabar la tinta en medio de un proyecto (¿Qué?)
        Estudiante 1: *¿Alguna vez se te acabó la tinta en medio de un proyecto?*
        Estudiante 2: *Sí, se me acabó la tinta en medio de un proyecto.*
        Estudiante 1: *¿Qué proyecto?*
        Estudiante 2: *Una composición para la clase de inglés el semestre pasado.*

1. descomponer el coche a la mitad del camino *(in the middle of the road)* (¿Dónde?)
2. romper algo valioso *(valuable)* (¿Qué?)
3. perder algo importante (¿Qué?)
4. apagar la computadora en medio de una tarea importante (¿Qué tarea fue?)
5. quedar en casa algo importante durante algún viaje (¿Qué?)
6. olvidar el nombre de alguien en el momento de hacer una presentación *(introduction)* (¿De quién?)
7. quemar *(burned)* la comida (¿Qué?)
8. olvidar el cumpleaños de alguien (¿Qué hiciste?)

11.35 **Excusas** Hay muchos problemas en la clase de arte. Con un compañero, túrnense para dar excusas y explicar lo que pasó. Usen los siguientes verbos.

acabar apagar caer descomponer olvidar perder quedar romper

Modelo ¿Por qué no estuviste en clase?
        Se me olvidó poner el despertador.
        Se me perdieron las llaves del coche.

1. ¿Por qué no tienes la tarea?
2. ¿Por qué no tienes el libro?
3. ¿Por qué no estudiaste para el examen?
4. ¿Por qué no terminaste la pintura?
5. ¿Por qué no llegó el modelo?
6. ¿Por qué llegó tarde el profesor?

¡Se me olvidó que tenemos un examen hoy!

Lectura

Antes de leer

Contesta las preguntas.

1. ¿Quién es tu artista favorito? ¿Por qué?
2. ¿Conoces a algún artista de España o Latinoamérica? ¿Quién? ¿Te gusta su arte?
3. En tu opinión ¿qué se necesita para ser artista?

A leer

Remedios Varo

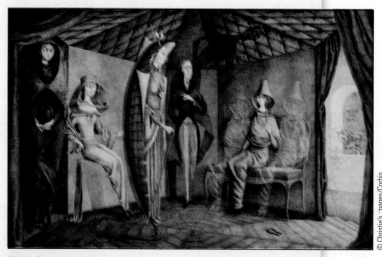

XX de Remedios Varo

© Christie's Images/Corbis

Una de las grandes artistas del siglo XX fue la pintora española Remedios Varo, nacida en 1908 en Anglés, España. Como muchos artistas, Remedios Varo **desarrolló** *developed* desde muy joven un interés por la pintura. Fue **apoyada** *supported* por su padre, un ingeniero que la enseñó a dibujar y le ayudó a ingresar a la Academia de San Fernando en Madrid cuando Remedios tenía quince años, a pesar de la oposición de su madre.

En la Academia de San Fernando, Remedios conoció a su futuro esposo, Gerardo Lizárraga, con quien se mudó a París cuando ambos finalizaron sus estudios en la Academia. Posteriormente se trasladaron a Barcelona, donde Remedios trabajó en publicidad.

[Una de las grandes artistas del siglo XX fue la pintora española Remedios Varo.]

El segundo esposo de Remedios Varo fue Benjamín Peret, un poeta que la introdujo a un grupo de artistas surrealistas encabezado por Andrés Bretón. El surrealismo tuvo un gran impacto en la obra de Varo a partir de ese momento.

La Guerra Civil española la hizo emigrar nuevamente a Francia, en donde **permaneció** hasta 1941, año de la invasión nazi. En ese año, Remedios se exilió definitivamente en México, país en el que se exiliaron muchos artistas europeos, incluyendo a Leonora Carrington, otra pintora surrealista que se hizo muy amiga de Remedios Varo. Fue en México que Varo pudo dedicarse por completo al arte, pintando sus mejores cuadros con el apoyo de su tercer marido, el austriaco Walter Gruen, un sobreviviente de los campos de concentración.

remained

Remedios Varo

© www.remediosvaro.org

La obra de Remedios Varo se distingue por un estilo muy característico en el que aparecen con frecuencia figuras humanas estilizadas. En sus cuadros se combinan elementos **oníricos** y

como de sueños

místicos con su gran interés científico y su búsqueda del conocimiento a través de la filosofía y la psicología. En sus obras también pueden verse recuerdos de la infancia de la pintora, como los horrores de la guerra.

Remedios regaló la mayoría de sus cuadros porque para ella el valor de la pintura estaba en el proceso de la creación artística. En 1963 la artista murió de un ataque cardiaco a la edad de 55 años.

Sources: Analitica.com; LatinArtMuseum.com

Comprensión

1. ¿Cuándo se interesó por el arte Remedios Varo? ¿Cómo la apoyó su padre?
2. ¿En qué países vivió Varo después de salir de España a consecuencia de la guerra?
3. ¿Cuántas veces se casó?
4. ¿Qué movimiento artístico la influenció más?
5. ¿Cuáles son algunos elementos de la obra de Remedios Varo?
6. ¿Qué hizo con la mayoría de sus cuadros?

Después de leer

Busca obras de Remedios Varo en Internet. ¿Cómo puedes describirlas? ¿Te gustan? ¿Por qué?

Sube a Share It! una foto de la obra de Remedios Varo que más te gusta y explica por qué te gusta.

Redacción

Write a simple analysis of a painting by a Hispanic artist.

Paso 1 Look at some paintings by Hispanic artists on the Internet and find one that you like. Find out a little bit about the artist: Where is he/she from? When was he/she born and if no longer living, when did he/she die? What is the artist's style? What themes are prevalent in his/her work?

 Look through the **Exploraciones del mundo hispano** in **Apéndice B** for names of Hispanic artists.

Paso 2 Look at the painting you have chosen. What is the name of the painting? When did the artist paint it? What is in the painting? What colors did the artist use?

© Tupungato/Shutterstock

Paso 3 Now think about why you like the painting. What drew you to it? What emotions does it evoke? What message do you think the artist wants to communicate?

Paso 4 Write an introductory paragraph about the artist you have chosen using the information you generated in **Paso 1**.

Paso 5 In a second paragraph describe the painting that you have chosen using the information in **Paso 2**. Remember that your reader is not looking at the painting, so be sure to give plenty of details.

Paso 6 Write a concluding paragraph in which you discuss your thoughts about the painting using the ideas you generated in **Paso 3**.

Paso 7 Edit your analysis:

1. Do you have smooth transitions between sentences? Between the two paragraphs?
2. Do verbs agree with the subject? Are they conjugated correctly?
3. Did you use the preterite and the imperfect appropriately?
4. Do adjectives agree with the people or items they describe?

Entrando en materia

¿Alguna vez has asistido a una exhibición en una galería? ¿Te gustó? ¿Por qué?

Nota de prensa *(Press release)*

Vas a leer una nota de prensa de una muestra de arte por inmigrantes latinoamericanos en Madrid. ¿Qué información piensas que se va a dar?

Muestra de arte latinoamericano "Acá nomás"

Madrid, 1 de octubre de 2010.

Con motivo del *Encuentro Ágora, América Latina, 100 voces diferentes, un compromiso común,* la Fundación Internacional y para Iberoamérica de Administración y Políticas Públicas (FIIAPP) organiza una muestra de artistas latinoamericanos residentes en Madrid, que tendrá lugar del 7 al 10 de octubre de 2010 en el pabellón Villanueva del Jardín Botánico de Madrid.

Bajo el título "Acá nomás", la muestra propone ofrecer un panorama de artistas de toda América Latina que han encontrado en Madrid una ciudad de inspiración y acogida donde pueden repensar sus raíces y desarrollar[1] nuevas facetas de su identidad. Su condición de migrantes les convierte en testigos privilegiados de los cambios que se vienen produciendo en sus países de origen y les ofrece elementos de juicio para contrastar las distintas[2] realidades sociales a ambos[3] lados del Atlántico.

La muestra de arte "Acá nomás" reúne a 15 artistas latinoamericanos, de diez nacionalidades diferentes. Esta exposición colectiva es el testimonio de migrantes latinos que, desde la distancia, miran su continente y proponen al nuevo hogar la inclusión en su cultura, migrantes que encuentran en el arte una presencia que lucha[4] por no perder su identidad y, a la vez, hacerse parte de ese hábitat presente.

En esta muestra se pueden encontrar abordajes[5] desde conceptos como la identidad, fragmentaciones que componen retratos, cartografías de sus contextos, la violencia, el deseo, la disociación y la mirada crítica y reflexiva sobre las ciudades; la relación entre los espacios urbanos y quienes los habitan.

Asimismo, los múltiples lenguajes artísticos presentes en la muestra de arte "Acá nomás", desde los más tradicionales, cruzando a través de la fotografía, la instalación, hasta la ilustración y el cómic son utilizados como herramientas[6] para acercarse a las problemáticas contemporáneas.

Source: La Fundación Internacional y para Iberoamérica de Administración y Políticas Públicas (FIIAPP)

© Broken mariposa, 2002. 117 x 87 cm. Acrylic on canvas. © Luis Arias Vera

Broken mariposa, por Luis Arias Vera

El conjunto[7] de reflexiones, conclusiones y propuestas[8] de todos estos artistas, cargado de[9] coincidencias y, sobre todo, de diferencias, es precisamente lo que colabora en la construcción de nuevos modelos sociales, integrales, inclusivos y sostenibles para el bienestar[10] y el desarrollo de todos. Son, en resumen, un espejo de América Latina.

Los 15 artistas invitados

Fernando Rubio (Colombia)
Carolina Belén Martínez (Argentina)
Natalia Granada (Colombia)
Alejandro Stock (Uruguay)
César Saldívar (México)

Luis Arias Vera (Perú)
Ana Blanco (Venezuela)
Flavia Totoro (Chile-México)
Juan Francisco Yoc (Guatemala)
Tomás Ochoa (Ecuador)

Ilustradores-Humor gráfico

Adriana Mosquera (Colombia)
Carlos Matera (Argentina)
Ulises Culebro (México)
Ómar Figueroa (Colombia)
Jorge Martínez (Cuba)

Contacto de prensa: Gorka Castillo
Comunicación Ágora, América Latina
Tel. +34 91 591 51 14

[1] *to develop* [2] *diferentes* [3] *both* [4] *struggles* [5] *approaches* [6] *tools* [7] *combination* [8] *suggestions* [9] *full of* [10] *well-being*

Comprensión

1. ¿Cómo se llama la exhibición, quién la organiza y de dónde son los 15 artistas?
2. ¿Cuáles son algunos temas que se ven en su arte?
3. ¿Qué tipos de arte se representan en la exhibición?

Más allá

Busca la obra de uno de los artistas que participaron en la exhibición y sube la imagen a Share It! Escribe un comentario sobre su obra: ¿cómo es? ¿cuáles son los temas? ¿te gusta? ¿por qué?

Las ventas ▶

Vocabulario

Sustantivos

la calidad	*quality*
la comisión	*commission*
la devolución	*return*
la línea	*style*
el proveedor	*wholesaler*
la temporada	*season*

Adjetivos

importado(a)	*imported*

Verbos

descubrir	*to discover*

Expresiones útiles

¿En qué le puedo servir?
How can I help you?

¿Qué talla usa?
What's your size?

Están en oferta.
They are on sale.

Aceptamos tarjeta de crédito.
We take credit cards.

Pase por la caja.
Go to the cash register.

Aquí está su vuelto.
Here is your change.

Gracias por su compra.
Thanks for shopping.

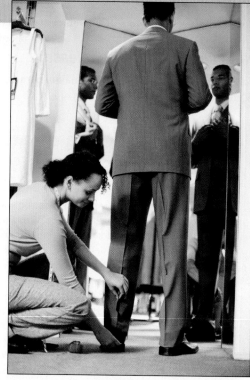

© Fuse/JupiterImages

DATOS IMPORTANTES

Educación: Estudios secundarios. Estudiantes universitarios preferiblemente. Se requiere buena presencia y buen servicio de atención al cliente

Salario: Entre $25 000 y $40 000 + comisiones y bonos

Dónde se trabaja: En centros comerciales, tiendas particulares, exposiciones de moda

Vocabulario nuevo Read each of the following answers carefully and write the question that was asked.

1. ¿—————————————?
   — Sí y también aceptamos cheques, si lo prefiere.

2. ¿—————————————?
   — Uso la mediana.

3. ¿—————————————?
   — Estoy buscando el departamento de ropa para niños.

Luis Collado, vendedor

© Cengage Learning

Luis Collado trabaja en una tienda de ropa. Es el vendedor estrella *(star)* de la tienda y hace diez años que trabaja para que todos los clientes compren ropa apropiada para su estilo y para cada estación. En el video vas a ver a Luis mientras ayuda a María Elisa, una señora que quiere comprar ropa para el trabajo.

Antes de ver

Muchos vendedores trabajan por comisión y reciben dinero extra por la ropa que venden. Algunos vendedores son muy amables, pero a otros realmente no les importa la atención al cliente. ¿Qué espera usted de un vendedor? ¿Qué preguntas le hace?

Comprensión

1. ¿Qué tipo de ropa busca la señora?
2. ¿En qué mes están?
3. ¿Qué tipo de ropa le muestra primero el vendedor?
4. ¿Qué se prueba la señora en el probador?
5. ¿Qué talla de pantalones usa la señora?
6. ¿Cómo quiere pagar la señora? ¿Por qué?
7. ¿Qué recibe la señora por ser una nueva cliente?

Después de ver

En parejas, representen a un vendedor de ropa y a un cliente potencial que quiere comprar algo pero no sabe qué. El vendedor le ayuda a decidir la ropa ideal según el estilo, el cuerpo y las necesidades del cliente (evento, ropa informal, fiesta, trabajo, etcétera). El cliente toma una decisión y compra o no la ropa.

11.36 **¿Qué piensas?** Usando los elementos indicados, escribe tus opiniones usando superlativos como el del modelo.

Modelo   arte / popular: la pintura, la escultura, la máscara
          La pintura es la más popular de las artes.

1. museo / grande: El Louvre, El Prado, El Museo Metropolitano
2. artista / talentoso: Pablo Picasso, Fernando Botero, Frida Kahlo
3. estilo / interesante: el abstracto, el paisaje, el retrato
4. escultura / conocido: *Venus de Milo, David, El pensador*
5. pintura / famoso: *La Mona Lisa* de Da Vinci, *La noche estrellada* de Van Gogh, *El Grito* de Munch
6. pintor / excéntrico: Salvador Dalí, Remedios Varo, Andy Warhol

11.37 **Descripciones** Completa las oraciones con la forma apropiada del participio pasado de los verbos entre paréntesis.

1. Frida Kahlo y Diego Rivera estaban _____ (casar).
2. Hay muchos libros _____ (escribir) sobre el arte latinoamericano.
3. Francisco Goya está _____ (morir).
4. La artesanía de Latinoamérica está _____ (hacer) a mano.
5. Carmen Lomas Garza es una artista _____ (conocer).
6. Diego Velázquez estaba _____ (interesar) en pintar la vida típica en España.
7. Hay varios cuadros de Pablo Picasso _____ (colgar) en los museos de Nueva York.
8. Mucha de la cerámica de las civilizaciones antiguas está _____ (romper).

11.38 **¡Qué día!** Usando el **se** accidental y el verbo entre paréntesis, explica lo que le pasó a Valentina ayer.

Modelo   Se levantó tarde. (olvidar)
          Se le olvidó poner el despertador.

1. Todas sus notas para la reunión se mojaron *(got wet)*. (caer)
2. Su bolígrafo no escribía y no pudo tomar notas en la reunión. (acabar la tinta)
3. Tampoco pudo tomar notas con su lápiz. (romper)
4. No tuvo los reportes para su jefe. (olvidar)
5. A la hora de almorzar no pudo comer nada. (quedar)
6. El coche se paró camino a su casa. (descomponer)
7. No pudo llamar a nadie con su celular. (apagar)
8. Cuando llegó a casa, no pudo entrar. (perder)

11.39 **Un pedido** Trabaja con un compañero. Uno de ustedes es vendedor y el otro es cliente. El cliente necesita ropa para un viaje a la playa. Mira la página del catálogo que aparece a continuación (below) y llama para hacer un pedido. Debes comprar tres prendas. El vendedor necesita ver el **Apéndice B** para contestar las preguntas del cliente y conseguir su información (nombre, teléfono, etcétera) y su tarjeta de crédito.

Modelo Estudiante 1: *Buenas tardes.*
Estudiante 2: *Buenas tardes. Necesito una camiseta de algodón azul en talla extra grande.*
Estudiante 1: *Lo siento. No la tenemos en talla extra grande.*
Estudiante 2: *¿Qué colores tienen en talla extra grande?*

C1050 Camiseta de algodón
Colores:
■ azul ■ negro
■ amarillo ■ beige
Tallas: P, M, G, XG
Precio: 25 €

C4325 Camisa con estampado hawaiano
Colores:
■ azul ■ rojo
■ verde
Tallas: P, M, G, XG
Precio: 35 €

B2219 Blusa de lunares
Colores:
■ blanco/ negro ■ negro/ rosado
■ rojo/blanco
Tallas: P, M, G, XG
Precio: 42 €

P6750 Pantalones cortos a rayas
Colores:
■ blanco/ azul ■ blanco/ verde
■ gris/negro ■ café/beige
Tallas: P, M, G, XG
Precio: 55 €

P7382 Pantalones cortos a cuadros
Colores:
■ azul/ verde ■ negro/ rojo
■ rosado/gris
Tallas: P, M, G, XG
Precio: 48 €

F9124 Falda con estampado de flores
Colores:
■ blanco/rosado (P, G, XG)
■ azul marino/rojo (P, M, XG)
■ anaranjado/amarillo (P, M, G, XG)
Tallas: P, M, G, XG
Precio: 57 €

© Cengage Learning

11.40 **A la moda** Con un compañero, van a decidir quién en la clase está más a la moda.

Paso 1 Con un compañero, completen las siguientes oraciones.

Alguien que está a la moda lleva...
Alguien que está a la moda no lleva...

Paso 2 Compartan sus ideas con el resto de la clase y decidan entre todos cuáles son las características de una persona a la moda.

Paso 3 Con tu compañero, decidan quién creen que está más a la moda en la clase y por qué. Repórtenle a la clase su decisión.

Vocabulario 1

2-26

En la tienda

la caja	*cash register*
el (dinero en) efectivo	*cash*
el número	*size (shoe)*
la oferta	*sale (event, reduction of prices)*
la prenda	*garment*
el probador	*dressing room*
la talla	*size (clothing)*
la tarjeta de crédito	*credit card*
las telas	*fabrics*
la venta	*sale (transaction)*

Telas

el algodón	*cotton*
la lana	*wool*
el lino	*linen*
la mezclilla	*denim*
la piel	*leather*
la seda	*silk*

Estilos

a cuadros	*plaid*
a rayas	*striped*
de lunares	*polka-dot*
estampado(a)	*patterned*

Verbos

elegir (i)	*to choose*
hacer juego	*to match*
probarse (ue)	*to try on*
quedar	*to fit*

Adjetivos

apretado(a)	*tight*
barato(a)	*cheap, inexpensive*
caro(a)	*expensive*
de marca	*name brand*
(estar) a la moda	*(to be) fashionable*
(estar) rebajado(a)	*(to be) on sale*
extra grande	*extra large*
grande	*large*
hecho(a) a mano	*handmade*
liso(a)	*solid*
mediano(a)	*medium*
pequeño(a)	*small*

Expresiones útiles

¡Qué bien te queda esa falda!	*That skirt really fits you well!*
¡Qué caros!	*How expensive!*
¡Qué color tan bonito!	*What a pretty color!*
¡Qué lindos zapatos!	*What pretty shoes!*
¡Qué pantalones tan elegantes!	*What elegant pants!*

Comparaciones

mayor	*older (age)*
mejor	*better*
menor	*younger*
peor	*worse*

Palabras adicionales

el descuento	*discount*
por ciento	*percent*

◀» Vocabulario 2

El arte

el arte abstracto	*abstract art*	la obra	*work (of art, literature, theater, etc.)*
el autorretrato	*self-portrait*		
la escultura	*sculpture*	el óleo	*oil painting*
la exhibición	*exhibit*	el paisaje	*landscape*
la galería	*gallery*	la paleta	*pallet*
el grabado	*engraving; print*	el pincel	*paintbrush*
la luz	*light*	la pintura	*painting*
la máscara	*mask*	el retrato	*portrait*
el mural	*mural*	la tinta	*ink*
la naturaleza muerta	*still life*		

Verbos

acabar	*to finish*	esculpir	*to sculpt*
apagar	*to turn off*	exhibir	*to exhibit*
apreciar	*to appreciate; to enjoy*	olvidar	*to forget*
		posar	*to pose*
descomponer	*to break down (a machine)*	quedar	*to remain (behind)*
diseñar	*to design*	romper	*to break*

Adjetivos

abstracto(a)	*abstract*	obscuro(a)	*dark*
claro(a)	*light, pale*	sencillo(a)	*simple*
complicado(a)	*complex*	surrealista	*surrealist*
cubista	*cubist*	tradicional	*traditional*
extraño(a)	*strange, odd*	vanguardista	*revolutionary; avant-garde*
impresionista	*impressionist*		

Diccionario personal

_____

_____

_____

_____

_____

_____

_____

_____

Learning Strategy

Use a good dictionary

While you should not look up every Spanish word that you
don't understand, a good bilingual dictionary is essential.
Ask your instructor for some recommendations for print
and online dictionaries that include complete entries,
idiomatic expressions and pronunciation. When you look
up an English word, be sure to choose the correct form,
such as a noun or an adjective. If the entry has a number
of definitions, cross-check the one you think you need in
the Spanish-English section to confirm your choice.

In this chapter you will learn how to:

- Talk about the future
- Talk about what you have done
- Discuss the environment
- Express your opinions and knowledge about the animal world and the environment
- Express doubt and certainty

¿Qué será de nuestro planeta?

© J.D. Dallet/age fotostock

La naturaleza nos ofrece las vistas más bellas del planeta y cada uno de sus componentes es vital para preservar el balance del medio ambiente.

El medio ambiente

la contaminación	contamination, pollution
la deforestación	deforestation
los desechos industriales	industrial waste
la ecología	ecology
el esmog	smog
la naturaleza	nature
el petróleo	oil
el reciclaje	recycling
los recursos naturales	natural resources

Los verbos

destruir	to destroy
preservar	to preserve
proteger	to protect

Otros lugares

la bahía	bay
el desierto	desert
el llano	plains
la pampa	grasslands
la península	peninsula
la selva	jungle
el valle	valley

Palabras adicionales

el árbol	tree
el cactus	cactus
la cascada	cascade, waterfall
la catarata	large waterfall
la Tierra	Earth

INVESTIGUEMOS LA GRAMÁTICA

The verb **destruir** is conjugated similarly to the verb **oír**.

La contaminación **destruye** la naturaleza.
Las compañías **destruyeron** el bosque.

A practicar

12.1 **Escucha y responde** Vas a escuchar una serie de ideas. Indica con el pulgar hacia arriba si la idea es lógica, y con el pulgar hacia abajo si es ilógica.

2-28

12.2 **Un poco de lógica** Decide cuál de las palabras completa la oración lógicamente.

1. Me encanta ir a la (costa / colina) y disfrutar del mar y de la arena.
2. En (el llano / la selva) hay muchos insectos y animales exóticos.
3. El (valle / cielo) está entre montañas.
4. Unas de las (cataratas / pampas) más impresionantes son las del Niágara y las de Iguazú.
5. En un (bosque / desierto) hay muchos árboles.
6. En medio del valle hay (una isla / un lago).
7. (Los desechos industriales / El petróleo) es un recurso natural no renovable.
8. Una península está rodeada *(surrounded)* por (el mar / las pampas) por tres lados.

12.3 **¿Cuál es diferente?** Trabaja con un compañero para decidir qué palabra no corresponde *(belongs)* a la lista. Expliquen por qué.

1. la montaña	el mar	el río	el lago
2. la costa	la bahía	la pampa	la península
3. el llano	las palmeras	el pasto	el árbol
4. las montañas	las colinas	la selva	el volcán
5. las cataratas	el medio ambiente	la ecología	la naturaleza
6. las olas	el mar	el valle	la arena

12.4 **Opiniones** Con un compañero, van a discutir si están de acuerdo o no con las siguientes afirmaciones, o si son verdaderas en el caso de ustedes. **¡OJO!** Deben explicar por qué.

1. Me preocupa la ecología y por eso reciclo plásticos, papeles y aluminio.
2. Utilizo el transporte público para usar menos gasolina.
3. La contaminación del aire es un gran problema en mi comunidad.
4. Uso toda el agua que quiero porque se puede procesar y reciclar.
5. No tiene ningún impacto en la ecología lo que una persona hace.
6. Una persona tiene el derecho de hacer lo que quiera con su propiedad privada.
7. Es importante conservar nuestros recursos naturales.

INVESTIGUEMOS LA MÚSICA

Look online for the song "¿Dónde jugarán los niños?" by the Mexican group Maná. Listen to the song and determine what the message is.

12.5 **Las descripciones** Trabaja con un compañero. Uno de ustedes (Estudiante 1) va a describirle el dibujo en esta página a su compañero (Estudiante 2), quien debe dibujar lo que escucha sin ver la ilustración. Al terminar comparen el original y el nuevo dibujo. Después el Estudiante 2 debe describir el dibujo en el **Apéndice B,** y el Estudiante 1 va a dibujarlo.

© Cengage Learning

Conexiones culturales
La diversidad geográfica

Cultura

Algunos artistas se dedican a plasmar *(to create)* los paisajes de su tierra. Estos artistas reciben el nombre de paisajistas. Uno de los paisajistas más famosos en la historia de México fue Gerardo Murillo (1875–1964). Murillo es más conocido como "Dr. Atl", que significa "agua" en náhuatl. En su juventud recibió una beca *(scholarship)* del gobierno mexicano para estudiar en Europa. Murillo consiguió un doctorado en Filosofía y Derecho de la Universidad de Roma en 1898. Su estancia en Europa influyó en él por el contacto que tuvo con el arte del Renacimiento *(Renaissance)* italiano y con el movimiento impresionista de ese tiempo. A su regreso comenzó a pintar activamente y a enseñar arte. En 1920 estudió vulcanología. Por su interés en los volcanes, los pintó en numerosos cuadros. Aquí aparece una reproducción de uno de sus paisajes. ¿Qué hay en el paisaje? ¿Conoces algún paisajista famoso de los Estados Unidos o de algún otro país?

Volcán Iztaccíhuatl

© Volcan Iztaccihuatl (oil on canvas), Atl, Dr. (Gerardo Murillo) (1875–1964) / Private Collection / Photo: © Michel Zabe / AZA INBA / The Bridgeman Art Library International

Investiga en Internet la leyenda relacionada con los volcanes Popocatépetl e Iztaccíhuatl.

Conexiones... a la geografía

Algunos parques nacionales en países donde se habla español son lugares espectaculares gracias a su localización. Entre los más bellos se encuentran los parques al sur de Argentina y Chile. Uno de los más conocidos es el Parque Nacional Los Glaciares, el cual es el segundo más grande de Argentina. Fue creado en 1937 y declarado Patrimonio de la Humanidad por la UNESCO en 1980. En Chile también hay numerosos parques nacionales, entre los que se distingue el Parque Nacional Torres del Paine, en la región antártica chilena. Aunque fue fundado en 1959, recibió su nombre actual en 1970, y en 1978 la UNESCO lo nombró Reserva Mundial de la Biosfera. En ambos parques pueden admirarse también algunos glaciares impresionantes. Los glaciares son masas de hielo compactado que tardan miles de años en formarse. Son una importante fuente de agua potable, pero la mayoría de los glaciares del mundo está desapareciendo a una velocidad alarmante.

Glaciar Perito Moreno, en la Patagonia argentina

© Pichugin Dmitry/Shutterstock

Elige un país hispano e investiga uno de sus parques nacionales ¿Qué características tiene? Comparte la información en Share It! y lee las descripciones de tus compañeros.

Busca otros parques nacionales y aprende más sobre El Salvador, Ecuador, Paraguay y Venezuela en la sección **Exploraciones del mundo hispano** en el **Apéndice A.**

Comparaciones

Biodiversidad es un término que se usa para referirse a la gran variedad de especies que habitan nuestro planeta. Gracias a la diversidad geográfica de algunos países, estos tienen también una enorme variedad de animales y plantas.

Embarcación de los Uros en el lago Titicaca

- El 25% de la tierra de Costa Rica está protegido a través de parques nacionales, mientras que solo el 15% de Venezuela está protegido. ¿Qué porcentaje del territorio de los Estados Unidos está protegido?
- Colombia tiene el segundo lugar en especies vegetales, con 49 000 especies diferentes. Solamente Brasil cuenta con más especies, pero tiene un territorio siete veces más grande que el de Colombia. ¿Cuántas especies vegetales hay en los Estados Unidos y cómo se compara al tamaño de Colombia?
- Colombia tiene el 19,4% de todas las aves *(birds)* del mundo. (África entera el 15%.) Otro país con una biodiversidad impresionante es Costa Rica, que tiene más variedades de aves (850) que los Estados Unidos y Europa juntos. ¿Cuántas especies de aves hay en los Estados Unidos?
- El volcán más alto del mundo está en la región entre Argentina y Chile: el Nevado Ojos del Salado. Tiene una altura de 6870 metros. ¿Cuál es el volcán más alto de Norteamérica y qué altura tiene?
- El lago navegable más alto del mundo es el lago Titicaca, entre Bolivia y Perú. ¿Sabes cuál es el lago más alto de Norteamérica?
- La catarata más alta del mundo es El Salto del Ángel en Venezuela. ¿Cuál es la segunda?
- El desierto de Atacama en Chile es el más seco del mundo. ¿Sabes cuál es el desierto más grande?

Comunidad

Elige un lugar en tu estado que te parezca muy importante conservar y diseña un cartel en español con los datos más importantes sobre el lugar. Después da razones para protegerlo.

Modelo *Es importante conservar la costa de Carolina del Norte para tener agua limpia...*

Panamá tiene áreas protegidas perfectas para bucear.

Exploraciones gramaticales

A analizar ▶

Rosa habla con sus amigos sobre sus planes para su viaje a Costa Rica. Después de ver el video lee parte de su conversación y observa las formas de los verbos.

Paula: ¿Cuándo van a ir?

Rosa: **Saldré** para México el día después de que terminen los exámenes finales, y **me quedaré** dos o tres días con mi familia. Luego mi hermano y yo **saldremos** para Costa Rica y **nos quedaremos** allí por dos semanas.

Nicolás: ¿**Se quedarán** en un lugar o piensan viajar a diferentes lugares?

Rosa: Todavía no tenemos planes concretos, pero queremos conocer todo lo que podamos en dos semanas, así que **estaremos** unos días en San José, luego **viajaremos** al Parque Nacional Santa Rosa. ¡Y, por supuesto, **iremos** a ver el volcán Arenal!

Santiago: ¡**Será** un viaje fantástico!

1. Based on the context of the conversation, what tense are the verbs in bold: past, present, or future?

2. Using the examples in the paragraph above and what you already know about verb conjugation, complete the following verb charts.

yo _____   nosotros _____   yo _____   nosotros _____

tú _____   vosotros necesitaréis   tú _____   vosotros estaréis

él, ella, usted _____   ellos, ellas, ustedes _____   él, ella, usted _____   ellos, ellas, ustedes _____

A comprobar

Future tense

1. You learned in **Capítulo 3** to express the future using the construction **ir + a +** infinitive. It is often used in spoken Spanish and generally refers to something that will happen in the near future. It is also common to use the present tense to express near future.

   Voy a pescar en el lago este fin de semana.
   I'm going to fish at the lake this weekend.

   Salgo para las montañas mañana.
   I'm leaving for the mountains tomorrow.

2. Another way to express what will happen is to use the future tense; however, it tends to be a little more formal and is generally used to refer to a more distant future. To form the future tense, add the endings to the infinitive

(rather than to the verb stem, as is done with most other verb tenses). Note that **-ar, -er,** and **-ir** verbs take the same endings.

hablar

yo	hablar**é**	nosotros(as)	hablar**emos**
tú	hablar**ás**	vosotros(as)	hablar**éis**
él, ella, usted	hablar**á**	ellos, ellas, ustedes	hablar**án**

volver

yo	volver**é**	nosotros(as)	volver**emos**
tú	volver**ás**	vosotros(as)	volver**éis**
él, ella, usted	volver**á**	ellos, ellas, ustedes	volver**án**

ir			
yo	iré	nosotros(as)	iremos
tú	irás	vosotros(as)	iréis
él, ella, usted	irá	ellos, ellas, ustedes	irán

El grupo **irá** a la isla primero.
*The group **will go** to the island first.*

The following are irregular stems for the future tense:

decir	**dir-**	querer	**querr-**
haber	**habr-**	saber	**sabr-**
hacer	**har-**	salir	**saldr-**
poder	**podr-**	tener	**tendr-**
poner	**pondr-**	venir	**vendr-**

Allí **podrán** ver el volcán.
*There **they will be able to** see the volcano.*

3. The future tense is also used to express probability or to speculate about present conditions. Verbs commonly used to speculate about conditions are **ser, estar, haber,** and **tener.** When speculating about present actions, use the future tense of **estar** with the present participle.

Si Octavio no está aquí, **estará** enfermo.
*If Octavio is not here, he **might be** sick.*

¿Quién **será**?
Who could it be? (Who might it be?)

Imagino que el presidente **tendrá** unos cincuenta años.
*I imagine the president **must be** about 50 years old.*

¿Qué hace Raúl en Argentina? ¿**Estará** esquiando?
*What is Raúl doing in Argentina? **Might** he **be** skiing?*

4. Remember that when using the verb **haber** to express the existence of something, it is used in its singular form regardless of whether it is followed by a singular or a plural noun.

Habrá 20 personas en la excursión.
*There **will be** 20 people on the excursion.*

A practicar

12.6 Predicciones para el futuro Lee las siguientes predicciones para el año 2050 y decide si estás de acuerdo o no. Explica tu respuesta.

1. El cielo será gris a consecuencia de la contaminación.
2. Los políticos crearán más leyes *(laws)* para proteger la naturaleza.
3. No dependeremos tanto del petróleo.
4. No existirán muchos de los animales que existen hoy en día.
5. Habrá menos agua potable en el mundo.
6. La gente tendrá menos aparatos eléctricos.
7. Los edificios se harán con materiales reciclados.
8. Los científicos podrán clonar animales que se extinguieron hace mucho tiempo.

Muchos animales estarán en peligro de extinción.

12.7 Nace un ecologista Toño quiere ser más ecologista en el año nuevo y hace una lista de sus resoluciones. Usa el futuro simple para completar las ideas.

1. Yo _____ (usar) menos electricidad y _____ (apagar) las luces al salir de un cuarto.
2. Yo les _____ (decir) a mis amigos que deben comprar solamente productos ecológicos.
3. En el supermercado mi esposa y yo _____ (pedir) solamente bolsas de papel o _____ (tener) bolsas de tela reusables.
4. Nosotros no _____ (conducir) un coche que consuma mucha gasolina; _____ (comprar) uno más económico.
5. Yo les _____ (explicar) a mis hijos que es importante reciclar y ellos _____ (aprender) a proteger el medio ambiente.
6. Yo no _____ (llevar) a mis hijos a la escuela en coche; nosotros _____ (poder) conversar mientras caminamos juntos a la escuela.

12.8 Después del curso Entrevista a un compañero sobre lo que hará después de terminar el curso (semestre, trimestre, etcétera). Pídele información adicional si da una respuesta positiva.

Modelo seguir estudiando el español (¿Dónde?)
    Estudiante 1: *¿Seguirás estudiando español?*
    Estudiante 2: *Sí, seguiré estudiando español.*
    Estudiante 1: *¿Dónde?*
    Estudiante 2: *Tendré otra clase en esta universidad.*

1. hacer un viaje (¿Adónde?)
2. buscar un trabajo (¿Qué tipo de trabajo?)
3. obtener un título *(diploma)* (¿En qué carrera *[major]*?)
4. volver a la universidad para el próximo curso (¿Qué clases tomará?)
5. salir con amigos para celebrar (¿Adónde?)
6. casarse (¿Cuándo?)
7. ir a visitar a su familia (¿Dónde?)
8. mudarse *(to move)* (¿Adónde?)

12.9 En el año 2050 Túrnense para hacer predicciones sobre el año 2050 en las siguientes categorías. Tu compañero te dirá también lo que piensa. Para la última, ustedes van a decidir otro tema. Sean originales.

Modelo la salud
    Estudiante 1: *Los científicos encontrarán una medicina para curar el cáncer.*
    Estudiante 2: *Es posible, pero habrá nuevas enfermedades.*

1. la escuela	3. la casa	5. las vacaciones	7. el dinero
2. el trabajo	4. la familia	6. los amigos	8. ¿?

12.10 ¿Qué pasará? Con un compañero, túrnense para explicar dónde están las personas y lo que están haciendo. Después expresen conjeturas sobre quiénes son, por qué están allí, cuál es la situación y cómo se sienten. Luego explica qué harán después.

Modelo *Ellos están en la playa y están tomando el sol. Seguramente ellos serán esposos y estarán de vacaciones en una isla. Imagino que será su primer aniversario y estarán muy felices. Más tarde saldrán a comer y a bailar.*

INVESTIGUEMOS LA MÚSICA
Find Mexican pop singer Paulina Rubio's song "Volverás" on the Internet and listen to it. What will her ex do?

1.

2.

3.

4.

5.

6.

A analizar

Rosa habla con sus amigos sobre los países que ha visitado en Centroamérica. Después de ver el video, lee parte de la conversación y observa los verbos en negritas. Luego contesta las preguntas al final.

> **Rosa:** ¿Alguno de ustedes **ha ido** a Costa Rica?
>
> **Santiago:** Nunca **he estado** en Centroamérica pero tengo muchas ganas de ir. ¿Tú **has visto** otros países en Centroamérica?
>
> **Rosa:** Sí. Mi hermano y yo **hemos viajado** a Guatemala, a Nicaragua y a Honduras y ahora queremos ir a Costa Rica. Todos los que **han ido,** dicen que es un país increíble con playas y bosques hermosos.

1. In **Capítulo 11** you learned to use the past participle with the verb **estar** to describe. In this conversation they are used with the verb **haber**. How is it conjugated?

2. Based on the context of the conversation, do you think the verbs express past, present, or future?

A comprobar

Present perfect

1. The present perfect is used to express actions that we have and have not done. It combines the present tense of the verb **haber** with the past participle.

haber			
yo	**he**	nosotros(as)	**hemos**
tú	**has**	vosotros(as)	**habéis**
él, ella, usted	**ha**	ellos, ellas, ustedes	**han**

2. You will remember from **Capítulo 11** that to form the regular past participles, you need to add **-ado** to the end of the stem of **-ar** verbs, and **-ido** to the stem of **-er** and **-ir** verbs.

hablar	habl**ado**
beber	beb**ido**
vivir	viv**ido**

The following verbs have accents in the past participles:

creer	**creído**	oír	**oído**
leer	**leído**	traer	**traído**

These are the irregular past participles you learned in **Capítulo 11.**

abrir	**abierto**	hacer	**hecho**
cubrir	**cubierto**	morir	**muerto**
decir	**dicho**	romper	**roto**
despertar	**despertado***	poner	**puesto**
devolver	**devuelto**	ver	**visto**
escribir	**escrito**	volver	**vuelto**

*Note the past participle of **despertar** becomes **despertado** when it is used in the present perfect.

3. When using the past participle with **estar,** it must agree in gender and number with the subject because it functions as an adjective. However, when using the participle with **haber,** it is part of the verb, and it does not agree with the subject.

> Ella **ha trabajado** mucho esta semana.
> Ellos **han ido** a la costa.

4. When using direct object, indirect object, or reflexive pronouns, they are placed in front of the conjugated form of **haber.**

> No **se** han despertado todavía.
> Ya **lo** he visto.

5. In Spanish, the present perfect is generally used as it is in English to talk about something that has happened or something that someone has done. It is usually either unimportant when it happened or it has some relation to the present.

> ¿Alguna vez **has ido** a las montañas?
> *Have you ever gone to the mountains?*

> **He perdido** el mapa y no sé dónde estamos.
> *I've lost the map and don't know where we are.*

6. The following expressions are often used with the present perfect:

alguna vez	*ever*
no... todavía	*not . . . yet, still . . . not*
nunca	*never*
recientemente	*recently*
ya	*already*

> **Ya** hemos ido a esa playa.
> *We have **already** been to that beach.*

> **No** han llegado **todavía.**
> *They have **not** arrived **yet.***

> **¿Alguna vez** has escalado una montaña?
> *Have you **ever** climbed a mountain?*

INVESTIGUEMOS LA GRAMÁTICA

In Spain it is much more common to use the present perfect rather than the preterite when referring to anything that happened that same day.

Hemos nadado en el mar esta mañana.
*We **swam** in the sea this morning.*

A practicar

12.11 **¿Son ecologistas?** Lee lo que dice Adela sobre sus actividades y las de sus amigos y familiares. Decide si las diferentes actividades son ecológicas o no. Explica tu respuesta.

1. Yo siempre he comprado agua en botellas de plástico.
2. Mis amigos y yo hemos empezado a reciclar papel.
3. Esta semana mis amigos han ido a la universidad en autobús cada día.
4. Mi hermano siempre se ha bañado por veinte minutos.
5. Este año mis padres han puesto un jardín con verduras al lado de la casa.
6. Mi tío siempre ha preferido tener un coche grande.
7. Mis padres y yo siempre hemos pedido bolsas de plástico en el supermercado.
8. Este verano he abierto las ventanas en vez de encender el aire acondicionado.

12.12 **¿Qué has hecho?** Con un compañero, completen las siguientes oraciones con información sobre sus experiencias personales.

Modelo Yo he ido a...
    Yo he ido a Puerto Rico. / Yo he ido a una isla.

1. He estado en...
2. He vivido en...
3. He roto...
4. He escrito...
5. He hecho...
6. He visto...
7. He comido...
8. He comprado...

12.13 De campamento Martín y su amigo Gerardo están en un campamento en la tundra argentina. Completa su historia con la forma necesaria del presente perfecto para cada verbo en paréntesis.

Este es nuestro quinto día de excursión. Hasta ahora, **(1.)** _____ (caminar) más de 100 kilómetros, pero no **(2.)** _____ (ver) ningún animal salvaje, excepto un grupo de castores *(beavers)* que **(3.)** _____ (destruir) muchos árboles. Es una lástima ver tantos árboles destruidos. Hace mucho frío por la noche y por eso yo no **(4.)** _____ (dormir) bien y me siento muy cansado. Además, yo tampoco **(5.)** _____ (comer) muy bien porque Gerardo trajo una comida enlatada *(canned)* horrible. Sin embargo, debo admitir que todos nosotros **(6.)** _____ (divertirse) mucho. A Gerardo le encanta la fotografía y **(7.)** _____ (tomar) muchas fotos para compartir a nuestro regreso. ¿Alguna vez **(8.)** _____ (hacer) tú este tipo de excursión?

12.14 ¿Quién lo ha hecho? Con un compañero, túrnense para preguntar y contestar quién ha hecho las siguientes actividades. Si pueden, mencionen otros datos sobre la persona.

Modelo cantar desde *(since)* su niñez
          Estudiante 1: *¿Quién ha cantado desde su niñez?*
          Estudiante 2: *Christina Aguilera.*

1. escribir más de quince novelas
2. recibir varios Premios Golden Globe
3. hacerse famoso como comediante
4. jugar para los Red Sox y los Twins
5. tener más de 70 canciones en la posición número uno en *Billboard*
6. vender más de 30 millones de álbumes
7. ganar las elecciones presidenciales dos veces
8. dirigir películas

  a. Christina Aguilera
  b. Sofía Vergara
  c. Carlos Santana
  d. Enrique Iglesias
  e. Alfonso Cuarón
  f. Michelle Bachelet
  g. George López
  h. Isabel Allende
  i. David Ortiz

12.15 Sondeo En grupos de tres o cuatro estudiantes hagan un sondeo para saber quién ha hecho las siguientes actividades. Túrnense para hacer las preguntas, y después repórtenle sus resultados a la clase.

Modelo trepar un árbol en un bosque
        ¿Quién ha trepado un árbol en un bosque?

1. hacer surf en el océano
2. ver una catarata
3. nadar en un lago
4. esquiar en las montañas

5. acampar en un bosque
6. ir de vacaciones a una isla
7. estar en un desierto
8. correr al lado del mar

12.16 En busca de... Pregúntales a ocho personas diferentes si alguna vez han hecho las siguientes actividades. Pídeles información adicional para reportársela a la clase. Recuerden que necesitan buscar a alguien que conteste que sí.

¿Alguna vez... ?

1. nadar en el mar (¿dónde?)
2. ver un volcán (¿dónde?)
3. ir a una isla (¿cuál?)
4. navegar en un río (¿en cuál?)

5. escalar una montaña (¿cuál?)
6. pescar en un lago (¿dónde?)
7. perderse en un bosque (¿qué hizo?)
8. estar en una selva (¿dónde?)

El volcán Cotopaxi en Ecuador

12.17 Este año Entrevista a tu compañero sobre lo que ha hecho este año.

Modelo leer un libro (¿cuál?)

    Estudiante 1: *¿Has leído un libro este año?*

    Estudiante 2: *Sí, he leído un libro.*

    Estudiante 1: *¿Cuál?*

    Estudiante 2: *Leí* Cien años de soledad.

1. hacer un viaje (¿adónde?)

2. escribir una carta (¿a quién?)

3. visitar a unos amigos o parientes (¿qué hicieron?)

4. mudarse *(to move)* (¿adónde?)

5. tener una fiesta (¿cuándo?)

6. comprar un coche (¿qué coche?)

7. ir a un concierto (¿de quién?)

8. encontrar un nuevo trabajo (¿dónde?)

 12.18 Hechos Con un compañero, túrnense para hablar de lo que han hecho con respecto a los siguientes temas. Ustedes deciden el último tema.

Modelo compras

    Estudiante 1: *Yo he comprado una casa.*

    Estudiante 2: *¿De veras? Yo he comprado un coche nuevo este año.*

1. estudios   5. comida

2. trabajos   6. deportes

3. viajes   7. hazañas *(feats)*

4. relaciones   8. ¿?

12.19 ¿Qué ha pasado? Trabaja con un compañero y túrnense para describir los dibujos. Deben explicar dónde están las personas y lo que ha pasado. Usen el presente perfecto y den muchos detalles.

Modelo *Ella está en la playa con un amigo. El amigo ha ido a nadar y ella se ha dormido y se ha quemado.*

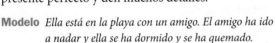

1.

2.

3.

4.

5.

6.

© Cengage Learning

Entrando en materia

El futuro del mundo son los niños, por eso es importante que aprendan a cuidar nuestro planeta desde pequeños. En tu opinión ¿a qué edad podemos empezar a enseñarles a los niños sobre el reciclaje? ¿Cuáles son tres ideas que se le pueden enseñar fácilmente a un niño acerca de reciclar?

Programa educativo para niños

◀)) Vas a escuchar un segmento de un programa de televisión acerca de cómo y qué
2-29 enseñarles a los niños.

Vocabulario útil

el envase	*container*
la envoltura	*packaging*
la pila	*battery*
el vidrio	*glass*

Comprensión

Decide si las ideas son ciertas o falsas según la información que escuchaste. Corrige las ideas falsas.

1. El Día Mundial del Reciclaje se celebra el 17 de mayo en todo el mundo.
2. Los niños están listos para aprender a separar el reciclaje a la edad de cinco años.
3. El mejor ejemplo para que los niños aprendan lo dan los padres.
4. El vidrio se debe poner en el contenedor azul.
5. Recuperar materiales significa que deben volver a utilizarse.
6. Una estrategia para reducir es comprar en envases de plástico.

Más allá

Los consejos que leíste son para enseñarles a niños pequeños. ¿Qué se debe hacer para informar a más adultos sobre el reciclaje? Escribe cinco ideas en Share It! y lee las recomendaciones de tus compañeros.

© auremar/Shutterstock

Lectura

Reading Strategy: Test your comprehension at the end of a reading.

The more actively you participate in a reading, the more you will get out of it. In **Capítulo 10** you learned to summarize each paragraph as you read. When you've finished reading, try creating a concise summary that explains the essence or main point of the text.

Estrategia

Use a good dictionary

Remember, do not look up every word that you don't understand, just the ones that are essential for comprehension.

Antes de leer

1. ¿Alguna vez has visitado un parque nacional? ¿Cuál?
2. ¿Puedes nombrar algunos parques nacionales famosos en los Estados Unidos? ¿Por qué es importante mantener los parques nacionales?

A leer

Los parques nacionales de Costa Rica y de Ecuador

Costa Rica fue uno de los primeros países en Latinoamérica en reconocer la importancia de la protección de los recursos naturales. Desde 1970 casi el 25% de su territorio ha sido declarado parque nacional o zona de protección.

Costa Rica es un país que se distingue por su respeto a la ecología y a la preservación del medio ambiente. Su sistema de parques nacionales refleja la preocupación

Una cascada en La Paz, Costa Rica

> [es un país que se distingue por su respeto a la ecología y a la preservación del medio ambiente]

por conservar la flora y la fauna del país. El éxito de sus parques nacionales es evidente al contemplar los hermosos paisajes de este país: cascadas cristalinas, playas, montañas y ríos para explorar, así como sitios arqueológicos e históricos.

Esto ha sido posible gracias a que los costarricenses consideran el **ambientalismo** una responsabilidad nacional. En este pequeño país existen 205 especies de mamíferos, 845 especies de aves, 160 especies de anfibios, 218 especies de reptiles y 1013 especies de peces de agua dulce.

environmentalism

Los parques nacionales de Costa Rica también son de gran importancia económica ya que se han convertido en importantes centros de atracción para los turistas que visitan Costa Rica. El país ha desarrollado una importante infraestructura hotelera para satisfacer la demanda de este turismo sin dañar al medio ambiente. Costa Rica es, sin duda, un ejemplo a seguir en materia de ecología.

Ecuador es otro país pequeño que también cuenta con una red importante de reservas ecológicas y parques nacionales públicos y privados. De entre

© Luis Louro/Shutterstock

todos sus parques, el más conocido es el Parque Nacional Galápagos, establecido en 1959. Se calcula que las islas se formaron **hace** más de ocho millones de años, pero fueron descubiertas apenas en 1535, accidentalmente. Por mucho tiempo las Galápagos fueron utilizadas por piratas ingleses como **escondite**. Las islas se hicieron famosas debido a Darwin, quien concibió su teoría de la evolución gracias a lo que observó en estas islas.

hace... años
years ago

hideout

Pelícanos en las islas Galápagos

En la actualidad el Parque Nacional Galápagos está compuesto por más de 30 islas y tiene una extensión de 693 700 hectáreas. En él abundan especies endémicas, es decir, que no existen en ninguna otra parte del mundo, por lo que tiene mucha importancia. Debido al delicado equilibrio de las islas, existen guías de **comportamiento** muy específicas para los visitantes. Por ejemplo, no es posible visitar las islas sin un guía especializado; no se debe acercar a ningún animal a menos de dos metros, para no alterar su comportamiento; no se debe introducir ningún organismo vivo, y jamás se deben comprar recuerdos que incluyan partes de animales. A pesar de estas rigurosas reglas, las Galápagos están en la lista de Patrimonio Universal en **peligro,** y hay quien piensa que eventualmente se prohibirá el acceso a los visitantes.

behavior

danger

Comprensión

1. ¿Qué porcentaje del territorio costarricense ocupan los parques nacionales y las zonas de protección?

2. ¿Cómo muestra Costa Rica el respeto por su tierra?

3. ¿Dónde es evidente el éxito de los parques nacionales?

4. ¿Por qué los parques nacionales tienen una gran importancia económica?

5. ¿Cuándo se estableció el Parque Nacional Galápagos?

6. ¿Por qué se hicieron famosas las Galápagos?

7. ¿Cuáles son dos reglas importantes que se deben seguir cuando se visitan las islas?

8. En tu opinión ¿tienen los Estados Unidos una estrategia de conservación similar a la de Costa Rica? Explica las semejanzas y diferencias.

Después de leer

Costa Rica es uno de los países latinoamericanos que más se esfuerza *(makes an effort)* por proteger su ecología. Escoge otro país de hispanohablantes e investiga lo que hacen sus habitantes para conservar la naturaleza. Luego, descríbele a la clase el área y los esfuerzos que se hacen para protegerla.

La vida en una granja no es fácil. Hay muchos animales que cuidar.

la ardilla

el águila

la jirafa

la granja

las ovejas

los conejos

las vacas

los cerdos

el pavo las gallinas

el gallo

los pollos

los patos

la tortuga

el pingüino

la rana

© Cengage Learning

INVESTIGUEMOS EL VOCABULARIO

Although a gender (**el** or **la**) is assigned to a species, we cannot assume the gender of the animal by the name. You can specify the gender of a specific animal by saying that it is **macho** *(male)*, or **hembra** *(female)*. For example, the generic term for *squirrel* is **la ardilla**, but we can talk about **una ardilla macho** or **una ardilla hembra**. For very common domesticated animals such as cats and dogs, it is common to change the ending: **perra, gata,** etc.; however, a few animals have different names, based on their gender:

caballo	yegua
toro	vaca
gallo	gallina

Los animales

la ballena	whale
la cebra	zebra
el cocodrilo	crocodile
el elefante	elephant
el gorila	gorilla
el jaguar	jaguar
el león	lion
la llama	llama
el lobo	wolf
el mono	monkey

el oso	bear
la serpiente	snake
el tiburón	shark
el tigre	tiger
el toro	bull
el venado	deer
el zorro	fox

Clasificaciones

los anfibios	amphibians
las aves	birds

los mamíferos	mammals
los peces	fish
los reptiles	reptiles

Palabras adicionales

cazar	to hunt
la caza	hunting
la jaula	cage
el peligro	danger
(de extinción)	(of extinction)
salvaje	wild

A practicar

12.20 **Escucha y responde** Escucharás algunas ideas sobre el hábitat de los animales. Si piensas que una idea es cierta, levanta la mano. Si es falsa, no hagas nada.

2-30

12.21 **Identificaciones** Decide a qué grupo corresponden los siguientes animales.

anfibio   ave   mamífero   pez   reptil

Modelo gorila *mamífero*

1. el cocodrilo
2. el pingüino
3. el zorro
4. el tiburón
5. el águila
6. la serpiente
7. la llama
8. la gallina
9. la ballena
10. la rana

12.22 **La personalidad de los animales** Observa la lista de descripciones y con un compañero decidan qué animales se asocian con cada descripción. Luego decidan si son verdaderos estos estereotipos de los animales o si son mentira. Expliquen por qué.

Modelo tonto
    el burro, la vaca

1. inteligente
2. loco
3. chistoso
4. sucio
5. limpio
6. leal *(loyal)*
7. perezoso
8. majestuoso

12.23 **Asociaciones** ¿Qué sabes de estos animales? Con un compañero, túrnense para relacionar un animal con una palabra de la lista y explicar le relación.

selva   bosque   mar   pasto   huevos
ratones   domesticado   salvaje   desierto

Modelo pandas – extinción
    Los pandas son animales en peligro de extinción. Hay muy pocos en el mundo.

1. osos
2. leones
3. zorros
4. delfines
5. tortugas
6. serpientes
7. coyotes
8. vacas

12.24 **Entrevista** Entrevista a un compañero con las siguientes preguntas.

1. Aparte de tus mascotas ¿cuál es tu animal favorito? ¿Por qué?
2. ¿Piensas que los derechos de los animales son importantes? ¿Por qué?
3. ¿Con qué frecuencia vas al zoológico? ¿Qué animales prefieres visitar?
4. ¿Te gustaría *(Would you like)* vivir con muchos animales en una granja? ¿Por qué?
5. ¿Te gustaría hacer un safari? ¿Por qué?
6. ¿Qué animales piensas que son los más inteligentes? ¿Por qué?
7. ¿Crees que los animales piensan y sienten? ¿Por qué lo crees?

12.25 **Donaciones** Imagina que un compañero y tú trabajan para el *World Wildlife Fund*. Uno de ustedes va a trabajar con la tabla en esta página, y el otro va a completar la tabla en el **Apéndice B.** Compartan la información para completarla y después decidan para qué animal deben hacer la siguiente campaña para recibir más donaciones.

ESPECIE	DONACIONES	PAÍS/ REGIÓN
1. Pingüino imperial	$200.340,00	Argentina/Chile/Antártica
2. El orangután	$1.050.450,00	
3. El jaguar	$503.789,00	
4. El oso frontino		Venezuela
5. El cóndor andino		Zonas montañosas de Sudamérica
6. El oso polar		

Conexiones culturales

El reino animal

Cultura

En todas las culturas, los animales han sido usados para protagonizar cuentos para niños, fábulas y otras historias. El escritor guatemalteco Augusto Monterroso utilizó animales para escribir fábulas modernas, muchas veces impregnadas de crítica social y de un humor cínico. Monterroso (1921–2003) nació en Honduras, pero su familia era de Guatemala, y allí creció. Debido a cuestiones políticas, tuvo que exiliarse en 1944. Al principio vivió en Chile y Bolivia, y finalmente se mudó a México, en donde vivió la mayor parte de su vida. Es famoso por sus cuentos cortos, y es también el autor del cuento más corto de la historia de la literatura universal.

La fábula del burro y la flauta

La siguiente fábula es una de las más conocidas de Monterroso.

Investiga en Internet otras fábulas hispanohablantes. Comparte una fábula en Share It!

El burro y la flauta

Tirada en el **campo** [field] estaba desde hacía tiempo una Flauta que ya nadie tocaba, hasta que un día un Burro que paseaba por ahí **resopló** [puffed] fuerte sobre ella haciéndola producir el sonido más dulce de su vida, es decir, de la vida del Burro y de la Flauta.

Incapaces de comprender lo que había pasado, pues la racionalidad no era su fuerte y ambos creían en la racionalidad, se separaron presurosos, avergonzados de lo mejor que el uno y el otro habían hecho durante su triste existencia.

En tu opinión ¿cuál es la crítica que hace el autor en esta fábula?

 Investigue quiénes son otros guatemaltecos famosos y aprenda más sobre Guatemala en **Exploraciones del mundo hispano** en el **Apéndice A.**

Comunidad

En muchas partes del mundo hispanohablante hay especies endémicas, es decir, especies que existen solamente en ese lugar. Habla con una persona de España o de algún país hispanoamericano y pregúntale qué especies son únicas de su país y si están protegidas.

El quetzal vive en las selvas de Centroamérica.

Comparaciones

Se calcula que existen de 5 a 50 millones de especies diversas en nuestro planeta, aunque hasta la fecha solo se han descrito alrededor de 1,4 millones.

El número total de especies conocidas en cada país es muy diferente. Algunos países son mucho más biodiversos que otros. Por ejemplo, en Colombia hay 1821 especies de aves, más que cualquier otro país del mundo, mientras que en Ecuador se encuentra el Parque Nacional Yasuní, la región con más biodiversidad en todo el planeta. ¿Sabes cuántas especies de aves habitan en los Estados Unidos?

La siguiente tabla muestra cinco países muy ricos por su cantidad de plantas, anfibios, reptiles y mamíferos. Investiga qué lugar ocupan los Estados Unidos en cada una de estas categorías. ¿Te sorprenden los resultados? ¿Por qué? ¿Puedes mencionar algunas especies que vivan solamente en el territorio de los Estados Unidos?

Se calcula que existen entre 5 y 50 millones de especies en nuestro planeta.

**Los países con más biodiversidad en el mundo
(País y número de especies)**

Plantas	Anfibios	Reptiles	Mamíferos
Brasil, 55 000	Brasil, 516	México, 707	Indonesia, 519
Colombia, 45 000	Colombia, 407	Australia, 597	México, 439
China, 30 000	Ecuador, 358	Indonesia, 529	Brasil, 421
México, 26 000	México, 282	Brasil, 462	China, 410
Australia, 25 000	Indonesia, 270	India, 433	Zaire, 409

Source: Instituto Nacional de Ecología, México

Conexiones... a la ecología

De acuerdo a la Unión Internacional para la Conservación de la Naturaleza (IUCN por sus siglas en inglés), un 40% de todos los organismos puede considerarse en peligro de extinción. Según el U.S. Fish and Wildlife Service, hay 1533 especies en peligro de extinción o amenazadas tan solo en los Estados Unidos (2014).

La siguiente lista es de varias especies de animales que están en peligro de extinción. Elige una y averigua: ¿Dónde vive este animal? ¿Por qué está en peligro? ¿Qué se debe hacer para preservarla? ¿Por qué se debe preservar? Repórtale a la clase lo que aprendiste.

Una iguana de las islas Galápagos

el axolotl	el murciélago gris
la tortuga gigante	el ocelote
el quetzal	el jaguar
la iguana de las islas Galápagos	el oso grizzly
el perico puertorriqueño	la ballena jorobada
la tortuga verde	el puma

A analizar

Camila habla con sus alumnos (*students*) sobre algunos animales en peligro de extinción. Después de ver el video, lee parte de su conversación y observa los verbos en negritas.

Camila:	Todos [estos animales] están en peligro de extinción. Quiere decir que es posible que algún día **no existan.**
Estudiante:	Pero no es justo que **se mueran.**
Camila:	Estoy de acuerdo... muchos animales ya no tienen donde vivir.
Estudiante:	No creo que puedan vivir en mi casa.
Camila:	Tienes razón... Es mejor que **estén** en la naturaleza.

© Cengage Learning

1. The verbs in bold are in the subjunctive. What verb form is similar?

2. Look at the expressions that precede the verbs in the subjunctive. What do they all have in common?

A comprobar

Subjunctive with impersonal expressions

Until now, all the verb tenses you have studied (present, preterite, imperfect, future, etc.) have been in the indicative. The indicative is an objective mood that is used to state facts and to talk about things that you are certain have occurred or will occur.

Las águilas están en peligro.   *Eagles are endangered.*

In contrast, the subjunctive is a subjective mood that is used to convey uncertainty, anticipated or hypothetical events, or the subject's wishes, fears, doubts, and emotional reactions.

Es terrible que las águilas desaparezcan.   *It is terrible (that) the eagles may disappear.*

The present subjunctive

1. You will notice that the subjunctive verb forms are very similar to formal commands. To form the present subjunctive, drop the **-o** from the first person **(yo)** present tense form and add the opposite ending. Add the **-er** endings for **-ar** verbs, and the **-ar** endings for **-er** and **-ir** verbs.

hablar		comer		vivir	
hable	hablemos	coma	comamos	viva	vivamos
hables	habléis	comas	comáis	vivas	viváis
hable	hablen	coma	coman	viva	vivan

2. Verbs that are irregular in the first person present indicative have the same stem in the present subjunctive.

> Es importante que **conduzcas** con cuidado porque hay venados.

3. Stem-changing **-ar** and **-er** verbs follow the same pattern as in the present indicative, changing in all forms except the **nosotros** and **vosotros** forms.

> Es bueno que **podamos** hacer algo, pero es necesario que todos **piensen** en el medio ambiente.

4. Stem-changing **-ir** verbs follow the same pattern as in the present indicative, however there is an additional change in the **nosotros** and **vosotros** forms. The additional stem change is similar to that in the third person preterite (**e → i** and **o → u**).

> Es mejor que nosotros **durmamos** en la casa y que los animales **duerman** afuera.

5. You will recall that the formal commands of verbs whose infinitives end in **-car, -gar,** and **-zar** have spelling changes. These same spelling changes occur in the subjunctive as well.

> Es necesario que todos **busquemos** una solución.

> Es malo que el gallo **empiece** a cantar tan temprano.

6. The subjunctive of the following verbs is irregular: **dar (dé), haber (haya), ir (vaya), saber (sepa),** and **ser (sea).** You will notice that once again the subjunctive form is similar to the formal command forms.

> Es imposible que **vayas** a la granja mañana.

> Es horrible que **haya** tantos animales en peligro de extinción.

7. Impersonal expressions do not have a specific subject and can include a large number of adjectives: **es bueno, es difícil, es importante, es triste,** etc. They can be negative or affirmative.

The following are impersonal expressions:

es buena/mala idea	es mejor	es recomendable
es horrible	es necesario	es ridículo
es imposible	es posible	es terrible
es increíble	es probable	es una lástima (*it's a shame*)
es justo (*it's fair*)	es raro	es urgente

8. When using an impersonal expression to convey an opinion or an emotional reaction, it is necessary to use the subjunctive with it. While in English the conjunction *that* is optional, in Spanish, it is necessary to use the **que** between the clauses.

> **Es importante que protejamos** a los animales.
> *It is important that we protect the animals.*

> **Es una lástima que haya** animales en peligro de extinción.
> *It's a shame (that) there are animals in danger of extinction.*

For complete verb charts of the stem-changing and irregular subjunctive verbs, please see Appendix H.

INVESTIGUEMOS LA GRAMÁTICA
When there is no specific subject, the infinitive is generally used after the impersonal expression.
Es imposible ver a todos los animales.
It is impossible to see all the animals.

A practicar

12.26 **Es lógico** Combina las dos columnas para crear ideas lógicas.

1. No es necesario que yo...
2. Es importante que todos nosotros...
3. Es urgente que el gobierno...
4. Es mejor que tú...
5. Es increíble que unos animales...

a. haga leyes (*laws*) para proteger la ecología.
b. se extingan rápidamente.
c. compre ropa o zapatos de piel.
d. pensemos en las otras criaturas que también viven en la tierra.
e. sigas las regulaciones de la caza.

12.27 ¿Es buena idea? Un amigo vive en un apartamento y va a adoptar una nueva mascota. Lee las siguientes afirmaciones, decide si son buenas ideas o no, y completa las oraciones con la forma necesaria del subjuntivo del verbo entre paréntesis.

(No) Es buena idea que él...

1. _____ (buscar) un animal de un refugio *(shelter)*.

2. _____ (decidir) si quiere un perro o un gato.

3. le _____ (pagar) un depósito al propietario *(owner)* del apartamento.

4. _____ (adoptar) un perro grande.

5. _____ (consultar) con su compañero de casa.

6. _____ (tener) prisa al tomar su decisión.

INVESTIGUEMOS LA MÚSICA

Joaquín Sabina is one of the more famous contemporary Spanish composers and musicians. Listen to his song "Es mentira." What are the lies mentioned in the song? Why does the person lie?

12.28 En un zoológico loco Con un compañero, miren el dibujo y túrnense para hablar sobre sus reacciones/recomendaciones, usando expresiones impersonales y el subjuntivo.

Modelo *Es raro que no haya hielo en la jaula de los pingüinos.*

© Cengage Learning

Para más información sobre Guinea Ecuatorial ve **Exploraciones del mundo hispano** en el **Apéndice A.**

12.29 El safari Un amigo va a hacer un safari en Guinea Ecuatorial. En parejas, túrnense para completar las siguientes ideas con sus recomendaciones. **¡OJO!** Recuerden que deben usar el subjuntivo.

1. Es buena idea que...   5. Es mala idea que...

2. Es necesario que...   6. Es probable que...

3. Es importante que...   7. Es imposible que...

4. Es recomendable que...   8. Es increíble que...

12.30 Consejos para un amigo Trabaja con un compañero para darle al menos seis consejos a una persona que piensa asistir a tu universidad. Usen expresiones impersonales diferentes y el subjuntivo. Después compartan los consejos con la clase.

Modelo *Es buena idea que viva cerca de la universidad.*

Exploraciones **gramaticales**

A analizar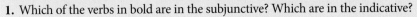

Camila habla con sus alumnos sobre algunos animales en peligro de extinción. Mira el video otra vez. Después lee parte de su conversación y observa los verbos en negritas.

> **Camila:** Es cierto que todos **son** animales, pero tienen algo más en común. Todos están en peligro de extinción... muchos animales ya no tienen donde vivir.
>
> **Estudiante:** Y no creo que **puedan** vivir en mi casa.
>
> **Camila:** Tienes razón. Dudo que **estén** felices viviendo en casas.
>
> **Estudiante:** Pues yo creo que **puedo** tener un gorila en el jardín de mi casa.
>
> **Camila:** No pienso que tu jardín **sea** el lugar adecuado para un gorila.

© Cengage Learning

1. Which of the verbs in bold are in the subjunctive? Which are in the indicative?
2. What expressions precede the verbs in the subjunctive? And in the indicative? How can you explain this difference?

A comprobar

Subjunctive with expressions of doubt

1. When expressing doubt or uncertainty about an action or a condition, you must use the subjunctive. The following are some common expressions of doubt that require the use of the subjunctive:

Dudar *(to doubt)* que	No estar seguro(a) que
No creer que	No ser cierto/verdad/
No pensar que	obvio/evidente que
No suponer	
(to suppose) que	

Dudo que la cebra **corra** más rápido que el león.
*I **doubt that** the zebra **runs** faster than the lion.*

No pensamos que los elefantes **duerman.**
*We **don't think that** the elephants **are sleeping.***

2. When using the expressions below to affirm a belief or express certainty, you must use the indicative.

Creer que	Estar seguro(a) que
Pensar que	Ser cierto/verdad/
Suponer que	obvio/evidente que

Creo que la preservación de la ecología **es** importante.
*I **believe that** the conservation of the ecology **is** important.*

Es obvio que necesitamos hacer algo.
*It **is obvious that we need** to do something.*

3. When using the verbs **pensar** and **creer** in a question, it is possible to use the subjunctive in the dependent clause as you are not affirming a belief.

¿Crees que **haya** suficiente comida para los animales?
*Do you think **there is** enough food for the animals?*

INVESTIGUEMOS LA GRAMÁTICA

While the expressions **negar** and **dudar** always require the subjunctive, there is variation in its use with **no negar** and **no dudar.** With these expressions, some speakers will use the subjunctive *(doubt)* or the indicative *(certainty)*, depending on the speaker's intention. You might prefer to use an expression of certainty like **estoy seguro(a)** or **es cierto** if you mean that you are completely sure about something.

A practicar

12.31 ¿Qué animal es? Lee los comentarios de los alumnos de Camila y decide a cuál de los animales se refiere cada uno.

el águila	el oso polar	la serpiente
el toro	**la tortuga**	**la vaca**

1. Creo que vive en el desierto.
2. Es obvio que produce leche.
3. Dudo que sea muy rápida.
4. No creo que le gusten las temperaturas muy altas.
5. No es cierto que le moleste el color rojo.
6. Pienso que es el símbolo de los Estados Unidos.

12.32 Oraciones incompletas Completa las oraciones con la frase apropiada. **¡OJO!** Algunas oraciones necesitan el subjuntivo y otras no.

1. Creo que el caballo...
   a. es un animal fuerte.   **b.** sea un animal fuerte.
2. Dudo que la tortuga...
   a. corre rápido.   **b.** corra rápido.
3. Supongo que las gallinas...
   a. tienen miedo del zorro.   **b.** tengan miedo del zorro.
4. Estoy seguro que el camello...
   a. no necesita agua.   **b.** no necesite agua.
5. No pienso que la oveja...
   a. come carne.   **b.** coma carne.
6. No es cierto que los pingüinos...
   a. saben volar *(to fly)*.   **b.** sepan volar.
7. No creo que el elefante...
   a. salta.   **b.** salte.
8. Es obvio que el cocodrilo...
   a. no puede sacar la lengua *(tongue)*.   **b.** no pueda sacar la lengua.

12.33 En clase Completa el siguiente párrafo con la forma apropiada del verbo entre paréntesis. **¡OJO!** Algunos verbos requieren el subjuntivo y otros el indicativo.

Miguel: Profesor, ¿es verdad que **(1.)** _____ (haber) muchos animales en peligro de extinción?

Profesor: Sí, es cierto. Es obvio que muchas personas no **(2.)** _____ (pensar) en el medio ambiente y no creen que sus acciones **(3.)** _____ (afectar) el mundo mucho. Yo creo que todos **(4.)** _____ (deber) hacer nuestra parte.

Miguel: Dudo que yo **(5.)** _____ (poder) cambiar las cosas *(make a difference)*.

Profesor: No creo que **(6.)** _____ (saber) todo lo que puedes hacer. Es cierto que tú **(7.)** _____ (ser) nada más una persona, pero hay muchas organizaciones que buscan voluntarios.

12.34 **En el reino de los animales** Trabaja con un compañero para decidir si son ciertas las siguientes oraciones. Luego usen las expresiones de duda para expresarle sus creencias *(beliefs)* a la clase. **¡OJO!** Usa el subjuntivo solo si tienes duda.

Modelo La cebra es blanca y negra.
Es obvio que la cebra es blanca y negra.
El pez puede vivir fuera del agua.
No creo que el pez pueda vivir fuera del agua.

1. El hipopótamo es carnívoro.
2. Se escucha a un león rugir *(to roar)* a cinco millas.
3. La boa vive en África.
4. Una tortuga puede vivir más de cien años.
5. A los gorilas les gusta tomar una siesta por la tarde.
6. Todos los osos duermen en el invierno.
7. El tigre es el más grande de los felinos.
8. Las rayas de cada cebra son únicas.
9. El gallo canta para despertar a las gallinas.
10. Algunas ardillas pueden medir *(measure)* hasta un metro.

12.35 **¿Qué piensas?** Usando las expresiones de duda, expresa tus opiniones acerca de las circunstancias en los dibujos.

Modelo *Es obvio que la niña quiere comprar el perro.*
Dudo que la madre le compre el perro.

1.
2.
3.
4.
5.
6.

© Cengage Learning

12.36 **En mi opinión** En grupos de tres, expresen sus opiniones sobre los siguientes temas usando el subjuntivo o el indicativo con las expresiones **(no) creer, (no) dudar, (no) pensar, (no) suponer, (no) estar seguro que** y **(no) ser cierto/evidente/verdad/obvio que.**

Modelo la crueldad con los animales
Pienso que el abuso de los animales es un crimen. Ellos no pueden protegerse.
No creo que las personas que son crueles con animales sean buenas personas.

1. ser vegetariano
2. la caza
3. la extinción de algunos animales
4. usar pieles de animales
5. la corrida de toros
6. los zoológicos
7. el problema de los gatos y perros callejeros *(stray)*
8. las peleas de gallos o de perros

Lectura

Antes de leer

1. ¿Conoces alguna historia sobre animales fantásticos? ¿Cuál?
2. ¿Cuáles son otros animales fantásticos de los que has oído?
3. ¿Por qué crees que hay historias sobre animales fantásticos?
4. ¿Piensas que existen o existieron? Explica por qué.

A leer

Animales fantásticos

Los animales han inspirado la creatividad y la imaginación de los hombres desde tiempos ancestrales, pero muchas veces lo que existe en la realidad parece más increíble que lo que puede hacer la imaginación, como se ve en la variedad y forma de algunos animales que viven en nuestro planeta. Cada año se descubren animales que parecen sacados de libros de ciencia ficción, en especial algunos organismos que viven en las profundidades de los océanos.

Una interpretación artística del Chupacabras

De la misma manera, por mucho tiempo se ha hablado de animales que nadie ha podido comprobar que existan. Algunos ejemplos conocidos son los de un tipo de dinosaurio que supuestamente vive en Escocia (el monstruo del lago Ness), el Yeti (el abominable hombre de las nieves), el de Sasquash (similar al Yeti, pero que habita supuestamente en el noroeste de los Estados Unidos), y el cada vez más célebre Chupacabras.

[se dice que es una mezcla de coyote o perro sin pelo, de rata, y hasta de canguro]

La historia del Chupacabras se inicia en los años 90, cuando empiezan a aparecer numerosos animales muertos sin **sangre,** como caballos, ovejas, **cabras,** gallinas y perros. El primer **avistamiento** del Chupacabras se reportó en Puerto Rico, pero en la actualidad hay personas que aseguran haberlo visto en lugares tan alejados como Argentina, Colombia y Chile. Sin embargo, la mayoría de los reportes siguen siendo de Puerto Rico, la República Dominicana, México y los Estados Unidos.

blood

goats/sighting

Según las personas que dicen haberlo visto, el Chupacabras es una mezcla de animales diferentes: se dice que es una mezcla de coyote o perro sin pelo, de rata, y hasta de canguro. Algunos le encuentran parecido con las gárgolas de la mitología europea. En lo que todos están de acuerdo, es en que el Chupacabras tiene forma humanoide y mide aproximadamente un metro de altura. También es un **hecho** que el interés acerca del Chupacabras ha dado como resultado una gran cantidad de publicidad y de artículos para el mercado: es fácil encontrar camisetas, tazas, libros y sombreros con la imagen del Chupacabras. Su existencia real seguirá siendo un misterio, pero su aparición en el cine, en la televisión, en los cómics, en videojuegos, en las leyendas urbanas y hasta en la música, no es ficticia.

fact

Comprensión

Contesta las preguntas según la lectura.

1. ¿Cuáles son algunos animales fantásticos?
2. ¿Cuándo y dónde comenzó la historia del Chupacabras? ¿Por qué?
3. ¿En qué países hay reportes de un animal como el Chupacabras?
4. ¿En qué productos se puede ver el Chupacabras hoy en día *(today)*?

Después de leer

En parejas, escriban una lista de otros animales que han despertado la imaginación de los humanos, y algunas películas o programas de televisión famosos que se inspiran en animales. Luego, escriban una idea para una película en la que un nuevo animal sea el protagonista de la historia. ¿Qué ocurre en la película? ¿Cómo termina?

© Ruslan Kudrin/Shutterstock

Redacción

An editorial in a newspaper is an opinion piece. Imagine that you work for a newspaper and have been asked to write an editorial in which you express your opinion on an animal issue or an environmental issue.

Estrategia

Use a good dictionary

When you look up the Spanish translation for an English word, pay attention to the parts of speech in order to choose the correct form. If the entry has a number of options, look up some of the words in the Spanish-English section to be sure that you choose the correct word.

Paso 1 Pick one of the following topics about which you have an opinion: water conservation, recycling, vegetarianism, hunting, or zoos. Or you may choose to come up with your own topic.

Paso 2 In order to write a good argument, it is important to think of both sides of the issue. Write down a list of pros and cons related to the issue.

Paso 3 Pick two of the items you wrote in **Paso 2** that support your view on the issue. Then jot down other ideas related to each of the points you have chosen.

> **Modelo** *El zoológico ayuda a educar a la gente.*
> *a. La gente puede observar los hábitos de los animales.*
> *b. La gente aprende a apreciar los animales.*
> *c. El zoológico tiene información sobre los animales.*

Paso 4 Write a topic sentence in which you express your opinion on the animal issue you have chosen to write about. Decide which of the points you chose in **Paso 3** you would like to begin your argument with, and then write your first paragraph using the information you generated. You may want to mention an opposing argument and refute it in your paragraph.

Paso 5 Write a transition sentence that will introduce your second point. You may think about using expressions such as **además de** *(besides)*, **por otra parte** *(moreover)*, or **aparte de** *(aside from)*.

Paso 6 Using the information you generated on the second point in **Paso 3,** write your second paragraph.

Paso 7 Write a concluding paragraph in which you restate your opinion and summarize your arguments. When restating your opinion, you should not use the same sentence you began your essay with. Instead, find another way to express your point of view.

Paso 8 Edit your paragraph:

1. Do all of the sentences in each paragraph support your topic sentence? If not, get rid of them.
2. Do you have smooth transitions between sentences and between paragraphs?
3. Do verbs agree with the subject? Are they conjugated correctly?
4. Did you use any expressions that require you to use the subjunctive?

Entrando en materia

¿Cuáles son algunos animales en peligro de extinción?

Bitácora (Blog)

Lee el siguiente artículo sobre algunos animales que están en peligro.

Cuatro especies animales en peligro de extinción en 2010

publicado el viernes 21 mayo 2010 por Me en: Animales Naturaleza EcoComunicados Información Peligro de Extinción

Esta es una de esas listas que nunca es inoportuno recordar: la de los animales más amenazados*, aquellos que están a un paso de extinguirse en la naturaleza y, en el caso de algunos, de desaparecer definitivamente de la faz de este planeta. Tal es el caso del rinoceronte de Java, el mamífero grande más raro de la Tierra y del que quedan 70 ejemplares en toda la Tierra.

threatened

El pingüino de Magallanes, bautizado en honor al explorador Fernando de Magallanes, con quien se encontró en 1520, vive en las costas de Argentina, Chile y las Islas Malvinas. Está amenazado por la pesca comercial y el cambio en las corrientes* oceánicas y en la temperatura del mar. El Fondo Mundial para la Naturaleza cree que estas pudieron ser las razones de que en el año 2009 cientos de estos pingüinos aparecieran muy enfermos o muertos en las playas de Río de Janeiro.

currents

Pingüinos de Magallanes en Argentina

© SDC/Shutterstock

La vaquita marina no es de las especies marinas más conocidas. De esta marsopa endémica de México no existen, de acuerdo con la organización Vaquita Marina, más de 600 individuos. Habita en el Golfo de California y la principal amenaza que enfrenta son las redes* pesqueras, en las que anualmente mueren atrapados entre 40 y 80 ejemplares.

nets

El murciélago* de Florida, *Eumops floridanus*, solo vive en el sur del estado estadounidense de Florida. Es uno de los murciélagos más grandes y raros, y las autoridades de Florida lo han clasificado como amenazado pues, de acuerdo con Bats Conservation International, la especie solo ha sido vista pocas veces desde 1960.

bat

Source: M.Salmerón, "Cinco especies animales en peligro de extinción en 2010," EcologíaBlog.com, 21 May 2010.

Comprensión

1. ¿Dónde vive el pingüino de Magallanes? ¿De dónde viene su nombre?
2. ¿Por qué se cree que cientos de estos pingüinos murieron en el 2009?
3. ¿Qué problemas enfrenta la vaquita marina? ¿Cuántas vaquitas marinas se cree que quedan?
4. ¿Por qué se considera que el murciélago de Florida está amenazado?

Más allá

Cada región del mundo tiene especies de animales que están en peligro de extinción, o especies que se han convertido en plagas y amenazan a otros animales. Elige a uno de estos animales e investiga su situación actual. En Share It! explica cuál es su situación y qué se debe hacer para corregir el problema.

La ingeniería ambiental ▶

Vocabulario

Sustantivos

la biodiversidad	*biodiversity*
el calentamiento	*warming*
la capa de ozono	*ozone layer*
el combustible	*fuel*
la energía	*energy*
el inversionista	*investor*
el molino de viento	*windmill*
el panel solar	*solar panel*

Adjetivos

contaminante	*pollutant*
destructivo(a)	*destructive*
híbrido(a)	*hybrid*
no renovable	*nonrenewable*
químico(a)	*chemical*
renovable	*renewable*
útil	*useful*

Verbos

ahorrar	*to save*
conservar	*to preserve*
proponer	*to propose*
recuperar	*to recuperate*

Expresiones útiles

Hay que aprovechar los recursos.
We should make use of the resources.

Se debe crear conciencia.
We should make people aware.

evitar el calentamiento global
to avoid global warming

invertir hoy para ganar mañana
(lit.) *to invest today to earn tomorrow;*
(fig.) *to act today to receive the benefits later*

© Jose Luis Pelaez Inc/Blend Images/Getty Images

DATOS IMPORTANTES

Educación: Estudios universitarios; Maestría en ingeniería con especialización en el medio ambiente

Salario: Entre $60 000 y $150 000, dependiendo de la agencia, la compañía y la experiencia

Dónde se trabaja: agencias del gobierno y privadas, agencias de conservación de recursos naturales, contructoras comprometidas a proteger el medio ambiente, agencias de regulaciones legales

Vocabulario nuevo Relaciona una de las palabras de la primera columna con una palabra de la segunda columna y explica la relación.

1.	los contaminantes	**a.**	la deforestación
2.	conservar	**b.**	los desechos industriales
3.	destructivo	**c.**	el esmog
4.	los químicos	**d.**	un recurso natural
5.	el petróleo	**e.**	preservar

Ramona Saldívar, ingeniera ambiental

Ramona Saldívar es ingeniera ambiental. Trabaja para una compañía que aprovecha los recursos renovables. En el video verás una presentación de la ingeniera Saldívar sobre un proyecto para ahorrar energía.

Antes de ver

Los trabajos relacionados con el medio ambiente tienen como meta *(goal)* reducir la contaminación. Algunas personas se dedican directamente a la limpieza del medio ambiente y otras, como los ingenieros ambientales, desarrollan *(develop)* máquinas para producir energía sin polución.

¿Qué problemas ambientales observas en la vida diaria? ¿Qué soluciones propones?

Comprensión

Hay que invertir hoy para ganar mañana.

1. ¿En qué tipo de ciudad vive la ingeniera Saldívar?
2. ¿Dónde quiere poner paneles solares compactos?
3. ¿Qué recurso renovable usará con esos paneles?
4. ¿Qué ahorrará la gente al usar estos paneles?
5. ¿Qué plan tiene la ingeniera para usar menos combustible?
6. ¿Qué instalará en las fábricas?
7. ¿Qué piensa el inversionista del plan?
8. ¿Qué piensa la ingeniera que ocurrirá si ellos realizan el proyecto?

Después de ver

En parejas, representen a un ingeniero ambiental que desarrolló un invento para proteger el medio ambiente. Mientras uno de ustedes explica qué es, cómo funciona y cuáles son los beneficios, el otro hace preguntas correspondientes para saber más sobre ese invento.

12.37 **Hablemos de mascotas** Completa la conversación con el presente perfecto
del verbo entre paréntesis.

Viviana: ¿Qué animales **(1.)** _____ (tener) tú de mascota?

Magda: Yo nunca **(2.)** _____ (adoptar) animales. Mi familia

siempre **(3.)** _____ (vivir) en apartamentos, así que no había

espacio para mascotas, ¿y tú?

Viviana: Yo **(4.)** _____ (tener) ratones, pollos, conejos, gatos,

perros y un pájaro, pero desde que mi esposo y yo nos mudamos a esta ciudad, no

(5.) _____ (volver) a adoptar mascotas. No tenemos tiempo para

cuidarlas, así que nosotros **(6.)** _____ (decidir) esperar. Yo siempre

(7.) _____ (decir) que no es justo tener una mascota si no tienes

tiempo para ella.

12.38 **En el zoológico** Éric va a ir al zoológico con su esposa y sus dos hijos mañana.
Completa las oraciones usando los verbos entre paréntesis en el futuro y da una
conclusión lógica.

Modelo Yo (comprar)...
Compraré comida para los animales.

1. Mi familia y yo (ir)...
2. Mi esposa (hacer)...
3. Los niños (poder)...
4. Mi hija (ver)...
5. Yo (tener)...
6. Todos (estar)...
7. Los animales (dormir)...
8. El zoológico (cerrarse)...

Les daré de comer a los monos.

12.39 **Viaje a Costa Rica** Fabricio va a hacer un viaje a Costa Rica con su amigo
Marcelo. Usa los diferentes elementos para completar sus comentarios. Debes
decidir entre el indicativo y el subjuntivo del verbo subrayado (_underlined_).
¡OJO! No olvides usar **que** en las oraciones.

Modelo no creo / Costa Rica / <u>tener</u> / desierto
No creo que Costa Rica tenga desierto.

1. es buena idea / yo / <u>llevar</u> / un traje de baño / para ir a la costa
2. supongo / <u>haber</u> / volcanes activos
3. es verdad / los costarricenses / <u>cuidar</u> / la naturaleza de su país
4. es posible / nosotros / <u>navegar</u> / en kayak / en el río Sarapiquí
5. no pienso / Marcelo / <u>conocer</u> / el Valle Central
6. no creo / Marcelo y yo / <u>viajar</u> / a la selva
7. es probable / yo / <u>ver</u> / muchos animales
8. es cierto / Costa Rica / <u>ofrecer</u> / muchas oportunidades para divertirse

12.40 **En contacto con la naturaleza** Habla con un compañero sobre sus experiencias con la naturaleza.

1. ¿Te gusta pasar tiempo en contacto con la naturaleza? ¿Por qué?

2. ¿Cuándo fue la última vez que estuviste en contacto con la naturaleza? ¿Dónde? ¿Qué hiciste?

3. ¿Alguna vez has visitado un parque nacional? ¿Cuál? ¿Qué viste en el parque?

4. ¿Adónde irás en el futuro para disfrutar de la naturaleza?

5. En tu opinión ¿es importante que hagamos algo para preservar la naturaleza? ¿Por qué?

6. ¿Crees que el esfuerzo *(effort)* de una persona es suficiente para lograr *(achieve)* un cambio? ¿Por qué?

12.41 **La granja** Mira uno de los dibujos y tu compañero va a mirar el otro en el **Apéndice B.** Túrnense para describir las granjas y encontrar las cinco diferencias.

© Cengage Learning

12.42 **¿Somos ambientalistas?** Van a descubrir quién es el más ecológico.

Paso 1 En grupos de tres escriban una lista de 5–7 actividades que se pueden hacer para preservar el medio ambiente.

Paso 2 Compartan su lista con el resto de la clase y decidan entre todos cuáles son las seis actividades más importantes.

Paso 3 En los grupos de tres, pregúntense para saber quiénes hacen las seis actividades. Descubran quién es el que hace más para preservar el medio ambiente de su grupo y repórtenle a la clase sus resultados.

🔊 Vocabulario 1
2-31

El medio ambiente *The environment*

el árbol	*tree*	la ecología	*ecology*
la arena	*sand*	el esmog	*smog*
el cactus	*cactus*	la naturaleza	*nature*
la cascada	*cascade, small waterfall*	la nube	*cloud*
		la ola	*wave*
la catarata	*large waterfall*	la palmera	*palm tree*
el cielo	*sky*	el pasto	*grass, pasture*
la contaminación	*contamination, pollution*	el petróleo	*oil*
		el reciclaje	*recycling*
la deforestación	*deforestation*	los recursos naturales	*natural resources*
los desechos industriales	*industrial waste*	el volcán	*volcano*

Lugares

la bahía	*bay*	la montaña	*mountain*
el bosque	*forest*	la pampa	*grasslands*
la colina	*hill*	la península	*peninsula*
la costa	*coast*	el río	*river*
el desierto	*desert*	la selva	*jungle*
la isla	*island*	la Tierra	*Earth*
el llano	*plains*	el valle	*valley*
el mar	*sea*		

Verbos

destruir	*to destroy*	proteger	*to protect*
preservar	*to preserve*		

Diccionario personal

_____

_____

_____

_____

_____

_____

_____

◀)) Vocabulario 2

Los animales

el águila (f.)	eagle		el mono	monkey
la ardilla	squirrel		el oso	bear
la ballena	whale		la oveja	sheep
la cebra	zebra		el pato	duck
el cerdo	pig		el pavo	turkey
el cocodrilo	crocodile		el pingüino	penguin
el conejo	rabbit		el pollo	chick
el elefante	elephant		la rana	frog
la gallina	hen		la serpiente	snake
el gallo	rooster		el tiburón	shark
el gorila	gorilla		el tigre	tiger
el jaguar	jaguar		el toro	bull
la jirafa	giraffe		la tortuga	turtle
el león	lion		la vaca	cow
la llama	llama		el venado	deer
el lobo	wolf		el zorro	fox

Clasificaciones

los anfibios	amphibians		los peces	fish
las aves	birds		los reptiles	reptiles
los mamíferos	mammals			

Palabras adicionales

cazar	to hunt		el macho	male
la caza	hunting		el peligro (de extinción)	danger (of extinction)
la granja	farm		salvaje	wild
la hembra	female			
la jaula	cage			

Diccionario personal

_____

_____

_____

_____

_____

_____

_____

_____

© Eduardo Longoni/picture-alliance/dpa/Newscom

Mario Benedetti
Biografía

Mario Benedetti (1920–2009) nació en Paso de los Toros, Uruguay. A los cuatro años su familia se mudó a Montevideo, donde asistió al Colegio Alemán de Montevideo y comenzó a escribir poemas y cuentos. A causa de problemas económicos tuvo que dejar la escuela y trabajar para ayudar a su familia, pero terminó sus estudios por su cuenta *(on his own)*. En 1949 publicó su primer libro de cuentos, por el cual recibió el Premio del Ministerio de Instrucción Pública. Así comenzó una larga carrera como escritor. Benedetti publicó más de 80 libros, incluyendo poemas, cuentos, novelas, ensayos y dramas. A causa de un golpe de estado *(coup)*, tuvo que salir de su país y vivió en el exilio por doce años en Argentina, Perú, Cuba y España. En 1983 finalmente pudo regresar al Uruguay, donde continuó escribiendo. Mario Benedetti recibió numerosos premios internacionales por su trabajo. Murió el 19 de mayo del 2009 y este día fue declarado luto nacional en Uruguay.

Antes de leer

1. ¿Crees que es importante aprender otros idiomas? ¿Por qué?
2. ¿Qué es lo más difícil de aprender otros idiomas?

El hombre que aprendió a ladrar

discouragement / to give up bark

Lo cierto es que fueron años de arduo y pragmático aprendizaje, con lapsos de **desaliento** en los que estuvo a punto de **desistir.** Pero al fin triunfó la perseverancia y Raimundo aprendió a **ladrar.** No a imitar ladridos, como suelen hacer los chistosos o se creen tales, sino verdaderamente a ladrar. ¿Qué lo había impulsado a ese

training

5 **adiestramiento?** Ante sus amigos se autoflagelaba con humor: "La verdad es que ladro por no llorar". Sin embargo, la razón más valedera era su amor casi franciscano hacia sus hermanos perros. Amor es comunicación.

¿Cómo amar entonces sin comunicarse?

Para Raimundo representó un día de gloria cuando su ladrido fue por fin

10 comprendido por Leo, su hermano perro, y (algo más extraordinario aún) él comprendió el ladrido de Leo. A partir de ese día, Raimundo

lay down

y Leo **se tendían** por lo general en
15 los atardeceres, bajo la glorieta, y dialogaban sobre temas generales. A pesar de su amor por los hermanos perros, Raimundo nunca había imaginado que Leo tuviera

astute

20 una tan **sagaz** visión de mundo.

© Zemfira/Shutterstock

simple

Por fin, una tarde se animó a preguntarle, en varios sobrios ladridos: Dime Leo, con toda franqueza: ¿qué opinas de mi forma de ladrar? La respuesta de Leo fue **escueta** y sincera: Yo diría que lo haces bastante bien, pero tendrás que mejorar. Cuando ladras, todavía se te nota el acento humano.

© Fundacion Mario Benedetti, c/o Guillermo Schavelzon & Asociados, Agencia Literaria, www.schavelzon.com

Investiguemos la literatura: la metáfora

A metaphor is a figure of speech in which an object or an idea is used in place of another, implying that there is a similarity between the two. For example, *The snake took every last thing I had.* The implication is that the person that took the things is like a snake. An extended metaphor is a metaphor that continues beyond the initial sentence; it can sometimes be an entire work.

Después de leer

A. Comprensión

1. ¿Por qué quiso aprender a ladrar Raimundo?
2. ¿Cuál fue el momento de gloria para Raimundo?
3. Según Leo ¿por qué todavía tiene que mejorar Raimundo?
4. Este cuento es una metáfora extendida. ¿Cuál es la comparación?

B. Conversemos

1. En el cuento se dice "Amor es comunicación". Explica la importancia de esta cita. ¿Estás de acuerdo? ¿Por qué?
2. ¿Piensas que tener un acento extranjero (*foreign*) es malo? ¿Por qué?

CAPÍTULO 13

Learning Strategy

Find ways to gain exposure to the language outside of the classroom

You can take many small steps to accelerate your progress in class. Listen to the songs in the **Investiguemos la música** suggestions. Watch a Spanish-language film. Read a magazine or newspaper published in Spanish. All of these activities will help you to increase your vocabulary. You will also become more familiar with structures and expressions used by native speakers and increase your cultural knowledge.

In this chapter you will learn how to:

- Talk about relationships
- Express desires and give recommendations
- Talk about popular culture
- Discuss emotional reactions to events

¿Es tu vida una telenovela?

© Alexander Tamargo/Getty Images

Las relaciones románticas pueden evolucionar de maneras muy diferentes, algunas más tradicionales que otras.

enamorarse
la cita
proponer matrimonio
el compromiso
la madrina
el padrino
la ceremonia
los recién casados
la luna de miel
dar a luz
estar embarazada
el nacimiento
¡Feliz aniversario!
25 años
las bodas de plata

© Cengage Learning

INVESTIGUEMOS EL VOCABULARIO

The function of **los padrinos** varies from one Spanish-speaking country to another. Their roles are generally different from those of the best man and maid of honor, and are often similar to that of godparents. For more information read **Tradiciones nupciales** on p. 460.

las bodas de oro	50th wedding anniversary
el divorcio	divorce
el noviazgo	engagement, courtship
la pareja	couple; partner
el (la) prometido(a)	fiancé(e)
la recepción	wedding reception
la relación	relationship
soltero(a)	single, unmarried
la unión libre	common-law union
viudo(a)	widowed

Verbos

abrazar	to hug
amar	to love
besar	to kiss
comprometerse (con)	to get engaged (to)
divorciarse (de)	to divorce
enamorarse (de)	to fall in love (with)
extrañar (a)	to miss (a person)
llevarse bien (mal)	to (not) get along
nacer	to be born
odiar	to hate

querer	to love
romper (con)	to break up (with)
separarse (de)	to separate (from)

Palabras adicionales

la adolescencia	adolescence
el estado civil	civil status
la juventud	youth
la madurez	maturity
la muerte	death
la niñez	childhood
la vejez	old age

A practicar

13.1 Escucha y responde Vas a escuchar una serie de afirmaciones. Levanta la mano si la afirmación te parece lógica. No hagas nada si la afirmación es ilógica.

2-33

INVESTIGUEMOS LA MÚSICA

Find the song "Amar y querer" online. The classic version is by José José, but there are other versions. Listen to it and explain the difference between **amar** and **querer**.

13.2 Diferencias Decide qué palabra no corresponde al grupo y explica por qué.

1. enamorarse | divorciarse | comprometerse | llevarse bien
2. la ceremonia | el anillo | comprometerse | proponer matrimonio
3. dar a luz | estar embarazada | extrañar | el nacimiento
4. romper | separarse | divorciarse | besar
5. el padrino | los novios | el noviazgo | la madrina
6. viudo | casado | el prometido | el novio

13.3 Un poco de lógica Con un compañero, relacionen las palabras de las dos columnas y expliquen la relación.

Modelo el anillo – el novio
El novio pone el anillo en la mano de la novia durante la ceremonia.

1. el nacimiento
2. la ceremonia
3. separarse
4. besar
5. la unión libre
6. la luna de miel
7. comprometerse
8. la adolescencia

a. la juventud
b. estar embarazada
c. el anillo de compromiso
d. la pareja
e. recién casados
f. divorciarse
g. los novios
h. los padrinos

INVESTIGUEMOS LA GRAMÁTICA

In Spanish, there are numerous verbs that consist of a root verb and a prefix, such as **conseguir**, which consists of the root of **seguir**, and **sonreír**, whose root is **reír**. The root of the verb **proponer** is **poner**; therefore, it is conjugated in the same way as **poner: propongo, propuse, he propuesto,** etc. Some other similar verbs are:

oponer	detener
posponer	mantener
suponer	obtener

13.4 Entrevista Con un compañero, túrnense para responder las preguntas. Den mucha información.

1. ¿Cuándo fue la última vez que fuiste a una boda? ¿Cómo y dónde fue la boda? ¿Había muchas personas? ¿Te gustó la ceremonia? ¿Hubo una fiesta después? ¿Qué había para comer y beber?

2. ¿Tienes un amigo que esté comprometido? ¿Por cuánto tiempo han sido novios? ¿Cuándo van a casarse?

3. ¿Has ido de luna de miel? ¿Adónde fuiste y por cuánto tiempo? Si no has ido, habla de la luna de miel de algún amigo o pariente, o de la luna de miel que quieres para ti si te casas un día.

13.5 La historia de una relación Trabaja con un compañero y túrnense para narrar los eventos de la relación en los dibujos de la página anterior. Usen el pretérito y el imperfecto y den muchos detalles.

13.6 Una relación La siguiente es una historia ilustrada de cómo evolucionó la relación entre Mercedes y Juan Sebastián. Trabaja con un compañero y túrnense para describir sus dibujos (numerados del 1 al 8) y completar la historia. Uno de ustedes va a describir las imágenes en esta página, y el otro las de el **Apéndice B**.

© Cengage Learning

Conexiones culturales

El cortejo

Comparaciones

Entre los jóvenes españoles, la palabra "cortejar" *(to court)* prácticamente ha caído en desuso, como la práctica misma de envolver a la persona amada en detalles que la harán caer en nuestros brazos.

No siempre fue así. Los llamados "tunos", jóvenes estudiantes de escasos recursos que aparecieron en el siglo XIII, se ganaban la vida entonando canciones en las tabernas. Por las noches utilizaban sus habilidades musicales para enamorar a sus doncellas. La costumbre estaba tan arraigada *(rooted)*, que muy posiblemente fue adoptada siglos después, con algunas variaciones, en las colonias españolas de Latinoamérica.

Tunos españoles

Actualmente en España solo quedan algunos grupos aislados de tunos. Se trata de jóvenes aficionados a la música y a la tradición y, sobre todo, a la vida nocturna. Ataviados *(Dressed)* con trajes de época y con una capa característica y acompañados de guitarras, recorren las calles en busca de mujeres a las que cortejar mientras interpretan canciones populares a puerta cerrada en un bar, o con una serenata a la intemperie *(outside)*.

Pero hoy en día los tunos son una excepción. Los jóvenes españoles prefieren decir "te quiero" a decir "te amo", ahora en España se habla mucho más de "ligar" *(to pick up)* que de "cortejar".

En casi todo el mundo, pues, el amor es hoy mucho menos romántico. Pero al mismo tiempo es más directo. Y, por lo tanto, más libre.

¿Cómo ha cambiado el cortejo en tu cultura? ¿Qué prácticas ya no se usan? ¿Qué nuevas prácticas hay?

Source: "El arte de cortejar alrededor de la planeta," Reader's Digest Argentina

INVESTIGUEMOS LA MÚSICA

Look online for the song "Amor a la antigua" by Mexican vocalist Pedro Fernández. According to Fernández, what are the things that make up old-fashioned love?

Investiga en Internet sobre los tunos de hoy en día. Puedes buscar con la palabra **tuna** y una ciudad universitaria de España como Granada, Sevilla o Salamanca.

Conexiones... a la música

La música es una de las formas favoritas de todas las culturas para hablar del amor. El siguiente es un fragmento de una canción clásica de la música mexicana, escrita por Consuelo Velázquez (1916–2005). ¿Cuál es el tono de la canción (triste, alegre, etcétera)? ¿Por qué? ¿Por qué crees que esta canción se hizo muy famosa?

La canción *Bésame mucho* habla del amor.

Bésame mucho
Bésame, bésame mucho
Como si fuera esta noche
La última vez.
Bésame, bésame mucho
Que tengo miedo a perderte
Perderte después.

Quiero tenerte muy cerca
Mirarme en tus ojos
Verte junto a mí.
Piensa que tal vez mañana
Yo ya estaré lejos
Muy lejos de aquí.

Estrategia

Gain Exposure to the Language
Listen several times to some songs in the **Investiguemos la música** suggestions throughout the textbook to improve your listening comprehension.

Cultura

Las relaciones personales pueden ser diferentes de país a país, especialmente donde hay una mezcla de culturas. En algunos países latinoamericanos las costumbres del cortejo reflejan la unión de creencias y tradiciones europeas con las indígenas. Un ejemplo de ello son los ritos de noviazgo quechuas en Perú, en donde algunas bodas, en la superficie, parecen ser la tradicional boda católica en la que hay una ceremonia y después se festeja la unión con música, comida y bailes. A consecuencia de la globalización, muchas de las bodas de esta región tienen elementos típicos occidentales, como una novia vestida de blanco y con un velo, o música que no es tradicional de la región, como un grupo de mariachi u otro tipo de música extranjera.

Un joven quechua

Sin embargo, todavía es posible ver bodas más tradicionales en algunas regiones quechuas. Las diferencias más grandes entre un matrimonio quechua y un matrimonio moderno en Perú o en Ecuador no se encuentran durante la celebración de la boda, sino en lo que ocurrió antes de ella. Muchos pueblos quechuas siguen una tradición inca llamada *sirvinakuy* que en quechua significa "servirse el uno al otro". Según esta tradición, los padres de la pareja hacen una alianza basada en los intereses de los jóvenes. Se dice que una pareja entra en un período de *sirvinakuy*, cuando uno de ellos se va a vivir a la casa de los padres del otro. Durante esta época la pareja vive y duerme junta, ayudando a los padres de él o de ella. La pareja no puede casarse hasta que tengan un hijo, comprobando así que pueden tener familia. Es entonces cuando finalmente se celebra la boda.

¿Cuáles son las ventajas y las desventajas de *sirvinakuy*? ¿Cómo se conocen las parejas dentro de tu cultura?

 En la sección **Exploraciones del mundo hispano** en el **Apéndice A** busca cuáles son otras comunidades indígenas del Perú e investígalas en Internet.

Comunidad

Entrevista a una persona hispana sobre alguna boda a la que haya asistido. Pregúntale sobre las tradiciones que usaron y lo que se hizo durante la boda. Después repórtale a la clase.

¿Cómo son las bodas hispanas?

A analizar

Santiago habla con Paula sobre como conoció a su novia. Mira el video. Después lee parte de su conversación y observa los verbos en negritas.

Paula:	Me cae bien tu novia. Por cierto, ¿cómo se conocieron?
Santiago:	**Nos conocimos** en la escuela primaria. Luego, en la escuela secundaria, **nos hablamos** más y **nos entendimos** mejor. Me acuerdo que **nos besamos** por primera vez la noche de la graduación. Empezamos a salir, y ahora que termine mis estudios **vamos a casarnos.**
Paula:	¡Qué emoción!

1. Who is the subject for each of the verbs in bold?

2. The word **nos** is an object pronoun. In the conversation above, who does it refer to?

A comprobar

Reciprocal verbs

1. In **Capítulo 6** you learned to use reflexive pronouns when the subject of the sentence does something to himself or herself.

> Ellos **se miran** en el espejo.
> *They **look at themselves** in the mirror.*

2. In English, the expressions *each other* and *one another* express reciprocal actions. In order to express a reciprocal action in Spanish, use the plural reflexives.

> Ellos **se miran** con amor.
> *They **look at each other** with love.*

3. Only the plural forms (**nos, os,** and **se**) are used to express a reciprocal action because the action must involve more than one person.

> Los novios **se besaron.**
> *The bride and groom **kissed each other.***

> Mi amiga y yo **nos escribimos.**
> *My friend and I **write to each other.***

4. It is usually evident from the context whether the verb is reflexive or reciprocal. If clarification is needed, **el uno al otro** can be used. The expression must agree with the subjects; however, if there are mixed sexes, the masculine form is used for both.

> Se lavaron el pelo **el uno al otro.**
> *They washed **each other's** hair.*

> Nos peinamos **la una a la otra.**
> *We did **each other's** hair.*

> Todos se respetan **los unos a los otros.**
> *They all respect **each other.***

5. When used in the infinitive form after another verb, the pronoun can be attached to the verb or placed in front of the conjugated verb.

> **Nos** vamos a amar para siempre.
> *We will love each other forever.*

> Quieren comprender**se.**
> *They want to understand each other.*

A practicar

13.7 **¿Lógico o ilógico?** Decide si las siguientes oraciones son lógicas o no.

1. Los amigos se escuchan.
2. Los amigos se hablan cuando hay un problema.
3. Los amigos se odian.
4. Los amigos se ayudan con frecuencia.
5. Los amigos normalmente no se entienden.
6. Los amigos se insultan.

13.8 **Pedro y Sara** Describe la evolución de la relación de Pedro y Sara usando los verbos recíprocos.

Modelo Pedro le escribió cartas de amor a Sara. Sara le escribió cartas de amor a Pedro.
Pedro y Sara se escribieron cartas de amor.

1. Pedro conoció a Sara en la fiesta. Sara conoció a Pedro en la fiesta.
2. Pedro le habló a Sara. Sara le habló a Pedro.
3. Pedro entendió bien a Sara. Sara entendió bien a Pedro.
4. Pedro empezó a llamar a Sara por teléfono. Sara empezó a llamar a Pedro por teléfono.
5. Pedro abrazó y besó a Sara. Sara abrazó y besó a Pedro.
6. Pedro se enamoró de Sara. Sara se enamoró de Pedro.
7. Pedro se casó con Sara. Sara se casó con Pedro.

13.9 **En la recepción** En parejas, túrnense para explicar lo que pasa en la recepción.
¡OJO! Algunos de los verbos son recíprocos y otros son reflexivos.

13.10 **Tu mejor amigo y tú** En parejas, usen las siguientes preguntas y túrnense para entrevistarse sobre su relación con su mejor amigo.

1. ¿Dónde y cuándo se conocieron tú y tu mejor amigo?
2. ¿Por qué se hicieron mejores amigos?
3. ¿Con qué frecuencia se hablan por teléfono?
4. ¿Con qué frecuencia se ven? ¿Dónde se encuentran?
5. ¿En qué ocasiones se dan regalos?
6. ¿Se ayudan con sus problemas?
7. ¿Se escriben por correo electrónico?
8. ¿Se pelean de vez en cuando?
9. ¿Alguna vez se han dejado de *(stopped)* hablar?

13.11 **Una historia de amor** En parejas, elijan una fotografía. Usando algunos de los verbos recíprocos indicados, narren la historia de amor de la pareja: ¿Dónde se conocieron? ¿Qué se dijeron? ¿Por qué se enamoraron? ¿Cómo va a ser su futuro? Luego léanle su historia a la clase para que sus compañeros decidan a cuál de las fotos corresponde.

| conocerse | besarse | enamorarse | comprometerse |
| casarse | separarse | hablarse | divorciarse |

A analizar

Santiago habla con Paula sobre sus planes para casarse. Después de ver el video lee parte de su conversación y observa los verbos en negritas.

> **Santiago:** Pues, yo prefiero tener una boda sencilla, pero María Luisa quiere que **tengamos** una boda grande y elegante. Nuestros amigos esperan que **haya** una gran fiesta después de la boda, pero yo quiero que **sea** pequeña y que **tengamos** una luna de miel fantástica. Mis padres quieren que **nos casemos** en la iglesia donde ellos se casaron, pero los padres de María Luisa piden que **nos casemos** en su jardín. ¡Creo que lo mejor sería escaparnos para casarnos!
>
> **Paula:** ¡Ay no! ¡Yo quiero asistir a tu boda!

1. The verbs in bold are subjunctive forms. What are the expressions that come before these verbs?
2. In the first sentence, how are the verb structures in **prefiero tener** different from those used in **quiere que tengamos**?

A comprobar

Subjunctive with expressions of desire

1. When expressing the desire to do something oneself, use a verb of desire such as **querer** or **preferir** followed by an infinitive.

    Prefiero ir a la recepción contigo.
    I prefer to go to the reception with you.

    Él quiere comprar un anillo para su novia.
    He wants to buy a ring for his girlfriend.

2. When expressing the desire for someone else to do something, you use a verb of influence plus **que** followed by the subjunctive.

    Prefiero que vayas a la recepción conmigo.
    I prefer (that) you go to the reception with me.

    Ella quiere que su novio le compre un anillo.
    She wants her boyfriend to buy a ring for her.

3. You will notice that when there are two different subjects and the verb in the main clause is in the indicative, the verb in the second clause (dependent clause) is in the subjunctive.

Main clause		Dependent clause
(Yo) Prefiero	que	(tú) **vayas** a la recepción conmigo.
Ella quiere	que	su novio le **compre** un anillo.

4. There are other verbs besides **querer** and **preferir** that express desire or influence. These verbs also require the use of the subjunctive when there are different subjects in the two clauses.

desear	*to desire*
esperar	*to hope, to wish*
insistir (en)	*to insist (on)*
mandar	*to order*
necesitar	*to need*
pedir	*to ask for, to request*
recomendar	*to recommend*
sugerir	*to suggest*

Edwin **espera que vayan** a Puerto Rico para la luna de miel.
Edwin hopes that they will go to Puerto Rico for the honeymoon.

Sus padres **recomiendan que viajen** a México.
His parents recommend (that) they travel to Mexico.

5. Ojalá is another way to express hope. This expression does not have a subject and therefore does not change forms. It always requires the use of the subjunctive in the dependent clause; however, the use of **que** is optional.

> **Ojalá (que)** los recién casados sean muy felices.
> *I hope (that) the newlyweds will be very happy.*

> **INVESTIGUEMOS EL VOCABULARIO**
>
> The word **ojalá** originated from the Arabic expression *God (Allah) willing*. There are many words of Arabic influence in Spanish due to the Muslim rule of Spain from 711 to 1492.

A practicar

13.12 **La recepción** Durante la recepción de una boda los invitados hicieron un brindis con sus deseos para los recién casados. Relaciona las dos columnas para averiguar *(find out)* cuáles fueron los deseos.

1. Ojalá que los novios...
2. Queremos que los padres de los recién casados...
3. Esperamos que el matrimonio de los nuevos esposos...
4. Yo le recomiendo a la novia que...
5. Sugerimos al novio que...
6. Yo insisto en que los invitados...

a. los ayuden durante su matrimonio.
b. hagan otro brindis por los novios.
c. siempre se amen.
d. le diga siempre la verdad a su esposo.
e. sea muy largo y muy feliz.
f. no vea fútbol cada fin de semana.

13.13 **El consejero matrimonial** Juanita y Pablo consultaron a un consejero matrimonial y tomaron notas de sus consejos, pero las notas están incompletas. Ayúdalos a completarlas usando los verbos en paréntesis en el subjuntivo.

Para el esposo:

Sinceramente, deseo que usted **(1.)** _____ (solucionar) sus problemas con su esposa.

Espero que **(2.)** _____ (ayudar) con los quehaceres de la casa.

Insisto en que usted **(3.)** _____ (mantener) una buena comunicación con su esposa.

Para la esposa:

Necesito que usted **(4.)** _____ (venir) a mi oficina dos veces por semana con su suegra.

Le pido que no le **(5.)** _____ (mentir) a su esposo.

Yo recomiendo que **(6.)** _____ (leer) mi libro sobre matrimonios con problemas.

Para los dos:

Les sugiero que **(7.)** _____ (encontrar) tiempo para salir juntos.

Les pido que no me **(8.)** _____ (pagar) con tarjeta de crédito.

Recomiendo que hablen con un consejero matrimonial.

13.14 **Entre la gente** Mira los dibujos y completa las oraciones de una manera lógica.

El hombre espera que...
La mujer quiere que...
Sus amigos desean que...

La chica desea que...
Los padres piden que...
El muchacho espera que...

La mujer insiste en que...
El hombre prefiere que...
El niño necesita que...

Las chicas esperan que...
Los chicos desean que...
Ojalá que...

13.15 **Expectativas** A veces las personas que nos rodean (*around us*) esperan algo de nosotros. Entrevista a un compañero de clase usando las siguientes preguntas.

1. ¿Qué te piden tus amigos que hagas?
2. ¿Qué quiere tu mejor amigo que hagas?
3. ¿Qué esperas tú que tus amigos hagan?
4. ¿Qué te recomienda el profesor de español?
5. ¿Qué le sugieres tú al profesor de español?
6. ¿Qué sugiere tu médico que hagas?
7. ¿Qué insiste tu jefe que hagas?
8. ¿Qué quieres tú que hagan tus compañeros de trabajo?

> **INVESTIGUEMOS LA MÚSICA**
>
> Find the song "A Dios le pido" by Colombian artist Juanes and listen to it. Make a list of the verbs in the subjunctive. What does he ask of God?

© Cengage Learning

13.16 **Preferencias** Con un compañero, hablen de lo que quieren que hagan sus amigos y familiares en las situaciones indicadas. **¡OJO!** Usen el subjuntivo.

Modelo Vas a casarte.
   Estudiante 1: *Quiero que mi novia se arregle muy bonita. ¿Y tú?*
   Estudiante 2: *Yo quiero que venga mi hermana de California.*

1. Es tu cumpleaños.
2. Estás enfermo.
3. Tu pareja te va a proponer matrimonio.
4. Acabas de *(just)* tener un bebé.
5. Tu pareja se va de viaje por dos semanas.
6. Acabas de mudarte a una casa nueva.

13.17 **Querida Teresa** Teresa trabaja para un periódico dando consejos a las personas que le escriben con sus problemas. Con un compañero, túrnense para hacer el papel *(role)* de Teresa y contesten las cartas con sus recomendaciones. Usen el subjuntivo y los siguientes verbos.

esperar   insistir   mandar   necesitar   pedir   recomendar   sugerir

Querida Teresa: Soy estudiante de inglés y quiero aprender a hablar bien. La clase es muy difícil y tengo malas notas en la clase. ¿Qué me recomienda? –Perdido

Querida Teresa: Mi esposo y yo hemos estado casados por 15 años, pero recientemente hemos tenido problemas. La semana pasada él mencionó la posibilidad de divorciarnos. Lo quiero mucho. ¿Qué debo hacer? –Casada y enamorada

Querida Teresa: Mi novio me propuso matrimonio y vamos a casarnos este verano. El problema es que no tenemos mucho dinero para la boda. ¿Qué podemos hacer? –Pobre y comprometida

Querida Teresa: Me han ofrecido un nuevo trabajo en otro estado. Es un muy buen trabajo y me van a pagar más, pero mi esposa no quiere que nos mudemos *(move)*. ¿Qué hago? –Entre la espada y la pared

Querida Teresa: Mi hija tiene 16 años y ahora está muy rebelde. No quiere ir a clases ni hacer la tarea. Sale con sus amigos y siempre llega muy tarde. Creo que está usando drogas. ¿Qué me sugiere? –Preocupada

---

13.18 **Todos tienen problemas** Con un compañero, van a hacer los papeles *(roles)* del consejero y del cliente. Escojan una de las fotos. El cliente debe explicar su problema y el consejero va a darle recomendaciones usando el subjuntivo y los verbos a continuación. Luego, escojan otra foto y cambien de papel.

esperar   insistir   mandar   necesitar   pedir   recomendar   sugerir

Entrando en materia

Uno de los eventos más importantes en la vida de muchas personas es su boda, y por eso la celebran con una gran fiesta y numerosos invitados. ¿Qué consejos le darías *(would you give)* a una persona que está planeando una boda?

Planeando una boda

◀)) Vas a escuchar a una experta en bodas dar una presentación.
2-34

Vocabulario útil

acompañar	*to accompany*	la herramienta	*tool*
anunciar	*to announce*	posteriormente	*later*
auto-invitarse	*to self-invite*	el presupuesto	*budget*
el costo	*cost, expense*	la utilidad	*usefulness*
enterarse	*to find out*		

Comprensión

1. ¿Acerca de qué es el curso que se ofrece?
2. ¿Qué se debe hacer antes de anunciar una boda en las redes sociales?
3. ¿Por qué es buena idea enviar un mensaje a las personas que no se va a invitar?
4. ¿Dónde se puede encontrar una lista de los servicios que se necesitan en una boda?
5. ¿Qué información puede dar su página de Internet después de escoger servicios?

Más allá

Imagínate que estás ayudando a planear un evento importante, como un gran cumpleaños, un aniversario o un funeral. Escribe una lista de ideas sobre los preparativos que deben hacerse antes, durante y después del evento. Compártelos en Share It! y lee las ideas de tus compañeros. ¿Qué evento es el más celebrado?

Una boda es un gran evento.

© iofoto/Shutterstock

Lectura

Antes de leer

¿Cuáles son algunas tradiciones relacionadas con una boda en los Estados Unidos?

A leer

Tradiciones nupciales

En muchos aspectos las bodas típicas en España y Latinoamérica son muy semejantes a las bodas que se realizan en los Estados Unidos: la novia lleva un vestido blanco con un velo mientras que el novio se viste de traje, los familiares y amigos de los novios asisten a la ceremonia y luego a una recepción, y la iglesia se decora con flores y velas. Sin embargo, hay algunas tradiciones que son particulares a ciertas regiones del mundo hispanohablante.

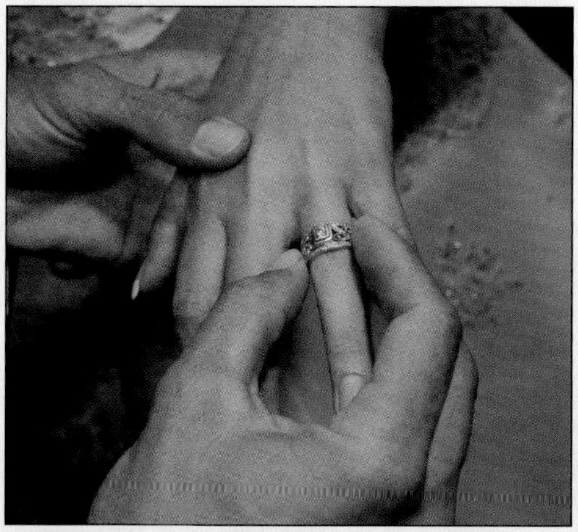

El anillo es un símbolo de amor

rope **El lazo:** Durante la ceremonia en México es tradicional que una pareja casada ponga un lazo en figura de ocho sobre la cabeza de los novios, representando la unión entre los dos. Los aztecas tenían una

tied práctica semejante en la que **amarraban** las puntas de las túnicas de los novios, pero no se sabe a ciencia cierta cuál es el origen de esta costumbre porque también forma parte de la ceremonia nupcial en España, Bolivia y Guatemala.

[hay algunas tradiciones que son particulares a ciertas regiones del mundo hispanohablante]

Las arras: En España, Venezuela, Panamá, Puerto Rico y México el novio le regala a la novia 13 arras, unas

coins **monedas** de oro que

to lack simbolizan la prosperidad y su promesa de que no le va a **faltar** nada. En algunos países, las familias de los novios también intercambian arras.

Hay semejanzas y diferencias en las tradiciones de bodas.

Los anillos: El anillo es un símbolo muy importante del amor que se tiene la pareja y representa la **fidelidad** que se prometen el uno al otro. En España y en la mayor parte de Latinoamérica se intercambian los anillos durante la ceremonia, pero en Argentina y Chile **se entregan** en una fiesta donde se celebra el compromiso de los novios. En Chile se lleva el anillo en la mano derecha hasta el día de la boda, cuando lo cambian a la mano izquierda.

faithfulness

are given

Los padrinos: El padrino es una figura muy importante en la boda, aunque su función varía un poco entre Latinoamérica y España. En España el padrino de la boda, quien lleva a la novia al altar, suele ser su padre, aunque es posible que sea otro familiar. En algunas comunidades él le regala **el ramo** de flores a la novia durante la ceremonia.

bouquet

En México hay entre cinco y ocho padrinos que **se encargan** de diferentes partes de la ceremonia. Los padrinos de lazo, por ejemplo, le ponen el lazo a la pareja durante la ceremonia, y las madrinas de ramo se encargan de los ramos de flores: uno para ofrecerle a la Virgen de Guadalupe y el otro que **se lanza** en la recepción. Típicamente los padrinos ayudan con los gastos económicos de la boda, por ejemplo, la madrina del pastel es responsable de comprar el pastel.

are responsible

is tossed

La procesión: En la mayoría de los países latinoamericanos el padre de la novia la lleva al altar para entregársela a su esposo, pero en Chile los padres y madres de los novios participan en la procesión y los acompañan junto al altar durante la ceremonia. En Argentina los acompañan el padre de la novia y la madre del novio solamente.

A pesar de las grandes semejanzas en las tradiciones que rodean las bodas, sobreviven algunas diferencias regionales que reflejan los valores culturales de cada grupo.

Sources: ArtículosInformativos.com.mx; Boston Bridal Shows; Bodas.net

Comprensión

Decide si las ideas son ciertas o falsas y corrige las ideas falsas.

1. En España y Latinoamérica generalmente la novia viste un vestido blanco.
2. Las arras son un símbolo de amor.
3. La costumbre de poner un lazo en forma del número ocho se originó entre los aztecas.
4. En los países hispanohablantes los padrinos y madrinas de una boda ayudan con los gastos.
5. En Chile y Argentina el anillo se entrega en una fiesta antes de la boda.
6. En toda Latinoamérica el padre entrega a la novia en el altar.

Después de leer

1. ¿Cuáles son otras tradiciones que has visto?
2. ¿Piensas que han cambiado las tradiciones en los últimos años? ¿Cómo?

En la televisión hay una gran variedad de programas para todos los gustos.

Mira, un documental sobre nuestro grupo de música favorito.

el adolescente

los adultos

los dibujos animados

la audiencia infantil

el reproductor de DVD

las revistas

el control remoto

la locutora

el noticiario

los concursos

el conductor

la pantalla

los audífonos

el ratón

el tablero

el MP3

el buscador

Exploraciones

La televisión		la televisión por satélite	satellite television	Verbos	
los anuncios comerciales	TV commercials	**La tecnología**		censurar	to censor
el canal	TV channel	el buscador	search engine	chatear	to chat
la clasificación	rating (for adults, for the whole family, etc.)	las redes sociales	social networks	hacer clic (en)	to click (on)
		la tableta	tablet	limitar	to limit
el patrocinador	sponsor			transmitir	to broadcast
la programación	programming	**El cine**			
la telenovela	soap opera	la butaca	seat		
el (la) televidente	television viewer	el éxito de taquilla	box office hit		
la televisión por cable	cable television	las golosinas	candy		
		las palomitas de maíz	popcorn		

© Cengage Learning

A practicar

13.19 **Escucha y responde** Escucha las palabras y decide si se relacionan con el cine o con la televisión. Indica con el pulgar hacia arriba si la idea se refiere al cine, y el pulgar hacia abajo si se refiere a la televisión.

2-35

13.20 ¿Cierto o falso? Decide si las oraciones son ciertas o falsas y corrige las ideas falsas.

1. C F Un locutor es una persona que habla en los anuncios de televisión o radio.
2. C F Generalmente las telenovelas son programas infantiles.
3. C F Los conductores de un programa de televisión son los choferes de los actores.
4. C F Los canales de televisión transmiten anuncios comerciales.
5. C F Cuando mandamos un correo electrónico escribimos con el ratón.
6. C F La clasificación de un programa de televisión depende del tipo de audiencia.

13.21 ¿Qué es? En parejas, túrnense para elegir una palabra de vocabulario y (para) explicársela a su compañero sin decírsela.

13.22 Relaciones Con un compañero, relacionen las dos columnas para crear ideas lógicas. Expliquen la relación entre las dos palabras.

Modelo transmitir   la televisión por cable
　　　　　*Algunos programas de televisión **se transmiten** solamente por televisión por cable.*

1. el ratón   **a.** los deportes
2. el locutor   **b.** los artículos
3. el patrocinador   **c.** los anuncios
4. los dibujos animados   **d.** las golosinas
5. las revistas   **e.** los programas infantiles
6. las palomitas de maíz   **f.** el tablero

13.23 Opiniones En grupos de tres, van a dar sus opiniones sobre las siguientes afirmaciones. ¿Están de acuerdo o no? Justifiquen sus respuestas.

1. La televisión es el medio de comunicación más importante.
2. Hay demasiados programas para adultos en horarios para toda la familia.
3. Es importante censurar el contenido de algunos programas de televisión.
4. La televisión hace que los televidentes no piensen ni sean creativos.
5. No se debe permitir que algunos patrocinadores se anuncien en televisión.
6. Prefiero ver las películas en DVD en mi casa en vez de ir al cine.

13.24 En familia Trabaja con un compañero para descubrir las cinco diferencias. Uno de ustedes mira este dibujo y el otro mira el dibujo en el **Apéndice B.** Túrnense para describir los dibujos y encontrar las cinco diferencias.

INVESTIGUEMOS LA MÚSICA

Listen to Guatemalan singer Ricardo Arjona's song "Frente al televisor." What is he watching on TV? Why is he watching television?

© Cengage Learning

Cultura

En años recientes, el cine latinoamericano ha producido películas excepcionales, muchas de las cuales han sido muy exitosas en los Estados Unidos. Por ejemplo, *El laberinto del fauno* (traducida al inglés como *Pan's Labyrinth*) es un filme dirigido por Guillermo del Toro, un cineasta mexicano que desde el inicio de su carrera ha creado películas con una temática relacionada con la Guerra Civil Española. *El laberinto del fauno* ganó 3 Óscares, además de haber ganado 68 premios internacionales y haber obtenido otras 58 nominaciones. Otro director de fama internacional es Alfonso Cuarón, cuya película *Gravity* ganó siete Óscares en el 2014, incluyendo el Óscar al mejor director.

El director Alfonso Cuarón

Elige una de las películas de la lista y mírala. Después escribe una crítica de la película. Usa las preguntas como guía: ¿Cuál es la trama *(plot)* de la película? ¿Cómo es la actuación en la película? ¿Piensas que la película tiene un mensaje social? ¿La recomiendas? ¿Por qué?

El secreto de sus ojos* (Argentina)   *Amores perros* (México)
Nueve reinas (Argentina)   *Voces inocentes* (México)
El hijo de la novia (Argentina)   *La nana* (Chile)
Frida (México)   *María llena de gracia* (Colombia)
El laberinto del fauno (México)   *La misma luna* (México – Estados Unidos)

Busca el nombre de un director hispano en la sección **Exploraciones del mundo hispano** en el **Apéndice A** e investiga en Internet sobre su vida y su filmografía. Comparte la información en Share It!

Estrategia

Gain Exposure to the Language

Watch a Spanish-language film. In addition to increasing your vocabulary, you will become more familiar with structures and expressions used by native speakers and increase your knowledge about the culture.

> **INVESTIGUEMOS EL VOCABULARIO**
>
> **¡De película!** is an expression that means that something is very cool, for example, *¡La fiesta estuvo de película!* Used as adjectives with **estar** or in an exclamation with **qué**, the following are some other ways to say that something is cool.
>
> | | |
> |---|---|
> | padre | (Mexico) |
> | guay | (Spain) |
> | chévere | (numerous countries in Latin America) |
> | copado | (Argentina, Uruguay) |
> | sólido | (Panama) |
> | bacán | (Chile) |
>
> **¡Qué padre!** *How cool!*
> *¡Ese coche* **está chévere***! That car is cool!*

*recibió el Óscar por La Mejor Película Extranjera en 2010

Comparaciones

En el mundo actual, en donde los sistemas de comunicación son excelentes, es muy común que un programa que fue exitoso en un país se adapte para producirse en otro país.

Por ejemplo, el programa de Betty la Fea era originalmente una telenovela colombiana. Fue tan exitosa que se hicieron nuevas versiones en varios países, incluyendo una versión en chino. La adaptación estadounidense se transmitió en un formato más típico del país, con episodios semanales en vez de diarios. Otro programa colombiano, *Nada más que la verdad* (Moment of Truth), fue adaptado para los televidentes estadounidenses.

> *Betty la fea* (Ugly Betty)
> *Nada más que la verdad* (The Moment of Truth)

Los siguientes son programas de la televisión hispana que se adaptaron de series originales estadounidenses:

> *100 mexicanos dijeron* (Family Feud)
> *La niñera* (The Nanny)
> *Amas de casa desesperadas* (Desperate Housewives)
> *Trato hecho* (Let's Make a Deal)

Betty la fea, de la telenovela colombiana

¿Creen que los programas tienen diferencias importantes cuando son adaptados a otro país? ¿Por qué?

Conexiones... a la economía

Cuando se piensa en productos de exportación de Latinoamérica, generalmente se piensa en productos como petróleo, materias primas y productos manufacturados. Sin embargo, un grupo de países hispanos exporta un número importante de productos menos tangibles: series de televisión y películas. Más allá del impacto económico, estas producciones llegan a tener también un fuerte impacto cultural debido a que se exhiben en muchos países. Gracias a las traducciones, muchas telenovelas se han visto en más de 130 países diferentes, con un público mucho mayor que el de habla hispana. Tan solo una empresa *(company)* de televisión, Televisa, ha ganado en un año casi tanto dinero como los ingresos *(income)* anuales de la BBC. El impacto económico de las telenovelas es comparable al de Hollywood en términos económicos.

Los países hispanos que más producciones de telenovela exportan son Argentina, Colombia, México y Venezuela, pero muchos otros han contribuido con producciones exitosas. Quizás el mercado de la telenovela latinoamericana sea mucho más exitoso que el de la telenovela estadounidense gracias a que su duración es breve (generalmente entre seis meses y un año) y a que su público no está limitado a amas de casa. De hecho, muchas veces se muestran en los mejores horarios por la noche.

Además del dinero que se gana a través de la venta de telenovelas a otros países, existen ganancias *(profits)* por venta de publicidad durante las emisiones, y por la venta de la idea de la novela para que sea adaptada a la cultura de países en otras regiones del mundo. Por si fuera poco, a estas ganancias se suman las que se reciben gracias a la comercialización de productos relacionados con cada telenovela.

Alicia Machado, actriz venezolana

Hoy en día se ha empezado a experimentar con la creación de webnovelas, es decir, producciones exclusivas para mostrarse en el Internet. ¿Tendrán éxito? ¿Cuál crees que sea el futuro de las telenovelas?

Comunidad

En la mayoría de las ciudades de los Estados Unidos es posible recibir al menos un canal de televisión en español. Elige un segmento de la programación (de unas 2 a 3 horas) y analízalo. ¿Qué tipo de programas hay? ¿Quiénes son los patrocinadores? ¿A qué audiencia se dirigen? ¿Te gustó alguno de los programas? ¿Por qué? ¿Crees que estos programas ayuden a la población hispana de la comunidad? ¿Por qué?

En los Estados Unidos recibimos canales de televisión en español.

A analizar ▶

Camila y Rodrigo hablan de sus planes para mañana.
Después de ver el video, lee parte de su conversación y
observa los verbos en negritas.

Camila: ¡Qué semana! Me alegra que por fin
sea el fin de semana y que **podamos**
relajarnos.

Rodrigo: Estoy de acuerdo. Por cierto, Óscar me llamó
hoy y quiere que asista a un partido de fútbol
mañana. ¿Te molesta que **vaya** con él?

Camila: Claro que no. Es más, creo que voy a
llamar a Vanesa a ver si quiere ir al cine conmigo.
Acaba de salir una nueva película que quiero ver,
Amor eterno, y sé que a ti no te gusta **ver** películas románticas.

1. All of the verbs in bold are subjunctive except for one. Which one is it?
2. Why do you think the verb form is not subjunctive?

A comprobar

Subjunctive with expressions of emotion

1. When expressing an emotion or feeling about
something, it is necessary to use the subjunctive if
there are two different subjects. Again, the verb in the
main clause is in the indicative, and the verb in the
dependent clause is in the subjunctive.

Main clause		Dependent clause
Me alegra	que	el programa **se transmita** por la noche.
Él tiene miedo de	que	el gobierno **censure** la programación.

2. Some verbs that express emotion are:

estar contento de	*to be glad; to be pleased*
estar triste de	*to be sad*
sentir	*to be sorry, to regret*
tener miedo de / temer	*to fear*

Temo que haya demasiados programas violentos.
I am afraid that there are too many violent programs.

Los niños **están contentos de** que su madre les
permita ver los dibujos animados.
*The children are glad that their mother allows them
to watch cartoons.*

3. Other verbs that express emotion are:

aburrir	*to bore*	**gustar**	*to like*
alegrar	*to make happy*	**molestar**	*to bother*
encantar	*to love*	**preocupar**	*to worry*
enojar	*to make angry*	**sorprender**	*to surprise*

You will recall that the verbs **gustar, encantar,** and
molestar require the use of the indirect object. The other
verbs in this list also require the use of the indirect object.

Al director **le** preocupa que los actores no lleguen a
tiempo.
The director is worried the actors won't arrive on time.

Me sorprende que haya tantos anuncios comerciales.
It surprises me that there are so many commercials.

4. If there is only one subject, the **que** is not necessary and the infinitive is used with the expression of emotion rather than the subjunctive.

> Estoy contento de **ayudar** con el documental.
> *I am happy to help with the documentary.*

> Sentimos no **poder** asistir al estreno.
> *We regret not being able to attend the debut.*

> **INVESTIGUEMOS LA GRAMÁTICA**
>
> In **Capítulo 9** you learned that the reflexive verbs **alegrarse, enojarse, preocuparse**, etc., are used to express a change in emotion or feeling. These verbs would also require the subjunctive. Notice that the preposition **de** is necessary before **que.**
>
> Me alegro de que **vayas** a casarte.
> *I am happy that you are going to get married.*

A practicar

13.25 Un poco de lógica Lee las siguientes oraciones y decide si las reacciones son lógicas o no. Corrige las oraciones ilógicas.

1. Me alegra que no transmitan mi programa favorito hoy.
2. A los productores les preocupa que el programa no tenga éxito.
3. Los padres temen que sus hijos miren dibujos animados.
4. A los actores les molesta que la compañía haya cancelado su programa.
5. Nos sorprende que el público se ría durante la serie cómica.
6. Elisa siente que el abuelo tenga cáncer.

13.26 En el foro Hoy están grabando una telenovela y hay muchas emociones en el foro *(set)*. Completa las oraciones con la forma apropiada del verbo entre paréntesis. **¡OJO!** Algunos verbos están en el subjuntivo y otros en el infinitivo.

1. Al director le enoja que los actores _____ (hacer) muchos errores y que _____ (tener) que repetir las escenas.
2. A Rosalía le preocupa que Pedro _____ (ir) a olvidar lo que tiene que decir.
3. A Bernardo le alegra _____ (poder) participar en la telenovela.
4. A Gustavo no le gusta que su papel *(part)* no _____ (ser) más importante.
5. A Vicente le encanta _____ (besar) a Lupita, pero a ella le molesta que él no _____ (cepillarse) los dientes.
6. A todos les sorprende que el director _____ (frustarse).

13.27 Oraciones incompletas Con un compañero, túrnense para completar las siguientes oraciones. **¡OJO!** Las oraciones deben tener dos sujetos.

1. Al profesor de español le molesta que...
2. Al presidente le preocupa que...
3. El patrocinador está triste de que...
4. Los niños se sienten mal de que...
5. A los estudiantes de español les sorprende que...
6. Mi familia está contenta de que...
7. A los reporteros les gusta que...
8. Los comediantes temen que...

> **INVESTIGUEMOS LA GRAMÁTICA**
>
> You learned in **Capítulo 9** that the reflexive form of the verb **sentir** means *to feel* and is used with an adverb or an adjective. This would also require the subjunctive if there are two subjects.
>
> **Me siento** mal de que no puedas ir al cine con nosotros.
> *I feel badly that you can't come to the movie theater with us.*

13.28 Hablando de la tele Trabaja con un compañero para expresar sus opiniones sobre la televisión.

| sorprender | gustar | molestar | preocupar | temer | enojar | aburrir |

Modelo alegrar

Estudiante 1: *Me alegra que haya una gran variedad de programas.*
Estudiante 2: *Me alegra que se puedan bloquear los programas inapropiados para los niños.*

13.29 Programas de televisión Con un compañero expliquen lo que pasa en los programas y las reacciones emocionales de los personajes.

Vocabulario útil:

el dragón *dragon*   **el extraterrestre** *extraterrestrial*   **la princesa** *princess*
engañar *to cheat on*   **el ladrón** *thief*   **el príncipe** *prince*

Modelo *El jugador corre a primera base. A sus compañeros de equipo les alegra que pueda correr tan rápido. Al otro jugador le preocupa que llegue a la base.*

1.

2.

3.

4.

5.

6.

© Cengage Learning

13.30 Los noticiarios Imagínate que escuchas las siguientes noticias en un noticiario. Con un compañero, túrnense para expresar una reacción. Usen el subjuntivo y una expresión de duda o de emoción, o una expresión impersonal.

Modelo Un ciudadano dice que vio un fantasma en la biblioteca.
        No creo que existan los fantasmas.
        Me sorprende que haya fantasmas en la biblioteca.
        Espero que el fantasma sea bueno.

1. Dos personas están heridas después de un accidente de coche.
2. Van a cancelar el Super Tazón (*Super Bowl*) este año.
3. Los científicos creen que han encontrado una cura para el cáncer.
4. Una niña de 6 años desapareció de su casa.
5. El presidente dice que la economía va a mejorar el próximo año.
6. Han descubierto que hay vida en el planeta Marte.
7. El departamento de salud va a empezar un estudio sobre los hábitos de los ratones.
8. Un prisionero escapó de la prisión estatal.

A analizar

Camila y Rodrigo hablan de lo que quieren ver en la tele. Mira el video. Después lee parte de su conversación y observa los verbos en negritas.

Rodrigo:	¿Qué quieres ver, mi amor?
Camila:	Quiero ver un programa que **sea** cómico.
Rodrigo:	Hay una película cómica que **parece** divertida. Comienza en una hora.
Camila:	¿No hay nada que **comience** ahora?
Rodrigo:	No, no hay ningún programa que **sea** cómico, pero hay un drama que **tiene** unos actores muy buenos.

You will notice that some of the verbs in bold are in the indicative and others are in the subjunctive. Using what you have already learned about the use of the subjunctive, what do you think determines this difference?

A comprobar

Subjunctive with adjective clauses

1. When using an adjective clause (underlined in the examples below) to describe something that the speaker knows exists the indicative is used.

   Quiero ver la telenovela <u>que **comienza** a las ocho</u>. En ese programa hay un conductor <u>que **es** muy cómico</u>.

2. However, when using an adjective clause (underlined in the examples below) to describe something that the speaker does not know exists or believes does not exist, the subjunctive is used.

   Quiero ver una telenovela <u>que **sea** intrigante</u>.
   I want to see a soap opera that is intriguing.

   ¿Hay un buen programa <u>que **comience** ahora</u>?
   Is there a good show that starts now?

   No hay ningún canal <u>que **tenga** un documental esta noche</u>.
   There is no channel that has a documentary tonight.

3. Some common verbs used with adjective clauses that can require either the subjunctive or the indicative are: **buscar, necesitar,** and **querer.**

   Busco un televisor que **tenga** una pantalla grande.
   I am looking for a television that has a big screen.

   Busco el televisor que **tiene** una pantalla grande.
   I am looking for a television that has a big screen.

In the first sentence the person does not have a specific television in mind and does not necessarily know if one exists, while in the second sentence he/she is looking for a specific television.

4. When asking about the existence of something, it is also necessary to use the subjunctive, as you do not know whether or not it exists.

   ¿Conoces a alguien que no **mire** la tele?
   Do you know anyone that doesn't watch TV?

   ¿Hay alguna película que **sea** romántica?
   Is there a romantic movie?

5. When using negative words, such as **nadie** or **ninguno,** to express doubt as to the existence of something, it is necessary to use the subjunctive in the adjective clause.

   No conozco a nadie que no **mire** la tele.
   I don't know anyone that doesn't watch TV.

   No hay ninguna película que **sea** romántica.
   There is no movie that is romantic.

INVESTIGUEMOS LA GRÁMATICA

When you do not have a specific person in mind or do not know if someone exists, it is not necessary to use the personal **a** in the main clause, except with **alguien** or **nadie.**

La estación de radio **busca un locutor** que pueda trabajar por la noche.

¿Conoces a alguien que busque trabajo?

A practicar

13.31 **¿Estás de acuerdo?** Lee las oraciones y decide si estás de acuerdo o no. Explica por qué.

1. Hoy en día no hay nadie que tenga televisor en blanco y negro.
2. La producción de programas de televisión es una profesión que paga bien.
3. Me aburren los anuncios comerciales que hay en la televisión.
4. Prefiero mirar programas que tengan mucha acción.
5. No hay ningún canal local que ofrezca buena programación.
6. Es importante que los niños no vean programas que tengan contenido para adultos.

13.32 **Un nuevo teléfono celular** Hoy en día se puede hacer mucho con los celulares, como mirar la tele, escuchar música y sacar fotos. Conjuga los verbos en el subjuntivo para completar las ideas. Después di si estás de acuerdo o no con la afirmación.

Quiero tener un teléfono celular que...

1. (poder) mandar documentos por fax
2. (grabar – *to record*) las conversaciones
3. (servir) para abrir y cerrar el coche automáticamente
4. (traducir) del inglés al español
5. (tener) una luz para poder usarla como una linterna
6. (ser) tan delgado como una tarjeta de crédito

13.33 **¿Qué buscas?** Explica lo que buscan las personas en los dibujos. **¡OJO!** Recuerda que necesitas usar el subjuntivo.

Modelo   *El muchacho busca un programa que sea cómico y que comience a las siete.*

1.

2.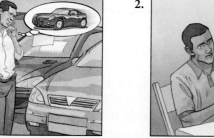

3.

4.

5.

© Cengage Learning

13.34 Un invento increíble Con un compañero, diseñen un invento y dibújenlo. Luego completen las siguientes oraciones para explicarle su invento a la clase.

Queremos inventar un(a) _____ que...
Nuestro invento tendrá _____ que...

Modelo *Queremos inventar un televisor que tenga un refrigerador con refrescos. Nuestro invento tendrá un microondas que esté conectado al televisor y que cocine mi comida mientras miro la tele. El televisor tendrá un control remoto que también sirva como teléfono.*

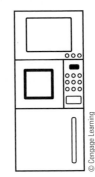

© Cengage Learning

13.35 Lo que quiero Con un compañero, completen las oraciones con sus preferencias personales.

Modelo Este fin de semana quiero ir a un lugar...
Estudiante 1: *Cuando (yo) salga este fin de semana quiero ir a un lugar que tenga buena música.*
Estudiante 2: *¿De veras? Yo quiero ir a un lugar que sea económico.*

1. Quiero ver una película que...
2. Quiero ir a un restaurante que...
3. Deseo comprar un coche que...
4. Espero tener un trabajo que...
5. En mis próximas vacaciones quiero ir a un lugar que...
6. Pienso comprar una casa que...
7. Quiero tener una mascota que...
8. En el futuro deseo tomar una clase que...

13.36 Quiero saber Con un compañero, túrnense para hacer y contestar las preguntas. Si responde positivamente, identifica a la persona a quien conoce y añade un poco más de información.

Modelo no tiene televisor
Estudiante 1: *¿Conoces a alguien que no tenga televisor?*
Estudiante 2: *No conozco a nadie que no tenga televisor. / Sí, mi abuelo no tiene televisor porque no le gusta la programación.*

¿Conoces a alguien que...?

1. mirar las telenovelas
2. no tener teléfono celular
3. nunca ir al cine
4. usar una tableta para hacer su tarea
5. leer historietas
6. chatear mucho por Internet
7. no saber usar una computadora
8. ver los noticiarios todos los días

No conozco a nadie que no tenga televisor.

© Monkey Business Images/Shutterstock

Lectura

Antes de leer

1. ¿Cuáles son las características generales de las telenovelas?
2. ¿Cuáles son dos telenovelas muy conocidas en los Estados Unidos?
3. ¿Conoces alguna telenovela latinoamericana? ¿En qué son diferentes a las de los Estados Unidos?
4. ¿Piensas que las telenovelas tengan algún valor?
5. En lo personal ¿te interesan las telenovelas?

A leer

Las telenovelas latinoamericanas: más que un entretenimiento

stations — Las telenovelas latinoamericanas son la columna vertebral de muchas **emisoras** de televisión en Latinoamérica. Se transmiten en todos los horarios y satisfacen la demanda de todas las audiencias. Quienes creen *glance* — que las telenovelas son solo para amas de casa deben echar un **vistazo** a los distintos subgéneros que han nacido en las últimas décadas: telenovelas históricas para los más intelectuales, telenovelas para niños, telenovelas de problemática social, y hasta telenovelas dirigidas a los hombres. Según los productores, este género promueve cambios sociales, ayuda a educar a la gente sobre temas de interés social, como el **SIDA**, la homosexualidad o la inmigración, y *AIDS* — hasta ha ayudado a salvar vidas.

> [este género promueve cambios sociales]

© Joe Cavaretta/MCT/Newscom

Las telenovelas latinoamericanas se transmiten en todo el mundo.

Las telenovelas latinoamericanas han evolucionado mucho desde su aparición. Al principio casi todas las telenovelas eran la típica historia de *Cinderella* — **Cenicienta,** en donde una mujer humilde se enamoraba de un amor imposible — *struggle* — generalmente un hombre rico de buena familia. La protagonista debía **luchar** contra innumerables desgracias, pero al final se quedaba con el hombre de sus sueños. Aunque todavía hoy en día se producen telenovelas de este tipo, también es cierto que se producen muchas otras con una temática más interesante que atrae a televidentes muy diversos. A veces se convierten en fenómenos sociales, como fue el caso del grupo musical RBD, creado en la telenovela *Rebelde,* y que hizo **giras** por todo el mundo, atrayendo multitudes y llenando estadios.

tours

    Una gran ventaja del formato de la telenovela latinoamericana es que tiene una duración limitada, generalmente alrededor de seis meses, lo que la hace mucho más versátil que la telenovela estadounidense. Es común que muchos de estos culebrones (otro nombre con que se conoce a las telenovelas) se traduzcan a docenas de otros idiomas y rompan récords de audiencia en países tan diferentes como Rusia, China y Rumania. Se transmiten en más de cien países alrededor del mundo y son considerados una gran fuente de empleo que promueve la economía de los países que las producen. **No sería de extrañar** que en el futuro cercano este formato empiece a atraer a mayor número de televidentes dentro de los Estados Unidos.

It wouldn't be surprising

Comprensión

1. ¿Cuáles son dos diferencias importantes entre las telenovelas de los Estados Unidos y las telenovelas latinoamericanas?

2. ¿Qué temas de interés social han tratado algunas telenovelas?

3. Según el texto ¿qué se creó *(created)* a partir de la telenovela *Rebelde*?

4. ¿Cómo afectan la economía las telenovelas?

5. En tu opinión ¿qué hace populares a estas historias en tantos países con culturas tan diferentes?

6. En tu opinión ¿de qué puede tratar una telenovela dirigida a niños?

7. ¿Conoces a alguien que vea telenovelas? Si contestas que sí ¿sabes por qué le gustan?

Después de leer

Investiga los temas de algunas de las novelas que se transmiten en la actualidad por los canales de televisión en español. ¿Tienen algún mensaje social?

"Más sabe el diablo" se transmitió en más de 70 países.

© Music4mix/Shutterstock

Redacción

Write a dramatic scene from a soap opera or a TV drama. It should be written as a script with stage directions in parentheses.

Paso 1 Think of a dramatic situation that would involve two people, such as a marriage proposal or a breakup. Then brainstorm where the scene would take place. Jot down some ideas such as where the two characters are, what is around them, and what they are doing.

Paso 2 Think about what might be said in a conversation of this nature and jot down some key sentences and questions along with some responses to those statements/questions.

Paso 3 Write a short paragraph in which you describe the scene using the information generated in **Paso 1.**

Paso 4 Using the information you generated in **Paso 2,** create a dramatic dialogue between the two characters. Because communication involves more than words, you will need to indicate gestures, tone, actions, etc., in parentheses.

Paso 5 Edit your script:

1. Are the stage directions clear?
2. Read the dialogue out loud. Does it flow? Does it seem "natural"?
3. Do adjectives agree with the person or object they describe?
4. Do verbs agree with the subject?
5. Did you use subjunctive forms where necessary?
6. Do you have a **personal a** where necessary? And indirect object pronouns?
7. Did you check your spelling, including accents?

Entrando en materia

Las fotonovelas son un pasatiempo popular que ha sobrevivido a pesar de la competencia de la programación en televisión por cable y satélite, de los DVDs, de las computadoras y de los éxitos de taquilla. ¿Cuál piensas que es la definición de una fotonovela?

Artículo informativo

Lee el artículo sobre las fotonovelas y contesta las preguntas que siguen.

El formato de la fotonovela se ha adaptado para hacer publicaciones educativas.

Como su nombre lo dice, las fotonovelas son novelas, pero están narradas visualmente a partir de fotografías. En México las fotonovelas tuvieron su origen en las historietas de siglo, las cuales eran versiones ilustradas de obras populares de la literatura europea. Algunas personas piensan que el origen de las fotonovelas está en la mercadotecnia[1] ya que, al parecer, se incluían pequeños segmentos ilustrados de relatos románticos en los paquetes de cigarrillos. Para saber cómo continuaba la historia, había que seguir comprándolos semana tras semana.

Desde el siglo XIX hasta hoy en día, las fotonovelas se publican en numerosos episodios. Estas historias eventualmente dieron forma a la serie original que se centró en la vida mexicana contemporánea. Popular hasta el día de hoy, la historieta moderna tiene objetivos tan variados como el entretenimiento, la educación y la política. El tiraje[2] de un ejemplar puede ser de hasta 250 mil copias, por lo que llegan a un enorme y variado

público de lectores. Debido al tiraje tan elevado, se puede hablar de que circulan en el país alrededor de 30 millones de historietas y fotonovelas cada mes.

Dentro de la comunidad mexicoamericana en los Estados Unidos la fotonovela tiene una manifestación distinta, donde proporciona un canal para que la comunidad exprese sus preocupaciones sociales a través de un lenguaje visual innovador. Activistas y grupos religiosos también han recurrido a la fotonovela como una herramienta[3] de organización para la difusión de información, la educación y el proselitismo.

Aunque las fotonovelas parecen simples, esta impresión es engañosa[4]. Los argumentos[5] tienden a ser melodramáticos, con temas como el ascenso social a la riqueza, los secretos de familia sobre amores prohibidos entre personas de diferentes clases sociales, etcétera. Más recientemente, los argumentos han tratado de temas sociales, o incluso de elementos sobrenaturales, como fantasmas[6].

Sources: Public Broadcasting Service; Crónica.com.mx © The Fotonovela Production Company. www.fotonovelacompany.com

[1]marketing   [2]print run   [3]tool   [4]deceiving   [5]plots   [6]ghosts

Comprensión

1. ¿Cómo se cree que se originaron las fotonovelas?
2. ¿Cuántas copias se llegan a publicar de cada fotonovela?
3. ¿Qué tipo de objetivos tiene la historieta moderna?
4. ¿En qué aspectos es diferente la fotonovela mexicoamericana?
5. ¿Cómo han usado las historietas algunos grupos religiosos o de activistas?

Más allá

Diseña el argumento *(plot)* para una fotonovela. Describe de cuatro a seis escenas diferentes que narren una breve historia. ¡No olvides incluir el diálogo para cada escena! Después, compártela en Share It! Lee las historias de tus compañeros. ¿Qué temas eligieron?

Los medios de comunicación

Vocabulario

Sustantivos

la cámara	*camera*
el (la) camarógrafo(a)	*camera person*
el (la) entrevistado(a)	*interviewee*
el foro	*set*
el guión	*script*
el maquillaje	*makeup*
el micrófono	*microphone*
el camerino	*dressing room*

Adjetivos

atento(a)	*attentive*
neutro(a)	*neutral*
presentable	*presentable*
puntual	*punctual*
simpático(a)	*appealing*

Verbos

despedirse	*to say goodbye*
guiar	*to guide*
presentarse	*to introduce yourself*

Expresiones útiles

salir al aire
to be on the air

seguir el guión
to follow the script

mirar fijo a la cámara
to look straight into the camera

Vamos a comerciales.
Let's go to commercials.

Los profesionales de la Comunicación pueden trabajar en la producción de programas para la televisión.

© John Stanmeyer/VII/Corbis

DATOS IMPORTANTES

Educación: Estudios universitarios o terciarios en comunicación y/o negocios

Salario: Entre $35 000 y $140 000, dependiendo de los años de experiencia, en un rango de 1 a 20 años.

Dónde se trabaja: En canales de televisión locales o nacionales, públicos o privados; en canales de televisión por cable o satélite

---

Vocabulario nuevo Completa las oraciones con la palabra apropiada de la lista de vocabulario.

1. _____ graba (*records*) la escena con su cámara.

2. Al final del programa el conductor _____.

3. Los actores se visten y se maquillan en sus _____.

4. Todos deben ser _____ y no llegar tarde al foro.

5. Si no usas _____ nadie te va a escuchar.

Ruth Baker, productora

Ruth Baker es productora de televisión. Trabaja en un canal privado de cable y está preparándose para un nuevo programa. En el video verás a Ruth dándole instrucciones a una persona.

Antes de ver

Los productores de programas de televisión trabajan detrás de las cámaras. Los televidentes no los ven, pero ellos hacen lo más importante de lo que vemos en TV. Las notas, el entretenimiento y el formato de los programas son idea de los productores. ¿Qué tipo de programas te interesa producir? ¿Qué ideas o qué formato nuevo te interesa presentar? ¿Cuántos actores o presentadores necesitas? Presenta ideas novedosas.

Comprensión

1. ¿A quién le da instrucciones Ruth?
2. ¿Dónde estará Ruth durante el programa?
3. ¿Qué ropa no le gusta a Jorge?
4. ¿Qué es lo primero que debe hacer Jorge al empezar el programa?
5. ¿Quién es el invitado de hoy?
6. ¿Qué tiene que hacer Jorge con la ropa durante el concurso?
7. ¿Quién participará en el concurso?
8. ¿Cuándo salen al aire?

Después de ver

En grupos de tres, representen a un productor de televisión dando instrucciones antes de la grabación de un programa. Las otras personas pueden ser actores, presentadores o personal técnico.

13.37 **La tele** Completa el párrafo con la forma apropiada del verbo entre paréntesis. **¡OJO!** Tendrás que usar el subjuntivo, el indicativo o el infinitivo.

Los Marino no quieren que su hijo Édgar **(1.)** _____ (ver) la tele mucho. Prefieren que **(2.)** _____ (pasar) más tiempo jugando afuera y leyendo. A Édgar le molesta que sus padres **(3.)** _____ (apagar) la tele después de una hora y que no le **(4.)** _____ (permitir) verla más. Esta noche él quiere **(5.)** _____ (ver) una película que **(6.)** _____ (empezar) a las ocho. Entonces Édgar les pide a sus padres que le **(7.)** _____ (dar) permiso para verla. Su padre le dice que sí, pero insiste en que **(8.)** _____ (terminar) su tarea primero. A Édgar le alegra **(9.)** _____ (poder) ver la película y promete terminar su tarea.

13.38 **Relaciones** Mira los dibujos y explica lo que pasa. Usa la forma recíproca de los verbos indicados en el presente del indicativo.

1.

amar, extrañar, escribir

2.

pelear, gritar *(to yell)*, mirar

3.

conocer, dar la mano, besar

4.

dar, decir

13.39 **Lo que se busca** Completa las oraciones con la forma apropiada del verbo entre paréntesis y con una conclusión lógica.

1. Al buscar una pareja algunas personas buscan a alguien que (ser)...
2. Al salir en una cita hay personas que buscan un lugar que (tener)...
3. Al casarse algunas parejas quieren tener una boda que (costar)...
4. Algunos recién casados prefieren vivir en un lugar que les (ofrecer)...
5. A veces, después de tener hijos, los padres necesitan un trabajo que les (permitir)...
6. Si la pareja se divorcia, es buena idea conseguir un abogado que (ser)...

13.40 **Una telenovela** Las siguientes fotos son de varias escenas de telenovelas. En parejas, elijan una e inventen los detalles. Piensen en lo siguiente: ¿Quiénes son los protagonistas? ¿Cuál es la trama? ¿Qué pasa en esta escena? ¿Cómo se va a resolver la situación? Usen diferentes ejemplos del subjuntivo en la descripción.

13.41 **¿Cuál es la pregunta?** Trabaja con un compañero. Uno de ustedes debe ver las preguntas en esta página, y el otro debe verlas en el **Apéndice B**. Es una competencia y el ganador *(winner)* es quien tenga más puntos. Obtienes puntos cuando adivinas la pregunta <u>exacta</u> que tiene tu compañero. Para ayudarte, tu compañero te va a decir la respuesta a la pregunta. Tienes tres oportunidades para adivinar cada pregunta.

Modelo ¿Qué es extrañar?
　　　　Estudiante 1: *Es cuando no estás con una persona y estás triste. Piensas mucho en*
　　　　　　　　　　la persona.
　　　　Estudiante 2: *¿Qué es extrañar?*

Puntos	Preguntas
10	¿Qué es la luna de miel?
20	¿Qué es divorciarse?
30	¿Qué es un soltero?
40	¿Qué es un nacimiento?
50	¿Qué hacemos en la adolescencia?
100	¿Qué es enamorarse?

13.42 **Y el premio es para...** Van a decidir cuál es el mejor programa de televisión.

Paso 1 Con un compañero, decidan cuáles son las características que hacen que un programa de televisión merezca *(deserves)* un premio *(award)*.

Paso 2 Compartan su lista de características con la clase y entre todos elijan 3 o 4.

Paso 3 Con tu compañero, hablen de algunos programas que piensan que reúnen las características. Decidan el programa que quieren nominar.

Paso 4 Todos los grupos van a nominar un programa y explicar por qué lo nominaron. Después la clase votará por el mejor programa de televisión.

🔊 Vocabulario 1
2-36

Relaciones personales

el anillo	*ring*	el padrino	*best man, godfather*
la ceremonia	*ceremony*	la pareja	*couple*
la cita	*date*	el (la) prometido(a)	*fiancé(e)*
el compromiso	*engagement*		
la luna de miel	*honeymoon*	la recepción	*wedding reception*
la madrina	*maid of honor, godmother*	el (la) recién casado(a)	*newlywed*
la muerte	*death*	soltero(a)	*single, unmarried*
el nacimiento	*birth*	la unión libre	*common-law union*
el noviazgo	*engagement, relationship*	viudo(a)	*widowed*

Verbos

abrazar	*to hug*	insistir (en)	*to insist (on)*
amar	*to love*	llevarse (bien/mal)	*to (not) get along*
besar	*to kiss*	mandar	*to order*
comprometerse (con)	*to get engaged (to)*	nacer	*to be born*
dar a luz	*to give birth*	odiar	*to hate*
desear	*to desire, to wish*	proponer matrimonio	*to propose matrimony*
divorciarse (de)	*to divorce*	querer	*to love*
enamorarse (de)	*to fall in love (with)*	romper (con)	*to break up (with)*
esperar	*to hope*	separarse (de)	*to separate (from)*
estar embarazada	*to be pregnant*	sugerir (ie)	*to suggest*
extrañar	*to miss*		

Palabras adicionales

la adolescencia	*adolescence*	la muerte	*death*
el estado civil	*civil status*	la niñez	*childhood*
la juventud	*youth*	la vejez	*old age*
la madurez	*maturity*		

Diccionario personal

_____

_____

_____

_____

_____

_____

◀))) Vocabulario 2
2-37

La televisión

el anuncio comercial	*commercial*
la audiencia	*audience*
el canal	*TV channel*
la clasificación	*rating (for adults, for the whole family, etc.)*
el concurso	*game show*
el (la) conductor(a)	*TV host*
el control remoto	*remote control*
el documental	*documentary*
los dibujos animados	*cartoons*

el (la) locutor(a)	*announcer*
el noticiario	*news*
el patrocinador	*sponsor*
la programación	*programming*
el reproductor de DVD	*DVD player*
la telenovela	*soap opera*
el (la) televidente	*television viewer*
la televisión por cable	*cable television*
la televisión por satélite	*satellite television*

La tecnología

los audífonos	*headphones*
el buscador	*search engine*
el MP3	*MP3 player*
la pantalla	*screen*
el ratón	*mouse*

las redes sociales	*social networks*
el reproductor de CDs	*CD player*
el tablero	*keyboard*
la tableta	*tablet*

El cine

la butaca	*seat*
el éxito de taquilla	*box office hit*
las golosinas	*candy*

las palomitas de maíz	*popcorn*

Verbos

censurar	*to censor*
chatear	*to chat*
hacer clic (en)	*to click (on)*

limitar	*to limit*
temer	*to fear*
transmitir	*to broadcast*

Palabras adicionales

el (la) adolescente	*adolescent*
el adulto	*adult*

infantil	*for children, childish*
la revista	*magazine*

Diccionario personal

_____

_____

_____

_____

CAPÍTULO 14

Learning Strategy

Think in Spanish

When speaking, try to think in Spanish and speak spontaneously rather than translating from English. If you find you need to use a word that you don't know, instead of saying it in English or looking it up in the dictionary, try explaining the concept using other Spanish words. With a little practice, this skill will become easier.

In this chapter you will learn how to:

- Discuss health issues with a doctor
- Discuss hypothetical situations
- Express opinions regarding world issues
- Tell what had happened prior to other events in the past

¿Qué haces en una emergencia?

© Stringer/Mexico/Reuters/Corbis

Los servicios de salud son muy importantes en todas las comunidades.

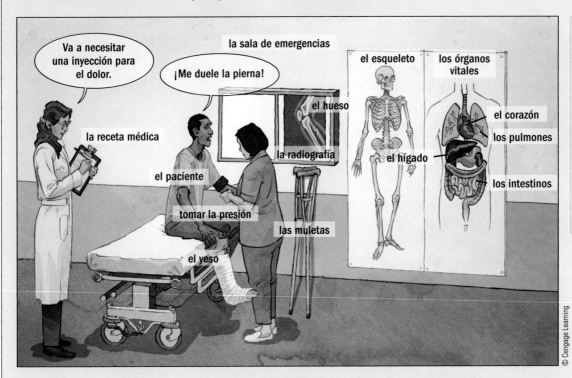

Va a necesitar una inyección para el dolor.

¡Me duele la pierna!

la sala de emergencias

la receta médica

el paciente

tomar la presión

el yeso

el hueso

la radiografía

las muletas

el esqueleto

los órganos vitales

el corazón

los pulmones

el hígado

los intestinos

© Cengage Learning

INVESTIGUEMOS LA GRAMÁTICA

The verb **doler**, like the verb **gustar**, requires the indirect object pronoun and is conjugated in the third person singular or plural in agreement with the subject. Remember to use the definite article rather than the possessive before parts of the body.

Me duelen los brazos.
My arms hurt.

Los síntomas	*Symptoms*
la alergia	*allergy*
la cortada	*cut*
el desmayo	*faint*
la diarrea	*diarrhea*
el dolor (de)	*pain (in)*
la náusea	*nausea*
la presión	*low/high*
baja/alta	*blood pressure*

Algunas enfermedades

el cáncer	*cancer*
la diabetes	*diabetes*
la gripe	*flu*
la hipertensión	*high blood pressure*
el insomnio	*insomnia*
la obesidad	*obesity*
el resfriado	*cold*
el SIDA	*AIDS*

Los medicamentos y procedimientos

la aspirina	*aspirin*
la cirugía	*surgery*
la curita	*small adhesive bandage*
las gotas	*drops*
la inyección	*shot*
el jarabe	*(cough) syrup*
la pastilla	*pill*
la silla de ruedas	*wheelchair*
la vacuna	*vaccination*
el vendaje	*bandage*

Verbos

cortarse	*to get a cut*
descansar	*to rest*
desmayarse	*to faint*
doler (ue)	*to hurt*
enfermarse	*to get sick*
estar mareado(a)	*to be dizzy*

estornudar	*to sneeze*
examinar	*to examine*
fracturarse	*to fracture*
recuperarse	*to recuperate, to recover*
respirar	*to breathe*
sangrar	*to bleed*
sentir naúseas	*to feel nauseous*
torcerse (ue)	*to twist, to sprain*
toser	*to cough*
vomitar	*to vomit*

Palabras adicionales

los primeros auxilios	*first aid*
la salud	*health*
la sangre	*blood*
el tratamiento	*treatment*

INVESTIGUEMOS EL VOCABULARIO

Remember that many words have similar forms in other parts of speech. Just as **doler** is a verb and **el dolor** is a noun, the verbs **estornudar, fracturar, desmayarse, enfermarse,** and **toser,** among many others, can become nouns: **el estornudo, la fractura, el desmayo, la enfermedad,** and **la tos.**

A practicar

14.1 **Escucha y responde** En un papel escribe "síntoma" y en otro "tratamiento". Vas a escuchar una serie de palabras del vocabulario. Levanta el papel correspondiente si la palabra que escuchas es un síntoma o un tratamiento.

2-38

14.2 La salud Escoge la opción más lógica para completar cada idea.

1. El _____ sirve para pensar y regular el sistema nervioso.

2. Un síntoma de los resfriados es la _____.

3. Le recomiendo tomar vitaminas si usted _____ con frecuencia.

4. El doctor _____ al paciente.

5. El órgano que sirve para respirar es _____.

6. Los paramédicos llevan en una _____ a un hombre que se rompió la pierna.

7. El paciente se sentó un momento porque estaba muy _____.

8. A veces las mujeres embarazadas sienten _____ en la mañana.

14.3 Asociaciones Con un compañero, relacionen las palabras de la primera columna con una opción de la segunda columna y expliquen la relación. Hay varias posibilidades.

Modelo obesidad   diabetes
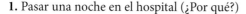
La obesidad es un factor que puede causar diabetes.

1. la inyección	**a.** el yeso
2. respirar	**b.** los pulmones
3. la presión alta	**c.** el hueso
4. la náusea	**d.** el vendaje
5. la cortada	**e.** la tos
6. la radiografía	**f.** la vacuna
7. la fractura	**g.** las pastillas
8. el resfriado	**h.** vomitar

14.4 Encuesta Trabajen en grupos de cuatro o cinco estudiantes para averiguar quiénes han tenido las experiencias de la lista. Acuérdense de hacer las preguntas adicionales y de tomar notas para después reportarle la información a la clase.

1. Pasar una noche en el hospital (¿Por qué?)

2. Tener gripe recientemente (¿Qué tratamiento siguió?)

3. Recibir una inyección (¿Cuándo?)

4. Fracturarse un hueso (¿Cómo?)

5. Administrar los primeros auxilios alguna vez (¿Por qué?)

6. Desmayarse alguna vez (¿Por qué?)

> **INVESTIGUEMOS LA MÚSICA**
>
> Listen to Spanish singers Joan Manuel Serrat and Joaquín Sabina's song "Pastillas para no soñar." What do they suggest that one do in order to live 100 years?

14.5 Diferencias Trabaja con un compañero. Uno mira el dibujo en esta página y el otro mira el dibujo en el **Apéndice B.** Túrnense para describir sus dibujos y encontrar las cinco diferencias.

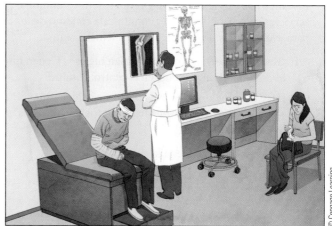

© Cengage Learning

Cultura

Hoy en día muchos problemas de salud son comunes en todas las regiones del mundo; ejemplos de estos problemas son las enfermedades del corazón, la diabetes y la obesidad. Sin embargo, no todas las personas siguen un tratamiento de medicina moderna. Algunas personas no confían *(trust)* en estos tratamientos, o sufren de alergias que no les permiten tomar ciertas medicinas. Otras personas no los toman porque no les han dado buenos resultados, o porque tienen más confianza en otros métodos que han ayudado a sus ancestros o conocidos a curarse. En algunas comunidades remotas de muchos países, y aún en las grandes ciudades, hay quienes prefieren seguir las recomendaciones de curanderos. Los curanderos son generalmente personas mayores que saben curar enfermedades a base de remedios naturales, como hierbas.

Los remedios naturales siempre han sido populares.

En el caso de México, la medicina tradicional indígena está reconocida en la Constitución Política del país como derecho cultural de los pueblos indígenas, y este reconocimiento incluye el respeto a la cosmovisión indígena, la cual reconoce al universo como una totalidad interconectada, y al cuerpo humano como al conjunto *(combination)* de mente *(mind)* y espíritu.

Los remedios van más allá del uso de plantas medicinales, e incluyen tratamientos terapéuticos como el uso de ciertos productos animales y minerales, masajes, limpias *(cleansings)* y otros ritos.

En la actualidad existe un movimiento para rescatar el conocimiento prehispánico acerca del uso de plantas para curar a la gente. El movimiento está apoyado por el gobierno y gracias a este apoyo se han abierto centros en donde se enseñan las bases de la medicina indígena.

¿Qué remedios o tratamientos naturales conoces? ¿Alguna vez has conocido a algún curandero? ¿Piensas que los remedios naturales son tan efectivos como la medicina tradicional de los hospitales? ¿Por qué?

> Investiga en Internet tratamientos naturales que son comunes en los países hispanohablantes. Comparte en Share It! algo interesante que descubriste y lee sobre los tratamientos que escogieron tus compañeros.

Comunidad

Investiga qué servicios de salud existen en tu comunidad. ¿Ofrecen estos servicios en español? Después comunícate con uno de los centros de salud para averiguar las respuestas a las siguientes preguntas:

1. ¿Reciben a personas que no hablan inglés? ¿Tienen intérpretes? ¿Qué idiomas habla el personal en el centro de salud?

2. ¿Hay documentos para pacientes que hablen español? Si los hay, pide algunas muestras. ¿De qué hablan estos documentos? ¿Son los mismos que se ofrecen en inglés?

Repórtale tus conclusiones a la clase.

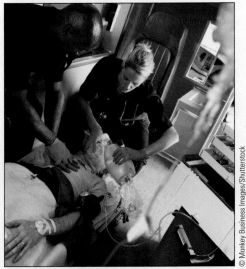

¿Qué servicios de salud existen en tu comunidad?

Comparaciones

No es secreto que la dieta de una persona afecta su salud. Tampoco es secreto que los cambios en nuestra sociedad han cambiado la manera en la que las personas se alimentan. El libro *Hungry Planet: What the World Eats* del fotógrafo Peter Menzel y la escritora Faith D'Aluisio, documenta visualmente la dieta semanal de 30 familias de diferentes países.

Observa las fotografías de las familias de estos dos países. ¿Son semejantes sus dietas? ¿Cuál piensas que es mejor? ¿Cuál se parece más a tu dieta? ¿En cuál de estos países piensas que hay más problemas de salud?

La familia Revises de Carolina del Norte, Estados Unidos

La familia Casales de Cuernavaca, México

Escoge un país hispanohablante en la sección **Exploraciones del mundo hispano** del **Apéndice A** e investiga las comidas tradicionales que se listan para ese país. ¿Son saludables?

Conexiones... a la filosofía

Con un compañero, lean los siguientes refranes para determinar lo que significan. ¿Hay refranes similares en inglés? Digan si están de acuerdo con estos refranes.

La naturaleza, el tiempo y la paciencia son tres grandes médicos.

Quien quiera vivir sano, coma poco y cene temprano.

A quien come muchos manjares *(delicacies)* no le faltarán enfermedades.

Gástalo en la cocina y no en medicina.

Donde entra el sol, no entra la enfermedad.

Échate a enfermar, verás quién te quiere bien o quién te quiere mal.

La salud no es conocida hasta que es perdida.

Entre salud y dinero, salud quiero.

Más vale prevenir que curar.

Más vale prevenir que curar.

A analizar

Nicolás no se siente bien y le pide consejos a Rosa. Después de ver el video, lee parte de su conversación y observa los verbos en negritas. Luego contesta las preguntas que siguen.

> **Nicolás:** ¡No puedo estar enfermo! Tengo un examen en la clase de Literatura Hispanoamericana el viernes. ¿Qué hago?
>
> **Rosa:** Yo **me quedaría** en casa y **dormiría** todo lo posible. **Tomaría** aspirina y **bebería** muchos líquidos. Si quieres, yo te llevo una sopa que mi madre siempre me preparaba cuando me sentía mal.
>
> **Nicolás:** ¡Gracias, Rosita! ¿Qué **haría** sin ti?
>
> **Rosa:** De nada, amigo.

1. The verbs in bold are in the conditional. How are they formed?
2. What is the infinitive of the irregular verb form **haría**?

A comprobar

Conditional

1. To form the conditional, add the following endings to the infinitive. Notice that all verbs take the same endings.

	hablar	**volver**	**ir**
yo	hablar**ía**	volver**ía**	ir**ía**
tú	hablar**ías**	volver**ías**	ir**ías**
él, ella, usted	hablar**ía**	volver**ía**	ir**ía**
nosotros(as)	hablar**íamos**	volver**íamos**	ir**íamos**
vosotros(as)	hablar**íais**	volver**íais**	ir**íais**
ellos, ellas, ustedes	hablar**ían**	volver**ían**	ir**ían**

2. Irregular verbs have the same stems in the conditional as they do in the future tense. The endings are the same as those for regular verbs.

decir	**dir-**	yo diría
hacer	**har-**	tú harías
poder	**podr-**	él podría
poner	**pondr-**	ella pondría
querer	**querr-**	ellos querrían
saber	**sabr-**	ellas sabrían
salir	**saldr-**	usted saldría
tener	**tendr-**	nosotros tendríamos
venir	**vendr-**	vosotros vendríais

3. The conditional is similar to the English construction *would* + verb.

> Yo **no tomaría** esa pastilla sin hablar con un médico.
> I **wouldn't take** that pill without talking with a doctor.
>
> Me dijo que **estaría** en la sala de emergencias.
> He told me he **would be** in the emergency room.

4. The conditional form of **haber** is **habría.** You will remember that there is only one form of the verb regardless of whether it is followed by a singular or plural noun.

> Pensé que **habría** más enfermeras.
> I thought there **would be** more nurses.

5. While the future is used to speculate about present conditions, the conditional is used for conjecture about past activities.

> ¿Por qué **no tomaría** las pastillas?
> Why **wouldn't he take** the pills? (**I wonder** why he **didn't take** the pills.)
>
> **Tendría** gripe.
> He **probably had** the flu.

6. The conditional is often used to demonstrate politeness or to soften a request.

> **Me gustaría** ver las radiografías.
> I **would like** to see the X-rays.
>
> ¿**Irías** al hospital conmigo?
> **Would you go** to the hospital with me?

A practicar

14.6 **Remedios** Imagina que tienes un hijo de cinco años. ¿Qué harías en los siguientes casos?

1. Tu hijo tiene un resfriado.

   a. Le prepararía comidas con vitamina C.

   b. Lo llevaría inmediatamente a la sala de emergencias.

2. Tu hijo se quema *(burn)* la mano en la estufa.

   a. Le pondría pasta de dientes en la quemadura.

   b. Sumergiría la mano en agua fresca.

3. Tu hijo tiene una cortada muy profunda.

   a. La limpiaría con jabón y un cepillo.

   b. Le aplicaría presión con un vendaje.

4. Tu hijo tiene mucha fiebre.

   a. Le daría agua o jugo.

   b. Le daría un baño caliente.

5. Tu hijo se rompe un brazo mientras juega en el parque.

   a. Le pondría hielo en el brazo.

   b. Movería el brazo para saber si le duele mucho.

6. A tu hijo le duele la garganta.

   a. Le daría antibióticos que tengo en casa.

   b. Le haría un té con limón y miel *(honey)*.

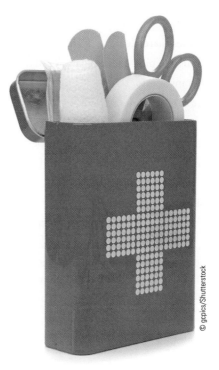

© gcpics/Shutterstock

14.7 **¿Es lógico?** Primero completa la oración con la forma apropiada del condicional. Después decide si la oración es lógica o no.

1. Tú _____ (poner) un vendaje en una cortada.

2. El doctor _____ (sacar) radiografías del hueso roto.

3. Una persona con diabetes _____ (estornudar) mucho.

4. Nosotros _____ (tomar) una aspirina para curar un dolor de estómago.

5. Las enfermeras _____ (poder) desmayarse al dar una inyección.

6. Yo _____ (venir) a la clase con una fiebre de 39 grados.

14.8 **En busca de...** Pregúntales a diferentes compañeros si harían las siguientes actividades si ganaran *(if they won)* la lotería. Pide información adicional para reportársela a la clase después. Recuerda que necesitas buscar a personas que contesten que sí.

Modelo comprar un coche nuevo (¿Por qué?)
        Estudiante 1: *¿Comprarías un coche nuevo?*
        Estudiante 2: *Sí, compraría un coche nuevo.*
        Estudiante 1: *¿Por qué?*
        Estudiante 2: *Porque mi auto se descompone con frecuencia.*

1. trabajar (¿Dónde?)

2. comprarles regalos a tus amigos (¿A quiénes?)

3. darles dinero a los necesitados (¿Para qué causas?)

4. seguir estudiando (¿Por qué?)

5. hacer un viaje (¿Adónde?)

6. salir a restaurantes muy caros (¿Qué comerías?)

7. tener una gran fiesta para todos tus amigos (¿Qué harían?)

8. poner parte del dinero en el banco (¿Cuánto?)

14.9 ¿Qué harías? Con un compañero, hablen de lo que harían en las siguientes situaciones.

Modelo   Tu doctor habla muy poco y no hace muchas preguntas.
Estudiante 1: *Le haría muchas preguntas.*
Estudiante 2: *Yo buscaría otro doctor.*

1. Te sientes mareado.

2. Un amigo te pide que le regales pastillas para el dolor.

3. Tienes insomnio.

4. Un amigo tiene un resfriado.

5. Estás con una amiga cuando de repente se desmaya.

6. Te rompes una pierna y tienes que llevar un yeso.

7. El médico te dice que tienes la presión alta.

8. Es la temporada de gripe.

9. Te duele mucho la cabeza.

10. Eres médico y tienes un paciente hipocondríaco.

14.10 ¿Qué pasaría? Mira los dibujos y explica lo que pasó. Después, usa el condicional para expresar una conjetura sobre cómo ocurrió.

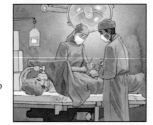

Modelo   *Los médicos operaron al paciente. El paciente tendría problemas cardíacos y necesitaría una cirugía para no morir.*

1.
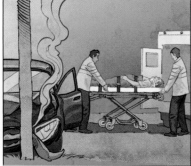

2.

3.

4.

5.

6.

A analizar

Nicolás habló con Rosa sobre su conversación con su madre. Mira el video otra vez. Después lee lo que dijo y observa los verbos en negritas.

> Acaba de llamar *(just called)* mi madre e hice el error de decirle que no me siento bien. Me dijo que estaba preocupada de que **tuviera** una enfermedad grave y que era importante que un médico me **examinara**. Recomendó que **fuera** inmediatamente. Creo que exagera un poco.

1. The verbs in bold are in the imperfect subjunctive. What is the stem for each of the verbs?
2. You have studied a variety of uses of the subjunctive. Look at each of the sentences, and explain why the subjunctive is required.

A comprobar

Imperfect subjunctive

1. In the last three chapters, you learned to use the present subjunctive. You will notice in the following examples that the verb in the main clause is in the present tense and that the verb in the dependent clause is in the present subjunctive.

Main clause	Dependent clause
Espero	que Clara **se recupere** pronto.
Es una lástima	que **tenga** un resfriado.

2. When the verb in the main clause is in the past (preterite or imperfect), the verb in the dependent clause must be in the imperfect subjunctive.

Main clause	Dependent clause
El médico le **recomendó**	que **tomara** unas pastillas.
Era necesario	que **usara** muletas.

3. The imperfect subjunctive is formed using the third person plural (**ellos, ellas, ustedes**) of the preterite. Eliminate the **-on** and add the endings as indicated. You will notice that the endings are the same, regardless of whether the verb ends in **-ar, -er,** or **-ir**. Verbs that are irregular in the preterite are also irregular in the imperfect subjunctive.

	hablar	tener	dormir
yo	hablar**a**	tuvier**a**	durmier**a**
tú	hablar**as**	tuvier**as**	durmier**as**
él, ella, usted	hablar**a**	tuvier**a**	durmier**a**
nosotros(as)	habl**áramos**	tuv**iéramos**	durm**iéramos**
vosotros(as)	hablar**ais**	tuvier**ais**	durmier**ais**
ellos, ellas, ustedes	hablar**an**	tuvier**an**	durmier**an**

*Notice that it is necessary to add an accent in the **nosotros** form.

4. The imperfect subjunctive form of **haber** is **hubiera.**

> No me gustó que **hubiera** tantas personas en la sala de espera.
> *I didn't like it that **there were** so many people in the waiting room.*

5. In general, the same rules that apply to the usage of the present subjunctive also apply to the past subjunctive.

To express an opinion using impersonal expressions:

> Era importante que **habláramos** con el médico.
> *It was important that we talk with the doctor.*

To express doubt:

El médico **dudaba** que **fuera** necesario operar.
The doctor doubted it would be necessary to operate.

To express desire:

El paciente no **quería** que le **pusieran** una inyección.
The patient did not want them to give him a shot.

To talk about the unknown using adjective clauses:

Leo **buscaba** un medicamento que no **causara** náusea.
Leo was looking for medication that wouldn't make him nauseous.

To express an emotion:

A Juana **le preocupaba** que su hijo **tuviera** gripe.
Juana was worried that her son had the flu.

6. When using an "if clause" to express what would happen in a hypothetical situation or a situation that is not likely or impossible, it is necessary to use the imperfect subjunctive and the conditional.

$$\underbrace{\text{si} \ + \ \text{imperfect subjunctive}}_{\textbf{dependent clause}} + \underbrace{\text{conditional}}_{\textbf{main clause}}$$

Si **tuviera** tiempo iría con el doctor.
*If **I had** time, I'd go to the doctor.*

A practicar

14.11 **Una visita al médico** Lee las siguientes oraciones y ponlas en un orden lógico.

1. _____ El doctor le dijo que tenía gripe y sugirió que tomara unas pastillas.

2. _____ Era necesario que pasara por la farmacia camino a la casa.

3. _____ Sandra no creía que tuviera nada serio, pero decidió ver al médico.

4. _____ Le sorprendió que el medicamento costara tanto.

5. _____ Buscó una clínica que estuviera cerca de su casa.

6. _____ Sandra se sentía mal y su esposo le sugirió que fuera al médico.

14.12 **Recomendaciones** Completa las oraciones con la forma apropiada del imperfecto del subjuntivo del verbo entre paréntesis.

1. Fui al médico ayer porque me sentía mal. Él me recomendó que (tomar) unas pastillas.

2. Mis hermanos quieren perder peso. Yo les sugerí que (comer) menos dulces.

3. Mi esposo y yo queremos dejar de fumar. Un amigo nos recomendó que no (salir) a lugares donde muchas personas fuman.

4. Mis hijos tienen fiebre. Yo les dije que (acostarse).

5. Mi amiga está embarazada. Su esposo le sugirió que (dejar) de trabajar.

6. Mi esposo tiene insomnio. Yo le recomendé que (leer) antes de acostarse.

14.13 **Todos opinan** Lee las situaciones y completa las oraciones de una forma lógica para indicar las reacciones y sugerencias de los amigos y familiares. **¡OJO!** Tendrás que usar el imperfecto del subjuntivo.

Modelo Virginia tuvo una entrevista de trabajo en el hospital.
Su esposo le sugirió que… *llevara un traje.*

1. Cecilia estaba muy enferma.
   a. Su médico le aconsejó que…
   b. Su madre temía que…
   c. Sus amigas esperaban que…

2. Donato tuvo un accidente de coche.
   a. El policía le pidió que…
   b. Sus padres preferían que…
   c. Su amigo le recomendó que…

14.14 **Consejos médicos** Los pacientes del doctor Orozco no llevaban una vida muy saludable. Con un compañero, túrnense para darles una recomendación del doctor a sus pacientes. Usen el imperfecto del subjuntivo.

Modelo Paulina siempre tenía mucho estrés en el trabajo.
Estudiante 1: *El doctor le recomendó que descansara más.*
Estudiante 2: *También le recomendó que buscara otro trabajo.*

1. José Luis y su esposa fumaban.
2. Magdalena comía muchos dulces.
3. Claudia y su hermano miraban la televisión seis horas al día.
4. Jaime usaba drogas.
5. Esmeralda bebía dos litros de soda todos los días.
6. Bety y Rosaura no hacían ejercicio.
7. Vicente solo dormía cinco horas cada noche.
8. Edwin y Nelson tomaban mucho alcohol.

14.15 **Se sienten mal** Con un compañero, miren las fotos y después túrnense para completar las oraciones correspondientes. ¡**OJO**! Algunas oraciones requieren el subjuntivo y otras el indicativo.

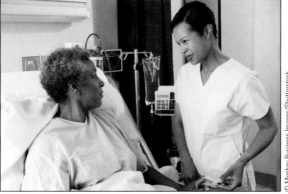

a. Era necesario que…
b. La paciente esperaba que…
c. La enfermera creía que…

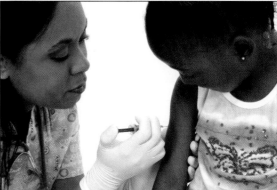

a. La niña tenía miedo de que…
b. La enfermera le recomendó que…
c. La niña le pidió que…

a. Era obvio que…
b. Le frustró que…
c. No conocía a nadie que…

a. La pareja quería que…
b. El doctor les dijo que…
c. Era importante que…

14.16 Si fuera así Completa las oraciones de forma original usando cada forma del imperfecto del subjuntivo.

1. Si tuviera el colesterol alto,

   a. comería…   **b.** tomaría…   **c.** debería…

2. Si un amigo estuviera muy enfermo, (yo)

   a. estaría…   **b.** lo llevaría…   **c.** iría…

3. Si yo fuera médico,

   a. sería…   **b.** tendría…   **c.** podría…

14.17 ¿Qué pasaría? Completa las oraciones con la forma apropiada del verbo entre paréntesis. Usa el imperfecto del subjuntivo y el condicional.

1. Algunas personas _____ (comprar) medicinas que no necesitan si los pacientes no _____ (necesitar) una receta médica para conseguirlas.

2. Si tú no _____ (sufrir) de alergias _____ (respirar) mejor.

3. Más personas _____ (poder) tener atención médica si el cuidado médico no _____ (ser) tan caro.

4. Si yo nunca _____ (enfermarse), no _____ (necesitar) gastar *(to spend)* dinero en medicinas.

5. Menos gente _____ (morir) si los científicos _____ (poder) encontrar una cura para el cáncer.

6. Si nosotros _____ (cuidarse) más, _____ (enfermarse) menos.

7. Si no _____ (haber) tantas personas en la sala de espera, yo no _____ (tener) que esperar mucho tiempo.

14.18 Lo que yo haría Con un compañero, hablen de lo que harían en las siguientes situaciones. Den muchos detalles.

Modelo ganar la lotería

Si ganara la lotería, iría de vacaciones a la República Dominicana porque tienen playas muy bonitas.

1. no tener que trabajar
2. vivir en otro lugar
3. ser famoso
4. poder viajar por el tiempo
5. encontrar una lámpara mágica y pedir un deseo
6. ser otra persona por un día
7. poder comer solo un tipo de comida
8. vivir hasta los 120 años

¿Qué harías si pudieras pedir un deseo?

© Fer Gregory/Shutterstock

Entrando en materia

¿Conoces la pirámide nutricional? En pocas palabras ¿qué es lo que recomienda?

Guías para la alimentación (diet)

🔊 Vas a escuchar un segmento de un documental sobre las acciones de varios países
2-39 latinoamericanos para mantener a su población sana. Escucha y después responde las preguntas.

Vocabulario útil

a largo plazo	*in the long run*	**destacarse**	*to stand out*	**fomentar**	*to encourage*
acorde a	*in agreement with*	**disponible**	*available*	**la grasa**	*fat (in food)*
el alimento	*food*	**el esfuerzo**	*effort*	**hacer daño**	*to harm*

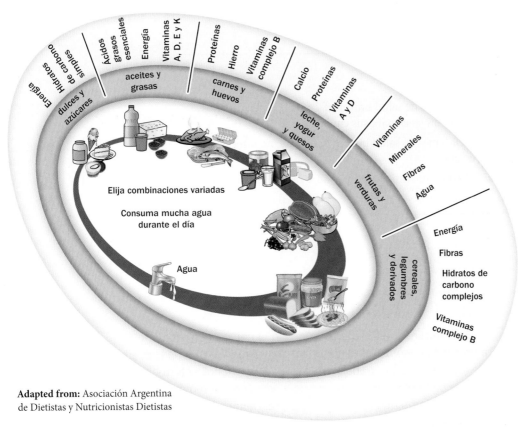

Adapted from: Asociación Argentina de Dietistas y Nutricionistas Dietistas

Comprensión

1. ¿Qué están haciendo algunos países latinoamericanos para mejorar la salud de sus habitantes?
2. ¿Cuáles son dos ejemplos de lo que recomienda la guía cubana?
3. ¿Cuál es el objetivo a largo plazo de la guía de la alimentación que se hizo en Cuba?
4. ¿Cuál es el nombre que se le dio a la guía de la alimentación argentina?
5. ¿Cuál es una diferencia entre el modelo argentino y la pirámide estadounidense?
6. ¿Cuál es un mensaje que propone el modelo argentino?

🖥️ Más allá

Diseña un modelo sencillo y realista para ayudar a estudiantes universitarios a tener una mejor alimentación. Trata de ser *(Try to be)* realista sobre la comida que se puede comprar donde vives y sobre los precios. Comparte tu modelo en Share It! y elige una idea de tus compañeros que te parezca muy buena.

Lectura

Reading Strategy: Overview (Part A)

In previous lessons you have learned multiple strategies to approach readings. This chapter reviews some of these strategies so you can keep practicing them.

1. Make notes while you read and use the margins to write down phrases or key words that summarize the main idea of each paragraph.
2. Read the first time(s) silently for comprehension. The last time, read out loud to remember words better and build pronunciation skills.
3. Identify the roots of words to increase your vocabulary and understanding. For example, you know the noun **resfriado.** What do you think the verb **resfriarse** means?
4. Make annotations as you read. Interacting with the text will allow you to understand it better. Create a simple code for your annotations, for example:

disagree = X　　new information = +
important to remember = !　　don't understand = ¿?

Antes de leer

1. ¿Qué crees que significa "ofrecer servicios de salud universal"? ¿Qué países hispanos piensas que tienen servicios de salud universal para sus ciudadanos?
2. ¿Crees que estos países gastan *(spend)* más en salud que los países que no ofrecen servicios de salud universal? ¿Por qué?
3. ¿De qué piensas que va a tratar el artículo? Anticipa un par de ideas sobre el artículo.

A leer

El valor de la salud

Como dice el refrán, nadie sabe cuánto vale la salud hasta que la pierde. Visto a un nivel económico la salud también tiene un gran impacto. El costo de los días que los trabajadores pierden por estar enfermos es enormo para cada país, pero las consecuencias son aún más grandes para los trabajadores que no tienen esta **prestación** y no reciben dinero si no trabajan. Claramente, mantener una buena salud es de primordial importancia para todos.

benefit

¿En qué países se enferma más la gente?

En un estudio de la comunidad europea se encontró que el número de **días tomados por enfermedad** varía de país a país. La conclusión más evidente fue que en los países del norte la gente toma muchos más días que en los países del sur de Europa. Por ejemplo, el 24% de los finlandeses y el 21.8% de los holandeses dijeron haber tomado al menos un día por enfermedad durante el último año, en contraste con el 6.7% de los griegos, el 8.5% de los italianos y el 11.8% de los españoles. Los hombres tomaron más días que las mujeres. ¿Será que las mujeres tienen mejor salud que los hombres?

sick days

[nadie sabe cuánto vale la salud hasta que la pierde]

Es posible argumentar que en los países en donde es más fácil conseguir un documento de "incapacidad", un día con **goce** de sueldo sin ir a trabajar, la gente toma más de estos días. En México si una persona está enferma por más de tres días debe ir a una clínica del Seguro Social y conseguir de su médico el documento de incapacidad. El médico especifica cuántos días se necesitan para recuperarse, y es **indispensable** presentar este papel para recibir el sueldo de los días que se faltó al trabajo. La compañía pagará el 75% del sueldo, y el Seguro Social pagará el 25%. Desafortunadamente, este servicio de salud se le ofrece solamente a una parte de la población empleada por empresas y otras organizaciones. En varios países latinoamericanos como Argentina, Chile, Costa Rica, Cuba y Uruguay, existe un programa universal de salud. Uruguay tiene uno de los mejores sistemas con servicios de Salud Pública para las personas que no pueden pagar y de Salud Privada para los que quieren comprar **seguros**. Los dos sistemas incluyen asistencia hospitalaria, cirugías y servicios de emergencia. Con este acceso se ha mejorado notablemente el servicio para las clases más pobres.

Ofrecer servicios de salud adecuados es uno de los grandes **retos** que enfrentan casi todos los países del mundo, y probablemente no haya una solución que funcione para todas las naciones.

benefit

essential

insurance

challenges

© Courtesy of Fernando Casas

Un hospital en la ciudad de Guadalajara, Jalisco, en México.

Source: http://www.afterhotel.com.uy/es/blog/95-el-sistema-de-salud-en-uruguay / http://internationalliving.com/2014/01/best-places-retire-overseas-affordable-efficient-health-care/

Comprensión

Lee las siguientes afirmaciones y decide si son ciertas o falsas. Corrige las oraciones falsas.

1. Según un estudio, los europeos del sur toman más días por enfermedad que los europeos del norte.
2. En Europa, los españoles son los que menos días faltan al trabajo por enfermedad.
3. Los hombres toman más días por enfermedad que las mujeres.
4. En México una incapacidad permite al empleado faltar el trabajo por enfermedad y recibir su sueldo.
5. En México existe el servicio de salud universal.

Después de leer

Escribe una lista de ideas sobre cómo se puede mejorar la salud de las personas en tu país. Después comparte tus ideas en Share It! y lee las de tus compañeros.

El español es un idioma que une a veintiún países.

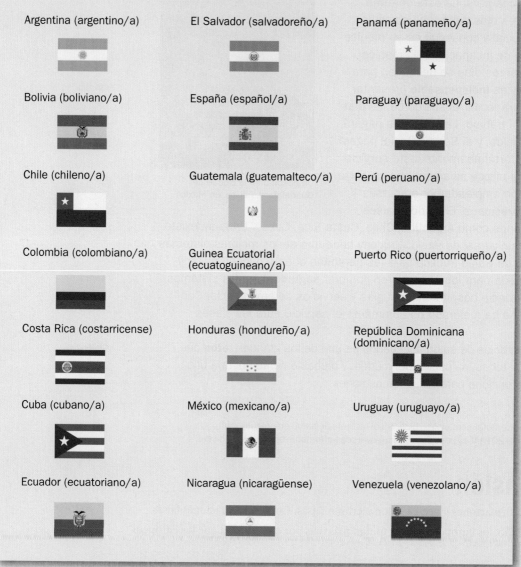

Argentina (argentino/a)

El Salvador (salvadoreño/a)

Panamá (panameño/a)

Bolivia (boliviano/a)

España (español/a)

Paraguay (paraguayo/a)

Chile (chileno/a)

Guatemala (guatemalteco/a)

Perú (peruano/a)

Colombia (colombiano/a)

Guinea Ecuatorial (ecuatoguineano/a)

Puerto Rico (puertorriqueño/a)

Costa Rica (costarricense)

Honduras (hondureño/a)

República Dominicana (dominicano/a)

Cuba (cubano/a)

México (mexicano/a)

Uruguay (uruguayo/a)

Ecuador (ecuatoriano/a)

Nicaragua (nicaragüense)

Venezuela (venezolano/a)

© Cengage Learning

La comunidad internacional

la beca	scholarship
el (la) ciudadano(a)	citizen
los derechos humanos	human rights
el desempleo	unemployment
la dictadura	dictatorship
la emigración	emigration
la globalización	globalization
el gobierno	government
la guerra	war
el idioma	language

la inmigración	immigration
el (la) inmigrante	immigrant
la ley	law
los organismos internacionales	international organizations
la paz	peace
el país	country
la pobreza	poverty
el (la) refugiado(a)	refugee
la riqueza	wealth
el tratado de comercio	trade agreement

Verbos

emigrar	emigrate
inmigrar	immigrate
mudarse	to move (to another place)
votar	to vote

A practicar

14.19 **Escucha y responde** Vas a escuchar una serie de ideas. Señala con el pulgar hacia arriba si la idea es lógica y hacia abajo si es ilógica.

2-40

14.20 **Nacionalidades** Escribe la nacionalidad de las siguientes personas según la información. **¡OJO!** Si no recuerdas en qué países están las ciudades, usa los mapas al final del libro.

Modelo Nayeli y Mario nacieron en La Habana. Son *cubanos*.

1. Sonia y su hijo son de Bogotá. Son _____.
2. Leticia y su madre nacieron en Tegucigalpa. Son _____.
3. Miguel ha vivido siempre en Panamá, donde nació. Es _____.
4. Mi familia y yo somos de Santo Domingo. Somos _____.
5. Tú naciste en Paraguay. Eres _____.
6. Mi esposa es de Quito. Ella es _____.
7. Marcela y todos sus abuelos nacieron en Guinea Ecuatorial. Son _____.
8. ¿Naciste en La Paz? Entonces eres _____ ¿no?

14.21 **Famosos** Observa la siguiente lista de personalidades hispanohablantes. Trabajen en grupos de tres para identificar la nacionalidad de cada persona y decir lo que saben de ellos.

1. Rigoberta Menchú
2. José Martí
3. Óscar Romero
4. Pablo Neruda
5. Franklin Díaz-Chang
6. Eva Perón
7. Carolina Herrera
8. David Ortiz
9. Rubén Blades

14.22 **Hablemos** Trabaja con un compañero para expresar sus experiencias y opiniones sobre las siguientes preguntas.

1. ¿Qué países conoces? ¿Qué países te gustaría visitar? ¿Por qué?
2. ¿Cuáles son tres ventajas de la inmigración? ¿Cuáles son tres desventajas?
3. ¿Hay inmigrantes en la historia de tu familia? ¿De dónde vinieron? ¿Por qué?
4. ¿Conoces a inmigrantes? ¿De dónde son? ¿En qué trabajan?
5. ¿Cuáles son las consecuencias de la globalización?

14.23 **El Mundial** Un amigo y tú quieren sorprender a todos sus amigos con fiestas para ver los juegos del Mundial de Fútbol. Uno de ustedes debe mirar la información en esta página y el otro debe mirar la información en el **Apéndice B**. Túrnense para completar las nacionalidades de sus amigos y el horario de los partidos. Al final encontrarán las cinco fechas cuando deberán tener las fiestas.

Preguntas posibles: *¿Cuál es la nacionalidad de Juan José?*
¿Cuándo es el juego número uno? / ¿Quiénes juegan el juego número uno?

Amigos

NOMBRE	Mundo	Jazmín	Marco	Pío		Marcelo	Yolanda
PAÍS	argentino		chileno	costarricense			

Horario de juegos

Juego 1	Brasil vs. Alemania		Juego 5		18 de junio
Juego 2		14 de junio	Juego 6	Perú vs. Costa Rica	
Juego 3		15 de junio	Juego 7		22 de junio
Juego 4	Honduras vs. Holanda		Juego 8	Ecuador vs. Francia	

¿Cuáles son los cinco partidos que van a ver y cuándo?

Conexiones culturales
Relaciones internacionales

Cultura

Si el mundo fuera un pueblo de 100 habitantes y reflejara proporcionalmente nuestro mundo actual, esto sería lo que veríamos:

60 habitantes serían asiáticos (20 chinos y 17 indios), 14 americanos (6 del norte y 8 del sur), 13 africanos, 12 europeos y una persona de Oceanía.

Habría 52 mujeres y 48 hombres.

89 serían heterosexuales y 11 homosexuales.

50.5 vivirían en el pueblo y 49.5 estarían esparcidos en el campo (countryside).

6 personas poseerían 59% de la riqueza total del pueblo (2 de ellos serían de los Estados Unidos).

50 habitantes vivirían con 2 dólares al día y 25 con solo 1 dólar al día.

25 consumirían el 75% de la energía total, los 75 otros consumirían el restante 25%.

17 no tendrían ni servicios médicos, ni vivienda adecuada, ni agua potable.

50 padecerían malnutrición.

20 habitantes controlarían el 86% del PNB (Producto Nacional Bruto) y 74% de las líneas telefónicas.

11 habitantes utilizarían un coche y dispondrían del 87% de todos los vehículos.

9 tendrían acceso a Internet.

1 tendría estudios universitarios.

La gente del pueblo tendría problemas para comunicarse porque unos 16 hablarían mandarín, 8 inglés, unos 7 hablarían español, 6 se comunicarían en ruso… y la mitad (half) de los habitantes hablarían otras lenguas.

Sources: http://www.sustainer.org/dhm_archive/index.php?display_article=vn338villageed

¿Te sorprende está información? ¿Por qué?

> Investiga en Internet cómo sería este pueblo en cuanto a edad, religión, ingresos y educación. Escribe en el buscador "Si el mundo fuera una aldea de 100 personas" + **edad, religión** o **educación**. Después comparte la información en Share It!

Conexiones... a la economía

El nuestro es un mundo en movimiento. Entre 1990 y 2013 el número de migrantes internacionales pasó de 150 millones a 230 millones, según las Naciones Unidas. Los Estados Unidos es un país que recibe a muchos inmigrantes, pero no es el único ni la región que más gente recibe. La Comunidad Europea ha sido el destino de la tercera parte de estos inmigrantes, seguida por Asia. En Europa, España es el país que más inmigrantes recibe cada año. América Latina ha recibido a casi 9 millones de personas.

Si se examinan los datos demográficos de estos inmigrantes, resaltan los siguientes datos:

- El grupo más grande es el de inmigrantes mayores de 65 años.
- Las islas Malvinas tienen uno de los porcentajes más altos de inmigrantes ya que el 69% de la población inmigró.
- Existe un país en el mundo donde el 100% de la población es inmigrante: El Vaticano

Identifica tres áreas sociales o económicas que sean afectadas por la inmigración. Explica los efectos con ejemplos concretos en los países que reciben inmigrantes y en los países que los pierden, ya sean efectos positivos o negativos.

Source: www.theguardian.com

El número de migrantes internacionales ha aumentado mucho.

Comparaciones

Se dice que una de las consecuencias más graves de la globalización es la desaparición de culturas. Esta consecuencia afecta en particular los idiomas en nuestro planeta. Los diferentes idiomas que existen son una forma palpable de las culturas que las hablan. Con la desaparición de idiomas, desaparece también gran parte de la diversidad cultural de los seres humanos. Se calcula que en el mundo existen en la actualidad unas seis mil lenguas, pero dentro de menos de cincuenta años el número se habrá reducido a la mitad *(half)*.

Aunque hay quienes dicen que un idioma está en peligro cuando el número de hablantes se reduce a menos de 50 000, algunos estudiosos consideran que un idioma está realmente en peligro cuando se observa que las nuevas generaciones dejan de usarlo. En contraste, un idioma hablado por unos cuantos cientos de personas podría no estar en peligro, si es el único idioma hablado por una comunidad entera y es necesario para su subsistencia.

Con la expansión de los medios de comunicación se ha acelerado el dominio de unos cuantos idiomas sobre todos los demás. De acuerdo a *Ethnologue*, el 94% de la población habla 389 idiomas (el 6% del total). El restante 6% de la población habla el restante 94% de las lenguas. Los tres idiomas más hablados en el mundo son chino, español e inglés.

Muchos grupos indígenas de América Latina y sus lenguas están amenazados.

Elige un país hispano en **Exploraciones del mundo hispano** en el **Apéndice A** y averigua *(find out)* cuántos idiomas se hablan en él. Después compara la información con el número de lenguas que se hablan en los Estados Unidos. ¿Cómo se pueden explicar las diferencias y semejanzas?

> **INVESTIGUEMOS LA MÚSICA**
>
> Listen to "Las Cruces de Tijuana," by the Spanish rock group Jarabe de Palo. What two places does he compare? Do you think his view of immigration is positive or negative? Why? What are key words that lead you to such a conclusion?

Comunidad

La inmigración es un fenómeno humano natural. Ha existido desde el principio de la humanidad, cuando grupos de nuestros ancestros se trasladaban de un lugar a otro para buscar mejores condiciones de vida. En el mundo en el que vivimos hay decenas de millones de seres humanos que dejan sus lugares de origen por diferentes motivos, entre ellos encontrar un mejor trabajo, huir *(to flee)* de la guerra, vivir en un clima más benigno, o estudiar. Aunque la mayor parte de la migración ocurre dentro de las fronteras de un mismo país (por ejemplo, la migración del campo a la ciudad), hay un número significativo de personas que se han desplazado a otros países y enfrentan grandes retos *(challenges)*.

Encuentra a una persona de un país hispano que haya inmigrado a los Estados Unidos y entrevístala: ¿De qué país es? ¿Por qué inmigró? ¿Hace cuánto tiempo vino? ¿Qué es lo más difícil de ser inmigrante?

La Pequeña Habana es un lugar importante para la comunidad cubana en los Estados Unidos.

Exploraciones **gramaticales**

A analizar

Rodrigo y Óscar hablan sobre sus razones para venir a los Estados Unidos. Mira el video y lee el párrafo que sigue. Observa las expresiones en negritas y los verbos que las siguen.

Óscar: ¿Alguna vez has vuelto a Colombia?

Rodrigo: Sí. **Cuando** tenía veinticinco años se murió mi abuela y regresé para el funeral. Fue entonces **cuando** conocí a Camila… Seguimos en contacto y al final ella decidió venir a estudiar aquí para estar más cerca. Desde entonces no hemos vuelto a Colombia, pero queremos regresar este año. **Cuando** ella termine el año escolar vamos a viajar a Colombia para ver a nuestras familias. Yo solo tengo dos semanas de vacaciones, pero ella piensa quedarse **hasta que** tenga que regresar a la escuela.

1. Each of the expressions in bold is related to time. Identify the expressions followed by the subjunctive. Considering what you know about the use of the subjunctive, why do you think the subjunctive was needed after these expressions?

2. Why do you think the others are followed by the indicative?

A comprobar

Subjunctive with adverbial clauses and conjunctions

1. An adverb tells when or how something is done. The following adverbial conjunctions of time require the subjunctive when referring to actions that have not yet occurred. With the exception of **antes (de) que,** which always requires the subjunctive, when referring to actions that have are already taken place or are habitual, they require the indicative.

antes (de) que	*before*	en cuanto	*as soon as*
cuando	*when*	hasta que	*until*
después (de) que	*after*	tan pronto (como)	*as soon as*

Indicative

Cuando se viaja por avión se tiene que mostrar la identificación.
*When one **travels** by plane, one has to show I.D.*

Se mudaron **tan pronto vendieron** su casa.
*They moved **as soon as** they **sold** their house.*

Subjunctive

Cuando salgas de viaje mañana, no olvides tu identificación.
*When **you leave** for your trip tomorrow, don't forget your I.D.*

Nos mudaremos **tan pronto como vendamos** nuestra casa.
*We will move **as soon as** we **sell** our house.*

2. **Antes (de) que, después (de) que,** and **hasta que** are often used with the infinitive if there is no change of subject. The **que** after the preposition is omitted.

Antes de poder hacerse ciudadano, Raimundo tiene que vivir en el país por tres años.
***Before being able** to become a citizen, Raimundo has to live in the country for three years.*

3. The following adverbs require the indicative when referring to something that is known or is definite. However, when referring to something that is unknown or indefinite, they require the subjunctive.

aunque	*although, even though, even if*
como	*as, how, however*
(a)donde	*where, wherever*

Quiero ir a África **aunque es** caro.
*I want to go to Africa **even though it is** expensive.*

Quiero ir a África **aunque sea** caro.
*I want to go to Africa **even if it is** expensive.*

4. The following conjunctions always require the subjunctive. Because they indicate that the action is contingent upon another action, the outcome is unknown.

a fin de que	in order that, so that
a menos que	unless
con tal (de) que	as long as; in order that, so that
en caso de que	in case
mientras (que)	as long as; provided that
para que	in order that, so that
siempre y cuando	as long as, provided that
sin que	without

No es posible entrar en el país **a menos que tengas** una visa.
*It is not possible to enter the country **unless** you **have** a visa.*

5. With the exception of **a menos que, mientras (que),** and **siempre y cuando,** the expressions above are often used with the infinitive if there is no change of subject. The **que** after the preposition is omitted.

Hay que luchar **para eliminar** la pobreza.
*It is necessary to fight **in order to eliminate** poverty.*

A practicar

14.24 ¿Quién sabe? Contesta las preguntas y explica tus respuestas.

1. ¿Quién sabe cuánto cuesta estudiar en otro país, Belinda o Walter?

   a. Belinda prefiere estudiar en otro país aunque <u>cuesta</u> mucho dinero.

   b. Walter prefiere estudiar en otro país aunque <u>cueste</u> mucho dinero.

2. ¿Quién sabe dónde hay libertad, Ernesto o Isabel?

   a. Ernesto quiere vivir donde <u>hay</u> libertad.

   b. Isabel quiere vivir donde <u>haya</u> libertad.

3. ¿Quién sabe si hay otras oportunidades en otra ciudad, Bárbara o Sebastián?

   a. Bárbara no quiere mudarse aunque <u>hay</u> oportunidades en otra ciudad.

   b. Sebastián no quiere mudarse aunque <u>haya</u> oportunidades en otra ciudad.

14.25 Antes y después Completa las oraciones con la forma apropiada del indicativo o del subjuntivo del verbo entre paréntesis. **¡OJO!** Presta atención a los tiempos verbales.

1. a. En cuanto _____ (encontrar) mi primer trabajo salí para celebrar con mis amigos.

   b. En cuanto _____ (encontrar) un buen trabajo voy a mudarme.

2. a. Cuando _____ (tener) diez años me gustaba jugar al fútbol.

   b. Cuando _____ (ser) mayor quiero tener hijos.

3. a. Después de que yo _____ (graduarse) de la escuela secundaria mi familia me hizo una fiesta.

   b. Mi familia estará muy feliz después de que yo _____ (graduarse) de la universidad.

4. a. Antes de que yo _____ (hacer) mi primer viaje tuve que trabajar para ganar el dinero necesario.

   b. Antes de que yo _____ (hacer) otro viaje es importante terminar mis estudios.

5. a. Tan pronto como _____ (terminar) el semestre pasado salí de vacaciones a la playa.

   b. Tan pronto como _____ (terminar) este semestre yo buscaré un trabajo.

14.26 La situación mundial Completa las oraciones añadiendo una de las expresiones indicadas y conjuga el verbo en la forma apropiada del presente del subjuntivo.

1. El nuevo presidente no quiere aprobar la nueva ley…

   a. (a fin de que/sin que) sus ministros le (dar) consejos.

   b. (antes de que/para que) el Congreso la (aprobar) primero.

2. Cada ciudadano debe votar…

   a. (para que/a menos que) se (escuchar) su voz *(voice)*.

   b. (sin que/a fin de que) su voto (poder) ayudar a mejorar la situación.

3. Los soldados irán a la guerra…

   a. (con tal de que/mientras que) (haber) justicia en el país.

   b. (a menos que/siempre y cuando) los presidentes (llegar) a un acuerdo primero.

14.27 ¿Cuándo? Con un compañero, completen las oraciones usando una de las siguientes expresiones adverbiales: **cuando, después de que, en cuanto, hasta que, tan pronto como. ¡OJO!** Presten atención al uso del indicativo y del subjuntivo. Intenten usar algunas de las expresiones conversacionales que aprendieron en el **Capítulo 13.**

Modelo Esta noche voy a acostarme…
> Estudiante 1: *Esta noche voy a acostarme después de que mis hijos se duerman.*
> Estudiante 2: *¿De veras? Yo voy a acostarme tan pronto como pueda.*

1. **a.** Siempre estudio…   **b.** Hoy pienso estudiar…

2. **a.** Esta mañana me levanté…   **b.** Mañana me levantaré…

3. **a.** Me gusta cenar…   **b.** Esta noche voy a cenar…

4. **a.** Compré mi primer coche…   **b.** Voy a comprar un coche nuevo…

5. **a.** Conseguí mi primer trabajo…   **b.** Buscaré un nuevo trabajo…

14.28 Destino España Rodolfo es argentino y quiere viajar a España. Usando algunas de las expresiones adverbiales (**a fin de que, en caso de que, para que**), explica por qué necesita los artículos de la lista.

Modelo la dirección de la embajada *(embassy)* argentina
> *Lleva la dirección de la embajada argentina en caso de que tengas alguna emergencia.*

1. una visa de turista   3. su currículum *(resumé)*   5. un traje

2. un par de zapatos cómodos   4. una maleta grande   6. yerba mate

14.29 Descripción de fotos Con un compañero, escojan una de las fotos y expliquen las circunstancias mencionando quiénes son las personas y lo que hacen. Usen algunas de las expresiones adverbiales y decidan si se requiere el indicativo o el subjuntivo.

a fin de que	a menos que	antes de que	para que	sin que
en caso de que	hasta que	aunque	cuando	después de que

© fotorobs/Shutterstock   © absolut/Shutterstock   © kojoku/Shutterstock

A analizar ▶

Rodrigo y Óscar hablan sobre sus razones para venir a los Estados Unidos. Mira el video otra vez. Después lee parte de la conversación y observa los verbos en negritas y los verbos que las siguen.

Rodrigo: Ya **había decidido** estudiar en Bogotá cuando un amigo me contó de una beca para poder estudiar en Nueva York. Me pareció una oportunidad interesante, solicité la beca… ¡y aquí estoy! […] ¿Y tú? ¿Por qué viniste a los Estados Unidos?

Óscar: Cuando tenía diez años, mi padre perdió su trabajo. Él tenía un amigo que dos años antes **se había mudado** a los Estados Unidos para trabajar en una compañía internacional. Se puso en contacto con su amigo y con su ayuda pudo conseguir un trabajo aquí.

1. You learned the present perfect in **Capítulo 12.** The verbs in bold are in the past perfect. How are these verbs formed?

2. These verbs are used to talk about specific times in the past. Does Rodrigo decide to study in Bogotá before or after finding out about the scholarship? Did the friend of Oscar's father move to the United States before or after his father lost his job? What can you determine about the past perfect from your answers?

A comprobar

Past perfect

1. Similar to the present perfect, the past perfect (also known as the **pluscuamperfecto**) combines the imperfect form of the verb **haber** with the past participle.

yo	había	nosotros(as)	habíamos
tú	habías	vosotros(as)	habíais
él, ella, usted	había	ellos, ellas, ustedes	habían

Habían inmigrado a México.
They had immigrated to Mexico.

¿Habías viajado a Europa antes?
Had you traveled to Europe before?

2. The past perfect is used to express a past action that already took place before another past action.

Camilo ya **había aprendido** inglés cuando se mudó a los Estados Unidos.
Camilo had already learned English when he moved to the United States.

Antes de hacerse ciudadano él **había establecido** la residencia.
Before becoming a citizen, he had established residency.

3. Remember the irregular past participles from **Capítulo 12:**

abrir	**abierto**	morir	**muerto**
decir	**dicho**	romper	**roto**
cubrir	**cubierto**	poner	**puesto**
despertar	**despierto**	ver	**visto**
escribir	**escrito**	volver	**vuelto**
hacer	**hecho**	devolver	**devuelto**

4. As with the present perfect, when using direct object, indirect object, or reflexive pronouns, they are placed in front of the conjugated form of **haber.**

No **se** habían mudado antes.
They hadn't moved before.

Ya **lo** habíamos visto.
We had already seen it.

A practicar

14.30 **¿Qué habían hecho?** Muchos latinos famosos han tenido una vida muy interesante. Relaciona el evento en la primera columna con el evento que ocurrió primero en la segunda columna.

1. _____ Julio Iglesias empezó a tocar la guitarra como terapia.

2. _____ Desi Arnaz hizo el papel de músico en el programa de televisión *I Love Lucy*.

3. _____ Carlos Santana empezó a tocar la guitarra a los ocho años.

4. _____ Shakira escribió su primera canción a los ocho años.

5. _____ Benicio del Toro tuvo su primer papel en la película *Big Top Pee-wee*.

6. _____ Óscar de la Renta trabajó para Elizabeth Arden por dos años.

a. Había escrito poesía desde los cuatro años.

b. Había dibujado para unas casas de moda en España.

c. Había tenido un accidente de coche.

d. Antes ya había tocado el violín.

e. Había dejado sus estudios de negocios para estudiar actuación.

f. Había tenido un grupo musical exitoso.

14.31 **Un poco de historia** Completa las oraciones con la forma apropiada del pluscuamperfecto del verbo indicado.

1. Antes de que Hernán Cortés llegara a México, él _____ (estar) en Cuba y en La Hispaniola.

2. Antes de que comenzara la Revolución cubana en 1956, el Che Guevara _____ (llegar) a la Isla.

3. Antes de que Puerto Rico llegara a ser un Estado Libre Asociado de los Estados Unidos en 1952, _____ (ser) una colonia española.

4. Antes de que el Canal de Panamá pasara a ser la responsabilidad de Panamá en 1999, los Estados Unidos lo _____ (controlar).

5. Antes de que Napoleón y sus tropas invadieran España en 1808, el rey Carlos IV y su hijo _____ (ir) a Francia a causa de una mentira de Napoleón.

6. Antes de que empezara la Guerra entre México y los Estados Unidos en 1846, Texas _____ (separarse) de México y _____ (formar) su propia república independiente.

7. Antes de que Guatemala, El Salvador, Nicaragua, Honduras y Costa Rica se establecieran como países, _____ (establecer) la República Federal de Centroamérica.

14.32 **Entrevista** Con un compañero, túrnense para preguntar si habían hecho las siguientes actividades antes de graduarse de la escuela secundaria. Añade (*Add*) detalles al contestarle a tu compañero.

Modelo viajar a Nueva York

    Estudiante 1: *Antes de graduarte de la escuela secundaria ¿habías viajado a Nueva York?*

    Estudiante 2: *Sí, había viajado a Nueva York. Fui con mi familia un verano. / No, no había viajado a Nueva York. Nunca he ido allí.*

1. comprar su primer coche

2. hacer un viaje solo

3. enamorarse

4. tener un accidente

5. asistir a una clase de español

6. empezar a trabajar

7. tomar un curso universitario

8. participar en algún equipo deportivo

14.33 **Una catástrofe** Con un compañero, observen la ilustración de un accidente que ocurrió en la calle, y mencionen todos los eventos que podrían haber pasado antes del accidente.

Modelo *Antes de que ocurriera el accidente, un hombre había comprado un periódico.*

Antes de que ocurriera el accidente…

14.34 **Un mal viaje** Norma salió de viaje ayer, pero tuvo un muy mal día. Con un compañero, túrnense para imaginarse lo que podría haber pasado antes para causar los siguientes eventos. Usen el pluscuamperfecto.

Modelo Norma llegó tarde al aeropuerto.
   Estudiante 1: *Se había despertado tarde.*
   Estudiante 2: *Se le habían perdido sus llaves.*

1. Norma no tenía su pasaporte cuando llegó al aeropuerto.
2. Norma llegó y no pudo abordar su vuelo.
3. Tomó otro vuelo después y su compañero de asiento se enojó con ella.
4. Cuando finalmente llegó a su destino, el agente de inmigración la detuvo *(detained)* dos horas.
5. Tuvo que ir a comprar ropa inmediatamente.
6. No comió nada en todo el día.
7. Cancelaron la conferencia a la que iba a asistir.
8. No tenía dinero para pagar la cuenta del hotel.
9. En el viaje de regreso no pudo dormir.
10. Cuando por fin llegó a casa, no encontró ningún mueble ni su televisión.

© CREATISTA/Shutterstock

Lectura

Antes de leer

Contesta las preguntas.

1. ¿Por qué emigra la gente? Menciona al menos cuatro razones.
2. ¿Conoces a algún inmigrante? ¿De dónde es? ¿Por qué dejó su país?
3. ¿Qué países crees que reciben más inmigrantes en el mundo? ¿Por qué?
4. ¿Sabes qué se necesita para inmigrar legalmente a los Estados Unidos?

A leer

Latinoamérica y la inmigración

Cuando se habla de inmigración, muchos piensan en los trabajadores agrícolas que inmigran a países como los Estados Unidos. Sin embargo, la inmigración ha ocurrido en todas las etapas de la historia, ha afectado a todos los sectores de la sociedad y no se ha limitado a trabajadores.

Una celebración menonita en Cuautémoc, México.

En países como Argentina, Chile y Uruguay, la mayor parte de la población desciende de inmigrantes europeos que llegaron a estas tierras en los siglos XVIII y XIX, buscando mejorar su vida. En el caso de Argentina, la inmigración europea se **promovió** *(promoted)* activamente, ya que se percibía como una forma de hacer progresar al país. Entre 1870 y 1914 llegaron al país alrededor de seis millones de extranjeros. Los nuevos inmigrantes se establecieron y **mezclaron** *(mixed)* su idioma y sus costumbres con los ya existentes, creando los diferentes sabores culturales de cada región que conocemos hoy.

Otro país que recibió un número significativo de inmigrantes fue Cuba, adonde llegaron aproximadamente 124 000 chinos entre 1853 y 1874 para trabajar en el campo. Esta inmigración se sumó a la de los españoles que se establecieron en la isla, y a la de los africanos que habían sido llevados en masa contra su voluntad para trabajar como esclavos.

A principios del siglo XX la Guerra Civil Española y la Primera y la Segunda Guerra Mundial trajeron como consecuencia una nueva **ola** de inmigrantes que

[la inmigración europea se promovió activamente]

huían de la violencia y de la pobreza que la guerra ocasionó en Europa. A Argentina llegaron numerosos grupos de **judíos.** México y Chile recibieron un gran número de exiliados políticos de España, muchos de ellos intelectuales, quienes se establecieron y fundaron escuelas y ayudaron a crear nuevas e importantes corrientes culturales que tuvieron impacto en la literatura, la educación y la cinematografía. Más tarde, en la década de los 70, las dictaduras militares de Argentina, Chile, Uruguay y Paraguay empujaron a miles de personas a abandonar su patria y a buscar asilo político en otros países hispanoparlantes, en particular en España y México. Históricamente, muchos latinoamericanos han preferido establecerse en países cuya cultura perciben como más cercana, y donde la lengua es un **vínculo** cultural.

Los grupos que huyeron a causa de guerras y persecución política buscaban más seguridad para ellos y sus familias. Afortunadamente, hoy en día, hay varios países latinoamericanos con índices de seguridad entre los más altos del mundo, como Chile y Uruguay. Según el índice de la Paz Global establecido por el Instituto para Economía y Paz (que usa indicadores como el número de crímenes, el respeto por los derechos humanos y el **gasto** militar), otros países latinoamericanos que se encuentran entre los 50 más seguros del mundo son Costa Rica y Argentina. Por su parte, España se sitúa en el lugar 25, por encima de Uruguay y Chile.

Aunque no es posible hablar en este reducido espacio de todos los grupos que han inmigrado y de sus razones para hacerlo, los ejemplos citados hacen evidente el impacto de la inmigración en las sociedades latinoamericanas. La migración es un fenómeno económico y social que continúa transformando la **faz** de todos los países del planeta.

wave

were fleeing

Jews

link

expense

cara

Comprensión

Decide si las afirmaciones son ciertas o falsas. Corrige las oraciones falsas.

1. En los siglos XVIII y XIX Argentina quiso aumentar la inmigración de Europa.
2. Los inmigrantes a Argentina no tuvieron efecto en la cultura del país.
3. Cuba es un país de gran diversidad cultural, debido a los numerosos inmigrantes.
4. La Guerra Civil Española creó una nueva ola de inmigración hacia Latinoamérica.
5. Las personas que emigraron a México huyendo de la Guerra Civil Española eran principalmente trabajadores sin mucha educación.
6. Muchas personas inmigraron a Chile, Argentina, Paraguay y Uruguay para escapar de las dictaduras.
7. Según el índice de la Paz Global, España no se considera un país seguro.
8. La inmigración es un fenómeno social que sigue cambiando la cultura de los países hispanohablantes.

Después de leer

España es uno de los países que recibe un gran número de inmigrantes. Investiga de dónde llegan estos inmigrantes y lo que hace el gobierno español para ayudarlos y fomentar la asimilación.

A narrative composition tells a story. You will write an article on a medical emergency or an international event that could appear in a newspaper.

Paso 1 Decide whether you would prefer to write about a medical emergency or an international event. You could choose to write about an event that has actually happened or invent one. Write a brief list of the chronological sequence of events.

Paso 2 Jot down a few sentences that someone involved in the event or who has witnessed it might say.

Paso 3 Write a topic sentence that presents what you are going to be writing about and that will grab your reader's interest.

> **Modelo** *Ayer ocurrió una tragedia en la biblioteca.*

© Yuri Arcurs/Shutterstock

Paso 4 Look back at your list of chronological events in **Paso 1**. Write three or four paragraphs that give the details of what happened. Using the sentences you created in **Paso 2,** be sure to add a quote or two from people interested in the event or involved in it where appropriate.

Paso 5 Write a concluding paragraph in which you give a final commentary or final statement that tells why the event is relevant or supposes what might be the results of the event.

Paso 6 Edit your article:

1. Is the information clearly organized in a logical sequence?
2. Do all of the sentences in each of the paragraphs support their topic sentences?
3. Did you include ample details?
4. Do you have verb and adjective agreement?
5. Did you use the past tenses (preterite, imperfect, past perfect) accurately?
6. Did you use subjunctive where necessary?

Entrando en materia

Imagina que vas a visitar una gran ciudad en cualquier parte del mundo. Aunque no existe una garantía para ser inmune a las emergencias los turistas muchas veces sufren de estos percances *(mishaps)*. ¿Qué precauciones puedes tomar para mantener tu salud y para enfrentar una emergencia médica? ¿y para mantener tu seguridad?

Información para turistas

Vas a leer un folleto con información para turistas. Después de leer contesta las preguntas.

Consejos para disfrutar su viaje. Con toda seguridad.

SEGURIDAD

- **Deje sus joyas y objetos de valor en la caja de seguridad del hotel.** No las necesita para conocer una ciudad y si no las lleva tampoco se las pueden quitar. Tampoco lleve demasiado dinero consigo y traiga solamente una tarjeta de crédito.

- **¡Preste atención!** Un **ladrón** siempre está buscando víctimas fáciles, que estén distraídas. Además, frecuentemente trabajan en parejas: mientras uno genera una distracción, el otro le roba sus pertenencias a la víctima. Siga su **sexto sentido** y **si algo le huele mal**, retírese de esa situación cuanto antes.

- **Mantenga todos los objetos de valor bien guardados,** incluyendo la cámara fotográfica. Si esta es demasiado grande, cuélguela diagonalmente, de modo que pase por debajo de su brazo.

- **No baje la guardia cuando se siente a comer en algún restaurante o café.** Este es un lugar favorito para los ladrones, ya que no son pocos los turistas **despistados** que dejan sus bolsos o pertenencias descuidados, en el suelo o en el respaldo de una silla.

- **Lleve en un bolsillo una cantidad apropiada de dinero para pagar.** No tenga todo su dinero en un solo lugar y no lo exhiba en público.

SALUD

- **Lo extenuante de un viaje,** el clima o el cambio en la alimentación pueden afectar nuestra salud. Por supuesto, es muy importante estar preparado. Lleve siempre toda la medicina que requiera. Es muy difícil comprar medicamentos en el **extranjero** sin una receta. Haga copias de su seguro médico y localice los servicios de emergencia más cercanos en cada una de las ciudades que visite. Estas sencillas precauciones podrían salvarle la vida.

- **Tome los primeros días con calma y descanse.** Su cuerpo necesita tiempo para adaptarse y recuperarse del estrés del viaje.

- **Un horario de comidas diferente y una dieta que no es la de siempre son elementos que pueden afectar el estómago de cualquier persona.** Aunque probar nuevas comidas es parte de la experiencia de viajar, hágalo en moderación, sobre todo los primeros días. Además, lleve siempre algunas medicinas básicas para el malestar estomacal.

pocket

thief

abroad

sixth sense / if something seems rotten

absent-minded

Comprensión

1. Según el texto ¿cuántas tarjetas de crédito se recomienda llevar en la cartera?
2. ¿Por qué trabajan en parejas los ladrones?
3. ¿Por qué los cafés y restaurantes son lugares favorecidos por los delincuentes?
4. ¿Qué se recomienda hacer para enfrentar mejor una emergencia médica?
5. ¿Qué se debe hacer los primeros días para sentirse mejor?
6. Según el texto ¿qué factores pueden causar problemas con el estómago?

Más allá

Escribe una lista de recommendaciones para turistas que van a visitar tu ciudad o región. Piensa en lo siguiente: ¿Hay zonas peligrosas? ¿Hay deportes o actividades que se practican en tu área que pueden ser peligrosos? ¿Hay fenómenos climáticos (tornados, huracanes, etcétera) que deban prevenirse *(be prepared for)*? Sube tus recomendaciones a Share It! y lee las recomendaciones de tus compañeros.

La medicina

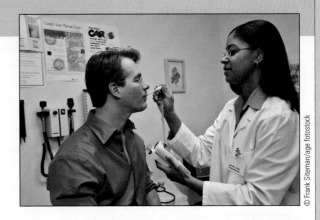

© Frank Siteman/age fotostock

Vocabulario

Especialistas

el (la) dermatólogo(a)	*dermatologist*
el (la) endocrinólogo(a)	*endocrinologist*
el (la) ginecólogo(a)	*gynecologist*
el (la) internista	*internist*
el (la) obstetra	*obstetrician*
el (la) oncólogo(a)	*oncologist*
el (la) ortopedista	*orthopedist*
el (la) otorrino(a)	*ear, nose, and throat specialist*
el (la) psiquiatra	*psychiatrist*
el (la) radiólogo(a)	*radiologist*
el (la) urólogo(a)	*urologist*

Sustantivos

la higiene	*hygiene*
la temperatura	*temperature*
el termómetro	*thermometer*

Verbos

atender	*to take care of*
auscultar	*to auscultate*
extraer	*to withdraw*
pesar	*to weigh*
revisar	*to check*

Expresiones útiles

¿Es alérgico a algún medicamento?
Are you allergic to any medication?

Necesito tomar su presión arterial.
I need to take your blood pressure.

Respire hondo.
Take a deep breath.

DATOS IMPORTANTES

Educación: Estudios universitarios o terciarios como enfermero registrado

Salario: Entre $40 000 y $100 000 (enfermería), dependiendo de los años de experiencia y del hospital o clínica, entre 1 y 20 años

Dónde se trabaja: En hospitales, clínicas privadas, laboratorios, escuelas, clubes deportivos

Vocabulario nuevo Completa las oraciones con la palabra apropiada de la lista de vocabulario.

1. Debes ver al _____ si tienes problemas con los pies.

2. El enfermero usa el termómetro para saber _____ del paciente.

3. El _____ es especialista en las enfermedades de las mujeres.

4. El médico _____ al paciente en un cuarto privado.

5. Una persona con cáncer debe consultar un _____.

Benjamín Dunn, enfermero

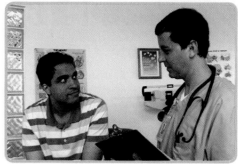

Benjamín Dunn es enfermero y trabaja en un hospital local. En el video verás a Benjamín atendiendo a un paciente.

Antes de ver

Los enfermeros trabajan constantemente para cuidar a los pacientes del hospital. Realizan muchas tareas y luego les dan el informe a los médicos. Los pacientes se sienten bien cuando los enfermeros son amables y cuidadosos. ¿Qué elementos interesantes encuentras en el trabajo de un enfermero? ¿Qué preguntas le harías a un enfermero con respecto a su trabajo? ¿Serías enfermero? ¿Por qué?

Comprensión

1. ¿Tiene fiebre el paciente?
2. ¿Dónde le duele?
3. ¿Había estado en el hospital antes?
4. ¿Cuánto pesa el paciente?
5. ¿Qué problema tuvo antes?
6. ¿Está comiendo mucho?
7. ¿Cómo está la presión arterial?
8. ¿Qué le da el enfermero para tomar?
9. ¿Para qué necesita una orden del médico?
10. ¿De dónde le va a extraer sangre?

Después de ver

Con un compañero, representen a un enfermero que está ayudando a un paciente. El enfermero debe hablarle al paciente sobre lo que le duele, cuándo empezó a sentirse mal y después darle recomendaciones.

14.35 **¿Por qué?** El asistente del doctor Navárez le hace muchas preguntas sobre los pacientes. Contesta las preguntas, usando el pluscuamperfecto del verbo entre paréntesis.

Modelo ¿Por qué operó a Leonor? (tener un accidente)
Porque había tenido un accidente.

1. ¿Por qué le puso un yeso en la pierna a Jaime? (romperse)
2. ¿Por qué le sacó radiografías del brazo a Gaby? (caerse)
3. ¿Por qué le puso una curita en la mano a Chuy? (cortarse)
4. ¿Por qué le hicieron una prueba de embarazo a la señora Núñez? (desmayarse)
5. ¿Por qué le puso un vendaje en la muñeca a Sabino? (torcerse)
6. ¿Por qué le examinó los ojos a Ernesto? (comenzar a perder la vista)

14.36 **Hablemos de doctores** Combina la primera columna con la segunda columna para completar las ideas lógicamente y cambia el verbo en paréntesis a la forma necesaria del presente del indicativo o del subjuntivo, según se necesite.

1. Cada mañana hablo con los primeros pacientes en cuanto …
2. Ana toma medicamentos sin que …
3. Visitaré Panamá antes de que …
4. Mis primos visitan una clínica en La Habana para que …
5. Inés va a llamar al hospital a fin de que …
6. Iremos al hospital tan pronto como …

a. la recepcionista le (dar) una cita.
b. los doctores me (operar).
c. un experto les (examinar) los ojos.
d. yo (llegar) al hospital.
e. la ambulancia (llegar) a nuestra casa.
f. su doctor se los (recetar).

14.37 **El pasado y el presente** Completa los siguientes comentarios con la forma apropiada del verbo entre paréntesis. Necesitarás usar el subjuntivo, el indicativo y el infinitivo. **¡OJO!** Algunos están en el presente y otros en el pasado.

1. En el pasado no había tantas personas que **(a.)** _____ (considerarse) obesas, pero hoy en día es un problema serio. Es posible que nuestra vida sedentaria **(b.)** _____ (ser) uno de los grandes factores, pero es obvio que la comida **(c.)** _____ (tener) un papel importante también. Ojalá (nosotros) **(d.)** _____ (poder) remediar este problema pronto.

2. No hay duda que hoy en día la gente **(a.)** _____ (vivir) con mucho estrés y no dudo que el estrés **(b.)** _____ (ser) una de las causas de nuestros problemas médicos. Es evidente que la mayor parte del estrés **(c.)** _____ (venir) de nuestros trabajos porque muchos jefes esperan que los empleados **(d.)** _____ (hacer) más. En el pasado la gente no se quejaba del estrés en el trabajo a menos que uno **(e.)** _____ (ser) jefe y que **(f.)** _____ (tener) muchas responsabilidades.

3. En el siglo XVII no había nadie que **(a.)** _____ (imaginarse) la posibilidad de exponer a la gente a una enfermedad para que (la gente) no **(b.)** _____ (enfermarse). Después de que Edward Jenner **(c.)** _____ (descubrir) que las personas podían inmunizarse contra la viruela *(smallpox),* empezaron a investigar las posibilidades. Hoy en día la mayoría de los niños reciben vacunas aunque **(d.)** _____ (haber) personas que prefieren que sus hijos no las **(e.)** _____ (recibir).

14.38 **Los idiomas** En grupos de tres o cuatro estudiantes respondan las siguientes preguntas.

1. ¿Por qué decidiste estudiar español?
2. ¿Habías estudiado español antes de entrar en la universidad? ¿Por cuánto tiempo?
3. ¿Era necesario que estudiaras un idioma para graduarte de la escuela secundaria?
4. ¿Piensas seguir con tus estudios de español cuando termine el semestre? ¿Por qué?
5. ¿Te gustaría aprender otro idioma aparte del español? ¿Cuál?
6. ¿Cuáles son las ventajas y las desventajas de aprender otro idioma?
7. En tu opinión ¿deberían los inmigrantes aprender el idioma del nuevo país dónde viven? ¿y los turistas? ¿Por qué?
8. ¿Cómo se puede ayudar a los inmigrantes a aprender el idioma de su nuevo país?

14.39 **Un diagnóstico** Imagínate que eres médico y que vas a consultar con otro médico sobre algunos pacientes. Trabaja con un compañero para completar la información. Uno va a mirar la información en esta página y el otro va a mirar la información en el **Apéndice B**.

Modelo Olivia Aragón   estornudos, ojos irritados
Estudiante 1: *Olivia Aragón estornuda mucho y tiene ojos irritados.*
Estudiante 2: *Debe tomar pastillas para las alergias y no salir al jardín en la primavera.*

Nombre	Síntomas	Remedio
Bruno Medina	la presión alta	
Lourdes Montes		hacer ejercicio
Saúl Reyes	tos, dolor de garganta (throat)	
Aranza Rivera		tomar un examen de embarazo
Ileana Castro	dolor de estómago, vómito	
Esteban Peña		tomar aspirina, descansar

14.40 **Un evento** La clase de español va a organizar un evento para recolectar fondos para mandar a una organización internacional que ayuda a personas que viven en la pobreza.

Paso 1 Escribe una lista de ideas para el tipo de evento que pueden tener. Después comparte tus ideas con un compañero de clase y decidan lo que quieran proponer.

Paso 2 Con tu compañero planeen los detalles del evento: ¿Cuándo lo van a tener y dónde? ¿Cómo lo van a promocionar? ¿Cómo van a conseguir el dinero para donar?

Paso 3 Compartan sus ideas y los detalles con el resto de la clase. Después la clase va a votar por el evento que más le guste.

🔊 Vocabulario 1
2-41

En el hospital

el corazón	*heart*
el esqueleto	*skeleton*
el hígado	*liver*
el hueso	*bone*
el intestino	*intestine*
el órgano vital	*vital organ*
el (la) paciente	*patient*
los primeros auxilios	*first aid*

el pulmón	*lung*
la radiografía	*x-ray*
la receta médica	*prescription*
la sala de emergencias	*emergency room*
la salud	*health*
la sangre	*blood*
el tratamiento	*treatment*
el yeso	*cast*

Los síntomas

la alergia	*allergy*
la cortada	*cut*
el desmayo	*faint*
la diarrea	*diarrhea*

el dolor	*pain*
la náusea	*nausea*
la presión baja/alta	*low/high blood pressure*

Algunas enfermedades

el cáncer	*cancer*
la diabetes	*diabetes*
la gripe	*flu*
la hipertensión	*high blood pressure*
el insomnio	*insomnia*

la obesidad	*obesity*
el resfriado	*cold*
el SIDA	*AIDS*

Los medicamentos y procedimientos

la aspirina	*aspirin*
la cirugía	*surgery*
la curita	*small adhesive bandage*
las gotas	*drops*
la inyección	*injection, shot*

el jarabe	*syrup (cough)*
la pastilla	*pill*
la silla de ruedas	*wheelchair*
la vacuna	*vaccine*
el vendaje	*bandage*

Verbos

cortarse	*to get a cut*
descansar	*to rest*
desmayarse	*to faint*
doler (ue)	*to hurt*
enfermarse	*to get sick*
estar mareado(a)	*to be dizzy*
estornudar	*to sneeze*
examinar	*to examine*
fracturarse	*to fracture*

recuperarse	*to recuperate, to recover*
respirar	*to breathe*
sangrar	*to bleed*
sentir náuseas	*to feel nauseous*
tomar la presión	*to take someone´s blood pressure*
torcerse (ue)	*to twist, to sprain*
toser	*to cough*
vomitar	*to vomit*

🔊 Vocabulario 2
2-42

Nacionalidades

argentino(a)	*Argentine*	hondureño(a)	*Honduran*
boliviano(a)	*Bolivian*	mexicano(a)	*Mexican*
chileno(a)	*Chilean*	nicaragüense	*Nicaraguan*
colombiano(a)	*Colombian*	panameño(a)	*Panamanian*
costarricense	*Costa Rican*	paraguayo(a)	*Paraguayan*
cubano(a)	*Cuban*	peruano(a)	*Peruvian*
dominicano(a)	*Dominican*	puertorriqueño(a)	*Puerto Rican*
ecuatoguineano(a)	*Ecuatorial Guinean*	salvadoreño(a)	*Salvadoran*
ecuatoriano(a)	*Ecuadorian*	uruguayo(a)	*Uruguayan*
español(a)	*Spanish*	venezolano(a)	*Venezuelan*
guatemalteco(a)	*Guatemalan*		

La comunidad internacional

la beca	*scholarship*	el (la) inmigrante	*immigrant*
el (la) ciudadano(a)	*citizen*	la ley	*law*
los derechos humanos	*human rights*	el organismo internacional	*international organization*
el desempleo	*unemployment*	el país	*country*
la dictadura	*dictatorship*	la paz	*peace*
la emigración	*emigration*	la pobreza	*poverty*
la globalización	*globalization*	el (la) refugiado(a)	*refugee*
el gobierno	*government*		
la guerra	*war*	la riqueza	*wealth*
el idioma	*language*	el tratado de comercio	*trade agreement*
la inmigración	*immigration*		

Verbos

emigrar	*emigrate*	mudarse	*to move (to another location)*
inmigrar	*immigrate*	votar	*to vote*

Adverbios

(a)donde	*where, wherever*	en cuanto	*as soon as*
a fin de que	*in order that, so that*	hasta que	*until*
a menos que	*unless*	mientras (que)	*as long as; provided that*
antes (de) que	*before*		
aunque	*although, even if*	para que	*in order that, so that*
con tal (de) que	*provided that*	siempre y cuando	*as long as*
cuando	*when*	sin que	*without*
después (de) que	*after*	tan pronto (como)	*as soon as*
en caso de que	*in case*		

Diccionario personal

_____

_____

Gregorio López y Fuentes

Biografía

Gregorio López y Fuentes (1899–1966) nació en la región de la Huasteca, en el estado mexicano de Veracruz, en una familia de comerciantes y campesinos *(farm workers)*. Estudió en la Escuela Nacional de Maestros en la Ciudad de México, donde posteriormente trabajó como maestro de literatura y más tarde como periodista. Después de varios intentos para publicar, encontró el éxito al escribir novelas sobre la Revolución Mexicana y la vida de los campesinos. Su primera novela, *El Vagabundo*, apareció en la revista *El Universal Ilustrado* en 1922, y en 1935 recibió el Premio Nacional Mexicano por su novela *La India*.

Antes de leer

1. ¿Alguna vez trabajaste mucho tiempo en algo que luego perdiste? ¿Qué? ¿Cómo reaccionaste?

2. ¿Qué pasa cuando un agricultor pierde toda su cosecha *(harvest)*?

3. En tu opinión o experiencia personal, ¿qué le piden a Dios las personas religiosas? ¿Qué tipo de respuesta crees que esperan estas personas de Dios? Explica.

Investiguemos la literatura: La ironía

Irony is a literary device in which the author creates an incongruity between what appears to be true and what is true. There are different types of irony, some of which include: dramatic irony in which there is a discrepancy between what the characters know and what the audience knows; situational irony in which there is a discrepancy between what is expected to happen and what really happens; and cosmic irony in which the universal forces (God, destiny, or fate) react contrary to what the character expects.

Una carta a Dios

La casa —única en todo el valle— estaba subida en uno de esos **cerros truncados** que, a manera de pirámides rudimentarias, dejaron algunas tribus

5 al continuar sus **peregrinaciones.**
Desde allí se veían las **vegas,** el río, rastrojos y, lindando con el corral, la **milpa,** ya a punto de **jilotear.** Entre las **matas** del maíz, el frijol con su

10 florecilla morada, promesa inequívoca de una buena **cosecha.**

flat-top hills

pilgrimages

plains

maíz / to form ears of corn

plantas

harvest

© argus/Shutterstock

Lo único que estaba haciendo falta a la tierra era una lluvia, cuando lo menos un fuerte **aguacero,** de esos que forman **charcos** entre los surcos. Dudar que llovería hubiera sido lo mismo que dejar de creer en la experiencia de quienes, por tradición enseñaron

15 a **sembrar** en determinado día del año.

Durante la mañana, Lencho —conocedor del campo, **apegado** a las viejas costumbres y creyente a puño cerrado— no había hecho más que examinar el cielo por el rumbo del noreste.

—Ahora sí que viene el agua, vieja.

20 Y la vieja, que preparaba la comida, le respondió:

—Dios lo quiera.

Los muchachos más grandes limpiaban de **hierba** la **siembra**, mientras que los más pequeños **correteaban** cerca de la casa, hasta que la mujer les gritó a todos:

—Vengan que les voy a **dar en la boca**…

25 Fue durante la comida cuando, como lo había asegurado Lencho, comenzaron a caer gruesas **gotas** de lluvia. Por el noreste se veían avanzar grandes montañas de nubes. El aire olía a **jarro** nuevo.

—Hagan de cuenta, muchachos —exclamaba el hombre mientras sentía la fruición de **mojarse** con el pretexto de recoger algunos **enseres** olvidados sobre una **cerca** de

30 piedra—, que no son gotas de agua las que están cayendo; son **monedas** nuevas; las gotas grandes son de a diez y las gotas chicas son de a cinco…

Y dejaba pasear sus ojos satisfechos por la milpa a punto de jilotear, adornada con las **hileras** frondosas del frijol, y entonces toda ella cubierta por la transparente cortina de la lluvia. Pero, de pronto, comenzó a soplar un fuerte viento y con las gotas

35 de agua comenzaron a caer **granizos** tan grandes como **bellotas.** Ésos sí parecían monedas de plata nueva. Los muchachos, exponiéndose a la lluvia, corrían a recoger las perlas heladas de mayor tamaño.

—Esto sí que está muy malo —exclamaba mortificado el hombre. —Ojalá que pase pronto…

40 No pasó pronto. Durante una hora el granizo **apedreó** la casa, la huerta, el monte, la milpa y todo el valle. El campo estaba blanco que parecía una **salina.** Los árboles, deshojados. El maíz **hecho pedazos.** El frijol, sin una flor. Lencho, con el alma llena de **tribulaciones.** Pasada la tormenta, en medio de los surcos, decía a sus hijos:

—Más hubiera dejado una nube de **langostas** … El granizo no ha dejado nada: ni

45 una sola mata de maíz dará una **mazorca,** ni una mata de frijol dará una **vaina** …

La noche fue de lamentaciones:

—¡Todo nuestro trabajo, perdido!

—¡Y ni a quién acudir!

—Este año pasaremos hambre…

50 Pero muy en el fondo espiritual de cuantos convivían bajo aquella casa solitaria en mitad del valle, había una esperanza: la ayuda de Dios.

—No te mortifiques tanto, aunque el mal es grande. ¡Recuerda que nadie se muere de hambre!

—Eso dicen: Nadie se muere de hambre…

Glosses (left margin):

shower / puddles
to plant
devoted
weeds / cultivated land
corrían
to hit
drops
earthen jar
to get wet / tools / fence
coins
rows
hailstones / acorns
hit
salt marsh
destruido
tristeza
locusts
ear of corn / pod

dawn

55   Y mientras llegaba el **amanecer,** Lencho pensó mucho en lo que había visto en la
iglesia del pueblo los domingos: un triángulo y dentro del triángulo un ojo, un ojo que
parecía muy grande, un ojo que, según le habían explicado, lo mira todo, hasta lo que
está en el fondo de las conciencias.

coarse

Lencho era un hombre **rudo** y él mismo solía decir que el campo embrutece,
60   pero no lo era tanto que no supiera escribir. Ya con la luz del día y aprovechando la
circunstancia de que era domingo, después de haberse afirmado en su idea de que sí

watches over

hay quien **vele** por todos, se puso a escribir una carta que él mismo llevaría al pueblo
para echarla al correo.

Era nada menos que una carta a Dios.

65   Dios —escribió— si no me ayudas, pasaré hambre con todos los míos, durante este
año: necesito cien pesos para volver a sembrar y vivir mientras viene la nueva cosecha,
pues el granizo…

Escribió / envelope / papel   **Rotuló** el **sobre** "A Dios", metió el **pliego** y, aun preocupado, se dirigió al pueblo.
stamp / mailbox   Ya en la oficina de correos, le puso un **timbre** a la carta y echó ésta en el **buzón.**

70   Un empleado, que era cartero y todo en la oficina de correos, llegó riéndose con
toda la boca ante su jefe: le mostraba nada menos que la carta dirigida a Dios. Nunca

residence   en su existencia de repartidor había conocido ese **domicilio.** El jefe de la oficina —gordo
amable / frowned   y **bonachón**— también se puso a reír, pero bien pronto **se le plegó el entrecejo** y,
mientras daba golpecitos en la mesa con la carta comentaba:

Faith   75   —**¡La fe!** ¡Quién tuviera la fe de quien escribió esta carta! ¡Creer como él cree!
¡Esperar con la confianza con que él sabe esperar! ¡Sostener correspondencia con
Dios!

Y, para no defraudar aquel tesoro de fe, descubierto a través de una carta que no
delivered   podía ser **entregada,** el jefe postal concibió una idea: contestar la carta. Pero una vez
will   80   abierta, se vio que contestarla necesitaba algo más que buena **voluntad,** tinta y papel.
He didn't give up /   **No por ello se dio por vencido:** exigió a su empleado una **dádiva,** él puso parte de su
donación / contribución   sueldo y a varias personas les pidió su **óbolo** "para una obra piadosa".

Fue imposible para él reunir los cien pesos solicitados por Lencho, y se conformó
con enviar al campesino cuando menos lo que había recibido: algo más que la mitad.
85   Puso los billetes en un sobre dirigido a Lencho y con ellos un pliego que no tenía más
que una palabra, a manera de firma: Dios.

Al siguiente domingo Lencho llegó a preguntar, más temprano que de costumbre,
dio   si había alguna carta para él. Fue el mismo repartidero quien **le hizo entrega** de la
carta, mientras que el jefe, con la alegría de quien ha hecho una buena acción, espiaba
scratched glass / oficina 90   a través de un **vidrio raspado,** desde su **despacho.**

Lencho no mostró la menor sorpresa al ver los billetes —tanta era su seguridad—
pero hizo un gesto de cólera al contar el dinero… ¡Dios no podía haberse equivocado,
ni negar lo que Lencho se le había pedido!

Inmediatamente, Lencho se acercó a la ventanilla para pedir papel y tinta. En
wrinkling   95   la mesa destinada al público, se puso a escribir, **arrugando** mucho la frente a causa
del esfuerzo que hacía para dar forma legible a sus ideas. Al terminar, fue a pedir un
punch   timbre, el cual mojó con la lengua y luego aseguró con un **puñetazo.**

En cuanto la carta cayó al buzón, el jefe de correos fue a recogerla. Decía:

"Dios: Del dinero que te pedí, sólo llegaron a mis manos sesenta pesos. Mándame
100 el resto, que me hace falta; pero, no me los mandes por conducto de la oficina de
correos, porque los empleados son muy ladrones. —Lencho".

Después de leer

A. Comprensión

1. ¿Cómo se sintió Lencho cuando comenzó a llover? ¿Por qué?
2. ¿Cuál fue el resultado de la tormenta?
3. ¿Cuál era la única esperanza de la familia?
4. ¿Qué decidió hacer Lencho?
5. ¿Cuál fue la reacción inicial del cartero y de su jefe?
6. ¿Por qué estaba sorprendido el jefe?
7. ¿Qué decidió hacer el jefe de correos?
8. ¿Cuál fue el problema del jefe? ¿Qué hizo al final?
9. ¿Por qué el jefe miraba mientras Lencho recogía la carta?
10. ¿Por qué Lencho no se sorprendió cuando vio el dinero?
11. ¿Cuál fue la reacción de Lencho cuando contó el dinero? ¿Qué hizo después?
12. ¿Cuál es la ironía del cuento?

B. Conversemos

1. ¿Qué habrías hecho si tú hubieras abierto la primera carta de Lencho?
2. ¿Cómo piensas que reaccionó el jefe de correos al abrir la segunda carta de Lencho?

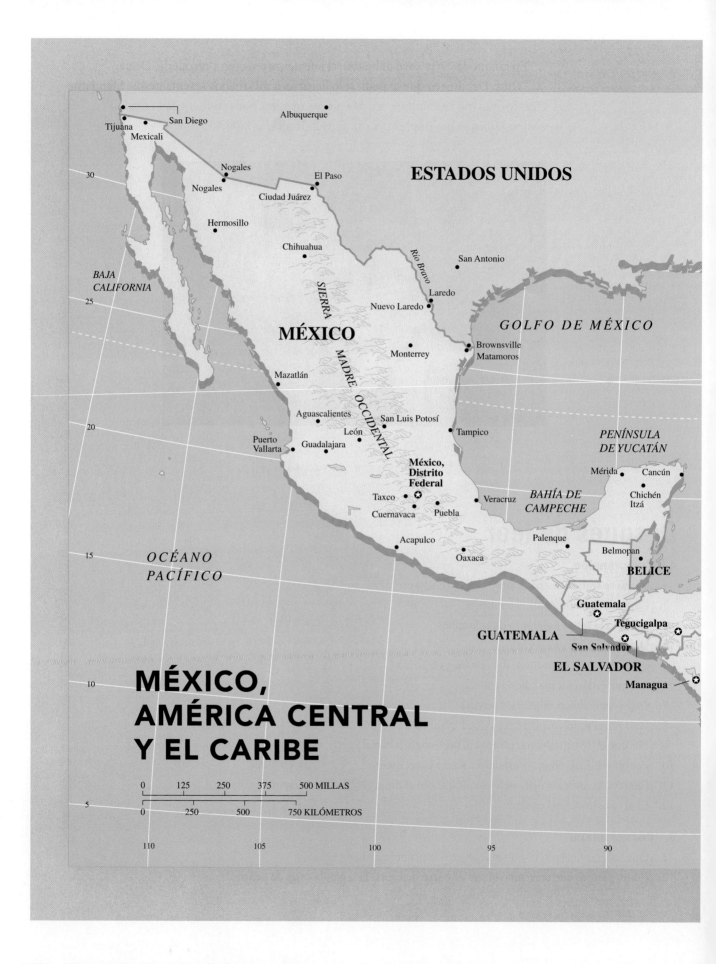

ESTADOS UNIDOS

Albuquerque

San Diego
Tijuana
Mexicali
Nogales
Nogales
El Paso
Ciudad Juárez
Hermosillo
Chihuahua
San Antonio
Río Bravo
BAJA CALIFORNIA
SIERRA
Laredo
Nuevo Laredo
GOLFO DE MÉXICO
MÉXICO
MADRE
Monterrey
Brownsville
Matamoros
Mazatlán
OCCIDENTAL
Aguascalientes
San Luis Potosí
PENÍNSULA DE YUCATÁN
León
Tampico
Puerto Vallarta
Guadalajara
México, Distrito Federal
Mérida
Cancún
Chichén Itzá
Taxco
Veracruz
BAHÍA DE CAMPECHE
Cuernavaca
Puebla
Acapulco
Palenque
OCÉANO PACÍFICO
Oaxaca
Belmopan
BELICE
Guatemala
Tegucigalpa
GUATEMALA
San Salvador
EL SALVADOR
Managua

MÉXICO, AMÉRICA CENTRAL Y EL CARIBE

0   125   250   375   500 MILLAS
0   250   500   750 KILÓMETROS

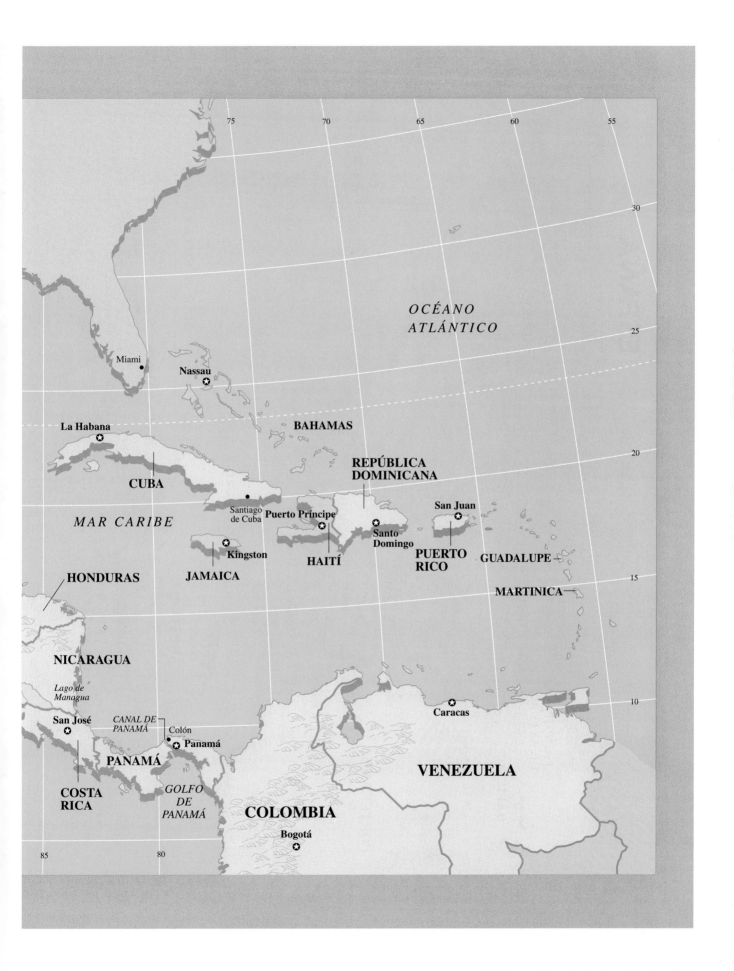

75 70 65 60 55

30

*OCÉANO
ATLÁNTICO*

25

Miami

Nassau

BAHAMAS

La Habana

**REPÚBLICA
DOMINICANA**

20

CUBA

San Juan

Santiago
de Cuba **Puerto Príncipe**

MAR CARIBE

**Santo
Domingo**

Kingston

**PUERTO
RICO** **GUADALUPE**

HAITÍ

HONDURAS

JAMAICA

MARTINICA

15

NICARAGUA

*Lago de
Managua*

10

Caracas

San José *CANAL DE
PANAMÁ* Colón **Panamá**

PANAMÁ

VENEZUELA

**COSTA
RICA** *GOLFO
DE
PANAMÁ*

COLOMBIA

Bogotá

85 80

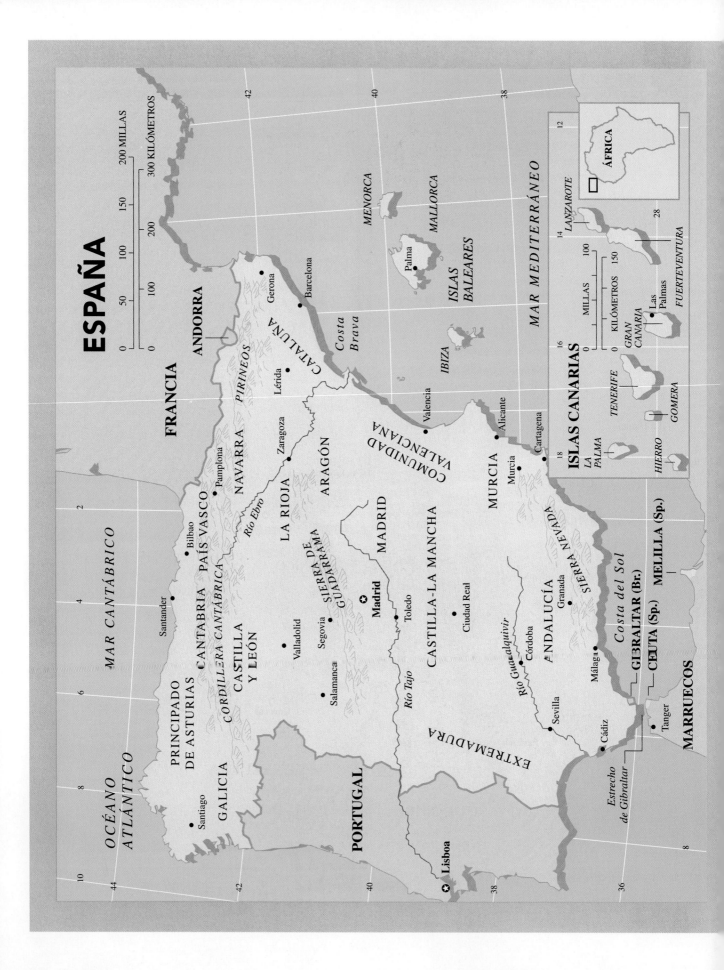

ESPAÑA

OCÉANO
ATLÁNTICO

MAR CANTÁBRICO

FRANCIA

ANDORRA

PIRINEOS

CATALUÑA

MENORCA

MALLORCA

ISLAS
BALEARES

MAR MEDITERRÁNEO

ÁFRICA

LANZAROTE

FUERTEVENTURA

ISLAS CANARIAS

GRAN
CANARIA

Las
Palmas

TENERIFE

GOMERA

LA
PALMA

HIERRO

200 MILLAS

300 KILÓMETROS

MILLAS

KILÓMETROS

Santander

Bilbao

PRINCIPADO
DE ASTURIAS

GALICIA

Santiago

CANTABRIA   PAÍS VASCO

CORDILLERA CANTÁBRICA

CASTILLA
Y LEÓN

Valladolid

Salamanca

Segovia

SIERRA DE
GUADARRAMA

NAVARRA

Pamplona

Río Ebro

LA RIOJA

ARAGÓN

Zaragoza

Lérida

Gerona

Barcelona

Costa
Brava

IBIZA

Palma

Valencia

COMUNIDAD
VALENCIANA

Alicante

Cartagena

MURCIA

Murcia

MADRID

Madrid

Toledo

CASTILLA-LA MANCHA

Ciudad Real

EXTREMADURA

PORTUGAL

Lisboa

Río Tajo

Río Guadalquivir

Córdoba

Sevilla

Cádiz

ANDALUCÍA

Granada

SIERRA NEVADA

Málaga

Costa del Sol

GIBRALTAR (Br.)

CEUTA (Sp.)   MELILLA (Sp.)

Estrecho
de Gibraltar

Tanger

MARRUECOS

42

40

38

2

4

6

8

10

44

42

40

38

36

8

12

14

16

18

28

AMÉRICA DEL SUR

ISLAS GALÁPAGOS

MAR CARIBE

OCÉANO ATLÁNTICO

BELICE
HONDURAS
NICARAGUA
EL SALVADOR
GUATEMALA
COSTA RICA
PANAMÁ

Lago de Managua

Barranquilla
Cartagena
Maracaibo
Lago de Maracaibo
San Cristóbal
Caracas
Río Orinoco

VENEZUELA

Medellín

⊛ Bogotá
Cali

COLOMBIA

Boa Vista

Georgetown
Paramaribo
GUAYANA
SURINAM
Cayena

GUAYANA FRANCESA

ECUADOR

⊛ Quito
ECUADOR
Guayaquil Cuenca
Iquitos

PERÚ

LOS ANDES

Río Amazonas

A M A Z O N A S

BRASIL

Machu Picchu
Lima ⊛
Ayacucho Cuzco
BOLIVIA

Brasilia ⊛

Lago Titicaca
⊛ La Paz Santa Cruz
Sucre
Potosí

Río Paraná

Río de Janeiro
São Paulo

CHILE

LOS ANDES

PARAGUAY
Asunción ⊛

Iguazú

Río Uruguay

OCÉANO PACÍFICO

Córdoba

Viña del Mar
Valparaíso
Santiago ⊛
Concepción

URUGUAY
Montevideo ⊛
ARGENTINA
Buenos Aires ⊛
Bahía Blanca
Río de la Plata

OCÉANO ATLÁNTICO

Viedma

ISLAS MALVINAS (Br.)

Estrecho de Magallanes
TIERRA DEL FUEGO

| 0 | 250 | 500 | 750 | 1,000 MILLAS |
| 0 | 500 | 1,000 | | 1,500 KILÓMETROS |

NIGERIA

ÁFRICA

Malabo ⊛
GUINEA ECUATORIAL
CAMERÚN
GABÓN

ÁFRICA

| 0 | MILLAS | 500 |
| 0 | KILÓMETROS | 750 |

Argentina ▶

INFORMACIÓN GENERAL

iLrn Para aprender más sobre Argentina, mira el video cultural en la mediateca (*Media Library*).

Nombre oficial: República Argentina

Nacionalidad: argentino(a)

Área: 2 780 400 km^2 (el país de habla hispana más grande del mundo, aproximadamente 2 veces el tamaño de Alaska)

Población: 42 611 000

Capital: Buenos Aires (f. 1580) (2 891 000 hab.)

Otras ciudades importantes: Córdoba, Rosario, Mendoza, Mar del Plata, San Miguel de Tucuman

Moneda: peso (argentino)

Idiomas: español (oficial), árabe, italiano, alemán

DEMOGRAFÍA

Alfabetismo: 97,2%

Religiones: católicos (92%), protestantes (2%), judíos (2%), otros (4%)

ARGENTINOS CÉLEBRES

Jorge Luis Borges
escritor, poeta (1899–1986)

Julio Cortázar
escritor (1914–1984)

Charly García
músico (1951–)

Ernesto "Che" Guevara
revolucionario (1928–1967)

Cristina Fernández
primera mujer presidenta (1953–)

Lionel Messi
futbolista (1987–)

Adolfo Pérez Esquivel
activista, Premio Nobel de la Paz (1931–)

Eva Perón
primera dama (1919–1952)

Joaquín "Quino" Salvador Lavado
caricaturista (1932–)

© Pablo H Caridad/Shutterstock

Puerto Madero es el antiguo puerto de Buenos Aires. Fue remodelado y ahora es un barrio (*neighborhood*) moderno y popular entre los porteños (los habitantes de Buenos Aires).

Investiga en Internet

La geografía: las cataratas del Iguazú, Parque Nacional Los Glaciares, la Patagonia, las islas Malvinas, las pampas

La historia: la inmigración, los gauchos, la Guerra Sucia, la Guerra de las Islas Malvinas, Carlos Gardel, Mercedes Sosa, José de San Martín

Películas: *Valentín, La historia oficial, Golpes a mi puerta, El secreto de sus ojos, Cinco amigas*

Música: el tango, la milonga, la zamba, la chacarera, Fito Páez, Soda Stereo

Comidas y bebidas: el asado, los alfajores, las empanadas, el mate, los vinos cuyanos

Fiestas: Día de la Revolución (25 de mayo), Día de la Independencia (9 de julio)

El Obelisco, símbolo de la ciudad de Buenos Aires

© meunierd/Shutterstock

© Alfredo Cerra/Shutterstock

El Glaciar Perito Moreno, en la Patagonia argentina, es el más visitado del país.

CURIOSIDADES

- Argentina es un país de inmigrantes europeos. A finales del siglo *(century)* XIX hubo una fuerte inmigración, especialmente de Italia, España e Inglaterra. Estas culturas se mezclaron *(mixed)* y ayudaron a crear la identidad argentina.

- Argentina se caracteriza por la calidad de su carne vacuna *(beef)* y por ser uno de los principales exportadores de carne *(meat)* en el mundo.

- El instrumento musical característico del tango, la música tradicional argentina, se llama *bandoneón* y es de origen alemán.

INFORMACIÓN GENERAL

Nombre oficial: Estado Plurinacional de Bolivia

Nacionalidad: boliviano(a)

Área: 1 098 581 km² (aproximadamente 4 veces el área de Wyoming, o la mitad de México)

Población: 10 461 000

Capital: Sucre (poder judicial) (284 000 hab.) y La Paz (sede del gobierno) (f. 1548) (835 000 hab.)

Otras ciudades importantes: Santa Cruz de la Sierra, Cochabamba, El Alto

Moneda: peso (boliviano)

Idiomas: español, quechua, aymará (Según la Constitución de 2009 el español y las 36 lenguas indígenas son todas oficiales.)

iLrn™ Para aprender más sobre Bolivia, mira el video cultural en la mediateca (*Media Library*).

DEMOGRAFÍA

Alfabetismo: 86,7%

Religiones: católicos (95%), protestantes (5%)

BOLIVIANOS CÉLEBRES

Jaime Escalante
ingeniero, profesor de
matemáticas (1930–2010)

Evo Morales
primer indígena elegido
presidente de Bolivia (1959–)

María Luisa Pacheco
pintora (1919–1982)

Edmundo Paz Soldán
escritor (1967–)

El Altiplano de Bolivia

© MP cz/Shutterstock

Investiga en Internet

La geografía: el lago Titicaca, Tiahuanaco, el salar de Uyuni

La historia: los incas, los aymará, la hoja de coca, Simón Bolívar

Música: la música andina, las peñas, la lambada, Los Kjarkas, Ana Cristina Céspedes

Comidas y bebidas: las llauchas, la papa (más de dos mil variedades), la chicha

Fiestas: Día de la Independencia (6 de agosto), Carnaval de Oruro (febrero o marzo), Festival de la Virgen de Urkupiña (14 de agosto)

La ciudad de Potosí fue muy importante, pues fue el principal abastecedor *(supplier)* de plata *(silver)* para España durante la Colonia.

El Salar de Uyuni

CURIOSIDADES

- Bolivia tiene dos capitales. Una de ellas, La Paz, es la más alta del mundo a 3640 metros (11 900 pies) sobre el nivel del mar *(sea)*.

- El lago Titicaca es el lago *(lake)* navegable más alto del mundo con una altura de más de 3800 metros (12 500 pies) sobre el nivel del mar.

- El Salar de Uyuni es el desierto de sal más grande del mundo.

- En Bolivia se consumen las hojas secas *(dried leaves)* de la coca para soportar mejor los efectos de la altura extrema.

- Bolivia es uno de los dos países de Sudamérica que no tiene costa marina.

Chile ▶

INFORMACIÓN GENERAL

iLrn Para aprender más sobre Chile, mira el video cultural en la mediateca (*Media Library*).

Nombre oficial: República de Chile

Nacionalidad: chileno(a)

Área: 756 102 km² (un poco más grande que Texas)

Población: 17 217 000

Capital: Santiago (f. 1541) (5 883 000 hab.)

Otras ciudades importantes: Valparaíso, Viña del Mar, Concepción

Moneda: peso (chileno)

Idiomas: español (oficial), mapuche, mapudungun, inglés

DEMOGRAFÍA

Alfabetismo: 95,7%

Religiones: católicos (70%), evangélicos (15%), testigos de Jehová (1%), otros (14%)

CHILENOS CÉLEBRES

Isabel Allende
escritora (1942–)

Michelle Bachelet
primera mujer presidente de Chile (1951–)

Gabriela Mistral
poetisa, Premio Nobel de Literatura (1889–1957)

Pablo Neruda
poeta, Premio Nobel de Literatura (1904–1973)

Violeta Parra
poetisa, cantautora (1917–1967)

Ana Tijoux
cantante (1977–)

Santiago está situada muy cerca de los Andes.

© Tifonimages/Shutterstock

© jorisvo/Shutterstock

La pintoresca ciudad de Valparaíso es Patrimonio de la Humanidad.

© Tomaz Kunst/Shutterstock

Los famosos moais de la isla de Pascua

CURIOSIDADES

- Chile es uno de los países más largos del mundo, pero también es muy angosto *(narrow)*. Gracias a su longitud, en el sur de Chile hay glaciares y fiordos, mientras que en el norte está el desierto más seco *(dry)* del mundo: el desierto de Atacama. La cordillera de los Andes también contribuye a la gran variedad de zonas climáticas y geográficas de este país.

- Es un país muy rico en minerales, en particular el cobre *(copper)*, que se exporta a nivel mundial.

- En febrero del 2010, Chile sufrió uno de los terremotos *(earthquakes)* más fuertes registrados en el mundo, con una magnitud de 8,8. En 1960 Chile también sufrió el terremoto más violento en la historia del planeta, con una magnitud de 9,4.

Colombia ▶

INFORMACIÓN GENERAL

Nombre oficial: República de Colombia

Nacionalidad: colombiano(a)

Área: 1 139 914 km² (aproximadamente 4 veces el área de Arizona)

Población: 45 746 000

Capital: Bogotá D.C. (f. 1538) (7 674 000 hab.)

Otras ciudades importantes: Medellín, Cali, Barranquilla, Bucaramanga

Moneda: peso (colombiano)

Idiomas: español (oficial), chibcha, guajiro y aproximadamente 90 lenguas indígenas

iLrn Para aprender más sobre Colombia, mira el video cultural en la mediateca (*Media Library*).

DEMOGRAFÍA

Alfabetismo: 90,4%

Religiones: católicos (90%), otros (10%)

COLOMBIANOS CÉLEBRES

Fernando Botero
pintor, escultor (1932–)

Tatiana Calderón Noguera
automovilista (1994–)

Gabriel García Márquez
escritor, Premio Nobel de Literatura
(1928–2014)

Lucho Herrera
ciclista, ganador del Tour de Francia y la
Vuelta de España (1961–)

Shakira
cantante, benefactora (1977–)

Sofía Vergara
actriz (1972–)

© rm/Shutterstock

Colombia tiene playas en el Caribe y en el océano Pacífico.

Cartagena es una de las ciudades
con más historia en Colombia.

Investiga en Internet

La geografía: los Andes, el Amazonas, Parque Nacional el Cocuy las playas de Santa Marta y Cartagena

La historia: los araucanos, Simón Bolívar, la leyenda de El Dorado, el Museo del Oro, las FARC

Películas: *María llena de gracia, Rosario Tijeras, Mi abuelo, mi papá y yo*

Música: la cumbia, el vallenato, Juanes, Carlos Vives, Aterciopelados

Comidas y bebidas: el ajiaco, las arepas, la picada, el arequipe, las cocadas, el café, el aguardiente

Fiestas: Día de la Independencia (20 de julio), Carnaval de Blancos y Negros en Pasto (enero), Carnaval del Diablo en Riosucio (enero, cada año impar)

Bogotá, capital de Colombia

CURIOSIDADES

- El 95% de la producción mundial de esmeraldas viene del subsuelo colombiano. Sin embargo, la mayor riqueza del país es su diversidad, ya que incluye culturas del Caribe, del Pacífico, del Amazonas y de los Andes.
- Colombia, junto con Costa Rica y Brasil, es uno de los principales productores de café en Latinoamérica.
- Colombia tiene una gran diversidad de especies de flores. Es el primer productor de claveles (*carnations*) y el segundo exportador mundial de flores después de Holanda.
- Colombia es uno de los países con mayor biodiversidad del mundo.

Costa Rica ▶

INFORMACIÓN GENERAL

Nombre oficial: República de Costa Rica

Nacionalidad: costarricense

Área: 51 100 km² (aproximadamente 2 veces el área de Vermont)

Población: 4 755 234

Capital: San José (f. 1521) (1 515 000 hab.)

Otras ciudades importantes: Alajuela, Cartago

Moneda: colón

Idiomas: español (oficial)

iLrn™ Para aprender más sobre Costa Rica, mira el video cultural en la mediateca (*Media Library*).

DEMOGRAFÍA

Alfabetismo: 96,3%

Religiones: católicos (76,3%), evangélicos y otros protestantes (15,7%), otros (4,8%), ninguna (3,2%)

COSTARRICENCES CÉLEBRES

Óscar Arias
político y presidente, Premio Nobel de la Paz (1949–)

Franklin Chang Díaz
astronauta (1950–)

Laura Chinchilla
primera mujer presidenta (1959–)

Carmen Naranjo
escritora (1928–2012)

Claudia Poll
atleta olímpica (1972–)

© Joe Ferrer/Shutterstock

El Teatro Nacional en San José es uno de los edificios más famosos de la capital.

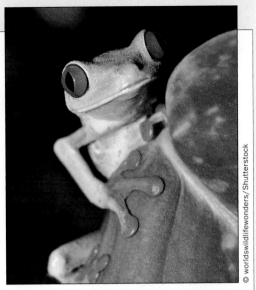

© worldswildlifewonders/Shutterstock

Costa Rica se conoce por su biodiversidad y respeto al medio ambiente.

🌐 **Investiga en Internet**

La geografía: Monteverde, Tortuguero, el Bosque de los Niños, el volcán Poás, los Parques Nacionales

La historia: las plantaciones de café, Juan Mora Fernández, Juan Santamaría

Música: El Café Chorale, Escats, Akasha

Comidas y bebidas: el gallo pinto, el café

Fiestas: Día de la Independencia (15 de septiembre), Fiesta de los Diablitos (febrero)

© Olaf Speier/Shutterstock

El Volcán Poás es un volcán activo de fácil acceso para el visitante.

CURIOSIDADES

- Costa Rica es uno de los pocos países del mundo que no tiene ejército *(army)*. En noviembre de 1949, 18 meses después de la Guerra *(War)* Civil, abolieron el ejército en la nueva constitución.

- Se conoce como un país progresista gracias a su apoyo *(support)* a la democracia, el alto nivel de vida de los costarricenses y la protección de su medio ambiente *(environment)*.

- Costa Rica posee una fauna y flora sumamente ricas. Aproximadamente una cuarta parte del territorio costarricense está protegido como reserva o parque natural.

- Costa Rica produce y exporta cantidades importantes de café, por lo que este producto es muy importante para su economía. Además, el café costarricense es de calidad reconocida *(recognized)* en todo el mundo.

Cuba ▶

INFORMACIÓN GENERAL

Nombre oficial: República de Cuba

Nacionalidad: cubano(a)

Área: 110 860 km² (aproximadamente el área de Tennessee)

Población: 11 047 251

Capital: La Habana (f. 1511) (2 116 000 hab.)

Otras ciudades importantes: Santiago, Camagüey

Moneda: peso (cubano)

Idiomas: español (oficial)

DEMOGRAFÍA

Alfabetismo: 99,8%

Religiones: católicos (85%), santería y otras religiones (15%)

CUBANOS CÉLEBRES

Alicia Alonso
bailarina, fundadora del Ballet
Nacional de Cuba (1920–)

Alejo Carpentier
escritor (1904–1980)

Nicolás Guillén
poeta (1902–1989)

Wifredo Lam
pintor (1902–1982)

José Martí
político, periodista, poeta (1853–1895)

Silvio Rodríguez
poeta, cantautor (1946–)

Juan Carlos Tabío
director de cine (1942–)

iLrn™ Para aprender más sobre Cuba, mira el video cultural en la mediateca (*Media Library*).

Catedral de la Habana

© Kamira/Shutterstock

La geografía: las cavernas de Bellamar, la Ciénaga de Zapata, la península de Guanahacabibes

La historia: los taínos, los ciboneyes, Fulgencio Batista, Bahía de Cochinos, la Revolución cubana, Fidel Castro

Películas: *Vampiros en La Habana, Fresa y chocolate, La última espera, Azúcar amargo*

Música: el son, Buena Vista Social Club, Celia Cruz, Pablo Milanés, Santiago Feliú, Alex Cuba

Comidas y bebidas: la ropa vieja, los moros y cristianos, el ron

Fiestas: Día de la Independencia (10 de diciembre), Día de la Revolución (1° de enero)

© Peeter Viisimaa/iStockphotos

Los autos viejos son una vista típica en toda la isla.

© Kamira/Shutterstock

El Morro, construído en 1589, para proteger la isla de invasores

CURIOSIDADES

- Cuba se distingue por tener uno de los mejores sistemas de educación del mundo, por su sistema de salud *(health)* y por su apoyo *(support)* a las artes.

- La población de la isla es una mezcla *(mix)* de los habitantes nativos (taínos), descendientes de esclavos africanos y europeos, mezcla que produce una cultura única.

- A principios *(beginning)* de la década de 1980, la nueva trova cubana (un movimiento musical) presentó al mundo entero la música testimonial.

- La santería es una religión que se originó en las islas del Caribe, especialmente en Cuba, y mezcla elementos religiosos de la religión yorubá de los esclavos de África, y elementos de la religión católica. El nombre de "santería" viene de un truco *(trick)* que los esclavos usaron para continuar adorando a los dioses *(gods)* en los que creían, burlando *(outsmarting)* la prohibición de los españoles. Así los esclavos fingían *(pretended)* que adoraban a los santos *(saints)* católicos, pero en realidad les rezaban *(prayed)* a los dioses africanos.

Ecuador ▶

INFORMACIÓN GENERAL

Nombre oficial: República del Ecuador

Nacionalidad: ecuatoriano(a)

Área: 283 561 km² (aproximadamente el área de Colorado)

Población: 15 654 411

Capital: Quito (f. 1556) (1 622 000 hab.)

Otras ciudades importantes: Guayaquil, Cuenca

Moneda: dólar (estadounidense)

Idiomas: español (oficial), quechua y otros idiomas indígenas

DEMOGRAFÍA

Alfabetismo: 91%

Religiones: católicos (95%), otros (5%)

ECUATORIANOS CÉLEBRES

Rosalía Arteaga
abogada, política, ex vicepresidenta
(1956–)

Jorge Carrera Andrade
escritor (1903–1978)

Oswaldo Guayasamín
pintor (1919–1999)

Jorge Icaza
escritor (1906–1978)

iLrn Para aprender más sobre Ecuador, mira el video cultural en la mediateca (*Media Library*).

© Marcos Aspiazu/Shutterstock

Las Peñas es un barrio muy conocido *(well-known)* de la ciudad de Guayaquil.

Investiga en Internet

La geografía: La selva amazónica, las islas Galápagos, Parque Nacional Cotopaxi

La historia: José de Sucre, la Gran Colombia, los indígenas tagaeri

Música: música andina, la quena, la zampoña, Fausto Miño, Daniel Betancourt, Michelle Cordero

Comida: la papa, el plátano frito, el ceviche, la fanesca

Fiestas: Día de la Independencia (10 de agosto), Fiestas de Quito (6 de diciembre)

El parque nacional más famoso de Ecuador es el de las Islas Galápagos.

La Basílica en Quito

CURIOSIDADES

- Este país tiene una gran diversidad de zonas geográficas como costas, montañas y selva *(jungle)*. Las famosas islas Galápagos son parte de Ecuador y presentan una gran diversidad biológica. A principios *(At the beginning)* del siglo XX, estas islas fueron usadas como prisión.

- Ecuador toma su nombre de la línea ecuatorial, que divide el planeta en dos hemisferios: norte y sur.

- La música andina es tradicional en Ecuador, con instrumentos indígenas como el charango, el rondador y el bombo.

- Ecuador es famoso por sus tejidos *(weavings)* de lana *(wool)* de llama y alpaca, dos animales de la región andina.

El Salvador

INFORMACIÓN GENERAL

Nombre oficial: República de El Salvador

Nacionalidad: salvadoreño(a)

Área: 21 041 km² (un poco más grande que Nueva Jersey)

Población: 6 125 512

Capital: San Salvador (f. 1524) (2 442 000 hab.)

Otras ciudades importantes: San Miguel, Santa Ana

Moneda: dólar (estadounidense)

Idiomas: español (oficial)

iLrn Para aprender más sobre El Salvador, mira el video cultural en la mediateca (*Media Library*).

DEMOGRAFÍA

Alfabetismo: 84,5%

Religiones: católicos (57,1%), protestantes (21%), otros (22%)

SALVADOREÑOS CÉLEBRES

Claribel Alegría
escritora (nació en Nicaragua pero se considera salvadoreña) (1924–)

Óscar Arnulfo Romero
arzobispo, defensor de los derechos humanos (1917–1980)

Alfredo Espino
poeta (1900–1928)

Cristina López
atleta, medallista olímpica (1982–)

El volcán de San Vicente

© moxelotle/iStockphoto

Investiga en Internet

La geografía: el bosque lluvioso (Parque Nacional Montecristo), el puerto de Acajutla, el volcán Izalco, los planes de Renderos

La historia: Tazumal, Acuerdos de Paz de Chapultepec, José Matías Delgado, FMLN, Ana María

Películas: *Romero*, *Voces inocentes*

Música: Taltipac, la salsa y la cumbia (fusión), Shaka y Dres

Comidas y bebidas: las pupusas, los tamales, la semita, el atole

Fiestas: Día del Divino Salvador del Mundo (6 de agosto), Día de la Independencia (15 de septiembre)

Una de las numerosas cascadas en el área de Juayua

La catedral en San Salvador

CURIOSIDADES

- El Salvador es el país más pequeño de Centroamérica pero el más denso en población.

- Hay más de veinte volcanes y algunos están activos.

- El Salvador está en una zona sísmica, por lo que ocurren terremotos *(earthquakes)* con frecuencia. En el pasado, varios sismos le causaron muchos daños *(damage)* al país.

- Entre 1979 y 1992, El Salvador vivió una guerra *(war)* civil. Durante esos años, muchos salvadoreños emigraron a los Estados Unidos.

- La canción de U2 "Bullet the Blue Sky" fue inspirada por el viaje a El Salvador que hizo el cantante Bono en los tiempos de la Guerra Civil.

España

INFORMACIÓN GENERAL

Nombre oficial: Reino de España

Nacionalidad: español(a)

Área: 505 992 km² (aproximadamente 2 veces el área de Oregón)

Población: 47 738 000

Capital: Madrid (f. siglo X) (6 574 000 hab.)

Otras ciudades importantes: Barcelona, Valencia, Sevilla, Toledo, Zaragoza

Moneda: euro

Idiomas: español (oficial), catalán, vasco, gallego

DEMOGRAFÍA

Alfabetismo: 97,7%

Religiones: católicos (94%), otros (6%)

ESPAÑOLES CÉLEBRES

Pedro Almodóvar
director de cine (1949–)

Rosalía de Castro
escritora (1837–1885)

Miguel de Cervantes Saavedra
escritor (1547–1616)

Penélope Cruz
actriz (1974–)

Lola Flores
cantante, bailarina de flamenco (1923–1995)

Federico García Lorca
poeta (1898–1936)

Antonio Gaudí
arquitecto (1852–1926)

Rafael Nadal
tenista (1986–)

Pablo Picasso
pintor, escultor (1881–1973)

(iLrn™) Para aprender más sobre España, mira el video cultural en la mediateca (*Media Library*).

La Plaza Mayor es un lugar con mucha historia en el centro de Madrid.

© Vinícius Tupinamba/Shutterstock

Arquitectura gótica en Barcelona

El Alcázar en la ciudad de Toledo

CURIOSIDADES

- España se distingue por tener una gran cantidad de pintores y escritores. En el siglo XX se destacaron *(stood out)* los pintores Pablo Picasso, Salvador Dalí y Joan Miró. Entre los clásicos figuran Velázquez, El Greco y Goya.

- El Palacio Real de Madrid presenta una arquitectura hermosa *(beautiful)*. Contiene pinturas de algunos de los artistas mencionados arriba. Originalmente fue un fuerte *(fort)* construido por los musulmanes en el siglo IX. Más tarde, los reyes de Castilla construyeron allí el Alcázar. En 1738, el rey Felipe V ordenó la construcción del Palacio Real, que fue la residencia de la familia real hasta 1941.

- Aunque el español se habla en todo el país, cada región de España mantiene viva su propia *(own)* lengua. De todos, el más interesante quizás sea el vasco, que es la única lengua de España que no deriva del latín y cuyo origen no se conoce.

- En la ciudad de Toledo se fundó la primera escuela de traductores en el año 1126.

- En Andalucía, una región al sur de España, se ve una gran influencia árabe por los moros que la habitaron de 711 a 1492, año en el que los reyes Católicos los expulsaron durante la Reconquista.

Guatemala ▶

INFORMACIÓN GENERAL

iLrn Para aprender más sobre Guatemala, mira el video cultural en la mediateca (*Media Library*).

Nombre oficial: República de Guatemala

Nacionalidad: guatemalteco(a)

Área: 108 890 km² (un poco más grande que el área de Ohio)

Población: 14 647 083

Capital: Ciudad de Guatemala (f. 1524) (2 945 000 hab.)

Otras ciudades importantes: Mixco, Villa Nueva Quetzaltenango, Puerto Barrios

Moneda: quetzal

Idiomas: español (oficial), K'iche', Mam, Q'eqchi'

DEMOGRAFÍA

Alfabetismo: 75,9%

Religiones: católicos (94%), protestantes (2%), otros (4%)

GUATEMALTECOS CÉLEBRES

Ricardo Arjona
cantautor (1964–)

Miguel Ángel Asturias
escritor (1899–1974)

Rigoberta Menchú
activista por los derechos humanos,
Premio Nobel de la Paz (1959–)

Carlos Mérida
pintor (1891–1984)

Augusto Monterroso
escritor (1921–2003)

Mujer tejiendo (*weaving*) en la región del departamento de Sololá

© SUETONE Emilio/age fotostock

Investiga en Internet

La geografía: el lago Atitlán, Antigua

La historia: los mayas, Efraín Ríos Mont, la matanza de indígenas durante la dictadura, quiché, el Popul Vuh, Tecun Uman

Películas: *El norte*

Música: punta, Gaby Moreno

Comida: los tamales, la sopa de pepino, fiambre, pipián

Fiestas: Día de la Independencia (15 de septiembre), Semana Santa (marzo o abril), Día de los Muertos (1 de noviembre)

Tikal, ciudad construida por los mayas

Vista del lago Atitlán

CURIOSIDADES

- Guatemala es famosa por la gran cantidad de ruinas mayas y por las tradiciones indígenas, especialmente los tejidos *(weavings)* de vivos colores.

- Guatemala es el quinto exportador de plátanos en el mundo.

- Antigua es una famosa ciudad que sirvió como la tercera capital de Guatemala. Es reconocida *(recognized)* mundialmente por su bien preservada arquitectura renacentista *(Renaissance)* y barroca. También es reconocida como un lugar excelente para ir a estudiar español.

- En Guatemala se encuentra Tikal, uno de los más importantes conjuntos *(ensembles)* arqueológicos mayas.

Guinea Ecuatorial ▶

INFORMACIÓN GENERAL

Nombre oficial: República de Guinea Ecuatorial

Nacionalidad: ecuatoguineano(a)

Área: 28 051 km² (aproximadamente el área de Maryland)

Población: 722 254

Capital: Malabo (f. 1827) (156 000 hab.)

Otras ciudades importantes: Bata, Ebebiyín

Moneda: franco CFA

Idiomas: español y francés (oficiales), fang, bubi

DEMOGRAFÍA

Alfabetismo: 94,2

Religiones: católicos y otros cristianos (95%), prácticas paganas (5%)

ECUATOGUINEANOS CÉLEBRES

Leoncio Evita
escritor del primer libro guineano y primera
novela africana en español (1929–1996)

Leandro Mbomio Nsue
escultor (1938–2012)

Eric Moussambani
nadador olímpico (1978–)

Donato Ndongo-Bidyogo
escritor (1950–)

María Nsué Angüe
escritora (1945–)

© Christine Nesbitt/AP Images

Niños jugando frente a una iglesia en Malabo

Investiga en Internet

La geografía: la isla de Bioko, el río Muni

La historia: los Bantú, los Igbo, los Fang

Música: Las Hijas del Sol, Betty Akna, Anfibio

Comidas y bebidas: la sopa banga, el pescado a la plancha, el puercoespín, el antílope, los vinos de palma, la malamba

Fiestas: Día de la Independencia (12 de octubre)

Mujeres pescando *(fishing)* en la playa

El bosque *(forest)* de la isla de Bioko

CURIOSIDADES

- Se cree que los primeros habitantes de esta región fueron pigmeos.

- Guinea Ecuatorial obtuvo su independencia de España en 1968 y es el único país en África en donde el español es un idioma oficial.

- Parte de su territorio fue colonizado por los portugueses y por los ingleses.

- Macías Nguema fue dictador de Guinea Ecuatorial hasta 1979.

- El país tiene una universidad, la Universidad Nacional de Guinea Ecuatorial, situada en la capital.

- Con el descubrimiento de reservas de petróleo y gas en la década de los años 90 se fortaleció *(strengthened)* considerablemente la economía.

- Guinea Ecuatorial tiene el más alto ingreso per cápita en África: 19,998 dólares. Sin embargo *(However)*, la distribución del dinero se concentra en unas pocas familias.

Honduras ▶

INFORMACIÓN GENERAL

Nombre oficial: República de Honduras

Nacionalidad: hondureño(a)

Área: 112 090 km² (aproximadamente el área de Pennsylvania)

Población: 8 598 561

Capital: Tegucigalpa (f. 1762) (1 324 000 hab.)

Otras ciudades importantes: San Pedro Sula, El Progreso

Moneda: lempira

Idiomas: español (oficial), garífuna

DEMOGRAFÍA

Alfabetismo: 85,1%

Religiones: católicos (97%), protestantes (3%)

HONDUREÑOS CÉLEBRES

Ramón Amaya Amador
escritor (1916–1966)

Carlos Mencia
comediante (1967–)

José Antonio Velásquez
pintor (1906–1983)

Lempira
héroe indígena (1499–1537)

David Suazo
futbolista (1979–)

iLrn™ Para aprender más sobre Honduras, mira el video cultural en la mediateca (*Media Library*).

Copán, declarado Patrimonio de la Humanidad (*World Heritage*) por la UNESCO

© Dave Rock/Shutterstock

El esnórquel es popular en Honduras.

Vista aérea de la isla Roatán en el Caribe hondureño

CURIOSIDADES

- Los hondureños reciben el apodo *(nickname)* de "catrachos", palabra derivada del apellido Xatruch, un famoso general que combatió en Nicaragua contra el filibustero William Walker.

- El nombre original del país fue Comayagua, el mismo nombre que su capital. A mediados del siglo XIX adoptó el nombre República de Honduras, y en 1880 la capital se trasladó *(moved)* a Tegucigalpa.

- Honduras basa su economía en la agricultura, especialmente en las plantaciones de banana, cuya comercialización empezó en 1889 con la fundación de la Standard Fruit Company.

- Se dice que en la región de Yoro ocurre el fenómeno de la lluvia *(rain)* de peces, es decir que, literalmente, los peces caen del cielo *(fall from the sky)*. Por esta razón, desde 1998 se celebra en el Yoro el Festival de Lluvia de Peces.

- En 1998, el huracán Mitch golpeó *(hit)* severamente la economía nacional, destruyendo gran parte de la infraestructura del país y de los cultivos. Se calcula que el país retrocedió 25 años a causa del huracán.

México

INFORMACIÓN GENERAL

Nombre oficial: Estados Unidos Mexicanos

Nacionalidad: mexicano(a)

Área: 1 964 375 km² (aproximadamente 4 1/2 veces el área de California)

Población: 120 386 655

Capital: México D.F. (f. 1521) (21 163 000 hab.)

Otras ciudades importantes: Guadalajara, Monterrey, Puebla, Tijuana

Moneda: peso (mexicano)

Idiomas: español (oficial), aproximadamente 280 otras lenguas amerindias

iLrn Para aprender más sobre México, mira el video cultural en la mediateca (*Media Library*).

DEMOGRAFÍA

Alfabetismo: 93,5%

Religiones: católicos (90,4%), protestantes (3,8%), otros (5,8%)

MEXICANOS CÉLEBRES

Carmen Aristegui
periodista (1964–)

Gael García Bernal
actor (1978–)

Alejandro González Iñarritu
director de cine (1963–)

Frida Kahlo
pintora (1907–1954)

Armando Manzanero
cantautor (1935–)

Rafa Márquez
futbolista (1979–)

Octavio Paz
escritor, Premio Nobel de Literatura (1914–1998)

Elena Poniatowska
periodista, escritora (1932–)

Diego Rivera
pintor (1886–1957)

Guillermo del Toro
cineasta (1964–)

Emiliano Zapata
revolucionario (1879–1919)

Teotihuacán, ciudad precolombina declarada Patrimonio de la Humanidad (*World Heritage*) la UNESCO.

© r9photos/Shutterstock

🌐 **Investiga en Internet**

La geografía: el cañón del Cobre, el volcán Popocatépetl, las lagunas de Montebello, Parque Nacional Cañón del Sumidero, la sierra Tarahumara, Acapulco

La historia: mayas, aztecas, toltecas, la conquista, la colonia, Pancho Villa, Porfirio Díaz, Hernán Cortés, Miguel Hidalgo, los Zapatistas

Películas: *Amores perros, Frida, Y tu mamá también, Babel, El laberinto del fauno, La misma luna*

Música: mariachis, ranchera, Pedro Infante, Vicente Fernández, Luis Miguel, Maná, Jaguares, Juan Gabriel, Thalía, Lucero, Julieta Venegas

Comidas y bebidas: los chiles en nogada, el mole poblano, el pozole, los huevos rancheros, el tequila (alimentos originarios de México: chocolate, tomate, vainilla)

Fiestas: Día de la Independencia (16 de septiembre), Día de los Muertos (1 y 2 de noviembre)

La Torre Latinoamericana, en la Ciudad de México, fue el primer rascacielos *(skyscraper)* del mundo construído exitosamente en una zona sísmica.

Puerto Vallarta

CURIOSIDADES

- La Ciudad de México es una de las ciudades más pobladas del mundo. Los predecesores de los aztecas fundaron la Ciudad sobre el lago *(lake)* de Texcoco. La ciudad recibió el nombre de Tenochtitlán, y era más grande que cualquier *(any)* capital europea cuando ocurrió la Conquista.

- Millones de mariposas *(butterflies)* monarcas migran todos los años a los estados de Michoacán y México de los Estados Unidos y Canadá.

- La Pirámide de Chichén Itzá fue nombrada una de las siete maravillas del mundo moderno.

- Los olmecas (1200 a.C–400 a.C) desarrollaron *(developed)* el primer sistema de escritura en las Américas.

Nicaragua ▶

INFORMACIÓN GENERAL

Nombre oficial: República de Nicaragua

Nacionalidad: nicaragüense

Área: 130 370 km² (aproximadamente el área del estado de Nueva York)

Población: 5 848 641

Capital: Managua (f. 1522) (2 132 000 hab.)

Otras ciudades importantes: León, Chinandega

Moneda: córdoba

Idiomas: español (oficial), misquito

Para aprender más sobre Nicaragua, mira el video cultural en la mediateca (*Media Library*).

DEMOGRAFÍA

Alfabetismo: 78%

Religiones: católicos (58%), evangélicos (22%), otros (20%)

NICARAGÜENSES CÉLEBRES

Ernesto Cardenal
sacerdote, poeta (1925–)

Rubén Darío
poeta, padre del Modernismo (1867–1916)

Violeta Chamorro
periodista, presidenta (1929–)

Bianca Jagger
activista de derechos humanos (1945–)

Ometepe, isla formada por dos volcanes

© rchphoto/iStockphoto

Investiga en Internet

La geografía: el lago Nicaragua, la isla Ometepe

La historia: los misquitos, Anastasio Somoza, Augusto Sandino, Revolución sandinista, José Dolores Estrada

Películas: *Ernesto Cardenal*

Música: polca, mazurca, Camilo Zapata, Carlos Mejía Godoy, Salvador Cardenal, Luis Enrique Mejía Godoy, Perrozompopo

Comidas y bebidas: los tamales, la sopa de pepino, el triste, el tibio, la chicha

Fiestas: Día de la Independencia (15 de septiembre)

Catedral de Granada

Isla del Maíz

CURIOSIDADES

- Nicaragua se conoce como tierra *(land)* de poetas y volcanes.

- La capital, Managua, fue destruída por un terremoto *(earthquake)* en 1972. A causa de la actividad sísmica no se construyen edificios altos.

- Las ruinas de León Viejo fueron declaradas Patrimonio de la Humanidad *(World Heritage)* en el año 2000. Es la ciudad más antigua de América Central.

- Es el país más grande de Centroamérica y tiene el lago más grande de la región, el lago Nicaragua, con más de 370 islas. La isla más grande, Ometepe, tiene dos volcanes.

Panamá

INFORMACIÓN GENERAL

Nombre oficial: República de Panamá

Nacionalidad: panameño(a)

Área: 75 420 km² (aproximadamente la mitad del área de Florida)

Población: 3 608 431

Capital: Panamá (f. 1519) (1 273 000 hab.)

Otras ciudades importantes: San Miguelito, David

Moneda: balboa, dólar (estadounidense)

Idiomas: español (oficial), inglés

iLrn Para aprender más sobre Panamá, mira el video cultural en la mediateca (*Media Library*).

DEMOGRAFÍA

Alfabetismo: 94,1%

Religiones: católicos (85%), protestantes (15%)

PANAMEÑOS CÉLEBRES

Joaquín Beleño
escritor y periodista (1922–1988)

Ricardo Miró
escritor (1883–1940)

Rubén Blades
cantautor, actor, abogado, político (1948–)

Omar Torrijos
militar, presidente (1929–1981)

© Manja/Shutterstock

El canal de Panamá es una de las principales fuentes *(sources)* de ingresos para el país.

Investiga en Internet

La geografía: el canal de Panamá

La historia: los Kuna Yala, la construcción del canal de Panamá, la dictadura de Manuel Noriega, Parque Nacional Soberanía, Victoriano Lorenzo

Películas: *El plomero, Los puños de una nación*

Música: salsa, Danilo Pérez, Edgardo Franco "El General", Nando Boom

Comidas y bebidas: el chocao panameño, el sancocho de gallina, las carimañolas, la ropa vieja, los jugos de fruta, el chicheme

Fiestas: Día de la Independencia (3 de noviembre)

© Courtesy of Margarita Casas

Una isla en el archipiélago de San Blas, lugar donde habitan los Kuna Yala

© Alfredo Maiquez/Shutterstock

La Ciudad de Panamá es famosa por sus rascacielos (*skyscrapers*).

CURIOSIDADES

- El canal de Panamá se construyó entre 1904 y 1914. Mide (*It measures*) 84 kilómetros de longitud y funciona con un sistema de esclusas (*locks*) que elevan y bajan los barcos (*boats*) porque los océanos Atlántico y Pacífico tienen diferentes elevaciones. Cada año cruzan unos 14 000 barcos o botes por el canal, el cual estuvo bajo control de los Estados Unidos hasta el 31 de diciembre de 1999. En promedio (*On average*), cada embarcación paga 54 000 dólares por cruzar el canal. La tarifa más baja la pagó un aventurero estadounidense, quien pagó 36 centavos por cruzar nadando en 1928.

- En la actualidad está construyéndose una ampliación al canal que permitirá que transiten por él barcos hasta tres veces más grandes que la máxima capacidad del canal actual.

- El territorio de los Kuna Yala se considera independiente. Para entrar a su territorio es necesario pagar una cuota (*fee*) y mostrar su pasaporte.

Paraguay ▷

INFORMACIÓN GENERAL

Nombre oficial: República del Paraguay

Nacionalidad: paraguayo(a)

Área: 406 750 km² (aproximadamente el área de California)

Población: 6 703 860

Capital: Asunción (f. 1537) (2 329 000 hab.)

Otras ciudades importantes: Ciudad del Este, San Lorenzo

Moneda: guaraní

Idiomas: español y guaraní (oficiales)

DEMOGRAFÍA

Alfabetismo: 93,9%

Religiones: católicos (90%), protestantes (6%), otros (4%)

PARAGUAYOS CÉLEBRES

Olga Blinder
pintora (1921–2008)

Arsenio Erico
futbolista (1915–1977)

Augusto Roa Bastos
escritor, Premio Cervantes de Literatura (1917–2005)

Berta Rojas
guitarrista (1966–)

iLrn™ Para aprender más sobre Paraguay, mira el video cultural en la mediateca (*Media Library*).

© Lukasz Kurbiel/Shutterstock

Ruinas de Misiones Jesuitas en Trinidad

Investiga en Internet

La geografía: las cataratas del Iguazú, los ríos Paraguay y Paraná, Parque Nacional Cerro Corá, la presa Itaipú, el Chaco

La historia: guaraníes, misiones jesuitas, la Guerra de la Triple Alianza, Alfredo Stroessner, Carlos Antonio López, José Félix Estigarribia

Películas: *Nosotros, Hamacas paraguayas, 7 cajas*

Música: polca, baile de la botella, arpa paraguaya, Perla, Celso Duarte

Comidas y bebidas: el chipá paraguayo, el surubí, las empanadas, la sopa paraguaya, el mate, el tereré

Fiestas: Día de la Independencia (14 de mayo), Verbena de San Juan (24 de junio)

El palacio presidencial en Asunción

Las cataratas de Iguazú, una de las siete maravillas naturales del mundo

CURIOSIDADES

- Por diversas razones históricas, Paraguay es un país bilingüe. Se calcula que el 90% de sus habitantes hablan español y guaraní, el idioma de sus habitantes antes de la llegada de los españoles. En particular, la llegada de los jesuitas tuvo importancia en la preservación del idioma guaraní. Actualmente se producen novelas y programas de radio en guaraní. Por otra parte, el guaraní ha influenciado notablemente el español de la región.

- Paraguay, igual que Bolivia, no tiene salida al mar *(sea)*.

- La presa *(dam)* de Itaipú es la mayor del mundo en cuanto a producción de energía. Está sobre el río Paraná y abastace *(provides)* el 90% del consumo de energía eléctrica de Paraguay y el 19% de Brasil.

Perú ▶

INFORMACIÓN GENERAL

iLrn™ Para aprender más sobre Perú, mira el video cultural en la mediateca (*Media Library*).

Nombre oficial: República del Perú

Nacionalidad: peruano(a)

Área: 1 285 216 km² (aproximadamente 2 veces el área de Texas)

Población: 30 147 935

Capital: Lima (f. 1535) (8 769 000 hab.)

Otras ciudades importantes: Callao, Arequipa, Trujillo

Moneda: nuevo sol

Idiomas: español, quechua y aymará (oficiales), otras lenguas indígenas

DEMOGRAFÍA

Alfabetismo: 92,9%

Religiones: católicos (81,3%), evangélicos (12,5%), otros (3,3%)

PERUANOS CÉLEBRES

Gastón Acurio
chef (1967–)

Alberto Fujimori
político y presidente (1938–)

Tania Libertad
cantante (1952–)

Claudia Llosa
directora de cine (1976–)

María Julia Mantilla
empresaria y presentadora de TV, ex Miss Universo (1984–)

Javier Pérez de Cuellar
secretario general de las Naciones Unidas (1920–)

Fernando de Szyszlo
pintor (1925–)

Mario Testino
fotógrafo (1954–)

César Vallejo
poeta (1892–1938)

Mario Vargas Llosa
escritor, político, Premio Nobel de Literatura (1936–)

Machu Picchu

© Mark Skalny/Shutterstock

Las calles de Cuzco

Investiga en Internet

La geografía: los Andes, el Amazonas, Machu Picchu, el lago Titicaca, Nazca

La historia: los incas, los aymará, el Inti Raymi, los uros, José de San Martín

Películas: *Todos somos estrellas, Madeinusa, La teta asustada*

Música: música andina, valses peruanos, jaranas, Gian Marco

Comidas y bebidas: la papa (más de 2000 variedades), la yuca, la quinoa, el ceviche, el pisco, anticuchos

Fiestas: Día de la Independencia (28 de julio)

La Plaza de Armas en Lima

CURIOSIDADES

- En Perú vivieron muchas civilizaciones diferentes que se desarrollaron *(developed)* entre el año 4000 a.C hasta principios *(beginning)* del siglo XVI. La más importante fue la civilización de los incas, que dominaba la región a la llegada de los españoles.

- Otra civilización importante fueron los nazcas, quienes trazaron figuras de animales que solo se pueden ver desde el aire. Hay más de 2000 km de líneas. Su origen es un misterio y no se sabe por qué las hicieron *(made)*.

- Perú es el país del mundo que tiene más platos típicos: 491.

- Probablemente la canción folclórica más famosa del Perú es "El Cóndor Pasa".

Puerto Rico ▶

INFORMACIÓN GENERAL

iLrn™ Para aprender más sobre Puerto Rico, mira el video cultural en la mediateca (*Media Library*).

Nombre oficial: Estado Libre Asociado de Puerto Rico (*Commonwealth of Puerto Rico*)

Nacionalidad: puertorriqueño(a)

Área: 13.790 km² (un poco menos que el área de Connecticut)

Población: 3 620 897

Capital: San Juan (f. 1521) (2 730 000 hab.)

Otras ciudades importantes: Ponce, Caguas

Moneda: dólar (estadounidense)

Idiomas: español, inglés (oficiales)

DEMOGRAFÍA

Alfabetismo: 94,1%

Religiones: católicos (85%), protestantes y otros (15%)

PUERTORRIQUEÑOS CÉLEBRES

Roberto Clemente
beisbolista (1934–1972)

Rosario Ferré
escritora (1938–)

Raúl Juliá
actor (1940–1994)

Ricky Martin
cantante, benefactor (1971–)

Rita Moreno
actriz (1931–)

Francisco Oller y Cestero
pintor (1833–1917)

Esmeralda Santiago
escritora (1948–)

Una calle en el Viejo San Juan

© Lori Froeb/Shutterstock

Investiga en Internet

La geografía: el Yunque, Vieques, El Morro, Parque Nacional Cavernas del Río Camuy

La historia: los taínos, Juan Ponce de León, la Guerra Hispanoamericana, Pedro Albizu Campos

Películas: *Lo que le pasó a Santiago, 12 horas, Talento de barrio*

Música: salsa, bomba y plena, Gilberto Santa Rosa, Olga Tañón, Daddy Yankee, Tito Puente, Calle 13, Carlos Ponce, Ivy Queen

Comidas y bebidas: el lechón asado, el arroz con gandules, el mofongo, los bacalaítos, la champola de guayaba, el coquito, la horchata de ajonjolí

Fiestas: Día de la Independencia de EE.UU. (4 de julio), Día de la Constitución de Puerto Rico (25 de julio)

CURIOSIDADES

- A los puertorriqueños también se los conoce como *(known as)* "boricuas", ya que antes de *(before)* la llegada de los europeos la isla se llamaba Borinquen.

- A diferencia de otros países, los puertorriqueños también son ciudadanos *(citizens)* estadounidenses, con la excepción de que no pueden votar en elecciones presidenciales de los Estados Unidos si no son residentes de un estado.

- El gobierno de Puerto Rico está encabezado por un gobernador.

- El fuerte *(fort)* de El Morro fue construido en el siglo XVI para defender el puerto de los piratas. Gracias a esta construcción, San Juan fue el lugar mejor defendido del Caribe.

República Dominicana ▶

INFORMACIÓN GENERAL

Nombre oficial: República Dominicana

Nacionalidad: dominicano(a)

Área: 48 670 km² (aproximadamente 2 veces el área de Vermont)

Población: 10 349 741

Capital: Santo Domingo (f. 1492) (2 191 000 hab.)

Otras ciudades importantes: Santiago de los Caballeros, La Romana

Moneda: peso (dominicano)

Idiomas: español

DEMOGRAFÍA

Alfabetismo: 90,1%

Religiones: católicos (95%), otros (5%)

DOMINICANOS CÉLEBRES

Juan Bosch
escritor (1909–2001)

Charytín
cantante y conductora (1949–)

Juan Pablo Duarte
héroe de la independencia (1808–1876)

Juan Luis Guerra
músico (1957–)

Óscar de la Renta
diseñador (1932–)

David Ortiz
beisbolista (1975–)

(iLrn™ Para aprender más sobre República Dominicana, mira el video cultural en la mediateca (*Media Library*).

© e2dan/Shutterstock

La plaza principal en Santo Domingo

Investiga en Internet

La geografía: Puerto Plata, Pico Duarte, Sierra de Samaná

La historia: los taínos, los arawak, la dictadura de Trujillo, las hermanas Mirabal, Juan Pablo Duarte

Películas: *Nueba Yol, Cuatro hombres y un ataúd*

Música: merengue, bachata, Wilfrido Vargas, Johnny Ventura, Milly Quezada

Comidas y bebidas: el mangú, el sancocho, el asopao, el refresco rojo, la mamajuana

Fiestas: Día de la Independencia (27 de febrero), Día de la Señora de la Altagracia (21 de enero)

Un vendedor de cocos en Boca Chica

Construido en 1976, Altos de Chavón es una recreación de un pueblo medieval de Europa.

CURIOSIDADES

- La isla que comparten *(share)* la República Dominicana y Haití, La Española, estuvo bajo control español hasta 1697, cuando la parte oeste *(western)* pasó a ser territorio francés.

- La República Dominicana tiene algunas de las construcciones más antiguas dejadas *(left)* por los españoles.

- Se cree que los restos de Cristóbal Colón están enterrados *(buried)* en Santo Domingo, pero Colón también tiene una tumba en Sevilla, España.

- En Santo Domingo se construyeron la primera catedral, el primer hospital, la primera aduana *(customs office)* y la primera universidad del Nuevo Mundo.

- Santo Domingo fue declarada Patrimonio de la Humanidad *(World Heritage)* por la UNESCO.

Uruguay

INFORMACIÓN GENERAL

iLrn™ Para aprender más sobre Uruguay, mira el video cultural en la mediateca (*Media Library*).

Nombre oficial: República Oriental del Uruguay

Nacionalidad: uruguayo(a)

Área: 176 215 km^2 (casi exactamente igual al estado de Washington)

Población: 3 333 000

Capital: Montevideo (f. 1726) (1 973 000 hab.)

Otras ciudades importantes: Salto, Paysandú, Punta del Este

Moneda: peso (uruguayo)

Idiomas: español (oficial)

DEMOGRAFÍA

Alfabetismo: 98%

Religiones: católicos (47,1%), protestantes (11%), otros (42%)

URUGUAYOS CÉLEBRES

Delmira Agustini
poetisa (1886–1914)

Mario Benedetti
escritor (1920–2009)

Jorge Drexler
músico, actor, médico (1964–)

Diego Forlán
futbolista (1979–)

José "Pepe" Mujica
presidente (1935–)

Julio Sosa
cantor de tango (1926–1964)

Horacio Quiroga
escritor (1878–1937)

Alfredo Zitarrosa
compositor (1936–1989)

Plaza Independencia, Montevideo (Palacio Salvo)

© VojtechVlk/Shutterstock

Carnaval de Montevideo

🌐 **Investiga en Internet**

La geografía: Punta del Este, Colonia

La historia: el Carnaval de Montevideo, los tablados, José Artigas

Películas: *Whisky, 25 Watts, Una forma de bailar, Joya, El baño del Papa, El Chevrolé, El viaje hacia el mar*

Música: tango, milonga, candombe, Jorge Drexler, Rubén Rada, La vela puerca

Comidas y bebidas: el asado, el dulce de leche, la faina, el chivito, el mate

Fiestas: Día de la Independencia (25 de agosto), Carnaval (febrero)

Colonia del Sacramento

CURIOSIDADES

● En guaraní, "Uruguay" significa "río *(river)* de las gallinetas". La gallineta es un pájaro de esta región.

● La industria ganadera *(cattle)* es una de las más importantes del país. La bebida más popular es el mate. Es muy común ver a los uruguayos caminando con el termo bajo el brazo, listo para tomar mate en cualquier lugar.

● Los descendientes de esclavos africanos que vivieron en esa zona dieron origen a *(gave rise to)* la música típica de Uruguay: el candombe.

● Uruguay fue el anfitrión *(host)* y el primer campeón de la Copa Mundial de Fútbol en 1930.

Venezuela ▶

INFORMACIÓN GENERAL

iLrn Para aprender más sobre Venezuela, mira el video cultural en la mediateca (*Media Library*).

Nombre oficial: República Bolivariana de Venezuela

Nacionalidad: venezolano(a)

Área: 912 050 km² (2800 km de costas) (aproximadamente 6 veces el área de Florida)

Población: 28 868 486

Capital: Caracas (f. 1567) (3 051 000 hab.)

Otras ciudades importantes: Maracaibo, Valencia, Maracay Barquisimeto

Moneda: bolívar

Idiomas: español (oficial), guajiro, wayuu y otras lenguas amerindias

DEMOGRAFÍA

Alfabetismo: 95,5%

Religiones: católicos (96%), protestantes (2%), otros (2%)

VENEZOLANOS CÉLEBRES

Andrés Eloy Blanco
escritor (1897–1955)

Simón Bolívar
libertador (1783–1830)

Hugo Chávez
militar, presidente (1954–2013)

Gustavo Dudamel
músico, director de
orquesta (1981–)

Lupita Ferrer
actriz (1947–)

Rómulo Gallegos
escritor (1884–1969)

Carolina Herrera
diseñadora (1939–)

© Vadim Petrakov/Shutterstock

El Salto Ángel, la catarata *(waterfall)* más alta del mundo

Investiga en Internet

La geografía: El Salto Ángel, la isla Margarita, el Amazonas Parque Nacional Canaima

La historia: los yanomami, el petróleo, Simón Bolívar, Francisco de la Miranda

Películas: *Punto y Raya, Secuestro Express*

Música: el joropo, Ricardo Montaner, Franco de Vita, Chino y Nacho, Carlos Baute, Óscar de León

Comidas y bebidas: el ceviche, las hallacas, las arepas, el carato de guanábana, el guarapo de papelón

Fiestas: Día de la Independencia (5 de julio), Nuestra Señora de la Candelaria (2 de febrero)

El Obelisco, en el centro de Plaza Francia en la ciudad de Caracas, fue en su momento la construcción más alta de la ciudad.

Isla Margarita, popular destino turístico

CURIOSIDADES

- El nombre de Venezuela ("pequeña Venecia") se debe a Américo Vespucio, quien llamó así a una de las islas costeras en 1499, debido a su aspecto veneciano.

- La isla Margarita es un lugar turístico muy popular. Cuando los españoles llegaron hace más de 500 años *(more than 500 years ago)*, los indígenas de la isla, los guaiqueríes, pensaron *(thought)* que eran dioses y les dieron *(gave)* regalos y una ceremonia de bienvenida. Gracias a esto, los guaiqueríes fueron los únicos indígenas del Caribe que tuvieron el estatus de "vasallos libres".

- En la época moderna Venezuela se destaca *(stands out)* por sus concursos *(contests)* de belleza y por su producción internacional de telenovelas.

- En Venezuela hay tres sitios considerados Patrimonio de la Humanidad *(World Heritage)* por la UNESCO: Coro y su puerto, el Parque Nacional de Canaima, y la Ciudad Universitaria de Caracas.

- En Venezuela habita un roedor *(rodent)* llamado chigüire que llega a pesar hasta 60 kilos.

Los Latinos en los Estados Unidos ▶

INFORMACIÓN GENERAL

Nombre oficial: Estados Unidos de América

Nacionalidad: estadounidense

Área: 9 826 675 km² (aproximadamente el área de China o 3,5 veces el área de Argentina)

Población: 318 892 103 (2010) (aproximadamente el 15% se consideran de origen hispano)

Capital: Washington, D.C. (f. 1791) (6 000 000 hab.)

Otras ciudades importantes: Nueva York, Los Ángeles, Chicago, Miami

Moneda: dólar (estadounidense)

Idiomas: inglés (oficial), español y más de 200 otros

(iLrn™) Para aprender más sobre Los Latinos en los Estados Unidos, mira el video cultural en la mediateca (*Media Library*).

DEMOGRAFÍA

Alfabetismo: 99%

Religiones: protestantes (51,3%), católicos (23,9%), mormones (1,7%), judíos (1,7%) y otros

HISPANOS CÉLEBRES DE ESTADOS UNIDOS

Christina Aguilera
cantante (1980–)

Julia Álvarez
escritora (1950–)

Marc Anthony
cantante (1969–)

César Chávez
activista por los derechos de los trabajadores (1927–1993)

Sandra Cisneros
escritora (1954–)

Junot Díaz
escritor (1968–)

Eva Longoria
actriz (1975–)

Soledad O'Brien
periodista, presentadora (1966–)

Ellen Ochoa
astronauta (1958–)

Edward James Olmos
actor (1947–)

Sonia Sotomayor
Juez Asociada de la Corte Suprema de Justicia de EE.UU. (1954–)

© Jeff Greenberg/The Image Works

La Pequeña Habana en Miami, Florida

Investiga en Internet

La geografía: regiones que pertenecieron a México, lugares con arquitectura de estilo español, Plaza Olvera, Calle 8, La Pequeña Habana

La historia: el Álamo, la Guerra Mexicoamericana, la Guerra Hispanoamericana, Antonio López de Santa Anna

Películas: *A Day without Mexicans, My Family, Stand and Deliver, Tortilla Soup*

Música: salsa, tejano (Tex-Mex), merengue, hip hop en español, Jennifer López, Selena

Comidas y bebidas: los tacos, las enchiladas, los burritos, los plátanos fritos, los frijoles, el arroz con gandules, la cerveza con limón

Fiestas: Día de la Batalla de Puebla (5 de mayo)

Un mural de Benito Juárez en Chicago, Illinois

El Álamo, donde Santa Anna derrotó *(defeated)* a los tejanos en una batalla de la Revolución de Texas.

CURIOSIDADES

- Los latinos son la primera minoría de Estados Unidos (más de 46 millones). Este grupo incluye personas que provienen de los veintiún países de habla hispana y a los hijos y nietos de estas que nacieron *(were born)* en los Estados Unidos. Muchos hablan español perfectamente y otros no lo hablan para nada. El grupo más grande de latinos es el de mexicanoamericanos, ya que territorios como Texas, Nuevo México, Utah, Nevada, California, Colorado y Oregón eran parte de México.

- Actualmente todas las culturas latinoamericanas están representadas en los Estados Unidos.

Partner Activities

Capítulo 1

1.5 **Correo electrónico** You and your partner are in charge of your school's Club Internacional. You have information for half of the new members on this page and your partner has the other half on page 5. Ask each other questions to complete the tables. You will need the following words: **arroba** (@) and **punto** *(dot)*.

> **Modelo** Estudiante 1: *¿Cuál es el correo electrónico de Pilar?*
> Estudiante 2: *pilybonita@uden.es → p-i-l-y-b-o-n-i-t-a,*
> *arroba, u-d-e-n, punto, e-s*

Nombre	Correo electrónico
1. Marina	marichiqui@ubbi.ar
2. Gabriel	
3. Alejandro	elmeroale@claro.mex
4. Valeria	

1.22 **La fila** Work with a partner to figure out the names of the people in the stands. One of you will look at this page, and the other will look at the picture on page 19. Take turns giving the name of a person and a description, so your partner will know who it is.

© Cengage Learning

1.37 Diferencias Working with a partner, one of you will look at the picture on this page, and the other will look at the picture on page 35. Take turns describing the pictures using the expression **hay,** numbers, and the classroom vocabulary. Find the eight differences.

Modelo Estudiante 1: *Hay una computadora.*
Estudiante 2: *Sí, y hay una silla.*
Estudiante 1: *No, no hay una silla.*

© Cengage Learning

Capítulo 2

2.5 Una familia You and your partner each have half of the information about the Navarro family. One of you will look at the drawing on this page, the other one will look at the drawing on page 41. Take turns asking the names of the different people.

Modelo Estudiante 1: *¿Cómo se llama el hermano de Sofía?*
Estudiante 2: *Se llama Miguel.*

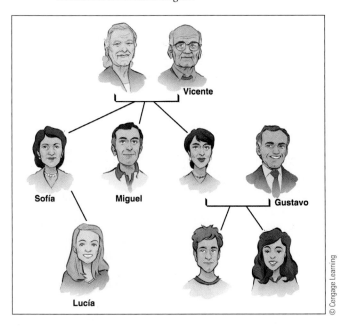

© Cengage Learning

2.23 **La graduación** In order to graduate, each student must take one class in each of the following categories: natural science, social science, math, humanities (**las humanidades**), and language. You and your partner must check the schedules of four students to determine which courses they have taken, and which ones they need. One of you will look at the information on this page and the other will look at page 55.

> **Modelo** Estudiante 1: *¿Tiene (has) Raúl Ruiz Costa una clase de ciencias naturales?*
> Estudiante 2: *Sí, Raúl tiene biología.*
> Estudiante 1: *¿Tiene Raúl una clase de humanidades?*
> Estudiante 2: *No, él necesita una clase de humanidades.*

Ramón Ayala Pérez	Andrea Gómez Ramos	Diana Salazar Casas	Hugo Vargas Díaz
arte		ingeniería	
química		física	
informática		alemán	
geografía		cálculo	
educación física			

2.41 **Datos personales** Working with a partner, look at the chart below while your partner looks at the chart on page 71. Take turns asking questions to fill in the missing information.

> **Modelo** *¿Cuántos años tiene Diego?* *Diego tiene veinte años.*
> *¿Qué parientes hay en la familia de Diego?* *Diego tiene dos hermanos.*
> *¿Qué clase tiene Diego?* *Diego tiene informática.*

Nombre	Edad	Familia	Clase
Diego	20	dos hermanos	informática
Alonso		una sobrina	
Magdalena			esquia
Cristina	30	cinco primos	
Pablo	62		
Gabriel	25		cálculo
Rufina		un esposo	alemán

Capítulo 3

3.5 **Los regalos** A friend sent a care package for the rest of your friends but forgot to label who everything was for, so you and a classmate need to clarify. One of you will look at the drawing on this page, and the other at the drawing on page 79.

> **Modelo** Estudiante 1: *¿Para quién (For whom) son los calcetines rojos?*
> Estudiante 2: *Los calcetines rojos son para Emilia.*

3.25 La tele En parejas túrnense para preguntar a qué hora son los programas y en qué canal son. Uno mira la programación y las preguntas aquí y el otro mira la página 93. *(With a partner, take turns asking what times the shows are on and on what channel. One will look at the guide and questions here, and the other will look at page 93).*

Modelo Estudiante 1: *¿A qué hora es* Vacaciones en familia?
Estudiante 2: Veredicto final *es a las dos de la tarde.*
Estudiante 1: *¿En qué canal es?*
Estudiante 2: *Es en Cine Canal.*

PROGRAMACIÓN ○ Películas ○ Especiales ○ Deportes ○ Nuevos

			14:00	14:30	15:00	15:30	16:00	16:30	17:00	17:30	18:00	18:30	19:00
Jueves 10 de agosto	Canal 5		Veredicto final			Será anunciada				Difícil de creer		Quiero amarte	
	Discovery Channel	Cable 35	MythBusters: Cazadores		Cazadores de Monstruos		Adictos	Adictos	Rides 3		Los Archivos del FBI		
	TNT	Cable 37	(:15)★★"Aprendiendo a Vivir" (1995) Peter Falk, D.B. Sweeney.					★ "Las Aventuras de Rocky y Bullwinkle" (2000)				Harry Potter	
	Cine Canal	Digital 482	"Vacaciones en Familia"		(:10)★★★"Las Ballenas de Agosto" (1987, Drama)				(16:55) "Durmiendo con el Enemigo"			Seducción	

¿A qué hora es... ?

1. El Chapulín Colorado
2. Dos Ilusiones
3. A los 30 Años
4. Gritos del Más Allá

3.41 Ocho diferencias Trabaja con un compañero. Uno mira la ilustración aquí y el otro mira la ilustración en la página 109. Túrnense para describir su ilustración y buscar las ocho diferencias. *(Work with a partner. One of you will look at the illustration on this page and the other will look at the illustration on page 109. Take turns describing the illustrations to find the eight differences.)*

© Cengage Learning

Capítulo 4

4.5 **Planes para el fin de semana** Trabaja con un compañero para descubrir cuáles son las actividades de Jazmín, Lila y Arturo durante el fin de semana y dónde las hacen. Uno de ustedes va a ver la información en esta página, y el otro va a ver la información en la página 115.

> **Modelo** Estudiante 1: *¿Qué hace Lila el sábado por la mañana?*
> Estudiante 2: *Lila corre.*
> Estudiante 1: *¿Dónde corre?*
> Estudiante 2: *En el gimnasio.*

	Jazmín	**Lila**	**Arturo**
sábado por la mañana		correr (el gimnasio)	
sábado por la tarde	caminar (el parque)		tomar fotos (el zoológico)
sábado por la noche	bailar (un club)	comer (un café)	
domingo por la mañana			buscar libros (la librería)

4.23 **Comparemos** Trabaja con un compañero. Uno de ustedes mira la casa en esta página mientras el otro mira la casa en la página 129. Túrnense para describir las casas y busquen las seis diferencias.

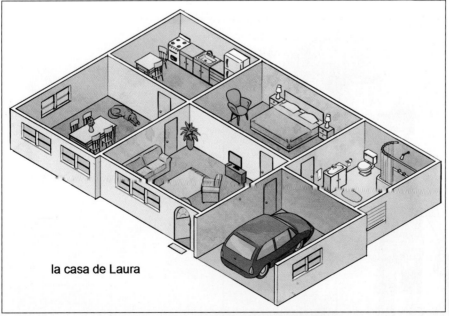

la casa de Laura

© Cengage Learning

4.37 **Seis diferencias** Trabaja con un compañero. Uno mira el dibujo aquí y el otro mira el dibujo en la página 145. Túrnense para describirlos y buscar seis diferencias.

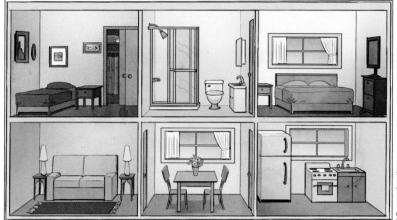

© Cengage Learning

Capítulo 5

5.6 **Los chismes (*gossip*)** Imagina que tu compañero y tú están intercambiando información sobre cómo están todos sus amigos. Uno de ustedes va a ver la tabla en esta página, y el otro va a ver la página 153. **¡OJO!** ¡Presta atención a la concordancia (*agreement*)!

Modelo Estudiante 1: *¿Cómo está Ramira?*
Estudiante 2: *Está contenta.*
Estudiante 1: *¿Por qué?*
Estudiante 2: *Porque va a ir de vacaciones a Venezuela.*

Nombre	¿Cómo está(n)?	¿Por qué?
Ramira	contento	Va a ir de vacaciones a Venezuela.
Emanuel y Arturo		Tienen mucha tarea.
Gisela		
Alex	avergonzado	
Karina e Iliana	enamorado	Sus novios son perfectos.
Gerardo		Va a tener varios exámenes difíciles.
Javier y Manuel	aburrido	

5.23 **Personas famosas** Trabaja con un compañero para completar la información. Uno de ustedes debe ver la tabla en esta página y el otro debe ver la tabla en la página 167. Túrnense para preguntar y responder.

Nombre	Profesión	País de origen
Alicia Alonso		Cuba
Óscar de la Renta	diseñador	
Andrea Serna		
Baruj Benacerraf	médico	Venezuela
Gabriela Mistral		Chile
Luis Federico Leloir	científico	

5.40 **Información, por favor** Trabaja con un compañero para completar la información. Uno debe mirar el gráfico en esta página y el otro debe mirar el gráfico en la página 183. Atención al uso de **ser** y **estar.**

Nombre	Profesión	Origen	Localización	Emoción
Carlota	pintora			alegre
Éric	arquitecto	Bogotá		
César			el café	
Paloma		Santiago		nerviosa
Samuel	escritor			ocupado
Camila		Montevideo	el teatro	

Capítulo 6

6.6 **Unos monstruos** Trabaja con un compañero. Uno debe mirar el dibujo aquí y el otro va a mirar el dibujo en la página 189. Túrnense para describir los monstruos y encontrar las cinco diferencias.

© Cengage Learning

6.25 **Actividades de verano** Los organizadores de los eventos de verano para una pequeña ciudad están intercambiando información sobre el equipo que necesitan y las actividades que tienen planeadas. Trabaja con un compañero para completar la información. Uno de ustedes debe ver la información en esta página y el otro debe ver la información en la página 203.

Evento	Lugar del evento	Equipo que tienen	Equipo/recursos que necesitan
1. Torneo de fútbol	la universidad		
2.		sacos de dormir	tiendas de campaña
3. Clases de natación		la piscina	
4.	el gimnasio de la preparatoria		raquetas
5. Torneo de voleibol			pelotas

6.41 **¿Qué hizo?** Dante es estudiante de secundaria pero no es muy aplicado *(dedicated)*. Con un compañero, túrnense para completar la información sobre lo que hizo *(what he did)* esta mañana. Uno de ustedes va a mirar la información en esta página y el otro va a mirar la página 219.

> Modelo   Estudiante 1: *¿Qué hizo a medianoche?*
> Estudiante 2: *Se acostó.*

12:00	acostarse
7:00	levantarse
7:30	
7:40	
8:00	cepillarse los dientes
8:55	
9:35	dormirse en clase
9:58	despertarse y correr a otra clase
10:10	
10:30	volver a clase
11:00	

Capítulo 7

7.6 **¿Cuánto cuesta?** Trabaja con un compañero. Uno de ustedes va a ver la información en esta página y el otro debe ver la página 227. Imagínense que están en dos supermercados diferentes en Chile. Llámense por teléfono para preguntar cuánto cuestan los productos de cada ilustración. Los precios que tu compañero necesita están abajo. Tomen notas y al final sumen *(add)* los totales. ¿Quién va a gastar más?

Tu compañero quiere comprar...

Tú quieres comprar...

1 kilo

500 gramos

500 gramos

250 gramos

3 kilos

Un ananás (piña) $1650
choclo (maíz), un kilo $1432
mantequilla ($522)
queso, un kilo $1725

plátanos, un kilo $439
uvas, un kilo, $811
crema, 200 gramos, $715
pan, $1150

7.24 **Comparemos** Trabaja con un compañero. Uno va a mirar el dibujo en esta página y el otro va a mirar el dibujo en la página 241. Túrnense para describir los dibujos y encontrar cinco diferencias.

© Cengage Learning

© Cengage Learning

7.41 **La fiesta** Tu compañero y tú están planeando una cena para unos amigos, pero los invitados tienen algunas restricciones en su dieta. Uno de ustedes mira la información en esta página y el otro mira la información en la página 257. Compartan la información sobre sus dietas y luego decidan qué van a servir del menú abajo.

> **aperitivo:** queso, totopos con salsa
>
> **primer plato:** ensalada con vinagreta, sopa de fideos *(noodles)*
>
> **segundo plato:** carne asada con papas fritas, fajitas con tortillas de maíz y verduras asadas
>
> **postre:** ensalada de frutas, pastel de chocolate
>
> **bebida:** té helado, limonada

Invitado	Restricción
Angélica	Es vegetariana.
Lucas	
Mateo	No puede consumir cafeína.
Regina	
Javier	Es intolerante a la lactosa.
Gisa	

Capítulo 8

8.6 **Compañeros de casa** Javier, Marcos y Emanuel decidieron vivir juntos y quieren organizarse para hacer los quehaceres de la casa que les gustan. Trabaja con un compañero para completar la tabla. Uno de ustedes va a ver la información en esta página, y el otro debe ver la información en la página 263. Primero completen el gráfico y después decidan quién va a hacer cada quehacer. Cada persona debe tener dos obligaciones.

Quehacer	Javier	Marcos	Emanuel	¿Quién va a hacerlo?
Lavar los platos	Le gusta.		No le gusta.	
Limpiar los baños		No le gusta.		
Trapear la cocina			No le gusta.	
Pasar la aspiradora	Le gusta.	No le gusta.	No le gusta.	
Cortar el césped	No le gusta.			
Regar las plantas		Le gusta.		

8.25 **Las actividades favoritas** Irma y Mario tienen que cuidar a varios niños todo el sábado. Irma quiere ir de excursión con la mitad de los niños, pero Mario quiere cuidarlos desde su casa porque tiene que trabajar. Trabaja con un compañero para saber qué actividades le gustan a los niños y después decidir cuáles son los niños que van a ir con Irma y quiénes se van a quedar con Mario. Un compañero debe mirar la tabla en la página 277.

> **Modelo** *¿Cuál es la actividad favorita de Manuela?*
> *¿A quién le gusta volar cometas?*

Niño	Actividad favorita	¿Con quién debe pasar el sábado?
Manuela	volar cometas	
	ir de paseo	
Nadia	nadar	
Alejandro	navegar por Internet	
	dibujar	
	trepar árboles	
Humberto	jugar juegos de mesa	

8.41 **Regalos** Tu compañero necesita comprar regalos para el cumpleaños de los hijos gemelos *(twins)* de un amigo (un niño y una niña). Encontró buenos regalos en un sitio web, pero no dan los precios. Tu compañero llama y pregunta cuánto cuestan los juguetes para decidir qué les va a comprar. Mira la lista de precios y contesta sus preguntas.

> **Modelo** *¿Cuánto cuesta el muñeco azul?*
> *Cuesta $32.*

© Cengage Learning

Capítulo 9

9.5 **Las tradiciones** Hay muchas tradiciones interesantes con las que las personas reciben el año nuevo. Trabaja con un compañero. Uno de ustedes va a ver la ilustración en esta página y el otro va a describir la ilustración en página 301. Describan sus ilustraciones (sin ver la otra) para encontrar las seis diferencias.

© Cengage Learning

9.22 **Contradicciones** Tu compañero y tú son testigos de un accidente, pero hay diferencias entre sus dos versiones. Uno de ustedes va a observar la ilustración en esta página y el otro va a observar la ilustración en la página 315. Encuentren las cinco diferencias.

9.39 **El periodista** Un periodista habla con un testigo sobre el accidente que vio. Trabaja con un compañero. Uno de ustedes es el periodista y hace las preguntas en la página 331, prestando atención al uso del pretérito o el imperfecto. El otro es el testigo y mira los dibujos en esta página para responder las preguntas.

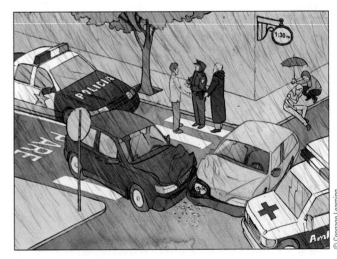

Capítulo 10

10.6 **¿Vamos por tren o por avión?** Tu compañero y tú están estudiando en Quito, Ecuador y quieren viajar este fin de semana. Deben decidir si van a viajar por avión a Cuenca, o por tren a Latacunga. Uno de ustedes puede ver la información para viajar por tren en esta página y el otro va a ver la información para viajar por avión en la página 337. Intercambien la información y tomen notas. Después van a ponerse de acuerdo *(agree)* en cómo van a viajar y a qué hora. Compartan toda la información antes de decidir.

TREN ECUADOR.COM

Ruta "Avenida de los volcanes", Quito–Machachi–El Boliche–Latacunga–Quito

Salida	Llegada	Regreso*	Precio por pasajero
4:20 AM	12:00 PM	3:30 PM	$38,00
8:00 AM	1:00 PM	3:30 PM	$40,00
10:00 AM	2:45 PM	5:45 PM	$44,95

*Regreso el mismo día

10.24 **¿Qué hotel elegir?** Tu compañero y tú están planeando unas vacaciones en Costa Rica y hablan por teléfono para decidir qué hotel elegir. Hay solamente dos hoteles que tienen habitaciones disponibles. Uno de ustedes va a mirar la información en esta página y el otro debe mirar la página 351. Pregúntense sobre los servicios y decidan al final en qué hotel van a quedarse.

Hotel Bellavista Monteverde

Descripción: 40 habitaciones, localizado en el centro de Monteverde, cerca de bancos y restaurantes.

Servicios: baño privado, televisor, Internet inalámbrico, cafetería abierta de 6:00 AM a 10:00 PM.

Precio: 115.000 colones (habitación doble/triple).

10.42 **En la agencia de viajes** Trabaja con un compañero. Uno de ustedes es el agente de viajes y mira la información en la página 367. El otro es el cliente y mira la información en esta página. El cliente llama al agente de viajes para comprar un boleto. El agente de viajes debe intentar encontrar el mejor boleto para el cliente y conseguir su información (nombre, teléfono, etcétera) y su tarjeta de crédito.

El cliente
Necesitas viajar a Santiago, Chile para una reunión el viernes por la mañana.

- Quieres viajar el jueves.
- Prefieres viajar por la tarde.
- No quieres tener escalas.
- Te gusta sentarte al lado de la ventanilla.
- No quieres pagar más de $750.

Capítulo 11

11.5 **Diferencias** Trabaja con un compañero para encontrar las ocho diferencias. Uno de ustedes va a mirar la ilustración en esta página y el otro va a mirar el dibujo en la página 375. Túrnense para describir la escena y encontrar las diferencias.

11.23 **Una exhibición de arte** Un museo local quiere montar una exhibición con obras de diferentes artistas hispanos, pero solo tiene el presupuesto *(budget)* para tres artistas diferentes. Tu compañero y tú deben compartir la información sobre los artistas y después decidir qué artistas presentar. Estén preparados para explicar por qué.

Artista	Medio	País	Año	Nombre del cuadro y estilo
1. Oswaldo Guayasamín		Ecuador		*El Presidente,* cubista
2. Mario Carreño			1981	*Mascarón de Proa,* surrealista
3. Joan Miró	pintura, escultura			
4. Marisol Escobar	escultura		2006	*El Padre Damian,* ecléctico
5. Diego Rivera		México	1928	
6. Roberto Matta	pintura	Chile		

11.39 **Un pedido** Trabaja con un compañero. Uno de ustedes es el vendedor y el otro es el cliente. El cliente necesita ropa para un viaje a la playa. Debe ver la información del catálogo en la página 405 y llamar para hacer un pedido. Necesita comprar tres prendas. El vendedor necesita ver esta página para contestar las preguntas del cliente y conseguir su información (nombre, teléfono, etcétera) y su tarjeta de crédito.

Modelo Estudiante 1: *Buenas tardes.*
Estudiante 2: *Buenas tardes. Necesito una camiseta de algodón azul en talla extra grande.*
Estudiante 1: *Lo siento. No la tenemos en talla extra grande.*
Estudiante 2: *¿Qué colores tienen en talla extra grande?*

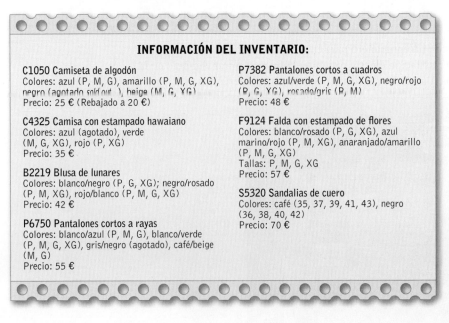

INFORMACIÓN DEL INVENTARIO:

C1050 Camiseta de algodón
Colores: azul (P, M, G), amarillo (P, M, G, XG), negro (agotado *sold out*), beige (M, G, XG)
Precio: 25 € (Rebajado a 20 €)

C4325 Camisa con estampado hawaiano
Colores: azul (agotado), verde (M, G, XG), rojo (P, XG)
Precio: 35 €

B2219 Blusa de lunares
Colores: blanco/negro (P, G, XG); negro/rosado (P, M, XG), rojo/blanco (P, M, G, XG)
Precio: 42 €

P6750 Pantalones cortos a rayas
Colores: blanco/azul (P, M, G), blanco/verde (P, M, G, XG), gris/negro (agotado), café/beige (M, G)
Precio: 55 €

P7382 Pantalones cortos a cuadros
Colores: azul/verde (P, M, G, XG), negro/rojo (P, G, YG), rosado/gris (P, M)
Precio: 48 €

F9124 Falda con estampado de flores
Colores: blanco/rosado (P, G, XG), azul marino/rojo (P, M, XG), anaranjado/amarillo (P, M, G, XG)
Tallas: P, M, G, XG
Precio: 57 €

S5320 Sandalias de cuero
Colores: café (35, 37, 39, 41, 43), negro (36, 38, 40, 42)
Precio: 70 €

© Cengage Learning

Capítulo 12

12.5 **Las descripciones** Trabaja con un compañero. Uno de ustedes (Estudiante 1) va a describirle el dibujo en la página 411 a su compañero (Estudiante 2) quien debe dibujar lo que escucha sin ver la ilustración. Al terminar comparen el original y el nuevo dibujo. Después el Estudiante 2 debe describir el dibujo en esta página, y el Estudiante 1 va a dibujarlo.

12.25 **Donaciones** Imagina que un compañero y tú trabajan para el *World Wildlife Fund*. Uno de ustedes va a trabajar con la tabla en esta página, y el otro va a completar la tabla en la página 425. Compartan la información para completarla, y después decidan para qué animal deben hacer la siguiente campaña para recibir más donaciones.

ESPECIE	DONACIONES	PAÍS/ REGIÓN
1. Pingüino imperial		
2. El orangután		Indonesia
3. El jaguar		Latinoamérica
4. El oso frontino	$129.467,00	
5. El cóndor andino	$871.034,00	
6. El oso polar	$1.209.654,00	El ártico

12.41 **La granja** Mira uno de los dibujos y tu compañero va a mirar el otro en la página 441. Túrnense para describir las granjas y encontrar las cinco diferencias.

13.6 **Una relación** La siguiente es una historia ilustrada de cómo evolucionó la relación entre Mercedes y Juan Sebastián. Trabaja con un compañero y túrnense para describir sus dibujos (numerados del 1 al 8) y completar la historia. Uno de ustedes va a describir las imágenes en esta página, y el otro las de la página 449.

13.24 **En familia** Trabaja con un compañero para descubrir las cinco diferencias. Uno de ustedes mira este dibujo y el otro mira el dibujo en la página 463. Túrnense para describirlos y encontrar las cinco diferencias.

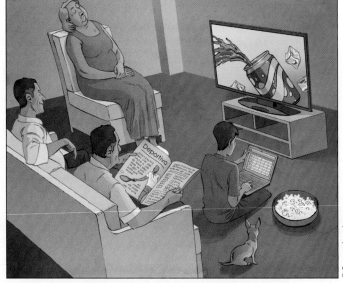

13.41 **¿Cuál es la pregunta?** Trabaja con un compañero. Uno de ustedes debe ver las preguntas en esta página, y el otro debe verlas en la página 479. Es una competencia y el ganador *(winner)* es quien tenga más puntos. Obtienes puntos cuando adivinas la pregunta <u>exacta</u> que tiene tu compañero. Para ayudarte, tu compañero te va a decir la respuesta a la pregunta. Tienes tres oportunidades para adivinar cada pregunta.

Modelo ¿Qué es extrañar?

> Estudiante 1: *Es cuando no estás con una persona y estás triste. Piensas mucho en la persona.*
>
> Estudiante 2: *¿Qué es extrañar?*

Puntos	Preguntas
10	¿Qué es el noviazgo?
20	¿Qué hay en una recepción?
30	¿Qué es la unión libre?
40	¿Qué hacemos en la vejez?
50	¿Quién es la prometida?
100	¿Qué es comprometerse?

Capítulo 14

14.5 **Diferencias** Trabaja con un compañero. Uno mira el dibujo en esta página y el otro mira el dibujo en la página 485. Túrnense para describir sus dibujos y encontrar las cinco diferencias.

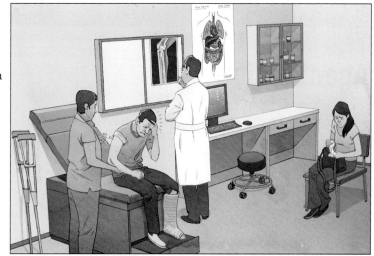

© Cengage Learning

14.23 **El Mundial** Un amigo y tú quieren sorprender a todos sus amigos con fiestas para ver los juegos del Mundial de Fútbol. Tu compañero debe mirar la información en la página 499. Túrnense para completar las nacionalidades de sus amigos y el horario de los partidos. Al final encontrarán las cinco fechas cuando deberán tener las fiestas.

Preguntas posibles: *¿Cuál es la nacionalidad de Juan José?*
¿Cuándo es el juego número uno? / ¿Quiénes juegan el juego número uno?

Amigos:

NOMBRE	Mundo	Jazmín	Marco	Pío	Marcelo	Yolanda
PAÍS		colombiana			ecuatoriano	paraguaya

Horario de juegos:

Juego 1		10 de junio	Juego 5	España vs. EEUU	
Juego 2	Colombia vs. México		Juego 6		19 de junio
Juego 3	Argentina vs. Chile		Juego 7	Bélgica vs. Paraguay	
Juego 4		16 de junio	Juego 8		24 de junio

¿Cuáles son los cinco partidos que deben ver y cuándo?

14.39 **Un diagnóstico** Imagínate que eres médico y que vas a consultar con otro médico sobre algunos pacientes. Trabaja con un compañero para completar la información. Uno va a mirar la información en esta página y el otro va a mirar la información en la página 515.

Modelo Olivia Aragón   estornudos, ojos irritados
Estudiante 1: *Olivia Aragón estornuda mucho y tiene ojos irritados.*
Estudiante 2: *Debe tomar pastillas para las alergias y no salir al jardín en la primavera.*

Nombre	Síntomas	Remedio
Bruno Medina		tomar pastillas, reducir el sodio
Lourdes Montes	falta de energía, insomnio	
Saúl Reyes		tomar jarabe para el resfriado
Aranza Rivera	náusea, mareos	
Ileana Castro		tomar antibióticos, quedarse en cama
Esteban Peña	dolor de cabeza, mareos	

Acentuación

In Spanish, as in English, all words of two or more syllables have one syllable that is stressed more forcibly than the others. In Spanish, written accents are frequently used to show which syllable in a word is the stressed one.

Words without written accents

Words without written accents are pronounced according to the following rules:

A. Words that end in a vowel (**a, e, i, o, u**) or the consonants **n** or **s** are stressed on the next to last syllable.

     tardes   capi**ta**les   **gran**de   es**tu**dia   **no**ches   **co**men

B. Words that end in a consonant other than **n** or **s** are stressed on the last syllable.

     bus**car**   ac**triz**   espa**ñol**   liber**tad**   ani**mal**   come**dor**

Words with written accents

C. Words that do not follow the two preceding rules require a written accent to indicate where the stress is placed.

     ca**fé**   sim**pá**tico   fran**cés**   na**ción**   José **Pé**rez

Words with a strong vowel (a, o, u) next to a weak vowel (e, i)

D. Diphthongs, the combination of a weak vowel (**i, u**) and a strong vowel (**e, o, a**), or two weak vowels, next to each other, form a single syllable. A written accent is required to separate diphthongs into two syllables. Note that the written accent is placed on the weak vowel.

     s**ei**s   estu**dia**   inter**ior**   **ai**re   **au**to   c**iu**dad
     re**ír**   **dí**a   **rí**o   ma**íz**   ba**úl**   veint**iún**

Monosyllable words

E. Words with only one syllable never have a written accent unless there is a need to differentiate it from another word spelled exactly the same. The following are some of the most common words in this category.

Unaccented	Accented	Unaccented	Accented
como *(like, as)*	cómo *(how)*	que *(that)*	qué *(what)*
de *(of)*	dé *(give)*	si *(if)*	sí *(yes)*
el *(the)*	él *(he)*	te *(you D.O., to you)*	té *(tea)*
mas *(but)*	más *(more)*	tu *(your)*	tú *(you informal)*
mi *(my)*	mí *(me)*		

F. Keep in mind that in Spanish, the written accents are an extremely important part of spelling since they not only change the pronunciation of a word, but may change its meaning and/or its tense.

     publico *(I publish)*   **público** *(public)*   **publicó** *(he/she/you published)*

Appendix D

Los verbos regulares

Simple tenses

	Present Indicative	Imperfect	Preterite	Future	Conditional	Present Subjunctive	Past Subjunctive	Commands
hablar (to speak)	hablo	hablaba	hablé	hablaré	hablaría	hable	hablara	
	hablas	hablabas	hablaste	hablarás	hablarías	hables	hablaras	habla (no hables)
	habla	hablaba	habló	hablará	hablaría	hable	hablara	hable
	hablamos	hablábamos	hablamos	hablaremos	hablaríamos	hablemos	habláramos	hablemos
	habláis	hablabais	hablasteis	hablaréis	hablaríais	habléis	hablarais	hablad (no habléis)
	hablan	hablaban	hablaron	hablarán	hablarían	hablen	hablaran	hablen
aprender (to learn)	aprendo	aprendía	aprendí	aprenderé	aprendería	aprenda	aprendiera	
	aprendes	aprendías	aprendiste	aprenderás	aprenderías	aprendas	aprendieras	aprende (no aprendas)
	aprende	aprendía	aprendió	aprenderá	aprendería	aprenda	aprendiera	aprenda
	aprendemos	aprendíamos	aprendimos	aprenderemos	aprenderíamos	aprendamos	aprendiéramos	aprendamos
	aprendéis	aprendíais	aprendisteis	aprenderéis	aprenderíais	aprendáis	aprendierais	aprended (no aprendáis)
	aprenden	aprendían	aprendieron	aprenderán	aprenderían	aprendan	aprendieran	aprendan
vivir (to live)	vivo	vivía	viví	viviré	viviría	viva	viviera	
	vives	vivías	viviste	vivirás	vivirías	vivas	vivieras	vive (no vivas)
	vive	vivía	vivió	vivirá	viviría	viva	viviera	viva
	vivimos	vivíamos	vivimos	viviremos	viviríamos	vivamos	viviéramos	vivamos
	vivís	vivíais	vivisteis	viviréis	viviríais	viváis	vivierais	vivid (no viváis)
	viven	vivían	vivieron	vivirán	vivirían	vivan	vivieran	vivan

Compound tenses

Present progressive

estoy		
estás	hablando	aprendiendo
está		viviendo
estamos		
estáis		
están		

Present perfect indicative

he		
has	hablado	aprendido
ha		vivido
hemos		
habéis		
han		

Past perfect indicative

había		
habías	hablado	aprendido
había		vivido
habíamos		
habíais		
habían		

Los verbos con cambios en la raíz

Infinitive / Present Participle / Past Participle	Present Indicative	Imperfect	Preterite	Future	Conditional	Present Subjunctive	Past Subjunctive	Commands
pensar *to think* e → ie pensando pensado	**pienso** **piensas** **piensa** pensamos pensáis **piensan**	pensaba pensabas pensaba pensábamos pensabais pensaban	pensé pensaste pensó pensamos pensasteis pensaron	pensaré pensarás pensará pensaremos pensaréis pensarán	pensaría pensarías pensaría pensaríamos pensaríais pensarían	**piense** **pienses** **piense** pensemos penséis **piensen**	pensara pensaras pensara pensáramos pensarais pensaran	**piensa (no pienses)** **piense** pensemos pensad (no penséis) **piensen**
acostarse *to go to bed* o → ue acostándose acostado	me **acuesto** te **acuestas** se **acuesta** nos acostamos os acostáis se **acuestan**	me acostaba te acostabas se acostaba nos acostábamos os acostabais se acostaban	me acosté te acostaste se acostó nos acostamos os acostasteis se acostaron	me acostaré te acostarás se acostará nos acostaremos os acostaréis se acostarán	me acostaría te acostarías se acostaría nos acostaríamos os acostaríais se acostarían	me **acueste** te **acuestes** se **acueste** nos acostemos os acostéis se **acuesten**	me acostara te acostaras se acostara nos acostáramos os acostarais se acostaran	acuéstate (**no te acuestes**) **acuéstese** acostémonos acostaos (no os acostéis) **acuéstense**
sentir *to feel* e → ie, i sintiendo sentido	**siento** **sientes** **siente** sentimos sentís **sienten**	sentía sentías sentía sentíamos sentíais sentían	sentí sentiste **sintió** sentimos sentisteis **sintieron**	sentiré sentirás sentirá sentiremos sentiréis sentirán	sentiría sentirías sentiría sentiríamos sentiríais sentirían	**sienta** **sientas** **sienta** **sintamos** **sintáis** **sientan**	**sintiera** **sintieras** **sintiera** **sintiéramos** **sintierais** **sintieran**	**siente (no sientas)** **sienta** **sintamos (no sintáis)** sentid **sientan**
pedir *to ask for* e → i, i pidiendo pedido	**pido** **pides** **pide** pedimos pedís **piden**	pedía pedías pedía pedíamos pedíais pedían	pedí pediste **pidió** pedimos pedisteis **pidieron**	pediré pedirás pedirá pediremos pediréis pedirán	pediría pedirías pediría pediríamos pediríais pedirían	**pida** **pidas** **pida** **pidamos** **pidáis** **pidan**	**pidiera** **pidieras** **pidiera** **pidiéramos** **pidierais** **pidieran**	**pide (no pidas)** **pida** **pidamos** pedid (no pidáis) **pidan**
dormir *to sleep* o → ue, u durmiendo dormido	**duermo** **duermes** **duerme** dormimos dormís **duermen**	dormía dormías dormía dormíamos dormíais dormían	dormí dormiste **durmió** dormimos dormisteis **durmieron**	dormiré dormirás dormirá dormiremos dormiréis dormirán	dormiría dormirías dormiría dormiríamos dormiríais dormirían	**duerma** **duermas** **duerma** **durmamos** **durmáis** **duerman**	**durmiera** **durmieras** **durmiera** **durmiéramos** **durmierais** **durmieran**	**duerme (no duermas)** **duerma** **durmamos** dormid (**no durmáis**) **duerman**

Los verbos con cambios de ortografía

Infinitive Present Participle Past Participle	Present Indicative	Imperfect	Preterite	Future	Conditional	Present Subjunctive	Past Subjunctive	Commands
comenzar (e → ie) to begin z → c before e comenzando comenzado	comienzo comienzas comienza comenzamos comenzáis comienzan	comenzaba comenzabas comenzaba comenzábamos comenzabais comenzaban	**comencé** comenzaste comenzó comenzamos comenzasteis comenzaron	comenzaré comenzarás comenzará comenzaremos comenzaréis comenzarán	comenzaría comenzarías comenzaría comenzaríamos comenzaríais comenzarían	**comience comiences comience comencemos comencéis comiencen**	comenzara comenzaras comenzara comenzáramos comenzarais comenzaran	comienza (**no comiences**) **comience comencemos** comenzad (**no comencéis**) **comiencen**
conocer to know c → zc before a, o conociendo conocido	**conozco** conoces conoce conocemos conocéis conocen	conocía conocías conocía conocíamos conocíais conocían	conocí conociste conoció conocimos conocisteis conocieron	conoceré conocerás conocerá conoceremos conoceréis conocerán	conocería conocerías conocería conoceríamos conoceríais conocerían	**conozca conozcas conozca conozcamos conozcáis conozcan**	conociera conocieras conociera conociéramos conocierais conocieran	conoce (**no conozcas**) **conozca conozcamos** conoced (**no conozcáis**) **conozcan**
pagar to pay g → gu before e pagando pagado	pago pagas paga pagamos pagáis pagan	pagaba pagabas pagaba pagábamos pagabais pagaban	**pagué** pagaste pagó pagamos pagasteis pagaron	pagaré pagarás pagará pagaremos pagaréis pagarán	pagaría pagarías pagaría pagaríamos pagaríais pagarían	**pague pagues pague paguemos paguéis paguen**	pagara pagaras pagara pagáramos pagarais pagaran	paga (**no pagues**) **pague paguemos** pagad (**no paguéis**) **paguen**
seguir (e → i, i) to follow gu → g before a, o siguiendo seguido	**sigo** sigues sigue seguimos seguís siguen	seguía seguías seguía seguíamos seguíais seguian	seguí seguiste siguió seguimos seguisteis siguieron	seguiré seguirás seguirá seguiremos seguiréis seguirán	seguiría seguirías seguiría seguiríamos seguiríais seguirían	**siga sigas siga sigamos sigáis sigan**	siguiera siguieras siguiera siguiéramos siguierais siguieran	sigue (**no sigas**) **siga sigamos** seguid (**no sigáis**) **sigan**
tocar to play, to touch c → qu before e tocando tocado	toco tocas toca tocamos tocáis tocan	tocaba tocabas tocaba tocábamos tocabais tocaban	**toqué** tocaste tocó tocamos tocasteis tocaron	tocaré tocarás tocará tocaremos tocaréis tocarán	tocaría tocarías tocaría tocaríamos tocaríais tocarían	**toque toques toque toquemos toquéis toquen**	tocara tocaras tocara tocáramos tocarais tocaran	toca (**no toques**) **toque toquemos** tocad (**no toquéis**) **toquen**

Los verbos irregulares

Infinitive Present Participle Past Participle	Present Indicative	Imperfect	Preterite	Future	Conditional	Present Subjunctive	Past Subjunctive	Commands
andar *to walk* andando andado	ando	andaba	anduve	andaré	andaría	ande	anduviera	
	andas	andabas	anduviste	andarás	andarías	andes	anduvieras	anda (no andes)
	anda	andaba	anduvo	andará	andaría	ande	anduviera	ande
	andamos	andábamos	anduvimos	andaremos	andaríamos	andemos	anduviéramos	andemos
	andáis	andabais	anduvisteis	andaréis	andaríais	andéis	anduvierais	andad (no andéis)
	andan	andaban	anduvieron	andarán	andarían	anden	anduvieran	anden
*dar *to give* dando dado	doy	daba	di	daré	daría	dé	diera	
	das	dabas	diste	darás	darías	des	dieras	da (no des)
	da	daba	dio	dará	daría	dé	diera	dé
	damos	dábamos	dimos	daremos	daríamos	demos	diéramos	demos
	dais	dabais	disteis	daréis	daríais	deis	dierais	dad (no deis)
	dan	daban	dieron	darán	darían	den	dieran	den
*decir *to say, tell* diciendo dicho	digo	decía	dije	diré	diría	diga	dijera	
	dices	decías	dijiste	dirás	dirías	digas	dijeras	di (no digas)
	dice	decía	dijo	dirá	diría	diga	dijera	diga
	decimos	decíamos	dijimos	diremos	diríamos	digamos	dijéramos	digamos
	decís	decíais	dijisteis	diréis	diríais	digáis	dijerais	decid (no digáis)
	dicen	decían	dijeron	dirán	dirían	digan	dijeran	digan
*estar *to be* estando estado	estoy	estaba	estuve	estaré	estaría	esté	estuviera	
	estás	estabas	estuviste	estarás	estarías	estés	estuvieras	está (no estés)
	está	estaba	estuvo	estará	estaría	esté	estuviera	esté
	estamos	estábamos	estuvimos	estaremos	estaríamos	estemos	estuviéramos	estemos
	estáis	estabais	estuvisteis	estaréis	estaríais	estéis	estuvierais	estad (no estéis)
	están	estaban	estuvieron	estarán	estarían	estén	estuvieran	estén
haber *to have* habiendo habido	he	había	hube	habré	habría	haya	hubiera	
	has	habías	hubiste	habrás	habrías	hayas	hubieras	he (no hayas)
	ha [hay]	había	hubo	habrá	habría	haya	hubiera	haya
	hemos	habíamos	hubimos	habremos	habríamos	hayamos	hubiéramos	hayamos
	habéis	habíais	hubisteis	habréis	habríais	hayáis	hubierais	habed (no hayáis)
	han	habían	hubieron	habrán	habrían	hayan	hubieran	hayan
*hacer *to make, to do* haciendo hecho	hago	hacía	hice	haré	haría	haga	hiciera	
	haces	hacías	hiciste	harás	harías	hagas	hicieras	haz (no hagas)
	hace	hacía	hizo	hará	haría	haga	hiciera	haga
	hacemos	hacíamos	hicimos	haremos	haríamos	hagamos	hiciéramos	hagamos
	hacéis	hacíais	hicisteis	haréis	haríais	hagáis	hicierais	haced (no hagáis)
	hacen	hacían	hicieron	harán	harían	hagan	hicieran	hagan

*Verbs with irregular *yo* forms in the present indicative

(*continued*)

Infinitive Present Participle Past Participle	Present Indicative	Imperfect	Preterite	Future	Conditional	Present Subjunctive	Past Subjunctive	Commands
ir *to go* **yendo** ido	voy vas va vamos vais van	iba ibas iba íbamos ibais iban	fui fuiste fue fuimos fuisteis fueron	iré irás irá iremos iréis irán	iría irías iría iríamos iríais irían	**vaya** **vayas** **vaya** **vayamos** **vayáis** **vayan**	fuera fueras fuera fuéramos fuerais fueran	ve (no vayas) vaya vamos (no vayamos) id (no vayáis) vayan
*oír *to hear* **oyendo** oído	**oigo** oyes oye oímos oís **oyen**	oía oías oía oíamos oíais oían	oí oíste oyó oímos oísteis oyeron	oiré oirás oirá oiremos oiréis oirán	oiría oirías oiría oiríamos oiríais oirían	oiga oigas oiga oigamos oigáis oigan	oyera oyeras oyera oyéramos oyerais oyeran	oye (no oigas) oiga oigamos oíd (no oigáis) oigan
poder (o → ue) *can, to be able* **pudiendo** podido	**puedo** **puedes** **puede** podemos podéis **pueden**	podía podías podía podíamos podíais podían	pude pudiste pudo pudimos pudisteis pudieron	podré podrás podrá podremos podréis podrán	podría podrías podría podríamos podríais podrían	**pueda** **puedas** **pueda** podamos podáis **puedan**	pudiera pudieras pudiera pudiéramos pudierais pudieran	puede (no puedas) pueda podamos poded (no podáis) puedan
*poner *to place, to put* poniendo **puesto**	**pongo** pones pone ponemos ponéis ponen	ponía ponías ponía poníamos poníais ponían	puse pusiste puso pusimos pusisteis pusieron	pondré pondrás pondrá pondremos pondréis pondrán	pondría pondrías pondría pondríamos pondríais pondrían	ponga pongas ponga pongamos pongáis pongan	pusiera pusieras pusiera pusiéramos pusierais pusieran	pon (no pongas) ponga pongamos poned (no pongáis) pongan
querer (e → ie) *to like* queriendo querido	**quiero** **quieres** **quiere** queremos queréis **quieren**	quería querías quería queríamos queríais querían	quise quisiste quiso quisimos quisisteis quisieron	querré querrás querrá querremos querréis querrán	querría querrías querría querríamos querríais querrían	**quiera** **quieras** **quiera** queramos queráis **quieran**	quisiera quisieras quisiera quisiéramos quisierais quisieran	quiere (no quieras) quiera queramos quered (no queráis) quieran
*saber *to know* sabiendo sabido	**sé** sabes sabe sabemos sabéis saben	sabía sabías sabía sabíamos sabíais sabían	supe supiste supo supimos supisteis supieron	sabré sabrás sabrá sabremos sabréis sabrán	sabría sabrías sabría sabríamos sabríais sabrían	**sepa** **sepas** **sepa** **sepamos** **sepáis** **sepan**	supiera supieras supiera supiéramos supierais supieran	sabe (no sepas) sepa sepamos sabed (no sepáis) sepan

*Verbs with irregular *yo* forms in the present indicative

(continued)

Infinitive Present Participle Past Participle	Present Indicative	Imperfect	Preterite	Future	Conditional	Present Subjunctive	Past Subjunctive	Commands
*salir *to go out* saliendo salido	salgo sales sale salimos salís salen	salía salías salía salíamos salíais salían	salí saliste salió salimos salisteis salieron	saldré saldrás saldrá saldremos saldréis saldrán	saldría saldrías saldría saldríamos saldríais saldrían	salga salgas salga salgamos salgáis salgan	saliera salieras saliera saliéramos salierais salieran	sal (no salgas) salga salgamos salid (no salgáis) salgan
ser *to be* siendo sido	soy eres es somos sois son	era eras era éramos erais eran	fui fuiste fue fuimos fuisteis fueron	seré serás será seremos seréis serán	sería serías sería seríamos seríais serían	sea seas sea seamos seáis sean	fuera fueras fuera fuéramos fuerais fueran	sé (no seas) sea seamos sed (no seáis) sean
*tener (e → ie) *to have* teniendo tenido	tengo tienes tiene tenemos tenéis tienen	tenía tenías tenía teníamos teníais tenían	tuve tuviste tuvo tuvimos tuvisteis tuvieron	tendré tendrás tendrá tendremos tendréis tendrán	tendría tendrías tendría tendríamos tendríais tendrían	tenga tengas tenga tengamos tengáis tengan	tuviera tuvieras tuviera tuviéramos tuvierais tuvieran	ten (no tengas) tenga tengamos tened (no tengáis) tengan
*traer *to bring* trayendo traído	traigo traes trae traemos traéis traen	traía traías traía traíamos traíais traían	traje trajiste trajo trajimos trajisteis trajeron	traeré traerás traerá traeremos traeréis traerán	traería traerías traería traeríamos traeríais traerían	traiga traigas traiga traigamos traigáis traigan	trajera trajeras trajera trajéramos trajerais trajeran	trae (no traigas) traiga traigamos traed (no traigáis) traigan
*venir (e → ie, i) *to come* viniendo venido	vengo vienes viene venimos venís vienen	venía venías venía veníamos veníais venían	vine viniste vino vinimos vinisteis vinieron	vendré vendrás vendrá vendremos vendréis vendrán	vendría vendrías vendría vendríamos vendríais vendrían	venga vengas venga vengamos vengáis vengan	viniera vinieras viniera viniéramos vinierais vinieran	ven (no vengas) venga vengamos venid (no vengáis) vengan
ver *to see* viendo visto	veo ves ve vemos veis ven	veía veías veía veíamos veíais veían	vi viste vio vimos visteis vieron	veré verás verá veremos veréis verán	vería verías vería veríamos veríais verían	vea veas vea veamos veáis vean	viera vieras viera viéramos vierais vieran	ve (no veas) vea veamos ved (no veáis) vean

*Verbs with irregular *yo* forms in the present indicative

Supplemental Structures

1. Perfect tenses

In **Capítulo 12** you learned that the perfect tense is formed by combining the present indicative of the verb **haber** with the past participle. Similarly, you learned in **Capítulo 14** that the past perfect is formed by combining the imperfect of the verb **haber** with the past participle. The future perfect and conditional perfect tenses are formed by combining the imperfect, future, and conditional of **haber** with the past participle.

Future perfect		Conditional perfect	
habré		habría	
habrás		habrías	
habrá	+ past	habría	+ past
habremos	participle	habríamos	participle
habréis		habríais	
habrán		habrían	

In general, the use of these perfect tenses parallels their use in English.

Para el año 2015, **habremos terminado** nuestros estudios aquí.
Yo lo **habría hecho** por ti.

By the year 2015, we will have finished our studies here.
I would have done it for you.

The present perfect subjunctive and past perfect subjunctive are likewise formed by combining the present subjunctive and past subjunctive of **haber** with the past participle.

Present perfect subjunctive		Past perfect subjunctive	
haya		hubiera	
hayas		hubieras	
haya	+ past	hubiera	+ past
hayamos	participle	hubiéramos	participle
hayáis		hubierais	
hayan		hubieran	

These tenses are used whenever the independent clause in a sentence requires the subjunctive and the verb in the dependent clause represents an action completed prior to the time indicated by the verb in the independent clause. If the time of the verb in the independent clause is present or future, the present perfect subjunctive is used; if the time is past or conditional, the past perfect subjunctive is used.

Dudo que lo **hayan leído.**
Si **hubieras llamado,** no tendríamos este problema ahora.

I doubt that they have read it.
If you had called, we would not have this problem now.

2. Past progressive tense

In **Capítulo 5** you learned that the present progressive tense is formed with the present indicative of **estar** and a present participle. The past progressive tense is formed with the imperfect of **estar** and a present participle.

The past progressive tense is used to express or describe an action that was in progress at a particular moment in the past.

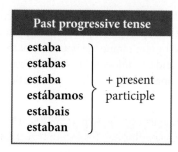

Past progressive tense	
estaba	
estabas	
estaba	+ present
estábamos	participle
estabais	
estaban	

Estábamos comiendo cuando llamaste.	*We were eating when you called.*
¿Quién **estaba hablando** por teléfono?	*Who was talking on the phone?*

Another past progressive tense can also be formed with the preterite of **estar** and the present participle. However, its use is of much lower frequency in Spanish.

3. Stressed possessive adjectives and pronouns

In **Capítulo 2** you learned to express possession using **de** or the possessive adjectives **mi(s), tu(s), su(s), nuestro(a, os, as), vuestro(a, os, as).** Possession may also be expressed using the stressed possessive adjectives equivalent to the English *of mine, of yours, of ours, of theirs.*

Stressed possessive adjectives and pronouns					
mío **míos**	**mía** **mías**	*my, (of) mine*	**nuestro** **nuestros**	**nuestra** **nuestras**	*our, (of) ours*
tuyo **tuyos**	**tuya** **tuyas**	*your, (of) yours*	**vuestro** **vuestros**	**vuestra** **vuestras**	*your, (of) yours*
suyo **suyos**	**suya** **suyas**	*its, his, (of) his hers, (of) hers your, (of) yours*	**suyo** **suyos**	**suya** **suyas**	*their, (of) theirs your, (of) yours*

A. As adjectives, the stressed possessives must agree in number and gender with the thing possessed.

Una amiga **mía** viene a visitarme hoy.	*A friend of mine is coming to visit me today.*
¿Qué hay en las maletas **suyas**, señor?	*What do you have in those suitcases of yours, sir?*
El coche **nuestro** nunca funciona.	*Our car never works.*

Note that stressed possessive adjectives *always* follow the noun they modify. Also note that the noun must be preceded by an article.

B. Stressed possessive adjectives can be used as possessive pronouns by eliminating the noun.

¿Dónde está **la suya,** señor?   *Where is yours, sir?*
El nuestro nunca funciona.   *Ours never works.*

Note that both the article and possessive adjective must agree in number and gender with the noun that has been eliminated.

C. A stressed possessive pronoun may be used without the article after the verb **ser.**

Esta maleta no es **mía,** señor.   *This suitcase is not mine, sir.*
¿Es **suya,** señora?   *Is it yours, ma'am?*

4. Present subjunctive of stem-changing verbs

A. Stem-changing **-ar** and **-er** verbs follow the same stem changes in the present subjunctive as in the present indicative. Note that the stems of the **nosotros** and **vosotros** forms do not change.

contar (ue)	
cuente	contemos
cuentes	contéis
cuente	cuenten

perder (ie)	
pierda	perdamos
pierdas	perdáis
pierda	pierdan

B. Stem-changing **-ir** verbs follow the same pattern in the present subjunctive, except for the **nosotros** and **vosotros** forms. These change **e → i** or **o → u.**

morir (ue)	
muera	muramos
mueras	muráis
muera	mueran

preferir (ie)	
prefiera	prefiramos
prefieras	prefiráis
prefiera	prefieran

pedir (i)	
pida	pidamos
pidas	pidáis
pida	pidan

5. Present subjunctive of verbs with spelling changes

As in the preterite, verbs that end in **-car, -gar,** and **-zar** undergo a spelling change in the present subjunctive in order to maintain the consonant sound of the infinitive.

A. **-car:**   **c** changes to **qu** in front of **e**

buscar: bus**que,** bus**ques,** bus**que...**

B. **-zar:**   **z** changes to **c** in front of **e**

almorzar: almuer**ce,** almuer**ces,** almuer**ce...**

C. **-gar:**   **g** changes to **gu** in front of **e**

jugar: jue**gue,** jue**gues,** jue**gue...**

D. **-ger:**   **g** changes to **j** in front of **a**

proteger: prote**ja,** prote**jas,** prote**ja...**

6. Irregular verbs in the present subjunctive

The following verbs are irregular in the present subjunctive:

dar	dé, des, dé, demos, deis, den
haber	haya, hayas, haya, hayamos, hayáis, hayan
ir	vaya, vayas, vaya, vayamos, vayáis, vayan
saber	sepa, sepas, sepa, sepamos, sepáis, sepan
ser	sea, seas, sea, seamos, seáis, sean

7. Past subjunctive and Conditional *Si* clauses

The past subjunctive of *all* verbs is formed by removing the **-ron** ending from the **ustedes** form of the preterite and adding the past subjunctive verb endings: **-ra, -ras, -ra, -ramos, -rais, -ran.** Thus, any irregularities in the **ustedes** form of the preterite will be reflected in all forms of the past subjunctive. Note that the **nosotros** form requires a written accent.

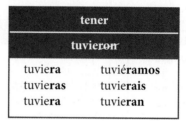

comprar	
comprar~~on~~	
compra**ra**	compr**áramos**
compra**ras**	compra**rais**
compra**ra**	compra**ran**

tener	
tuvier~~on~~	
tuvie**ra**	tuvi**éramos**
tuvie**ras**	tuvie**rais**
tuvie**ra**	tuvie**ran**

ser	
fuer~~on~~	
fue**ra**	fu**éramos**
fue**ras**	fue**rais**
fue**ra**	fue**ran**

An alternate form of the past subjunctive uses the verb endings **-se, -ses, -se, -semos, -seis, -sen.** This form is used primarily in Spain and in literary writing.

A. The past subjunctive has the same uses as the present subjunctive, except that it generally applies to past events or actions.

Insistieron en que **fuéramos.**	*They insisted that we go.*
Era imposible que lo **terminaran** a tiempo.	*It was impossible for them to finish it on time.*

B. In Spanish, as in English, conditional sentences express hypothetical conditions usually with an *if*-clause: *I would go if I had the money.* Since the actions are hypothetical and one does not know if they will actually occur, the past subjunctive is used in the *if*-clause.

Iría a Perú si **tuviera** el dinero.	*I would go to Peru if I had the money.*
Si **fuera** necesario, pediría un préstamo.	*If it were necessary, I would ask for a loan.*

C. Conditional sentences in the present use either the present indicative or the future tense. The present subjunctive is never used in *if*-clauses.

Si me **invitas,** iré contigo.	*If you invite me, I'll go with you.*

Grammar Guide

For more detailed explanations of these grammar points, consult the Index on pages 619–622 to find the places where these concepts are presented.

ACTIVE VOICE (La voz activa) A sentence written in the active voice identifies a subject that performs the action of the verb.

Juan	cantó	la canción.
Juan	*sang*	*the song.*
subject	**verb**	**direct object**

In the sentence above Juan is the performer of the verb **cantar.**

(*See also* **Passive Voice.**)

ADJECTIVES (Los adjetivos) are words that modify or describe **nouns** or **pronouns** and agree in **number** and generally in **gender** with the nouns they modify.

Las casas **azules** son **bonitas.**
*The **blue** houses are **pretty.***

Esas mujeres **mexicanas** son mis **nuevas** amigas.
*Those **Mexican** women are my **new** friends.*

- **Demonstrative adjectives (Los adjetivos demostrativos)** point out persons, places, or things relative to the position of the speaker. They always agree in **number** and **gender** with the **noun** they modify. The forms are: **este, esta, estos, estas / ese, esa, esos, esas / aquel, aquella, aquellos, aquellas.** There are also neuter forms that refer to generic ideas or things, and hence have no gender: **esto, eso, aquello.**

Este libro es fácil.	*This book is easy.*
Esos libros son difíciles.	*Those books are hard.*
Aquellos libros son pesados.	*Those books (**over there**) are boring.*
Eso es impotante.	*That is important.*

Demonstratives may also function as **pronouns,** replacing the **noun** but still agreeing with it in **number** and **gender:**

Me gustan esas blusas verdes.	*I like those green blouses.*
¿Cuáles, **estas?**	*Which ones, **these**?*
No. Me gustan **esas.**	*No. I like **those**.*

- **Stressed possessive adjectives (Los adjetivos posesivos tónicos)** are used for emphasis and follow the noun that they modifiy. These adjectives may also function as pronouns and always agree in **number** and in **gender.** The forms are: **mío, tuyo, suyo, nuestro, vuestro, suyo.** Unless they are directly preceded by the verb **ser,** stressed possessives must be preceded by the **definite article.**

Ese perro pequeño es **mío.**	*That little dog is **mine**.*
Dame el **tuyo;** el **nuestro** no funciona.	*Give me **yours; ours** doesn't work.*

- **Possessive adjectives (Los adjetivos posesivos)** demonstrate ownership and always precede the **noun** that they modify.

La señora Elman es **mi** profesora.	*Mrs. Elman is **my** professor.*
Debemos llevar **nuestros** libros a clase.	*We should take **our** books to class.*

ADVERBS (Los adverbios) are words that modify **verbs, adjectives,** or other adverbs and, unlike **adjectives,** do not have **gender** or **number.** Here are examples of different classes of adverbs:

Practicamos **diariamente.**	*We practice **daily.*** (adverb of frequency)
Ellos van a salir **pronto.**	*They will leave **soon.*** (adverb of time)
Jennifer está **afuera.**	*Jennifer is **outside.*** (adverb of place)
No quiero ir **tampoco.**	*I don't want to go **either.*** (adverb of negation)
Paco habla **demasiado.**	*Paco talks **too much.*** (adverb of quantity)
Esta clase es **extremadamente** difícil.	*This class is **extremely** difficult.* (modifies adjective)
Ella habla **muy** poco.	*She speaks **very** little.* (modifies adverb)

AGREEMENT (La concordancia) refers to the correspondence between parts of speech in terms of **number, gender,** and **person.** Subjects agree with their verbs; articles and adjectives agree with the nouns they modify, etc.

Toda**s** la**s** lengua**s** son interesante**s**.	*All languages are interesting.* (number)
Ella es bonit**a**.	*She is pretty.* (gender)
Nosotros somos de España.	*We are from Spain.* (person)

ARTICLES (Los artículos) precede nouns and indicate whether they are definite or indefinite persons, places, or things.

- **Definite articles (Los artículos definidos)** refer to particular members of a group and are the equivalent of *the* in English. The definite articles are: **el, la, los, las.**

El hombre guapo es mi padre.	*The handsome man is my father.*
Las mujeres de esta clase son inteligentes.	*The women in this class are intelligent.*

- **Indefinite articles (Los artículos indefinidos)** refer to any unspecified member(s) of a group and are the equivalent of *a(n)* and *some.* The indefinite articles are: **un, una, unos, unas.**

Un hombre vino a nuestra casa anoche.	*A man came to our house last night.*
Unas niñas jugaban en el parque.	*Some girls were playing in the park.*

CLAUSES (Las cláusulas) are subject and verb combinations; for a sentence to be complete it must have at least one main clause.

- **Main clauses** (Independent clauses) **(Las cláusulas principales)** communicate a complete idea or thought.

Mi hermana va al hospital.	*My sister goes to the hospital.*

- **Subordinate clauses** (Dependent clauses) **(Las cláusulas subordinadas)** depend upon a main clause for their meaning to be complete.

Mi hermana va al hospital	cuando está enferma.
My sister goes to the hospital	*when she is ill.*
main clause	**subordinate clause**

In the sentence above, *when she is ill* is not a complete idea without the information supplied by the main clause.

COMMANDS (Los mandatos) (*See* **Imperatives.**)

COMPARISONS (Las comparaciones) are statements that describe one person, place, or thing relative to another in terms of quantity, quality, or manner.

- **Comparisons of equality (Las formas comparativas de igualdad)** demonstrate an equal share of a quantity or degree of a particular characteristic. These statements use a form of **tan** or **tanto(a)(s)** and **como.**

Ella tiene **tanto** dinero **como** Elena.	*She has **as much** money **as** Elena.*
Fernando trabaja **tanto como** Felipe.	*Fernando works **as much as** Felipe.*
Jim baila **tan** bien **como** Anne.	*Jim dances **as well as** Anne.*

- **Comparisons of inequality (Las formas comparativas de desigualdad)** indicate a difference in quantity, quality, or manner between the compared subjects. These statements use **más/menos... que** or comparative **adjectives** such as **mejor/peor, mayor/ menor.**

México tiene **más** playas **que** España.	*Mexico has **more** beaches **than** Spain.*
Tú hablas español **mejor que** yo.	*You speak Spanish **better than** I.*

(*See also* **Superlative statements.**)

CONJUGATIONS (Las conjugaciones) are the forms of the verb as they agree with a particular subject or person.

Yo bailo los sábados.	*I dance on Saturdays.* (1st-person singular)
Tú bailas los sábados.	*You dance on Saturdays.* (2nd-person singular)
Ella baila los sábados.	*She dances on Saturdays.* (3rd-person singular)
Nosotros bailamos los sábados.	*We dance on Saturdays.* (1st-person plural)
Vosotros bailáis los sábados.	*You dance on Saturdays.* (2nd-person plural)
Ellos bailan los sábados.	*They dance on Saturdays.* (3rd-person plural)

CONJUNCTIONS (Las conjunciones) are linking words that join two independent clauses together.

Fuimos al centro **y** mis amigos compraron muchas cosas.
*We went downtown, **and** my friends bought a lot of things.*

Yo quiero ir a la fiesta, **pero** tengo que estudiar.
*I want to go to the party, **but** I have to study.*

CONTRACTIONS (Las contracciones) in Spanish are limited to preposition/article combinations, such as **de + el = del** and **a + el = al,** or preposition/pronoun combinations such as **con + mí = conmigo** and **con + ti = contigo.**

DIRECT OBJECTS (Los objetos directos) in sentences are the direct recipients of the action of the verb. Direct objects answer the questions *What?* or *Whom?*

¿Qué hizo?   *What did she do?*
Ella hizo **la tarea.**   *She did her **homework.***
Y luego llamó **a su amiga.**   *And then called **her friend.***

(*See also* **Pronoun, Indirect Object, Personal *a*.**)

EXCLAMATORY WORDS (Las palabras exclamativas) communicate surprise or strong emotion. Like interrogative words, exclamatory words also carry accents.

¡Qué sorpresa!   ***What** a surprise!*
¡Cómo canta Miguel!   ***How well** Miguel sings!*

(*See also* **Interrogatives.**)

GERUNDS (Los gerundios) in Spanish refer to the present participle. In English gerunds are verbals (based on a verb and expressing an action or a state of being) that function as nouns. In most instances where the gerund is used in English, the infinitive is used in Spanish.

(El) **Ser** cortés no cuesta nada.   ***Being** polite is not hard.*
Mi pasatiempo favorito es **viajar.**   *My favorite pasttime is **traveling.***
Después de **desayunar,** salió de la casa. *After **eating** breakfast, he left the house.*

(*See also* **Present Participle.**)

IDIOMATIC EXPRESSIONS (Las frases idiomáticas) are phrases in Spanish that do not have a literal English equivalent.

Hace mucho frío.   *It is very cold.* (Literally, *It makes a lot of cold.*)

IMPERATIVES (Los imperativos) represent the mood used to express requests or commands. It is more direct than the **subjunctive** mood. Imperatives are commonly called commands and fall into two categories: affirmative and negative. Spanish speakers must also choose between using formal commands and informal commands based upon whether one is addressed as **usted** (formal) or **tú** (informal).

Habla conmigo.   **Talk** to me. (informal, singular, affirmative)
No me hables.   **Don't talk to me.** (informal, singular, negative)
Hable con la policía.   **Talk** to the police. (formal, singular, affirmative)
No hable con la policía.   **Don't talk** to the police. (formal, singular, negative)
Hablen con la policía.   **Talk** to the police. (formal, plural, affirmative)
No hablen con la policía   **Don't talk** to the police. (formal, plural, negative)
Hablad con la policía.   **Talk** to the police. (informal [Spain], plural, affirmative)
No habléis con la policía.   **Don't talk** to the police. (informal [Spain], plural, negative)

(*See also* **Mood.**)

IMPERFECT (El imperfecto) The imperfect tense is used to make statements about the past when the speaker wants to convey the idea of 1) habitual or repeated action, 2) two actions in progress simultaneously, or 3) an event that was in progress when another action interrupted. The imperfect tense is also used to emphasize the ongoing nature of the middle of the event, as opposed to its beginning or end. Age and clock time are always expressed using the imperfect.

Cuando María **era** joven, ella **cantaba** en el coro.
*When María **was** young, she **used to sing** in the choir.*

Aquel día **llovía** mucho y el cielo **estaba** oscuro.
*That day **it was raining** a lot and the sky **was** dark.*

Juan **dormía** cuando sonó el teléfono.
*Juan **was sleeping** when the phone rang.*

(*See also* **Preterite.**)

IMPERSONAL EXPRESSIONS (Las expresiones impersonales) are statements that contain the impersonal subjects of *it* or *one*.

Es necesario estudiar.	*It is necessary to study.*
Se necesita estudiar.	*One needs to study.*

(*See also* **Passive Voice.**)

INDEFINITE WORDS (Las palabras indefinidas) are **articles, adjectives, nouns** or **pronouns** that refer to unspecified members of a group.

Un hombre vino.	*A man came.* (indefinite article)
Alguien vino.	*Someone came.* (indefinite noun)
Algunas personas vinieron.	*Some people came.* (indefinite adjective)
Algunas vinieron.	*Some came.* (indefinite pronoun)

(*See also* **Articles.**)

INDICATIVE (El indicativo) The indicative is a mood, rather than a tense. The indicative is used to express ideas that are considered factual or certain and, therefore, not subject to speculation, doubt, or negation.

Josefina **es** española.	*Josefina is Spanish.*
(present indicative)	
Ella **vivió** en Argentina.	*She lived in Argentina.*
(preterite indicative)	

(*See also* **Mood.**)

INDIRECT OBJECTS (Los objetos indirectos) are the indirect recipients of an action in a sentence and answer the questions *To whom?* or *For whom?* In Spanish it is common to include an indirect object **pronoun** along with the indirect object.

Yo **le** di el libro **a Sofía.**	*I gave the book **to Sofía.***
Sofía **les** guardó el libro **a sus padres.**	*Sofía kept the book **for her parents.***

(*See also* **Direct Objects** and **Pronouns.**)

INFINITIVES (Los infinitivos) are verb forms that are uninflected or **not conjugated** according to a specific **person.** In English, infinitives are preceded by *to: to talk, to eat, to live.* Infinitives in Spanish end in **-ar (hablar), -er (comer),** and **-ir (vivir).**

INTERROGATIVES (Las formas interrogativas) are used to pose questions and carry accent marks to distinguish them from other uses. Basic interrogative words include: **quién(es), qué, cómo, cuánto(a)(s), cuándo, por qué, dónde, cuál(es).**

¿**Qué** quieres?	*What do you want?*
¿**Cuándo** llegó ella?	*When did she arrive?*
¿De **dónde** eres?	*Where are you from?*

(*See also* **Exclamatory Words.**)

MOOD (El modo) is like the word *mode*, meaning *manner* or *way*. It indicates the way in which the speaker views an action, or his/her attitude toward the action. Besides the **imperative** mood, which is simply giving commands, there are two moods in Spanish: the **subjunctive** and the **indicative.** Basically, the subjunctive mood communicates an attitude of uncertainty toward the action, while the indicative indicates that the action is certain or factual. Within each of these moods there are many **tenses.** Hence you have the present indicative and the present subjunctive, the present perfect indicative and the present perfect subjunctive, etc.

- **Indicative mood (El indicativo)** is used to talk about actions that are regarded as certain or as facts: things that happen all the time, have happened, or will happen. It is used in contrast to situations where the speaker is voicing an opinion, doubts, or desires.

Yo **quiero** ir a la fiesta.	*I want to go to the party.*
¿**Quieres** ir conmigo?	*Do you want to go with me?*

- **Subjunctive mood (El subjuntivo)** indicates a recommendation, a statement of uncertainty, or an expression of opinion or emotion.

Yo recomiendo que tú **vayas** a la fiesta.	*I recommend that **you go** to the party.*
Dudo que **vayas** a la fiesta.	*I doubt that **you'll go** to the party.*
No creo que **vayas** a la fiesta.	*I don't believe that **you'll go** to the party.*
Si **fueras** a la fiesta, te divertirías.	*If **you were to go** to the party, you would have a good time.*

- **Imperative mood (El imperativo)** is used to make a command or request.

¡**Ven** conmigo a la fiesta!	***Come** with me to the party!*

(*See also* **Mood, Indicative, Imperative,** *and* **Subjunctive.**)

NEGATION (La negación) takes place when a negative word, such as **no,** is placed before an affirmative sentence. In Spanish, double negatives are common.

Yolanda va a cantar esta noche.	*Yolanda will sing tonight.* (affirmative)
Yolanda **no** va a cantar esta noche.	*Yolanda will **not** sing tonight.* (negative)
Ramón quiere algo.	*Ramón wants something.* (affirmative)
Ramón **no** quiere **nada.**	*Ramón **doesn't** want **anything.*** (negative)

NOUNS (Los sustantivos) are persons, places, things, or ideas. Names of people, countries, and cities are proper nouns and are capitalized.

Alberto	*Albert* (person)
el pueblo	*town* (place)
el diccionario	*dictionary* (thing)

ORTHOGRAPHY (La ortografía) refers to the spelling of a word or anything related to spelling, such as accentuation.

PASSIVE VOICE (La voz pasiva), as compared to **active voice (la voz activa),** places emphasis on the action itself rather than the subject (the person or thing that is responsible for doing the action). The passive **se** is used when there is no apparent subject.

Luis vende los coches.	*Luis sells the cars.* (active voice)
Los coches **son vendidos por** Luis.	*The cars **are sold by** Luis.* (passive voice)
Se venden los coches.	*The cars **are sold.*** (passive voice)

(*See also* **Active Voice.**)

PAST PARTICIPLES (Los participios pasados) are verb forms used in compound tenses such as the **present perfect.** Regular past participles are formed by dropping the **-ar** or **-er/-ir** from the **infinitive** and adding **-ado** or **-ido.** Past participles are generally the equivalent of verb forms ending in *-ed* in English. They may also be used as **adjectives,** in which case they agree in **number** and **gender** with their nouns. Irregular past participles include: **escrito, roto, dicho, hecho, puesto, vuelto, muerto, cubierto.**

Marta ha **subido** la montaña.	*Marta has **climbed** the mountain.*
Hemos **hablado** mucho por teléfono.	*We have **talked** a lot on the phone.*
La novela **publicada** en 1995 es su mejor novela.	*The novel **published** in 1995 is her best novel.*

PERFECT TENSES (Los tiempos perfectos) communicate the idea that an action has taken place before now (present perfect) or before a moment in the past (past perfect). The perfect tenses are compound tenses consisting of the auxiliary verb **haber** plus the **past participle** of a second verb.

Yo **he comido.**	*I **have eaten.*** (present perfect indicative)
Antes de la fiesta, yo ya **había comido.**	*Before the party **I had already eaten.*** (past perfect indicative)
Yo espero que **hayas comido.**	*I hope that **you have eaten.*** (present perfect subjunctive)
Yo esperaba que **hubieras comido.**	*I hoped that **you had eaten.*** (past perfect subjunctive)

PERSON (La persona) refers to changes in the subject pronouns that indicate if one is speaking (first person), if one is spoken to (second person), or if one is spoken about (third person).

Yo hablo.	*I speak.* (1st-person singular)
Tú hablas.	*You speak.* (2nd-person singular)
Ud./Él/Ella habla.	*You/He/She speak(s).* (3rd-person singular)
Nosotros(as) hablamos.	*We speak.* (1st-person plural)
Vosotros(as) habláis.	*You speak.* (2nd-person plural)
Uds./Ellos/Ellas hablan.	*They speak.* (3rd-person plural)

PERSONAL A (La *a* personal) The personal **a** refers to the placement of the preposition **a** before a person or a pet when it is the **direct object** of the sentence.

Voy a llamar **a** María.	*I'm going to call María.*
El veterinario curó **al** perro.	*The veterinarian treated the dog.*

PREPOSITIONS (Las preposiciones) are linking words indicating spatial or temporal relations between two words.

Ella nadaba **en** la piscina.	*She was swimming **in** the pool.*
Yo llamé **antes de** las nueve.	*I called **before** nine o'clock.*
El libro es **para** ti.	*The book is **for** you.*
Voy **a** la oficina.	*I'm going **to** the office.*
Jorge es **de** Paraguay.	*Jorge is **from** Paraguay.*

PRESENT PARTICIPLE (El participio del presente) is the Spanish equivalent of the *-ing* verb form in English. Regular participles are created by replacing the infinitive endings (**-ar, -er/-ir**) with **-ando** or **-iendo.** They are often used with the verb **estar** to form the present progressive tense. The present progressive tense places emphasis on the continuing or progressive nature of an action. In Spanish, the participle form is referred to as a gerund.

Miguel está **cantando** en la ducha.	*Miguel is **singing** in the shower.*
Los niños están **durmiendo** ahora.	*The children are **sleeping** now.*

(*See also* **Gerunds**)

PRETERITE (El pretérito) The preterite tense, as compared to the **imperfect tense,** is used to talk about past events with specific emphasis on the beginning or the end of the action, or emphasis on the completed nature of the action as a whole.

Anoche yo **empecé** a estudiar a las once y **terminé** a la una.
*Last night I **began** to study at eleven o'clock and **finished** at one o'clock.*

Esta mañana **me desperté** a las siete, **desayuné, me duché** y **vine** al campus para las ocho.
*This morning **I woke up** at seven, **I ate breakfast, I showered,** and **I came** to campus by eight.*

PRONOUNS (Los pronombres) are words that substitute for **nouns** in a sentence.

Yo quiero **este.**	*I want **this one.*** (demonstrative—points out a specific person, place, or thing)
¿Quién es tu amigo?	***Who** is your friend?* (interrogative—used to ask questions)
Yo voy a llamar**la.**	*I'm going to call **her.*** (direct object—replaces the direct object of the sentence)
Ella va a dar**le** el reloj.	*She is going to give **him** the watch.* (indirect object—replaces the indirect object of the sentence)
Juan **se** baña por la mañana.	*Juan bathes **himself** in the morning.* (reflexive—used with reflexive verbs to show that the agent of the action is also the recipient)
Es la mujer **que** conozco.	*She is the woman **that** I know.* (relative—used to introduce a clause that describes a noun)
Nosotros somos listos.	***We** are clever.* (subject—replaces the noun that performs the action or state of a verb)

SUBJECTS (Los sujetos) are the persons, places, or things which perform the action of a verb, or which are connected to a description by a verb. The **conjugated** verb always agrees with its subject.

Carlos siempre baila solo.	***Carlos** always dances alone.*
Colorado y **California** son mis estados preferidos.	***Colorado** and **California** are my favorite states.*
La cafetera produce el café.	*The **coffee pot** makes the coffee.*

(*See also* **Active Voice.**)

SUBJUNCTIVE (El subjuntivo) The subjunctive mood is used to express speculative, doubtful, or hypothetical situations. It also communicates a degree of subjectivity or influence of the main clause over the subordinate clause.

No creo que **tengas** razón.	*I don't think that **you're** right.*
Si yo **fuera** el jefe, les pagaría más a mis empleados.	*If I **were** the boss, I would pay my employees more.*
Quiero que **estudies** más.	*I want **you to study** more.*

(*See also* **Mood, Indicative.**)

SUPERLATIVE STATEMENTS (Las frases superlativas) are formed by adjectives or adverbs to make comparisons among three or more members of a group. To form superlatives, add a definite article **(el, la, los, las)** before the comparative form.

Juan es **el más alto** de los tres.	*Juan is **the tallest** of the three.*
Este coche es **el más rápido** de todos.	*This car is **the fastest** of them all.*
En mi opinión, ella es **la mejor** cantante.	*In my opinion, she is **the best** singer.*

(*See also* **Comparisons.**)

TENSES (Los tiempos) refer to the manner in which time is expressed through the verb of a sentence.

Yo estudio.	*I study.* (present tense)
Yo estoy estudiando.	*I am studying.* (present progressive)
Yo he estudiado.	*I have studied.* (present perfect)
Yo había estudiado.	*I had studied.* (past perfect)
Yo estudié.	*I studied.* (preterite tense)
Yo estudiaba.	*I was studying.* (imperfect tense)
Yo estudiaré.	*I will study.* (future tense)

VERBS (Los verbos) are the words in a sentence that communicate an action or state of being.

Helen **es** mi amiga y ella **lee** muchas novelas.	*Helen **is** my friend and she **reads** a lot of novels.*

- **Auxiliary verbs (Los verbos auxiliares)** or helping verbs **haber, ser,** and **estar** are used to form the passive voice, compound tenses, and verbal periphrases.

Estamos estudiando mucho para el examen mañana.	***We are** studying a lot for the exam tomorrow. (verbal periphrases)*
Helen **ha** trabajado mucho en este proyecto.	*Helen **has** worked a lot on this project. (compound tense)*
La ropa **fue** hecha en Guatemala.	*The clothing **was** made in Guatemala. (passive voice)*

- **Reflexive verbs (Los verbos reflexivos)** use reflexive **pronouns** to indicate that the person initiating the action is also the recipient of the action.

Yo **me afeito** por la mañana.	*I shave (myself) in the morning.*

- **Stem-changing verbs (Los verbos con cambios de raíz)** undergo a change in the main part of the verb when conjugated. To find the stem, drop the **-ar, -er,** or **-ir** from the **infinitive: dorm-, empez-, ped-.** There are three types of stem-changing verbs: **o** to **ue, e** to **ie** and **e** to **i.**

dormir: Yo d**ue**rmo en el parque.	*I sleep in the park.* (**o** to **ue**)
empezar: Ella siempre emp**ie**za su trabajo temprano.	*She always starts her work early.* (**e** to **ie**)
pedir: ¿Por qué no p**i**des ayuda?	*Why don't you ask for help?* (**e** to **i**)

Functional Glossary

Asking questions
Question words

¿Adónde? To where?
¿Cómo? How?
¿Cuál(es)? Which? What?
¿Cuándo? When?
¿Cuánto/¿Cuánta? How much?
¿Cuántos/¿Cuántas? How many?
¿Dónde? Where?
¿Para qué? For what reason?
¿Por qué? Why?
¿Qué? What?
¿Quién(es)? Who? Whom?

Requesting information

¿Cómo es su (tu) profesor(a) favorito(a)? What's your favorite professor like?
¿Cómo se (te) llama(s)? What's your name?
¿Cómo se llama? What's his/her name?
¿Cuál es su (tu) facultad? What's your school/department?
¿Cuál es su (tu) número de teléfono? What's your telephone number?
¿De dónde es (eres)? Where are you from?
¿Dónde hay...? Where is/are there . . .?
¿Qué estudia(s)? What are you studying?

Asking for descriptions

¿Cómo es...? What is . . . like?
¿Cómo son...? What are . . . like?

Asking for clarification

¿Cómo? What?
Dígame (Dime) una cosa. Tell me something.
Más despacio. More slowly.
No comprendo./No entiendo. I don't understand.
¿Perdón? Pardon me?
¿Qué? Otra vez, por favor. What? One more time, please.
Repita (Repite), por favor. Please repeat.
¿Qué significa...? What does . . . mean?

Asking about and expressing likes and dislikes

¿Te (le) gusta(n)? Do you like it (them)?
No me gusta(n). I don't like it (them).
Sí, me gusta(n). Yes, I like it (them).

Asking for confirmation

... ¿de acuerdo? . . . agreed? (*Used when some type of action is proposed.*)
... ¿no? . . . isn't that so? (*Not used with negative sentences.*)
... ¿no es así? . . . isn't that right?
... ¿vale? . . . okay?
... ¿verdad? ¿cierto? . . . right?
... ¿está bien? . . . OK?

Complaining

Es demasiado caro/cara (costoso/costosa). It's too expensive.
No es justo. It isn't fair.
¡No, hombre/mujer! No way!
No puedo esperar más. I can't wait anymore.
No puedo más. I can't take this anymore.

Expressing belief

Es cierto/verdad. That's right./That's true.
Estoy seguro/segura. I'm sure.
Lo creo. I believe it.
No cabe duda de que... There can be no doubt that . . .
No lo dudo. I don't doubt it.
No tengo la menor duda. I haven't the slightest doubt.
Tiene(s) razón. You're right.

Expressing disbelief

Hay dudas. There are doubts.
Es poco probable. It's doubtful/unlikely.
Lo dudo. I doubt it.
No lo creo. I don't believe it.
Estás equivocado(a). You're wrong.
Tengo mis dudas. I have my doubts.

Expressing frequency of actions and length of activities

¿Con qué frecuencia...? How often . . .?
de vez en cuando from time to time
durante la semana during the week
frecuentemente frequently
los fines de semana on the weekends
nunca never
por la mañana/por la tarde/por la noche in the morning/afternoon/evening
siempre always
todas las tardes/todas las noches every afternoon/evening
todos los días every day
Hace un año/dos meses/tres semanas que... for a year/two months/three weeks

Listening for instructions in the classroom

Abran los libros en la página... Open your books to page . . .
Cierren los libros. Close your books.
Complete (Completa) (Completen) la oración. Complete the sentence.
Conteste (Contesta) (Contesten) en español. Answer in Spanish.
Escriban en la pizarra. Write on the board.
Formen grupos de... estudiantes. Form groups of . . . students.
Practiquen en parejas. Practice in pairs.
¿Hay preguntas? Are there any questions?
Lea (Lee) en voz alta. Read aloud.
Por ejemplo... For example . . .
Preparen... para mañana. Prepare . . . for tomorrow.
Repita (Repite), (Repitan) por favor. Please repeat.
Saquen el libro (el cuaderno, una hoja de papel). Take out the book (the notebook, a piece of paper).

Greeting and conversing
Greetings

Bien, gracias. Fine, thanks.
Buenas noches. Good evening.
Buenas tardes. Good afternoon.
Buenos días. Good morning.
¿Cómo está(s)? How are you?
¿Cómo le (te) va? How is it going?
Hola. Hi.
Mal. Bad./Badly.
Más o menos. So so.
Nada. Nothing.
No muy bien. Not too well.
¿Qué hay de nuevo? What's new?
¿Qué tal? How are things?
Regular. Okay.
¿Y usted (tú)? And you?

Introducing people

¿Cómo se (te) llama(s)? What is your name?
¿Cómo se llama(n) él/ella/usted(es)/ellos/ellas? What is (are) his/her, your, their name(s)?
¿Cuál es su (tu) nombre? What is your name?
El gusto es mío. The pleasure is mine.
Encantado(a). Delighted.
Igualmente. Likewise.
Me llamo... My name is . . .
Mi nombre es... My name is . . .
Mucho gusto. Pleased to meet you.
Quiero presentarle(te) a... I want to introduce you to . . .
Se llama(n)... His/Her/Their name(s) is/are . . .

Entering into a conversation

Escuche (Escucha). Listen.
(No) Creo que... I (don't) believe that . . .
(No) Estoy de acuerdo porque... I (don't) agree because . . .

Pues, lo que quiero decir es que... Well, what I want to say is . . .

Quiero decir algo sobre... I want to say something about . . .

Saying goodbye

Adiós. Goodbye.

Chao. Goodbye.

Hasta la vista. Until we meet again.

Hasta luego. See you later.

Hasta mañana. Until tomorrow.

Hasta pronto. See you soon.

Chatting

(Bastante) bien. (Pretty) well, fine.

¿Cómo está la familia? How's the family?

¿Cómo le (te) va? How's it going?

¿Cómo van las clases? How are classes going?

Fenomenal. Phenomenal.

Horrible. Horrible.

Mal. Bad(ly).

No hay nada de nuevo. There's nothing new.

¿Qué hay de nuevo? What's new?

¿Qué tal? How's it going?

Reacting to comments

¡A mí me lo dice(s)! You're telling me!

¡Caray! Oh! Oh no!

¿De veras?/¿De verdad? Really? Is that so?

¡Dios mío! Oh, my goodness!

¿En serio? Seriously? Are you serious?

¡Estupendo! Stupendous!

¡Fabuloso! Fabulous!

¡No me diga(s)! You don't say!

¡Qué barbaridad! How unusual! Wow! That's terrible!

¡Qué bien! That's great!

¡Qué desastre! That's a disaster!

¿Qué dijo (dijiste)? What did you say?

¡Qué gente más loca! What crazy people!

¿Qué hizo (hiciste)? What did you do?

¡Qué horrible! That's horrible!

¡Qué increíble! That's amazing!

¡Qué lástima! That's a pity! That's too bad!

¡Qué mal! That's really bad!

¡Qué maravilla! That's marvelous!

¡Qué pena! That's a pain! That's too bad!

¡Ya lo creo! I (can) believe it!

Extending a conversation using fillers and hesitations

A ver... Let's see . . .

Buena pregunta... That's a good question . . .

Bueno... Well . . .

Es que... It's that . . .

Pues... no sé. Well . . . I don't know.

Sí, pero... Yes, but . . .

No creo. I don't think so.

Expressing worry

¡Ay, Dios mío! Good grief!

¡Es una pesadilla! It's a nightmare!

¡Eso debe ser horrible! That must be horrible!

¡Pobre! Poor thing!

¡Qué espanto! What a scare!

¡Qué horror! How horrible!

¡Qué lástima! What a pity!

¡Qué mala suerte/pata! What bad luck!

¡Qué terrible! How terrible!

¡Qué triste! How sad!

¡Qué pena! What a shame!

Expressing agreement

Así es. That's so.

Cierto./Claro (que sí)./Seguro. Certainly. Sure(ly).

Cómo no./Por supuesto. Of course.

Correcto. That's right.

Es cierto/verdad. It's true.

Eso es. That's it.

(Estoy) de acuerdo. I agree.

Exacto. Exactly.

Muy bien. Very good. Fine.

Perfecto. Perfect.

Probablemente. Probably.

Expressing disagreement

Al contrario. On the contrary.

En absoluto. Absolutely not. No way.

Es poco probable. It's doubtful/not likely.

Incorrecto. Incorrect.

No es así. That's not so.

No es cierto. It's not so.

No es verdad. It's not true.

No es eso. That's not it.

No está bien. It's no good/not right.

No estoy de acuerdo. I don't agree.

Todo lo contrario. Just the opposite./ Quite the contrary.

Expressing sympathy

Es una pena. It's a pity.

Lo siento mucho. I'm very sorry.

Mis condolencias. My condolences.

¡Qué lástima! What a pity!

Expressing obligation

Necesitar + *infinitive* To need to . . .

(No) es necesario + *infinitive* It's (not) necessary to . . .

(No) hay que + *infinitive* One must(n't) . . ., One does(n't) have to . . .

(Se) debe + *infinitive* (One) should (ought to) . . .

Tener que + *infinitive* To have to . . .

In the hospital
Communicating instructions

Aplicar una pomada. Apply cream/ ointment.

Bañarse con agua fría/caliente. Take a bath in cold/hot water.

Lavar la herida. Wash the wound.

Llamar al médico. Call the doctor.

Pedir información. Ask for information.

Poner hielo. Put on ice.

Poner una tirita/una venda. Put on a Band-Aid®/a bandage.

Quedarse en la cama. Stay in bed.

Sacar la lengua. Stick out your tongue.

Tomar la medicina/las pastillas después de cada comida (dos veces al día/antes de acostarse). Take the medicine/the pills after each meal (two times a day/ before going to bed).

Describing symptoms

Me duele la cabeza/la espalda, etc. I have a headache/backache, etc.

Me tiemblan las manos. My hands are shaking.

Necesito pastillas (contra fiebre, mareos, etc.). I need pills (for fever, dizziness, etc.).

Necesito una receta (unas aspirinas, un antibiótico, unas gotas, un jarabe). I need a prescription (aspirin, antibiotics, drops, cough syrup).

Invitations
Extending invitations

¿Le (Te) gustaría ir a... conmigo? Would you like to go to . . . with me?

¿Me quiere(s) acompañar a...? Do you want to accompany me to . . .?

¿Quiere(s) ir a...? Do you want to go to . . .?

Si tiene(s) tiempo, podemos ir a... If you have time, we could go to . . .

Accepting invitations

Sí, con mucho gusto. Yes, with pleasure.

Sí, me encantaría. Yes, I'd love to.

Sí, me gustaría mucho. Yes, I'd like to very much.

Declining invitations

Lo siento mucho, pero no puedo. I'm very sorry, but I can't.

Me gustaría, pero no puedo porque... I'd like to, but I can't because . . .

Making reservations and asking for information

¿Dónde hay...? Where is/are there . . .?

¿El precio incluye...? Does the price include . . .?

Quisiera reservar una habitación... I would like to reserve a room . . .

Opinons
Asking for opinions

¿Cuál prefiere(s)? Which do you prefer?

¿Le (Te) gusta(n)...? Do you like . . .?

¿Le (Te) interesa(n)...? Are you interested in . . .?

¿Qué opina(s) de...? What's your opinion about . . .?

¿Qué piensa(s)? What do you think?

¿Qué le (te) parece(n)? How does/ do . . . seem to you?

Giving opinions

Creo que... I believe that . . .
Es bueno. It's good.
Es conveniente. It's convenient.
Es importante. It's important.
Es imprescindible. It's indispensable.
Es mejor. It's better.
Es necesario./Es preciso. It's necessary.
Es preferible. It's preferable.
Me gusta(n)... I like . . .
Me interesa(n)... I am interested in . . .
Me parece(n)... It seems . . . to me. (They seem . . . to me.)
Opino que... It's my opinion that . . .
Pienso que... I think that . . .
Prefiero... I prefer . . .

Adding information

A propósito/De paso... By the way . . .
Además... In addition . . .
También... Also . . .

Negating and contradicting

¡Imposible! Impossible!
¡Jamás!/¡Nunca! Never!
Ni hablar. Don't even mention it.
No es así. It's not like that.
No está bien. It's not right.

Making requests

¿Me da(s)...? Will you give me . . .?
¿Me hace(s) el favor de...? Will you do me the favor of . . .?
¿Me pasa(s)...? Will you pass me . . .?

¿Me puede(s) dar...? Can you give me . . .?

¿Me puede(s) traer...? Can you bring me . . .?

¿Quiere(s) darme...? Do you want to give me . . .?

Sí, cómo no. Yes, of course.

In a restaurant
Ordering a meal

¿Está incluida la propina? Is the tip included?

Me falta(n)... I need . . .

¿Me puede traer..., por favor? Can you please bring me . . .?

¿Puedo ver la carta/el menú/la lista de vinos? May I see the menu/the wine list?

¿Qué recomienda usted? What do you recommend?

¿Qué tarjetas de crédito aceptan? What credit cards do you accept?

Quisiera hacer una reservación para... I would like to make a reservation for . . .

¿Se necesitan reservaciones? Are reservations needed?

¿Tiene usted una mesa para...? Do you have a table for . . .?

Tráigame la cuenta, por favor. Please bring me the check/bill.

Shopping
Asking how much something costs and bargaining

¿Cuánto cuesta...? How much is . . .?
El precio es... The price is . . .
Cuesta alrededor de... It costs around . . .
¿Cuánto cuesta(n)? How much does it (do they) cost?
De acuerdo. Agreed. All right.
Es demasiado. It's too much.
Es una ganga. It's a bargain.

No más. No more.
No pago más de... I won't pay more than . . .
solo only
última oferta final offer

Describing how clothing fits

Me queda(n) bien/mal. It fits (They fit) me well/badly.

Te queda(n) bien/mal. It fits (They fit) you well/badly.

Le queda(n) bien/mal. It fits (They fit) him/her/you well/badly.

Getting someone's attention

Con permiso. Excuse me.
Discúlpeme. Excuse me.
Oiga (Oye). Listen.
Perdón. Pardon.

Expressing satisfaction and dissatisfaction

El color es horrible. The color is horrible.

El modelo es aceptable. The style is acceptable.

Es muy barato(a). It's very inexpensive.
Es muy caro(a). It's very expensive.
Me gusta el modelo. I like the style.

Thanking

De nada./Por nada./No hay de qué. It's nothing. You're welcome.

¿De verdad le (te) gusta? Do you really like it?

Estoy muy agradecido(a). I'm very grateful.

Gracias. Thanks./Thank you.

Me alegro que le (te) guste. I'm glad you like it.

Mil gracias. Thanks a lot.

Muchas gracias. Thank you very much.

Muy amable de su (tu) parte. You're very kind.

Spanish-English Vocabulary

This vocabulary includes all the words and expressions listed as active vocabulary in **Exploraciones**. The number following the definition refers to the chapter in which the word or phrase was first used actively. For example, an entry followed by **13** is first used actively in **Capítulo 13**. Nouns that end in **-o** are maculine and in **-a** are feminine unless unless otherwise indicated.

All words are alphabetized according to the 1994 changes made by the Real Academia: **ch** and **ll** are no longer considered separate letters of the alphabet.

Stem-changing verbs appear with the vowel change in parentheses after the infinitive: **(ie), (ue), (i), (ie, i), (e, i), (ue, u),** or **(i, i).** Most cognates, conjugated verb forms, and proper nouns used as passive vocabulary in the text are not included in this glossary.

The following abbreviations are used:

adj. adjective	*n.* noun	*dem.* demonstrative	*prep.* preposition	*form.* formal	*s.* singular
adv. adverb	*pl.* plural	*dir. obj.* direct object	*pron.* pronoun	*indir. obj.* indirect object	*subj.* subject
art. article	*pp.* past participle	*f.* feminine	*refl.* reflexive	*interj.* interjection	*v.* verb
conj. conjunction	*poss.* possessive	*f.* feminine		*m.* masculine	

A

a to, at; **a causa de** on account of; **a cuadros** checkered; plaid (11); **a fin de que** so that (14); in order that (14); **a la derecha de** to the right of (4); **a la izquierda de** to the left of (4); **a lo largo (de)** along; **a lunares** polka-dotted; **a menos que** unless (14); **a menudo** frequently, often; **a pesar de** in spite of; **a propósito** by the way; **a rayas** striped (11); **a tiempo completo** full-time; **a tiempo** on time (10); **al horno** baked (7); **al igual que** like; **al lado (de)** alongside (of); beside, next to (4); **al mes** per month
abajo *adv.* below; **abajo de** under
abogado(a) lawyer (5); attorney
abordar to board (10); **pase** *m.* **de abordar** boarding pass (10)
abrazar (c) to hug (13)
abrigo coat (3)
abril *m.* April (3)
abrir to open (3)
abstracto(a) abstract (11); **arte** *m.* **abstracto** abstract art (11)
abuelo(a) grandfather/grandmother (2)
aburrido(a) bored (5); boring (1)
aburrir to bore (8); **aburrirse** to become bored (9)
acabar to finish (11); **acabar de** (+ *inf.*) to have just (*done something*)
acampar to go camping
acaso perhaps
acción *f.* action
aceite *m.* oil
aceituna olive
aceptar to accept
acera sidewalk (9)
acercarse (qu) to approach
acompañar to accompany
acondicionado(a): aire acondicionado *m.* air-conditioning
acontecimiento event
acostarse (ue) to lie down (6); to go to bed (6)
actividad activity
actor *m.* actor (5)
actriz *f.* actress (5)
actual current
acuerdo agreement; **de acuerdo** agreed, all right; **estar de acuerdo** to agree
adelgazar (c) to lose weight
además besides; furthermore; in addition
adiós goodbye (1)
adolescencia adolescence (13)
adolescente *m. f.* adolescent (13)
¿adónde? to where? (4)
aduana customs (10)
adulto adult (13)

aéreo(a) *adj.* air; **línea aérea** airline
aeropuerto (internacional) airport (4); (international) airport (10)
afeitarse to shave (6)
aficionado(a) fan (6)
afuera *adv.* outside
agente *m. f.* agent; **agente de aduana** customs official; **agente de seguridad** security agent (10); **agente de viajes** travel agent (5)
agosto August (3)
agradecido(a) grateful
agresivo(a) aggressive (1)
agua *f.* (*but* **el agua**) water
aguacate *m.* avocado
águila *f.* (*but* **el águila**) eagle
ahí there
ahora now (3) (6); **hasta ahora** up to now, so far
ajedrez *m.* chess (8)
ajo garlic
alberca swimming pool
albergue estudiantil *m.* youth hostel
alegrarse to become happy (9)
alegre happy (5)
alemán *m.* German (*language*) (2)
alergia allergy (14)
alfombra carpet (4); rug
algo something
algodón *m.* cotton (11)
alguien someone, somebody
aliviar to relieve, alleviate
allá over there
allí there
almacén *m.* department store
almohada pillow
almorzar (ue) (c) to have lunch (4)
almuerzo lunch (7)
aló hello (*telephone response in some countries*)
alojamiento lodging (10)
alojarse to lodge, to stay (*in a hotel*) (10)
alpinismo mountain climbing; **hacer alpinismo** to climb mountains (6)
alquilar to rent (4)
alto(a) high; tall (1); **presión** *f.* **alta** high blood pressure (14)
amable kind (1)
amar to love (13)
amarillo(a) yellow (3)
ambiente *m.* atmosphere, environment
ambulancia ambulance (9)
amigo(a) friend (2)
amo(a) de casa homemaker (5)
anaranjado(a) orange (3)
ándale there you go
andar to walk; **andar en** to ride (8); **andar en bicicleta** to ride a bike (6)

andén *m.* platform (10)
anfibio amphibian (12)
anfitrión(-ona) host
anillo ring (13)
animado(a) excited; **dibujos animados** cartoons (13)
aniversario (wedding) anniversary (9)
anoche last night (6)
ante todo first of all, first and foremost
anteayer the day before yesterday
anterior before, prior
antes previously; **antes de** (+ *inf.*) before (*doing something*) (6); **antes (de) que** before (14)
antipático(a) unfriendly (1)
anuncio comercial commercial (13)
añadir to add
año year; **Año Nuevo** New Year (3); **el año pasado** last year; **los quince años** girl's fifteenth birthday celebration (9); **tener... años** to be . . . years old (2)
apagar (gu) to turn off (11)
aparcamiento parking lot
apartamento apartment (4)
aplicarse (qu) to apply
apreciar to appreciate; to enjoy (11)
aprender (a +*inf.***)** to learn (*to do something*) (3)
apretado(a) tight (11)
aprobar (ue) to approve
aquel(la) *adj.* that (over there); *pron.* that (one) (over there)
aquello *pron.* that (one)
aquellos(as) *adj.* those (over there); *pron.* those (over there)
aquí here; **hasta aquí** up to now, so far
árbol *m.* tree (12); **trepar un árbol** to climb a tree (8)
ardilla squirrel (12)
arena sand (12)
argentino(a) Argentine (14)
armario closet, armoire (4)
arquitecto(a) architect (5)
arreglar to arrange; **arreglarse** to fix oneself up (6); to get ready (6)
arriba up (with)
arroz *m.* rice (7)
arte *m.* art (2); **arte abstracto** abstract art (11); **arte dramático** theater; **artes marciales** *f. pl.* martial arts; **bellas artes** *f. pl.* fine arts
arterial: presión *f.* **arterial** blood pressure
artesanías handicrafts
artículo article; **artículos de limpieza** cleaning materials
asado(a) grilled (7)
ascensor *m.* elevator (10)

así like this, thus, in this manner; **así es** that's so; **así que** thus, therefore; **¿no es así?** isn't that so?

asiento seat (10)

asistente *m. f.* **de vuelo** flight attendant (5)

asistir (a) to attend (3)

aspiradora vacuum cleaner; **pasar la aspiradora** to vacuum (8)

aspirante *m. f.* job candidate

aspirina aspirin (14)

asustado(a) scared (5)

asustarse to become frightened (9)

atender (ie) a to wait on; to attend to; to pay attention to (*other people*)

aterrizar (c) to land (10)

ático small attic apartment

atlético(a) athletic (1)

atletismo track and field (6)

atracción *f.* attraction; **parque** *m.* **de atracciones** amusement park

atrasado(a) late; **estar atrasado(a)** to be late

atravesar (ie) to cross (9)

atropellar to run over (9)

atún *m.* tuna

audiencia audience (13)

audífonos headphones (13)

auditorio auditorium (2)

aumento increase

aunque although, though

auto car

autorretrato self-portrait (11)

auxilio help; **primeros auxilios** first aid (14)

ave *f.* (*but* **el ave**) poultry; bird (12)

avergonzado(a) embarrassed (5)

avión *m.* plane

ayer yesterday (6)

ayudar to help (2)

ayuntamiento city hall

azafata *f.* flight attendant

azúcar *m.* sugar (7)

azul blue (3)

B

bádminton *m.* badminton (6)

bahía bay (12)

bailar to dance (2)

bailarín/bailarina dancer

bajar de to get out of (*a vehicle*) (9)

bajo(a) short (1); **presión** *f.* **baja** low blood pressure (14)

ballena whale (12)

balneario spa

balón *m.* (volley)ball

baloncesto basketball

banco bank (4)

bandera flag (1)

banderines streamers (9)

bañarse to bathe, to take a bath; to shower (*Mex.*) (6)

bañera bathtub (4)

baño bath; bathtub; bathroom (4); **traje de baño** bathing suit

bar *m.* bar (4)

barato(a) inexpensive, cheap (11)

barbilla chin

barco ship, boat

barrer to sweep (8)

básquetbol *m.* basketball (6)

bastante rather

basura trash, garbage, litter (8); **bote** *m.* **de basura** trashcan (8); **sacar (qu) la basura** to take the trash out (8)

batido(a) whipped

bautizo baptism (9)

beber to drink (3)

bebida drink (7)

beca scholarship (14)

béisbol *m.* baseball (6)

bellas artes *f. pl.* fine arts

beneficios benefits

besar to kiss (13)

biblioteca library (2)

bibliotecario(a) librarian

bicicleta bicycle; **andar en bicicleta** to ride a bike (6)

bien fine (1); well; **llevarse bien** to get along well (13); **pasarlo bien** to have a good time; **¡qué bien te queda esa falda!** that skirt really fits you well! (11); **sentirse (e, i) bien** to feel well

billete *m.* ticket

biología biology (2)

birth nacimiento (13)

bisabuela great grandmother

bisabuelo great grandfather

blanco(a) white (3); **vino blanco** white wine (7)

blusa blouse (3)

bluyíns *m., pl.* blue jeans (3)

boca mouth (6)

bocadillo snack (9)

boda wedding (9)

boleto ticket (10)

bolígrafo pen (1)

boliviano(a) Bolivian (14)

bolsa bag; purse (3); handbag

bolso bag; beach bag; purse; handbag

bombero(a) firefighter; **estación** *f.* **de bomberos** fire station

bonito(a) pretty (1); **¡qué color tan bonito!** what a pretty color! (11)

borracho(a) drunk (5)

borrador *m.* (chalk) eraser

bosque *m.* forest (12); wood(s)

bota boot (3)

bote *m.* **de basura** trashcan (8)

botella bottle

botones *m. f., sing. pl.* bellhop (10)

brazo arm (6)

brindar to toast (9)

brindis *m.* toast (*with a drink*) (9)

brócoli *m.* broccoli (7)

bucear con tubo de respiración to snorkel

bucear to scuba dive (6)

buen/bueno(a) good (1); **buen provecho** enjoy your meal; **buenas noches** good night (1); **buenas tardes** good afternoon (1); **buenos días** good morning (1); **hace buen tiempo** it's nice weather (3); **¡que tengas un buen día!** have a nice day! (1)

bufanda scarf (3)

buscador *m.* search engine (13)

buscar (qu) to look for (2)

butaca seat (*theater*) (13)

C

caballero gentleman

caballo horse (2); **montar a caballo** to ride horseback

cabello hair

caber to fit; **no cabe duda** there can be no doubt

cabeza head (6); **me duele la cabeza** I have a headache

cabo: al fin y al cabo after all; when all is said and done

cada each, every

cadera hip

caer(se) to fall (9); **caer bien (mal)** to like (dislike) a person (8)

café *m.* coffee (7); café (4); brown (3); **tomar café** to drink coffee

cafetera coffee maker (4)

cafetería cafeteria (2)

caja cash register (11)

calabacita zucchini

calabaza squash; pumpkin

calcetines *m. pl.* socks (3)

calefacción *f.* heat

caliente warm, hot

calle *f.* street (4)

calor *m.* warmth; heat; **hace calor** it's hot; **tener (mucho) calor** to be (very) hot (2)

calvo(a) bald (1)

cama bed (4); **cama matrimonial** double bed; **coche** *m.* **cama** sleeping car (10); **hacer la cama** to make the bed (8)

camarero(a) (hotel) maid (10)

camarón *m.* shrimp (7)

cambiar to change

cambio change; **en cambio** on the other hand

camilla stretcher (9)

caminar to walk (2)

camisa shirt (3)

camiseta T-shirt (3)

campo field (6)

cáncer *m.* cancer (14)

cancha court (*sports*) (6)

cansado(a) tired (5)

cantante *m. f.* singer (5)

cantar to sing (2)

cara face (6)

¡caray! oh!; oh no!

cariñoso(a) loving (1)

carne *f.* meat (7); **carne de res** beef; **carne de vacuno** beef

carnicería butcher shop

caro(a) expensive (11); **¡qué caro(a)!** how expensive! (11)

carretera highway (9)

carrito toy car (8)

carta letter (4); menu; *pl.* playing cards (8)

cartel *m.* poster (1)

cartera billfold, wallet

casa house

casarse (con) to get married to (9)

cascada waterfall (*small*) (12)

caso: en caso (de) (que) in case (that) (14)

catarata waterfall (12)

catorce fourteen (1)

catsup *f.* ketchup (7)

causa cause; **a causa de** on account of

causar to cause

caza hunting (12)

cazar (c) to hunt (12)

CD *m.* CD; **reproductor de CDs** CD player (13)

cebolla onion (7)

cebra zebra (12)

ceja eyebrow

celebrar to celebrate (9)

celos *m. pl.* jealousy; **tener celos** to be jealous

celoso(a) jealous (5)

cena dinner (7)

cenar to eat dinner (7)

censurar to censor (13)

centro center; **centro comercial** shopping center; **centro estudiantil** student center (2); **centro de negocios** business center (10)

cepillarse to brush (6)

cerca (de) close (to) (4)

cerdo pork (7); pig (12)

ceremonia ceremony (13)

cereza cherry

cero zero (1)

cerrar (ie) to close (4); to shut

cerro hill
certeza certainty
cerveza beer (7)
césped *m.* lawn; **cortar el césped** to mow the lawn (8)
ceviche (cebiche) *m. raw fish marinated in lime juice*
chalet *m.* villa
champán *m.* champagne (9)
champú *m.* shampoo (6)
chao Bye (1)
chaqueta jacket (3)
charlar to chat
charlatán(-ana) gossipy
chatear to chat (*online*) (8)
cheque *m.* check; **cheque de viaje** traveler's check; **cheque de viajero** traveler's check
chico(a) child; *adj.* small (11)
chileno(a) Chilean (14)
chimenea fireplace
chismear to gossip
chiste *m.* joke (8)
chocar (qu) (con) to crash (*into something*) (9)
ciclista *m. f.* cyclist (9)
cielo sky (12)
cien/ciento one hundred (1) (7); **cien mil** (one) hundred thousand; **cien millones** (one) hundred million; **ciento uno** one hundred one (1) (7); **por ciento** percent (11)
ciencias *f. pl.* science; **ciencias naturales** natural science (2); **ciencias políticas** political science (2); **ciencias sociales** social science (2)
científico(a) scientist (5)
cierto(a) *adj.* sure, certain, true; *adv.* certainly, surely; **¿cierto?** right?
cinco five (1)
cincuenta fifty (1)
cine *m.* movie theater (4); cinema
cintura waist
cinturón *m.* belt; **cinturón de seguridad** safety (seat) belt (10)
cirugía surgery (14)
cita date (13)
ciudadano(a) citizen (14)
claro(a) *adj.* sure; clear; light, pale (11); *adv.* certainly, surely; **claro que no** of course not; **claro que sí** certainly, surely, of course
clase *f.* class; **compañero(a) de clase** classmate (2); **primera clase** first class (10); **salón** *m.* **de clases** classroom (1); **segunda clase** second class (10)
clasificación *f.* rating (13)
clic: hacer clic (en) to click on (13)
cliente *m. f.* client
clínica clinic
club *m.* club (4)
coche *m.* car; **coche cama** sleeping car (10)
cochera garage (4)
cocina kitchen (4); **papel de cocina** paper towel
cocinar to cook (2)
cocinero(a) cook
cocodrilo crocodile (12)
coctel *m.* cocktail (7)
codo elbow (6)
cognado cognate
cola line, queue; **hacer cola** to stand in line
coleccionar to collect
colegio school (*secondary*)
colgar (ue) to hang (8)

colina hill (12)
collar *m.* necklace
colmo height; **¡esto es el colmo!** this is the last straw!
colombiano(a) Colombian (14)
color *m.* color; **¡qué color tan bonito!** what a pretty color! (11)
columna vertebral spinal column
comedor *m.* dining room (4)
comenzar (ie) (c) to begin (4); to start
comer to eat (3)
comercial: anuncio comercial commercial (13); **centro comercial** shopping center (4)
comerciante *m. f.* merchant
comercio: tratado de comercio trade agreement (14)
comestibles *m. pl.* groceries
cometa kite (8)
cómico(a) funny (1); **tira cómica** comic strip (8)
comida meal; food (7); lunch (7)
como like, as; **como consecuencia** as a consequence; **como resultado** as a result
¿cómo? how? (4); what?; **¿cómo está usted?** how are you? (*form.*) (1); **¿cómo estás?** how are you? (*fam.*) (1); **cómo no** of course
cómoda chest of drawers; bureau
cómodo(a) comfortable (3)
compañero(a) companion, significant other, partner; **compañero(a) de clase** classmate (2); **compañero(a) de cuarto** roommate
comparado(a) con compared with
compartir to share
competencia competition
competir (i, i) to compete (4)
completar to complete; to fill out
completo(a) complete; **a tiempo completo** full-time; **pensión** *f.* **completa** full board
complicado(a) complex (11)
comprar to buy (2)
comprender to understand (3)
comprobante *m.* voucher, credit slip
comprometerse (con) to get engaged (to) (13)
compromiso engagement (13)
computación: ciencias de la computación computer science
computadora computer (1)
con with; **con mucho gusto** with pleasure; **con tal (de) que** provided (that) (14)
concluir (y) to conclude
concurso contest; game show (13)
conducir (zc) to drive (5)
conductor(a) driver (9); TV host (13)
conejo rabbit (12)
conexión *f.* connection (10)
conferencia lecture; **sala de conferencias** conference center (10)
confundido(a) confused (5)
conjunto outfit
conmigo with me
conocer (zc) to know; to be acquainted with (5)
conocimiento knowledge
consecuencia consequence; **como consecuencia** as a consequence
conseguir (i, i) to get, obtain
consejero(a) adviser
conserje *m. f.* concierge
conservador(a) conservative (1)
construir (y) to build, construct
consultar to look up (a webpage,

a text, etc.); to consult
consultorio doctor's office
contabilidad *f.* accounting
contable *m. f.* accountant
contador(a) accountant (5)
contaminación pollution; contamination (12)
contar (ue) to count; to tell (a story) (8)
contener (*like* **tener**) to contain
contento(a) happy (5)
contestar to answer
contra against
contradecir to contradict
contrario(a) opposite, contrary; **al contrario** on the contrary; **al contrario de** unlike
control *m.* control; **control de pasaporte** passport control; **control de seguridad** security check; **control remoto** remote control (13)
copa wine glass (7)
corazón *m.* heart (14)
corbata tie (3)
cordero lamb
cordillera mountain range
correcto(a) that's right
correo mail; post office (4); **oficina de correos** post office
correr to run (3); **pista de correr** track
cortacésped *m.* lawnmower (8)
cortar to cut (8); **cortarse** to cut (oneself) (6) (14); **cortar el césped** to cut, to mow the lawn (10)
cortina curtain (4)
corto(a) short (1); **pantalones** *m. pl.* **cortos** shorts
cosa thing
costa coast (12)
costar (ue) to cost (4)
costarricense *m. f.* Costa Rican (14)
costoso(a) expensive
crédito credit; **tarjeta de crédito** credit card (11)
creer to believe (3); to think
crema cream (7); **crema batida** whipped cream
cremoso(a) creamy
criminología criminology (2)
cruce *m.* crosswalk (9)
crucigrama *m.* crossword puzzle
cruel cruel (1)
cruzar (c) to cross (9)
cuaderno notebook (1)
cuadro square; painting (4); picture (4); **a cuadros** checkered; plaid (11)
¿cuál(es)? which? (4)
cuando when
¿cuándo? when? (1)
cuanto: en cuanto as soon as (14)
¿cuánto(a)? how much? (4)
¿cuántos(as)? how many? (4)
cuarenta forty (1)
cuarto quarter (*of an hour*); room; **cuarto de baño** bathroom; **cuarto oscuro** darkroom
cuarto(a) *adj.* fourth (4)
cuatro four (1)
cuatrocientos(as) four hundred (7)
cubano(a) Cuban (14)
cubierto(a) covered
cubiertos *m. pl.* table setting; cutlery
cubista *m. f.* cubist (11)
cuchara soupspoon (7)
cucharita teaspoon
cuchillo knife (7)
cuello neck (6)

cuenta bill *(restaurant)* (7); check
cuento story (8)
cuerda jumping rope (8)
cuero leather
cuerpo body
cuidado care; **tener (mucho) cuidado** to be (very) careful (2)
cuidar (de) to take care (of)
culpa fault
cultivar el jardín to garden *(flowers)*
cumpleañero(a) birthday boy (girl)
cumpleaños *m. sing., pl.* birthday (3) (9); **fiesta de cumpleaños** birthday party
curita small adhesive bandage (14)
cuyo(a), cuyos(as) whose

D

dama lady; *pl.* checkers (8)
dañado(a) damaged; **estar dañado(a)** to be damaged (9)
dañar to damage (9)
dar to give (5); **dar a luz** to give birth (13); **darse cuenta de** to realize; **dar la vuelta** to take a walk or a ride (8)
de of, from; **de acuerdo** agreed, all right; **¿de dónde eres tú?** where are you *(fam.)* from? (1); **¿de dónde?** from where? (4); **de lunares** with polka dots (11); **de moda** fashionable (11); **de nuevo** new; again; **de paso** by the way; **de repente** suddenly (9); **¿de veras?** really, is that so?; **de verdad** really; **del mismo modo** similarly
debajo (de) below; under (4)
deber (+ inf.) should/ought to (*do something*) (3)
décimo(a) tenth (4)
decir to say, to tell (5); **querer decir** to mean
declarar to declare; **algo que declarar** something to declare
decorar to decorate (9)
dedo finger (6); **dedo del pie** toe (6)
definido(a) definite
deforestación *f.* deforestation (12)
dejar to leave; **dejar una propina** to leave a tip (7)
delante (de) in front (of)
delantero(a) front
delgado(a) thin (1)
demasiado(a) too, too much
dentro (de) inside (of) (4)
dependiente(a) clerk (5)
deportes *m. pl.* sports; **practicar (qu) deportes** to play sports (2)
deportivo(a) related to sports, sporting
deprimido(a) depressed (5)
derecha right; **a la derecha (de)** to the right (of) (4)
derecho law; right; **derechos humanos** human rights (14); **seguir (i) derecho** to go straight (10)
desacuerdo disagreement
desayunar to eat breakfast (7)
desayuno breakfast (7)
descansar to rest (14)
descomponer to break down (*a machine*) (11)
descuento discount (11)
desear to wish (2) (13); to desire (13); to want
desechos industriales industrial waste (12)
desembarcar (qu) to deplane
desempleado(a) unemployed
desempleo unemployment (14)
desfile *m.* parade (9)
deshacer la maleta to unpack one's suitcase
desierto desert (12)

desmayarse to faint (14)
desmayo faint (14)
despacio slowly
despedida farewell; **despedida de soltera** bridal shower; **despedida de soltero** bachelor party
despedir (i, i) to fire; **despedirse** to say goodbye
despegar (gu) to take off (10)
despejado(a) clear *(weather)* (3)
despertador *m.* alarm clock (6)
despertarse (ie) to wake up (6)
después then, next; **después de (que)** after (14); **después de (+ inf.)** after *(doing something)* (6)
destino destination
destruir (y) to destroy (12)
desván *m.* attic
detergente *m.* **para platos** dish detergent
detrás (de) in back (of); behind (4)
devolver (ue) to return *(something)* (4)
día *m.* day (3); **al día** per day; **día de santo** saint's day; **día feriado** holiday (3); **¡que tengas un buen día!** have a nice day! (1); **todos los días** every day (3)
diabetes *f.* diabetes (14)
diario(a) daily
diarrea diarrhea (14)
dibujar to draw (8)
dibujos animados cartoons (13)
diccionario dictionary (1)
diciembre *m.* December (3)
dictadura dictatorship (14)
diecinueve nineteen (1)
dieciocho eighteen (1)
dieciséis sixteen (1)
diecisiete seventeen (1)
diente *m.* tooth (6)
diez ten (1)
diferencia difference; **a diferencia de** unlike; in contrast to
diferente different; **diferente de** unlike
dinero money (4); **el dinero en efectivo** cash (11)
Dios *m.* God; **Dios mío** oh, my goodness
dirección *f.* direction; address (4)
discoteca nightclub (4)
disculparse to excuse oneself
diseñador(a) designer (5)
diseñar to design (11)
disfrutar to enjoy (9)
disponible available (10)
distraerse to get distracted (9)
diversión *f.* entertainment; hobby, pastime
divertido(a) funny (5); fun
divertirse (ie, i) to have fun (6)
divorciarse (de) to divorce (13)
doblar to bend; to turn (10)
doble double (10); **habitación doble** double room
doce twelve (1)
docena dozen
documental *m.* documentary (13)
doler (ue) to hurt (14); **me duele la cabeza** I have a headache
dolor *m.* pain (14); ache
doméstico(a) domestic, household
domingo *m.* Sunday (3)
dominicano(a) Dominican (14)
dominó *sing.* dominos (8)
donde where
¿dónde? where? (1) (4); **¿de dónde?** from where? (4); **¿de dónde eres tú?** where are you *(fam.)* from? (1)
dormir (ue, u) to sleep (4); **dormirse (ue, u)** to fall asleep (6); **saco de dormir** sleeping bag (6)

dormitorio bedroom (4)
dos two (1)
doscientos(as) two hundred (7)
dramático(a) dramatic; **arte** *m.* **dramático** theater
ducha shower (4)
ducharse to shower (6)
duda doubt; **no cabe duda** there can be no doubt
dudar to doubt (12)
dudoso(a) doubtful
dulce sweet; **salsa de tomate dulce** tomato sauce; ketchup; *n. pl.* candies (9)
durazno peach (7)
duro(a) tough, hard

E

ecología ecology (12)
economía economics; economy (2)
económico(a) *adj.* economical; inexpensive; **ciencias económicas** economics; **hotel** *m.* **económico** inexpensive hotel
ecuatoguineano Equatorial Guinean (14)
ecuatoriano(a) Ecuadorian (14)
edificio building (4)
efectivo cash (11); **el dinero en efectivo** cash (11)
eficiente efficient
egoísta selfish (1)
ejemplo example; **por ejemplo** for example
ejercicio exercise; **ejercicios aeróbicos** aerobics
el *def. art. m.* the; **el cual(es)** which, whom; **el que** that, which, whom, the one
él *sub. pron.* he
elefante *m.* elephant (12)
elegante elegant; **¡qué pantalones tan elegantes!** what elegant pants! (11)
elegir (i, i) (j) to elect; to choose (11)
ella she
embarazada pregnant; **estar embarazada** to be pregnant (13)
embargo: sin embargo nevertheless; however
emergencia: sala de emergencias emergency room (14)
emigración *f.* emigration (14)
emigrar to emigrate (14)
emisora de radio radio station
empatar to tie *(score)*
empezar (ie) (c) to begin (4); **empezar a** to begin to do something (4); to start; **para empezar** to begin with
empresa firm, business; **administración** *f.* **de empresas** business and management
en in; on; at; **en cambio** on the other hand; **en caso (de) (que)** in case (that) (14); **en conclusión** in conclusion; **en particular** in particular; **en principio** in principle; **en resumen** in summary; **en suma** in conclusion; **en venta** on sale; **en voz alta** aloud
enamorado(a) (de) in love *(with)* (5)
encantado(a) delighted; nice to meet you (1)
encantador(a) enchanting
encantar to love, to be delighted (8)
encender (ie) to turn on (4)
encerrar (ie) to lock up
encima (de) on top (of) (4)
encontrar (ue) to find (4)
enero January (3)
enfermero(a) nurse (5)
enfermo(a) sick (5)
enfrente (de) in front (of) (4)
engordar to gain weight
enojado(a) angry (5)
enojarse to become angry (9)

ensalada salad (7)
enseñar to teach (2)
entender (ie) to understand (4)
entonces then, next
entrada entrance; cover charge; ticket (6)
entrar to enter
entre among; between (4)
entregar (gu) to hand in, hand over
entremés *m.* appetizer (7)
entrenador(a) coach
entrenar to train, to coach
entreplanta loft
entrevista interview (5)
entusiasta enthusiastic
envolver (ue) to wrap
equipaje *m.* luggage (10); **facturar equipaje** to check luggage (10); **reclamo de equipaje** baggage claim (10); **revisión** *f.* **de equipaje** luggage screening (10)
equipo team (6); equipment (6); **equipo escolar** school supplies
equivocado(a) wrong (5)
equivocarse (qu) to make a mistake
escala layover (10); **hacer escala** to make a stop, layover
escalera stairs (7)
escoba broom (8)
escolar *adj.* school; **equipo escolar** school supplies
escondidas *f.* hide and seek (8)
escribir (un mensaje) to write (a message) (3)
escritor(a) writer (5)
escritorio desk; teacher's desk (1)
escuchar to listen (2)
escuela school (4)
esculpir to sculpt (11)
escultura sculpture (11)
ese(a) *adj.* that; *pron.* that (one)
esmog *m.* smog (12)
eso *pron.* that (one); **por eso** therefore
esos(as) *adj.* those; *pron.* those
espalda back (6)
espanto fright
España Spain
español *m.* Spanish (*language*)
español(a) *m.* (*f.*) native of Spain; *adj.* Spanish (14)
espejo mirror
espera: sala de espera waiting room (10)
esperar to hope (for) (13); to expect; to wait (9)
espinaca spinach
esponja sponge
esposo(a) husband/wife; spouse (2)
esqueleto skeleton (14)
esquí acuático *m.* water-skiing
esquiar to ski (2); **esquiar en el agua** to water ski (6); **esquiar en tabla** to snowboard (6)
esquina corner (9)
estación *f.* station; season; **estación de autobuses** bus station; **estación de bomberos** fire station; **estación de ferrocarril** train station; **estación de policía** police station
estacionarse to park (9)
estadio stadium (2)
Estados Unidos United States
estadounidense *m. f.* citizen of the United States
estampado(a) patterned (11)
estante *m.* shelf
estar to be (4); **¿cómo está usted?** how are you (*form.*)? (1); **¿cómo estás?** how are you (*fam.*)? (1); **estar embarazada** to be pregnant (13); **estar atrasado(a)** to

be late; **estar dañado(a)** to be damaged (9); **estar de acuerdo** to agree; **estar de moda** to be in style; **estar herido(a)** to be injured (9); **estar mareado(a)** to be dizzy (14); **está lloviendo** it's raining; **está nevando** it's snowing; **está nublado** it is cloudy (3); **está despejado** it is clear (3); **fuera de** outside of (4)
estatura height
este(a) *adj.* this; *pron.* this (one)
estilográfico(a): pluma estilográfica fountain pen
estirarse to stretch (6)
esto *pron.* this (one); **¡esto es el colmo!** this is the last straw!
estómago stomach (6)
estornudar to sneeze (14)
estornudo sneeze (14)
estos(as) adj. these
éstos(as) *pron.* these
estrecho strait
estreñimiento constipation
estudiante *m. f.* student (1)
estudiantil *adj.* student; **albergue estudiantil** *m.* youth hostel; **centro estudiantil** student center (2)
estudiar to study (2)
estudio efficiency apartment, studio
estufa stove (4)
exacto(a) exactly
examen *m.* exam (2); **examen médico** medical examination
examinar to examine (14)
excursión: ir de excursión to hike (6)
excusarse to make an excuse
exhibición *f.* exhibition (11)
exhibir to exhibit (11)
éxito success; **éxito de taquilla** box office hit (13); **tener (mucho) éxito** to be (very) successful (2)
expresión *f.* expression; **expresión oral** speech (2)
extinción: peligro de extinción danger of extinction (12)
extranjero: al extranjero abroad
extranjero(a) foreigner
extrañar to miss (13)
extraño strange, odd (11)
extremidad *f.* extremity
extrovertido(a) extrovert

F

fábrica factory
fácil easy (1)
facturar equipaje to check luggage (10)
facultad *f.* school, college
falda skirt (3); **¡qué bien te queda esa falda!** that skirt really fits you well! (11)
falta lack
famoso(a) famous (1)
farmacéutico(a) pharmacist
farmacia pharmacy (4)
fascinante fascinating
fascinar to fascinate, be fascinated by (8)
favor *m.* favor; **por favor** please
febrero February (3)
fecha date (*calendar*) (3)
felicitar to congratulate (7)
feliz happy (5); **ponerse feliz** to become happy
feo(a) ugly (1)
ferrocarril *m.* railroad; **estación** *f.* **de ferrocarril** train station
festejado(a) guest of honor
festejar to entertain, to celebrate
festejo party, celebration (9)

festival *m.* festival
festivo: día *m.* **festivo** holiday
fiambre *m.* luncheon meat, cold cut
fiebre *f.* fever
fiesta party; **fiesta de canastilla** baby shower; **fiesta de cumpleaños** birthday party; **fiesta sorpresa** surprise party
filosofía philosophy (2); **filosofía y letras** liberal arts
fin *m.* end; **fin de semana** weekend (3); **a fin de que** so (that), in order that (14); **al fin y al cabo** after all; when all is said and done; **por fin** finally
final *m.* end; **al final** in the end
finalmente finally
física physics (2)
físico(a) physical
flan *m.* flan (7)
flojo(a) loose
flor *f.* flower (4); **de flores** floral, flowered
forma shape; **mantenerse** (*like* **tener**) **en forma** to stay fit, keep in shape
foto *f.* photo(graph); **revelar fotos** to develop photos; **sacar (qu) fotos** to take photos
fotógrafo(a) photographer (5)
fracturarse to fracture (14)
francés *m.* French (*language*) (2)
frase *f.* phrase
fregadero kitchen sink (4)
fregar (ie) (gu) to mop; to scrub
frente a facing
frente *f.* forehead
fresa strawberry (7)
fresco(a) fresh, cool; **hace fresco** it's cool (*weather*)
frijol *m.* bean
frío(a) cold; **hace frío** it's cold (*weather*); **tener (mucho) frío** to be (very) cold (2)
frito(a) fried (7)
frustrado(a) frustrated (5)
frustrarse to become frustrated (9)
fruta fruit (7)
frutería fruit store
fuego fire; **fuegos artificiales** fireworks (9)
fuera (de) outside (of) (4)
fútbol *m.* soccer (6); **fútbol americano** football
futbolista *m. f.* football (soccer) player

G

gafas *pl.* glasses; **gafas de sol** sunglasses
galería gallery (11)
gallina hen (12)
gallo rooster (12)
gamba shrimp
gana desire, wish; **tener ganas de** (+ *inf.*) to feel like (*doing something*) (2)
ganar to earn (5); to win
ganga bargain
garganta throat; **dolor** *m.* **de garganta** sore throat; **inflamación** *f.* **de la garganta** strep throat
gastar to spend
gato(a) cat (2)
gemelo(a) twin
general: por lo general generally
generalmente generally
generoso(a) generous (1)
gente *f.* people
geografía geography (2)
gerente *m. f.* manager
gimnasio gym(nasium) (2)
gis *m.* chalk

globalización f. globalization (14)
globo balloon (9)
gobierno government (14)
golf m. golf (6)
golfo gulf
golosina candy (13)
goma (pencil) eraser
gordo(a) fat (1); plump
gorila gorilla (12)
gorra cap
gorro cap (3)
gota drop (14)
grabado engraving (11); print (11)
grabadora tape recorder
gracias thanks, thank you
gracioso(a) funny; charming
graduación f. graduation (9)
gran/grande great; big (1); large (11)
granja farm (12)
gripe f. flu (14)
grupo group; **grupo de música** music group (9); band (9)
guante m. glove (3)
guapo(a) handsome (1)
guardar to keep; to put away (8)
guatemalteco(a) Guatemalan (14)
guerra war (14)
guisante m. pea
gustar to like; to please; to be pleasing; **me gusta** I like (3); **le gusta** he/she likes (3); **te gusta** you (*fam. sing.*) like (3)
gusto pleasure; taste; **con mucho gusto** with pleasure; **mucho gusto** nice to meet you (1)

H

habitación f. room (4) (10); **habitación doble** double room; **habitación sencilla** single room; **servicio a la habitación** room service (10)
hablar to talk (2); to speak; **hablar por teléfono** to talk on the phone (2)
hacer to do (5); to make (5); **hace buen tiempo** the weather is nice (3); **hace calor** it's hot (3); **hace fresco** it's cool (*weather*) (3); **hace frío** it's cold (*weather*) (3); **hace mal tiempo** the weather is bad (3); **hace sol** it's sunny (3); **hace viento** it's windy (3); **hacer alpinismo** to climb mountains (6); **hacer clic (en)** to click on (13); **hacer juego** to match (11); **hacer la cama** to make the bed (8); **hacer la maleta** to pack one's suitcase; **hecho(a) a mano** handmade (11); **¿qué tiempo hace?** what's the weather like?
hambre f. hunger; **tener (mucha) hambre** to be (very) hungry (2)
hamburguesa hamburger (7)
hasta until; **hasta ahora** up to now, so far; **hasta aquí** up to now, so far; **hasta hace poco** until a little while ago; **hasta luego** see you later (1); **hasta mañana** see you tomorrow (1); **hasta pronto** see you soon (1); **hasta que** until
hay there is/are (1); **hay que** (+ *inf.*) one should (+ *verb*); it's necessary to (+ *verb*); **¿qué hay de nuevo?** what's new? (1)
helada frost
helado ice cream (7)
hembra female (12)
herida wound
herido(a): estar herido(a) to be injured (9)
hermanastro(a) stepbrother/stepsister
hermano(a) brother/sister (2); **medio(a) hermano(a)** half brother/half sister (2)
hermoso(a) beautiful

hielo ice; **patinar sobre hielo** to ice skate
hierba grass
hígado liver (14)
hijastro(a) stepson/stepdaughter
hijo(a) son/daughter (2)
hipertensión f. hypertension; high blood pressure (14)
historia history (2); **historia médica** medical history
hogar m. home
hoja de papel piece of paper
hola hello (1)
holandés(esa) Dutch
hombre m. man (1)
hombro shoulder (6)
hondureño(a) Honduran (14)
honesto(a) honest (1)
hora time (*of day*)
hornear to bake (7)
horno oven (4); **al horno** baked (7)
hospital m. hospital (4)
hostal m. hostel
hotel m. hotel (4); **hotel económico** inexpensive hotel; **hotel de lujo** luxury hotel; **hotel de primera clase** first-class hotel
hoy today (3) (6)
huelga strike
hueso bone (14)
huésped m. f. guest (10)
huevo egg (7)

I

ida: de ida one-way; **de ida y vuelta** round-trip
idealista idealist (1)
identificación f. identification
idioma m. language (14)
iglesia church (4)
igual equal; **al igual que** like
igualmente likewise
impaciente impatient (1)
impermeable m. raincoat (3)
importancia importance
importante important
importar to be important (8)
imposible impossible
imprescindible indispensable
impresionante impressive
impresionista impressionist (11)
impresora printer
impuesto tax
incluido(a) included
incluir (y) to include
incorrecto(a) not right, incorrect
infantil childish, for children (13)
inferior lower
infinitivo infinitive
inflamación f. **de la garganta** strep throat
informática computer science (2)
ingeniería engineering (2)
ingeniero(a) engineer
inglés m. English (*language*)
inicialmente initially
inmigración f. immigration (14)
inmigrar to immigrate (14)
inodoro toilet (4)
insistir (en + *inf.*) to insist (*on*) (13)
insomnio insomnia (14)
inteligente intelligent (1)
interesado(a) interested (5)
interesante interesting (1)
interesar to interest, be interested in (8)
internacional international; **aeropuerto internacional** international airport

(10); **organismo internacional** international organization (14)
Internet inalámbrico m. wireless Internet (10)
interno(a) internal
intestino intestine (14)
introvertido(a) introvert
invierno winter (3)
invitación f. invitation (9)
invitado(a) guest (9)
inyección f. injection (14); shot; **poner(le) una inyección** to give (him/her) an injection
ir to go (2); **irse** to leave, go away (6); **ir de excursión** to hike (6); **ir de pesca** to go fishing (6)
isla island (12)
italiano Italian (2)
izquierda left; **a la izquierda (de)** to the left (of) (4)

J

jabón m. soap (6); **jabón para platos** dish soap (8)
jade m. jade; **objeto de jade** jade object
jaguar m. jaguar (12)
jamás never (6)
jamón m. ham (7)
jarabe m. cough syrup (14)
jardín m. yard; garden (4); **jardín botánico** botanical garden; **cultivar el jardín** to garden (*flowers*)
jardinería gardening; **hacer jardinería** to do yardwork (8)
jaula cage (12)
jirafa giraffe (12)
joven (*pl.* **jóvenes**) young (1)
jubilado(a) retired
judía verde green bean
juego game; **juego de mesa** board game (8); **hacer** *irreg.* **juego** to match (11)
jueves m. Thursday (3)
jugar (ue, u) (gu) to play (4); **jugar a los bolos** to go bowling (8)
jugo juice (7)
juguete m. toy (8)
juicio judgment
julio July (3)
junio June (3)
junto a beside, next to
jurar to swear, give one's word
justo(a) fair
juventud f. youth (13)

K

kiosco kiosk, stand

L

la f. the; *d.o.* her/it/you (*form. sing.*)
labio lip
laboratorio laboratory (2)
lado side; **al lado (de)** alongside (of); beside, next to (4)
lago lake (6)
lámpara lamp (4)
lana wool (11)
langosta lobster
lápiz m. (*pl.* **lápices**) pencil(s) (1)
largo(a) long (1); **a lo largo (de)** along
las f. pl. the; *d.o. pron.* you (*form. pl.*) them
lástima pity
lavabo bathroom sink (4)
lavadora washing machine (4)

lavandería laundry, laundry room
lavaplatos *m. sing., pl.* dishwasher (4)
lavar(se) to wash (6); **lavar platos** to do dishes (8); **lavar ropa** to do laundry (8)
le *i.o.* you (*form. sing.*); to/for him, her, it; **le presento a...** I'd like to introduce you (*form.*) to . . . (1)
leal loyal
lección *f.* lesson
leche *f.* milk (7)
lechería dairy store
lechuga lettuce (7)
leer to read (3)
lejos (de) far (from) (4)
lengua language (2); tongue; **lenguas modernas** modern languages; **sacar (qu) la lengua** to stick out one's tongue
lentes *m. pl.* glasses (3)
león *m.* lion
les *i.o. pron.* to, for you (*form. pl.*), them
letras: filosofía y letras liberal arts
levantar to lift; **levantarse** to get up (6); **levantar pesas** to lift weights (6)
ley *f.* law (14)
liberal liberal (1)
libra pound
libre free; **unión** *f.* **libre** common-law union (13)
librería bookstore (2)
libro book (1)
licuado smoothie made with fruits, juices, and ice
limitar to limit (13)
límite *m.* **de velocidad** speed limit (9)
limón *m.* lemon; lime
limpiador *m.* liquid cleaner; **limpiador para el hogar** all-purpose cleaner
limpiar to clean (2)
limpieza: artículos de limpieza cleaning materials
limpio(a) clean
lindo(a) pretty; **¡qué lindos zapatos!** what pretty shoes! (11)
línea aérea airline
lino linen (11)
liquidación *f.* sale
liso(a) solid (*color*) (11)
lista list
litera bunk (bed)
literatura literature (2)
litro liter
llama llama (12)
llamar to call (2); **llamarse** to be called/named; **me llamo...** my name is . . . (1)
llano plains (12)
llave *f.* key (10)
llegada arrival (10)
llegar (gu) to arrive (2)
lleno(a) full
llevar to take (3); to carry (3); to wear (3); to take along (7); **llevar puesto** to be wearing (3)
llevarse bien/mal to (not) get along (13)
llover (ue) to rain (4); **está lloviendo** it's raining; **llueve** it is raining, it rains (3)
lluvia rain
lo *m. d.o.* you (*form. sing.*); him,/it; **lo cual** which; **lo que** what, which; **lo siento (mucho)** I'm (very) sorry
lobo wolf (12)
loco(a) crazy (5); **volverse loco(a)** to go crazy
locutor(a) announcer (13)
los *def. art. m. pl.* the; *d.o.* them/you (*form. pl.*)
lucha fight, struggle

luchar to fight, struggle
lucir (zc) to wear; to show off, sport (*wear*)
luego then, next (6); **hasta luego** see you later (1)
lugar *m.* place; **tener lugar** to take place
lujo luxury; **de lujo** luxurious (10); **hotel** *m.* **de lujo** luxury hotel
luna de miel honeymoon (13)
lunar: de lunares polka-dotted (11)
lunes *m.* Monday (3)
luz *f.* (*pl.* **luces**) light (11); **dar a luz** to give birth (13)

M

macho male (12)
madrastra stepmother
madre *f.* mother (2)
madrina godmother (13)
maestro(a) teacher; **maestro(a) de ceremonias** master of ceremony
maíz *m.* corn (7); **palomitas de maíz** popcorn (13)
mal *adv.* badly; bad (1), not well; **hace mal tiempo** the weather is bad (3); **llevarse mal** to not get along (13); **sentirse (e, i) mal** to feel bad, ill
mal, malo(a) bad (1)
maleta suitcase (10); **deshacer la maleta** to unpack one's suitcase; **hacer la maleta** to pack one's suitcase
maletero porter
mamá mother (2)
mamífero mammal (12)
manantial *m.* spring (of water)
mandar to order (13); **mandar (un mensaje)** to send (a message) (2)
mandato command
manejar to drive (2)
manera way
manguera hose (8)
mano *f.* hand (6); **equipaje** *m.* **de mano** hand luggage (10); **hecho(a) a mano** handmade (11)
mantel *m.* tablecloth
mantenerse (*like* tener) **en forma** to stay fit, keep in shape
mantequilla butter (7)
manzana apple (7)
mañana tomorrow (3) (6); morning; **de la mañana** A.M.; **hasta mañana** see you tomorrow (1); **por la mañana** in the morning (3)
mapa *m.* map (1)
maquillarse to put on make-up (6)
mar *m.* sea (12)
maravilla marvel, wonder
marca: de marca name brand (11)
marcador *m.* marker
marcharse to leave, to go away
marcial: artes marciales *f. pl.* martial arts
mareado dizzy; **estar mareado(a)** to be dizzy (14)
marearse to feel dizzy
mareo dizziness; **tener mareos** to be dizzy
mariscal *m. raw shellfish marinated in lime juice*
mariscos shellfish
marrón brown
martes *m.* Tuesday (3)
marzo March (3)
más more; plus (*in mathematical functions*); **más que** more than; **más tarde** later (6)
máscara mask (11)
masticar (qu) to chew
matemáticas *pl.* mathematics (2)

materia course, subject
matrimonial: cama matrimonial double bed
matrimonio: marriage **proponer matrimonio** to propose marriage (13)
mayo May (3)
mayonesa mayonnaise (7)
mayor older (11); **el/la mayor** the oldest
me *d.o., i.o. pron.* me
mecánico(a) mechanic (5)
media stocking
mediano(a) medium (11)
medianoche *f.* midnight (3)
medias *pl.* panty hose
medicamento medication
médico(a) *adj.* medical; **examen** *m.* **médico** medical examination; **historia médica** medical history; **receta médica** prescription (14)
médico(a) *n.* doctor (5)
medio(a) half; **medio(a) hermano(a)** half brother/half sister (2); **media pensión** half board (*breakfast and one other meal*)
mediodía *m.* noon (3)
mejilla cheek
mejillón *m.* mussel
mejor better (11); **el/la mejor** the best
melón *m.* melon (7)
menor younger (11); **el/la menor** the youngest
menos less; minus (*in mathematical functions*); **menos que** less than; **a menos que** unless (14)
mentir (ie, i) to lie (4)
menudo: a menudo frequently, often (6)
mercado market
merecer (zc) to deserve
merendar (ie) to eat a snack
merienda snack
mermelada jam
mes *m.* month
mesa table; **poner la mesa** to set the table (8); **recoger (j) la mesa** to pick up the table (8); to clear the table (8)
mesero(a) (*Mex.*) (*restaurant*) waitperson; waiter (5)
meseta plateau
mesita coffee table (4); end table; **mesita de noche** night table
metro subway
mexicano(a) Mexican (14)
mezclilla denim (11)
mezquita mosque (4)
mi my
microondas *m.* microwave (4)
miedo fear; **tenerle miedo a** to be afraid of (*person*); **tener (mucho) miedo** to be (very) afraid (2)
miel *f.* honey; **luna de miel** honeymoon (13)
miembro member
mientras while (6)
miércoles *m.* Wednesday (3)
mil one thousand (7); **cien mil** (one) hundred thousand; **dos mil** two thousand (7)
millón *m.* million (7); **cien millones** (one) hundred million
mío(a) mine
mirar (la tele) to watch (TV) (2); to look (at)
misa mass
mismo(a) same; **del mismo modo** similarly
mochila backpack (1)
moda fashion, style; **de moda** fashionable (11); **estar de moda** to be in style (11); **pasado(a) de moda** out of style

modelo *m. f.* model (5)
moderno(a) modern; **lenguas modernas** modern languages
modista dressmaker
modo way; **del mismo modo** similarly
molestar to bother (8), be bothered by
mono monkey (12)
montaña mountain (12)
montañoso(a) mountainous
montar to climb; get on; **montar a** to ride (an animal) (6)
morado(a) purple (3)
moreno(a) dark-skinned/dark-haired (1), brunette
morir (ue, u) to die (4)
mostaza mustard (7)
mostrador *m.* counter (10)
mostrar (ue) to show (8)
moto(cicleta) motorcycle (8)
mover (ue) to move (*something*)
MP3 *m.* MP3 (13)
mucho(a) much; many; a lot (2); **lo siento (mucho)** I'm (very) sorry; **mucho gusto** nice to meet you (1)
mudarse to move (14)
muebles *m. pl.* furniture
muerte *f.* death (13)
muerto(a) dead; **naturaleza muerta** still life (11)
mujer *f.* woman (1); **mujer policía** police officer (5)
multa fine (9); ticket (9)
municipalidad *f.* city hall
muñeca wrist
muñeco(a) doll (8)
mural *m.* mural (11)
muscular muscular; **dolor** *m.* **muscular** muscle ache
museo museum (4)
música music (2)
músico(a) musician (5)
muslo thigh (6)
muy very (1)

N

nacer (zc) to be born (13)
nacionalidad *f.* nationality
nada nothing (1)
nadar to swim (2)
nadie no one, nobody
naipes *m. pl.* (playing) cards
naranja orange (7) (8)
nariz *f.* nose (6)
natación swimming (6)
natural natural; **recursos naturales** natural resources (12)
naturaleza nature (12); **naturaleza muerta** still life (11)
navegar (gu) a la vela to sail; **navegar el Internet** to surf the web (8)
Navidad Christmas (3)
necesario(a) necessary
necesitar to need (2)
negar (ie) (gu) to deny, to negate
negocio business (4); **negocios** *pl.* business (2); **centro de negocios** business center (10)
negro(a) black (3)
nevar (ie) to snow (4); **está nevando** it's snowing; **nieva** it is snowing, it snows (3)
ni... ni neither . . . nor
nicaragüense *m. f.* Nicaraguan (14)
niebla fog
nieto(a) grandson/granddaughter (2)
nieve *f.* snow

nilón *m.* nylon
ningún/ninguno(a) none, not any
niñera babysitter (8)
niñez *f.* childhood (13)
no no; **¿no?** isn't that so?; **¿no es así?** isn't that right?; **no obstante** however
noche *f.* night; **de la noche** P.M.; **mesita de noche** night table; **por la noche** in the evening (3)
nombre *m.* name
noreste *m.* northeast
normalmente normally (6)
noroeste *m.* northwest
norte *m.* north
norteamericano(a) North American
nos *d.o.* us; *i.o.* to/for us; *refl. pron.* ourselves; **nos vemos** see you later (1)
nosotros(as) *subj. pron.* we
nota grade (2); **nota adhesiva** sticky note; **sacar (qu) una buena/mala nota** to get a good/bad grade
noticiario news (13)
novecientos(as) nine hundred (7)
novelista *m. f.* novelist
noventa ninety (1)
noviazgo engagement (13); relationship (13)
noviembre *m.* November (3)
novio(a) groom/bride; fiancé(e); boyfriend/girlfriend (2); *pl.* bride and groom (9)
nube *f.* cloud (12)
nublado(a) cloudy; **está nublado** it is cloudy (3)
nuboso(a) cloudy
nuera daughter-in-law
nuestro(a) *poss.* our
nueve nine (1)
nuevo(a) new; **Año Nuevo** New Year (3); **de nuevo** new; again; **¿Qué hay de nuevo?** What's new? (1)
número number; size (*shoe*) (11)
nunca never (6)

O

o or; **o...o** either . . . or
obesidad *f.* obesity (14)
objeto object; **objeto directo** direct object; **objeto indirecto** indirect object
obligación *f.* obligation
obra work (*of art, literature, theater, etc.*) (11)
obscuro(a) dark (11)
obstante: no obstante however
obstinado(a) obstinate, stubborn
obtener to get
obvio(a) obvious
océano ocean
ochenta eighty (1)
ocho eight (1)
ochocientos(as) eight hundred (7)
octubre *m.* October (3)
ocupado(a) busy (5)
ocurrir to occur
odiar to hate (13)
oferta offer; sale (event, reduction of prices) (11)
oficina office (4); **oficina de correos** post office
oficio occupation
oído inner ear
oír to hear (5)
ojalá (que) I hope (that)
ojo eye

ola wave (12)
óleo oil painting (11)
oler (ue) to smell
olfato sense of smell
olla de cerámica ceramic pot
olvidar to forget (11)
once eleven (1)
onomástico saint's day
opinar to give one's opinion
opinión *f.* opinion
optimista *m., f.* optimist (1)
oración *f.* sentence
orden *f.* order (7)
ordenador *m.* computer
ordenar to tidy up (8); to straighten up (8)
oreja (*outer*) ear (6)
organismo internacional international organization (14)
organizar (c) to organize, to tidy up
órgano organ; **órgano vital** vital organ (14)
orgulloso(a) (de) proud (of)
origen *m.* origin
oro gold
os *d.o.* (*Sp.*) you (*fam. pl.*); *i.o.* (*Sp.*) to/for you (*fam. pl.*); *refl. pron.* (*Sp.*) your-selves (*fam. pl.*)
oscuro(a) dark; **cuarto oscuro** darkroom
osito teddy bear (8)
oso bear (12)
otoño autumn (3)
otro(a) other; **otra vez** again; **por otra parte** moreover; on the other hand
oveja sheep (12)

P

pachanga (rowdy) party
paciente patient (1) (14)
padrastro stepfather (2)
padre *m.* father (2); *pl.* parents
padrino best man, godfather (13)
pagar (gu) to pay; **pagar y marcharse** to check out (10)
página page
país *m.* country (14)
paisaje *m.* landscape (11)
pájaro bird
palabra word
palacio palace
paleta pallet (11)
palmera palm tree (12)
palomitas de maíz popcorn (13)
pampa grasslands (12)
pan *m.* bread (7)
panadería bakery
panameño(a) Panamanian (14)
pantalla screen (13)
pantalones *m. pl.* pants (3); **pantalones cortos** shorts (3)
papá *m.* father (2)
papa potato (7)
papel *m.* paper (1); **hoja de papel** piece of paper; **papel de cocina** paper towel
paperas mumps
paquete package (4)
para for; in order to; to (*in the direction of*); **para empezar** to begin with; **para que** so (that) (14); **¿para qué?** for what reason?
parada stop (10)
paraguas *m. sing., pl.* umbrella (3)
paraguayo(a) Paraguayan (14)
paramédico paramedic (9)
parcial partial; **a tiempo parcial** part-time
PARE: pasarse una señal de PARE to run a STOP sign (9)
parecer (zc) to seem

parecerse a to look like; to be similar/like
pared *f.* wall
pareja pair; couple (2) (13); partner (2)
pariente relative (2)
párpado eyelid
parque *m.* park (4); **parque de atracciones** amusement park
parquímetro parking meter (9)
parte *f.* part; **por otra parte** moreover; on the other hand
particular: en particular in particular
partido match; game (*sports*) (6)
pasa raisin
pasado(a) past; last; **el año pasado** last year; **la semana pasada** last week (6); **pasado(a) de moda** out of style
pasaje *m.* ticket (*transportation*)
pasajero(a) passenger (10)
pasaporte *m.* passport (10); **control de pasaporte** passport control
pasar to pass; to happen; **pasar la aspiradora** to vacuum (8); **pasarlo bien** to have a good time; **pasar por seguridad** to go through security (10); **pasar tiempo** to spend time (8); **pasarse un semáforo en rojo** to run a red light (9); **pasarse una señal de PARE** to run a STOP sign (9); **¿qué pasa?** what's going on? (1)
pase: pase *m.* **de abordar** boarding pass (10)
pasear to walk
paseo: ir de paseo to go for a walk (8)
pasillo hallway; aisle (10)
paso: de paso by the way
pasta de dientes toothpaste (6)
pastel *m.* pastry; cake (7) (9)
pastelería pastry shop
pastilla pill (14)
pasto grass, pasture (12)
patín *m.* skate
patinar to skate (6); **patinar en hielo** to ice skate (6); **patinar sobre ruedas** to roller-skate, roller-blade
patineta skateboard (8)
patio patio (4); courtyard; yard; flower garden
pato duck (12)
patrulla police car (9)
pavo turkey (7) (12)
paz *f.* peace (14)
pecho chest (6)
pedagogía pedagogy; **ciencias de la pedagogía** education
pedir (i, i) to ask for (4); to request
peinarse to comb/style one's hair (6)
pelear to fight (8); to argue (8)
película movie (4); film
peligro (de extinción) danger (of extinction) (12)
pelirrojo(a) red-haired (1)
pelo hair (6)
pelota ball (6)
península peninsula (12)
pensar (ie) to think (4); to intend
peor worse (11); **el/la peor** the worst
pepinillo pickle (8)
pepino cucumber (7)
pequeño(a) small (1)
pera pear
perder (ie) to lose (4); to miss (a flight, a train) (10)
perdón *m.* pardon
perdonarse to excuse oneself
perezoso(a) lazy (1)

periodismo journalism (2)
periodista *m. f.* journalist (5)
permiso permission (8)
pero *conj.* but
perro dog (2)
persona person
peruano(a) Peruvian (14)
pesa weight; **levantar pesas** to lift weights (6)
pesadilla nightmare
pésame *m. sing.* condolences
pesar to weigh
pesar: a pesar de in spite of
pesca: ir de pesca to go fishing (6)
pescadería fish store, fish market
pescado fish (*food*) (7)
pescar (qu) to fish (6)
pesimista *adj. m. f.* pessimist (1)
pestaña eyelash
petróleo oil (12)
pez *m.* (*pl.* **peces**) fish (2)
piano piano; **tocar (qu) el piano** to play the piano
picar (qu) to snack
pico mountain peak
pie *m.* foot (6)
piel *f.* skin; leather (11)
pierna leg (6)
pijama *m. sing.* pajamas (3)
piloto *m. f.* pilot (5)
pimienta pepper (7)
pincel *m.* paintbrush (11)
ping-pong *m.* ping-pong; **jugar al ping-pong** to play ping-pong (6)
pingüino penguin (12)
pintor(a) painter (5)
pintura paint
piña pineapple (7)
piñata piñata (9)
Pirineos Pyrenees
piscina swimming pool (4)
piso apartment; floor (*of a building*) (4)
pista (de correr) track
pizarra chalkboard (1)
plancha iron (8)
planchar to iron (8); **tabla de planchar** ironing board (8)
planta plant (4); floor (*building*)
plata silver
plátano banana (7)
platillo saucer
plato plate; dish; **detergente** *m.* **para platos** dish detergent; **jabón** *m.* **para platos** dish soap (8); **lavar platos** to wash the dishes (8); **plato principal** main dish (7)
playa beach (4)
plaza city square (4)
pluma (estilográfica) (fountain) pen
pobre poor (1)
pobreza poverty (14)
poco(a) little, few (2); **hasta hace poco** until a little while ago
poder (ue) to be able to (4)
policía *f.* police (*force*); **estación** *f.* **de policía** police station
policía *m.* police officer (5); **mujer** *f.* **policía** police officer (5)
poliéster *m.* polyester
político(a) *n.* politician (5); *adj.* political; **ciencias políticas** political science (2)
pollo chicken (7); chick (12)
pomada cream; ointment
poner to put, place; to put on; to put up; **poner la mesa** to set the table (8); **poner(le) una inyección** to give (him/

her) an injection; **ponerse** to get (+ *adj.*); to become (+ *adj.*); **ponerse feliz** to become happy; **ponerse la ropa** to put on clothing (6); **ponerse triste** to become sad
por by; through; because of; due to; on account of; times (*in mathematical functions*); **por adelantado** in advance; **por ciento** percent (11); **por ejemplo** for example; **por eso** therefore; **por favor** please; **por fin** finally; **por lo general** generally; **por otra parte** moreover; on the other hand; **por otro lado** on the other hand; **¿por qué?** why? (1); **por supuesto** of course; **por último** lastly, finally
porque because
portero door attendant
posada inn; *pl.* nine-day celebration before Christmas
posar to pose (11)
posesivo(a) possessive
postre *m.* dessert (7)
postura posture
práctica activity; practice
practicar (qu) to practice; **practicar deportes** to play sports (2)
prado meadow
precio price
precioso(a) precious; lovely; beautiful
preferible preferable
preferir (ie, i) to prefer (4)
pregunta question
preguntar to ask (2)
preguntón(-ona) inquisitive
prenda garment (11); article of clothing
preocupación *f.* worry
preocupado(a) worried (5)
preocuparse to worry
preposición *f.* preposition
presentar to introduce; **le presento a...** I'd like to introduce you (*form.*) to . . . (1); **te presento a...** I'd like to introduce you (*fam.*) to . . . (1)
preservar to preserve (12)
presidente *m. f.* president
presión *f.* **arterial** blood pressure; **presión alta/baja** high/low blood pressure (14); **tomar la presión** to take someone's blood pressure (14)
prestar to lend (8)
pretérito preterite
previamente previously
primavera spring (3)
primer, primero(a) first; **hotel** *m.* **de primera clase** first-class hotel; **primera clase** first class (10); **Primera Comunión** *f.* First Communion; **primeros auxilios** first aid (14)
primo(a) cousin (2)
principal main; **plato principal** main dish (7)
principio beginning; principle; **al principio** at the beginning; **en principio** in principle
prisa hurry, haste; **tener (mucha) prisa** to be in a (big) hurry (2)
privado(a) private
probablemente probably
probador *m.* dressing room (11); fitting room
probar(se) (ue) to try (on) (11); to test
problema *m.* problem
problemático(a) problematic
profesión *f.* profession
profesor(a) professor (1)
profundo(a) deep
programación *f.* programming (13)

programador(a) programmer
prohibir to prohibit
prometer to promise
prometido(a) fiancé(e) (13)
pronombre *m.* pronoun
pronto soon (6); **hasta pronto** see you soon (1); **tan pronto como** as soon as (14)
propina tip; **dejar una propina** to leave a tip (7)
proponer (matrimonio) to propose (marriage) (13)
propósito: a propósito by the way
propuesta proposal
proteger (j) to protect (12)
protesta protest
provecho: buen provecho enjoy your meal
prueba test
psicología psychology (2)
psicólogo(a) psychologist (5)
público(a) public; **funcionario(a) público(a)** public official
puerta door (1); **puerta de salida** gate (10)
puerto port, harbor
puertorriqueño(a) Puerto Rican (14)
puesto de trabajo position, job
pulgar *m.* thumb
pulmón *m.* lung (14)
pulpo octopus
pulsera bracelet
punto point
pupitre *m.* student desk (1)

Q

que that, which; than; **¡que tengas un buen día!** have a nice day (1)
¡qué! what!; **¡qué bien te queda esa falda!** that skirt really fits you well! (11); **¡qué caro(a)!** how expensive! (11); **¡qué color tan bonito!** what a pretty color! (11); **¡qué lindos zapatos!** what pretty shoes! (11); **¡qué pantalones tan elegantes!** what elegant pants! (11)
¿qué? what? (1); **¿qué hay de nuevo?** what's new? (1); **¿qué pasa?** what's going on? (1); **¿qué tal?** how's it going? (1); **¿qué tiempo hace?** what's the weather like?
quedar to remain (11); to fit (11); **quedarse** to stay (10); **¡qué bien te queda esa falda!** that skirt really fits you well! (11)
quedarle to fit
quehacer *m.* chore (8)
quejarse to complain
quemadura de sol sunburn
querer to want (4), to love (7) (13); **querer decir** to mean; **quisiera** I would like
queso cheese (7)
quien(es) who, whom
¿quién(es)? who? (1) (4)
química chemistry (2)
quince fifteen (1); **los quince años** girl's fifteenth birthday celebration (9)
quinceañera girl celebrating her fifteenth birthday (9)
quinientos(as) five hundred (7)
quitarse to take off (*clothing*)
quizá(s) perhaps

R

racional rational
radio: emisora de radio radio station
radiografía X-ray (14)
raíz *f.* (*pl.* **raíces**) root
rana frog (12)
rápido fast

raqueta racket (6)
ráquetbol *m.* racquetball
raro(a) strange
ratón *m.* mouse (2)
raya stripe; **a rayas** striped (11)
rayos X X-rays; **sacar (qu) rayos X** to take X-rays
razón *f.* reason; **no tener razón** to be wrong; **tener razón** to be right (2)
realista realist (1)
rebajado(a) on sale (11); **estar rebajado(a)** to be on sale (11)
recepción *f.* reception (desk) (10); wedding reception (13)
recepcionista *m. f.* desk clerk; receptionist (10)
receta médica prescription (14)
rechazar (c) to decline, reject
recibir to receive (3); **recibir un regalo** to receive a gift (3)
recibo receipt
reciclaje *m.* recycling (12)
recién casado(a) newlywed (13)
recinto campus
reclamo de equipaje baggage claim (10)
recoger (j) la mesa to clear the table (8); to pick up the table (8)
recomendación *f.* recommendation
recomendar (ie) to recommend
recordar (ue) to remember (4)
recreación *f.* recreation; **sala de recreación** rec room
recuperarse to recover (14)
recursos naturales natural resources (12)
red *f.* net
redacción *f.* writing (2)
redes *f. pl.* **sociales** social networks (13)
refresco soda (7)
refrigerador *m.* refrigerator (4)
refugiado(a) refugee (14)
regalo gift (3); **recibir un regalo** to receive a gift (3)
regar (ie) (gu) to water (8)
regatear to bargain
registrarse to register (10)
regla ruler
regresar (a casa) to return (home) (2)
regular so-so (1); okay
reír (í, i) to laugh (4)
relación *f.* relationship
relacionado(a) related
relámpago lightning
rellenar to fill out
reloj *m.* clock (1); watch
remediar to remedy
remedio remedy
remoto: control *m.* **remoto** remote control (13)
renunciar to resign
reparar to repair
repente: de repente suddenly (9)
repetir (i, i) to repeat (4)
representante *m. f.* representative
reproductor: reproductor de CDs CD player (13); **reproductor de DVDs** DVD player (13)
reptil *m.* reptile (12)
res: carne de res beef
resaca hangover
reservación *f.* reservation
resfriado cold (*illness*) (14)
resguardo voucher; credit slip
residencia residence hall (2)
resistir to resist
resolución *f.* resolution
resolver (ue) to solve

respiración *f.* breathing; **bucear con tubo de respiración** to snorkel
respirar to breathe (14)
responder to respond
responsabilizar (c) to make (someone) responsible
responsable responsible
respuesta reply, answer
restaurante *m.* restaurant (4)
resultado result; **como resultado** as a result
resultar (de/en) to result (in)
resumen *m.* summary
retrasado(a) delayed (10)
retrato portrait (11)
revelar fotos to develop photographs
revisar to inspect
revisión *f.* **de equipaje** luggage screening (10)
revisor *m.* controller
revista magazine (13)
rezar (c) to pray (4)
rico(a) rich (1); delicious
riñón *m.* kidney
río river (12)
riqueza wealth (14)
rocoso(a) rocky
rodilla knee (6)
rojo(a) red (3); **pasarse un semáforo en rojo** to run a red light (9)
romántico(a) romantic
romper(se) to break (9) (11); **romper con** to break up with (relationship) (13)
ropa clothes; clothing; **lavar ropa** to do laundry (8)
ropero closet
rosado(a) pink (3); **vino rosado** rosé wine
rotulador *m.* marker
rubio(a) blond(e) (1)
rueda wheel; **patinar sobre ruedas** to roller-skate, roller-blade
rutina routine

S

sábado *m.* Saturday (3)
saber to know (*facts, how to do something*) (5)
sabroso(a) delicious
sacar (qu) to take (out); **sacar fotos** to take photographs; **sacar la basura** to take the trash out (8); **sacar la lengua** to stick out one's tongue; **sacar una buena/mala nota** to get a good/bad grade; **sacar rayos X** to take X-rays
saco suit coat; sport coat; **saco de dormir** sleeping bag
sacudidor *m.* duster (8)
sacudir to dust (8)
sal *f.* salt (7)
sala living room (4); **sala de conferencias** conference center (10); **sala de emergencias** emergency room (14); **sala de espera** waiting room (10); **sala de recreación** rec room; **sala de recreo** rec room
salado(a) salty
salchicha sausage
salida departure (10); **puerta de salida** gate (10)
salir to leave, to go out; **salir (a + *inf.*)** to go out (to do something) (8)
salmón *m.* salmon
salón *m.* living room; sitting room; hall; **salón de clases** classroom (1)
salsa de tomate (dulce) tomato sauce; ketchup
saltar to jump (8)
salud *f.* health (5) (14)
saludar to greet (7)

saludo greeting
salvadoreño(a) Salvadorian (14)
salvaje wild
sandalia sandal (3)
sandía watermelon
sándwich *m.* sandwich (7)
sangrar to bleed (14)
sangre *f.* blood
sano(a) healthy
santo saint; saint's day (9); **día** *m.* **de santo** saint's day
sastre *m.* tailor
satisfacción *f.* satisfaction
satisfecho(a) full (*stomach*); satisfied
sauna *m.* sauna (10)
secadora dryer (4)
secar(se) (qu) to dry (oneself) (6); to dry (8)
secretario(a) secretary (5)
sed *f.* thirst; **tener (mucha) sed** to be (very) thirsty (2)
seda silk (11)
seguir (i, i) to follow (5); **seguir (i) derecho** to go straight (10)
segundo(a) second; **segunda clase** second class (10)
seguridad *f.* security; **agente de seguridad** security agent (10); **cinturón** *m.* **de seguridad** safety (seat) belt (10); **control de seguridad** security check; **pasar por seguridad** to go through security (10)
seguro(a) *adj.* sure (5); *adv.* certainly; surely
seis six (1)
seiscientos(as) six hundred (7)
selva jungle (12); **selva tropical** tropical rain forest
semáforo stoplight; **pasarse un semáforo en rojo** to run a red light (9)
semana week (3); **fin de semana** weekend (3); **semana pasada** last week (6)
semestre semester (2)
sencillo(a) single (*room*) (10); simple (11); **habitación** *f.* **sencilla** single room
sensacional sensational
sensible sensitive
sentarse (ie) to sit (down)
sentido sense
sentir (ie, i) to feel; **lo siento (mucho)** I'm (very) sorry; **sentirse bien** to feel well; **sentirse mal** to feel bad, ill
señal *f.* sign; **pasarse una señal de PARE** to run a STOP sign (9)
separarse (de) to separate (from) (13)
septiembre *m.* September (3)
ser *m.* **humano** human being
ser to be (1); **¿de dónde eres tú?** where are you (*fam.*) from? (1); **yo soy de...** I'm from . . . (1)
serenata serenade (9)
serio(a) serious (1)
serpiente *f.* snake (12)
servicio a la habitación room service (10)
servicios utilities
servilleta napkin (7)
servir (i, i) to serve (4)
sesenta sixty (1)
setecientos(as) seven hundred (7)
setenta seventy (1)
si if, whether
sí yes
sicología psychology
sicólogo(a) psychologist
SIDA *m. sing.* AIDS (14)
siempre always (6); **casi siempre** almost always (6); **siempre y cuando** as long as (14)

sierra mountain range
siete seven (1)
silla chair (1)
sillón *m.* armchair (4)
sin without; **sin embargo** nevertheless; however; **sin que** without (14)
sino but (rather), instead; **sino (que)** *conj.* but
sobre on; on top of; over; about
sobremesa after-dinner conversation
sobrino(a) nephew/niece (2)
social social; **redes** *f. pl.* **sociales** social networks (13)
sociología sociology
sofá *m.* couch (4)
sol *m.* sun; **gafas de sol** sunglasses; **hace sol** it's sunny; **quemadura de sol** sunburn
solicitar to apply
solicitud *f.* application (5); want ad (5)
solidaridad *f.* solidarity
solo only
soltero(a) single person; unmarried person (13); **despedida de soltera** bridal shower; **despedida de soltero** bachelor party
solución *f.* solution
solucionar to solve
sombrero hat (3)
sombrilla beach umbrella
sonreír (i, i) to smile (4)
soñar (ue) to dream (*about*) (4)
sopa soup (7)
sorprenderse to be surprised (9)
sorprendido(a) surprised (5)
sorpresa surprise; **fiesta sorpresa** surprise party
sostener to support
sótano basement
su *poss.* your (*form. sing., pl.*); his; her; its; their
subir to go up, to take something up (10); **subir a** to get into (*a vehicle*) (9)
sucio(a) dirty (8)
suegro(a) father-in-law/mother-in-law (2)
sueldo salary (5)
suelo floor
sueño dream; sleep; **tener (mucho) sueño** to be (very) sleepy (2)
suerte *f.* luck; **tener (mucha) suerte** to be (very) lucky (2)
suéter *m.* sweater (3)
sugerencia suggestion
sugerir (ie, i) to suggest (13)
suma sum; summary; **en suma** in conclusion
súper super (*used as prefix*)
superar to overcome
superior superior; upper
supermercado supermarket (4)
supersticioso(a) superstitious
supuesto: por supuesto of course
sur *m.* south
sureste *m.* southeast
suroeste *m.* southwest
surrealista *m. f.* surrealist (11)
suspender to fail

T

tabla: esquiar en tabla to snowboard (6); **tabla de planchar** ironing board (8)
tablero keyboard (13)
tacto touch
tal vez perhaps
tal: ¿qué tal? how's it going? (1); **con tal (de) que** provided that (14)
taller *m.* workshop; garage
también also (1); in addition
tan so; **tan... como** as . . . as; **tan pronto como** as soon as (14); **¡qué color tan bonito!** what a pretty color! (11); **¡qué**

pantalones tan elegantes! what elegant pants! (11)
tanto(a) *adj.* so much; *pl.* so many; **tanto(s)/ tanta(s)... como** as many . . . as
tapete *m.* throw rug
taquilla ticket window (10); box office; **éxito de taquilla** box office hit (13)
tarde *adv.* late (6)
tarde *f.* afternoon; **de la tarde** P.M.; **más tarde** later (6); **por la tarde** in the afternoon (6)
tarea homework
tarjeta de crédito credit card (11)
tarta pie
taza cup
tazón *m.* soup bowl
te *d.o.* you (*fam. sing.*); *i.o.* to/for you (*fam. sing.*); *refl.* yourself; **te presento a...** I'd like to introduce you (*fam.*) to . . . (1)
té *m.* tea, afternoon tea
teatro theater (2) (4)
techo ceiling
técnico(a) technician
tejer to knit (8)
tela fabric
teléfono telephone; **teléfono celular** cell phone (8)
telenovela soap opera (13)
televidente *m. f.* television viewer (13)
televisión *f.* television (*medium*); **televisión por satélite** satellite television (13)
televisor *m.* television set (1)
temblar (ie) to shake; **me tiemblan las manos** my hands are shaking
temer to fear
temperatura temperature
templo temple (4)
temprano early (6)
tenedor *m.* fork (7)
tener to have; **tener que** (+ *inf.*) to have to (+ *verb*) (2); **no tener razón** to be wrong; **¡que tengas un buen día!** have a nice day (1); **tener (mucha) hambre** to be (very) hungry (2); **tener (mucha) prisa** to be in a (big) hurry (2); **tener (mucha) sed** to be (very) thirsty (2); **tener (mucha) suerte** to be (very) lucky (2); **tener (mucho) calor** to be (very) hot (2); **tener (mucho) cuidado** to be (very) careful (2); **tener (mucho) éxito** to be (very) successful (2); **tener (mucho) frío** to be (very) cold (2); **tener (mucho) miedo** to be afraid of (2); **tener (mucho) sueño** to be (very) sleepy (2); **tener celos** to be jealous; **tener ganas de** (+ *inf.*) to feel like (*doing something*) (2); **tener lugar** to take place; **tener mareos** to be dizzy; **tener razón** to be right (2); **tener... años** to be . . . years old (2); **tenerle miedo a** to be afraid of (*person*)
tenis *m.* tennis (6); tennis shoes (3)
terminar to finish (3) (9)
ternera veal
terraza terrace
testigo *m. f.* witness
textura texture
tiburón *m.* shark (12)
tiempo time; weather; **a tiempo** on time (10); **a tiempo completo** full-time; **a tiempo parcial** part-time; **hace buen tiempo** the weather is nice (3); **hace mal tiempo** the weather is bad (3); **pasar tiempo** to spend time (8); **¿Qué tiempo hace?** What's the weather like?

tienda shop; store (4); **tienda de campaña** camping tent (6)
tierno(a) tender
Tierra Earth (*planet*) (12)
tierra land, earth
tigre *m.* tiger (12)
tinta ink (11)
tinto: vino tinto red wine (7)
tintorería dry cleaners
tío(a) uncle/aunt (2)
tiza chalk
toalla towel (6); **toalla de papel** paper towel
tobillo ankle (6)
tocador *m.* dressing table
tocar (qu) to touch; **tocar (el piano)** to play (*the piano*) (8); to touch
tocino bacon
todavía still (6)
todo(a) all, every; **todos los días** every day (6)
tomar to take (2); **tomar (café)** to drink (coffee) (2); **tomar la presión** to take someone's blood pressure (14)
tomate *m.* tomato (7); **salsa de tomate (dulce)** tomato sauce; ketchup
tonto(a) dumb (1)
topografía topography
torcerse (ue) (z) to twist (14)
tormenta storm
toro bull (12)
toronja grapefruit
torre *f.* tower
tortuga turtle (12)
toser to cough (14)
totopos *pl.* tortilla chips (7)
trabajador(a) *adj.* hardworking (1)
trabajador(a) social social worker (5)
trabajar to work (2)
trabajo work; job (5); **solicitud** *f.* **de trabajo** job application
tradicional traditional (11)
traductor(a) translator
traer to bring (5)
traidor(a) traitorous
traje *m.* suit (3); **traje de baño** swimming suit (3)
tranquilo(a) tranquil; calm
transicional transitional
transmitir to broadcast (13)
transporte *m.* transportation (10)
trapeador *m.* mop (8)
trapear to mop (8)
trapo dust cloth; rag (8); cloth (8)
tratado de comercio trade treaty (14)
tratamiento treatment (14)
trece thirteen (1)
treinta thirty (1)
tren *m.* train
trepar (un árbol) to climb (a tree) (8)
tres three (1)
trescientos(as) three hundred (7)
trimestre quarter (2)
triple triple (10)
triste sad (5); **ponerse triste** to become sad
tronco trunk
tropezar (ie) (c) to trip (9)
tropical tropical; **selva tropical** tropical rain forest
trucha trout

trueno thunder
tú *subj. pron.* you (*fam. sing.*); **¿de dónde eres tú?** where are you (*fam.*) from? (1); **¿y tú?** and you (*fam.*)? (1)
tu(s) *poss.* your (*fam. sing.*)
tubo: bucear con tubo de respiración to snorkel
tuna cactus fruit
turista *m. f.* tourist (10)

U

ubicación *f.* location
último(a) final; last; **por último** lastly; finally
un/uno(a) a, an, one (1)
único(a) unique; only
unión *f.* **libre** common-law union (13)
universidad *f.* university
unos(as) some
urgente urgent
uruguayo(a) Uruguayan (14)
usado(a) used
usar to use (2)
usted *subj. pron.* you (*form. sing.*); **¿cómo está usted?** how are you (*form.*)? (1); **¿y usted?** and you (*form.*)? (1)
usualmente usually
uva grape (7)

V

vaca cow (12)
vacaciones *f. pl.* vacation
vacuna vaccine (14)
vacunar to vaccinate
vacuno: carne de vacuno beef
vagón *m.* car, wagon (10)
valer to be worth; to cost; **¿vale?** okay?
valiente valiant, courageous
valle *m.* valley (12)
valor *m.* value
vanguardista *m. f.* revolutionary (11); avant-garde (11)
varicela chicken pox
varios several (2)
vaso glass
veinte twenty (1)
veinticinco twenty-five (1)
veinticuatro twenty-four (1)
veintidós twenty-two (1)
veintinueve twenty-nine (1)
veintiocho twenty-eight (1)
veintiséis twenty-six (1)
veintisiete twenty-seven (1)
veintitrés twenty-three (1)
veintiuno twenty-one(1)
vejez *f.* old-age (13)
vela candle (9)
velocidad: límite *m.* **de velocidad** speed limit (9)
vena vein
venado deer (12)
venda bandage
vendaje *m.* bandage (14)
vendedor(a) salesperson (5)
vender to sell (3)
venezolano(a) Venezuelan (14)
venir to come (5)
venta sale (transaction) (11); **en venta** on sale

ventana window (1); **limpiador para ventanas** window cleaner
ventanilla window (10)
ver to see (5); **verse** to see to see oneself (6); **a ver** let's see; **nos vemos** see you later (1)
verano summer (3)
verbo verb
verdad *f.* truth; **¿verdad?** right?; **de verdad** really
verde green (3)
verduras *f. pl.* vegetables
vestido dress (3)
vestirse (i, i) to get dressed (6)
veterinaria veterinary medicine
veterinario(a) veterinarian (5)
vez *f.* time; **a veces** sometimes (6); **de vez en cuando** from time to time; **dos veces** two times, twice
viajar to travel (2)
viaje *m.* trip; **agente de viajes** travel agent (5); **cheque** *m.* **de viaje** traveler's check; **viaje todo pagado** all-inclusive trip
viajero(a) traveler; **cheque** *m.* **de viajero** traveler's check
videojuego videogame (8)
viejo(a) old (1)
viento wind; **hace viento** it's windy
viernes *m.* Friday (3)
VIH *m.* HIV
vinagre *m.* vinegar
vino wine; **vino blanco** white wine (7); **vino rosado** rosé wine; **vino tinto** red wine (7)
visa visa (10)
visitar to visit
vista view; sight
viudo(a) widower/widow (13)
vivienda housing
vivir to live (3)
volar (ue) to fly (8)
volcán *m.* volcano (12)
voleibol *m.* volleyball (6)
voleibolista *m. f.* volleyball player
volver (ue) to return; to come back (4); **volverse loco(a)** to go crazy
vomitar to vomit (14)
vosotros(as) *subj. pron.* you (*fam. pl.*) (*Sp.*)
votar to vote (14)
voz *f.* voice; **en voz alta** aloud
vuelo flight (10); **asistente** *m. f.* **de vuelo** flight attendant
vuestro(a) *poss.* your (*fam. sing.*) (*Sp.*)

Y

y and; **¿y tú?** and you (*fam.*)? (1); **¿y usted?** and you (*form.*)? (1)
ya already (6); **ya no** no longer (6)
yerno son-in-law
yeso cast (14)
yo I; **yo soy de...** I'm from . . . (1)
yogur yogurt (7)

Z

zanahoria carrot (7)
zapatilla slipper
zapato shoe (3); **¡qué lindos zapatos!** what pretty shoes! (11)
zona area
zoológico zoo (4)
zorro fox (12)

Vocabulario 1

🔊 1-8
Saludos

bien	*fine*
Buenas noches.	*Good night.*
Buenas tardes.	*Good afternoon.*
Buenos días.	*Good morning.*
¿Cómo estás (tú)?	*How are you? (informal)*
¿Cómo está (usted)?	*How are you? (formal)*
gracias	*thank you*
hola	*hello*
mal	*bad*
nada	*nothing*
¿Qué hay de nuevo?	*What's new?*
¿Qué pasa?	*What's going on?*
¿Qué tal?	*How's it going?*
regular	*so-so*
¿Y tú?	*And you? (informal)*
¿Y usted?	*And you? (formal)*

Presentaciones

Encantado(a).	*Nice to meet you.*
Me llamo...	*My name is . . .*
Mucho gusto.	*Nice to meet you.*
Le presento a...	*I'd like to introduce you to . . . (formal)*
Te presento a...	*I'd like to introduce you to . . . (informal)*

Despedidas

Adiós.	*Goodbye.*
Chao.	*Bye.*
Hasta luego.	*See you later.*
Hasta mañana.	*See you tomorrow.*
Hasta pronto.	*See you soon.*
Nos vemos.	*See you later.*
¡Que tengas un buen día!	*Have a nice day!*

El salón de clases

la bandera	*flag*
el bolígrafo	*pen*
el cartel	*poster*
la computadora	*computer*
el cuaderno	*notebook*
el diccionario	*dictionary*
el escritorio	*teacher's desk*
el (la) estudiante	*student*
el lápiz	*pencil*
el libro	*book*
el mapa	*map*
la mesa	*table*
la mochila	*backpack*
el papel	*paper*
la pizarra	*chalkboard*
el (la) profesor(a)	*professor*
la puerta	*door*
el pupitre	*student desk*
el reloj	*clock*
el salón de clases	*classroom*
la silla	*chair*
el televisor	*television set*
la ventana	*window*

Gramática

Gender and number of nouns

1. A noun is a person, place, or thing. In order to make a noun plural, add an **-s** to words ending in a vowel. Add **-es** to words ending in a consonant, unless that consonant is **-z** in which case the **-z** changes to **-c** before adding **-es.** (lápiz ▶ lápices)

2. Some nouns lose an accent mark or gain an accent mark when they become plural. (examen → exámenes) You will learn more about accents in **Capítulo 2.**

3. Nouns have gender (masculine / feminine) whether or not they refer to people. In general, if they are not referring to people, nouns that end in **-o** are masculine, and nouns that end in **-a** are feminine. Exceptions include **el** día (m.), **el** mapa (m.), **el** problema (m.), **la** mano (f.), **la** foto (f.), and **la** moto (f.).

Definite and indefinite articles

1. Definite articles mean *the*, and are used to refer to specific nouns or nouns already mentioned. They agree in gender and number with the noun they modify.

	masculino	femenino
singular	**el**	**la**
plural	**los**	**las**

2. Indefinite articles mean *a, an* or *some*, and are used to refer to non-specific nouns or nouns not yet mentioned. They also agree in gender and number with the noun they modify.

	masculino	femenino
singular	**un**	**una**
plural	**unos**	**unas**

Hay

1. **Hay** means *there is* when followed by a singular noun and *there are* when followed by a plural noun.

Hay un libro en el pupitre.
There is a book on the desk.

Hay veinte estudiantes en la clase.
There are twenty students in the class.

Palabras adicionales

¿De dónde eres tú?	*Where are you from?*
hay	*there is/there are*
Yo soy de...	*I am from . . .*

Palabras interrogativas

¿Dónde?	*Where?*
¿Cuándo?	*When?*
¿Cuántos(as)?	*How many?*
¿Qué?	*What?*
¿Quién?	*Who?*
¿Por qué?	*Why?*

Los números

uno	*one*		**nueve**	*nine*
dos	*two*		**diez**	*ten*
tres	*three*		**once**	*eleven*
cuatro	*four*		**doce**	*twelve*
cinco	*five*		**trece**	*thirteen*
seis	*six*		**catorce**	*fourteen*
siete	*seven*		**quince**	*fifteen*
ocho	*eight*		**dieciséis**	*sixteen*
			diecisiete	*seventeen*
			dieciocho	*eighteen*
			diecinueve	*nineteen*
			veinte	*twenty*
			veintiuno	*twenty-one*
			veintidós	*twenty-two*
			veintitrés	*twenty-three*
			veinticuatro	*twenty-four*
			veinticinco	*twenty-five*
			veintiséis	*twenty-six*
			veintisiete	*twenty-seven*
			veintiocho	*twenty-eight*
			veintinueve	*twenty-nine*
			treinta	*thirty*

Vocabulario 2

🔊 1-9

Adjetivos para describir la personalidad

aburrido(a)	*boring*
agresivo(a)	*aggressive*
amable	*kind*
antipático(a)	*unfriendly*
atlético(a)	*athletic*
bueno(a)	*good*
cariñoso(a)	*loving*
cómico(a)	*funny*
conservador(a)	*conservative*
cruel	*cruel*
egoísta	*selfish*
famoso(a)	*famous*
generoso(a)	*generous*
honesto(a)	*honest*
idealista	*idealist*
impaciente	*impatient*
inteligente	*intelligent*
interesante	*interesting*
liberal	*liberal*
malo(a)	*bad*
optimista	*optimist*
paciente	*patient*
perezoso(a)	*lazy*
pesimista	*pessimist*
pobre	*poor*
realista	*realist*
rico(a)	*rich*
serio(a)	*serious*
simpático(a)	*nice*
sociable	*sociable*
tímido(a)	*timid, shy*
tonto(a)	*dumb*
trabajador(a)	*hardworking*

Adjetivos para describir el aspecto físico

alto(a)	*tall*
bajo(a)	*short*
bonito(a)	*pretty*
calvo(a)	*bald*
delgado(a)	*thin*
feo(a)	*ugly*
gordo(a)	*fat*
grande	*big*
guapo(a)	*good-looking*
joven	*young*
moreno(a)	*dark-skinned/ dark-haired*
pelirrojo(a)	*red-haired*
pequeño(a)	*small*
rubio(a)	*blond(e)*
viejo(a)	*old*

Otros adjetivos

corto(a)	*short (length)*
difícil	*difficult*
fácil	*easy*
largo(a)	*long*

Gramática

Subject pronouns

1. The subject pronouns in Spanish are **yo, tú, él, ella, usted, nosotros/nosotras, vosotros/vosotras, ellos, ellas,** and **ustedes.**

2. **Tú** and **usted (Ud.)** both mean *you*. **Tú** is informal, **usted** is formal.

3. The subject pronouns **nosotros, vosotros,** and **ellos** must be made feminine when referring to a group of only females (**nosotras, vosotras, ellas**). If there is a mixed-gender group, the subject pronouns remain in the masculine form.

4. **Vosotros** and **ustedes** both mean *you* (plural). **Vosotros** is used in Spain with a familiar group of people, and **ustedes** is always used to address a group formally. In Latin America, it is also used to address a familiar group.

Ser

1. The verb **ser** means *to be,* and its forms are as follows:

yo *(I)*	**soy**	nosotros / nosotras *(we)*	**somos**
tú *(you)*	**eres**	vosotros / vosotras *(you, plural)*	**sois**
usted *(you)*	**es**	ustedes *(you, plural)*	**son**
él *(he)* / ella *(she)*	**es**	ellos / ellas *(they)*	**son**

2. **Ser** is used when describing someone's traits (tall, intelligent, etc.) and to say where someone is from.

Adjective agreement

1. Adjectives describe a person, place, or thing. In Spanish, adjectives must agree in gender and number with the nouns that they modify.

2. If a singular masculine adjective ends in **-o**, the ending must be changed to **-a** when modifying a feminine noun (**alto → alta**).

3. If a singular masculine adjective ends in **-a** or **-e**, it does not need to be changed when modifying a feminine noun (**idealista, paciente**).

4. If a singular masculine adjective ends in a consonant, it does not need to be made feminine, unless the ending is **-or,** in which case you would add an **-a** (**trabajador → trabajadora**).

5. Once you have made the adjective agree in gender, you must make it also agree in number. To modify plural nouns, you add **-s** to adjectives that end in vowels or **-es** to adjectives that end in consonants (**bajos, liberales**).

Verbos

ser	*to be*

Palabras adicionales

el hombre	*man*
la mujer	*woman*
muy	*very*
el (la) niño(a)	*child*
pero	*but*
un poco	*a little*
también	*also*
y	*and*

Vocabulario 1

🔊 1–14

La familia

el (la) abuelo(a)	grandfather / grandmother
el (la) amigo(a)	friend
el (la) esposo(a)	spouse
el (la) hermanastro(a)	stepbrother / stepsister
el (la) hermano(a)	brother / sister
el (la) hijo(a)	son / daughter
la madrastra	stepmother
la madre (mamá)	mother
el (la) medio(a) hermano(a)	half brother / half sister
el (la) nieto(a)	grandson / granddaughter
el (la) novio(a)	boyfriend / girlfriend
el padrastro	stepfather
el padre (papá)	father
la pareja	couple; partner
el pariente	relative
el (la) primo(a)	cousin
el (la) sobrino(a)	nephew / niece
el (la) suegro(a)	father-in-law / mother-in-law
el (la) tío(a)	uncle / aunt

Las mascotas

el caballo	horse
el (la) gato(a)	cat
el pájaro	bird
el (la) perro(a)	dog
el pez	fish
el ratón	mouse

Los verbos

ayudar	to help
bailar	to dance
buscar	to look for
caminar	to walk
cantar	to sing
cocinar	to cook
comprar	to buy
desear	to wish
enseñar	to teach
escuchar	to listen
esquiar	to ski
estudiar	to study
hablar (por teléfono)	to talk (on the phone)
limpiar	to clean
llamar	to call
llegar	to arrive
mandar (un mensaje)	to send (a message)
manejar	to drive
mirar (la tele)	to look, to watch (TV)
nadar	to swim
necesitar	to need
practicar (deportes)	to practice; to play (sports)
preguntar	to ask
regresar (a casa)	to return (home)
tomar (café)	to take; to drink (coffee)
trabajar	to work
usar	to use
viajar	to travel

Gramática

Possessive adjectives

1. The possessive adjectives in Spanish are as follows:

mi(s)	my	nuestro(a)(s)	our
tu(s)	your	vuestro(a)(s)	your (plural, informal)
su(s)	his, her, its, your (formal)	su(s)	their, your (plural, informal or formal)

2. Possessive adjectives, like other adjectives, must agree in gender and number with the nouns that they modify. **Nuestro** and **vuestro** are the only possessive adjectives that need to change for gender.

> **Nuestra familia** es muy grande. **Our family** is very big.
> **Mis primos** son jóvenes. **My cousins** are young.

3. In Spanish, the 's does not exist. Instead, if you want to be more specific about who something belongs to, it is necessary to use **de.**

> Elena es la hija **de** Juan.
> *Elena is Juan's daughter.*

4. When **de** is followed by **el** in Spanish, you form the contraction **del.**

> Anita es una amiga **del** profesor.
> *Anita is the professor's friend.*

Regular *-ar* verbs

1. The verbs presented on the left are in the *infinitive* form. This form identifies the action, and is translated as *to (do something)* in English. (**Bailar** means <u>to</u> dance.)

2. Verbs in the infinitive form need to be conjugated when you are identifying the person who is doing the action. Regular **-ar** verbs are all conjugated in the same way. To form a present tense verb, the **-ar** is dropped from the infinitive and an ending is added that reflects the subject (the person doing the action).

nadar

yo	**-o**	nad**o**	nosotros(as)	**-amos**	nad**amos**
tú	**-as**	nad**as**	vosotros(as)	**-áis**	nad**áis**
él / ella / usted	**-a**	nad**a**	ellos / ellas / ustedes	**-an**	nad**an**

3. When using two verbs together that are dependent upon each other, the second verb remains in the infinitive.

> Los estudiantes **necesitan estudiar.**
> *The students need to study.*

However, both verbs are conjugated if they are not dependent on each other.

> Mi primo **trabaja, practica** deportes y **estudia** en la universidad.
> *My cousin works, plays sports, and studies at the university.*

4. Place the word **no** before the conjugated verb to make a statement negative.

> Mis padres **no** toman café.
> *My parents **don't** drink coffee.*

5. To form a yes/no question, you simply use intonation to raise your voice and place the subject after the conjugated verb. There is no need for a helping word in Spanish.

> ¿**Cocinas tú** bien?
> *Do you cook well?*

Vocabulario 2

 1–15

Las materias académicas

el alemán	German
el álgebra	algebra
el arte	art
la biología	biology
el cálculo	calculus
las ciencias naturales	natural science
las ciencias políticas	political science
las ciencias sociales	social science
la criminología	criminology
la economía	economy
la educación física	physical education
la expresión oral	speech
la filosofía	philosophy
la física	physics
el francés	French
la geografía	geography
la geometría	geometry
la historia	history
la informática	computer science
la ingeniería	engineering
el inglés	English
el italiano	Italian
las lenguas	languages
la literatura	literature
las matemáticas	mathematics
la música	music
los negocios	business
el periodismo	journalism
la psicología	psychology
la química	chemistry
la redacción	writing
el teatro	theater
la veterinaria	veterinary medicine

Los lugares en la universidad

el auditorio	auditorium
la biblioteca	library
la cafetería	cafetoria
el centro estudiantil	student center
el estadio	stadium
el gimnasio	gymnasium
el laboratorio	laboratory
la librería	bookstore
las residencias	residence halls

Expresiones con *tener*

tener... años	to be . . . years old
tener (mucho) calor	to be (very) hot
tener (mucho) cuidado	to be (very) careful
tener (mucho) éxito	to be (very) successful
tener (mucho) frío	to be (very) cold
tener ganas de + infinitive	to feel like doing something

Gramática

The verb *tener*

1. The verb **tener** means *to have*, and its forms are as follows:

yo	**tengo**	nosotros(as)	**tenemos**
tú	**tienes**	vosotros(as)	**tenéis**
él / ella / usted	**tiene**	ellos / ellas / ustedes	**tienen**

2. The verb **tener** can also mean *to be* when used in certain expressions. See **expresiones con *tener*** in the left-hand column of this page.

> Mi mejor amiga **tiene** diecinueve años.
> *My best friend **is** nineteen years old.*

> Yo siempre **tengo** hambre antes del almuerzo.
> *I **am** always hungry before lunch.*

3. As you remember from **Capítulo 2,** other than adjectives of quantity, adjectives are generally placed behind the noun they modify. However, there are some other exceptions. **Bueno** and **malo** are often used in front of the noun they modify, and they drop the **o** when used in front of a masculine singular noun.

> La señora es una **buena** profesora.
> *The woman is a **good** teacher.*

> Es un **mal** día.
> *It is a **bad** day.*

Adjective Placement

1. In Spanish, adjectives are generally placed after the noun they describe.

> La química no es una clase **fácil**.
> *Chemistry is not an **easy** class.*

2. Adjectives such as **mucho, poco,** and **varios** that indicate quantity or amount are placed in front of the object.

> Tengo **varias** clases los jueves, pero no tengo clase los viernes.
> *I have **several** classes on Thursdays, but I don't have class on Fridays.*

3. When using more than one adjective to describe a noun, use commas between adjectives and **y** (*and*) before the last adjective.

> Mis clases son largas, difíciles **y** aburridas.
> *My classes are long, difficult, **and** boring.*

tener (mucha) hambre	to be (very) hungry
tener (mucho) miedo	to be (very) afraid
tener (mucha) prisa	to be in a (big) hurry
tener que + infinitive	to have to do something
tener (mucha) razón	to be right
tener (mucha) sed	to be (very) thirsty
tener (mucho) sueño	to be (very) sleepy
tener (mucha) suerte	to be (very) lucky

Palabras adicionales

el (la) compañero(a) de clase	classmate
el examen	exam
mucho	a lot
la nota	grade
poco	few
el semestre	semester
la tarea	homework
el trimestre	quarter
varios	several

Vocabulario 1

🔊 1–20

La ropa y los accesorios

el abrigo	coat
la blusa	blouse
los bluyines	blue jeans
la bolsa	purse
las botas	boots
la bufanda	scarf
los calcetines	socks
la camisa	shirt
la camiseta	T-shirt
la chaqueta	jacket
la corbata	tie
la falda	skirt
el gorro	cap
los guantes	gloves
el impermeable	raincoat
los lentes	glasses
los pantalones	pants
los pantalones cortos	shorts
el paraguas	umbrella
la pijama	pajamas
las sandalias	sandals
el sombrero	hat
el suéter	sweater
los tenis	tennis shoes
el traje	suit
el traje de baño	swimming suit
el vestido	dress
los zapatos	shoes

El tiempo

Está despejado.	It is clear.
Está nublado.	It is cloudy.
Hace buen tiempo.	The weather is nice.
Hace calor.	It's hot.
Hace fresco.	It is cool.
Hace frío.	It's cold.
Hace mal tiempo.	The weather is bad.
Hace sol.	It's sunny.
Hace viento.	It is windy.
Llueve.	It rains. / It is raining.
Nieva.	It snows. / It is snowing.

Las estaciones

el invierno	winter
el otoño	fall
la primavera	spring
el verano	summer

Los verbos

abrir	to open
aprender (a + infinitive)	to learn (to do something)
asistir (a)	to attend
beber	to drink
comer	to eat
comprender	to understand
correr	to run
creer	to believe
deber	should, ought to
decidir	to decide
escribir	to write
leer	to read
recibir (un regalo)	to receive (a gift)
vender	to sell
vivir	to live

Palabras adicionales

cómodo(a)	comfortable
llevar	to wear, to carry; to take
llevar puesto(a)	to be wearing

Gramática

The verb *gustar*

1. The Spanish equivalent of *I like* is **me gusta**, which literally means *it pleases me*. The expression **me gusta** (*I like*) is followed by singular nouns.

   > **Me gusta** la clase.
   > *I like the class. (The class pleases me.)*

   > **No me gusta** la pizza.
   > *I don't like pizza. (Pizza doesn't please me.)*

2. When followed by a plural noun, the verb becomes **gustan.**

   > **No me gustan** los exámenes.
   > *I don't like exams.*

   > **Me gustan** el francés y el italiano.
   > *I like French and Italian.*

3. When followed by a verb or a series of verbs, the singular form **gusta** is used.

   > A Julio **le gusta** practicar deportes y leer.
   > *Julio likes to play sports and read.*

4. **Gustar** can also be used to ask about or indicate what other people like.

me gusta(n)	I like
nos gusta(n)	we like
te gusta(n)	you like
os gusta(n)	you like (plural, Spain)
le gusta(n)	he/she likes
les gusta(n)	they, you (plural) like

5. When using **gustar** with a noun, you must use the definite article as well.

   > No me gusta **el** invierno.
   > *I don't like winter.*

6. To clarify who he or she is, it is necessary to use an **a** in front of the name.

   > **A Marta** le gusta correr.
   > *Marta likes to run.*

7. To express different degrees, use the terms **mucho** (*a lot*), **poco** (*a little*), and **para nada** (*not at all*).

   > No me gusta trabajar **para nada.**
   > *I don't like working **at all.***

Regular *-er* and *-ir* verbs

1. Regular **-er** and **-ir** verbs follow a pattern very similar to that of regular **-ar** verbs.

2. The endings for regular **-er** verbs are as follows:

comer

yo	**-o**	com**o**	nosotros(as)	**-emos**	com**emos**
tú	**-es**	com**es**	vosotros(as)	**-éis**	com**éis**
él / ella / usted	**-e**	com**e**	ellos / ellas / ustedes	**-en**	com**en**

3. The endings for regular **-ir** verbs are as follows:

vivir

yo	**-o**	viv**o**	nosotros(as)	**-imos**	viv**imos**
tú	**-es**	viv**es**	vosotros(as)	**-ís**	viv**ís**
él / ella / usted	**-e**	viv**e**	ellos / ellas / ustedes	**-en**	viv**en**

Expresiones importantes

me gusta	I like
te gusta	you like
le gusta	he/she likes
nos gusta	we like
os gusta	you (plural) like (Spain)
les gusta	they, you (plural) like

Vocabulario 2

🔊 1-21

Los días de la semana

el lunes	Monday
el martes	Tuesday
el miércoles	Wednesday
el jueves	Thursday
el viernes	Friday
el sábado	Saturday
el domingo	Sunday

Los meses

enero	January
febrero	February
marzo	March
abril	April
mayo	May
junio	June
julio	July
agosto	August
septiembre	September
octubre	October
noviembre	November
diciembre	December

Los verbos

| ir | to go |
| terminar | to finish |

Palabras adicionales

ahora	now
el Año Nuevo	New Year
el cumpleaños	birthday
el día	day
el día feriado	holiday
la fecha	date
el fin de semana	weekend
hoy	today
mañana	tomorrow
la medianoche	midnight
el mediodía	noon
Navidad	Christmas
la semana	week
por la mañana / tarde / noche	in the morning / afternoon / evening
todos los días	every day

Gramática

The verb *ir*

1. The verb **ir** means *to go*:

voy	vamos
vas	vais
va	van

2. To tell where someone is going, it is necessary to use the preposition **a** *(to)*. When asking where someone is going, the preposition **a** is added to the word **dónde (adónde).** When **a** is followed by the definite article **el,** you must use the contraction **al.**

¿**Adónde** van?
(To) **Where** *are they going?*

Mis amigos van **al** museo.
*My friends are going **to the** museum.*

3. It is common to use the verb **ir** in the present tense to tell where someone is going at that moment.

Mi amiga **va** a la universidad ahora.
*My friend **is going** to the university now.*

4. The verb **ir** is used in a variety of expressions.

ir de compras *to go shopping*
ir de excursión *to go hiking*
ir de paseo *to go for a walk*
ir de viaje *to take a trip*

Ir + a + infinitive

1. Similar to English, the verb **ir** can be used to talk about the future. To tell what someone is going to do use the structure **ir + a + infinitive.**

El viernes **vamos a bailar.**
On Friday we're going to dance.

Miguel **va a estudiar** este fin de semana.
Miguel is going to study this weekend.

2. To ask what someone is going to do, use the verb **hacer** in the question. When responding, the verb **hacer** is not necessary.

¿Qué vas a hacer (tú)?
What are you going to do?

(Yo) Voy a estudiar (trabajar, comer, etcétera).
I am going to study (work, eat, etc.).

Vocabulario 1

🔊 1-26

Los lugares

el aeropuerto	airport
el banco	bank
el bar	bar
el café	cafe
la calle	street
el centro comercial	mall
el cine	movie theater
el club	club
el correo	post office
la discoteca	nightclub
el edificio	building
la escuela	school
la farmacia	pharmacy
el hospital	hospital
el hotel	hotel
la iglesia	church
el mercado	market
la mezquita	mosque
el museo	museum
el negocio	business
la oficina	office
el parque	park
la piscina	swimming pool
la playa	beach
la plaza	city square
el restaurante	restaurant
la sinagoga	synagogue
el supermercado	supermarket
el teatro	theater
el templo	temple
la tienda	store
el zoológico	zoo

Los verbos

almorzar	to have lunch
alquilar	to rent
costar	to cost
depositar	to deposit
devolver	to return (something)
dormir	to sleep
encontrar	to find
estar	to be
jugar	to play
llover	to rain
morir	to die
poder	to be able to
recordar	to remember
rezar	to pray
soñar (con)	to dream (about)
volver	to come back

Palabras adicionales

la carta	letter
el dinero	money
el paquete	package
la película	movie

Gramática

Stem changing verbs (o → ue)

1. Most of the verbs that appear in the **verbos** section of vocabulary to the left are stem-changing verbs. That means there is a change in the stem or the root of the verb. All of the endings are the same as other **-ar**, **-er**, and **-ir** verbs.

2. **Poder** is an **o → ue** stem-changing verb. Notice that **o** changes to **ue** in all forms except **nosotros** and **vosotros**.

puedo	podemos
puedes	podéis
puede	**pue**den

3. The verb **jugar** follows the same pattern, but its stem changes from **u → ue**:

juego	jugamos
juegas	jugáis
juega	**jue**gan

Estar with prepositions

1. **Estar** means *to be* and is used to talk about position or location. Its forms are as follows:

estoy	estamos
estás	estáis
está	están

2. You will always use **estar** when using any of the prepositions listed on the left of this page.

El café **está entre** la farmacia y la biblioteca.
The coffee shop is (located) between the pharmacy and the library.

3. Note that most of the prepositional phrases listed in this chapter include the word **de**. Remember to form the contraction **del** when **de** is followed by the definite article **el**.

Vivo lejos **del** supermercado.
I live far from the supermarket.

Las preposiciones

a la derecha de	to the right of
al lado de	beside, next to
a la izquierda de	to the left of
cerca de	near
debajo de	under
dentro de	inside
detrás de	behind
en	in, on, at
encima de	on top of
enfrente de	in front of
entre	between
fuera de	outside
lejos de	far from

Vocabulario 2

🔊 1–27

Habitaciones de la casa

el baño	bathroom
la cochera	garage
la cocina	kitchen
el comedor	dining room
el dormitorio	bedroom
el jardín	garden
el patio	patio
la sala	living room

Muebles, utensilios y aparatos electrodomésticos

la alfombra	carpet
el armario	closet, armoire
la bañera	bathtub
la cafetera	coffee maker
la cama	bed
las cortinas	curtains
el cuadro	painting, picture
la ducha	shower
el espejo	mirror
la estufa	stove
la flor	flower
el fregadero	kitchen sink
el horno	oven
el (horno de) microondas	microwave (oven)
el inodoro	toilet
la lámpara	lamp
el lavabo	bathroom sink
la lavadora	washer
el lavaplatos	dishwasher
la mesita	coffee table
las plantas	plants
el refrigerador	refrigerator
la secadora	dryer
el sillón	armchair
el sofá	couch

Los verbos

cerrar	to close
comenzar (a)	to begin (to do something)
competir	to compete
empezar (a)	to begin (to do something)
encender	to turn on
entender	to understand
mentir	to lie
nevar	to snow
pedir	to ask for
pensar	to think
perder	to lose
preferir	to prefer
reír	to laugh
repetir	to repeat
querer	to want
servir	to serve
sonreír	to smile

Gramática

Interrogatives

1. In most questions:
   - the subject is placed after the verb.
   - the question word is often the first word of the question.
   - it is not necessary to have a helping word such as *do* or *does*.
   - it is necessary to have an inverted question mark at the beginning of the questions and another question mark at the end.

2. Prepositions (**a, con, de, en, por, para,** etc.) cannot be placed at the end of the question. They must be in front of the question word.

   > ¿**Con** quién estudias?
   > ***With** whom do you study?*

Stem-changing verbs e → ie and e → i

1. Most of the verbs that appear in the **verbos** section of vocabulary to the left are stem-changing verbs. That means there is a change in the stem or the root of the verb. All of the endings are the same as other **-ar, -er,** and **-ir** verbs.

2. **Querer** is an **e → ie** stem-changing verb. Notice that **i** changes to **ie** in all forms except **nosotros** and **vosotros.**

qu**ie**ro	queremos
qu**ie**res	queréis
qu**ie**re	qu**ie**ren

3. The **e → ie** stem-changing verbs **comenzar** and **empezar** are followed by the preposition **a** when used with an infinitive.

3. **Quién** and **cuál** must agree in number with the noun that follows, and **cuánto** and **cuántos** must agree in gender with the preceding noun.

4. There are two ways to express *What?* or *Which?*: When asking *which,* use **qué** in front of a noun and **cuál** in front of a verb or with the preposition **de.** When asking *what,* use **cuál** with the verb **ser** with the exception of the question ¿**Qué es?** *(What is it?).* Use **qué** with all other verbs.

   > ¿**Qué** electrodomésticos necesitas?
   > *What (Which) appliances do you need?*

   > ¿**Cuáles** de los libros te gustan más?
   > *Which of the books do you like the most?*

   > **Empieza a** llover.
   > *It's starting to rain.*

4. **Pedir** is an **e → i** stem-changing verb. Note that **pedir** means to ask *for* something or to order, where as **preguntar** means to ask a question. Here are the forms of **pedir:**

p**i**do	pedimos
p**i**des	pedís
p**i**de	p**i**den

5. The verbs **reír** and **sonreír** require accents on the **í** in the conjugated forms.

   > Los niños **sonríen** en la foto.
   > *The children smile in the photo.*

Palabras adicionales

el apartamento	apartment
la dirección	address
la habitación	room
el mueble	furniture
la planta baja	ground floor
el (primer) piso	(first) floor

Palabras interrogativas

¿adónde?	to where?
¿cómo?	how?
¿cuál(es)?	which?
¿cuándo?	when?
¿cuánto(a)?	how much?
¿cuántos(as)?	how many?
¿de dónde?	from where?
¿dónde?	where?
¿por qué?	why?
¿qué?	what?
¿quién(es)?	who?

Vocabulario 1

🔊 1–32

Los estados de ánimo y otras expresiones con el verbo *estar*

aburrido(a)	bored
alegre	happy
asustado(a)	scared
avergonzado(a)	embarrassed
borracho(a)	drunk
cansado(a)	tired
celoso(a)	jealous
confundido(a)	confused
contento(a)	happy
deprimido(a)	depressed
divertido(a)	entertained; in a good mood
enamorado(a) (de)	in love (with)
enfermo(a)	sick
enojado(a)	angry
equivocado(a)	wrong
feliz	happy
frustrado(a)	frustrated
interesado(a)	interested
loco(a)	crazy
nervioso(a)	nervous
ocupado(a)	busy
preocupado(a)	worried
sano(a)	healthy
seguro(a)	sure
sorprendido(a)	surprised
triste	sad

Palabras adicionales

la salud	health

Gramática

Estar with adjectives and present progressive

1. Remember that **estar** is an irregular verb:

estar

estoy	estamos
estás	estáis
está	están

2. Apart from indicating location, the verb **estar** is also used to express an emotional, mental, or physical condition.

   Mis padres **están** felices.
   My parents are happy.

3. The verb **estar** is also used with present participles to form the present progressive. The present progressive is used to describe actions in progress. To form the present participle, add **-ando** (**-ar** verbs) or **–iendo** (**-er** and **-ir** verbs) to the stem of the verb.

   El profesor **está hablando** con Tito ahora.
   The professor is talking to Tito now.

4. The present participle of the verb **ir** is **yendo.** However, it is much more common to use the present tense of the verb when the action is in progress.

5. When the stem of an **-er** or an **-ir** verb ends in a vowel, **-yendo** is used instead of **-iendo.**

   leer – le**yendo**   oír – o**yendo**

6. Stem-changing **-ir** verbs have an irregular present participle. An **e** in the stem becomes an **i,** and an **o** in the stem becomes a **u.**

   mentir – m**i**ntiendo   dormir – d**u**rmiendo

7. In the present progressive, the verb **estar** must agree with the subject; however, you will notice that the present participle does NOT agree in gender (masculine/feminine) or number (singular/plural) with the subject.

   Mis hijos están estudiando inglés.
   My children are studying English.

Ser and *estar*

1. The verb **ser** is used in the following ways:
   a. to describe characteristics of people, places, or things

   La profesora **es** inteligente.
   The professor is intelligent.

   b. to identify a relationship, occupation, or nationality

   Mi novia **es** peruana.
   My girlfriend is Peruvian.

   c. to express origin

   Yo **soy** de Bolivia.
   I am from Bolivia.

   d. to express possession

   El libro **es** de Álvaro.
   The book belongs to Álvaro.

   e. to tell time and give dates

   Son las dos.
   It **is** two o'clock.

2. The verb **estar** is used in the following ways:
   a. to indicate location

   Ella **está** en la casa.   She **is** in the house.

   b. to express an emotional, mental, or physical condition

   Mi madre **está** enferma hoy.
   My mother is sick today.

   c. in the present progressive

   Estoy estudiando.   *I am studying.*

3. It is important to realize that the use of **ser** and **estar** with some adjectives can change the meaning of the adjectives. The use of **ser** indicates a characteristic or a trait, while the use of **estar** indicates a condition. Some common adjectives that change meaning are: **aburrido(a), alegre, feliz, bueno(a), malo(a), guapo(a), listo(a),** and **rico(a).**

   Carlos **es** aburrido.
   Carlos is boring. (personality)

   Graciela **está** aburrida.
   Graciela is bored. (present condition)

Vocabulario 2

🔊 1-33

Las profesiones

el (la) abogado(a)	lawyer
el actor	actor
la actriz	actress
el (la) agente de viajes	travel agent
el amo(a) de casa	homemaker
el (la) arquitecto(a)	architect
el (la) asistente de vuelo	flight attendant
el bailarín/ la bailarina	dancer
el (la) cantante	singer
el (la) científico(a)	scientist
el (la) cocinero(a)	cook
el (la) consejero(a)	adviser
el (la) contador(a)	accountant
el (la) dependiente	clerk
el (la) deportista	athlete
el (la) diseñador(a)	designer
el (la) enfermero(a)	nurse
el (la) escritor(a)	writer
el (la) fotógrafo(a)	photographer
el (la) ingeniero(a)	engineer
el jefe/la jefa	boss
el (la) maestro(a)	elementary/high school teacher
el (la) mecánico(a)	mechanic
el (la) médico(a)	doctor
el (la) mesero(a)	waiter
el (la) modelo	model
el (la) músico(a)	musician
el (la) periodista	journalist
el (la) piloto	pilot
el (la) pintor(a)	painter
el policía/la mujer policía	police officer
el (la) político(a)	politician
el (la) psicólogo(a)	psychologist
el (la) secretario(a)	secretary
el (la) trabajador(a) social	social worker
el (la) vendedor(a)	salesperson
el (la) veterinario(a)	veterinary

Palabras adicionales

el (la) cliente	client
la entrevista	interview
la solicitud	application; want ad
el sueldo	salary
el trabajo	job

Los verbos

conducir	to drive
conocer	to know, to be acquainted with
dar	to give
decir	to say, to tell
ganar	to earn
hacer	to do, to make
oír	to hear
poner	to put; to set
saber	to know (facts; how to do something)
salir	to go out, to leave
seguir	to follow
traer	to bring
venir	to come
ver	to see

Gramática

Verbs with changes in the first person

1. The following verbs have irregular first person forms:

poner → pongo   conducir → conduzco
salir → salgo   dar → doy
traer → traigo   ver → veo

2. The following verbs are not only irregular in the first person form, but also have other changes:

decir
digo	decimos
dices	decís
dice	dicen

venir
vengo	venimos
vienes	venís
viene	vienen

seguir
sigo	seguimos
sigues	seguís
sigue	siguen

oír
oigo	oímos
oyes	oís
oye	oyen

Saber and conocer

1. *Saber* and *conocer* are irregular in the first person form.

saber
sé	sabemos
sabes	sabéis
sabe	saben

conocer
conozco	conocemos
conoces	conocéis
conoce	conocen

2. While the verbs **saber** and **conocer** both mean *to know*, they are used in different contexts. **Saber** is used to express knowledge of facts or information as well as skills. **Conocer** is used to express acquaintance or familiarity with a person, place or thing.

Ana **conoce** Chile.   (*familiarity*)
Ana **sabe** dónde está Chile.   (*fact*)

3. When using **saber** to mean to *know how to do something*, it is followed by the infinitive.

El profesor **sabe** enseñar.
*The professor **knows how to** teach.*

4. When expressing knowledge or familiarity with general concepts or subjects, the verb **conocer** is used.

El artista conoce el arte prehispánico.
*The artist **knows** (is familiar with) pre-Hispanic art.*

La enfermera conoce la medicina.
*The nurse **knows** (is familiar with) medicine.*

5. Remember to use the *personal a* with **conocer** when referring to a person or a pet.

Conozco al piloto.   *I **know** the pilot.*

Vocabulario 1

🔊 1–37

Los verbos reflexivos

acostarse (ue)	to lie down; to go to bed
afeitarse	to shave
arreglarse	to fix oneself up; get ready
bañarse	to bathe; to shower (Mex.)
cepillarse	to brush
cortarse	to cut
despertarse	to wake up
divertirse	to have fun
dormirse	to fall asleep
ducharse	to shower
estirarse	to stretch
irse	to leave, to go away
lavarse	to wash
levantarse	to get up
maquillarse	to put on make-up
peinarse	to comb or style one's hair
ponerse (la ropa)	to put on (clothing)
quitarse (la ropa)	to take off (clothing)
secarse	to dry oneself
sentarse	to sit down
verse	to look at oneself
vestirse	to get dressed

Las partes del cuerpo

la boca	mouth
el brazo	arm
la cabeza	head
la cara	face
el codo	elbow
el cuello	neck
el dedo	finger
el dedo (del pie)	toe
el diente	tooth
la espalda	back
el estómago	stomach
el hombro	shoulder
la mano	hand
el muslo	thigh
la nariz	nose
el ojo	eye
la oreja	ear
el pecho	chest
el pelo	hair
el pie	foot
la pierna	leg
la rodilla	knee
el tobillo	ankle

Adverbios

a menudo	often
a veces	sometimes
ahora	now
antes de + infinitive	before (doing something)
después de + infinitive	after (doing something)
hoy	today
luego	later
mañana	tomorrow
más tarde	later
mientras	while
normalmente	normally, usually
(casi) nunca	(almost) never
pronto	soon
(casi) siempre	(almost) always

Gramática

Reflexive verbs

1. Reflexive verbs are verbs whose subject also receives the action performed. Simply put, they describe what one does to oneself. In Spanish, these verbs are characterized by the reflexive pronoun **se** that follows the infinitive form of the verb. Many of the verbs used to talk about daily routine are reflexive verbs.

2. Reflexive verbs are conjugated like regular verbs, except that the reflexive pronoun **se** must also be changed to reflect the subject.

levantarse

me levanto	**nos** levantamos
te levantas	**os** levantáis
se levanta	**se** levantan

3. The reflexive pronoun can always go in front of the conjugated verb. If you are using two verbs, it will precede the first verb.

   Nos lavamos las manos antes de comer.
   We wash our hands before eating.

   Paula **se está estirando.**
   Paula is stretching.

4. When using a reflexive verb with the infinitive, you can attach the pronoun to the infinitive.

Adverbs of time and frequency

1. One of the functions of an adverb is to tell when an action occurs. The following common adverbs of time may be used either before or after the action:

ahora	luego	pronto
a menudo	mañana	todos los días
hoy	más tarde	

2. The following adverbs of time usually come before the verb:

a veces*	(casi) siempre
mientras*	todavía
normalmente	ya
(casi) nunca	ya no

*If using a subject in the sentence, these adverbs are placed in front of the subject.

When using a reflexive verb with the present participle, you can attach the pronoun to the present participle, but you must then add an accent to maintain the original stress. The pronoun will still always agree with the subject.

   ¿**Vas a ducharte** antes de salir?
   Gilberto **está poniéndose** la ropa en su habitación.

5. Verbs may be reflexive or nonreflexive depending on who receives the action.

   Roberto **se lava.**
   Roberto **lava** a su perro.

6. Use the definite article rather than the possessive adjective after a reflexive verb.

   Mariana **se cepilla** los dientes.

7. Using a reflexive pronoun changes the meaning of some verbs.

   Vivián **se va** porque está enojada con su novio.
   Vivian left because she was angry at her boyfriend.

   Mi prima **va** a la iglesia a las diez.
   My cousin goes to church at ten.

3. To say what someone does before or after another activity, use the expressions **antes de** + *infinitive* and **después de** + *infinitive*.

   Antes de acostarse, mi hijo lee un libro.
   Before going to bed, my son reads a book.

When using a verb after a preposition, such as **de**, it is necessary to use the infinitive. **Antes** and **después** can be used without the preposition **de** and followed by a conjugated verb; however, the meaning changes slightly, and they are translated as *beforehand* and *afterwards*, respectively.

   Me ducho y después me acuesto.
   I shower and afterwards I go to bed.

4. When saying how often you do something, use the word **vez**.

   Me cepillo los dientes **dos veces al día.**
   *I brush my teeth **twice a day**.*

Notice that the adverbial expression comes after the activity.

todavía	still
todos los días	every day
ya	already
ya no	no longer

Palabras adicionales

el champú	shampoo
la pasta de dientes	toothpaste
el despertador	alarm clock
el jabón	soap
tarde	late
temprano	early
la toalla	towel

Vocabulario 2

◀))) 1-38

Los deportes

el atletismo	track and field
el bádminton	badminton
el básquetbol	basketball
el béisbol	baseball
el fútbol	soccer
el fútbol americano	American football
el golf	golf
la natación	swimming
el tenis	tennis
el voleibol	volleyball

El equipo

el equipo	equipment, team
el patín	skate
la pelota	ball
la raqueta	racquet
la red	net
el saco de dormir	sleeping bag
la tienda de campaña	camping tent

Verbos

acampar	to go camping
andar en bicicleta	to ride a bicycle
bucear	to scuba dive
esquiar en el agua	to water-ski
esquiar en tabla	to snowboard
hacer alpinismo	to climb mountains
ir de excursión	to hike
ir de pesca	to go fishing
jugar al ping-pong	to play ping-pong
levantar pesas	to lift weights
montar a	to ride (an animal)
patinar	to skate
patinar en hielo	to ice skate
pescar	to fish

Palabras adicionales

el (la) aficionado(a)	fan (of a sport)
anoche	last night
ayer	yesterday
el campo	field
la cancha	court
la entrada	ticket
el lago	lake
el partido	game
la semana pasada	last week

Gramática

The preterite

1. The preterite is used to discuss actions completed in the past. To form the preterite of regular **-ar** verbs, add these endings to the stem of the verb.

ballar

yo	bail**é**	nosotros(as)	bail**amos**
tú	bail**aste**	vosotros(as)	bail**asteis**
él / ella / usted	bail**ó**	ellos / ellas / ustedes	bail**aron**

José **viajó** a México.　　　　José **traveled (did travel)** to Mexico.

2. The preterite endings for regular **-er** and **-ir** verbs are identical. They are as follows:

beber / vivir

yo	beb**í** / viv**í**	nosotros(as)	beb**imos** / viv**imos**
tú	beb**iste** / viv**iste**	vosotros(as)	beb**isteis** / viv**isteis**
él / ella / usted	beb**ió** / viv**ió**	ellos / ellas / ustedes	beb**ieron** / viv**ieron**

¿**Escribiste** tú una carta?　　　　**Did you write** a letter?

3. **-Ar** and **-er** verbs that have stem changes in the present tense do not change in the preterite tense. You will learn about stem-changing **-ir** verbs below.

4. Verbs ending in **-car**, **-gar**, and **-zar** have spelling changes in the **yo** form in the preterite. Notice that the spelling changes preserve the original sound of the infinitive for **-car** and **-gar** verbs.

> car → **qué**　　**Busqué** el libro. **I looked for** the book.
>
> gar → **gué**　　**Llegué** tarde a la fiesta. **I arrived** late to the party.
>
> zar → **cé**　　**Empecé** a estudiar español el año pasado. **I started** studying Spanish last year.

5. The third person singular and plural of **oír** and **leer** also have spelling changes when conjugated in the preterite tense. These verbs carry accents in all forms of the preterite except for the third person plural.

> oír → **oyó, oyeron**　　　　leer → **leyó, leyeron**

Stem-changing verbs in the preterite

1. **-Ir** verbs that have stem changes in the present tense also have stem changes in the preterite. The third person singular and plural change **e → i** and **o → u**.

pedir

pedí	pedimos
pediste	pedisteis
p**i**dió	p**i**dieron

dormir

dormí	dormimos
dormiste	dormisteis
d**u**rmió	d**u**rmieron

Mi hermano **pidió** pollo, pero yo **pedí** la sopa.
*My brother **ordered** chicken, but I ordered soup.*

2. Other common stem-changing verbs:

conseguir (i)	morir (u)	repetir (i)	servir (i)
divertirse (i)	preferir (i)	seguir (i)	vestirse (i)

Vocabulario 1

🔊 2–5

Frutas

el durazno	*peach*
la fresa	*strawberry*
la manzana	*apple*
el melón	*melon*
la naranja	*orange*
la piña	*pineapple*
el plátano	*banana*
la sandía	*watermelon*
las uvas	*grapes*

Verduras

el brócoli	*broccoli*
la cebolla	*onion*
la lechuga	*lettuce*
el maíz	*corn*
la papa	*potato*
el pepino	*cucumber*
el tomate	*tomato*
la zanahoria	*carrot*

Lácteos y otros alimentos

la catsup	*ketchup*
el cereal	*cereal*
la crema	*cream*
el huevo	*egg*
el jamón	*ham*
la leche	*milk*
la mantequilla	*butter*
la mayonesa	*mayonnaise*
la mermelada	*jam*
la mostaza	*mustard*
el pan	*bread*
el pepinillo	*pickle*
el queso	*cheese*
el yogur	*yogurt*

Verbos

hornear	*to bake*

Palabras adicionales

la rebanada	*slice*

Los números

cien	*100*
ciento uno	*101*
doscientos	*200*
trescientos	*300*
cuatrocientos	*400*
quinientos	*500*
seiscientos	*600*
setecientos	*700*
ochocientos	*800*
novecientos	*900*
mil	*1000*
dos mil	*2000*
un millón	*1 000 000*

Gramática

Irregular verbs in the preterite

1. There are a number of verbs that are irregular in the preterite. **Ser** and **ir** have the same forms in the preterite.

ser/ir

fui	fuimos
fuiste	fuisteis
fue	fueron

2. The verbs **dar** and **ver** have similar conjugations in the preterite.

dar

di	dimos
diste	disteis
dio	dieron

ver

vi	vimos
viste	visteis
vio	vieron

3. Other irregular verbs can be divided into three groups. Notice that there are no accents on these verbs and that they all take the same endings (with the exception of the 3rd person plural of the verbs with **j** in the stem).

Verbs with *u* in the stem: tener

tuve	tuv**imos**
tuv**iste**	tuv**isteis**
tuv**o**	tuv**ieron**

Verbs with *i* in the stem: venir

vine	vin**imos**
vin**iste**	vin**isteis**
vin**o**	vin**ieron**

Verbs with *j* in the stem: traer

traj**e**	traj**imos**
traj**iste**	traj**isteis**
traj**o**	traj**eron**

Other verbs with **u** in the stem: **andar** (**anduv-**), **estar** (**estuv-**), **poder** (**pud-**), **poner** (**pus-**), **saber** (**sup-**) and **tener** (**tuv-**)

Other verbs with **i** in the stem: **hacer** (**hic-**) and **querer** (**quis-**)

Other verb with **j** in the stem: **conducir** (**conduj-**), **decir** (**dij-**), **producir** (**produj-**) and **traducir** (**traduj-**)

4. The preterite tense of **hay** is **hubo**.

> **Hubo** mucha información para estudiar.

Por and *para* and prepositional pronouns

1. **Por** and **para** can both be translated as *for* in English, but they have different uses in Spanish. **Por** is used to indicate:

a. cause, reason, or motive *(because of, on behalf of)*
> Nos tuvimos que poner los abrigos **por** el frío.

b. duration, period of time *(during, for)*
> El presidente habló **por** una hora y media.

c. exchange *(for)*
> Mi padre pagó diez mil dólares **por** el coche.

d. general movement through space *(through, around, along, by)*
> Pasamos **por** el parque porque es más bonito.

e. expressions:

por ejemplo	*for example*
por eso	*that's why*
por favor	*please*
por fin	*finally*
por supuesto	*of course*

2. **Para** is used to indicate:

a. goal or purpose *(in order to, used for)*
> Fueron al cine **para** ver una película.
> *They went to the movie theater **to** see a film.*

b. recipient *(for)*
> La abuela preparó la comida **para** sus nietos.
> *The grandmother prepared the food **for** her grandchildren.*

c. destination *(to)*
> Vamos **para** la playa este verano.
> *We're going **to** the beach this summer.*

d. deadline *(for, due)*
> Tenemos que leer el texto **para** el lunes.
> *We have to read the text **for** Monday.*

e. contrast to what is expected
> **Para** estar a dieta, come mucho.
> ***For** being on a diet, he eats a lot.*

f. expressions:

para colmo	*to top it all off*
para nada	*not at all*
para siempre	*forever*
para variar	*for a change*

3. After a preposition, use the same pronoun that you use as a subject pronoun, except for **yo** and **tú**. **Yo** becomes **mí** after a preposition, and **tú** becomes **ti**.
> La habitación grande es **para ti**.
> *The large room is **for you**.*

4. Instead of **mí** or **ti** with **con**, **conmigo** and **contigo** are used.
> ¿Puedo ir **contigo**?
> *Can I go with you?*

> ¡Claro que sí! Puedes venir **conmigo**.
> *Of course! You can come with me.*

Vocabulario 2

🔊 2–6

Los utensilios

la copa	wine glass
la cuchara	spoon
el cuchillo	knife
el mantel	tablecloth
el plato	plate
el plato hondo	bowl
la servilleta	napkin
la taza	cup
el tazón	serving bowl
el tenedor	fork
el vaso	glass

La comida

el arroz	rice
el azúcar	sugar
la bebida	drink
el café	coffee
el camarón	shrimp
la carne	meat
el cerdo	pork
la cerveza	beer
el coctel	cocktail
la ensalada	salad
el entremés	appetizer
el flan	flan
la fruta	fruit
la hamburguesa	hamburger
el helado	ice cream
el jugo	juice
la naranja	orange
el pastel	cake
el pavo	turkey
el pescado	fish
la pimienta	pepper
el pollo	chicken
el postre	dessert
el refresco	soda
la sal	salt
el sándwich	sandwich
la sopa	soup
los totopos	tortilla chips
el vino blanco	white wine
el vino tinto	red wine

Verbos

cenar	to eat dinner
dejar (una propina)	to leave (a tip)
desayunar	to eat breakfast
felicitar	to congratulate
llevar	to take along
querer	to love
saludar	to greet

Palabras adicionales

al horno	baked
el almuerzo	lunch
asado(a)	grilled
la cena	dinner
la comida	food, lunch
la cuenta	bill
el desayuno	breakfast
frito(a)	fried
la orden	order
el plato principal	main dish

Gramática

Direct object pronouns I

1. Direct object pronouns are used to replace the direct object, or the noun that receives the action of the verb. In Spanish, the direct object pronoun must agree in gender and number with the noun that it replaces.

    Esteban dejó **la propina.**
    Esteban left the tip. (Tip is the direct object.)

    Esteban **la** dejó.
    *Esteban left it. (**La,** to reflect the feminine gender of **la propina.**)*

2. Here are the direct object pronouns for the third person:

	singular	plural
masculino	**lo** *it, him, you*	**los** *them, you*
femenino	**la** *it, her, you*	**las** *them, you*

Direct object pronouns II

1. The direct object pronouns outlined above are only for the third person. Here are all of the direct object pronouns:

	singular	plural
first person	**me** *me*	**nos** *us*
second person	**te** *you*	**os** *you (plural)*
third person	**lo / la** *it, him, her, you*	**los / las** *them, you (plural)*

3. Note that the direct object pronoun is placed before the conjugated verb.

    ¿Comiste el pescado?
    Did you eat the fish?

    Sí, **lo** comí.
    Yes, I ate it.

    ¿Hiciste la tarea?
    Did you do the homework?

    La estoy haciendo ahora.
    I am doing it now.

4. The direct object pronoun can also be attached to the infinitive or the present participle. An accent is necessary when adding the pronoun to the end of the present participle.

    ¿Quieres ver**los** mañana?
    Do you want to see them tomorrow?

    Lo está preparando. / Está preparándo**lo.**
    She is preparing it.

2. The following verbs are frequently used with direct object pronouns:

ayudar	escuchar	querer
buscar	felicitar	saludar
conocer	invitar	ver
creer	llamar	visitar
encontrar	llevar	

Vocabulario 1

🔊 2-11

La limpieza

la basura	trash, garbage, litter
el bote de basura	trash can
el cortacésped	lawnmower
la escoba	broom
el jabón para platos	dish soap
la manguera	hose
la plancha	iron
el quehacer	chore
el sacudidor	duster
la tabla de planchar	ironing board
el trapeador	mop
el trapo	cloth, rag

Verbos

barrer	to sweep
colgar (ue)	to hang
cortar (el césped)	to cut, to mow (the lawn)
guardar	to put away
hacer la cama	to make the bed
lavar platos	to wash the dishes
lavar ropa	to do laundry
ordenar	to tidy up, to straighten up
pasar la aspiradora	to vacuum
planchar	to iron
poner la mesa	to set the table
recoger (la mesa)	to pick up (to clear the table)
regar (ie)	to water
sacar la basura	to take the trash out
sacudir	to dust
secar	to dry
trapear	to mop

Adjetivos

limpio(a)	clean
sucio(a)	dirty

Palabras negativas

nadie	no one, nobody
nada	nothing
nunca	never
jamás	never
tampoco	neither, either
ningún (ninguno), ninguna	none, any
ni... ni	neither . . . nor

Palabras indefinidas

alguien	someone, somebody
algo	something
siempre	always
también	also
algún (alguno), alguna	some
o... o	either . . . or

Gramática

The imperfect

1. To conjugate regular verbs in the imperfect, add the following endings to the stem:

-ar verbs trabajar	-er/-ir verbs vivir
trabaj**aba**	viv**ía**
trabaj**abas**	viv**ías**
trabaj**aba**	viv**ía**
trabaj**ábamos**	viv**íamos**
trabaj**abais**	viv**íais**
trabaj**aban**	viv**ían**

2. Only three verbs have irregular imperfect forms:

ser	ir	ver
era	iba	veía
eras	ibas	veías
era	iba	veía
éramos	íbamos	veíamos
erais	ibais	veíais
eran	iban	veían

3. There are no stem-changing verbs in the imperfect. Except for the three verbs mentioned above, all conjugations are regular.

4. The imperfect of the verb **haber (hay)** is **había**.

5. The imperfect is used to tell what one used to do in the past. Phrases such as **siempre, todos los días, todos los años, con frecuencia,** a menudo, normalmente, generalmente, a veces, etc. may elicit the use of the imperfect.

> Cuando era niña, hacía mi tarea **todos los días.**
> *When I was young, I did (used to do) my homework **every day.***

> Mi hermana **siempre hacía** su cama.
> *My sister **always made (used to make)** her bed.*

6. The imperfect is also used to describe an action in progress at a particular moment in the past where there is no emphasis on when the action began or ended. It is also possible to use the imperfect with the helping verb **estar** and a present participle.

> El año pasado, mi tío **trabajaba** en Puerto Rico.
> *Last year my uncle **was working** in Puerto Rico.*

> A las dos de la mañana, mi familia y yo **estábamos durmiendo.**
> *At two in the morning, my family and I **were sleeping.***

Indefinite and negative words

1. Indefinite and negative words are listed on the left-hand side of this page.

2. In Spanish, it is correct to use a double negative. When using a negative expression after a verb, be sure to put **no** before the verb.

> Jaime **no** estudia **nunca**.
> **No** tengo **ninguna** camisa limpia.

3. **Nadie, jamás, nunca,** and **tampoco** can all be placed before the verb. **Nada** can go before the verb only if it is used as the subject.

> Andrés no quiere ir, y yo **tampoco** quiero ir.
> *Andrés doesn't want to go, and I don't want to go either.*

> **Nada** es mejor que la familia.
> *Nothing is better than family.*

4. The words **ningún** and **algún** are used before singular masculine nouns. The words **ninguno** and **alguno** must agree in gender and number with the nouns that they modify.

> ¿Tienes **algunos amigos** que puedan venir con nosotros?
> No tengo **ninguna idea** dónde está la escoba.

While it is correct to use **algunos(as)** in front of a noun, it is much more common to use **unos(as)** or to omit the article. **Algunos(as)** tends to be used more frequently as a pronoun: **Necesito plantas para el jardín. ¿Tiene algunas?**

Vocabulario 2

🔊 2–12

Juegos y juguetes

el ajedrez	chess
el carrito	toy car
las cartas	playing cards
el chiste	joke
la cometa	kite
el cuento	story
la cuerda	(jumping) rope
las damas	checkers
el dominó	dominos
las escondidas	hide and seek
la historieta	comic book
el juego de mesa	board game
la motocicleta	motorcycle
la (el) muñeca(o)	doll
el osito	teddy bear
la patineta	skateboard
el videojuego	video game

Verbos

aburrir	to bore
andar en	to ride
caer (bien / mal)	to like / dislike a person
chatear	to chat (online)
contar (ue)	to tell (a story); to count
dar la vuelta	to take a walk or a ride
dibujar	to draw
encantar	to really like, to enjoy immensely
fascinar	to fascinate
hacer jardinería	to garden
importar	to be important
interesar	to interest
ir de paseo	to go for a walk
jugar a los bolos	to go bowling
molestar	to bother
mostrar (ue)	to show
navegar el Internet	to surf the web
pasar tiempo	to spend time
pelear	to fight; to argue
portarse (bien / mal)	to behave (well / badly)
prestar	to lend
salir (a + infinitive)	to go out (to do something)
saltar	to jump
tejer	to knit
tocar (el piano / la guitarra)	to play (the piano / the guitar)
trepar (un árbol)	to climb (a tree)
volar	to fly

Palabras adicionales

el juguete	toy
la niñera	baby-sitter
el permiso	permission
el teléfono celular	cell phone

Gramática

Indirect object pronouns

1. An indirect object pronoun indicates **to whom** or **for whom** an action takes place.

> Marcos siempre **les** dice la verdad a sus padres.
> *Marcos always tells the truth **to his parents.***

2. In Spanish, the indirect object pronoun must always be used when mentioning the indirect object, even though it may seem redundant. This is true even if you clarify or emphasize the indirect object pronoun using the preposition **a**.

> Lola **les** sirvió la cena **a su familia.**
> *Lola served dinner **to her family.***

> Mis amigos **me** dieron el dinero **a mí.**
> *My friends gave the money **to me.***

3. The indirect object pronouns are:

yo **me**	nosotros(as) **nos**
tú **te**	vosotros(as) **os**
él / ella **le**	ellas / ellos **les**
usted	ustedes

4. An indirect object pronoun can be placed before a conjugated verb or attached to the end of an infinitive or present participle.

> **Te** voy a comprar una muñeca.
> *I'm going to buy a doll **for you.***

Double object pronouns

1. When using both indirect and direct object pronouns with the same verb, the indirect object pronoun comes before the direct object pronoun.

> —Me gusta tu suéter.
> *I like your sweater.*

> —Gracias. Mi abuela **me lo** tejió.
> *Thanks. My grandmother knitted it for me.*

2. When using double object pronouns, the pronouns must always be placed together. Just as when they are used individually, they may be placed before a conjugated verb or attached to the end of the present participle or infinitive. When adding the two pronouns to a present participle or infinitive, an accent must also be added.

Mi hermana está contándo**les** un cuento
*My sister is telling **them** a story.*

5. The following verbs are frequently used with indirect object pronouns:

contar (ue)	pedir
dar	preguntar
decir	prestar
devolver (ue)	preguntar
mostrar (ue)	servir

6. The verb **gustar** is always conjugated with an indirect object pronoun. The following verbs work just like **gustar:**

> **aburrir** *to bore*
> **caer (bien/mal)** *to like/dislike a person*
> **encantar** *to really like, to enjoy immensely*
> **fascinar** *to fascinate*
> **importar** *to be important*
> **interesar** *to interest*
> **molestar** *to bother*

> No **les** gusta limpiar.
> *They don't like to clean. (Cleaning is not pleasing **to them**.)*

> A Julián **le** fascina hacer jardinería.
> *Julián really likes gardening (Gardening is fascinating **to Julián**.)*

¿Te gusta este osito? **Te lo** voy a regalar para tu cumpleaños.
*Do you like this teddy bear? I am going to give **it to you** for your birthday.*

¿La lección? No la oí. El profesor ya **estaba dándosela** a la clase cuando yo entré.
*The lesson? I didn't hear it. The teacher was already **giving it to the class** when I entered.*

3. When using a double object pronoun, the third person indirect object pronouns (**le, les**) change to **se** before the third person direct object pronouns.

> Laura no tiene dinero. **Se lo** prestó a su amigo.
> *Laura doesn't have any money. She lent it to her friend.*

Vocabulario 1

🔊 2–16

En la fiesta

los banderines	streamers
los bocadillos	snacks
el brindis	toast
el champán	champagne
el desfile	parade
los dulces	candies
el festejo	party, celebration
los fuegos artificiales	fireworks
los globos	balloons
el grupo de música	music group/band
la invitación	invitation
el invitado	guest
los novios	bride and groom
el pastel	cake
la piñata	piñata
la quinceañera	girl celebrating her fifteenth birthday
el regalo	gift
la serenata	serenade
la vela	candle

Las celebraciones

el aniversario	anniversary
el bautizo	baptism
la boda	wedding
el cumpleaños	birthday
la graduación	graduation
las posadas	nine-day celebration before Christmas
los quince años	a girl's fifteenth birthday celebration
el santo	saint's day

Verbos

brindar	to toast
casarse (con)	to get married (to)
celebrar	to celebrate
cumplir años	to be/to turn years old
decorar	to decorate
disfrutar	to enjoy
romper	to break
terminar	to finish

Gramática

A comparison of the preterite and the imperfect

1. The **imperfect** is used in the following situations:

a. to describe past actions in progress

Miguel **trabajaba** el viernes por la noche, y no pudo venir a la fiesta.
Miguel was working Friday night, and couldn't come to the party.

b. to describe habitual actions in the past

Al regresar de la escuela, siempre **comíamos** un bocadillo.
When we got home from school, we always used to eat a snack.

c. to describe conditions, people, and places in the past

Cuando **era** joven, mi abuela **era** muy bonita.
When she was young, my grandmother was very pretty.

d. to give the background information or details when telling a story

Hacía mal tiempo y **llovía** el día que tuve mi accidente.
The weather was bad and it was raining the day I had my accident.

2. The **preterite** is used in the following situations:

a. to describe completed actions in the past

Mi familia y yo **fuimos** a México el año pasado.
My family and I went to Mexico last year.

b. to narrate the main events of a story

José **entró** en el salón, **buscó** a sus amigos y **empezó** a hablar con María.
José came into the room, looked for his friends, and started talking to María.

Uses of the preterite and the imperfect

When relaying a past event, the actions can usually be expressed in one of three ways:

1. Two simultaneous actions: When talking about two actions that are going on at the same time in the past, use the imperfect, as both actions are *in progress*.

Mientras Juan **preparaba** los bocadillos, Pilar **ponía** las decoraciones.
While Juan was preparing the snacks, Pilar was putting up decorations.

2. A series of completed actions: When listing a series of events that occurred, use the preterite.

Primero **mandamos** invitaciones. Después **compramos** globos y velas. Por fin **hicimos** el pastel.
First we sent invitations. Then we bought balloons and candles. Finally we made the cake.

3. One action in progress when another begins: In the past when an action is in progress and a second action begins or is completed, both the preterite and the imperfect are used. The imperfect is used for the action in progress and the preterite is used for the new action that began or interrupted the first action.

Mis amigos **estaban** en la cocina cuando yo **llegué.**
My friends were in the kitchen when I arrived.

Vocabulario 2

🔊 2-17

En la calle

la acera	sidewalk
la ambulancia	ambulance
la camilla	stretcher
la carretera	highway
el (la) ciclista	cyclist
el (la) conductor(a)	driver
el cruce	crosswalk
la esquina	corner
el límite de velocidad	speed limit
la multa	fine, ticket
el paramédico	paramedic
el parquímetro	parking meter
la patrulla	police car
el peatón (la peatona)	pedestrian
el poste	post
el puente	bridge
el semáforo	traffic light
la señal	sign
el servicio de emergencias	emergency service
el (la) testigo	witness

Los verbos

aburrirse	to become bored
alegrarse	to become happy
asustarse	to become frightened
atravesar (ie)	to cross
atropellar	to run over
bajar de	to get out of (a vehicle)
caer(se)	to fall
chocar (con)	to crash (into something)
cruzar	to cross
dañar	to damage
distraerse	to get distracted
enojarse	to become angry
esperar	to wait
estacionarse	to park
frustrarse	to become frustrated
pasarse un semáforo en rojo	to run a red light
pasarse una señal de PARE	to run a stop sign
sentirse	to feel
sorprenderse	to be surprised
subir a	to get into (a vehicle)
tropezar (ie)	to trip

Expresiones adicionales

de repente	suddenly
estar dañado(a)	to be damaged
estar herido(a)	to be injured

Gramática

Preterite and imperfect with emotions and mental states

1. When describing emotions or mental states in the past, use the same guidelines as with past actions. To express that someone was feeling a certain way over time, use the imperfect. To express that someone felt a certain way during a specific period, or reacted emotionally to something, use the preterite.

> Nora **estaba contenta** porque hacía sol.
> Nora **was happy** because it was sunny.

> Mi primo **estuvo enfermo** por dos meses.
> My cousin **was ill** for two months.

> El Señor López **se enojó** cuando vio la ventana rota.
> Mr. López **got angry** when he saw the broken window.

2. The following verbs are generally used in the preterite, as they describe a specific change in emotion or feeling:

aburrirse	asustarse	frustrarse
alegrarse	enojarse	sorprenderse

3. The verb **sentirse** (e → ie) is used to express how one feels.

> **Me sentí deprimida** después de la película porque era muy triste.
> **I felt depressed** after the movie because it was very sad.

> ¿**Te sentías** cansado anoche?
> **Were you feeling** tired last night?

4. Use **ponerse** in the preterite followed by an adjective to express a change in emotion.

> Cecilia **se puso** nerviosa porque no podía encontrar su tarea.
> Cecilia **became** nervous because she couldn't find her homework.

5. Verbs that express mental states function similarly to action verbs; using them in the imperfect implies an ongoing condition, whereas using them in the preterite indicates the beginning or completion of the condition.

	Imperfect	Preterite
conocer	to know, to be acquainted with	to meet
saber	to know (about)	to find out
haber	there was/were (descriptive)	there was/there were (occurred)
poder	was able to (circumstances)	succeeded in
no poder	was not able to (circumstances)	failed to
querer	wanted	tried to
no querer	didn't want	refused to

Preterite and imperfect: A summary

1. To summarize, the **preterite** is used to express:

   a. a past action or a series of actions that are completed as of the moment of reference.

   > Anoche **fui** al cine y **vi** una buena película.
   > Last night, I **went** to the movies and **saw** a good movie.

   b. an action that is beginning or ending

   > **Empezó** a llover a las cuatro de la tarde.
   > It **began** to rain at four in the afternoon.

   c. a change of condition or emotion

   > Esteban **se frustró** con el examen y no lo terminó.
   > Esteban **got frustrated** with the exam and didn't finish it.

2. The **imperfect** is used to express:

   a. an action in progress with no emphasis on the beginning or end of the action

   > Los estudiantes **estaban trabajando** duro.
   > The students **were working** hard.

   b. a habitual action

   > Siempre **salía** con mis amigos, pero ahora solo salimos un día la semana.
   > I always **used to go** out with my friends, but now we only go out one day a week.

   c. a description of a physical or mental condition

   > Javier **se sentía** feliz con su novia.
   > Javier **felt** happy with his girlfriend.

   d. other descriptions such as, time, date, and age

   > Mi madre **tenía** diez años en 1970.
   > My mom **was** ten years old in 1970.

Vocabulario 1

🔊 2-21

De viaje

a tiempo	on time
la aduana	customs
el asiento	seat
el boleto	ticket
la conexión	connection
el equipaje	luggage
el equipaje de mano	hand luggage
la llegada	arrival
el (la) pasajero(a)	passenger
el pasaporte	passport
el pasillo	aisle
la primera clase	first class
retrasado(a)	delayed
la sala de espera	waiting room
la salida	departure
la segunda clase	second class
la ventanilla	window

En el aeropuerto

el aeropuerto internacional	international airport
el (la) agente de seguridad	security agent
el cinturón de seguridad	safety (seat) belt
la escala	layover
la maleta	suitcase
el mostrador	counter
el pase de abordar	boarding pass
la puerta (de salida)	gate (departure)
el reclamo de equipaje	baggage claim
la revisión de equipaje	luggage screening
la visa	visa
el vuelo	flight

En la estación de tren

el andén	platform
el coche cama	sleeping car
la litera	bunk
la parada	stop
el (la) revisor(a)	controller
la taquilla	ticket window
el vagón	car, wagon

Los verbos

abordar	to board
aterrizar	to land
despegar	to take off
doblar	to turn
facturar equipaje	to check luggage
pasar por seguridad	to go through security
perder	to miss (a flight, a train)
seguir derecho	to go straight

Gramática

Relative pronouns and adverbs

1. The relative pronouns **que** and **quien** are used to combine two sentences with a common noun or pronoun into one sentence. When used as relative pronouns, **que** and **quien** do not carry accents.

> El vuelo estaba retrasado. El vuelo despegó a las nueve, no a las ocho.
>
> El vuelo **que** estaba retrasado despegó a las nueve, no a las ocho.

2. **Que** is the most commonly used relative pronoun. It can be used to refer to people or things.

> El tren tiene un coche cama **que** es muy pequeño.

3. In English, the relative pronoun can sometimes be omitted; in Spanish, however, it must be used.

> Los boletos **que** compraste son para primera clase.
>
> *The tickets (that) you bought are for first class.*

4. **Quien(es)** refers only to people and is used after a preposition (**a, con, de, para, por, en**).

> El agente de seguridad es la persona **con quien** debes hablar.

5. **Quien(es)** may replace **que** when the dependent clause is set off by commas.

> Andrés y Julián, **quienes** viajaron en primera clase, no se sentaron con nosotros.

6. When referring to places, you will need to use the relative adverb **donde**, without an accent.

> La parada **donde** debes esperar está al otro lado de la calle.
>
> *The stop where you should wait is on the other side of the street.*

Formal and *nosotros* commands

Commands, or **mandatos** in Spanish, are used to tell someone to do something. You do not use the subject when giving a command.

1. Formal commands are used with people you would address with **usted** or **ustedes**. To form these commands, drop the **-o** from the present tense first person (**yo** form) and add the opposite ending (**-e(n)** for **-ar** verbs, and **-a(n)** for **-er** and **-ir** verbs).

	trabajar	tener	dormir
usted	trabaje	tenga	duerma
ustedes	trabajen	tengan	duerman

> **Aborden** el avión a tiempo.
> *Board the plane on time.*

2. Negative formal commands are formed by placing **no** before the verb.

> **No traigan** demasiado equipaje.
> *Don't bring too much luggage.*

3. Infinitives that end in **-car** and **-gar** have spelling changes in order to maintain the same sound as the infinitive. Infinitives that end in **-zar** also have a spelling change.

> tocar → to**que**(n)   almorzar → almuer**ce**(n)
> llegar → lle**gue**(n)

> **Escojan** los asientos de ventanilla, si es posible.
> *Choose window seats if it's possible.*

4. These verbs have irregular command forms:

dar	**dé (den)**
estar	**esté(n)**
ir	**vaya(n)**
saber	**sepa(n)**
ser	**sea(n)**

> **Sea** paciente con los empleados.
> *Be patient with the employees.*

5. To make suggestions with *Let's*, use commands in the **nosotros** form. **Nosotros** commands are very similar to formal commands. Add **-emos** for **-ar** verbs, and **-amos** for **-er** and **-ir** verbs.

> **Almorcemos** antes de irnos.
> *Let's eat lunch before leaving.*

6. Note the irregular verbs in number 4. They follow a similar pattern for **nosotros** commands, but they use the **nosotros** endings.

> **Seamos** tranquilos. No vamos a llegar tarde.
> *Let's be calm. We're not going to arrive late.*

7. **Ir** has two different forms. While it is possible to use **vayamos**, the present tense **vamos** is often used with affirmative commands and **vayamos** with negative commands.

8. **-Ar** and **-er** verbs with stem changes do <u>not</u> change in **nosotros** command. However, **-ir** verbs do stem change.

> **Juguemos** cartas mientras esperamos.
> *Let's play cards while we wait.*
>
> **Pidamos** algo para tomar.
> *Let's order something to drink.*

Vocabulario 2

🔊 2–22

El hotel

el alojamiento	lodging
el ascensor	elevator
el (la) botones	bellhop
el (la) camarero(a)	housekeeping
el centro de negocios	business center
las escaleras	stairs
el (la) gerente	manager
la habitación	room
el (la) huésped	guest
el Internet inalámbrico	wireless Internet
la llave	key
la recepción	reception (desk)
el (la) recepcionista	receptionist
la sala de conferencias	conference center
el sauna	sauna
el servicio a la habitación	room service
el transporte	transportation
el (la) turista	tourist

Verbos

alojarse	to lodge, to stay (in a hotel)
bajar	to go down, to take something down
pagar (y marcharse)	to check out
quedarse	to stay
registrarse	to register
subir	to go up, to take something up

Palabras adicionales

la clase turista	economy class
disponible	available
doble	double
de lujo	luxurious
sencillo(a)	single
triple	triple

Gramática

Informal commands

1. Informal commands are used with anyone you would address using **tú**, such as family members or friends. To form the affirmative informal (**tú**) commands, use the third person singular (**él/ella**) of the present tense.

Tiende la cama. *Make the bed. (Note that stem-changing verbs keep their changes in the informal command forms.)*

2. The following verbs have irregular forms for the affirmative informal commands:

decir **di**	ir **ve**	salir **sal**	tener **ten**
hacer **haz**	poner **pon**	ser **sé**	venir **ven**

3. When forming negative informal commands, use the formal **usted** commands and add an **–s.**

Verb	*Usted* command	Negative *tú* command
comer	coma	**no comas**
tener	tenga	**no tengas**
ir	vaya	**no vayas**

No **pongas** la maleta en la cama.
*Don't **put** the suitcase on the bed.*

4. In Spain, the **ustedes** commands are formal. To give commands to two or more friends or family members, they use **vosotros** commands. **Vosotros** affirmative commands are formed by dropping the **–r** from the infinitive and replacing it with **–d.** Negative commands are formed by using the base of the **usted** commands and adding the **vosotros** ending (**-éis, -áis**).

Verb	Affirmative *vosotros* command	Negative *vosotros* command
hablar	**hablad**	**no habléis**
ir	**id**	**no vayáis**
poner	**poned**	**no pongáis**

No **uséis** el ascensor, **subid** por las escaleras. *Don't **use** the elevator, **go up** the stairs.*

Commands with pronouns

1. When using affirmative commands, the pronouns are attached to the end of the verb.

No sé dónde está la llave. **Búsquenla** por favor.
*I don't know where the key is. **Look for it** please.*

Allí está el botones. **Llámalo.**
*There is the bellhop. **Call him.***

2. When using negative commands, the pronouns are placed directly before the verb.

El huésped está durmiendo. No **lo moleste.**
*The guest is sleeping. Don't **bother him.***

3. When adding the pronoun(s) creates a word of three or more syllables, an accent is added to the syllable where the stress would normally fall.

lava	lávalos
limpia	límpiala
da	dámelo

Vocabulario 1

🔊 2-25

En la tienda

la caja	cash register
el (dinero en) efectivo	cash
el número	size (shoe)
la oferta	sale (event, reduction of prices)
la prenda	garment
el probador	dressing room
la talla	size (clothing)
la tarjeta de crédito	credit card
la venta	sale (transaction)

Telas

el algodón	cotton
la lana	wool
el lino	linen
la mezclilla	denim
la piel	leather
la seda	silk

Estilos

a cuadros	plaid
a rayas	striped
de lunares	with polka dots
de moda	fashionable
estampado(a)	patterned

Verbos

elegir (i)	to choose
hacer juego	to match
probarse (ue)	to try on
quedar	to fit

Adjetivos

apretado(a)	tight
barato(a)	cheap, inexpensive
caro(a)	expensive
chico(a)	small
de marca	name brand
(estar) de moda	fashionable
(estar) rebajado(a)	on sale
grande	large
hecho(a) a mano	handmade
liso(a)	solid
mediano(a)	médium

Expresiones útiles

¡Qué bien te queda esa falda!	That skirt really fits you well!
¡Qué caros!	How expensive!
¡Qué color tan bonito!	What a pretty color!
¡Qué lindos zapatos!	What pretty shoes!
¡Qué pantalones tan elegantes!	What elegant pants!

Comparaciones

mayor	older (age)
mejor	better
menor	younger
peor	worse

Palabras adicionales

el descuento	discount
por ciento	percent

Gramática

Constructions with *se*

1. The pronoun **se** is used when the subject is not known or not relevant. When **se** is used, the verb is conjugated in the third person form, either singular or plural, depending on the noun.

   Se habla español en la clase.
   *Spanish **is spoken** in class.*

   En esta tienda, solo **se venden** zapatos de marca.
   *In this store, only name brand shoes **are sold.***

2. When the verb is not used with a noun, it is conjugated in the third person singular form. The pronoun **se** translates to *one, you* or *they* in English.

   Se dice que es mejor no usar una tarjeta de crédito.
   ***They say** it is better not to use a credit card.*

   Se paga en la caja.
   ***One pays** at the cash register.*

3. When using a verb such as **deber** or **poder** that is followed by an infinitive and a noun, the verb is conjugated in agreement with the noun because it is the subject. If there is no noun, then the verb is conjugated in the singular form.

   Se pueden ver los nuevos vestidos en la vitrina.
   ***One can** see the new dresses in the display window.*

Comparisons

1. Comparisons of equality:

   a. to compare equal qualities use **tan** + adjective/adverb + **como**

   La camisa es **tan barata como** la falda.
   The shirt is as cheap as the skirt.

   b. to compare equal quantities, use **tanto(s) / tanta(s)** + noun + **como**

   Katia tiene **tanta ropa como** su hermana.
   Katia has as many clothes as her sister.

   c. to compare equality in actions, use verb + **tanto como**

   Mis amigos van de compras **tanto como** trabajan.
   My friends go shopping as much as they work.

2. Comparisons of inequality:

   a. to express that one thing is greater than another, use **más** + adjective/adverb/noun + **que**

   Los pantalones negros me quedan **más apretados que** los azules.
   The black pants are tighter on me than the blue ones.

   b. to express that one thing is less than another, use **menos** + adjective/ adverb/ noun + **que**

   Este suéter de lana es **menos cómodo que** el suéter de algodón.
   This wool sweater is less comfortable than the cotton sweater.

   c. to compare unequal actions, use verb + **más que / menos que**

   Pilar gasta **más que** gana.
   Pilar spends more than she earns.

3. The following adjectives and adverbs do not use **más** or **menos** in their constructions:

   bueno/bien → **mejor** *better*
   joven → **menor** *younger*
   malo/mal → **peor** *worse*
   viejo (age of a person) → **mayor** *older*

   Cecilia tiene amigos que son **menores que** ella.

4. Superlatives are used when someone or something is referred to as the most, the least, the best, etc. This is expressed through the following construction:

   article **(el, la, los, las)** + noun (optional) **+ más / menos** + adjective

   Héctor es **el más guapo** del grupo.
   Héctor is the most handsome in the group.

   La prenda que tienes es **la menos cara** de la tienda.
   The garment that you have is the least expensive of the store.

   As with the other comparisons, when using **bueno/bien, malo/mal, joven,** and **viejo** (age), you must use the irregular constructions **mejor, peor, menor,** and **mayor**.

   Esta tienda tiene **las mejores** rebajas.

5. The preposition **de** is often used with superlatives to express *in* or *of*.

Vocabulario 2

🔊 2-26

El arte

el arte abstracto	abstract art
el autorretrato	self-portrait
la escultura	sculpture
la exhibición	exhibit
la galería	gallery
el grabado	engraving; print
la luz	light
la máscara	mask
el mural	mural
la naturaleza muerta	still life
la obra	work (of art, literature, theater, etc.)
el óleo	oil painting
el paisaje	landscape
la paleta	pallet
el pincel	paintbrush
la pintura	painting
el retrato	portrait
la tinta	ink

Verbos

acabar	to finish
apagar	to turn off
apreciar	to appreciate; to enjoy
descomponer	to break down (a machine)
diseñar	to design
esculpir	to sculpt
exhibir	to exhibit
olvidar	to forget
posar	to pose
quedar	to remain (behind)
romper	to break

Adjetivos

abstracto(a)	abstract
claro(a)	light, pale
complicado(a)	complex
cubista	cubist
extraño(a)	strange, odd
impresionista	impressionist
obscuro(a)	dark
sencillo(a)	simple
surrealista	surrealist
tradicional	traditional
vanguardista	revolutionary; avant-garde

Gramática

Estar with the past participle

1. The past participle is formed by changing the verb as follows:

-**ar** verb → add -**ado**   diseñado, apagado
-**er** / -**ir** verb → add –**ido**   vendido, esculpido

The following verbs are the irregular past participles:

abrir	**abierto**	hacer	**hecho**
cubrir	**cubierto**	morir	**muerto**
decir	**dicho**	romper	**roto**
despertar	**despierto**	poner	**puesto**
devolver	**devuelto**	ver	**visto**
escribir	**escrito**	volver	**vuelto**

2. The past participle can be used as an adjective to show condition. You have already learned some of them, such as **aburrido, cansado,** and **muerto.** Like other adjectives, they must agree in gender and number with the nouns they describe.

> El museo está **abierto** todos los días menos lunes.
> *The museum is **open** every day except Monday.*

> Carlos tiene unos cuadros **pintados** por Picasso.
> *Carlos has paintings **painted** by Picasso.*

3. They are often used with the verb **estar;** however they can also be placed after the noun they describe.

> Las obras **esculpidas** por Señor Ramos **están conocidas** por todos.
> *The works sculpted by Mr. Ramos are familiar to everyone.*

Se to indicate accidental occurrences

1. In **Exploraciones gramaticales 1,** you learned to use the pronoun **se** in order to indicate that the subject is either unknown or unimportant. Use the following construction with **se** to indicate unintentional or accidental occurrences:

se + indirect object pronoun + verb

> **Se me perdieron** los libros.
> *I (accidentally) lost the books.*

Notice that the verb agrees with the subject (**los libros**). The indirect object pronoun (**me**) identifies who is affected by this action.

2. The following are common verbs used with this construction:

acabar	olvidar
apagar	perder
caer	quedar
descomponer	romper

> A Rodrigo **se le acabó** la pintura antes de terminar el mural.
> *Rodrigo ran out of paint before finishing the mural.*

> Jugábamos en la casa y **se nos rompió** la escultura de mamá.
> *We were playing in the house, and **we** (accidentally) **broke** Mom's sculpture.*

Vocabulario 1

🔊 2–31

El medio ambiente

el árbol	tree
la arena	sand
el cactus	cactus
la cascada	cascade, waterfall (small)
la catarata	waterfall
el cielo	sky
la contaminación	contamination, pollution
la deforestación	deforestation
los desechos industriales	industrial waste
la ecología	ecology
el esmog	smog
la naturaleza	nature
la nube	cloud
la ola	wave
la palmera	palm tree
el pasto	grass, pasture
el petróleo	oil
el reciclaje	recycling
los recursos naturales	natural resources
el volcán	volcano

Lugares

la bahía	bay
el bosque	forest
la colina	hill
la costa	coast
el desierto	desert
la isla	island
el llano	plains
el mar	sea
la montaña	mountain
la pampa	grasslands
la península	peninsula
el río	river
la selva	jungle
la Tierra	Earth
el valle	valley

Verbos

destruir	to destroy
preservar	to preserve
proteger	to protect

Gramática

Future tense

1. Things that are going to happen in the near future can be expressed in the present tense or using the construction ir + a + an infinitive.

   Salgo para las montañas.
   I'm leaving for the mountains today.

   Vamos a visitar la selva.
   We are going to visit the jungle.

2. Another way to express what will happen is to use the future tense; however, it tends to be a little more formal and is generally used to refer to a more distant future. To form the future tense, add the following endings to the infinitive. In the future tense, -ar, -er, and -ir verbs take the same endings.

proteger

Subject	Ending	Verb form
yo	-é	protegeré
tú	-ás	protegerás
él / ella / usted	-á	protegerá
nosotros(as)	-emos	protegeremos
vosotros(as)	-éis	protegeréis
ellos / ellas / Uds.	-án	protegerán

Ellos **protegerán** el medio ambiente.
They will protect the environment better.

The following are irregular stems for the future tense:

decir	dir-	querer	querr-
haber	habr-	saber	sabr-
hacer	har-	salir	saldr-
poder	podr-	tener	tendr-
poner	pondr-	venir	vendr-

¿**Podrá** venir con nosotros?
Will he be able to come with us?

3. The future tense is also used to express probability or to speculate about present conditions.

   A Julio le gusta el fútbol. **Tendrá** boletos para el partido este sábado.
   Julio likes soccer. He might have tickets for the game this Saturday.

4. Remember that when using the verb **haber** to express the existence of something, it is used in its singular form regardless of whether it is followed by a singular or plural noun.

   Habrá 20 personas en la excursión.
   There will be 20 people on the excursion.

Present Perfect

1. The present perfect is used to express actions that we have and have not done. It combines the present tense of the verb **haber** with the past participle.

haber

he	hemos
has	habéis
ha	han

2. Remember, to form past participles, you add -ado to the stem of an -ar verb, and -ido to the stem of an -er or -ir verb. The past participles **creído, leído, oído,** and **traído** all carry accents. Note the remaining irregular forms listed here:

abierto	hecho	roto
dicho	muerto	visto
devuelto	puesto	vuelto
escrito		

3. When using the participle with **haber,** it is part of the verb, and it does not agree with the subject.

   Raquel no **ha visto** la bahía.
   Raquel hasn't seen the bay.

4. When using direct object, indirect object, or reflexive pronouns, they are placed in front of the conjugated form of **haber.**

   Ya **los** hemos devuelto.
   We have already returned them.

5. In Spanish, the present perfect is generally used as it is in English to talk about something that has happened or something that someone has done. It is usually either unimportant when it happened or it has some relation to the present.

6. The following expressions are often used with the present perfect: **alguna vez, no...todavía, nunca, recientemente,** and **ya.**

Vocabulario 2

🔊 2-32

Los animales

el águila (f.)	eagle
la ardilla	squirrel
la ballena	whale
la cebra	zebra
el cerdo	pig
el cocodrilo	crocodile
el conejo	rabbit
el elefante	elephant
la gallina	hen
el gallo	rooster
el gorila	gorilla
el jaguar	jaguar
la jirafa	giraffe
el león	lion
la llama	llama
el lobo	wolf
el mono	monkey
el oso	bear
la oveja	sheep
el pato	duck
el pavo	turkey
el pingüino	penguin
el pollo	chick
la rana	frog
la serpiente	snake
el tiburón	shark
el tigre	tiger
el toro	bull
la tortuga	turtle
la vaca	cow
el venado	deer
el zorro	fox

Clasificaciones

los anfibios	amphibians
las aves	birds
los mamíferos	mammals
los peces	fish
los reptiles	reptiles

Palabras adicionales

cazar	to hunt
la caza	hunting
la granja	farm
la hembra	female
la jaula	cage
el macho	male
el peligro (de extinción)	danger (of extinction)
salvaje	wild

Gramática

Subjunctive with impersonal expressions

Until now, all the verb tenses you have studied have been in the indicative. The indicative is an objective mood that is used to state facts and to talk about things that you are certain have occurred or will occur.

> **Las águilas están en peligro.**   *Eagles are endangered.*

In contrast, the subjunctive is a subjective mood that is used to convey uncertainty, anticipated or hypothetical events, or the subject's wishes, fears, doubts, and emotional reactions.

> **Es terrible que las águilas desaparezcan.**
> *It is terrible (that) the eagles may disappear.*

1. You will notice that the subjunctive verb forms are very similar to formal commands. To form the present subjunctive, drop the **-o** from the first person (**yo**) present tense form and add the opposite ending. Add the **-er** endings for **-ar** verbs, and the **-ar** endings for **-er** and **-ir** verbs.

   hablar: hable, hables, hable, hablemos, habléis, hablen
   comer: coma, comas, coma, comamos, comáis, coman
   escribir: escriba, escribas, escriba, escribamos, escribáis, escriban

   > Es bueno que las tortugas **naden** en el mar y no en un acuario.
   > *It's good that the turtles swim in the sea and not in an aquarium.*

2. Verbs that are irregular in the first person present indicative have the same stem in the present subjunctive.

   > Es importante que **tengamos** paciencia.   *It's important that we have patience.*

3. Stem-changing **-ar** and **-er** verbs follow the same pattern as in the present indicative, changing in all forms except the **nosotros** and **vosotros** forms.

   > Es necesario que tú **pienses** en el medio ambiente.   *It's necessary that you think of the environment.*

4. Stem-changing **-ir** verbs follow the same pattern as in the present indicative, however there is an additional change in the **nosotros** and **vosotros** forms. The additional stem change is similar to that in the third person preterite. (e → i and o → u)

   > Es terrible que no **durmamos** mejor.   *It's terrible that we don't sleep better.*

5. You will recall that the formal commands of verbs whose infinitives end in **-car, -gar,** and **-zar** have spelling changes. These same spelling changes occur in the subjunctive as well. There is also a spelling change for verbs ending in **-ger;** change the **g** to **j** and add the subjunctive ending.

   > Es recomendable que **lleguemos** a tiempo.   *It's recommended that we arrive on time.*

6. The subjunctive of the following verbs is irregular: **dar (dé), haber (haya), ir (vaya), saber (sepa),** and **ser (sea).** You will notice that once again the subjunctive form is similar to the formal command forms.

   > Es ridículo que Jorge no **sepa** más de los animales que viven en esta parte del país.
   > *It's ridiculous that Jorge doesn't know more about the animals that live in this part of the country.*

7. Impersonal expressions do not have a specific subject and can include a large number of adjectives: **es bueno, es difícil, es importante, es triste,** etc. They can be negative or affirmative.

8. Note that the **que** is required as a conjunction between the main clause and the dependent (subjunctive) clause, even though it may be omitted in English.

   > **Es una lástima que no podamos** hacer más.   *It's a shame (that) we can't do more.*

Subjunctive with expressions of doubt

1. When expressing doubt or uncertainty about an action or a condition, you must use the subjunctive. The following are some common expressions of doubt that require the use of the subjunctive:

   > Dudar que, No creer que, No pensar que, No suponer que, No estar seguro(a) que, No ser cierto/verdad/obvio/evidente que

   > **No es cierto que vayamos** a ayudar las águilas con este programa de preservación.
   > *It's not certain that we are going to help the eagles with this preservation program.*

   > **No creo que haya** ovejas en esta granja.   *I don't think that there are sheep on this farm.*

2. When using the following expressions to affirm a belief or express certainty, you must use the indicative.

   > Creer que, Pensar que, Suponer que, Estar seguro(a) de que, Ser cierto/verdad/obvio/evidente que

   > **Inés está segura de que hay** elefantes en este zoológico.

3. When using the verbs **pensar** and **creer** in a question, it is possible to use the subjunctive in the dependent clause as you are not affirming a belief:

   > ¿Crees que **haya** suficiente comida para los animales?
   > *Do you think there is enough food for the animals?*

Vocabulario 1

🔊 2-36

Relaciones personales

el anillo	ring
la ceremonia	ceremony
la cita	date
el compromiso	engagement
la luna de miel	honeymoon
la madrina	maid of honor, godmother
la muerte	death
el nacimiento	birth
el noviazgo	engagement, relationship
el padrino	best man, godfather
la pareja	couple
el (la) prometido(a)	fiancé(e)
la recepción	wedding reception
el (la) recién casado(a)	newlywed
soltero(a)	single, unmarried
la unión libre	common-law union
viudo(a)	widowed

Verbos

abrazar	to hug
amar	to love
besar	to kiss
comprometerse (con)	to get engaged (to)
dar a luz	to give birth
desear	to desire, to wish
divorciarse (de)	to divorce
enamorarse (de)	to fall in love (with)
esperar	to hope
estar embarazada	to be pregnant
extrañar	to miss
insistir (en)	to insist (on)
llevarse (bien/mal)	to (not) get along
mandar	to order
nacer	to be born
odiar	to hate
proponer matrimonio	to propose marriage
querer	to love
romper (con)	to break up (with)
separarse (de)	to separate (from)
sugerir (ie)	to suggest

Palabras adicionales

la adolescencia	adolescence
el estado civil	civil status
la juventud	youth
la madurez	maturity
la muerte	death
la niñez	childhood
la vejez	old age

Gramática

Reciprocal verbs

1. In **Capítulo 6** you learned to use reflexive pronouns when the subject of the sentence does something to himself or herself.

> Ellos **se miran** en el espejo.
> They **look at themselves** in the mirror.

2. In English the expressions *each other* and *one another* express reciprocal actions. In order to express a reciprocal action in Spanish, use the plural reflexives.

> Ellos **se miran** con amor.
> They **look at each other** with love.

3. Only the plural forms (**nos, os,** and **se**) are used to express reciprocal actions as the action must involve more than one person.

> Paco y Carlota **se vieron** en la fiesta.
> Paco and Carlota **saw each other** at the party.

> Mi primo y yo **nos abrazamos.**
> My cousin and I **hugged each other.**

Subjunctive with expressions of desire

1. When expressing the desire to do something, you use a verb of desire or influence such as **querer** or **preferir** followed by an infinitive.

> Prefiero tener un noviazgo corto.
> I prefer to have a short engagement.

2. When expressing the desire for someone else to do something, you use a verb of influence plus **que** followed by the subjunctive.

> Prefiero que tengamos un noviazgo corto.
> I prefer that we have a short engagement.

3. You will notice in the sample sentence above that when there are two different subjects and the verb in the main clause is in the indicative, the verb in the second clause is in the subjunctive.

4. There are other verbs besides **querer** and **preferir** that express desire or influence. These verbs also require the use of the subjunctive when there are different subjects in the two clauses.

4. It is usually evident by context whether the verb is reflexive or reciprocal. However, if there is need for clarification, **el uno al otro** can be used. The expression must agree with the subject(s); however, if there are mixed sexes, the masculine form is used for both.

> En mi familia, nos cuidamos **los unos a los otros.**
> In my family, we all care for **each other.**

5. When used in the infinitive form after another verb, the pronoun can be attached to the verb or placed in front of the conjugated verb.

> Vamos a ver**nos** todos los días.
> We are going to see each other every day.

> Mariana y Jorge no **se** quieren hablar.
> Mariana and Jorge don't want to talk to each other.

desear	mandar	recomendar
esperar	necesitar	sugerir
insistir (en)	pedir	

> Rogelio **recomienda que vayamos** a la recepción juntos.
> Rogelio **recommends that we go** to the reception together.

5. **Ojalá** is another way to express hope. This expression does not have a subject and therefore does not change forms. It always requires the use of the subjunctive in the dependent clause; however, the use of **que** is optional.

> **Ojalá (que)** los recién casados se diviertan en su luna de miel.
> **I hope (that)** the newlyweds have fun on their honeymoon.

Vocabulario 2

🔊 2-37

La televisión

el anuncio comercial	*commercial*
la audiencia	*audience*
el canal	*TV channel*
la clasificación	*rating (for adults, for the whole family, etc.)*
el concurso	*game show*
el conductor	*TV host*
el control remoto	*remote control*
el documental	*documentary*
los dibujos animados	*cartoons*
el (la) locutor(a)	*announcer*
el noticiario	*news*
el patrocinador	*sponsor*
la programación	*programming*
el reproductor de DVDs	*DVD player*
la telenovela	*soap opera*
el televidente	*television viewer*
la televisión por cable	*cable television*
la televisión por satélite	*satellite television*

La tecnología

los audífonos	*headphones*
el buscador	*search engine*
el MP3	*MP3 player*
la pantalla	*screen*
el ratón	*mouse*
las redes sociales	*social networks*
el reproductor de CDs	*CD player*
el tablero	*keyboard*
la tableta	*tablet*

El cine

la butaca	*seat*
el éxito de taquilla	*box office hit*
las golosinas	*candy*
las palomitas de maíz	*popcorn*

Verbos

censurar	*to censor*
chatear	*to chat*
hacer clic (en)	*to click (on)*
limitar	*to limit*
transmitir	*to broadcast*

Palabras adicionales

adolescente	*adolescent*
adulto	*adult*
infantil	*for children, childish*
la revista	*magazine*

Gramática

The subjunctive with expressions of emotion

1. When expressing an emotion or feeling about something, it is necessary to use the subjunctive if there are two different subjects. Again, the verb in the main clause is in the indicative, and the verb in the second clause is in the subjunctive.

> **Tengo miedo de**   **que**   **haya** demasiada información falsa en la televisión.
> Main Clause   Dependent Clause

2. Some verbs that express emotion are:

estar contento de	**sentir**
estar triste de	**tener miedo de / temer**

3. Other verbs that express emotion are:

aburrir	**enojar**	**preocupar**
alegrar	**gustar**	**sorprender**
encantar	**molestar**	

You will recall that the verbs **gustar, encantar,** and **molestar** require the use of the indirect object. The other verbs in this list also require the use of the indirect object.

> Al productor **le preocupa que nadie vaya** a patrocinar su programa.
> *The producer is worried that nobody is going to sponsor his program.*

4. If there is only one subject, the **que** is not necessary and the infinitive is used with the expression of emotion rather than the subjunctive.

> **Me molesta leer** una revista con artículos tan infantiles.
> *It bothers me to read a magazine with such childish articles.*

The subjunctive with adjective clauses

1. When using an adjective clause to describe something that the speaker knows exists the indicative is used.

> Quiero comprar las golosinas <u>que **son** de chocolate.</u>
> *I want to buy the sweets that are chocolate.*

2. However, when using an adjective clause to describe something that the speaker does not know exists or believes does not exist, the subjunctive is used.

> Necesitamos una actriz <u>que **sea** talentosa.</u>   *We need an actress who is talented.*

3. Some common verbs used with adjective clauses that can require either the subjunctive or the indicative are: **buscar, necesitar,** and **querer.**

> Busco un televisor que **tenga** una pantalla grande.
> Busco el televisor que **tiene** una pantalla grande.

In the first sentence the person does not have a specific television in mind and does not necessarily know if one exists, while in the second sentence he/she is looking for a specific television.

4. When asking about the existence of something, it is also necessary to use the subjunctive, as you do not know whether or not it exists.

> En tu familia, ¿hay alguien que no **tenga** una computadora?

5. When using a negative statement in the main clause, it also necessary to use the subjunctive.

> No hay nadie que no **tenga** una computadora.

Vocabulario 1

🔊 2–41

En el hospital

el corazón	heart
el esqueleto	skeleton
el hígado	liver
el hueso	bone
el intestino	intestine
el órgano vital	vital organ
el (la) paciente	patient
los primeros auxilios	first aid
el pulmón	lung
la radiografía	x-ray
la receta médica	prescription
la sala de emergencias	emergency room
la salud	health
la sangre	blood
el tratamiento	treatment
el yeso	cast

Los síntomas

la alergia	allergy
la cortada	cut
el desmayo	faint
la diarrea	diarrhea
el dolor	pain
la náusea	nausea
la presión baja/ alta	low/high blood pressure

Algunas enfermedades

el cáncer	cancer
la diabetes	diabetes
la gripe	flu
la hipertensión	high blood pressure
el insomnio	insomnia
la obesidad	obesity
el resfriado	cold
el SIDA	AIDS

Los medicamentos y procedimientos

la aspirina	aspirin
la cirugía	surgery
la curita	small adhesive bandage
las gotas	drops
la inyección	injection, shot
el jarabe	syrup (cough)
la pastilla	pill
la silla de ruedas	wheelchair
la vacuna	vaccine
el vendaje	bandage

Verbos

cortarse	to get a cut
descansar	to rest
desmayarse	to faint
doler (ue)	to hurt
enfermarse	to get sick
estar mareado	to be dizzy
estornudar	to sneeze
examinar	to examine
fracturarse	to fracture
recuperarse	to recuperate, to recover
respirar	to breathe
sangrar	to bleed
sufrir náuseas	to feel nauseous
tomar la presión	to take someone´s blood pressure
torcerse (ue)	to twist, to sprain
toser	to cough
vomitar	to vomit

Gramática

Conditional

1. To form the conditional, add the following endings to the infinitive. Notice that all verbs take the same endings.

hablar	**volver**	**ir**
hablar**ía**	volver**ía**	ir**ía**
hablar**ías**	volver**ías**	ir**ías**
hablar**ía**	volver**ía**	ir**ía**
hablar**íamos**	volver**íamos**	ir**íamos**
hablar**íais**	volver**íais**	ir**íais**
hablar**ían**	volver**ían**	ir**ían**

2. The irregular stems for the conditional are the same as the irregular stems for the future tense (see **Capítulo 12**). The endings are the same as the regular forms of the conditional.

> ¿Qué **harías** con un millón de dólares?
> *What would you do with a million dollars?*

> Yo **querría** viajar.
> *I would want to travel.*

3. The conditional is similar to the English construction *would* + verb.

> Yo no **iría** a la sala de emergencias.
> *I **wouldn't go** to the emergency room.*

Imperfect Subjunctive

1. In the last three chapters, you learned to use the present subjunctive. When the verb in the main clause is in the past (preterite or imperfect), the verb in the dependent clause must be in the imperfect subjunctive.

> **Era** necesario que le **pusieran** un yeso a Tomás.

2. The imperfect subjunctive is formed using the third person plural (**ellos, ellas, ustedes**) of the preterite. Eliminate the **-on** and add the endings as indicated. Endings are the same, regardless of whether the verb ends in **-ar, -er,** or **-ir.** Verbs that are irregular in the preterite are also irregular in the imperfect subjunctive.

hablar	**tener**	**dormir**
hablar**a**	tuvier**a**	durmier**a**
hablar**as**	tuvier**as**	durmier**as**
hablar**a**	tuvier**a**	durmier**a**
hablár**amos**	tuviér**amos**	durmiér**amos**
hablar**ais**	tuvier**ais**	durmier**ais**
hablar**an**	tuvier**an**	durmier**an**

*Notice that it is necessary to add an accent in the **nosotros** form.

4. The conditional form of **haber** is **habría.** You will remember that there is only one form of the verb regardless of whether it is followed by a singular or plural noun.

> Creí que **habría** más vacunas necesarias antes de viajar.
> *I thought **there would be** more necessary vaccinations before traveling.*

5. The conditional is also used for conjecture about past activities.

> ¿Por qué **no le pondrían** un vendaje a Cristina?
> *Why **wouldn't they put** a bandage on Cristina?*
> *(I **wonder** why **they didn't put** a bandage on Cristina.)*

6. The conditional is often used to demonstrate politeness or to soften a request.

> ¿**Me daría** usted una aspirina?
> ***Would you please give me** an aspirin?*

3. The imperfect subjunctive form of **haber** is **hubiera.**

4. In general, the same rules that apply to the usage of the present subjunctive also apply to the past subjunctive.

· To express an opinion using impersonal expressions

· To express doubt

· To express desire

· To express an emotion

· To talk about the unknown using adjective clauses

5. When using an "if clause" to express what would happen in a hypothetical situation or a situation that is not likely or impossible, it is necessary to use the imperfect subjunctive and the conditional.

si + imperfect subjunctive + conditional

> **Si no estuviera** enferma, **iría** al concierto con ustedes.
> ***If I weren't** sick, **I would go** to the concert with you all.*

Vocabulario 2

🔊 2–42

Nacionalidades

argentino	*Argentine*
boliviano	*Bolivian*
chileno	*Chilean*
colombiano	*Colombian*
costrricense	*Costa Rican*
cubano	*Cuban*
dominicano	*Dominican*
ecuatoguineano	*Equatorial Guinean*
ecuatoriano	*Ecuadorian*
español	*Spanish*
guatemalteco	*Guatemalan*
hondureño	*Honduran*
mexicano	*Mexican*
nicaragüense	*Nicaraguan*
panameño	*Panamanian*
paraguayo	*Paraguayan*
peruano	*Peruvian*
puertorriqueño	*Puerto Rican*
salvadoreño	*Salvadoran*
uruguayo	*Uruguayan*
venezolano	*Venezuelan*

La comunidad internacional

la beca	*scholarship*
el (la) cuidadano(a)	*citizen*
los derechos humanos	*human rights*
el desempleo	*unemployment*
la dictadura	*dictatorship*
la emigración	*emigration*
la globalización	*globalization*
el gobierno	*government*
la guerra	*war*
el idioma	*language*
la inmigración	*immigration*
la ley	*law*
el organismo internacional	*international organization*
el país	*country*
la paz	*peace*
la pobreza	*poverty*
el (la) refugiado(a)	*refugee*
la riqueza	*wealth*
el tratado de comercio	*trade agreement*

Verbos

emigrar	*emigrate*
inmigrar	*immigrate*
mudarse	*to move (to another location)*
votar	*to vote*

Adverbios

a fin de que	*in order that, so that*
a menos que	*unless*
antes (de) que	*before*
aunque	*although, even if*
con tal (de) que	*provided that*
después (de) que	*after*
en caso de que	*in case*
en cuanto	*as soon as*
hasta que	*until*
para que	*in order that, so that*
siempre y cuando	*as long as*
sin que	*without*
tan pronto (como)	*as soon as*

Gramática

Subjunctive with adverbial clauses and conjunctions

1. The following adverbial conjunctions always require the subjunctive. Because they indicate that the action is contingent upon another action, the outcome is unknown: **a fin de que, antes (de) que, a menos que, con tal (de) que, en caso de que, mientras (que), para que, siempre y cuando, sin que**

> Aníbal cambió de trabajo **para que** su esposa pudiera estar con su familia.
> *Aníbal changed jobs **so that** his wife could be with his family.*

2. With the exception of **a menos que, mientras (que)** and **siempre y cuando,** the expressions above are often used with the infinitive if there is no change of subject. The **que** after the preposition is omitted.

> Los políticos tuvieron que trabajar mucho **para cambiar** esa ley.
> *The politicians had to work hard **in order to change** that law.*

3. The following adverbial conjunctions of time require the subjunctive when referring to actions that have not yet occurred. When referring to actions that are already taking place or are habitual, they require the indicative: **cuando, después (de) que*, en cuanto, hasta que*, tan pronto, (como)**

> ***Después (de) que** and **hasta que** are often used with the infinitive if there is no change of subject. Again, the **que** after the preposition is omitted.

Present indicative

> **Tan pronto como recibo** mi cheque, le mando dinero a mi familia.
> *As soon as I receive my check, I send money to my family.*

Subjunctive

> **Cuando tengamos** los recursos necesarios, nos mudaremos a los Estados Unidos.
> *When we have the necessary resources, we will move to the United States.*

4. The following adverbial conjunctions require the indicative when referring to something that is known or is definite. However, when referring to something that is unknown or indefinite, they require the subjunctive: **aunque, como, (a)donde.**

> Mi familia va de viaje **aunque hay** una guerra muy cerca de su destino.
> *My family is taking a trip **even though there is** a war near their destination.*

> Mi familia va de viaje **aunque haya** una guerra muy cerca de su destino.
> *My family is taking a trip **even if there may be** a war near their destination.*

Past perfect

1. Similar to the present perfect, the past perfect (also known as the **pluscuamperfecto**), combines the imperfect form of the verb **haber** with the past participle: **había, habías, había, habíamos, habíais, habían.**

> **Habían obtenido** su visa antes de salir.   ***They had obtained** their visa before leaving.*

2. The past perfect is used to express a past action that already took place before another past action.

> Camilo ya **había aprendido** inglés cuando llegó a los Estados Unidos.
> *Camilo **had** already **learned** English when he arrived in the United States.*

3. Remember the irregular past participles from **Capítulo 12: abierto, cubierto, dicho, escrito, hecho, muerto, puesto, roto, visto vuelto, devuelto.**

4. As with the present perfect, when using direct object, indirect object, or reflexive pronouns, they are placed in front of the conjugated form of **haber.**

> Cuando llegaron a la casa, ya **nos habíamos mudado.**
> *When they arrived at the house, **we had** already **moved.***

Learning Strategies

Capítulo 1: Hola, ¿qué tal?

Study frequently
When learning a foreign language it is important to study every day. Aside from any written homework you may have, plan to spend some time each day learning the current vocabulary. For most students, it is more effective to study for 15-20 minutes three times a day than to spend a full hour on the subject. It might also be a lot easier for you to find time to study if you break it into smaller periods of time.

How did you apply this strategy? _____

_____

How useful did you find this strategy? Why? _____

_____

_____

Capítulo 2: ¿Cómo es tu vida?

Listen to and repeat vocabulary
When studying vocabulary, take time to listen to and repeat the pronunciation of the words. It will help your pronunciation, which in turn will help you learn to spell the words properly. You may click on the vocabulary in the eBook to hear it pronounced or you may want to download the audio files onto your MP3 player or cell phone, so they will be more accessible.

How did you apply this strategy? _____

_____

How useful did you find this strategy? Why? _____

_____

_____

Capítulo 3: ¿Qué tiempo hace hoy?

Understand before moving on
Learning a foreign language is like learning math; you will continue to use what you have already learned and will build upon that knowledge. Therefore, if you find you don't understand something, make an appointment to see your instructor or a tutor right away in order to get some extra help. For help with grammar topics, you can also watch the tutorials in iLrn.

How did you apply this strategy? _____

_____

How useful did you find this strategy? Why? _____

_____

_____

Capítulo 4: ¿Dónde vives?

Participate

Participate in class. You cannot learn another language simply by observing. You must be willing to use the language actively, and to learn from the mistakes you make.

How did you apply this strategy? _____

_____

How useful did you find this strategy? Why? _____

_____

Capítulo 5: ¿Estás feliz en el trabajo?

Guess intelligently

When you are listening to audio recordings or your instructor, or when watching a video, make intelligent guesses as to the meaning of words you do not know. Use context, intonation, and if possible, visual clues such as gestures, facial expressions and images to help you figure out the meaning of words.

How did you apply this strategy? _____

_____

How useful did you find this strategy? Why? _____

_____

Capítulo 6: ¿Cómo pasas el día?

Study with a partner

Study with a friend or form a study group. Not only will you benefit when someone in your group understands a concept that you may have difficulty with, but you can also increase your own understanding by teaching others who need extra help. Group study will provide you with more opportunities to speak and listen to Spanish as well.

How did you apply this strategy? _____

_____

How useful did you find this strategy? Why? _____

_____

Capítulo 7: ¿Qué te gusta comer?

Try a variety of memorization techniques

Use a variety of techniques to memorize vocabulary and verbs until you find the ones that work best for you. Some students learn better when they write the words, others learn better if they listen to recordings of the words while looking over the list, and still others prefer to rely on flashcards.

How did you apply this strategy? _____

_____

How useful did you find this strategy? Why? _____

_____

Capítulo 8: ¿Qué haces dentro y fuera de la casa?

Review material from previous chapters
Because you continue to use vocabulary, verbs, and grammar that you learned in past chapters, it is important to review this material. Make flashcards for each chapter and review them often, go back to the **Exploraciones de repaso** section in earlier chapters to be sure you can still do the activities, and complete the **Hora de reciclar** activities in your *Student Activities Manual* or iLrn.

How did you apply this strategy? _____

_____

How useful did you find this strategy? Why? _____

_____

Capítulo 9: ¿Qué pasó?

Remember that Spanish and English have different structures
Grammar is an essential part of any language. While it is helpful to understand and compare basic concepts of the English language such as pronouns and direct objects, it is important to learn the new structures and avoid translating directly from English to Spanish.

How did you apply this strategy?_____

_____

How useful did you find this strategy? Why? _____

_____

Capítulo 10: ¿Adónde vas a viajar?

Use Spanish every time you talk in class
Try to use Spanish for all your classroom interactions, not just when called on by the instructor or answering a classmate's question in a group activity. Don't worry that your sentences may not be structurally correct; the important thing is to begin to feel comfortable expressing yourself in the language. You might even initiate a conversation with your instructor or another classmate before or after class.

How did you apply this strategy? _____

_____

How useful did you find this strategy? Why? _____

_____

Capítulo 11: ¿Es la moda arte?

Find ways to use your language in real-life settings
Seek out international students from Spanish-speaking countries or, if possible, visit a local restaurant or shop where you may have the opportunity to initiate a conversation with native speakers of Spanish. Explore opportunities to travel or to study abroad. Using the language in different social interactions will help to increase your proficiency as well as your confidence.

How did you apply this strategy? _____

_____

How useful did you find this strategy? Why? _____

_____

Capítulo 12: ¿Qué será de nuestro planeta?

Use a good dictionary
While you should not look up every Spanish word that you don't understand, a good bilingual dictionary is essential. Ask your instructor for some recommendations for print and online dictionaries that include complete entries, idiomatic expressions and pronunciation. When you look up an English word, be sure to choose the correct form, such as a noun or an adjective. If the entry has a number of definitions, cross-check the one you think you need in the Spanish-English section to confirm your choice.

How did you apply this strategy? _____

_____

How useful did you find this strategy? Why? _____

_____

_____

Capítulo 13: ¿Es tu vida una telenovela?

Find ways to gain exposure to the language outside of the classroom
You can take many small steps to accelerate your progress in class. Listen to the songs in the **Investiguemos la música** suggestions. Watch a Spanish-language film. Read a magazine or newspaper published in Spanish. All of these activities will help you to increase your vocabulary. You will also become more familiar with structures and expressions used by native speakers and increase your cultural knowledge.

How did you apply this strategy? _____

_____

How useful did you find this strategy? Why? _____

_____

_____

Capítulo 14: ¿Qué haces en una emergencia?

Think in Spanish
When speaking, try to think in Spanish and speak spontaneously rather than translating from English. If you find you need to use a word that you don't know, instead of saying it in English or looking it up in the dictionary, try explaining the concept using other Spanish words. With a little practice, this skill will become easier.

How did you apply this strategy? _____

_____

How useful did you find this strategy? Why? _____

_____

_____